The Persian Gulf in History

Edited by
Lawrence G. Potter

palgrave
macmillan

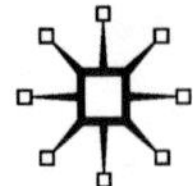

THE PERSIAN GULF IN HISTORY

First published in hardcover in 2009 by PALGRAVE MACMILLAN® in the United States – a division of St. Martin's Press LLC, 175 Fifth Avenue, New York, NY 10010.

Where this book is distributed in the UK, Europe and the rest of the world, this is by Palgrave Macmillan, a division of Macmillan Publishers Limited, registered in England, company number 785998, of Houndmills, Basingstoke, Hampshire RG21 6XS.

Palgrave Macmillan is the global academic imprint of the above companies and has companies and representatives throughout the world.

ISBN: 978-0-230-61282-2

Library of Congress Cataloging-in-Publication

The Persian Gulf in history / edited by Lawrence G. Potter.
p. cm.
Includes bibliographical references and index.
ISBN 1-4039-7245-1
1. Persian Gulf Region—History. I. Potter, Lawrence G.

DS326.P4745 2008
953.6—dc22 2008021284

A catalogue record of the book is available from the British Library.

Design by Macmillan Publishing Solutions

First PALGRAVE MACMILLAN paperback edition: May 2010

Transferred to Digital Printing in 2010

Printed in the United States of America.

Contents

PART II: THE GULF AND THE INDIAN OCEAN

PART III: THE ROLE OF OUTSIDERS

List of Tables

List of Maps and Figures

Maps

Figures

Acknowledgments

This book grew out of a conference held in Limassol, Cyprus, in October 2004. It was organized by Gulf/2000 (http://gulf2000.columbia.edu), a major international research and documentation project on the Persian Gulf states based at Columbia University, with the support and cooperation of The Centre for World Dialogue (CWD) in Nicosia (http://www.worlddialogue.org). We are most grateful to the CWD for its wonderful hospitality, which facilitated what many participants felt was one of the most productive conferences they had ever attended. It was to our knowledge the first ever held on the history of the Persian Gulf in all historical periods and included scholars from every littoral state, as well as Europe and the United States. The discussions there contributed substantially to the making of this book. We greatly regret that the CWD president, Hossein Alikhani, passed away in March 2008 and will not see this book. I very much appreciate the cooperation and contributions of the colleagues that made possible this project in international collaboration. I would like to extend special gratitude to Haideh Sahim, who supervised the transliteration, and for her advice and forbearance during the course of this project. The excellent work of the indexer, Lisa Rivero, has enhanced the usefulness of this book. The outstanding map designed by M.R. Izady is also much appreciated. The steady support and encouragement of Gary Sick, the Executive Director of Gulf/2000, was above all critical to the success of the conference and this book. We all owe him our thanks.

Lawrence Potter

Note on Transliteration

Since this book is aimed at a wide readership we have tried to simplify the spelling of Arabic and Persian words, and have forgone diacritical marks in the text. The system of transliteration employed will leave some, especially Iranists, unsatisfied, as it does not make allowance for pronunciation. In this book the initial *ain* has been dropped (thus Shah Abbas not ‘Abbas), diphthongs have been rendered as *-ai* (Husain) and *-aw* (Faw), the *izafa* (*ezafeh*) is rendered by *-i*, short vowels are rendered as u (not o) and i (not e), and Persian words take a final *-a* and not *-eh* (thus *Shahnama*). In the case of proper names, those already familiar in an anglicized version have been retained (e.g., Tehran, Safavids, Saddam Hussein). Since there is no universally accepted system of transliteration some compromise has been necessary.

INTRODUCTION

Lawrence G. Potter

Until now the Persian Gulf has been regarded as a border zone of the Middle East, on the periphery of cultures and empires, and as such the Gulf region, which includes the present-day countries of Bahrain, Iran, Iraq, Kuwait, Oman, Qatar, Saudi Arabia, and the United Arab Emirates, has not received the attention it deserves from historians. This volume, however, will focus on the unifying factors that have historically led to this region's distinctiveness, and not on the divisions that have arisen with modern statehood. For the first time, the Gulf will be viewed as a civilizational unit that should be studied in its own right over a long period of time.[1]

The unique identity of the Persian Gulf has been well defined since antiquity. Based on the archaeological record, Daniel Potts concludes that the Gulf "cannot be viewed as a mere appendage of, for example, Mesopotamia or Iran . . . From a very early date, the region has had an identity which was apparent to its neighbours as it was to its inhabitants."[2]

The Gulf world is set apart from the rest of the Middle East by physical barriers—mountains to the north and east, marshes at its head, and forbidding deserts to the south. In the past, people living on the shores of the Gulf had closer relations with one another than with those living in the interior, which is typical of littoral societies.[3] For millennia it was an integrated region characterized by the constant interchange of people, commerce, and religious movements. Before the modern era, peoples of the region shared a maritime culture based on pearling, fishing, and long-distance trade, and were part of an interlinked system that included agricultural villages and oases that sustained the caravan trade.

The Gulf has always been a key international trade route connecting the Middle East to India, East Africa, Southeast Asia, and China. Its orientation was outward, toward the Indian Ocean, and its society reflected this. A cosmopolitan, mercantile, and tolerant society developed here, which thrived in spite of the lack of local resources. The mobility of these people and their assets differed markedly from that of the oasis-based agricultural peasant societies that arose in the interior of neighboring states. Historically, regional powers, including states based on the Iranian plateau or the powers that controlled parts of the Arabian Peninsula or Mesopotamia, rarely exercised effective political control over the Gulf littoral.

REGIONAL IDENTITY

The subject of this book is the Gulf, *khalij*, in Persian and Arabic, and its people, the Khalijis. The literal English translation, "Gulfies," may be regarded as derogatory by some and has been avoided here. For convenience, the term "Khaliji" is sometimes invoked to draw a distinction between dwellers on the Iranian or Arabian coasts and those living in the interior. Although peoples living on the Gulf littoral had a similar lifestyle and often had intense economic and social relations, this does not mean that they shared a common identity. Rather, in premodern times, identity in the Middle East was local. In the twentieth century, factors such as tribe, locality, ethnicity, and religion have been increasingly overtaken by state citizenship as the primary source of identity. The issue of identity as Arab or Persian or gradations thereof is complicated and is a subject of dispute among scholars studying the region. This essay only seeks to point out the issue, not resolve it.

Tribes were the key to forming modern states in the Arabian Peninsula, and the dynasties presently ruling there are all of tribal origin. Until the mid-twentieth century in Iran and up to the present time in Iraq, tribalism has also played an important role. Language has also served as a source of difference and, sometimes, division. Arabic, a Semitic language, is spoken in Iraq and in the Arabian Peninsula. Iran has an Aryan heritage, and its official language, Persian, is an Indo-European tongue. However, people along the Iranian littoral south of Bushehr often speak Arabic, which also predominates in the southwestern Iranian province of Khuzistan. On the southern shore, especially in Bahrain and Dubai, expatriate communities of Iranians speak Persian. In post–World War II Bahrain, the British diplomat Sir Rupert Hay reported that "the Persians can, nearly all, speak Arabic fluently, but few Arabs will admit to a knowledge of Persian."[4] "A British Political Agent in Muscat, writing at the turn of the century, spoke of 14 languages that might be heard every day in the *suqs* of Muscat and Matrah."[5] This bilingualism was common and led to a mutual tolerance that typified society in the Gulf.

The religious history of the Gulf has yet to be written. In a general sense Shiism unified Iran, Wahhabism unified Saudi Arabia, and Ibadism unified Oman. Although Iran today is a Shi'i state and the Arabian peninsula is largely Sunni, there are significant pockets of Sunnis along the Iranian coastline from Kangan to Minab and many Shi'is reside in Bahrain,[6] Kuwait, the UAE (especially Dubai), and Oman. Oman forms the only Ibadi state in the world. Historically, there were often outsiders—Banyans from India, Zoroastrians, Jews,[7] and Europeans—who also formed part of the human mix in the Gulf and were usually there for commercial purposes. In the Gulf region religious tolerance and intermingling has been the norm in port cities for centuries. A Portuguese visitor in 1549 commented that in Hormuz, God was celebrated four times a week—by the Muslims on Friday, the Jews on Saturday, the Christians on Sunday, and the Hindus on Monday.[8]

In the twentieth century the historical unity of Gulf society was shattered. On the Arab side, British intervention led to the drawing of borders and the creation of new states. As part of the modernization process these states were determined to create national histories and assert control over their Gulf littoral. After the British withdrawal in 1971, there was a period of about two decades in which regional states (notably Iran and Saudi Arabia) themselves dominated the area, followed by renewed superpower intervention, this time by the United States. Today regional states face a common set of political and economic problems, including regime security, the challenge of radical Islam, sectarian differences, management of petroleum resources, and preparation for life after oil. The major role played by external powers also seems likely to continue.

REWRITING THE HISTORY OF THE GULF

The arrival of oceans as a suitable subject of study is highlighted in a recent series of articles in *The American Historical Review*.[9] As the introduction notes, "No longer outside time, the sea is being given a history, even as the history of the world is being retold from the perspective of the sea."[10] Much of the history of the Indian Ocean—and by extension the Persian Gulf—since the early modern period has been treated from the standpoint of the intrusion and domination of external powers: the Portuguese in the sixteenth century, the Dutch in the seventeenth, and the English from the late eighteenth. The great European trading companies that operated in the region, the English East India Company (founded in 1600), the Dutch East Indies Company (founded in 1602), and the French Compagnie Française des Indes (founded in 1664), all left voluminous records that have been mined by historians. These materials, in light of the paucity of local records from the Gulf, have left an image of a region focused on maritime trade and resistance to or collaboration with foreign intruders. However, "contrary to the situation elsewhere in Asia the Europeans did not establish settlements dominated by Europeans that later grew into enclaves with their own jurisdictional rights and authority," according to Floor. The Europeans were always very much in the minority and were quite dependent on the local powers.[11] As we are reminded in a wide-ranging review article, "many important aspects of European-Asian interaction in maritime Asia cannot be understood if we maintain an analytic separation of European intrusion and Asian response; they emerged in highly contingent and specific ways from the interactions, the congruences and mutual adaptations, of specific facets of the European and various Asian civilizations."[12]

Writing the history of the Persian Gulf has long been the preserve of outsiders, until recently primarily that of the British, who dominated the region for 150 years. Such writers were mainly interested in the Gulf for strategic reasons and were largely confident of the benevolence of Britain's imperial imprint.[13] More recently, a few notable works have appeared that focus on the indigenous peoples.[14] In Iran and the states of the Arabian Peninsula, there is frustration among a new generation of historians that others have long had a monopoly on interpreting the region's history. By the 1970s a new generation of historians had arisen on the Arab side of the Gulf who criticized the British for imposing new boundaries and fragmenting the Gulf's unity. They also accused the British of altering the traditional Gulf economy, by taking over most of the long-distance trade while relegating native dhows or sailing craft to the peddler trade in smaller ports.[15] Since the revolution, Iranian historians have tended to emphasize the pernicious effects of the Europeans in the Gulf, while criticizing their own government for not resisting more strongly.[16]

What the British characterized as "piracy" in the eighteenth and nineteenth centuries, for example, and used to justify their intervention, could be regarded as lawful resistance to foreign intrusion and a cultural response to maritime competition.[17] "Piracy" could alternatively be described as "maritime warfare," or as a transference to the sea of the tribal conflict and levying of tolls for protection (*khuwa*) which was prevalent on land. The idea that their ancestors were pirates, and that it was necessary for the British to intervene to safeguard the trade of the Gulf, is particularly repellent to the ruling shaikhs of what is now the UAE.[18]

In all of the present territorial disputes in the Gulf, such as that between Iran and Iraq and between Iraq and Kuwait over their common borders, much of the key documentary evidence was produced by British civil servants in the late nineteenth and early twentieth centuries.[19] There is an acute shortage of available local records and histories in Arabic and Persian. It is surprising, for example, that so far the Iranian government has not produced more historical documents to buttress their claim of ownership of the islands of Abu Musa and Greater and Lesser Tunb.

History Used and Abused

Governments in the region have sought to use history to create or to reinforce a feeling of national identity and bolster their own legitimacy. They favor national histories that sharply differentiate one state from its neighbors. This has often involved rewriting the past. In line with the tendency in Arabic and Iranian historiography to focus on the deeds of great men (*rijal va muluk*), all of these states have overemphasized the role of personality to the exclusion of social and historical factors shaping events. This has led to personality cults around figures such as Ibn Sa'ud, Saddam Hussein and the Pahlavi shahs of Iran. But whether they are royal, secular or Islamic, governments have demonstrated that control over the interpretation of the past is an important tool in maintaining authority and legitimacy: history is important.[20]

Until now, an inability to conceptualize the Gulf's history as a whole has resulted in scholarly attention being focused on small pieces of it. In the Western academic system, students may specialize in Iran, the Arabian Peninsula, or Iraq and learn Arabic or Persian. But very rarely will a historian of Iran have an interest in the history of Saudi Arabia or vice versa. For this reason no one has yet written a satisfactory and comprehensive history of the Gulf.[21] What is needed is a new historical approach in which the unit of study is the Persian Gulf in its entirety.[22]

Brides of the Sea

Any history of the Persian Gulf will necessarily focus on its port cities, those "brides of the sea" that connected the Gulf region to the Indian Ocean and the wider world.[23] Persian Gulf ports were mostly small and, with the exception of Basra and Hormuz at its height, did not themselves constitute a significant market. Their main function, as at Bushehr, was to forward goods to the interior, or to redistribute them to minor regional ports.[24] The rise and fall of ports in the Gulf has been a feature throughout its history, having to do with both changing geographical as well as political conditions.[25] André Wink remarks that "the historical study of the Indian Ocean is, to a very considerable degree, the study of changing landscapes,"[26] and this is also true of the Gulf.

The major ports at the head of the Gulf were located far up an inland river, the Shatt al-Arab: Basra is 72 miles upstream from its mouth, Khurramshahr (formerly Muhammara) is 52 miles inland, and the newer port of Bandar Shahpur (renamed Bandar Khomeini after the revolution), located on the Khur Musa inlet, is 40 miles up the channel. Such rivers and inlets, however, often silted up. The Shatt al-Arab, with a shallow entrance, was notorious for its wrecks and dangerous currents and was considered "one of the most dangerous waterways in Asia."[27] Because of this goods bound for Basra were commonly offloaded at Muscat or Siraf for further transport by smaller ships. This is similar to the situation at the Red Sea, where goods would be transferred at Shihr or Aden for shipment further north.[28]

Port cities on the southern shore such as Dubai, Sharjah, and Ras al-Khaimah are located on small inlets (*khurs*), known in English as creeks, with the same problem.[29] Silting led to the decline of Sharjah as a port, whereas the decision to dredge Dubai Creek in the late 1950s led to the port's runaway success.[30] As Lienhardt observes, "the shifting of the sands of the coast, blocking some ports and eating others away, is perhaps a reason why the coastal towns as we know them have had such a short history."[31]

There has always been a major port at the head (northern end) of the Gulf. Thus Ubulla, the port for Basra under the Abbasids, was the former Apologus of Sasanian times.[32] The most important Gulf ports up to the twentieth century were always on the Iranian coast, probably because the water is deeper there. Over time their location shifted eastward: from Rishahr on the Bushehr peninsula in the Umayyad period (661–750 C.E.) to Siraf (850–1000), Kish (1000–1300), and Hormuz (1300–1600). Bandar Abbas was the most important port from 1622 to the mid-eighteenth century, when it was replaced by Bushehr. After about 1900 Bushehr was increasingly eclipsed by Khurramshahr, which was the leading Iranian port by World War II. This suggests a certain interchangeability, where port traffic was affected by the rate of customs duties as well as by the political situation: for example during troubles at Bandar Abbas in the late eighteenth century, the European trading companies transferred operations to Basra or Bushehr.

The relative importance of ports on the Arab side also shifted. Thus Julfar was the most important port on the Trucial coast from the early Islamic era until the eighteenth century when it was superseded by nearby Ras al-Khaimah, a base of the Qawasim rulers, and Abu Dhabi was developed by the Bani Yas tribal confederation.[33] By the early twentieth century Ras al-Khaimah had been eclipsed by Sharjah as the largest port on the Trucial Coast.[34] In Oman, the city of Qalhat, which thrived from the thirteenth to sixteenth century, was superseded by Suhar and eventually by Muscat as the leading port.

The difficulty of communication with the interior before modern times—especially prior to the coming of the telegraph in the 1860s—served to isolate the Iranian littoral from major cities such as Shiraz, Isfahan or Tehran. For example, Bushehr is 182 miles from Shiraz and in the 1890s it took five or six days to travel this route.[35] On the other hand, by sea Bushehr is 170 miles from Kuwait and 190 miles from Manama.[36] With a good wind, the sailing time from Bushehr to Kuwait was 22 hours and from Bushehr to Manama 24 hours.[37] In his autobiography, Easa Saleh Al-Gurg, an Arab from Lingeh whose family moved to Dubai after World War I (where he became a leading businessman and diplomat), relates a family tradition of Friday dinners when relatives from Sharjah and Ras al-Khaimah would cross the Gulf in time for the evening prayer and, after dinner, return to the Arabian shore, arriving around midnight.[38] Today, Iranian smugglers from Bandar Abbas who sell sheep and goats in Khasab, on the Musandam peninsula of Oman, and bring back cigarettes to Bandar Abbas can make the trip in as little as 45 minutes in a fast boat.[39]

Also crucial is the subject of port-hinterland relations. Iranian ports were cut off from the major cities on the plateau by the Zagros Mountains, and connections with the interior were via a few difficult passes, for example, those behind Bushehr and Lingeh. The cities on the coast thus depended extensively on imports to sustain what seem like impossibly large populations, if we accept that at its height in the tenth century Siraf was almost as large as Shiraz[40] and Hormuz once held up to 40,000 people.[41] Recent work on the Bushehr hinterland has helped reveal how the city was provisioned in the Sasanid period.[42] Insecurity in the hinterland could have a severe effect on the ports. Attacks by Mongol tribesmen around 1300 on the original city of Hormuz, located on the mainland near Minab, led to a move to the island of Jarun, subsequently renamed Hormuz. The major reason for the fall of Bushehr, which had been an independent Arab shaikhdom from 1750 to 1850, was that it lost control over its hinterland and could not resist Qajar advances.[43]

A Hybrid Culture

One characteristic of port cities in the Gulf and the Indian Ocean was the varied human mix: "port functions, more than anything else, made a city cosmopolitan, a word which does not necessarily mean 'sophisticated' but rather hybrid. A port city is open to the

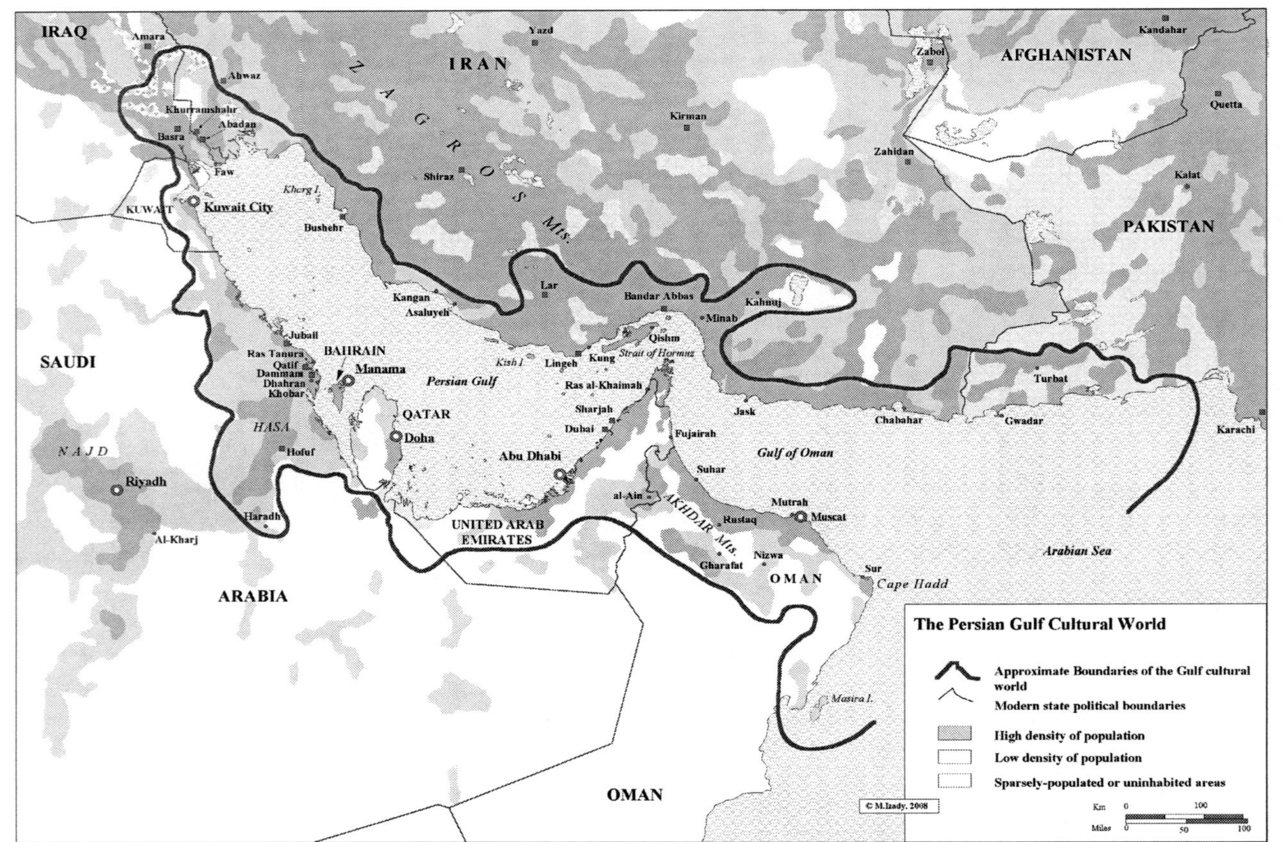

Map 0.1 The Persian Gulf Cultural World.

world, or at least to a varied section of it. In it races, cultures, and ideas as well as goods from a variety of places jostle, mix, and enrich each other and the life of the city."[44]

In the Gulf ports a hybrid Arab-Persian culture flourished. According to the tenth-century geographer Muqaddasi, Persian was spoken in the port of Suhar (modern Oman), while in Aden and Jidda the majority of people were Persian but their language was Arabic.[45] At the same time in Khuzistan the people "often blend their Persian with the Arabic . . . You do not find them speaking in Persian without changing to Arabic; and when they speak in one of the two languages you would not realize they knew the other one well."[46] Hormuz in medieval travel accounts was legendary for its human diversity, and the descriptions of port cities in Lorimer's great compendium of the early twentieth century make their hybrid nature very clear.

During his visit to Bandar Lingeh in 1863, Lewis Pelly notes that "the wealthier class are Persianised Arabs," although the bulk of the population appeared to be African.[47] This is a reminder of the large role that slavery played in the Gulf, especially in the nineteenth century, and the fact that many pearl divers were slaves.[48] At the time of his visit to the same city in 1889–90, George Curzon remarked that "the population of the place is partly Arab, partly Persian, partly African, partly that nameless hybrid mixture that is found in every maritime town east of Port Said."[49]

Another characteristic of Gulf ports was their transient population.[50] They would be teeming with foreign and local merchants during the trading season, but become ghost towns when the hot weather set in. Muscat, for example, was notorious for its torrid summers, and its weather took a deadly toll on British diplomats stationed there. Those who could, moved to the seaside or inland spring towns. Likewise, in Bandar Abbas, anyone who could, took off for the inland hills or mountains, notably the town of Isin, 16 kilometers to the north. Many Gulf Arabs traditionally summered in Shiraz on the Iranian plateau; others preferred the rainy monsoon weather in Bombay or, more recently, Dhofar. This population shift was not unique to the Gulf but was also characteristic of the Red Sea ports.[51]

The Gulf World Defined

As scholars have moved beyond nation-states to formulate histories based on the great oceans of the world, there is often a question of how to define the topic and structure research.[52] As one scholar has remarked, "historians of contemporary times who choose to focus on the ocean, or on any one of its coastal regions, have to confront the problem of where the coast ends and the hinterland begins and how much of the hinterland is relevant to an understanding of the coast and the ocean."[53] Studies of port cities in Asia have tended to focus on themes such as city-hinterland relationships, morphogenesis, and interactions between indigenous and foreign elites,[54] which are pointers to the way Gulf ports might be explored. Studies of the Indian Ocean have also focused on networks of commercial exchange, religious diffusion, and resistance to imperial powers, all fruitful avenues of research.

"Most current categories of social analysis were initially developed to understand land-based societies," according to Kären Wigen. "How those categories need to be transformed by perspectives from the sea—and how far they can be stretched, bent, and reworked to accommodate ocean-centered realities—is perhaps the most important unresolved agenda."[55] In the case of the Persian Gulf, like the Mediterranean, defining the research area is not an issue, for it is a clearly defined body of water.

While the Persian Gulf is part of a region we today call the Middle East, it also constitutes a world of its own, a geographically and culturally distinct region (see map 0.1).[56] As is the case with the Black Sea, regions "are about connections: profound and durable linkages among people and communities that seem to mark off one space from another." The Gulf world from the earliest times has been characterized by a dense web of economic and social connections.[57] How shall we define the boundaries of the Gulf world?[58] In the north, it is hemmed in by the great marshes of southern Iraq and the swampy lowlands of the Iranian province of Khuzistan.[59] The coastline at the head of the Gulf is composed of river deltas, marshes, and mud flats and was known to ancient Mesopotamian cultures as the "Sealand." The southern foothills of the Zagros Mountains, which rise in Iran north of Ahwaz, abruptly mark the northern boundary of the Gulf world.

Along the Iranian coast, littoral society inhabits a narrow, salty coastal plain between the Zagros Mountains and the sea.[60] The coastal zone in Iran forms part of what the Iranians call the *garmsir,* or "hot lands," as opposed to the *sardsir,* or "cold lands" of the high plateau.[61] The garmsir roughly corresponds to the realm of the date palm. North of Bandar Lingeh and 190 miles distant, at an altitude of about 3,000 feet, lies Lar, located south of the main Zagros range. This salient of territory has often had connections with the Gulf world and should be counted as its northern fringe.[62] The Lar princes, for example, played a major role in controlling the Persian Gulf ports, especially Bandar Abbas, during the Safavid period.[63] The Lar area is known for its Sunni population, many of whom migrated to the Arab side of the Gulf over the past century.

Just as the Iranian coast is bounded by barren limestone and sandstone mountain ranges, the Arabian coast is hemmed in by deserts and salt flats (*sabkha*).[64] From the Shatt al-Arab all the way to the Musandam Peninsula at the mouth of the Gulf, the coastline is made up of sand and gravel plains and is everywhere below 200 meters in altitude. In Oman, the Jabal Akhdar Mountains, rising to 10,000 feet, cut off the coast from inland areas. The Arabian shoreline is backed by desert, including the awesome Rub' al-Khali, which in places continues down to the water's edge. There are some mangrove swamps, especially on the coast between Abu Dhabi and Dubai, similar to those on the Iranian side around the Clarence Strait (between Qishm island and the mainland). There are no rivers, but there are a number of inlets or *khurs* where settlements have been founded, such as at Dubai and Sharjah. Kuwait, surrounded by sandy desert, has the largest bay and the finest natural harbor in the Gulf.[65]

People of the Dhow

The key determinant of the Gulf's trading seasons was the annual cycle of monsoon winds.[66] From the Arabic *mawsim,* meaning "season," the monsoon referred to the regular periods of northeast and southwest winds that blew across the Indian Ocean. These winds resulted from the difference in temperature of the sea and the continental landmass of Asia. "The seasonal monsoons, blowing in opposite directions, determine the patterns of winds, ocean currents and rainfall, and it is within this rhythm of nature that Arabians travelling between India, Southern Arabia and East Africa came into contact with different cultures, races, religions and ideas. The *longue durée* or long rhythms of the climate, agriculture and seaborne activity determined basic social attitudes in terms of diet, technology and what goods the Arabians traded."[67] The dates when it was safe for dhows to sail were established with great precision. Hourani, for example, has reconstructed the likely schedule of the voyages between the Gulf and China that were made in the Abbasid period, the round trip taking a year and a half.[68] From the fall equinox through the winter, ships from the Gulf and India caught the northeast monsoon and sailed down to the East African coast. From the spring equinox to the summer the winds reversed, and the southwest monsoon carried the ships back. Alan Villiers, the intrepid Australian seaman, sailed in one such dhow on the eve of World War II and told the tale in the great classic *Sons of Sinbad.*[69] The long layover in the ports led to marriage and liaisons between Arab sailors and local women, and extensive business and social connections, and helped to create a "brotherhood of the sea" that tied together the Indian Ocean basin.

The sailing season dovetailed nicely with other aspects of the Gulf economy. Thus dates, the major product of the Gulf, were harvested from plantations along the Shatt al-Arab in August and September,[70] just in time for loading the dhows that would sail from Kuwait. Summer in the Gulf, when the dhows were laid up, was the time that the water was warm enough for pearling, so those who wanted to could sail in the winter and work the pearl beds in the summer. Pearling, which occupied a large part of the Gulf's population and produced much of its wealth, was however physically punishing, and the life of a diver was often a short one.[71]

The Environment's Effects

The physical environment has played a profound role in shaping society in the Gulf. The setting is well described by the British politician and journalist L. S. Amery, in his foreword to Arnold Wilson's classic history:

> A certain aroma of romance hangs round the name of the Persian Gulf, but those who know the region best are probably least disposed to regard it in a romantic light. It is an area of bleak coasts, torrid winds, and pitiless sunshine. The amenities of life are few and far between. Nature is in her fiercest humour and man has done little to improve upon her handiwork. The population is scanty, the standard of living low. Towns are few and insanitary; villages little more than clusters of mud huts. To a casual visitor it might seem a mere backwater to which civilization has scarcely penetrated.[72]

Similar climatic conditions led to similar material culture, architecture, dress, and diet among the people of the Gulf littoral. The primary diet always consisted of fish and dates, as confirmed by travelers such as Marco Polo and Ibn Battuta.[73] The climate may have also led to similar medical conditions, as explored in a pioneering work on the medical history of the Persian Gulf by Dr. Iraj Nabipour.[74]

The geography and climate of the Gulf have also had a profound effect upon the pattern of settlement. Here a distinction should be made between a port and a harbor. "Most ports have poor harbours, and many fine harbours see few ships. Harbour is a physical concept, a shelter for ships; port is an economic concept, a centre of land-sea exchange, which requires good access to a hinterland even more than to a sea-linked foreland."[75] With the exception of Kuwait Bay, there were few good harbors in the Gulf. The main port cities in southern Iran—Bushehr, Lingeh, and Bandar Abbas—all had anchorages far out at sea. According to a visitor, in the early twentieth century, "none of these [Persian] ports, though much business is done there, possesses an apology even for a wharf, jetty or landing place of any sort or description."[76] On the Arabian coast, even in Kuwait, deep-water steamers had to anchor a mile offshore.[77] The major Saudi oil terminal at Ras Tanura extends some 9 miles into the sea, another indication of the very shallow shoreline. Muscat, located outside the Gulf proper but well integrated into the Gulf world, has a good but small protected harbor.

Shortage of Water and Wood

The shortage of fresh water has always been a serious issue on the Gulf littoral, in light of the scanty rainfall and high temperatures. However, local people overcame the problem of transportation of water. In the sixteenth century, the great island emporium of Hormuz—which had virtually no water—required over 300 *terradas* (small boats) per day to bring water from the neighboring island of Qishm.[78] Drinking water for

Kuwait was provided by special water dhows that brought it from the Shatt al-Arab, until desalination facilities were built in the early 1950s.[79] In towns along the Persian coast, including Bandar Abbas, Bandar Lingeh, and Bushehr, cisterns (*birka*) for collecting the scanty rainwater were in widespread use.[80] In Bahrain, people obtained fresh water from underwater springs near shore.

Two inventions attributed to Iranian ingenuity provided successful strategies for dealing with the extreme climate.[81] The underground aqueduct, known in Persian as *qanat* or *kariz* and in Arabic as *falaj* (pl. *aflaj*), constructed in the mountain foothills, made settled life possible on much of the Iranian plateau and in highland areas of northern Oman. Aflaj were also built in the Hasa region of eastern Arabia, Qatif, Khobar, and Bahrain. Another Iranian invention, the *badgir* or windcatcher, was in widespread use in cities on both sides of the Gulf, especially Bandar Abbas and the Al Bastakiya neighborhood of Dubai (where they are known as *barjeel*), as well as in Bahrain, Qatar, and throughout the UAE.[82]

One of the most significant limitations was the lack of wood. Although this was a shipbuilding society, the wood to build them was usually imported from India (or East Africa) and cut according to the instructions of the dhow-builders in Kuwait and other places.[83] The lack of wood was undoubtedly one reason that Iran did not have a navy until the twentieth century. In the seventeenth and early eighteenth century, the Ya'rubid dynasty in Oman resorted to Indian shipyards to build their navy.[84] Even the Ottomans were unable to establish a shipyard at Basra and had to build ships on the upper Euphrates.[85]

The lack of wood also affected the architecture and town structure. The ceilings of houses on both sides of the Gulf were made of mangrove poles obtained from East Africa, which determined the size of the rooms.[86] Thus the cargo of poles collected by Villiers' dhow was used to build a palace in Riyadh. Such poles were also widely used on the Iranian side of the Gulf, for example, in the fortress at Siraf, built in the early twentieth century.

Housing for most people along the Arab coast and southern Iranian littoral consisted of simple huts made of palm fronds (Arabic, *barasti;* Persian, *kapar*). These were the most effective adaptation to a hot, damp climate.[87] In Dubai, many people lived in *barasti* houses well into the 1960s,[88] and in Oman, until the mid-1970s or later.[89] "These houses were the nearest thing to a bedouin tent among the settled people: they could if necessary be dismantled and removed to another place," according to Lienhardt.[90]

More substantial buildings on the coast were constructed of coral rock (Arabic *farush* or *hasa*; Persian *sang-i marjan*). The mining of this coral from shallow water on the Arab side was a dangerous occupation that took place mainly in the summer months.[91] The reason that much of the great fortress that the Portuguese built on Hormuz in the sixteenth century survives is that it was built of locally mined coral, whereas most other historic forts in Iran were built of mud and are crumbling today.[92]

A CULTURE OF MIGRATION

An obvious difference between the littoral areas and other parts of the Middle East was the absence of a settled peasantry (except in Bahrain, Qatif/Ahsa, and Oman) and the low level of urbanization in the Gulf. Whereas most people in Iran and Arabia were tied to the land and oasis-based agriculture, the Khalijis were tied to the sea, and they could easily move if dissatisfied. In a region where boats and not land constituted capital, it was easy to sail away and reestablish themselves elsewhere and there was little a ruler could do to stop this. To cite a well-known example, when in 1910 Shaikh Mubarak of Kuwait demanded higher payments, the three leading pearl fishermen deserted with their several hundred boats, which was a crippling blow to the local economy and the prestige of the shaikh. They defected to Bahrain and stayed there until the shaikh made concessions to ensure their return.[93]

It was common for tribes to migrate, both over their home range (Arabic, *dira*) on land and from one side of the Gulf to the other. For example, drought conditions in the interior helped push Arabian tribes toward the coast in the late eighteenth century, where new dynasties and states were founded: the Al Sabah established themselves in Kuwait in the 1750s, while those under the leadership of the Al Khalifa migrated to Zubara (on the northwest coast of Qatar) in 1766 and ultimately came to rule over Bahrain in 1782. The most important feature of new towns such as Kuwait, Qatar, Zubara, and Bahrain is that they were free ports with no customs taxes, and as such attracted regional merchants.[94]

There was also the pull factor of favorable ecological conditions on the Iranian coast, which, when unprotected, attracted Arab settlers. In the eleventh century many Arabs moved from the Omani coast to southern Iran where they established the city of (old) Hormuz. In the period after Nadir Shah's death in 1747, a decades-long political struggle ensued in Iran during which there was no strong central government and the southern ports were largely autonomous. The German traveler Carsten Niebuhr, who visited the region in the 1760s, remarked that "the Arabs possess all the sea-coast of the Persian empire, from the mouths of the Euphrates, nearly to those of the Indus."[95] Some tribesmen, notably the Qawasim, were based at Sharjah and Ras al-Khaimah on the Arab shore but also governed Bander Lingeh, one of the most important Persian ports. They freely moved back and forth until the Tehran government, in line with its policy of reclaiming its own Gulf littoral, ultimately evicted them in 1887.[96]

This movement is exemplified by the Hawla or Hawala, groups of Sunni Arabs that migrated from Oman and the eastern coast of the Arabian peninsula to the Iranian side of the Gulf, between Bushehr and Bandar Abbas, probably starting in the eighteenth century.[97] They eventually returned to the Arab side, especially after the discovery of oil and the imposition of restrictive economic policies by Reza Shah in the 1930s. In the early 1900s Hawala were living in the UAE, Qatar, Bahrain, Hasa and on the island of Sirri.[98] Such Hawala, who were bilingual and at ease on either side of the Gulf, were Khalijis par excellence.

Since the arrival of the Najdis and their Bedouin culture in the eighteenth century, the tradition of the Arab tribal shaikh as the first among equals, bound to consult his tribesmen before taking action, militated against the rise of autocratic shaikhs. Political differences led to tribal splits and the formation of new tribes, not enforced allegiance. There was also something else in the Gulf that was lacking in other areas: the hope of striking it rich and the incentive to work hard to do so. The prospect of finding a valuable pearl, however improbable, gave hope to the poor pearl divers and sent them back to the pearl beds, year after year until they collapsed physically.[99] Significantly, nobody owned the pearl beds and anyone from the region was free to fish them and perhaps find his fortune. Likewise, the prospect of profitable voyages induced thousands of men to depart the Gulf annually in dhows throughout the Indian Ocean. There was uncertainty of reward, but hope that it would be forthcoming.[100] All this was very different from the poor peasants in Persian villages or Bedouin tribesmen trying to wrest a livelihood from the Arabian deserts. However, life was not necessarily rosy for people in the Gulf. Sailors and pearlers were not paid a salary but only received a share of the hoped-for profits. High levels of debt that effectively restricted one's freedom of action were common at all levels of society from the pearl divers to the sea captains (*nakhudas*).

If one thing characterized the Gulf and south Arabia, it was the constant emigration of people to other parts of the Indian Ocean basin. Because of poor ecological conditions the Gulf region could not support all its people, so migration became a way of life. "The people of Oman . . . have always needed to develop outside their own land if they are to rise above the lowest economic levels," according to John Wilkinson. "Almost to exist, therefore, they have traditionally operated overseas."[101] Aside from the Gulf proper the Hadhramawt, in southwest Arabia (present-day Yemen), was historically a large exporter of manpower, including merchants, mercenaries, and religious luminaries. The Hadhrami diaspora throughout the Indian Ocean, from the Malay world to southwest India to East Africa, has recently begun to attract scholars' attention.[102]

Society in the Gulf

Who, then, are the Khalijis? Historically, they are the descendants of the Ichthyophagi, the "fish eaters" that lived all around the coasts of East Africa, the Gulf ("Erythraean Sea"), southern Iran, and India who were mentioned by Greek and Latin writers. Like the Ichthyophagi, they share a similar lifestyle but not a common identity, except perhaps in the eyes of outsiders. There are, for example, clear differences between those living in the northern and southern Gulf on both sides: on the Arab side historians have discerned a "Greater Bahrain" and a "Greater Oman," while on the Iranian shore societies differ in Bushehr and Bandar Abbas. In some historical periods, however, when both sides of the Gulf were ruled by the same Arab shaikhs or tribes, the sense of common identity may have been stronger. Thus the kingdom of Hormuz included Qalhat (in Oman)[103] as virtually a second capital, and later Bahrain was ruled by Iran. Oman leased large portions of the Iranian coast around Bandar Abbas, while the Qawasim tribe controlled ports such as Bandar Lingeh, Sharjah, and Ras al-Khaimah. Clearly, much more research must be done before any conclusions can be reached about the nature of identity in the Persian Gulf.

The preoccupation of the Khalijis, past and present, has been business.[104] Probably due to limited local resources, Gulf residents have been renowned merchants since ancient times, when trade routes linked the Sealand (southern Mesopotamia), Dilmun (Bahrain), Magan (Oman), and the Indus area. As illustrated by Villiers, in modern times merchant families arose in the Gulf that dispatched family members to far-flung parts of the Indian Ocean to manage their interests there; a web of such merchants knitted together the trade of the Indian Ocean and operated efficiently in the absence of European interference, down to World War II.[105] The success of Dubai today as an El Dorado of commerce and tourism rests on this solid precedent. As M. R. Izady suggests, "the modern glittering shopping malls of Dubai, Sharjah, Abu Dhabi, Kish, Manama, and the like are just a modern version of what centuries ago the commercial centers such as Hormuz, Cong, Cameron, Basra, Siraf, Khat/Qatif, Suhar, and Muscat must have looked like."[106]

Life along the Gulf littoral, and on the sea itself, strongly influenced the literature, folk beliefs, and religious practices of the Khalijis and set them apart from those living inland. The severe climate also wrought havoc with people's mental health. The mental universe of the coastal dwellers was explored in the writings of the prominent Iranian author Ghulam-Husain Sa'idi (d. 1985) in his anthropological study, *Ahl-i Hava* (People of the Wind, 1966), and his novel, *Tars va Larz* (Fear and Trembling, 1968).[107] For Sa'idi and most other Iranians, the Persian Gulf coast was an unfamiliar and isolated area remote from the world of urban Iran. There, the influence of Africa, Arabia, and India was strong. The most characteristic local ritual was that of the *zar* cults, which were of African origin but were also prevalent in Oman and East Africa.[108] More recently, the leading Iranian contemporary writer Moniru Ravanipur (b. 1954) has portrayed the beliefs, superstitions, and lifestyle of her native village of Jofreh near Bushehr, in the novel *Ahl-i Gharq* (The Drowned, 1989).[109]

Another unique marker of Khaliji culture is its music, in which the songs of the pearl divers form an important musical tradition.[110] Each year the great Arab pearling fleets left port to the sounds of this music with its drumming "imbued with mystical, religious and symbolic meanings" and designed to strengthen the will of the divers as they headed off on their hazardous occupation.[111] "In every boat, whether pearling boat or cargo boat, there used to be a *naham,* a chanter. Some shipmasters vie to get first-class *nahams* and pay them well . . . The *naham* had a great influence on the sailors. They would take up their gruelling work with strength and vigour and, if the *naham* was really good, forget about their hardships."[112]

The Indian Connection

Any consideration of what distinguishes the Khalijis from other Middle Easterners must highlight their historic ties with India. (Countries in North Africa and the Levant, in contrast, were more closely tied to the Mediterranean and Europe). Since the first recorded trading voyages thousands of years ago, India has always been the primary trading partner with the Gulf and indeed the source of supplies, such as foodstuffs and wood, that were critical to the survival and prosperity of the Khalijis. The main exports of the Gulf were pearls, dates, and horses, which found ready markets there. Indian currency was used in the Gulf down to the twentieth century. The great prosperity of Basra and Hormuz was to a large extent based on the India trade. Bushehr was known as the "darvaza-yi Hind," or Gateway of India. By the time of World War I, the mail streamer from Bombay to Basra took only seven to eight days to make the passage.[113]

On a cultural and political level, Persia had a huge amount of interaction with South Asia in the period 1500–1900, as demonstrated by Juan Cole.[114] He notes in particular the linguistic affinity, with Persian widely taught and understood in India, as well as being the official language of the Mughal Empire. Indeed, since the population of the Indian subcontinent in 1600 (estimated at 120 million) dwarfed that of Persia itself (estimated at four to five million), there were many more Persian speakers in India than in Persia or the Gulf.[115] There were also religious groups in India that maintained close ties to Iran, such as Shi'i dynasties in the Deccan, Zoroastrians, and Isma'ilis.

Protecting the Indian Frontier

The major aim of both Portugal and Britain in the Gulf was to protect their Indian frontier. After Britain became a territorial power in India in the late eighteenth century, and especially after it abolished the Mughal dynasty in 1858 and assumed direct rule, political and security ties with India were the most important fact of life in the Gulf. The major rationales for British involvement were to put an end to the piracy, slavery, and the arms trade that flourished there and disrupted maritime traffic on the route to India. These concerns led Britain to establish control over the Gulf after the 1820s and establish political ties with ruling shaikhs. Britain enforced a maritime truce and instituted a system of indirect rule identical to the one it had developed in India since the late eighteenth century, as explained by James Onley.[116] Officials from the Indian Political Service served as its representatives there, with the top official, the Resident, based at Bushehr and assisted by officers posted around the Gulf.

Britain also relied on Indian manpower to police the Gulf. Twice in the nineteenth century when London sought to stymie Persian incursions against Herat, it mounted expeditions to the Gulf to threaten and punish the shah. In such cases, Indian troops were considered suitable for duty. Thus, after the Persian army besieged Herat in 1837, the Indian navy occupied Kharg Island from June 1838 until March 1842.[117] When the Persian army beseiged Herat in May 1856 and later occupied it, a Persian Expeditionary Force occupied Kharg and Bushehr in December and Muhammara was captured the following March. By this time one-third of the Bombay Army had been sent to Persia, endangering security in India. The war was settled by the Treaty of Paris (March 4, 1857), and the last imperial troops did not leave Persian soil until February 1858.[118]

The policing actions and small wars undertaken by Britain in the Gulf in the nineteenth century were minor affairs compared with the commitment of Indian forces on the side of Britain in two world wars. Some 600,000 Indian troops were sent to Mesopotamia to secure the Ottoman vilayets of Basra and Baghdad during World War I. "This enormous outpouring of men and material from India transformed much of Mesopotamia, above all the province of Basra, into a de facto Indian colony," according to Thomas R. Metcalf.[119] This was the only time in history that India directly controlled southern Iraq.

ARABS, PERSIANS, AND KHALIJIS

In reconstructing the history of the region, it is not fruitful to engage in polemics such as whether the proper name should be the Persian Gulf or the Arabian Gulf. One recent book even flaunted the title *The Ottoman Gulf*, as a reminder that the Ottomans were players in the region in the sixteenth and again in the late nineteenth and early twentieth centuries.[120] (The Ottomans themselves referred to it as the Gulf of Basra.) As Jean Aubin recommended back in 1953, there should not be a hegemonic Iranian or Arab historiography that improperly "iranizes" or "arabizes" the littoral population and its culture.[121] The Gulf region has always been a mixed one ethnically, linguistically, and religiously and should not be considered a mere annex of either the Iranian or Arab world.

As is evident from the chapters in this book, the Gulf has been united under the same political leadership only rarely in history, notable indigenous examples being the Sasanians in the pre-Islamic period and the kingdom of Hormuz in the post-Mongol period. Hormuz, indeed, is an excellent example of a thalassocracy (sea rule, from the Greek *thalassa,* sea), as first described by Thucydides in the fifth century B.C. The amirs of Kish in the twelfth century C.E. and the Qawasim in the nineteenth century are other examples of the type of local maritime polities that typically controlled and contested parts of the Gulf. The usual situation has been for powerful city-states or port cities to rise and fall, with none dominating the others. In the era of imperial intrusion, although the Portuguese in the sixteenth century controlled the area around the Strait of Hormuz they infrequently ventured into the upper Gulf. Only the British, in the nineteenth and early twentieth centuries, dominated the entire Gulf. The situation today resembles that which has prevailed for the past 500 years, in which an imperial hegemon—now the United States—tries to maintain stability thanks to naval superiority but is not able to exert complete control over the regional states.

THE IRANIAN ELEMENT IN THE GULF

Most of the history written about the Gulf after the coming of Islam tends to privilege the Arab element at the expense of the Iranian.[122] Iranians, in fact, are often denigrated for their fear of the sea or lack of nautical ability. The opinion of Curzon represents a harsh consensus:

> Brave and victorious as the Persians have shown themselves at different epochs on land, no one has ever ventured so far to belie the national character as to insinuate that they have betrayed the smallest proficiency at sea. It would be difficult, and perhaps impossible, in the history of the world to find a country possessing two considerable seaboards, and admirably suited for trade, which has so absolutely ignored its advantages in both respects, and which has never in modern times either produced a navigator, or manned a merchant fleet, or fought a naval battle.[123]

One of the major reasons for this line of thinking is the historic lack of interest by Iranian dynasties in projecting their power into the Gulf. Despite Sasanian domination of the Gulf, evidence of a Sasanian navy is lacking. During the Abbasid period, major voyages launched from Basra, Siraf, and Suhar to as far as China were organized by merchants in the port cities. As Hourani reminds us, the Abbasids aimed to meld Arab and Iranian together in one Islamic society, in which for hundreds of years Arabic was the language of scholarship. Thus the great Muslim geographers of the tenth century, even if Persian, wrote in Arabic. It is therefore perhaps not unusual that there is more literary mention of Arabs than Persians in the sea trade.[124] However, it is clear that Persians continued to play an active role in the Gulf and beyond. Many of the nautical terms in widespread usage in the Indian Ocean were Persian, such as *nakhuda* (captain), *bandar* (port), and *shahbandar* (port master). Likewise many of the names of captains in the tenth-century *Aja'ib al-Hind*, a collection of sea stories collected by a captain from Siraf, were Persian.[125] A glittering succession of independent port cities on the Iranian side—Siraf, Kish, and Hormuz—dominated the Gulf from the ninth to the seventeenth centuries.

It was not until the Safavid period that Iranian governments sought a naval arm in the Gulf, and not until the time of Reza Shah that they began to acquire it in earnest. The fact that Persian kings did not have a navy meant that they could not prevent Albuquerque's conquest of Hormuz in 1515, and in order to evict the Portuguese they had to depend on English ships of the East India Company in 1622. Numerous Safavid requests for ships or naval transport so that they could attack Oman or the Portuguese were refused. It was not until the 1740s that an Iranian ruler, Nadir Shah, sought to control the Gulf.[126] His attempt to build a navy met familiar obstacles: refusal on the part of the English and the Dutch to sell him ships and a lack of wood to construct them himself, excepting what could be imported from India or obtained at great effort from the Caspian forests. Although he had a Persian admiral, most of the seamen in his fleet were Arabs, with some Baluchis and Indians.[127]

The early Qajar monarchs were not particularly interested in the Gulf or able to assert themselves there; they were preoccupied with threats from Russia in the northwest and the reconquest of Herat in the northeast. The Persian government was content to let the British provide security in the Gulf, although it was periodically rebuffed in requests for naval assistance to retake Bahrain. Not until 1888 did the Tehran government finally acquire a modern warship to patrol Gulf waters.[128] In a similar manner neither the contemporary Wahhabis in Arabia nor the Ottomans made a serious effort to exert control in the Gulf.

The Name Game

The rise of pan-Arabism in the post–World War II period and the sharpening of political tensions between Iran and Arab states have led to an unfortunate lexical struggle over the proper name of the Gulf.[129] The same impulse has led Iranians to restore the classical name (Arvand Rud) of the Shatt al-Arab, the waterway forming the border between Iran and Iraq.[130] It has also led some modern Iranian historians to emphasize the eternal Persian nature of the Gulf and deemphasize its hybridity. In a similar manner, Arab states now insist on using the term "Arabian Gulf."

What, in fact, does the historical record show? According to Potts, the name "Persian Gulf" probably came into use at the time of Darius I (522–486 B.C.). "In older Mesopotamian cuneiform sources it had always been the Lower Sea and in one case the 'Sea of Magan,' but around 500 B.C. the Greek geographer Hecataeus . . . used the term *Persikos kolpos,* i.e. Persian Gulf, for the first time in a written source."[131] Herodotus (fifth century B.C.) refers to the modern Red Sea as "the Arabian Gulf,"[132] and the wider region including the Persian Gulf, Red Sea, Arabian Sea, and Gulf of Oman was the "Erythraean Sea" as described in the famous *Periplus of the Erythraean Sea* (about second century A.D.).[133] The earliest Islamic text on seafaring in the Indian Ocean uses the Arabic term *Bahr Fars,* "Sea of Fars," which came into general use.[134] Much later accounts of the Portuguese use the term Persian Gulf (*Sino Persico*), and this term was subsequently employed by European mapmakers, and used by the British, for the past two centuries.[135] All the extensive publications of the British on the region until recent years used the term "Persian Gulf."

A campaign to replace the term "Persian Gulf" with "Arabian Gulf" or "Arab Gulf" was carried out by President Gamal Abdel Nasser of Egypt starting in the 1950s in his bid to promote pan-Arabism and oppose Iranian hegemony in the region. After the revolution in Iraq in 1958, the Baathist regime took up the campaign with gusto in an attempt to cultivate influence in the shaikhdoms of the Gulf and among ethnic Arabs in the southwest Iranian province of Khuzistan (now referred to as Arabistan).[136] A report in *The Times* of August 5, 1958 (only three weeks after the coup overthrowing the monarchy), recorded an Iranian protest that the new government of Abd al-Karim Qasim had decided to start using the term "Arabian Gulf" instead of "Persian Gulf."[137] "By 1968, however, all Arab states, including the Gulf Emirates passed laws and issued decrees making the use of the term 'Arabian Gulf' compulsory in all communications with the outside world."[138] Subsequent usage in Gulf Cooperation Council (GCC) communiqués of the term Arabian Gulf has continued to anger the post-revolutionary government in Tehran.

Compromise suggestions, for example, that the body of water be referred to as the "Islamic Gulf," have not been embraced by either side. While many Arabs would apparently accept the term "the Gulf" without a specific referent (as in GCC), the Iranians insist that the full historic name be used. After the National Geographic Society in Washington published a new edition of their world atlas in late 2004 adding in parentheses the term "Arabian Gulf" under the term "Persian Gulf," as an alternative secondary name already familiar to many, Iranians both in Iran and abroad raised a firestorm of protest and insisted that the term be withdrawn. The society updated its online maps to include a summary of the dispute and a statement that the waterway was "historically and most commonly known as the Persian Gulf."[139] At present, the term "Persian Gulf" is recognized by the United Nations and by the U.S. State Department, although the Defense Department began occasional use of the term "Arabian Gulf" in September 1987 in deference to its Arab allies during the Iran-Iraq War.[140] The U.S. Air Force and U.S. Army now use "Persian Gulf" almost exclusively, whereas the U.S. Navy (whose Fifth Fleet is headquartered in Bahrain) uses "Arabian Gulf."

What is clear is that there will be no resolution of this issue as the competing nationalisms of both sides will not permit any compromise. Just as other geographic areas carry dual designations (such as the English Channel for Britons and La Manche for the French, the Falklands/Malvinas islands off South America or the body of water between Japan and Korea (Sea of Japan/East Sea), the terms "Arabian" and "Persian" Gulf will continue to be used as symbols of regional rivalry.

CONCLUSION

"The Gulf is not oil. The Gulf is its people and its land," Kuwaiti historian Muhammad Rumaihi reminds readers. "So it was before the discovery of oil, and so it will remain when the oil disappears. Oil is no more than a historical phase in this part of the Arab world—and a rather short one at that."[141] Although the contemporary world is riveted on the price of oil and the stability of the Gulf due to dependence on its oil and gas, in this book oil hardly figures at all. Rather, the important role the Gulf has played in history, its outward orientation toward the Indian Ocean, and the distinct culture of its inhabitants, the Khalijis, as well as their interactions with outsiders, have formed its subject. What persists is the unique role the Khalijis have carved out for themselves in marketing their only valuable local resource—first pearls and now oil.

The Persian Gulf's continued strategic significance is not in doubt: it is a key source of the world's energy and was the location of a revolution and three major wars at the end of the twentieth century. It may well be the venue of future conflicts. There is every indication, in short, that the Gulf will continue to play a critical international role in the twenty-first century. It is vital for both outsiders and insiders to better understand its past and to account for prevailing present-day attitudes about the region. This book represents an unprecedented international collaborative effort that seeks to address these important issues, set an agenda for future research, and help reframe our understanding of the Gulf.

NOTES

1. I would like to express my sincere thanks to several colleagues who read an earlier version of this chapter and provided helpful comments and corrections: Richard Bulliet, M. R. Izady, Rudi Matthee, Shahnaz Nadjmabadi, J. E. Peterson, and Haideh Sahim. In addition, Willem Floor and Ahmad Ashraf provided help along the way, and Karen Rohan offered valuable editorial suggestions. Needless to say neither they nor the participants at the conference on which this book is based necessarily agree with my conclusions.
2. D. T. Potts, *The Arabian Gulf in Antiquity,* vol. 2, *From Alexander the Great to the Coming of Islam* (Oxford: Clarendon Press, 1990), 349–50.
3. "Location on the shore transcends differing influences from an inland that is very diverse, both in geographic and cultural terms, so that the shore folk have more in common with other shore folk thousands of kilometers away on some other shore of the ocean than they do with those in their immediate hinterland. Surat and Mombasa have more in common with each other than they do with inland cities such as Nairobi or Ahmadabad." Michael N. Pearson, "Littoral Society: The Concept and the Problems," *Journal of World History* 17, no. 4 (2006): 353–54.
4. Rupert Hay, *The Persian Gulf States* (Washington, D. C.: The Middle East Institute, 1959), 148.
5. John Peterson, "Oman's Diverse Society: Northern Oman," *Middle East Journal* 58, no. 1 (2004): 34.

> The Political Agent enumerated the languages as: *Arabic* spoken by natives; *Persian* by some natives of Persia who have settled recently in Oman for trade purposes as well as by some families who are of Persian extraction and whose residence dates from the Persian occupation of Muscat; *Baluchi* by the Baluch fishermen and others who form the majority of the servant class throughout State; *English* by the Political Agent and his staff, as well as certain Goanese and other merchants; *French* by the French Consul and certain Belgian arms merchants; *Swahili* by Negro slaves and their relatives; *Somali* by natives of Somaliland who visit Oman's shores yearly in search of dates, etc.; *Hindustani* by the large bulk of the educated population; *Sindi* by Hindu merchants from Sind and by the Khoja community who have within the last century settled in Oman and are rapidly coming to be regarded as part of the Arab population; *Gujarati* by a number of Hindu traders from the southern part of Bombay Presidency, residence of some of whom in Oman dates back for 150 years and possibly more; *Portuguese* or *Goanese* by the Goanese population, merchants, domestic servants, etc., who number a dozen souls or more; *Pushtu* by Baluch and Afghan arms' dealers who are still to be met with occasionally in bazaars; *Armenian* and *Turkish* by Armenian merchants and secretaries and by a few Turkish soldiers who having deserted from the Turkish army operating in Yemen have migrated east, and taken service under the sympathetic ruler of Oman.

W. G. Grey, "Trade and Races of Oman," *Quarterly Journal of the Mythic Society* 2, no. 2 (January 1911), p. 4. Somali, Portuguese, and Armenian could probably be deleted from today's list.

6. Juan R. I. Cole, "Rival Empires of Trade and Imami Shi'ism in Eastern Arabia, 1300–1800," *International Journal of Middle East Studies* 19, no. 2 (1987): 177–203. In this important article, Cole traces how "the Baharina [indigenous Shi'i Arabs of Bahrain] gradually traded the radical, egalitarian Isma'ilism of the ninth through 11th century Carmathian movement for a more quietist version of Shi'ism—the Twelver or Imami branch—which Sunni rulers considered less objectionable" (p. 178).
7. Walter J. Fischel, "The Region of the Persian Gulf and its Jewish Settlements in Islamic Times," in *Alexander Marx Jubilee Volume,* English Section (New York: The Jewish Theological Seminary of America, 1950), 204–29.
8. Cited below, page 221.
9. AHR Forum, "Oceans of History," *The American Historical Review* 111, no. 3 (June 2006): 717–80. These articles treat the history of the Atlantic, the Pacific, and the Mediterranean; notably, the Indian Ocean is absent.
10. Kären Wigen, "Introduction," ibid., 717.
11. Willem Floor, *The Persian Gulf: A Political and Economic History of Five Port Cities 1500–1730* (Washington, D.C.: Mage, 2006), 601.
12. John E. Wills, Jr., "Maritime Asia, 1500–1800: The Interactive Emergence of European Domination," *American Historical Review* 98, no 1 (February 1993): 84–5.
13. A good example is J. B. Kelly, *Britain and the Persian Gulf 1795–1880* (Oxford: Clarendon Press, 1968; repr. 1991).
14. A source of inspiration for this book is the work of Braudel on the Mediterranean (Fernand Braudel, *The Mediterranean and the Mediterranean World in the Age of Philip II,* 2 vols., trans. Siân Reynolds, 2nd. rev. ed. [New York: Harper and Row, 1975]). Only one recent book by a scholar from the Gulf has embraced a Braudelian approach to the area (M. Reda Bhacker, *Trade and Empire in Muscat and Zanzibar: Roots of British Domination* [London: Routledge, 1992]). Braudel's insights have now been applied to the Indian Ocean: see K. N. Chaudhuri, *Trade and Civilisation in the Indian Ocean: An Economic History from the Rise of Islam to 1750* (Cambridge: Cambridge University Press, 1985) and *Asia Before Europe: Economy and Civilisation of the Indian Ocean from the Rise of Islam to 1750* (Cambridge: Cambridge University Press, 1990); also Michael Pearson, *The Indian Ocean,* Seas in History (London: Routledge, 2003). The French historian Jean Aubin set the standard for investigating the history of the Persian Gulf with many studies highlighting the role of Hormuz. See especially "Les princes d'Ormuz du XIIIe au XVe siècle," *Journal Asiatique* 241 (1953): 77–137 and "Le royaume d'Ormuz au début du XVIe siècle," *Mare Luso-Indicum* II (1973): 77–179. A concise and helpful overview of the expansion of merchants and Islam in the Indian Ocean is provided by Patricia Risso in *Merchants and Faith: Muslim Commerce and Culture in the Indian Ocean,* New Perspectives on Asian History (Boulder, CO: Westview Press, 1995). Another ambitious effort to tie together the modern history of the western Indian Ocean is by Beatrice Nicolini, *Makran, Oman and Zanzibar: Three-Terminal Cultural Corridor in the Western Indian Ocean (1799–1856),* Islam in Africa 3 (Leiden, Netherlands: Brill, 2004). An Iranian scholar, Mohammad Bagher Vosoughi [Muhammad Baqir Vusuqi], has recently produced a stream of publications on the Persian Gulf in the medieval period. For example, see *Tarikh-i muhajirat-i aqvam dar Khalij-i Fars* [The History of the Emigration of Peoples in the Persian Gulf] (Shiraz: Intisharat-i Danishnama-yi Fars, 1380/2002). The numerous works of Willem Floor on the Gulf from about 1500 to 1800 contain a wealth of valuable detail and must also be mentioned. See especially *The Persian Gulf: A Political and Economic History of Five Port Cities 1500–1730* and *The Persian Gulf: The Rise of the Gulf Arabs; The Politics of Trade on the Persian Littoral, 1747–1792* (Washington, D.C.: Mage, 2006 and 2007).
15. Khaldoun Hasan al-Naqeeb, *Society and State in the Gulf and Arab Peninsula: A Different Perspective,* trans. L. M. Kenny (London and New York: Routledge for the Centre

for Arab Unity Studies, 1990); Assem Dessouki, "Social and Political Dimensions of the Historiography of the Arab Gulf," in *Statecraft in the Middle East: Oil, Historical Memory, and Popular Culture,* ed. Eric Davis and Nicolas Gavrielides (Miami: Florida International University Press, 1991), 92–115 (with citations of relevant works).

16. Muhammad Ali Khan Sadid al-Saltana, *Tarikh-i Masqat va Uman, Bahrain va Qatar va ravabit-i anha ba Iran* (1933), ed. A. Iqtidari (Tehran, Iran: Dunya-yi kitab, 1370/1991).
17. See the thoughtful discussion in Patricia Risso, "Cross-Cultural Perceptions of Piracy: Maritime Violence in the Western Indian Ocean and Persian Gulf Region during a Long Eighteenth Century," *Journal of World History* 12 (2001): 293–319.
18. Sultan Muhammad Al-Qasimi, *The Myth of Arab Piracy in the Gulf,* 2nd ed. (London: Routledge, 1988). The most thorough treatment is Charles E. Davies, *The Blood-Red Arab Flag: An Investigation into Qasimi Piracy 1797–1820* (Exeter, UK: University of Exeter Press, 1997).
19. Especially J. G. Lorimer, *Gazetteer of the Persian Gulf, Oman and Central Arabia* (Calcutta, India: Superintendent Government Printing, 1908 and 1915; repr. Gerrards Cross, Buckinghamshire, UK: Archive Editions, 1986), in 9 volumes.
20. Several collections of old maps of the Gulf have been published: see Dejanirah Couto, Jean-Louis Bacqué-Grammont, and Mahmoud Taleghani, eds., *Historical Atlas of the Persian Gulf (Sixteenth to Eighteenth Centuries)* (Turnhout, Belgium: Brepols, 2006); Sultan bin Muhammad Al-Qasimi, ed., *The Gulf in Historic Maps 1478–1861,* 2nd ed. (Leicester, UK: Thinkprint Ltd., 1999); Mohammad-Reza Sahab et al., eds., *Persian Gulf: Atlas of Old and Historical Maps (3000 B.C.–2000 A.D.),* 2 vols. (Tehran, Iran: Center for Documents and Diplomatic History with the Cooperation of Tehran University, 2005).
21. For decades the standard history has been Arnold T. Wilson, *The Persian Gulf: An Historical Sketch from the Earliest Times to the Beginning of the Twentieth Century* (London: George Allen and Unwin, 1928; repr. 1959). This can be supplemented with Alvin J. Cottrell, ed., *The Persian Gulf States: A General Survey* (Baltimore: The Johns Hopkins University Press, 1980). A new treatment in Persian is Muhammad Baqir Vusuqi, *Tarikh-i Khalij-i Fars va mamalik-i hamjavar* [The History of the Persian Gulf and its Bordering Territories] (Tehran, Iran: Intisharat-i Samt, 1384/2005). A book by Svat Soucek, *The Persian Gulf: Its Past and Present* (Costa Mesa, CA: Mazda Publishers, 2008) appeared just as this book went to press.
22. In the vicinity of the Gulf we have recent books on the history of the Black Sea and the Caspian Sea, which, like the Gulf, have recently become the focus of international attention and competition for petroleum resources: Charles King, *The Black Sea: A History* (Oxford: Oxford University Press, 2004) and Guive Mirfendereski, *A Diplomatic History of the Caspian Sea: Treaties, Diaries, and Other Stories* (New York: Palgrave, 2001). The Red Sea—a historical competitor of the Persian Gulf as a conduit between Europe and Asia—is another body of water that deserves further research. The Society for Arabian Studies has recently carried out a Red Sea Project. Published proceedings to date include: P. Lunde and A. Porter, eds., *Trade and Travel in the Red Sea Region,* Society for Arabian Studies, Monograph No. 2/B.A.R. International Series 1269 (Oxford: Archaeopress, 2004); Janet Starkey, ed., *People of the Red Sea,* Society for Arabian Studies, Monograph No. 3/B.A.R. International Series 1395 (Oxford: Archaeopress, 2005); and Janet Starkey, Paul Starkey, and Tony Wilkinson, eds., *Natural Resources and Cultural Connections of the Red Sea,* Society for Arabian Studies, Monograph No. 5/B.A.R. International Series 1661 (Oxford: Archaeopress, 2007).
23. Material on the largest Arab port cities (Kuwait, Manama, Doha, Abu Dhabi, Dubai, Sharjah, Ras al-Khaimah, Muscat, and Mutrah) is collected in Richard Trench, ed., *Arab Gulf Cities,* 4 vols. (Slough, UK: Archives Editions, 1994). See now Nelida Fuccaro, *Histories of City and State in the Persian Gulf: Manama Since 1800* (Cambridge: Cambridge University Press, 2009). This important rethinking of the history of the Gulf focuses on urbanism and indigenous populations, as opposed to tribalism and external influences that have traditionally dominated scholarship of the region.
24. Floor, *Five Port Cities,* 1–2.

25. Lawrence Potter, "The Port of Siraf: Historical Memory and Iran's Role in the Persian Gulf," in *Proceedings of the International Congress of Siraf Port* (Bushehr, Iran: Bushehr Branch of Iranology Foundation, 2005), 28–49.
26. André Wink, "From the Mediterranean to the Indian Ocean: Medieval History in Geographic Perspective," *Comparative Studies in Society and History* 44 (2002): 418.
27. R. J. Barendse, *The Arabian Seas: The Indian Ocean World of the Seventeenth Century* (Armonk, NY: M. E. Sharpe, 2002), 40.
28. Michel Tuchscherer, "Trade and Port Cities in the Red Sea – Gulf of Aden Region in the Sixteenth and Seventeenth Century," in *Modernity and Culture: From the Mediterranean to the Indian Ocean,* ed. Leila Tarazi Fawaz and C. A. Bayly (New York: Columbia University Press, 2002), 29.
29. Peter Lienhardt, *Shaikhdoms of Eastern Arabia* (New York: Palgrave, 2001), 116–17.
30. Frauke Heard-Bey, *From Trucial States to United Arab Emirates,* new ed. (London: Longman, 1996), 258–59.
31. Lienhardt, *Shaikhdoms of Eastern Arabia*, 117.
32. Basra lay 12 miles from the Tigris and was connected by two canals. (G. Le Strange, *The Lands of the Eastern Caliphate: Mesopotamia, Persia, and Central Asia from the Moslem Conquest to the Time of Timur* (Cambridge: Cambridge University Press, 1905; repr. Lahore: Al-Biruni, 1977), 44.
33. John C. Wilkinson, *The Imamate Tradition of Oman,* Cambridge Middle East Library (Cambridge: Cambridge University Press, 1987), 47.
34. Lorimer, *Gazetteer,* vol. 9, 1761–62. At this time Sharjah had a population of about 15,000.
35. Naval Intelligence Division, British Admiralty, *Persia,* Geographical Handbook Series ([Oxford: Oxford University Press?], 1945), 545 and George N. Curzon, *Persia and the Persian Question,* vol. 2 (London: Longmans, Green, 1892; repr. London: Frank Cass, 1966), 198.
36. Lorimer, *Gazetteer,* vol. 7, 339.
37. My thanks to Dr. Iraj Nabipour for consulting old sailors in Bushehr to determine this information.
38. Easa Saleh Al-Gurg, *The Wells of Memory: An Autobiography* (London: John Murray, 1998), 4–5.
39. "Iranian Smugglers Thrive Across Hormuz," Reuters (Khasab, Oman), May 7, 2000 (online).
40. According to Istakhri, cited in Le Strange, *Lands of the Eastern Caliphate*, 258. Excavations in the 1970s revealed that the walls of Siraf enclosed an area of more than 250 hectares (see David Whitehouse, "Excavations at Siraf: Sixth Interim Report," *Iran* 12 [1974]: 2.)
41. Here I accept the reasoning of Floor, who suggests 40,000 as the maximum population of Hormuz in the winter season. (Floor, *Five Port Cities*, 16.) Others commonly cite a figure of 50,000 at the beginning of the sixteenth century proposed by Jean Aubin in "Le royaume d'Ormuz," 150.
42. R. A. Carter, K. Challis, S. M. N. Priestman, and H. Tofighian, "The Bushehr Hinterland: Results of the First Season of the Iranian-British Archaeological Survey of Bushehr Province, November–December 2004," *Iran* 44 (2006): 63–103.
43. Stephen R. Grummon, "The Rise and Fall of the Arab Shaykhdom of Bushire: 1750–1850," (PhD diss., Johns Hopkins University, 1985), 98–99.
44. Rhoads Murphey, "On the Evolution of the Port City," in *Brides of the Sea: Port Cities of Asia from the 16th–20th Centuries,* ed. Frank Broeze (Kensington, Australia: New South Wales University Press, 1989), 225.
45. Al-Muqaddasi, *The Best Divisions for Knowledge of the Regions: A Translation of* Ahsan al-Taqasim fi Ma'rifat al-Aqalim, trans. B. A. Collins and M. H. al-Tai (Reading, UK: Garnet Publishing for The Centre for Muslim Contribution to Civilisation, 1994), 89.
46. Ibid., 371.
47. Lewis Pelly, "Visit to Lingah, Kishm, and Bunder Abbass," *Journal of the Royal Geographical Society of London* 34 (1864): 252. I am grateful to William Beeman for providing a copy of this article.

48. Vanessa Martin, "Slavery and Black Slaves in Iran in the Nineteenth Century," in *The Qajar Pact: Bargaining, Protest and the State in Nineteenth-Century Persia* (London: I. B. Tauris, 2005), 150–69; Thomas M. Ricks, "Slaves and Slave Traders in the Persian Gulf, 18th and 19th Centuries: An Assessment," *Slavery and Abolition* 9, no. 3 (1988): 60–70.
49. Curzon, *Persia and the Persian Question*, 409.
50. There is a good discussion of this concerning Hormuz in Floor, *Five Port Cities*, 17.
51. Tuchscherer, "Trade and Port Cities in the Red Sea – Gulf of Aden Region," 32.
52. Jerry H. Bentley, "Sea and Ocean Basins as Frameworks of Historical Analysis," *Geographical Review* 89, no. 2 (April 1999): 215–24.
53. Ibid., 234–35.
54. Peter Reeves, Frank Broeze, and Kenneth McPherson, "Studying the Asian Port City," in Broeze, *Brides of the Sea*, 35.
55. Kären Wigen, "Introduction," in *Seascapes: Maritime Histories, Littoral Cultures, and Transoceanic Exchanges*, ed. Jerry H. Bentley, Renate Bridenthal, and Kären Wigen, Perspectives on the Global Past (Honolulu: University of Hawai'i Press, 2007), 17.
56. This thesis is developed by M. R. Izady in "The Gulf's Ethnic Diversity: An Evolutionary History," in *Security in the Persian Gulf: Origins, Obstacles, and the Search for Consensus*, ed. Lawrence G. Potter and Gary G. Sick (New York: Palgrave, 2002), 33–90.
57. King, *The Black Sea*, 7.
58. For excellent maps by Dr. Izady illustrating the cultural boundaries, languages, and religions of the Gulf world, see the website of the Gulf/2000 project located at http://gulf2000.columbia.edu/maps.shtml.
59. See Emma Nicholson and Peter Clark, eds., *The Iraqi Marshlands: A Human and Environmental Study*, 2nd ed. (London: Politico's Publishing, 2002) and the website, http://www.Edenagain.org. Also Naval Intelligence Division, British Admiralty, *Iraq and the Persian Gulf*, Geographical Handbook Series ([Oxford: Oxford University Press?], 1944), chaps. 7 and 9.
60. For a detailed description see W. B. Fisher, "Physical Geography," in *The Cambridge History of Iran*, vol. 1, *The Land of Iran*, ed. W. B. Fisher (Cambridge: Cambridge University Press, 1968), 3–110; British Admiralty, *Persia;* and the appendixes in Cottrell, *The Persian Gulf States*, 541–666.
61. Xavier de Planhol, "Garmsir and Sardsir," *Encyclopædia Iranica* 10 (2001): 316–17.
62. Refer to the excellent article, "Lar, Laristan," by Jean Calmard in *The Encyclopedia of Islam*, new ed., 5 (1986), 665–76. See now Muhammad Baqir Vusuqi, Manuchihr Abidi Rad, Sadiq Rahmani, and Kiramat-Allah Taqavi, *Tarikh-i mufassal-i Laristan* [Comprehensive History of Laristan], 2 vols. (Tehran: Hamsaya, 1385/2006).
63. Floor, *Five Port Cities*, 282–84, 296–99, 321–22.
64. Sources: Admiralty, *Iraq Handbook;* W. B. Fisher, *The Middle East: A Physical, Social and Regional Geography*, 6th ed. (London: Methuen, 1971), 465–73.
65. See here, Admiralty, *Iraq Handbook*, 149–50.
66. See Chapter 11, "Braving the Winds," in Dionisius A. Agius, *Seafaring in the Arabian Gulf and Oman: The People of the Dhow* (London: Kegan Paul, 2005), 191–201. Matthee notes, for example, that there was a narrow window of opportunity for trading in Basra: ships departing from Goa in May, with intermediate stops, would arrive in Basra in July and had to depart again for India not later than October. Unfortunately, this corresponded with the hot summer months (see below, page 109).
67. Agius, *Seafaring in the Arabian Gulf and Oman*, 204.
68. George F. Hourani, *Arab Seafaring in the Indian Ocean in Ancient and Early Medieval Times*, revised and expanded edition by John Carswell (Princeton, NJ: Princeton University Press, 1995), 69–79.
69. Alan Villiers, *Sons of Sinbad* (New York: Charles Scribner's Sons, 1940; repr. 1969). This book has now been republished with a new introduction by William Facey, Yacoub Al-Hijji, and Grace Pundyk (London: Arabian Publishing, 2006). A marvelous selection of his photos has appeared as *Sons of Sindbad: The Photographs; Dhow Voyages with the Arabs in 1938–39 in the Red Sea, round the Coasts of Arabia, and to Zanzibar and Tanganyika; Pearling in the Gulf; And the Life of the Shipmasters and Mariners on Kuwait,*

selected and introduced by William Facey, Yacoub Al-Hijji, and Grace Pundyk (London: Arabian Publishing, 2006). A brief account of his voyage from the Gulf to East Africa is contained in "Some Aspects of the Arab Dhow Trade," *The Middle East Journal* 2 (1948): 399–416.

70. Agius, *Seafaring in the Arabian Gulf and Oman,* 114.
71. See Robert Carter, "The History and Prehistory of Pearling in the Persian Gulf," *Journal of the Economic and Social History of the Orient* 48, no. 2 (2005): 139–209; Saif Marzooq al-Shamlan, *Pearling in the Arabian Gulf: A Kuwaiti Memoir,* rev. ed., trans. Peter Clark (London: The London Centre of Arab Studies, 2001); and Richard LeBaron Bowen, Jr., "The Pearl Fisheries of the Persian Gulf," *Middle East Journal* 5 (1951): 161–80.
72. Wilson, *The Persian Gulf,* ix.
73. Henry Yule, trans. and ed., *The Book of Ser Marco Polo the Venetian Concerning the Kingdoms and Marvels of the East,* 3rd ed. (London: John Murray, 1902; repr. 1929), vol. 1, 107–08 (at Hormuz they ate dates, salt-fish, and onions) and vol. 2, 450 (at Qalhat they ate dates and salt fish); *The Travels of Ibn Battuta A.D. 1325–1354,* vol. 2, Second Series No. CXVII, trans. H. A. R. Gibb (Cambridge: Cambridge University Press for the Hakluyt Society, 1962), 400 (at Hormuz they ate fish and dried dates imported from Oman and Basra).
74. Iraj Nabipur is a physician practicing in Bushehr. See his *Pishdaramadi bar tarikh-i pizishki-yi Khalij-i Fars* [Introduction to the Medical History of the Persian Gulf] (Bushehr: Intisharat-i Danishgah-i Ulum-i Pizishki va Khadamat-i Bihdashti-Darmani-yi Bushihr, 1386/2007), with illustrations. See also his earlier work, *Maktab-i Pizishki-yi Bandar-i Siraf* [The Medical School of the Port of Siraf] (Bushehr: Danishgah-i Ulum-i Pizishki va Khadamat-i Bihdashti-Darmani-yi Bushehr, 1384/2005).
75. Murphey, "On the Evolution of the Port City," in *Brides of the Sea,* 230–32.
76. C. M. Cursetjee, *The Land of the Date: A Recent Voyage from Bombay to Basra and Back, Fully Descriptive of the Ports and Peoples of the Persian Gulf and the Shat'-el-Arab, their Conditions, History and Customs. 1916–1917* (1918; new ed. Reading, UK: Garnet, 1994), 17.
77. Admiralty, *Iraq Handbook,* 149.
78. Floor, *Five Port Cities,* 20–23.
79. Villers, "Some Aspects of the Arab Dhow Trade," 399 and Yacoub Al-Hijji, *Old Kuwait: Memories in Photographs* (Kuwait: Center for Research and Studies on Kuwait, 1997), 93, 96.
80. Curzon, *Persia and the Persian Question,* vol. 2, 409 and Cursetjee, *Land of the Date,* 62.
81. See Hans E. Wulff, "The Qanats of Iran," *Scientific American* 218 (1968): 94–105 and Dale R. Lightfoot, "The Origin and Diffusion of Qanats in Arabia: New Evidence from the Northern and Southern Peninsula," *The Geographical Journal* 166, no. 3 (2000): 215–26.
82. See Anne Coles and Peter Jackson, *Windtower* (London: Stacey International, 2007).
83. Ya'qub Yusuf al-Hijji, *The Art of Dhow-building in Kuwait* (London: The London Centre of Arab Studies in association with the Centre for Research and Studies on Kuwait, 2001), 38–41.
84. See below, page 216.
85. See below, page 109.
86. Villiers, *Sons of Sinbad,* chap. 12, "Delta of Misery," 223–46 and "Some Aspects of the Arab Dhow Trade," 414.
87. Charles Belgrave, *The Pirate Coast* (Beirut, Lebanon: Librairie du Liban, 1960, repr. 1972), 192.
88. Heard-Bey, *From Trucial States to United Arab Emirates,* 247.
89. Personal communication from J. E. Peterson.
90. Lienhardt, *Shaikhdoms of Eastern Arabia,* 118.
91. Richard LeBaron Bowen, Jr., "Marine Industries of Eastern Arabia," *The Geographical Review* 41 (1951): 393–95.
92. Pedro Teixeira mentions the mining of this coral rock (which he calls *sang-i mahi*) near Hormuz in the sixteenth century. See *The Travels of Pedro Teixeira; with His "Kings of*

Harmuz," and Extracts from his "Kings of Persia," ed. William F. Sinclair and Donald Ferguson (Hakluyt Society, 1902; repr. Nendeln/Liechtenstein: Kraus Reprint, 1967), 233–34.

93. Salwa Alghanim, *The Reign of Mubarak Al-Sabah: Shaikh of Kuwait 1896–1915* (London: I. B. Tauris, 1998), 146–48.
94. Hala Fattah, *The Politics of Regional Trade in Iraq, Arabia, and the Gulf 1745–1900* (Albany: State University of New York Press, 1997), 25–28.
95. M. Niebuhr, *Travels through Arabia, and Other Countries in the East,* trans. Robert Heron (Edinburgh, 1792; reprint, Reading, UK: Garnet Publishing, 1994), vol. 2, 137.
96. Lawrence G. Potter, "The Consolidation of Iran's Frontier on the Persian Gulf in the Nineteenth Century," in *War and Peace in Qajar Persia: Implications Past and Present,* ed. Roxane Farmanfarmaian (London: Routledge, 2008), 125–48.
97. John R. Perry, *Karim Khan Zand: A History of Iran, 1747–1779,* Publications of the Center for Middle Eastern Studies, no. 12 (Chicago: University of Chicago Press, 1979), 152.
98. Lorimer, *Gazeeteer,* vol. 8, 754–55.
99. "Ahmad: A Kuwaiti Pearl Diver" by Nels Johnson, in *Struggle and Survival in the Modern Middle East,* ed. Edmund Burke, III (Berkeley: University of California Press, 1993), 91–99.
100. On the mindset of the sailors, see Villiers, "Some Aspects of the Arab Dhow Trade," 407–8, 416.
101. Wilkinson, *The Imamate Tradition of Oman,* 69.
102. Ulrike Freitag and William G. Clarence-Smith, eds., *Hadhrami Traders, Scholars and Statesmen in the Indian Ocean, 1750s–1960s* (Leiden, Netherlands: Brill, 1997); Linda Boxberger, *On the Edge of Empire: Hadhramawt, Emigration, and the Indian Ocean, 1880s–1930s* (Albany: State University of New York Press, 2002); Ulrike Freitag, *Indian Ocean Migrants and State Formation in Hadhramaut: Reforming the Homeland* (Leiden, Netherlands: Brill, 2003); and Engseng Ho, *The Graves of Tarim: Genealogy and Mobility across the Indian Ocean* (Berkeley: University of California Press, 2006).
103. Mohammed Redha Bhacker and Bernadette Bhacker, "Qalhat in Arabian History: Context and Chronicles," *The Journal of Oman Studies* 13 (2004): 11–55.
104. See Izady, "Gulf's Ethnic Diversity," 39–40.
105. Villiers, "Some Aspects of the Arab Dhow Trade," 405. Villers mentions as an example a large family based in Kuwait; a very informative portrait of a similar family based in Bushehr and Bahrain is provided by James Onley, in "Transnational Merchants in the Nineteenth-Century Gulf: The Case of the Safar Family," in *Transnational Connections and the Arab Gulf,* ed. Madawi Al-Rasheed (London; Routledge, 2005), 59–89.
106. Izady, "Gulf's Ethnic Diversity," 77–78.
107. *Ahl-i Hava* (Tehran: Mu'assisa-yi Mutali'at va Tahqiqat-i Ijtima'i, Intisharat 36, Monograph 8, Chapkhana-yi Danishgah, 1345/1966) has not been translated. See Gholam-Hossein Sa'edi, *Fear and Trembling,* trans. Minoo Southgate (Washington, D. C.: Three Continents Press, 1984), and commentary in the translater's introduction.
108. Beatrice Nicolini, "Some Thoughts on the Magical Practice of the Zar along the Red Sea in the Sudan," in Starkey, *People of the Red Sea,* 157–61.
109. This has not yet been translated into English. See Nasrin Rahimieh, "Magical Realism in Moniru Ravanipur's *Ahl-e gharq,*" *Iranian Studies* 23 (1990): 61–75.
110. Nasser Al-Taee, "'Enough, Enough, Oh Ocean': Music of the Pearl Divers in the Arabian Gulf," *Middle East Studies Association Bulletin* 39, no. 1 (2005): 19–30.
111. Ibid., 20.
112. Al-Shamlan, *Pearling in the Arabian Gulf,* 111–12.
113. Cursetjee, *The Land of the Date,* 13.
114. Juan R. I. Cole, "Iranian Culture and South Asia, 1500–1900," in *Iran and the Surrounding World: Interactions in Culture and Cultural Politics,* ed. Nikki R. Keddie and Rudi Matthee (Seattle: University of Washington Press, 2002), 15–35.
115. Cole, "Iranian Culture and South Asia," 16.

116. James Onley, *The Arabian Frontier of the British Raj: Merchants, Rulers, and the British in the Nineteenth-Century Gulf* (Oxford: Oxford University Press, 2007).
117. Kelly, *Britain and the Persian Gulf,* chap. 8, "The Egyptian and Persian Crises, 1837–1841," 290–353.
118. Kelly, *Britain and the Persian Gulf,* chap. 11, "The Persian War 1856–1857," 452–99.
119. Thomas R. Metcalf, *Imperial Connections: India in the Indian Ocean Arena, 1860–1920* (Berkeley: University of California Press, 2007), 89–101 (quote is on page no. 89).
120. Frederick F. Anscombe, *The Ottoman Gulf: The Creation of Kuwait, Saudi Arabia, and Qatar* (New York: Columbia University Press, 1997).
121. Aubin, "Les princes d'Ormuz," 128. This idea is endorsed by Nadjmabadi, below page 129.
122. It might be pointed out that there is some question as to what "Arab" identity constituted in the pre-Islamic period. See Michael G. Morony, "The Arabisation of the Gulf," in *The Arab Gulf and the Arab World,* ed. B. R. Pridham (London: Croom Helm, 1988), 3–28.
123. Curzon, *Persia and the Persian Question,* vol. 2, 388.
124. Hourani, *Arab Seafaring in the Indian Ocean,* 65.
125. This is pointed out by Hourani in *Arab Seafaring in the Indian Ocean,* 65–68. Refer to Buzurg ibn Shahriyar, *Kitab ajaib al-Hind,* trans. and ed. by G. S. P. Freemen-Grenville as *The Book of the Wonders of India: Mainland, Sea and Islands* (London: East-West Publications, 1981).
126. See "The Persian Navy in the Persian Gulf during the Eighteenth Century," chap. 1 in Floor, *The Rise of the Gulf Arabs.*
127. L. Lockhart, *Nadir Shah: A Critical Study Based Mainly upon Contemporary Sources* (London, 1938; repr. Jalandhar, India: Asian Publishers, 1993), 222.
128. Potter, "The Consolidation of Iran's Frontier on the Persian Gulf," 132–33.
129. The best article on the subject is C. Edmund Bosworth, "The Nomenclature of the Persian Gulf," in Cottrell, *The Persian Gulf States,* xvii–xxxiv; reprinted in *Iranian Studies* 30, nos. 1–2 (1997): 77–94.
130. M. Kasheff, "Arvand-Rud," in *Encyclopædia Iranica* 2 (1987): 679–81.
131. See below, page 39.
132. Bosworth, "The Nomenclature of the Persian Gulf," xix.
133. Ibid., xviii–xix.
134. Ibid., xxii.
135. Ibid., xxxiii.
136. Charles Tripp, *A History of Iraq* (Cambridge: Cambridge University Press, 2000), 165.
137. "Persian Protest to Iraq" (Reuters), *The Times,* August 5, 1958, 6. My thanks to James Onley for sharing this.
138. S. H. Amin, *Political and Strategic Issues in the Persian-Arabian Gulf* (Glasgow: Royston Limited, 1984), 82. See his section on the controversy on pages 81–85.
139. See press release, "National Geographic statement on Eighth Edition Atlas, Dec. 30, 2004," on their Web site at http://press.nationalgeographic.com/pressroom/ (accessed October 16, 2008).
140. "State Department Says it's the Persian, not Arabian, Gulf," Associated Press, September 1, 1987 (online).
141. Muhammad Rumaihi, *Beyond Oil: Unity and Development in the Gulf,* trans. James Dickens (London: Al Saqi Books, 1986), 11.

Part I

Gulf History and Society

Chapter 1

The Archaeology and Early History of the Persian Gulf

D. T. Potts

In antiquity the Persian Gulf region was culturally diverse, containing at least four major regions and many more subregions. These included (a) southern Iran, from the Shatt al-Arab to the Strait of Hormuz, certainly not a homogenous area and one which is frustratingly understudied; (b) southernmost Mesopotamia; (c) northeastern Arabia (modern Eastern Province of Saudi Arabia and Kuwait), Bahrain, and Qatar, in whose material culture we can recognize enough similarities to justify such a geographical grouping; and (d) southeastern Arabia, the modern UAE, and, although technically outside the Gulf (except for Ras Musandam), Oman.

Our knowledge of the Arabian littoral and its offshore islands (Failaka, Bahrain, and the Abu Dhabi islands) is infinitely greater than that of its Persian counterpart. In spite of the fact that archaeological research in Iran has a much longer history than it does in eastern Arabia, the vast majority of surveys and excavations have been conducted in continental Iran rather than along the coast. Little survey or excavation has been conducted on the Iranian Coast[1] and offshore islands, with the exception of Tul-e Peytul (ancient Liyan), near modern Bushehr, where a large mound with Elamite occupation was sounded in 1913[2]; Kharg Island, where a French expedition excavated part of a Nestorian monastic complex and surveyed numerous other pre-Islamic tombs and monuments in 1959 and 1960[3]; Siraf, where an important site of the Sasanian and early Islamic era was excavated from 1966 to 1973[4]; and Kish Island, where a limited survey and soundings were carried out in the mid-1970s[5] . We have some notices in Greek and Latin sources on this coast and on some of the major islands (e.g., Qishm),[6] but these, although interesting, are of limited value.

In contrast, archaeological excavations in Kuwait, eastern Saudi Arabia, Bahrain, Qatar, the UAE, and Oman, which began with the opening of a few tombs on Bahrain in 1879,[7] have gathered in intensity during the past fifty years, particularly in the last two decades. We now have not only a large number of excavated sites from all periods but also a significant number of radiocarbon dates and detailed ceramic, metallurgical, faunal, numismatic, and other analyses. In comparison with Mesopotamia, southwestern Iran, or South Arabia, the number of indigenous written sources is small, yet their absence is certainly made up for by a robust archaeological sequence.

In this chapter I shall deal with the pre-Sasanian record of human occupation in the four major regions (a–d) defined above. As indicated already, the archaeological, epigraphic, and literary sources available for each region differ markedly in quantity and quality. On the one hand the trends and developments discernible in one region are not always documented in another, while on the other hand certain developments transcend the boundaries of these regions. Overall, however, the Persian Gulf constitutes a coherent region with a historical identity comparable to Mesopotamia, Egypt, or the Indus Valley.

The Earliest Populations

Many who work on the Persian Gulf region may not have considered where the original populations actually came from, but there are several reasons why this should be studied. In the first place, there is no evidence to suggest continuity in population and occupation from the Middle (ca. 70,000–35,000 years ago) and Upper Palaeolithic (ca. 35,000–10,000 years ago)periods, when the earliest stone tools probably began to appear on sites in the region,[8] to the mid-Holocene period, that is, ca. 6000 B.C., when we see a marked increase in the size and number of archaeological sites along the coast and in the interior of eastern Arabia. These two facts suggest that we should not assume that hominids have lived continuously in the area.

Several factors may account for the discontinuity we see in the archaeological evidence. To start with, however, we should briefly review the geomorphology and historical hydrology of the Persian Gulf.[9] Worldwide sea levels during the last glacial maximum (ca. 70,000–17,000 B.P. [before present]) were as much as 120 meters lower than they are today. Hence, there was no Persian Gulf at all during the Late Pleistocene era.[10] Rather, the combined effluent of the Euphrates, Tigris, and Karun rivers formed a palaeo-river that drained into the Arabian Sea at the Strait of Hormuz. After 17,000 B.P., when the Flandrian Transgression began (and worldwide sea levels began to rise again), the valley through which this river ran gradually filled, reaching approximately modern levels by about 7000 B.P. Subsequently, sea levels have fluctuated in a fairly minor way, sometimes by as much as ± 1.5 meters relative to modern levels.[11]

The impact of these fluctuations on human populations around the Gulf would have varied. In the southern Gulf, certain areas along the flat coast of the UAE, which are now hills, were demonstrably islands, some islands off the coast of Abu Dhabi were in fact attached to the mainland, and some sites located inland from the modern coast (such as Tell Abraq) were actually close to the shoreline.[12] Further north, however, we can see evidence of more dramatic changes. Thus, for example, during the sixth millennium B.C., the trough between Bahrain and the eastern seaboard of Saudi Arabia was probably not yet full of water, meaning that Bahrain was still part of continental Arabia and not yet an island.[13] Significantly, the island of Failaka, in the bay of Kuwait, was submerged until about 2000 B.C.[14] This is supported, moreover, by the absence of any cultural remains of earlier date on Failaka, in spite of the fact that the bay of Kuwait itself has evidence of sixth-millennium B.C. occupation at several points (e.g. H3) along its shores.[15] How changing sea levels may have affected Kharg Island, or the bay of Bushehr and its peninsula, we do not know.

The infilling of the Persian Gulf will have submerged any Pleistocene and early Holocene archaeological sites that may have been close to the palaeoriver. Still, we might expect to find such evidence on what would have been higher terraces located farther back from the actual floodplain. On the Iranian side, archaeological survey has simply not been extensive enough to determine whether there is any such evidence. Certainly there is Palaeolithic occupation in the interior of Fars[16] and further north in the western Zagros (from Khurramabad northwards),[17] but this does not necessarily prove that human occupation occurred further south. In southernmost Iraq, an abundance of game (waterfowl, fish, mammalian fauna) in the riverine environment is likely to have been a magnet for early hunter-gatherer groups, but millennia of siltation and marsh formation have effectively blanketed any pre-Holocene remains which might have existed.[18] In northeastern Arabia, all along the Arabian shelf, there is a curious absence of any Palaeolithic occupation, despite the presence of numerous sites in western and central Arabia on the Arabian shield[19]; in the UAE, as noted above; and in southern Oman[20] and Yemen.[21]

Subsistence and Social Organization in the Sixth and Fifth Millennium B.C.

The earliest evidence of occupation on the shores of the Persian Gulf dates to ca. 6000–5500 B.C., a time considered as a climatic "optimum" across much of western Asia and followed by an onset of aridity in about 4000 B.C.[22] Elsewhere in the region, agriculture (with an emphasis on barley and wheat), domestic animal husbandry (concentrating on sheep, goats, and cattle), and sedentary, village life (characterized by mudbrick or stone architecture, the use of lime plaster, groundstone, and ceramics) were already well established by this time.[23] The resource base and environmental conditions of the Persian Gulf differed from those on the plains of northern Mesopotamia or in the intermontane valleys of the Zagros.[24] Marine resources were abundant. Fish,[25] shellfish,[26] green turtles (*Chelonia mydas*),[27] and marine mammals (e.g., dugong[28]) provided protein, and the abundance of these resources prompted sedentary and seasonal occupation on the coast (sometimes alternating with a retreat to the higher elevations during the winter).[29] An outstanding example of one such community, excavated at Jabal al-Buhais in the interior of Sharjah, has recently been published in lavish detail. Not only does it illustrate the sort of material culture used by a typical mid-Holocene population in this region, but the discovery there of a cemetery containing hundreds of individuals at a site known as BHS 18 has also given us a fascinating glimpse of health, diet, pathology, nutrition, morbidity rates, and demography among one such group of early Arabians.[30]

In a low-rainfall environment without perennial rivers, cereal cultivation required well irrigation, and wheat and barley were cultivated, probably in a *bustan* arrangement wherein the shade of the date palm was used to shelter the cereal crops, using water raised from hand-dug wells.[31] The absence of rivers and springs was thus not an insuperable difficulty, particularly in an area as rich in groundwater (aquifers) as eastern Arabia.[32]

As neither wheat nor barley occurred naturally this far south, both species must have been introduced there.[33] Interestingly, we see the use of chaff in the earliest, indigenous pottery known in the region (the coarse, handmade redwares of the Eastern Province of Saudi Arabia), which was a by-product of cultivated, not imported, cereals.[34] Nor were sheep, goats, and cattle native to the region.[35] The fact that the earliest stone tools in Qatar, dating to the sixth and fifth millennium B.C., show strong similarities to the Levantine blade-arrowhead tradition[36] has prompted some scholars to suggest a movement of people from the southern Levant into the east Arabian littoral, together with their already domesticated sheep, goats, and cattle. Certainly those sites of this period in eastern Saudi Arabia, the UAE, and Oman, which have been excavated (and are not just known from surface finds), always yield bones of domesticated sheep, goats, and cattle. While early researchers were liable to classify such sites as the campsites of hunters and gatherers, primarily due to the predominance of finely pressure-flaked, barbed, and tanged arrowheads in the stone-tool inventory,[37] it is more accurate to categorize the societies that created such sites as herders who supplemented their diet by doing a bit of hunting, rather than hunters who did a bit of herding. The distinction is important, for, first and foremost, these people lived on the marine resources available in the Gulf and on the secondary products provided by their livestock. Fleece, hair, and milk products complemented the marine protein available from fish, shellfish, and marine mammals; and the terrestrial protein derived from mammals such as gazelle, oryx, and wild camel. Just as importantly, as we know from ethnographic studies in the region, sheep and goats are able to drink brackish water, which is unpotable for human groups, and convert it into potable milk that can be either drunk as is or turned into a variety of cheese-and yogurt-related products. Having a herd is thus tantamount to having a mobile water-purification system.[38] Yet to slaughter one's sheep and goats for their meat is obviously to destroy this capacity and to cut off the supply of secondary products. Hence, hunting wild fauna provides a meat supply without endangering the capital represented by a group's herd.

Ubaid Contact

Since the late 1960s, when diagnostic sherds of the so-called Ubaid type were found at a number of sites in the Eastern Province of Saudi Arabia,[39] the relationship between southern Mesopotamia and the Gulf region has been much discussed. In brief, sherds of well-fired (or sometimes over-fired) buffware with geometric decoration in black manganese paint—a characteristic of the initial, sedentary occupation of southern Iraq (e.g., at sites Tell Oueilli, Ur, and the eponymous Tell al-Ubaid)—have been found at sites on the coasts of Kuwait (H3); eastern Saudi Arabia (Abu Khamis, Dosariyyah, Ain Qannas); Bahrain (al-Markh); Qatar (Khor, Ras Abaruk, al-Da'asa); and the UAE (Jazirat al-Hamra [Ras al-Khaimah], al-Madar [Umm al-Qaiwain], Hamriyah [Sharjah], Marawah, and Dalma islands [Abu Dhabi]).

The Ubaid period in Mesopotamia[40] comprises five phases (Ubaid 0–4), extending from sometime prior to 6000 B.C. to about 4000 B.C., with a terminal or post-Ubaid phase lasting until ca. 3800 B.C. Thus, the evidence of contact between the population residing at the head of the Gulf and the inhabitants of the Arabian coasts must be seen in a broad chronological context and not viewed as something necessarily sudden or intense. The earliest Ubaid sherds found in the Persian Gulf come from H3 in Kuwait and date to Ubaid 2–3 times, while most of the sherds from further south date to Ubaid 3–4 times. Various explanations have been advanced to account for this north-south contact, ranging from seasonal fishing expeditions to traders in search of pearls. Certainly the contact seems to have been waterborne, for most of the sites are on the coast (the exception being those in eastern Saudi Arabia), and H3 has now yielded important fragments of reed-impressed bitumen that represent the remains of bitumen-caulked boats.[41]

Except for those inhabiting what is today northeastern Saudi Arabia, the native populations of the Gulf region did not apparently undergo much culture change as a result of these contacts. Sites in Saudi Arabia show a local, coarse, chaff-tempered redware alongside the imported Ubaid sherds, suggesting that some attempt was made to adopt the technology and culture of ceramics. But this was not to last, and an indigenous ceramic tradition did not develop in the region until the third millennium B.C. Apart from the use of ceramics, however, it is arguable whether the culture of southern Mesopotamia in the sixth and fifth millennia B.C. was very different from that of eastern Arabia or southern Iran. Because of the marshes that, in recent times, have covered much of southernmost Iraq, we have no archaeological evidence of this period south of Eridu, where, to be sure, mudbrick architecture was already in use, as is seen from the foundation of the site and where the residents were agriculturalists.[42] In the Gulf, on the other hand, the coastal dwellers probably lived, for the most part, in *barastis*, palm-frond houses well suited to the warm, humid climate of the region,[43] which left a distinctive signature, in the form of postholes, in the ground. Lithic industries, intensive fish and shellfish use, and herding are a hallmark of the Arabian sites, but as we have no excavated sites in the southern portion of Iraq to compare, it would be unwise to envisage a culture there that was technologically much further advanced or socially more highly organized than that along the coasts of Iran and Arabia. The contrasts in subsistence strategy, which to be sure were real, should not necessarily be interpreted as markers of profound sociological differences.

Mesopotamia and the Persian Gulf: First Contacts Attested in the Written Record

The fourth millennium in eastern Arabia is very poorly documented.[44] An aceramic dugong- butchering site on the island of Akab (Umm al-Qaiwain) provides one of the only excavated assemblages.[45] Interestingly, long tubular beads that are perforated at either end have been found there, which find parallels in fourth-millennium Mesopotamia.[46] The paucity of excavated sites, however, is probably not an indication of a genuine hiatus in human occupation. Were one able to get C14 dates for many of the unexcavated lithic sites in the region, occupation throughout the fourth millennium would almost certainly be apparent, as it is all along the coast of Oman.[47] In Mesopotamia, on the other hand, there is a wealth of evidence, but again, all of this derives from much further north than our area of concern. What is significant, however, is the fact that in the very earliest protocuneiform texts from Uruk, the southern Mesopotamian site at which writing seems to have been invented, the toponym DILMUN occurs.[48] This is a name that we can later, without hesitation, identify with Bahrain and the adjacent portion of eastern Saudi Arabia. References to a Dilmun axe in the Archaic metals list; to a Dilmun tax collector; and to officials involved with Dilmun, all suggests contact at this time as well as a degree of organization in Dilmun itself, which is belied by the paucity of archaeological evidence from this period (ca. 3400–3000 B.C.).

The dearth of archaeological evidence on Bahrain during the early third millennium stands in contrast to the situation in eastern Saudi Arabia, where sites such as Tarut Island, Abqayq, and Umm an-Nussi have yielded considerable numbers of imported Mesopotamian ceramic vessels of Early Dynastic I–II date (ca. 2900–2350 B.C.),[49] suggesting that the main population centers of Dilmun, at this time, may have lain on the mainland and not on Bahrain. Late Early Dynastic royal inscriptions from Tello (ancient Girsu, in the city-state of Lagash) attest to the import of copper (from Oman) and wood "of foreign lands" (teak from western India?) from Dilmun.[50] As neither Bahrain nor eastern Saudi Arabia was endowed with such raw materials, it appears as if Dilmun was already exercising a role that it enjoyed throughout its later history, much like Bahrain in the historic era (and more recently Dubai), that is, that of middleman in transshipping goods from further afield to ports in southern Iraq.

Magan and the Hafit and Umm an-Nar Cultures

The copper sent by Dilmun to Mesopotamia at this time almost certainly came from Oman, where the Hajar Mountains represent a source exploited intermittently from the fourth millennium B.C. to the modern day.[51] Around 3000 B.C. a type of above-ground, circular tomb, built of unworked stone with a dome-like shape and keyhole entrance, appeared in southeastern Arabia. Known as the Hafit tombs (after Jabal Hafit, near Al-Ain, where the first examples were excavated),[52] these monuments are effectively the only evidence we have of early third millennium occupation in the region.[53] Importantly, they have yielded evidence of collective burial, involving small numbers of individuals (families? kin groups?),[54] copper weaponry (daggers), and imported Mesopotamian pottery of the Jamdat Nasr type (named after the type site of the same name in south-central Iraq).

Within a few centuries, however, the cultural landscape of the Oman peninsula had changed radically, for while the tradition of collective burial persisted, now often involving hundreds of individuals interred over a century or more (e.g., at Tell Abraq, Hili, Unar 1–2 at Shimal, Umm an-Nar island),[55] major innovations appear as well. Circular fortifications, somewhat like Martello towers,[56] built of mudbrick or stone (or a combination of both) appear at various sites (e.g., Hili 8, Tell Abraq, Bidya, and Baat in the interior of Oman).[57] A refined ceramic industry,[58] possibly owing much technological inspiration (or even manufacture) to immigrant Iranian potters, an ever-expanding metallurgical repertoire,[59] and a sizable industry in the manufacture of soft-stone (steatite, chlorite, or chloritite) vessels,[60] all mark the so-called Umm an-Nar culture.

Moreover, beginning in the twenty-fourth century, Akkadian royal inscriptions (and later Ur III economic texts) refer to southeastern Arabia as Sumerian *Magan* (Akkadian *Makkan*), a region against which at least two Old Akkadian monarchs (Manishtushu and Naram-Sin) campaigned.[61] Until Cypriot copper began to be readily available in Mesopotamia in the eighteenth century B.C.,[62] Magan was the chief source of copper for the city-states of the south (e.g., Ur, Lagash). Omani soft-stone vessels have been found at sites in southern Mesopotamia (Ur), eastern Arabia (Tarut), Bahrain (Saar tombs, Qalat al-Bahrain settlement), Iran (Susa, Tul-e Peytul, Tepe Yahya), and the Indus Valley (Mohenjo-Daro). Conversely, imported ceramics of Iranian (black-on-grey and burnished greyware [Kirman, Baluchistan],[63] Kaftari-ware [Fars]),[64] and Harappan (black-slipped storage jars, painted vessels) origin,[65] as well as Harappan or Harappan-inspired seals (Ur, Susa, Qalat al-Bahain, Tell Abraq, Ras al-Jinz)[66] and genuine Harappan weights (Shimal, Tell Abraq),[67] indicate that there was considerable Arabian Sea–Persian Gulf and intra-Gulf traffic in the late third millennium B.C.

By this point in time, there seems to have been a very real divergence, in social-evolutionary terms, on the Arabian side of the Gulf from the social patterns we can see in Iran or southern Mesopotamia. There are several indications of a strong, kin-based society in Magan. The iconography of two people holding hands appears on a seal from Ras al-Jinz and on a tomb relief at Hili.[68] The Umm an-Nar tombs are entirely collective, showing no sign of any distinction between elites and nonelites in death. And although there are a few references to a *lugal-Magan*, or "king" of Magan, the account of Manishtushu's campaign, in which he crossed the Lower Sea—as the Persian Gulf was known in the Mesopotamian sources (appearing once in the Ur III period [2100–2000 B.C.] as the "Sea of Magan")—and subjugated thirty-two cities and their "lords" (*en*) before advancing to the metal mines and quarrying black stone (diorite, gabbro) in the mountains which he loaded on ships and sent back to Agade, does not suggest the existence of a unitary state. Unlike Mesopotamia, with its city-states united by the Akkadians under a central government,[69] or Iran, which, at least in the Elamite areas of Khuzistan and Fars, seems to have been a confederation of numerous groups and regions,[70] Magan appears to have been a society consisting of fishermen and herders along the coast— oasis-based strongholds, exemplified by the circular fortification towers on the coast and in the interior— and transhumant pastoralists, who probably moved seasonally between the coasts and the mountains.

During the last century of the third millennium B.C., when the Third Dynasty of Ur ruled over Mesopotamia, direct trade between Ur and Magan was instituted, often involving a merchant named Lu-enlilla, some of whose texts were excavated by Sir Leonard Woolley at Ur.[71] Textiles of the coarsest grade were routinely sent to Magan[72] in exchange for commodities such as copper and ivory, the latter being an Indian product that was being sold onward by a middleman.

On the other hand, Dilmun appears to have been structured differently with a true primate settlement system in which Qalat al-Bahrain, covering an area measuring 400 × 700 meters and 8 meters high, or roughly 15 ha., dominated the main island of Bahrain with only a few secondary settlements (e.g., Saar, Diraz) existing alongside it. Moreover, Dilmun appears to have been a far more mercantile society and one less engaged in primary production. Transshipping wood, copper, ivory, carnelian, and, eventually, tin (from Afghanistan, via Melukhkha [Indus Valley or Harappan civilization])[73] generated considerable wealth, as reflected in the accounts of the *alik Tilmun*, or Dilmun traders, from Old Babylonian Ur.[74] Significantly, the pattern of burial on Bahrain and in eastern Saudi Arabia was completely different from that in Magan. Instead of collective burials, which were used on a community-wide basis, the Dilmunites practiced individual inhumation, sometimes in conspicuously grand grave chambers covered with an earthen mantle (hence the great fields of over 150,000 burial mounds on Bahrain which still survive). In these, however, they placed relatively few objects, obviously loathe to take wealth out of circulation.[75]

By the late third millennium B.C. (and much earlier in Mesopotamia) many parts of the Near East had developed a sealing device with distinctive iconography. In some cases this took the form of a cylinder seal, in others a stamp seal. In the Persian Gulf different seal types were developed in Dilmun and Magan. In Dilmun a circular, usually a stone stamp seal with a raised, perforated back (known as a "boss") was used. The iconography of the earliest seals (so-called Persian Gulf seals), dating to the last two or three centuries of the third millennium B.C., is limited to fauna (bulls, snakes, scorpions) and flora. Most of the known examples come from Bahrain,[76] but specimens have also been found at Tell Abraq in the UAE, on Tarut island and at Dhahran in eastern Saudi Arabia, on Failaka (probably old when they reached the island), and, most interestingly, at Ur. A small number of the seals from Failaka and Ur are distinguished by the fact that, in addition to the usual animals (almost always a bull) they bear short texts written in Harappan characters.[77] As the Harappan script has not been deciphered,[78] we cannot say for sure what such texts signify, but some scholars believe these short inscriptions of four or five signs might be personal names added to the seals to identify their owner. Interestingly, the sequence of signs found on the seals from the Gulf and Ur is never replicated on any of the several thousand seals known from sites in the Indus Valley itself. This has led some scholars to speculate that the names, if they are indeed that, are not Harappan names, but may be in other languages (e.g., a Semitic language such as Amorite or Akkadian, attested in some of the cuneiform texts found on Bahrain).[79] A Harappan presence in the Gulf region[80] was mentioned above, and it is possible that Harappans married into some of the local groups with whom they traded. This might explain why someone with a strong Harappan identity, but of mixed parentage and bearing a non-Harappan name, had a seal with an unorthodox Harappan inscription on it.

Far fewer seals of a late third millennium date have come to light in the area of ancient Magan, and these are heterogeneous, consisting of triangular prism-shaped seals decorated on all three sides,[81] circular and square or rectangular stamp seals,[82] and even cylinder seals.[83]

Dilmun in the Late Third and Early Second Millennium B.C.

The collapse of the Ur III state around 2000 B.C. may have reverberated somewhat in the Gulf region, and the same may have been true of the collapse of the Harappan civilization a century later. Yet, apart from a cessation of references to direct trade between Ur and Magan, it is difficult to gauge the real effects of these geopolitical reversals in neighboring states. Certainly there is evidence in the cuneiform sources from the Isin-Larsa and Old Babylonian periods (ca. 2000–1700 B.C.) of renewed contact between Ur, one of southern Mesopotamia's most important outlets to the Persian Gulf (though not on the Gulf itself, in much the same way as Basra is not) and Dilmun, which continued to supply copper to merchants like Ea-nasir of Ur. Limited references also attest to links between Dilmun and Susa,[84] and the probable presence of Dilmun pottery (typical red-ridged storage jars) at Tul-e Peytul (ancient Liyan), along with Elamite inscriptions there, would suggest that Liyan was an important gateway for contact between the highlands of Fars (ancient Anshan) and the Gulf region.[85] The presence of Late Harappan pottery (Micaceous Redware) at Saar and Tell Abraq, almost certainly originating in Gujarat, suggest ongoing maritime trade between Dilmun and the Late Harappan world.[86] At the same time, overland caravans, probably used for diplomatic rather than commercial purposes, are known to have traveled between the important city-state of Mari on the Euphrates (near the modern Syrian-Iraqi frontier) and Dilmun.[87]

During the late third and early second millennium B.C. Qalat al-Bahrain continued to be inhabited,[88] Saar was a flourishing, planned settlement (with streets and houses laid out to a design repeated throughout the settlement),[89] and the temple at Barbar, with its impressive oval retaining wall of limestone ashlars, continued to be in use.[90] Evidence from the east Arabian mainland is less abundant and consists mainly of tombs excavated near Dhahran airport.[91] One important initiative that should be mentioned, however, was the foundation of an apparent satellite settlement by Dilmun on the Kuwaiti island of Failaka. As mentioned above, Failaka did not begin to emerge from the waters of the Gulf until ca. 2000 B.C. Shortly thereafter a settlement with houses made of coral-rock (Ar. *farush*)[92] was founded on virgin soil and the fact that the ceramics and small finds found there are entirely in the style of what we know from Bahrain strongly suggests that the colonists came from Dilmun.[93]

One of the most distinctive hallmarks of Dilmunite material culture in the early second millennium is the "Dilmun" stamp seal, a circular stamp seal with a raised, perforated boss much like its "Persian Gulf" predecessor, but with a much more varied iconography including humans and a range of motifs not seen in the earlier group.[94] Hundreds of such seals have been excavated on Bahrain and Failaka, and a handful have been found at sites in southwestern Iran (Susa) and the UAE (Mazyad, near Jabal Hafit). Among the many decorative elements found on these seals are several which are particularly identifiable with the region, including gazelle, date palms, and single-masted boats with upturned prow and stern.

The Wadi Suq Period in Oman (2000–1300 B.C.)

In comparison with the Umm an-Nar period, the early second millennium occupation of southeastern Arabia is much less well-represented. Twenty-five years ago some scholars attributed this to processes such as nomadization, perhaps attendant upon the domestication of the camel (*Camelus dromedarius*), decline triggered by economic collapse in Mesopotamia at the end of the Old Babylonian period, or a shift away from sedentary settlement precipitated by climatic change.[95] We still have very few settlements from the period ca. 2000–1300 B.C.,[96] despite the relatively large number of collective burials (no longer circular, but mainly long, narrow chambers with rounded ends, or roughly oval).[97] There is a palpable devolution in ceramics, from a technological point of view, although the metals industry continued to flourish—large quantities of weaponry, socketed spear/lanceheads and swords now dominate, and arrowheads become common, often with simple marks such as X on the flattened surface of the midrib.[98] We now know, furthermore, that the camel was not domesticated until the Iron Age,[99] and we have very equivocal climatic data, so the sorts of explanations in vogue in the 1970s are no longer tenable. Some settlements, like Tell Abraq, do show continuity of occupation,[100] as well as ceramics imported from Bahrain[101] and seal impressions of a type known in post-Harappan contexts in Gujarat.[102] However, there can be no denying the general paucity of settlement remains at this time.

On Failaka and Bahrain we can certainly chart stylistic changes in the ceramic assemblage,[103] but it is not so clear that this equates to a major break in the occupational or cultural sequences there. We are here, in Mesopotamian terms, in what has often been termed a "Dark Age," following the Hittite conquest of Babylonia, and prior to the full flowering of the Kassite state. Certainly much work remains to be done on this period.

Kassites, Elamites, and Dilmun

By the middle or third quarter of the second millennium B.C. the situation becomes much clearer. Whereas the earliest occupation on Failaka may have had the hallmarks of colonization from the south (Dilmun), the next phase of occupation on the island is just as easily identified as an influx from the north, this time from Mesopotamia. By this point in time the Kassites, an alien group possibly originating in northwestern Iran or the east Tigris region, had come to power.[104] The ceramic evidence from Failaka, coupled with a few seals and cuneiform inscriptions,[105] shows us that Kassite material culture suddenly appeared on the island, lasting into the final centuries of the second millennium.

On Bahrain the evidence is even clearer. Here we have more Kassite texts, which confirm that Dilmun was under Kassite political control.[106] This evidence is buttressed by an unprovenanced cylinder seal in the British Museum which refers to its owner's great-grandfather as *shakkanakku*, usually translated as "governor," of Dilmun.[107] Moreover, two letters excavated at Nippur,[108] one of the holiest cities in Mesopotamia, were written by a governor of Dilmun, Ili-ippashra, to his friend and probably fellow Kassite bureaucrat, Ili-liya. Ili-liya, a nickname for Enlil-kidinni, is attested in texts from the reigns of Burnaburiash II (1359–1333 B.C.) and Kurigalzu II (1332–1308 B.C.) so we can safely place these letters in the second half of the fourteenth century B.C. These important letters name the two chief deities of Dilmun, Inzak and Meskilak; report on the depredations of the Ahlamu, a Semitic-speaking group of nomads or semisedentary nomads who had been stealing dates right off of the trees in Dilmun; and speak of dreams predicting the destruction of the palace. While the Kassites were in control of Dilmun and presumably Failaka, their Elamite contemporaries were in control of the northern Iranian coast,[109] as demonstrated by several inscriptions from Tul-e Peytul dating to the reigns of Humban-Numena (ca. 1350–1340 B.C.), Kutir-Nahhunte, and Shilhak-Inshushinak (late fourteenth/early thirteenth centuries B.C.).[110]

Kassite rule ended abruptly in around 1225 B.C. when the Assyrian king Tukulti-Ninurta I (1243–1207 B.C.) defeated his Kassite counterpart Kashtiliashu IV (1232–1225 B.C.). The Assyrians, however, did not project their power into the Gulf. Rather, the ceramics from Failaka and Bahrain suggest that the Second Dynasty of the Sealand, the name given in Babylonian sources to a dynasty that arose in southernmost Iraq in the late second millennium B.C.,[111] was involved in the region after the fall of the Kassites and not the Elamites or Assyrians.[112] The only real sign of contact between the Gulf region and Elam in this period consists of a typical Middle Elamite, faience cylinder seal from Tell Abraq and possibly a few sherds with Elamite-looking profiles.[113]

Iron Age Dilmun and the Assyrian Empire

Over the next few centuries we have no historical information on events in the Gulf whatsoever. At Qalat al-Bahrain there is evidence of continuity in occupation,[114] but there is little if anything from Failaka, mainland eastern Arabia, or the coast of southern Iran that dates to the period between ca. 1200 and 800 B.C., and there is only slightly more information to be found in the UAE, where the Iron Age I occupation at Tell Abraq and several other sites (e.g., Kalba) can be linked to the first centuries of the first millennium B.C.[115] By contrast, the developed Iron Age (Iron Age II) in the region, from ca. 800–550 B.C., is abundantly represented through graves, an expansion of settlement (e.g., Tell Abraq, Rumeilah, Muweilah, Bida Bint Saud, al-Madam) that almost certainly reflect the growth of new water-management techniques,[116] abundant metal weaponry, and clearly differentiated ceramic traditions, seals, and stone vessels.[117] A temple complex seems to be present at the site of Bithnah, in the mountains of Fujairah, where evidence of a snake cult is strong as well.[118] Once again we see clear distinctions in the material culture of Dilmun and Magan.

Beginning with the reign of Sargon II (721–705 B.C.), the number of references to the Gulf region in Assyrian sources increases.[119] After describing his military exploits against Babylonia and Elam, Sargon says that "Uperi, king of Dilmun, who lives (*lit.* "whose camp is situated") like a fish, thirty *beru* [double hours, a unit of travel time] away in the midst of the sea of the rising sun, heard of my lordly might and brought his gifts" (Annals, Khorsabad palace, Salons II, V, and XIII, year 13, §41). Similar inscriptions elsewhere in Sargon's palace at Khorsabad (ancient Dur-Sharrukin) boast of the gifts sent by Uperi and probably one of his descendants named Ahundara/Hundaru upon their hearing of the might of the gods Assur, Nabu, and Marduk, thus making it clear that no actual conquest of Dilmun was involved. Moreover, they strongly suggest the existence of a kingship or at least a chiefly lineage in control of Dilmun during the late eighth century B.C. That a ruler of Dilmun should voluntarily choose to send gifts to the great king of Assyria at this time is hardly surprising, given how the other neighbors of Assyria had suffered at its hands. Interestingly, Ran Zadok has shown that the names Uperi and Ahundara/Hundaru are both Elamite,[120] and this is the first indication of any sort of link between Elam and Dilmun since the Susa texts of the earlier second millennium B.C. attesting to traffic in copper between the regions.

In the reign of Sargon's son and successor, Sennacherib (704–681 B.C.), we again hear of gifts being brought from Dilmun to the Assyrian court. This time, the dust of Babylon, a city destroyed by Sennacherib, was carried by the Euphrates all the way to Dilmun, according to a text from the *bit akitu* or "temple of the New Year's feast" at Assur (*ARAB* ii §438). From Dilmun came "workmen levied from their land, carriers of the head-pad, bronze spades, and bronze wedges, tools (which they use for) the work of their country, in order to (help) demolish Babylon."

During the reign of Esarhaddon (680–669 B.C.) a change can be detected in Assyrian relations with Dilmun. In one badly preserved text from Assur, Esarhaddon boasts of imposing tribute on a king of Dilmun called Qana (a West Semitic name). Beyond this, we have no insight into what brought about this state of affairs.

A much more complex relationship between Dilmun and Assyria is evident in the reign of Esarhaddon's son, Assurbanipal (668–627 B.C.). Three letters from Bel-ibni, Assurbanipal's governor in the province of the Sealand (southernmost Iraq), contain important allusions to Dilmun.[121] In one case (ABL 458), reference is made to Bel-ibni's having sent Idru, the messenger of Hundaru, king of Dilmun, to the Assyrian palace with the tribute of Bahrain. In another (ABL 791), Bel-ibni questions Hundaru's loyalty, suspecting him of making common cause with Assyria's great enemy, Nabu-bel-shumate, a Chaldaean outlaw/insurgent who, in Assyria's eyes, was an enemy of the state.[122] Like his father, Merodach-Baladan, Nabu-bel-shumate sought and was frequently given shelter by the Elamites, and Bel-ibni seemed to feel that Dilmun might have been doing the same. We also have a letter (*AAA* XX.C) from Assurbanipal to Hundaru, in which the Assyrian monarch asks, rhetorically to be sure, "Dost thou not know that I for my part am giving thee the kingdom of Tilmun, wherein thou shalt dwell, (wherein) thou shalt live under my protection? So in this wise shall my interests be guarded."

One final text of Assurbanipal's, the so-called Ishtar slab inscription from Nineveh (now unfortunately lost),[123] refers to the fact that Assurbanipal received annual tribute from Hundaru of Dilmun and Pade, king of Qade, as well as from kings of Kuppi and Hazmani, which may have lain outside of the Gulf region. Qade can easily be identified with Magan (Oman) thanks to the later trilingual Achaemenid inscriptions from Naqsh-i Rustam (DNa §3) and Susa (DSe 16, DSaa 31) in Iran where Qade and Maka, the Old Persian form of Magan, are equated. Moreover, Assurbanipal says that Pade lived in the capital of Qade, which he calls Iskie, and this is unquestionably Izki, in the interior of Oman, reputed in oral tradition to be the oldest town in the Sultanate.[124]

Several Iron Age sites in southeastern Arabia including Muweilah (Sharjah), Bida Bint Saud, and Rumeilah (both near Al-Ain, in the interior of Abu Dhabi), have columned buildings which recall those of the Iranian Iron Age at Hasanlu, Godin Tepe, and Nush-i Jan in the Iranian Zagros.[125] Moreover, certain ceramics—bridge-spouted vessels—of clear Iranian inspiration or manufacture or both, appear on both Bahrain and in southeastern Arabia,[126] while some of the bronze weaponry in Oman compares closely with that known in Iron Age Iran. Just how these connections were established, and what they signified, let alone what were the function(s) of the columned buildings, remains an open question.

THE NEO-BABYLONIAN PERIOD

After the fall of the Assyrian empire in 612 B.C. we have ample evidence of Babylonian contact (in the Neo-Babylonian period) with the northern and central Gulf region, via ceramics and seals found on Failaka and Bahrain. In addition, Failaka has yielded intriguing evidence of a possible Babylonian establishment on the island. In 1953 a fragment of a large piece of ashlar masonry bearing the text "palace of Nebuchadnezzar, king of Babylon," was found.[127] Although this was long thought to have been carried there later (though precisely how is a mystery), the discovery of an inscribed bronze bowl[128] on Failaka bearing a dedication to Shamash (the Babylonian sun god) from Nebuchadnezzar (604–562 B.C.) makes it much more likely that there was indeed a Babylonian presence, specifically linked to Nebuchadnezzar, on the island. Even more importantly, the bronze bowl says Shamash "dwells in the *é-kara*," therby giving us the name of his temple, and a temple by this name appears in a Neo-Assyrian list of temples in Dilmun,[129] making it probable that these texts relate to a real Babylonian presence on Failaka. Moreover, a stone slab with an Aramaic inscription of a fifth/fourth century B.C. date in which the word *ekara* can be read has been found on Failaka.[130]

The final piece of evidence that suggests some degree of Neo-Babylonian hegemony in the northern or central Gulf region dates to 544 B.C., that is, only five years before Cyrus the Great's entry into Babylon. It is a private account in which reference is made to the brother of the *bel pihati Dilmun*, normally translated as "administrator" (whether civil, military, or commercial remains uncertain in this context) of Dilmun.

The Achaemenid Presence

The impact of the Achaemenid Empire on the Persian Gulf has long been debated.[131] While the conquests of Cyrus the Great, Cambyses, Darius I, and Xerxes, to name the most well-known Achaemenids, forged an empire that stretched from the Aegean to Central Asia and the borders of India, the extent of Achaemenid interest in the Persian Gulf is less well-documented. Herodotus twice refers to the inhabitants of the "islands in the Erythraean Sea," in one case saying that they formed part of the fourteenth satrapy[132] under Darius I (*Hist.* 3.89), and in another that they fought with Xerxes at the battle of Doriscus (*Hist.* 7.80). The continued existence of the fourteenth satrapy unit in the fourth century B.C. is confirmed by Arrian who says that on his voyage up the Persian Gulf (following the conquest of India), Alexander's admiral Nearchus (discussed later in the chapter) encountered Mazenes, the "hyparch of the country" (Arrian, *Indica* 34.1) or "hyparch of the province" (Arrian, *Indica* 36.1) on Oaracta (Qishm) (Strabo, *Geog.* 16.3.7).

An Achaemenid presence further north on the coastal plain of Iran is shown by Strabo's (*Geog.* 15.3.3) reference to a Persian palace "on the coast near Taocê." Taocê has long been identified with Islamic Tawwaj[133] and Elamite Tam(uk)ka(n), a place mentioned in a number of Persepolis fortification texts.[134] Whether the place is identical to the Achaemenid site at Borazjan, near Tawwaj, where a pavilion of finely masoned ashlars in the style of Pasargadae (and hence dating to the reign of Cyrus the Great) was excavated by an Iranian team before the revolution,[135] is unclear.

Failaka, in particular Tell Khazneh, has yielded numerous examples of horse-and-rider terracotta figurines,[136] a figurine type well-attested at Susa and in Babylonia during the Achaemenid era, and excavations at Qalat al-Bahrain have brought to light numerous local imitations of Achaemenid "tulip bowls" as well as a glass stamp seal showing a royal hero in Persian dress with a sphinx and winged bull, all motifs known from the Achaemenid "court style" of glyptic.[137] The reuse of the large building complex of the early second millennium at Qalat al-Bahrain during the Achaemenid period is well-attested by the material excavated there by Danish archaeologists. The finds include some intriguing evidence of snake veneration, consisting of the bodies of sea *(Hydrophis lapemoides)* and rat snakes *(H. ventromaculatus)* that had been carefully wrapped in cloth bags, placed in bowls, and deposited under the floors of two different rooms.[138] Whether Failaka and Bahrain were included among the islands of the fourteenth satrapy we do not know, but it is certainly possible, judging from the Achaemenid-related finds from Qalat al-Bahrain, that the island was ruled by some sort of governor, if not a full-fledged satrap who was resident in the main building complex there.

In the Oman peninsula, material links with the Achaemenid world consist of short swords[139] and certain ceramic types (s-carinated bowls, tulip bowls). Just as important, moreover, is the fact that three of Darius I's (521–486 B.C.) own inscriptions give Qade as the Akkadian form of Old Persian Maka, clearly the cognate form of the older Akkadian *Makkan* (Sumerian *Magan*) which, as noted above, links this toponym with southeastern Arabia via the name of its capital, Iskie (i.e., Izki). Thus, from the time of Darius onwards, Maka or southeastern Arabia was part of the Persian Empire. Six of the Persepolis fortification texts,[140] moreover, use the Elamite form, Makkash. Two of these (PF 679 and 680) record the disbursement of wine to Irdumasda, satrap of Makkash, and in one case this occurred at Tamukkan, that is Taocê. Presumably the wine was distributed before Irdumasda embarked by boat on a trip back to his post somewhere in Oman. Four more texts (PF 1545, 2050; PFa 17, 29) record the disbursement of beer and flour rations for people going to or coming from Makkash. In one case, the flour was supplied to sixty-two men and their servants, all of whom were described as "Arabians," a strong indication that the destination, that is, Maka/Makkash, lay on the Arabian side of the Gulf (even though Arab settlement on the Iranian side of the Gulf, well-attested from the early Islamic to the modern era, may already date to this early period).

In describing the subject peoples of Darius I, Herodotus (*Hist.* 3.93) refers to the Mykoi, and these are certainly the inhabitants of Maka. Similarly, Xerxes lists the Maciya, an Old Persian gentilic from the toponym Maka, among the peoples "who dwell by the sea and dwell across the sea" (Daiva inscription), and Herodotus says the Mykoi fought with Xerxes at Doriscus in 480 B.C. (*Hist.* 7.68).

Interestingly, it was probably during the reign of Darius I that the Persian Gulf came to be referred to in this way. In older Mesopotamian cuneiform sources it had always been the Lower Sea, and in one case the "Sea of Magan," but around 500 B.C. the Greek geographer Hecataeus (excerpted by the later Byzantine writer Stephen of Byzantium)[141] used the term *Persikos kolpos*, that is, Persian Gulf, for the first time in a written source.

ALEXANDER'S EXPLORATION AND THE SELEUCIDS

In 325 B.C. Alexander sent a fleet under the command of Nearchus the Cretan from the mouth of the Indus River to Susa that was charged with exploring the coast of Iran. Convinced of Arabia's great wealth, Alexander dispatched three more naval expeditions a year later, all of which set out from Babylon.[142] The first, under Archias of Pella, got as far as Bahrain, known in Greek sources as Tylos (cf. Akkadian *Tilmun*, Sumerian *Dilmun*) or Tyrus (Arrian, *Anab.* 7.20.7). The second expedition, led by Androsthenes, also visted Tylos and its sister island Arados (modern Muharraq, just to the north of the main island of Bahrain, on which a place called Arad still exists), and is said to have sailed part way round the Arabian Peninsula. The third expedition, under Hieron, went all the way to Heroöpolis in Egypt, before returning to Babylon. These expeditions gathered an enormous amount of geographical, ethnographic, and botanical data, which was excerpted by later writers like Eratosthenes, Theophrastus, Strabo, Pliny, and Arrian, who have given us a description of the southern coast of Iran[143]; detailed descriptions of the flora of Tylos (Bahrain)[144]; a list of names of tribes and towns in eastern Arabia[145]; and the first detailed account of pearling in the Persian Gulf.[146]

Thereafter Alexander embarked on a program of colonization, founding an unnamed city[147] in southernmost Iraq, possibly near modern Kufa, and a second city, which Pliny calls Alexandria (Alexandria-on-the-Tigris) and which was probably meant to serve as an entrepôt at the head of the Persian Gulf to supersede Teredon, which had been founded by Nebuchadnezzar. After Alexander's death in 323 B.C. his Seleucid successors established a maximum of nine further colonies in the northern Gulf. At the head of the Gulf (perhaps near the mouth of the Tigris), was Seleucia-on-the-Erythraean Sea, a town which may have been sited with long-distance, Indian trade in mind. Further down the Iranian coast we find Antiochia-in-Persis, a settlement usually located at Rishahr, on the Bushehr Peninsula,[148] which was colonized by Greeks from Magnesia-ad-Maeandrum in Asia Minor according to a text of 205 B.C. found there. Badly damaged by flood, Alexandria-on-the-Tigris was refounded as Antiochia by Antiochus IV in 166 or 165 B.C. Later the town would have an illustrious career as a major economic center under the name Spasinou Charax (discussed later in the chapter). Finally, three more towns—Arethusa, Larisa, and Chalcis—are mentioned by Pliny (*Nat. Hist.* 6.159) but their locations are unknown, as is the location of Artemita in Arabia, mentioned by Cl. Ptolemy.

Of all these settlements the most important was probably Alexandria/Antiochia. This has been seen as the intended base for a Seleucid navy in the Gulf and as the new emporium for Babylonia's trade with India and the East. It was probably also the capital of the "satrapy of the Erythraean Sea,"[149] mentioned in 221 B.C. Whether or not a Seleucid navy was stationed permanently in the Gulf is, however, debatable. It is certain that, on occasion, ships were available and were used, as in the case of the return of Antiochus III from India in 205 B.C. (Polybius, *Hist.* 13.9). Antiochus sailed to eastern Arabia, possibly from Antiochia-in-Persis, in order to deal with the inhabitants of Gerrha, a rich trading city on the mainland (possibly the large, walled site of Thaj west of present-day Jubail). Polybius tells us that, after speaking with the Gerrhans, Antiochus sailed to Tylos, and then to Seleucia-on-the-Tigris in Babylonia (*Hist.* 13.9.4–5). All of this bespeaks the availability of ships, but this does not prove that Seleucid vessels were stationed off Qalat al-Bahrain or Failaka on a regular basis, as sometimes suggested.[150]

There is, however, archaeological evidence of significant Seleucid influence in the region. Of Antiochia-in-Persis we can say little since Rishahr remains unexcavated, but a decree sent to the "kinsmen and friends" at Magnesia by the citizens of Antiochia makes it clear that the Persian colony had the institutions of a Greek *polis*, complete with a representative council (*boule*).[151] On Failaka, where Danish and later French archaeologists worked in the 1950s and 1980s, a small, square fortification and several small Greek temples have been excavated, along with an important stele inscribed with forty-four lines of Greek,[152] and although the text contains a letter from one Anaxarchos to the inhabitants of Ikaros (the Greek name of Failaka),[153] replete with interesting references to gymnastic games and sanctuaries, there is no hint that the settlement there was constituted as a full-fledged *polis.*[154] On Bahrain, occupation of the large town at Qalat al-Bahrain continued throughout this period, and numerous burials have been excavated containing typical Hellenistic pottery and, in some cases, remarkably well-preserved wooden coffins.[155]

Several dozen smaller sites in northeastern Saudi Arabia, as well as the large, walled site of Thaj, built entirely of cut ashlar masonry, have common Hellenistic ceramics along with much local pottery and much glazed pottery that was probably manufactured in southwestern Iran or southern Babylonia or in both. Thaj has also yielded several Greek coins and at least one stamped Rhodian amphora handle.[156]

In southeastern Arabia there is little evidence from the Seleucid period outside of Mleiha, a sprawling settlement in the interior of Sharjah where a small number of Greek black-glazed sherds and a few stamped Rhodian amphora handles have been found among large amounts of local wares, mudbrick houses, and monumental, semi-subterranean tombs.[157]

Sites on the Arabian mainland and offshore islands have also yielded objects characteristic of the interior and southwestern corner of Arabia, including beehive-shaped, alabaster bottles with lids topped by handles in the form of a crouching lion[158] and small, cubical incense burners,[159] suggesting that overland trade, practiced since the Iron Age with the help of the domesticated camel,[160] was a factor in the local economy as well. Indeed Gerrha, the city visited by Antiochus the Great, was noted as an emporium for incense, and it may have been the city's wealth and economic importance which prompted the Seleucid emperor to make a special call on its inhabitants.[161] Gerrhan incense (ultimately of South Arabian origin) was exported to Babylonia (Strabo, *Geog.* 16.3.3), and Gerrhan merchants were said to mix with Minaean traders at Petra and in Palestine (Agatharchides, *Geog. Graeci Minores* §87). Gerrhan incense, obtained in Palestine, is mentioned in two of the Zenon papyri dating to 261 B.C. (P. Cairo Zen. 59536) and 260–258 B.C. (P. Cairo Zen. 59009), and Gerrhan traders—one named Temellatos (i.e., Taym-allat) and the other Kasmaios[162]—are attested on the Greek island of Delos in 146/5 B.C. and 141/0 B.C. We also have at least one typical

Nabataean sherd from a painted bowl excavated at Thaj, along with several Nabataean coins,[163] as well as two rock-cut, monumental tombs on Kharg Island, off the coast of Iran, which have been compared with Nabataean funerary architecture, suggestive of contact between northeastern and northwestern Arabia. One of the Kharg tombs, however, contained an inscription in Jewish Aramaic, dated to ca. A.D. 50, as well as graffiti of a menorah and a boat,[164] suggesting a more complex ethnic and religious mix in the region at this time. Jewish communities are well documented in southern Iraq during the period.[165]

Thaj, and a small number of associated sites in the northeast Arabian area (al-Hinna, Ayn Jawan, Qatif, Dhahran), provide us with a corpus of roughly fifty texts from this period.[166] Written in South Arabian characters, the texts are in a north Arabian dialect known as Hasaitic (after the modern name of the region, al-Hasa). This is most probably the language in which the letter to Antiochus III from the Gerrhans was written, since Antiochus required an interpreter to understand it (Polybius, *Hist.* 13.9.4). Most of these texts are found on tomb stelae, naming the deceased, one or more ancestors, and sometimes a kin or tribal affiliation. In addition, locally minted coin issues with the name of the solar deity Shams, written in South Arabian, have been attributed to this area.[167] These use as their model the tetradrachms of Alexander the Great and, later, of a diademed Seleucid sovereign.[168] Interestingly, when Antiochus III visited Gerrha he is said to have been given 500 talents of silver, along with 1,000 talents of frankincense, and 200 talents of *stacte*, a superior type of myrrh. The fact that small numbers of coins of this type minted by a king named Abyatha have turned up on Failaka and at Mektepini and Gordion suggests that they got there via Antiochus' army.[169] Antiochus returned to Babylonia, it can easily be argued, via Ikaros (Failaka), after which he headed to Asia Minor, hence the distribution of these exotic coins (which scarcely circulated outside of the Arabian peninsula otherwise) so far to the north.

CHARAX AND THE PALMYRENE PRESENCE

The Seleucids had little luck in controlling any part of southern Iran and by the 140s B.C. the Parthians had expanded into Khuzistan and southern Babylonia.[170] Yet it was not Parthia but the small kingdom of Characene in southern Iraq that exerted most influence in the Gulf. Aspasine (Gr. Hyspaosines), who had been satrap of the Erythraean Sea under Antiochus VII (Pliny, *Nat. Hist.* 6.31.138), seized power amidst the collapse of Seleucid authority in the east and established himself as king by 127 B.C., refounding Alexandria/Antiochia as Spasinou Charax.[171] A Greek dedicatory inscription from Bahrain honoring Hyspaosines and his wife Thalassia names Kephisodoros as *strategos* of Tylos and of the islands.[172] Since we know that Aspasine died in 124 B.C., and that he only assumed the title "king" in 127 B.C., this gives us a fairly precise date for his subjugation of Bahrain. The anonymous *Periplus of the Erythraean Sea*, a Greek mariner's handbook written around A.D. 60–75 which sets out the sailing conditions, ports, and main products along the route between Alexandria in Egypt and the ports of western and southern India, calls Spasinou Charax and its port of Apologos the main emporium in the Persian Gulf.[173] Moreover, Charax and a number of other cities in southern Iraq, including Vologesias and Forat, were linked by direct caravan routes with Palmyra in Syria.[174] Thus, goods from the Mediterranean flowed eastward to Charax via Palmyra and then on to India via the Gulf, just as goods from India flowed westward in the opposite direction. Charax is specifically mentioned in nine inscriptions from Palmyra and Umm al-Amad dating to between A.D. 50/1 (or 70/1) and 193. In many ways, therefore, this "Characene corridor" was a southerly alternative to the better-known transcontinental Silk Route.

Because of the profitable trade that it generated Charax was, for the most part, left to its own devices by the Parthians, the major dynasty ruling Iran from the mid-third century B.C. (though in western Iran only from the 140s B.C.) to ca. A.D. 224 They do not seem to have meddled in its affairs until much later. In A.D. 131, as we know from an honorific inscription found at Palmyra, a Palmyrene citizen named Yarhai served as the satrap of the *Thilouanoi*, that is, the inhabitants of Thiloua/os (Tylos) for the king of Charax, Meredat. Coins issued by Meredat in A.D. 142 identify him as *basileus Oman*.[175] A text from Palmyra dated to A.D. 157 refers to "the merchants who have returned from Scythia [viz. India] in the fleet of Honainu (HNYNW), son of Haddudan (HDWDN)" and, as noted above, the latest Palmyrene caravan inscription mentioning Charax dates to A.D. 193.

Archaeologically, we have evidence from the first and early second century A.D. of a major site, possibly ancient Omana, at ed-Dur on the coast of Umm al-Qaiwain.[176] Contemporary finds are known from Mleiha, in Sharjah[177]; the tombs[178] and Qalat of Bahrain[179]; graves in eastern Saudi Arabia[180]; and a squatter settlement in the Seleucid fortress on Failaka. A rich mix of imports has been found on these sites. Numismatic evidence includes small numbers of late Seleucid, Characene, Elymaean, Parthian, Persid, Kushan, and Indian coins.[181] Roman glass has been found in sizable quantities at both ed-Dur[182] and Mleiha. Western, Roman ceramics (*terra sigillata*),[183] amphora fragments inscribed with incuse letters[184]; Indian red-polished ware; and Namord ware from Kerman or Baluchistan[185] have also been recovered.

This is a period in which a sizable production of local coinage occurred, mainly in southeastern Arabia. At Mleiha a coin mold was discovered[186] while at ed-Dur hundreds of coins have been found both in hoards and scattered across the surface of the site. Like the earlier coinage from this region, these later issues are modeled on those of Alexander the Great, but the obverse head of Heracles is now much more debased than in the earlier issues, while the seated figure of Zeus on the reverse is sometimes abstracted into a stick figure, and the coin legends are in Aramaic.[187] The name of a king called Abi'el is repeated on most of this coinage, albeit often defectively written, and sometimes with a patronymic. The circulation of these coins, many of which are in base metal while some are in silver, was limited almost entirely to northeastern and southeastern Arabia, although at least one example has appeared in South Arabia. At Mleiha, the small, square fort with which the coin mold was associated may have been the seat of Abi'el's domain.

Late Parthian involvement in the affairs of the Gulf has often been inferred from the accounts of Ardashir's conquest of southern Iran (e.g., in the *Karnamak i Ardashir i Papakan*, Tabari and Ibn al-Athir), which refer to a Parthian vassal king named Haftanboxt (Haftavad of Ferdowsi's *Shahnama*) who ruled along the "coasts of the Persian Sea."[188] However, there has been too little archaeological work in coastal Iran to identify any of his "numerous castles." Similarly, in describing Ardashir's campaigns against Oman, Bahrain, and Yamama, the historians Tabari, Dinawari, and Ibn al-Athir say that he encountered and defeated a ruler named Sanatruq in northeastern Arabia. Some scholars have suggested a confusion made by a copyist between the toponym *Hatta*, a designation for a district in eastern Saudi Arabia, and *Hatra*, in northern Iraq, where Sanatruq (SNTRWQ) was a name attested in the ruling dynasty.[189] The name Sanatruq, however, was also attested in Adiabene (a kingdom and later satrapy of Parthia, located in the area of the Greater and Lesser Zab rivers in northeastern Iraq) and we should not exclude the possibility that a Parthian vassal by this name ruled over the district of Bahrain (by which the mainland, and not the island, is meant in the Arabic sources) during the early third century A.D.

With the rise of Ardashir in the first half of the third century, and the founding of the great Sasanian dynasty that ruled Persia from A.D. 224 to A.D. 642 , the Persian Gulf, so long a corridor of Characene and Palmyrene trade with the East, became a "Sasanian lake."[190] Almost a century after Ardashir's campaigns, eastern Arabia was devastated by Shapur II,[191] and although there are lacunae in the history of Sasanian political domination in the region, Sasanian control is amply documented in Bahrain (northeastern Arabia) and Mazun (southeastern Arabia),[192] in the centuries that preceded the coming of Islam.[193]

Conclusion

Neither the natural resources nor the environment of the Persian Gulf has changed appreciably over the course of the past 6,000 years. Indeed it could be argued that until the development of the cultured pearl and the beginnings of the oil industry, the local economic imperatives in the Persian Gulf were extremely stable. With respect to transshipment or transit trade, the nonlocal commodities changing hands did vary through time, and the organizational means by which they were moved certainly evolved. The administrative arrangements of Lu-Enlila at Ur were a far cry from those of the Dutch or English East India Companies several thousand years later, and the political involvements of neighboring states changed constantly.

The Persian Gulf has over millennia been characterized by contacts, often trade ties with and sometimes political domination by, neighboring states. Foreign trade has always played an important role in providing items not indigenous to the area, and local products such as pearls, dates, horses, and metals were exchanged for goods from far afield, including Iraq, Iran, East Africa, India, China, and the East Indies. A characteristic of long standing was the region's commercial relations with Mesopotamia. In every historical period there was an important port (whose name varied) at the head of the Gulf. Free trade more than political domination was in the interest of the Mesopotamian dynasties, and the Gulf peoples often enjoyed autonomy, for example in the centuries between the fall of the Achaemenids and the rise of the Sasanids.

In antiquity the Persian Gulf possessed highly developed spiritual as well as commercial traditions. For example, there is the religious significance of Dilmun and its deities in Mesopotamian literature. Much later, Failaka was accorded high regard as an isle of cult sanctuaries by the Greeks who accompanied Alexander. Both Judaism and Zoroastrianism were practiced during the Sasanian period. Nestorian Christianity was an integrating force that for three centuries brought the inhabitants of eastern Arabia, Mesopotamia, and southwestern Iran into close relations and helped unite a region that would later embrace Islam.

Throughout the entire period discussed here, the Persian Gulf constitutes a coherent region with remarkable stability in the identities of its subregions: southern Iran, southern Iraq, northeastern Arabia, and southeastern Arabia. In spite of linguistic and demographic changes over the course of six millennia, much of the archaeological record reflects those strong identities. Moreover, the subplots one can detect throughout the long history of this area—intra-Gulf relationships, particular attachments to particular resources and subsistence strategies—seem to have been remarkably consistent, notwithstanding those clear changes at a macropolitical or macroeconomic level which have been documented above. If any lesson is to be derived from these observations, then, it is that a longitudinal history of a region reveals patterns which more detailed studies of narrower slices of time simply cannot expose.

Abbreviations

(NB: titles of journals are italicized whereas those of a monograph series are not)

AAE *Arabian Archaeology & Epigraphy*
ABL R. F. Harper, *Assyrian and Babylonian letters belonging to the Kouyunjik Collections of the British Museum* Chicago: University of Chicago Press, 1892–1914.
BAR British Archaeological Reports
BBVO Berliner Beiträge zum Vorderen Orient (Berlin: Reimer Verlag, 1982–present)
CNIP Carsten Niebuhr Institute Publications (Copenhagen: Museum Tusculanum, 1986–present)
DNa trilingual inscription *a* on the tomb of Darius I at Naqsh-i Rustam
DSe trilingual inscription *e* of Darius I at Susa
DSaa Akkadian inscription *aa* of Darius I at Susa
EW *East and West*
JA *Journal Asiatique*
JAOS *Journal of the American Oriental Society*
JASP Jutland Archaeological Society Publications
JCS *Journal of Cuneiform Studies*
JOS *Journal of Oman Studies*
JRAS *Journal of the Royal Asiatic Society*
MASP Finkbeiner, U., ed. *Materialien zur Archäologie der Seleukiden- und Partherzeit im südlichen Babylonien und im Golfgebiet.* Tübingen: Wasmuth.
MDP Mémoires de la Délégation (Archéologique) en Perse (Paris: Geuthner, 1900–present)
Or *Orientalia*
PF siglum for texts from the Persepolis fortification
PFIC D. T. Potts, H. Al Naboodah, and P. Hellyer, eds. 2003. *Archaeology of the United Arab Emirates: Proceedings of the First International Conference on the Archaeology of the UAE* (London: Trident).
PSAS *Proceedings of the Seminar for Arabian Studies*
TAVO Tübinger Atlas des vorderen Orients (Weisbaden: Ludwig Reichert Verlag, 1972–present)
TMO Travaux de la Maison de l'Orient (Lyon: Maison de l'Orient, 1980–present)
ZA *Zeitschrift für Assyriologie*

Notes

1. For sites in the interior of Laristan, see R. Pohanka, *Burgen und Heiligtümer in Laristan, Südiran* (Vienna, Austria: Sitzungsber. d. Österreichische Akad. d. Wiss., phil.-hist. Kl. 466 [= Veröffentlichungen der Iranischen Kommission 19], 1986); D. Schön, *Laristan - eine südpersische Küstenprovinz* (Vienna: Sitzungsber. d. Österreichische Akad. d. Wiss., phil.-hist. Kl. 553 [= Veröffentlichungen der Iranischen Kommission 24], 1990). In 2004 D. Kennet, University of Durham, began a survey program around Minab, inland from the Strait of Hormuz.
2. M. Pézard, *Mission à Bender Bouchir* (MDP 15, 1914); D. Whitehouse and A. G. Williamson, "Sasanian Maritime Trade," *Iran* 11 (1973): 29–49; D. Whitcomb, "Bushire and the Angali Canal," *Mesopotamia* 22 (1987): 311–36. New survey work was conducted around Bushehr and its hinterland in 2004. See R. A. Carter, K. Challis, S. M. N. Priestman, and H. Tofighian, "The Bushehr Hinterland: Results of the First Season of the Iranian-British Archaeological Survey of Bushehr Province, November–December 2004," *Iran* 44 (2006): 63–103.

3. M.-J. Steve, *L'île de Kharg: Une page de l'histoire du Golfe persique et du monachisme oriental* (Neuchâtel: Civilisations du Proche-Orient Série I, Archéologie et environnement 1, 2003).
4. See e.g. D. Whitehouse, *The Congregational Mosque and Other Mosques from the Ninth to the Twelfth Centuries* (London: British Institute of Persian Studies [= Siraf III], 1980); N. M. Lowick, *The Coins and Monumental Inscriptions* (London: British Institute of Persian Studies [= Siraf XV], 1985); M. Tampoe, *Maritime Trade between China and the West: An Archaeological Study of the Ceramics from Siraf (Persian Gulf), 8th to 15th Century A.D.* (Oxford: BAR International Series 555, 1989).
5. D. Whitehouse, "Kish," *Iran* 14 (1976): 146–47.
6. See, for example, W. Tomaschek, *Topographische Erläuterung der Küstenfahrt Nearchs vom Indus bis zum Euphrat* (Vienna, Austria: Sitzungsberichte der Kais. Akad. d. Wiss. in Wien, phil.-hist. Cl. 121 (1890), 1–88; A. Berthelot, "La côte méridionale de l'Iran d'après les géographes grecs" in *Mélanges offerts à M. Octave Navarre par ses élèves et ses amis* (Toulouse, France: Edouard Privat, 1935), 11–24. D. T. Potts, "The Islands of the XIVth Satrapy," in *Draya tya hacâ Pârsâ aitiy: Essays on the Archaeology and History of the Persian Gulf Littoral,* ed. K. Abdi (Oxford: Archaeopress, in press).
7. H. Rawlinson, "Notes on Capt. Durand's Report upon the Islands of Bahrain," *JRAS* 12 (1880): 13–39.
8. Since the 1920s claims have been made for the discovery of Palaeolithic stone tools at numerous sites in eastern Arabia, but most of these proved to be incorrect. More recently, evidence has begun to mount and, with the benefit of modern methods of lithic study, it now seems that there are indeed sites of Palaeolithic date in the Oman peninsula (e.g., S. McBrearty, "Earliest stone tools from the Emirate of Abu Dhabi, United Arab Emirates," in *Fossil Vertebrates of Arabia,* ed. P. J. Whybrow and A. Hill (New Haven, CT and London: Yale University Press, 1999), 373–88. Recently, archaeologists working in Abu Dhabi have discovered more tools of Palaeolithic type at Barakah, in western Abu Dhabi and at Jabal Faya, in the interior of Sharjah.
9. K. Lambeck, "Shoreline Reconstructions for the Persian Gulf since the Last Glacial Maximum," *Earth and Planetary Science Letters* 142 (1996): 43–57; J. T. Teller, K. W. Glennie, N. Lancaster, and A. K. Singhvi, "Calcareous Dunes of the United Arab Emirates and Noah's flood: The Postglacial Reflooding of the Persian (Arabian) Gulf," *Quaternary International* 68–71 (2000): 297–308.
10. Pleistocene is the term given to the geological era extending from ca. 1.8 million to 10,000 years ago. Holocene refers to the period since the end of the Pleistocene and hence encompasses our own era.
11. R. Dalongeville and P. Sanlaville, "Confrontation des datations isotopiques avec les donnés géomorphologiques et archéologiques: A propos des variations relatives du niveau marin sur la rive arabe du Golfe persique," in *Chronologies in the Near East,* ed. O. Aurenche, J. Évin, and F. Hours (Oxford: BAR International Series 379 (1987), 568–83; P. Sanlaville, R. Dalongeville, J. Évin, and R. Paskoff, "Modification du tracé littoral sur la côte arabe due Golfe persique en relation avec l'archéologie," in *Déplacements des lignes de rivage en Méditerranée* (Paris: Éditions du CNRS, 1987), 211–22.
12. R. Dalongeville, "L'environnement du site de Tell Abraq," in *A Prehistoric Mound in the Emirate of Umm al-Qaiwain: Excavations at Tell Abraq in 1989,* D. T. Potts (Copenhagen, Denmark: Munksgaard, 1990), 139–40; R. Boucharlat, R. Dalongeville, A. Hesse, and M. Millet, "Occupation humaine et environnement au 5e et au 4e millénaire sur la côte Sharjah-Umm al-Qaiwain (UAE)," *AAE* 2 (1991): 93–106; P. Bernier, R. Dalongeville, B. Dupuis, and V. de Medwecki, "Holocene Shoreline Variations in the Persian Gulf: Example of the Umm al-Qowayn Lagoon (UAE)," *Quaternary International* 29–30 (1995): 95–103.
13. See Lambeck (note 9).
14. R. Dalongeville, "Présentation physique générale de l'île de Failaka," in Y. Calvet and J. Gachet, eds., *Failaka fouilles françaises 1986–1988* (TMO 18, 1990), 39.

15. See for example, R. Carter, H. Crawford, S. Mellalieu, and D. Barrett, "The Kuwait-British Archaeological Expedition to As-Sabiyah: Report on the First Season's Work," *Iraq* 61 (1999): 43–58.
16. For example M. Piperno, "Jahrom, a Middle Palaeolithic Site in Fars, Iran," *EW* 22 (1972): 183–97; M. Piperno, "Upper Palaeolithic Caves in Southern Iran: Preliminary report," *EW* 24 (1974): 9–13; M. Rosenberg, *Paleolithic Settlement Patterns in the Marv Dasht, Fars Province, Iran* (Ann Arbor, MI: University Microfilms, 1988).
17. See generally P. E. L. Smith, *Paleolithic Archaeology in Iran* (Philadelphia, PA: American Institute of Iranian Studies, Monograph 1, 1986).
18. D. T. Potts, *Mesopotamian Civilization: The Material Foundations* (Ithaca, NY: Cornell University Press, 1997), 52; J. Zarins, "The Early Settlement of Southern Mesopotamia: A Review of Recent Historical, Geological, and Archaeological Research," *JAOS* 112 (1992): 55–77.
19. J. Zarins, "Archaeological and Chronological Problems within the Greater Southwest Asian Arid Zone, 8500–1850 b.c.," in *Chronologies in Old World Archaeology*, ed. R. W. Ehrich, 3rd ed. (Chicago: University of Chicago Press, 1992), 42–62.
20. For example P. Biagi, "An Early Palaeolithic Site Near Saiwan (Sultanate of Oman)," *AAE* 5 (1994): 81–88.
21. H. Amirkhanov, "Research on the Palaeolithic and Neolithic of Hadramaut and Mahra," *AAE* 5 (1994): 217–28; H. Amirkhanov, *The Paleolithic in South Arabia* [in Russian] (Moscow: Nauka, 1991); N. M. Whalen and K. E. Schatte, "Pleistocene Sites in Southern Yemen," *AAE* 8 (1997): 1–10.
22. The literature on this topic is vast, but see A. G. Parker, G. Preston, H. Walkington, and M. J. Hodson, "Developing a Framework of Holocene Climatic Change and Landscape Archaeology for the Lower Gulf Region, Southeastern Arabia," *AAE* 18 (2007): 125–30. Also U. Neff, S. J. Burns, A. Mangini, M. Mudelsee, D. Fleitmann, and A. Mattar, "Strong Coherence between Solar Variability and the Monsoon in Oman between 9 and 6 k yr Ago," *Nature* 411 (2001): 290–93.
23. See for example O. Bar-Yosef and R. H. Meadow, "The Origins of Agriculture in the Near East," in *Last hunters, First Farmers: New Perspectives on the Prehistoric Transition to Agriculture,* ed. T. D. Price and A. B. Gebauer (Santa Fe, NM: School of American Research Press, 1995), 39–94.
24. S. Cleuziou and M. Tosi, "Hommes, climats et environnements de la Péninsule arabique à l'Holocène," *Paléorient* 23 (1998): 121–35.
25. For example, M. Beech, "The Development of Fishing in the UAE: A Zooarchaeological Perspective," PFIC (2003), 290–308, with bibliography. Also M. Beech, *In the Land of the Icthyophagi: Modelling Fish Exploitation in the Arabian Gulf and Gulf of Oman from the 5th Millennium B.C. to the Late Islamic Period* (Oxford: British Archaeological Reports International Series 1217 [=Abu Dhabi Islands Archaeological Survey Monograph 1], 2004.
26. For example, E. Glover, "Molluscan Evidence for Diet and Environment at Saar in the Early Second Millennium B.C.," *AAE* 6 (1995): 157–79.
27. J. Frazier, "Prehistoric and Ancient Historic Interactions between Humans and Marine Turtles," in *The Biology of Sea Turtles*, vol. 2, ed. P. L. Lutz, J. A. Musick, and J. Wyneken (Boca Raton, FL: CRC Press, 2003), 3–6.
28. H. Jousse, M. Faure, C. Guérin, and A. Prieur, "Exploitation des ressources marines au cours des Ve-IVe millénaires: Le site à dugongs de l'île d'Akab (Umm al-Qaiwain, Émirats Arabes Unis)," *Paléorient* 28 (2002): 43–60; H. Jousse and C. Guérin, "Les dugongs (Sirenia, Dugongidae) de l'Holocène ancien d'Umm al-Qaiwain (Émirats Arabes Unis)," *Mammalia* 67 (2003): 337–47.
29. See for example, W. Lancaster and F. Lancaster, "Tribe, Community and the Concept of Access to Resources: Territorial Behaviour in South-East Ja'alan," in *Mobility and Territoriality: Social and Spatial Boundaries among Foragers, Fishers, Pastoralists and Peripatetics,* ed. M. J. Asimov and A. Rao (Oxford and Providence, RI: Berg, 1992), 343–63; J. C. Wilkinson, *Water and Tribal Settlement in South-Eastern Arabia* (Oxford: Clarendon Press, 1977).

30. H.-P. Uerpmann, M. Uerpmann, and S. A. Jasim, eds., *Funeral Monuments and Human Remains from Jebel al-Buhais* (Sharjah, UAE and Tübingen, Germany: Department of Culture and Information and Kerns Verlag, 2006). For the human remains, see H. Kiesewetter, "Analyses of the Human Remains from the Neolithic Cemetery at al-Buhais 18" (Excavations 1996–2000), 2006, 103–380.
31. S. Cleuziou and L. Costantini, "Premiers éléments sur l'agriculture protohistorique de l'Arabie oriental," *Paléorient* 6 (1980): 245–51.
32. J. M. Marsh, I. Sagaby, and R. R. Sooley, "A Groundwater Resources Databank in the Kingdom of Saudi Arabia," *Journal of the Geological Society of London* 138 (1981): 599–602.
33. D. T. Potts, "Contributions to the Agrarian History of Eastern Arabia II. The Cultivars," *AAE* 5 (1994): 236–75.
34. G. Willcox and M. Tengberg, "Preliminary Report on the Archaeobotanical Investigations at Tell Abraq with Special Attention to Chaff Impressions in Mud Brick," *AAE* 6 (1995): 129–38.
35. H.-P. Uerpmann, "Problems of archaeo-zoological research in Eastern Arabia," in P. M. Costa and M. Tosi, eds., *Oman Studies: Papers on the Archaeology and History of Oman* (Rome: Serie Orientale Roma 63, 1989), 164; M. Uerpmann, H.-P. Uerpmann, and S. A. Jasim, "Stone Age Nomadism in SE Arabia: Palaeo-Economic Considerations on the Neolithic Site of Al-Buhais 18 in the Emirate of Sharjah, UAE," *PSAS* 30 (2000): 229–34; H. Kallweit, "Remarks on the Late Stone Age in the UAE," PFIC (2003): 61–63.
36. H. Kapel, *Atlas of the Stone Age Cultures of Qatar* (JASP 6, 1967), 18.
37. See generally M. Uerpmann, "Structuring the Late Stone Age of Southeastern Arabia," *AAE* 3 (1992): 65–109; R. H. Spoor, "Human Population Groups and the Distribution of Lithic Arrowheads in the Arabian Gulf," *AAE* 8 (1997): 143–60.
38. Lancaster and Lancaster, "Tribe, Community and the Concept of Access to Resources," 345.
39. The bibliography on this topic is long. For earlier material and a good overview of the problem see M. Uerpmann and H.-P. Uerpmann, "'Ubaid Pottery in the Eastern Gulf – New Evidence from Umm al-Qaiwain (UAE)," *AAE* 7 (1996): 125–39.
40. Again, there is an enormous bibliography on this topic. For the most recent statement see J. Oates, "Ubaid Mesopotamia revisited," in K. von Folsach, H. Thrane, and I. Thuesen, eds., *From Handaxe to Khan: Essays Presented to Peder Mortensen on the Occasion of His 70th birthday* (Aarhus, Denmark: Aarhus University Press, 2004), 87–104 with extensive bibliography.
41. R. Carter, "Ubaid-Period Boat Remains from As-Sabiyah: Excavations by the British archaeological expedition to Kuwait," *PSAS* 32 (2002): 13–30. Also J. Connan, R. Carter, H. Crawford, M. Tobey, A. Charrié-Duhaut, D. Jarvie, P. Albrecht, and K. Norman, "A Comparative Geochemical Study of Bituminous Boat Remains from H3, As-Sabiyah (Kuwait), and RJ-2, Ra's al-Jinz (Oman)," *AAE* 16 (2005): 21–66.
42. For more background on Mesopotamia in the Ubaid period, see the papers in E. F. Henrickson and I. Thuesen, eds., *Upon This Foundation: The 'Ubaid Reconsidered* (Copenhagen, Denmark: CNIP, 1989), 10; R. Matthews, *The Early Prehistory of Mesopotamia: 500,000 to 4,500 b.c.* (Turnhout, Belgium: Brepols, 2000).
43. Cf. W. Dostal, *The Traditional Architecture of Ras al-Khaimah (North)* (Wiesbaden, Germany: TAVO, Beheft B 54, 1983).
44. M. Uerpmann, "The Dark Millennium: Remarks on the Final Stone Age in the Emirates and Oman," PFIC, 74–81.
45. Jousse, Faure, Guérin, and Prieur, "Exploitation des ressources marines au cours des Ve-IVe millénaires"; Jousse and Guérin, "Les dugongs (Sirenia, Dugongidae) de l'Holocène ancien d'Umm al-Qaiwain (Émirats Arabes Unis)."
46. A. Prieur and C. Guérin, "Découverte d'un site préhistorique d'abattage de dugongs à Umm al-Qaiwain (Emirats Arabes Unis)," *AAE* 2 (1991): Figs. 4–5.
47. P. Biagi, "A Radiocarbon Chronology for the Aceramic Shell-Middens of Coastal Oman," *AAE* 5 (1994): 17–31.

48. R. K. Englund, "Dilmun in the Archaic Uruk Corpus," in *Dilmun: New studies in the Archaeology and Early History of Bahrain*, ed. D. T. Potts, BBVO 2 (1983), 35–37; H. J. Nissen, "Ortsnamen in den archaischen Texten aus Uruk," *Or* 54 (1985): 226–33.
49. D. T. Potts, *Miscellanea Hasaitica* (CNIP 9, 1989); J. Zarins, "Eastern Saudi Arabia and External Relations: Selected Ceramic, Steatite and Textual evidence—3500–1900 b.c.," in *South Asian Archaeology 1985*, ed. K. Frifelt and P. Sørensen (Copenhagen, Denmark: Scandinavian Institute of Asian Studies Occasional Paper 4, 1989): 74–103.
50. The texts can be found in several different compilations. Perhaps the most convenient source for all of the texts relating to Dilmun (and Magan) is W. Heimpel, "Das untere Meer," *ZA* 77 (1987): 22–91.
51. The literature on copper ores and copper metallurgy in Oman is large. For a convenient source with full bibliography, see now L. R. Weeks, *Early Metallurgy of the Persian Gulf: Technology, Trade and the Bronze Age World* (Boston and Leiden, Netherlands: Brill, 2003).
52. D. T. Potts, "Eastern Arabia and the Oman Peninsula during the Late Fourth and Early Third Millennium B.C.," in *Ǧamdat Nasr: Period or Regional Style?*, ed. U. Finkbeiner and W. Röllig (Wiesbaden, Germany: TAVO, Beiheft B 62, 1986), 121–70.
53. Occupation at the settlement of Hili 8 may have begun around 3000 B.C., coeval with the Hafit tomb tradition, but I have queried the C14 dates and suggested these may have been run on charcoal from timber that was already old when it was used. For the arguments, see D. T. Potts, "Re-writing the Late Prehistory of Southeastern Arabia: A Reply to Jocelyn Orchard," *Iraq* 59 (1997): 63–71.
54. The argument has been made for the later Umm an-Nar graves and would apply to the Hafit graves as well since these are also collective, albeit involving fewer individuals. See K. W. Alt, W. Vach, K. Frifelt, and M. Kunter, "Familienanalyse in kupferzeitlichen Kollektivgräbern aus Umm al-Nar, Abu Dhabi," *AAE* 6 (1995): 65–80.
55. There is a very large bibliography on Umm an-Nar tombs. For a recent discussion with extensive bibliography see S. Blau, "Fragmentary Endings: A Discussion of 3rd-Millennium b.c. Burial Practices in the Oman Peninsula," *Antiquity* 75 (2001): 557–70. On the skeletal remains in these tombs and what they can tell us, see S. Blau, "Limited yet informative: Pathological alterations observed on human skeletal remains from third and second millennia B.C. collective burials in the United Arab Emirates," *International Journal of Osteoarchaeology* 11 (2001): 173–205.
56. Named after Mortella on Corsica, these round towers are attested as early as the fifteenth century. They became particularly popular in the Napoleonic era. With a height of up to 12 meters and extremely thick walls, these towers could withstand cannon fire. An elevated surface near the top served as a gun platform. See S. Sutcliffe, *Martello Towers* (Newton Abbot: David and Charles, 1972).
57. D. T. Potts, "Before the Emirates: An archaeological and historical account of developments in the region c. 5000 B.C. to 676 A.D.," in *United Arab Emirates: A New Perspective*, ed. I. Al Abed and P. Hellyer (London: Trident, 2001), 40 with earlier bibliography.
58. S. Méry, *Les céramiques d'Oman et l'Asie moyenne: Une archéologie des échanges à l'Âge du Bronze* (Paris: Éditions du CNRS, 2000).
59. Weeks, *Early Metallurgy of the Persian Gulf.*
60. H. David, "Styles and Evolution: Soft Stone Vessels during the Bronze Age in the Oman Peninsula," *PSAS* 26 (1996): 31–46.
61. All of the relevant texts can be found in W. Heimpel, "Das untere Meer," *ZA* 77 (1987): 22–91.
62. A. Millard, "Cypriot Copper in Babylonia, c. 1745 B.C.," *JCS* 25 (1973): 211–13.
63. See, for example, D. T. Potts, *Ancient Magan: The Secrets of Tell Abraq* (London: Trident, 2000); D. T. Potts, "Tepe Yahya, Tell Abraq and the chronology of the Bampur sequence," *Iranica Antiqua* 38 (2003): 1–24.
64. D. T. Potts, "Anshan, Liyan and Magan c. 2000 B.C.," in *Yeki bud, yeki nabud: Essays on the Archaeology of Iran in Honor of William M. Sumner*, ed. N. Miller and K. Abdi (Los Angeles: Cotsen Institute of Archaeology, 2003), 156–59.
65. S. Méry, *Les céramiques d'Oman et l'Asie moyenne: Une archéologie des échanges à l'Âge du Bronze* (Paris: Éditions du CNRS, 2000).

66. P. Amiet, *L'âge des échanges inter-iraniens, 3500–1700 avant J.-C.* (Paris: Notes et documents des Musées de France 11, 1986), 150; S. Cleuziou, G. Gnoli, C. Robin, and M. Tosi, "Cachets inscrits de la fin du IIIe millénaire av. notre ère à Ras' al-Junayz, Sultanat d'Oman," *Comptes Rendus de l'Académie des Inscriptions & Belles-Lettres 1994* (1994): 453–68. S. Cleuziou and M. Tosi, *In the Shadow of the Ancestors: The Prehistoric Foundations of the Early Arabian Civilization in Oman* (Muscat: Ministry of Heritage and Culture, 2007).
67. See most recently S. Ratnagar, "Theorizing Bronze-Age Intercultural Trade: The Evidence of the Weights," *Paléorient* 29 (2003): 79–92.
68. S. Cleuziou, "Early Bronze Age Trade in the Gulf and the Arabian Sea: The Society behind the Boats," PFIC (2003), 145.
69. See generally M. Liverani, *Akkad, the First World Empire: Structure, Ideology, Traditions* (Padua: Sargon, 1993).
70. See generally D. T. Potts, *The Archaeology of Elam: Formation and Transformation of an Ancient Iranian State* (Cambridge: Cambridge University Press, 1999).
71. These texts have been much discussed. See, for example, A. L. Oppenheim, "The Seafaring Merchants of Ur," *JAOS* 74 (1954): 6–17.
72. H. Waetzoldt, *Untersuchungen zur neusumerischen Textilindustrie* (Rome: Studi Economici e Tecnologici 1, 1972), 72.
73. For the trade in copper and tin through the Persian Gulf, see Weeks, *Early Metallurgy of the Persian Gulf.*
74. For the classic discussion, see W. F. Leemans, *Foreign Trade in the Old Babylonian Period* (Leiden, Netherlands: Studia et Documenta ad Iura Orientis Antiqui Pertinentia 6, 1960).
75. These issues have been discussed by several authors including C. C. Lamberg-Karlovsky, "Death in Dilmun," in *Bahrain Through the Ages: The Archaeology,* ed. H. A. Al Khalifa and M. Rice (London: Kegan Paul International, 1986), 163–65.
76. See most recently, with earlier bibliography, H. Crawford, *Early Dilmun Seals from Saar: Art and Commerce in Bronze Age Bahrain* (Ludlow, UK: Archaeology International, 2001).
77. R. H. Brunswig, Jr., A. Parpola, and D. T. Potts, "New Indus type and related seals from the Near East," in *Dilmun: New Studies in the Archaeology and Early History of Bahrain,* ed. D. T. Potts (BBVO 2, 1983), 101–15.
78. See in general A. Parpola, *Deciphering the Indus Script* (Cambridge: Cambridge University Press, 1994).
79. See, for example, J.-J. Glassner, "Dilmun, Magan, and Meluhha: Some Observations on Language, Toponymy, Anthroponymy and Theonymy," in *The Indian Ocean in Antiquity,* ed. J. E. Reade (London: Kegan Paul International, 1996), 235–50; J. Glassner, "Dilmun et Magan: La place de l'écriture," in *Languages and Cultures in Contact: At the Crossroads of Civilizations in the Syro-Mesopotamian Realm,* ed. K. Van Lerberghe and G. Voet, Orientalia Lovaniensia Analecta 96 (Leuven, Belgium: Peeters Press en Departement Ossterse Studies, [2000]), 141–42; D. T. Potts with S. Blau, "Identities in the East Arabian Region," *Mediterranean Archaeology* 11 (1998): 27–38.
80. This topic has been addressed by numerous scholars. See, for example, B. Vogt, "Bronze Age Maritime Trade in the Indian Ocean: Harappan Traits on the Oman Peninsula," in *The Indian Ocean in Antiquity,* Reade, 107–32; U. Franke-Vogt, "The Harappans and the West: Some Reflections on Meluhha's relations to Magan, Dilmun and Mesopotamia," *Bulletin of Archaeology, the University of Kanazawa* 20 (1993): 72–101; D. T. Potts, "South and Central Asian elements at Tell Abraq (Emirate of Umm al-Qaiwain, United Arab Emirates), c. 2200 B.C–A.D. 400," in *South Asian Archaeology 1993,* vol. 2, ed. A. Parpola and P. Koskikallio (Helsinki, Finland: Annales Academiæ Scientiarum Fennicæ B 271, 1994), 615–28.
81. G. Weisgerber, "Archäologische und archäometallurgische Untersuchungen in Oman," *Beiträge zur allgemeine und vergleichende Archäologie* 2 (1980): 86, Abb. 15.
82. S. Cleuziou and M. Tosi, "Evidence for the Use of Aromatics in the Early Bronze Age of Oman: Period III at RJ-2 (2300–2200 B.C.)," in *Profumi d'Arabia,* ed. A. Avanzini (Rome: Saggi di Storia Antica, 1997), 11, Fig. 11.

83. J. N. Benton, *Excavations at Al Sufouh: A Third Millennium Site in the Emirate of Dubai* (Turnhout, Belgium: Brepols, 1996), 165 and Fig. 197.
84. L. de Meyer, "Een Tilmoenit te Suse," *Orientalia Gandensia* 3 (1966): 115–17; M. Lambert, "Tablette de Suse avec cachet du Golfe," *Revue d'Assyriologie* 70 (1976): 71–72.
85. Potts, "Anshan, Liyan and Magan c. 2000 B.C."
86. Potts, "South and Central Asian elements at Tell Abraq," 617; R. A. Carter, "Saar and its external relations: New evidence for interaction between Bahrain and Gujarat during the early second millennium B.C.," *AAE* 12 (2001): 183–201.
87. J. Eidem and F. Højlund, "Trade or Diplomacy? Assyria and Dilmun in the Eighteenth Century B.C.," *World Archaeology* 24 (1993): 441–48.
88. F. Højlund and H. H. Andersen, *Qala'at al-Bahrain,* vol. 1, *The Northern City Wall and the Islamic Fortress* (JASP 30/1, 1994); F. Højlund and H. H. Andersen, *Qala'at al-Bahrain,* vol. 2, *The Central Monumental Buildings* (JASP 30/2, 1997).
89. J. Moon and R. G. Killick, "A Dilmun residence on Bahrain," in *Beiträge zur Kulturgeschichte Vorderasiens: Festschrift für Rainer Michael Boehmer,* ed. U. Finkbeiner, R. Dittmann, and H. Hauptmann (Mainz, Germany: Von Zabern, 1995), 413–38; H. Crawford, R. Killick, and J. Moon, *The Dilmun Temple at Saar* (London: Kegan Paul International, 1997). R. Killick and J. Moon, eds., *The Early Dilmun Settlement at Saar* (Ludlow, UK: London-Bahrain Archaeological Expedition Saar Excavation Report 3, 2005).
90. H. H. Andersen and F. Højlund, *The Barbar Temples* (JASP 48, 2004). Danish archaeologists have recently begun new excavations at the Barbar temple: see F. Højlund, P. Bangsgaard, J. Hansen, N. Haue, P. Kjærum, and D. D. Lund, "New Excavations at the Barbar Temple, Bahrain," *AAE* 16 (2005): 105–28.
91. J. Zarins, "Excavations at Dhahran South: The Tumulus Field (208–92); A preliminary Report," *Atlal* 8 (1984): 25–54.
92. The mining of "dead coral rock" is well-described in R. LeB. Bowen, "Marine industries of Eastern Arabia," *Geographical Review* 41 (1951): 393–95.
93. F. Højlund, *Failaka/Dilmun, the Second Millennium Settlements,* vol. 2, *The Bronze Age Pottery* (JASP 17/2, 1987). For a good overview of the later French excavations of Bronze Age remains on Failaka between 1983 and 1988, see Y. Calvet, "Agarum, une île de la civilisation de Dilmoun," in G. Galliano, ed., *L'île de Failaka, archéologie du Koweït* (Lyon, France: Musée des Beaux Arts, 2005), 41–61.
94. See P. Kjærum, *Failaka/Dilmun, the Second Millennium Settlements,* vol. 1, *The Stamp and Cylinder Seals* (JASP 17/1, 1983). H. Crawford, *Early Dilmun Seals from Saar* (Ludlow, UK: London-Bahrain Archaeological Expedition Saar Excavation Report 1, 2001).
95. S. Cleuziou, "Oman Peninsula in the early 2nd millennium b.c.," in *South Asian Archaeology 1979,* ed. H. Härtel (Berlin, Germany: Dietrich Reimer, 1981), 279–93.
96. For a recent overview of the period with earlier bibliography see C. Velde, "Wadi Suq and Late Bronze Age in the Oman peninsula," PFIC (2003), 101–14.
97. For a good introduction see B. Vogt, "State, Problems and Perspectives of Second Millennium b.c. Funerary Studies in the Emirate of Ras al-Khaimah (UAE)," in *Arabia and Its Neighbours: Essays on Prehistorical and Historical Developments: Essays Presented in Honour of Beatrice de Cardi,* ed. C. Phillips, D. T. Potts, and S. Searight (Turnhout, Belgium: Brepols, 1998), 273–90.
98. The literature on the metals industry of the period is large. See, for example, A. B. al-Shanfari and G. Weisgerber, "A Late Bronze Age Warrior Burial from Nizwa, Oman," in *Oman Studies: Papers on the Archaeology and History of Oman,* ed. P. M. Costa, and M. Tosi (Rome: Serie Orientale Roma, 1989), 17–30; G. Weisgerber, "Archäologisches Fundgut des 2. Jahrtausends v. Chr. in Oman - Möglichkeiten einer chronologischen Gliederung?," in *Golf-Archäologie,* ed. K. Schippmann, A. Herling, and J. -F. Salles (Buch am Erlbach, Germany: Internationale Archäologie 6 (1991), 321–30; P. Magee, "The Chronology and Regional Context of Late Prehistoric Incised Arrowheads in Southeastern Arabia," *AAE* 9 (1998): 112–17; D. T. Potts, "Some Issues in the Study of the Pre-Islamic Weaponry of Southeastern Arabia," *AAE* 9 (1998): 182–208.

99. M. Uerpmann, "Remarks on the Animal Economy of Tell Abraq (Emirates of Sharjah and Umm al-Qaywayn, UAE)," *PSAS* 31 (2001); 227–34.
100. D. T. Potts, *A Prehistoric Mound in the Emirate of Umm al-Qaiwain: Excavations at Tell Abraq in 1989* (Copenhagen, Denmark: Munksgaard, 1990); D. T. Potts, *Further Excavations at Tell Abraq: The 1990 Season* (Copenhagen, Denmark: Munksgaard, 1991); D. T. Potts, *Ancient Magan: The Secrets of Tell Abraq* (London: Trident, 2000).
101. P. Grave, D. T. Potts, N. Yassi, W. Reade, and G. Bailey, "Elemental Characterisation of Barbar Ceramics from Tell Abraq," *AAE* 7 (1996): 177–87.
102. D. T. Potts, "Post-Harappan Seals and Sealings from the Persian Gulf," *Man and Environment* 30/2 (2005): 108–11.
103. See, for example, M. Kervran, P. Mortensen, and F. Hiebert, "The Occupational Enigma of Bahrain between the 13th and the 8th Century b.c.," *Paléorient* 13 (1987): 77–93.
104. See generally J. A. Brinkman, *Materials and Studies for Kassite History*, vol. 1 (Chicago: The Oriental Institute, 1976).
105. J. -J. Glassner, "Inscriptions cunéiformes de Failaka," in *Failaka fouilles françaises 1983*, ed. J.-F. Salles (TMO 9, 1984), 31–50.
106. B. André-Salvini and P. Lombard, "La découverte épigraphique de Qal'at al-Bahreïn: Un jalon pour la chronologie de la phase Dilmoun moyen dans le Golfe arabe," *PSAS* 27 (1997): 165–70; J. Eidem, "Cuneiform Inscriptions," in *Qala'at al-Bahrain*, vol. 2, 76–80.
107. J. A. Brinkman, "A Kassite seal mentioning a Babylonian governor of Dilmun," *NABU* (1993/4): 89–90 [= note 106]. The seal is illustrated in J. Reade, "Commerce or Conquest: Variations in the Mesopotamia-Dilmun Relationship," in *Bahrain Through the Ages: The Archaeology*, ed. H. A. Al Khalifa and M. Rice (London: Kegan Paul International, 1986), Fig. 137.
108. A. Goetze, "The Texts Ni. 615 and Ni. 641 of the Istanbul Museum," *JCS* 6 (1952): 142–45; P. B. Cornwall, "Two Letters from Dilmun," *JCS* 6 (1952): 137–41.
109. D. T. Potts, "Elamites and Kassites in the Persian Gulf," *Journal of Near Eastern Studies* 65 (2006): 111–19.
110. For all of the texts see F. W. König, *Die elamischen Königsinschriften* (Graz: Archiv für Orientforschung, 1965), Beiheft 16; D. T. Potts, *The Archaeology of Elam: Formation and Transformation of an Ancient Iranian State* (Cambridge: Cambridge University Press, 1999).
111. So-called because this is the term given to this short dynasty in a Babylonian text known as Kinglist A. On the Second Dynasty of the Sealand. See J. A. Brinkman, *A Political History of Post-Kassite Babylonia, 1158–722 B.C.* (Rome: Analecta Orientalia 43, 1968): 149–57.
112. F. Højlund, "Dilmun and the Sealand," *Northern Akkad Project Reports* 2 (1989): 9–14.
113. Potts, *A Prehistoric Mound in the Emirate of Umm al-Qaiwain*, Figs. 46.1, 47.2, 87.1–2, 90.6, 98.8, 105.8 (pottery) and 150–51 (seal).
114. M. Kervran, P. Mortensen, and F. Hiebert, "The Occupational Enigma of Bahrain between the 13th and the 8th Century B.C.," *Paléorient* 13 (1987): 77–93.
115. P. Magee and R. Carter, "Agglomeration and Regionalism: Southeastern Arabia between 1400 and 1100 B.C.," *AAE* 10 (1999): 161–79.
116. Older literature generally refers to the appearance of *qanat* or *falaj*-type irrigation, but more recent studies suggest this is a misnomer. See R. Boucharlat, "Les galeries de captage dans la péninsule d'Oman au premier millénaire avant J.-C.: Questions sur leurs relations avec les galeries du plateau iranien," in *Irrigation et drainage dans l'Antiquité: Qanats et canalisations souterraines en Iran, en Égypte et en Grèce*, Persika 2, ed. P. Briant (Paris: Thotm, 2001), 157–83; R. Boucharlat, "Iron Age Water-Draining Galleries and the Iranian 'qanat'," PFIC (2003), 162–72.
117. The literature on the Iron Age of the Oman peninsula is now enormous. See, for example, P. Magee, "The Chronology of the Southeast Arabian Iron Age," *AAE* 7 (1996): 240–52; P. Magee, "Settlement Patterns, Polities and Regional Complexity in the Southeast Arabian Iron Age," *Paléorient* 24 (1999): 49–60; J. Córdoba, "Villages of Shepherds

in the Iron Age: The Evidence of Al Madam (AM1 Thuqaibah Sharjah, UAE)," PFIC (2003), 174–80; and for older bibliography on many sites, M. Mouton and W. Y. al-Tikriti, eds., *The Architectural Remains of the Iron Age Sites in the UAE and Oman* (Lyon, France: Maison de l'Orient, 2001) (CD-ROM).

118. A. Benoist, "An Iron Age II Snake Cult in the Oman Peninsula: Evidence from Bithnah (Emirate of Fujairah)," *AAE* 18 (2007): 34–54.
119. All of the sources can be found in W. Heimpel, "Das untere Meer," *ZA* 77 (1987): 22–91.
120. R. Zadok, *The Elamite onomasticon* (Naples, Italy: Annali dell'Istituto Orientale di Napoli, Supplement 40, 1984), 13, 16.
121. Much literature exists on this correspondence. See for example, H. H. Figulla, "Der Briefwechsel Bêl-ibni's: Historische Urkunden aus der Zeit Asurbanipals," *Mitteilungen der Vorderasiatisch-Ägyptischen Gesellschaft* 17, 1912): 1–104.
122. See, for example, F. Malbran-Labat, "Nabû-bêl-šumâte, prince du Pays-de-la-Mer," *JA* 163 (1975): 7–37.
123. R. Campbell Thompson and M. E. L. Mallowan, "The British Museum excavations at Nineveh, 1931–32," *Annals of Archaeology and Anthropology* 20 (1933): 96.
124. D. T. Potts, "The Location of Iz-ki-e," *Revue d'Assyriologie* 79 (1985): 75–76; D. T. Potts, "From Qadê to Mazûn: Four Notes on Oman, c. 700 B.C. to 700 A.D.," *Journal of Oman Studies* 8 (1985): 81–83.
125. R. Boucharlat and P. Lombard, "Le bâtiment G de Rumeilah (Oasis d'Al Ain). Remarques sur les salles à poteaux de l'âge du Fer en péninsule d'Oman," *Iranica Antiqua* 36 (2001): 213–38; D. Stronach, "From Cyrus to Darius: Notes on art and architecture in early Achaemenid palaces," in *The Royal Palace Institution in the First Millennium B.C.: Regional Development and Cultural Interchange between East and West,* ed. I. Nielsen (Athens, Greece: Monographs of the Danish Institute at Athens, vol. 4 (2001), 97. P. Magee, "Columned Halls, Power and Legitimisation in the Southeast Arabian Iron Age," PFIC (2003), 182–91.
126. See, for example, S. Kroll, "Zu den Beziehungen eisenzeitlicher bemalter Keramikkomplexe in Oman und Iran," in *Golf-Archäologie*, 315–20.
127. A. J. Ferrara, "An Inscribed Stone Slab of Nebuchadrezzar," *JCS* 27 (1975): 231–32.
128. J.-J. Glassner, "Inscriptions cunéiformes de Failaka," in *Failaka fouilles françaises 1983,* ed. J.-F. Salles (TMO 9, 1984), 46.
129. E. Ebeling, "Ekara," *Reallexikon der Assyriologie* 2 (1938): 320.
130. M. Sznycer, "Une inscription araméenne de Tell Khazneh," in *Failaka fouilles françaises 1984–1985,* ed. Y. Calvet and J.-F. Salles (TMO 12, 1986), 275.
131. See, for example,. H. Schiwek, "Der Persische Golf als Schiffahrts - und Seehandelsroute in achämenidischer Zeit und in der Zeit Alexanders des Grossen," *Bonner Jahrbücher* 162 (1962): 4–97; J.-F. Salles, "Les Achéménides dans le Golfe arabo-persique," in *Achaemenid History IV. Centre and Periphery,* ed. H. Sancisi-Weerdenburg and A. Kuhrt (Leiden: Nederlands Instituut voor het Nabije Oosten, 1990), 111–30.
132. Potts, "The Islands of the XIVth Satrapy". Also D. T. Potts, "Achaemenid interests in the Persian Gulf," in *The World of Achaemenid Persia,* ed. J. Curtis and St. J. Simpson (London: British Museum and Iran Heritage Foundation, in press).
133. At least since the late eighteenth century. See B. d'Anville, "Recherches géographiques sur le Golfe persique, et sur les bouches de l'Euphrate et du Tigre," *Mémoires de littérature, tirés des registres de l'Académie Royale des Inscriptions et Belles-Lettres* 30 (1764): 161. Cf. W. Tomaschek, "Topographische Erläuterung der Küstenfahrt Nearchs vom Indus bis zum Euphrat," in *Sitzungsberichte der Kais. Akad. d. Wiss. in Wien, phil.-hist. Cl.* 121 (1890), 64; P. Schwarz, *Iran im Mittelalter nach den arabischen Geographen*, vol. 1 (Leipzig, Germany: Harrassowitz, 1896), 66.
134. R. Hallock, "The Elamite texts from Persepolis," in *Akten des vierundzwanzigsten internationalen Orientalisten-Kongresses München,* ed. H. Franke (Wiesbaden, Germany: Steiner, 1959), 177–79; D. Metzler, "Ptolemaios' Geographie und die Topographie der Persepolis Fortification Tablets," in *XIX. Deutscher Orientalistentag,* ed. W. Voigt (Wiesbaden, Germany: ZDMG Supplement 3/2, 1977), 1057–60.

135. A. A. Sarfaraz, "Borazjan," *Iran* 11 (1973): 188–89.
136. J.-F. Salles, "Tell Khazneh: Les figurines en terre cuite," in *Failaka fouilles françaises 1984–1985*, ed. Y. Calvet and J.-F. Salles (TMO 12, 1986), 143–200.
137. P. Kjærum, "Stamp Seals and Seal Impressions," in *Qala'at al-Bahrain*, vol. 2, *The central monumental buildings*, F. Højlund and H. H. Andersen (JASP 30/2, 1997), 163–64 and Fig. 734. Also D. T. Potts, "Differing modes of contact between India and the West: Some Achaemenid and Seleucid examples," in *Memory as History: The Legacy of Alexander in India*, ed. H. P. Ray and D. T. Potts (New Delhi, India: Aryan Books, 2007), 122–30.
138. D. T. Potts, "Revisiting the Snake Burials of the Late Dilmun Building Complex on Bahrain," *AAE* 18 (2007): 55–74.
139. D. T. Potts, "Some Issues in the Study of the Pre-Islamic Weaponry of Southeastern Arabia," *AAE* 9 (1998): 194 and Fig. 10.
140. R. T. Hallock, *Persepolis Fortification Tablets* (Chicago: Oriental Institute Publications no. 92, 1969).
141. A. Meineke, *Stephani Byzantii Ethnicorum quae supersunt*, vol. 1 (Berlin: Reimer, 1849), 396.
142. See in general P. Högemann, *Alexander der Große und Arabien* (Munich: Zetemata, 1985), 82.
143. Tomaschek, "Topographische Erläuterung der Küstenfahrt Nearchs vom Indus bis zum Euphrat," 1–88; A. Berthelot, "La côte méridionale de l'Iran d'après les géographes grecs," in *Mélanges offerts à M. Octave Navarre par ses élèves et ses amis* (Toulouse, France: Edouard Privat, 1935), 11–24.
144. See, for example, H. Bretzl, *Botanische Untersuchungen des Alexanderzuges* (Leipzig, Germany: Teubner, 1903).
145. S. B. Miles, "Note on Pliny's Geography of the East Coast of Arabia," *JRAS* 10 (1878): 157–72.
146. Theophrastus, *De Lapidibus* §36; Athenaeus, *Deipnosophistai* 3.146.
147. There is an enormous literature on this subject but all of the primary sources are conveniently catalogued with commentary by V. Tscherikower, *Die hellenistischen Städtegründungen von Alexander dem Grossen bis auf die Römerzeit* (Leipzig, Germany: Philologus Supplementband 19/1, 1927); G. M. Cohen, *The Seleucid Colonies: Studies in Founding, Administration and Organization* (Wiesbaden, Germany: Steiner, 1978).
148. At least since W. W. Tarn, "Ptolemy II and Arabia," *Journal of Egyptian Archaeology* 15 (1929): 11.
149. Again, a much discussed topic. On the city generally see G. Le Rider, "Un atelier monétaire dans la province de la mer Erythrée?," *Revue Numismatique 1965* (1965): 36–43.
150. For example, J.-F. Salles, "The Arab-Persian Gulf under the Seleucids," in *Hellenism in the East*, ed. A. Kuhrt and S. Sherwin-White (London: Duckworth, 1987), 103; J.-F. Salles, "Antique Maritime Channels from the Mediterranean to the Indian Ocean," in *From the Mediterranean to the China Sea: Miscellaneous Notes*, ed. C. Guillot, D. Lombard and R. Ptak (Wiesbaden, Germany: Harrassowitz, 1998), 56.
151. S. Sherwin-White and A. Kuhrt, *From Samarkhand to Sardis: A New Approach to the Seleucid Empire* (London: Duckworth, 1993), 166.
152. The reading of the inscription in places has been somewhat contentious, not helped by the deterioration of the stone since its original discovery. For the most recent edition, with earlier bibliography, see F. Canali de Rossi, *Iscrizioni del estremo Oriento Greco: un repertorio* (Bonn: Inschriften griechischer Städte aus Kleinasien 65, 2004). For a full report on the architecture on Failaka, see K. Jeppesen, *Ikaros, the Hellenistic Settlements*, vol. 3, *The Sacred Enclosure in the Early Hellenistic Period* (JASP 16/3, 1989). For an overview of the French excavations see O. Callot, J. Gachet-Bizollon and J.-F. Salles, "Ikaros, de la conquête d'Alexandre au 1er siècle avant J.-C.," in *L'île de Failaka, archéologie du Koweït*, ed. G. Galliano (Lyon, France: Musée des Beaux Arts, 2005), 63–93. For inscriptions from Failaka mentioning an Athenian officer named Soteles, see P.-L. Gatier, "Sôtélès l'Athénien," *AAE* 18 (2007): 75–79.

153. J. Teixidor, "À propos d'une inscription araméenne de Failaka," in *L'Arabie préislamique et son environnement historique et culturel,* ed. T. Fahd (Leiden, Netherlands: Travaux du Centre de Recherche sur le Proche-Orient et la Grèce antique de l'Université des Sciences Humaines de Strasbourg, 10, 1989), 169–71, has suggested that the name of a temple on the island—*é-kara*—discussed above, is actually at the root of the name Ikaros, given in Greek sources to Failaka.
154. Several stamped Rhodian amphora handles have been found on Failaka as well as numerous mold-made, terracotta figurines showing females wearing typical Greek drapery. See H. E. Mathiesen, *Ikaros, the Hellenistic Settlements,* vol. 1, *The Terracotta Figurines* (JASP 16/1, 1982); J. B. Connelly, "Votive Offerings from Hellenistic Failaka: Evidence for Herakles Cult," in *L'Arabie préislamique et son environnement historique et culturel,* ed. T. Fahd (Leiden, Netherlands: Travaux du Centre de Recherche sur le Proche-Orient et la Grèce antique de l'Université des Sciences Humaines de Strasbourg 10, 1989), 145–58.
155. See, for example, S. T. Jensen, "Tylos Burials from Three Different Sites on Bahrain," *AAE* 14 (2003): 127–63; J. Littleton, "Unequal in Life? Human Remains from the Danish Excavations of Tylos Tombs," *AAE* 14 (2003): 164–93; K. C. MacDonald, "The Domestic Chicken in the Tylos Burials of Bahrain," *AAE* 14 (2003): 194–95; S. F. Andersen, H. Strehle, M. Tengberg, and M. I. Salman, "Two Wooden Coffins from the Shakhoura Necropolis, Bahrain," *AAE* 15 (2004): 219–28.
156. For Thaj with earlier bibliography, see D. T. Potts, "The Sequence and Chronology of Thaj," MASP (1993), 87–110.
157. R. Boucharlat and M. Mouton, "Mleiha (3e s. avant J.-C. - 1er/2e s. après J.-C.)," in *Materialien zur Archäologie der Seleukiden- und Partherzeit im südlichen Babylonien und im Golfgebiet,* ed. U. Finkbeiner (Tübingen, Germany: Wasmuth, 1993), 219–50, with earlier bibliography.
158. J. Hassell, "Alabaster Beehive-Shaped Vessels from the Arabian Peninsula: Interpretations from a Comparative Study of Characteristics, Contexts and Associated Finds," *AAE* 8 (1997): 245–81.
159. M. Shea, "The Small Cuboid Incense Burners of the Ancient Near East," *Levant* 15 (1983): 76–109.
160. M. Uerpmann, "Remarks on the Animal Economy of Tell Abraq (Emirates of Sharjah and Umm al-Qaywayn, UAE)," *PSAS* 31 (2001): 232.
161. M. Huth and D. T. Potts, "Antiochus in Arabia," *American Journal of Numismatics,* 2nd series 14 (2003): 73–81.
162. On their names, cf. T. Fahd, "Gerrhéens et Ǧurhumites," in *Studien zur Geschichte und Kultur des Vorderen Orients: Festschrift für Bertold Spuler zum siebzigsten Geburtstag,* ed. H. R. Roemer and A. Noth (Leiden, Netherlands: Brill, 1981), 69.
163. D. T. Potts, "Nabataean Finds from Thaj and Qatif," *AAE* 2 (1991): 138–44. For a Nabataean coin (Aretas IV, 9 B.C–A.D.40) from ed-Dur, see E. Haerinck, "International Contacts in the Southern Persian Gulf in the late 1st Century B.C./1st Century A.D.: Numismatic Evidence from ed-Dur (Emirate of Umm al-Qaiwain, UAE)," *Iranica Antiqua* 33 (1998): 289. D. T. Potts, "The Circulation of Foreign Coins within Arabia and of Arabian Coins Outside the Peninsula in the Pre-Islamic era," in *Coinage of the Caravan Kingdoms,* ed. P. Van Alfen and M. Huth (New York: American Numismatic Society, in press).
164. M.-J. Steve, *L'île de Kharg: Une page de l'histoire du Golfe persique et du monachisme oriental* (Neuchâtel: Civilisations du Proche-Orient Série I, Archéologie et environnement 1, 2003), 59–68.
165. A. Oppenheimer, *Babylonia Judaica in the Talmudic period* (Wiesbaden, Germany: Beihefte zum TAVO B 47, 1983).
166. C. Robin, trans., in *The Arabian Gulf in Antiquity,* vol. 2, D. T. Potts (Oxford: Clarendon Press, 1990), 76–79. For a linguistic appraisal see C. Robin, *L'Arabie antique de Karib'îl à Mahomet* (Aix-en-Provence: Édisud [= *Revue du Monde Musulman et de la Méditerranée* 61], 1991–93), 136–37; M. C. A. Macdonald, "Reflections on the Linguistic Map of Pre-Islamic Arabia," *AAE* 11 (2000): 42; M. C. A. Macdonald, "Ancient North

Arabian," in *The Cambridge Encyclopedia of the World's Ancient Languages,* ed. R. D. Woodard (Cambridge: Cambridge University Press, 2004), 488–533.

167. C. Robin, "Monnaies provenant de l'Arabie du nord-est," *Semitica* 24 (1974): 83–125; O. Callot, "Les monnaies dites 'arabes' dans le nord du Golfe arabo-persique à la fin du IIIème siècle avant notre ère," in *Failaka fouilles françaises 1986–1988,* ed. Y. Calvet and J. Gachet (TMO 18, 1990), 221–40; C. Arnold-Biucchi, "Arabian Alexanders," in *Mnemata: Papers in Memory of Nancy M. Waggoner,* ed. W. E. Metcalf (New York: American Numismatic Society, 1991), 101–15.
168. D. T. Potts, *The Pre-Islamic Coinage of Eastern Arabia* (CNIP 14, 1991), 30–32; D. T. Potts, *Supplement to the Pre-Islamic Coinage of Eastern Arabia* (Copenhagen, Denmark: CNIP, 1994), 16, 13, 16–17.
169. M. Huth and D. T. Potts, "Antiochus in Arabia," *American Journal of Numismatics* 14 (2002): 73–81.
170. D. T. Potts, *The Archaeology of Elam: Formation and Transformation of an Ancient Iranian State* (Cambridge: Cambridge University Press, 1999), 384–91.
171. While there is a large literature on this topic, see now M. Schuol, *Die Charakene: Ein mesopotamisches Königreich in hellenistisch-parthischer Zeit* (Stuttgart, Germany: Oriens et Occidens 1, 2000).
172. P.-L. Gatier, P. Lombard and K. al-Sindi, "Greek Inscriptions from Bahrain," *AAE* 13 (2002): 223–33.
173. Of several editions of the *Periplus,* the most recent and authoritative is L. Casson, *The Periplus Maris Erythraei: Text with Introduction, Translation, and Commentary* (Princeton, NJ: Princeton University Press, 1989); for the date see C. Robin, "L'Arabie du Sud et la date du *Périple de la mer Erythrée* (nouvelles données)," *JA* 279 (1991): 1–30.
174. The Palmyrene caravan trade with the cities of Characene is discussed with full bibliography in D. T. Potts, "The Roman relationship with the *Persicus sinus* from the rise of Spasinou Charax (127 B.C.) to the reign of Shapur II (A.D. 309–379)," in *The Early Roman Empire in the East,* ed. S. E. Alcock (Oxford: Oxbow Monograph 95, 1997), 94–97.
175. The expansion of Characene influence in the lower Gulf was first discussed in D. T. Potts, "Arabia and the kingdom of Characene," in *Araby the Blest,* ed. D. T. Potts, (CNIP 7, 1988), 137–67.
176. Many articles have appeared on ed-Dur. For a good introduction to the materials recovered at the site with earlier bibliography see E. Haerinck, *Excavations at ed-Dur (Umm al-Qaiwain, United Arab Emirates),* vol. 2, *The Tombs* (Leuven, Belgium: Peeters, 2001).
177. R. Boucharlat and M. Mouton, "Mleiha (3e s. avant J.-C. - 1er/2e s. après J.-C.)," in *Materialien zur Archäologie der Seleukiden- und Partherzeit im südlichen Babylonien und im Golfgebiet,* ed. U. Finkbeiner (Tübingen, Germany: Wasmuth, 1993), 219–50.
178. A. Herling and J.-F. Salles, "Hellenistic Cemeteries in Bahrain," MASP (1993), 161–82; S. F. Andersen, "The Chronology of the Earliest Tylos Period on Bahrain," *AAE* 13 (2002): 234–45; S. T. Jensen, "Tylos Burials from Three Different Sites on Bahrain," *AAE* 14 (2003): 127–63.
179. P. Lombard and M. Kervran, "Les niveaux 'Hellénistiques' du Tell de Qal'at al-Bahrain: Données préliminaires," MASP (1993), 127–60.
180. D. T. Potts, "Northeastern Arabia in the later pre-Islamic Era," in *Arabie orientale, Mésopotamie, et Iran méridional de l'âge du fer au début de la période islamique,* ed. R. Boucharlat and J.-F. Salles (Lyon, France: Éditions recherche sur les civilisations, 1984), 85–144; D. T. Potts, "The Sequence and Chronology of Thaj," MASP (1993), 87–110; D.T. Potts, "The Sequence and Chronology of Ayn Jawan," MASP (1993), 111–26.
181. C. J. Howgego and D. T. Potts, "Greek and Roman Coins from Eastern Arabia," *AAE* 3 (1992): 183–89; E. Haerinck, "International Contacts in the Southern Persian Gulf in the Late 1st Century B.C./1st Century A.D.: Numismatic Evidence from ed-Dur (Emirate of Umm al-Qaiwain, UAE)," *Iranica Antiqua* 33 (1998): 273–302; E. Haerinck, "The Shifting Pattern of Overland and Seaborne Trade in SE-Arabia: Foreign Pre-Islamic Coins from Mleiha (Emirate of Sharjah, UAE)," *Akkadica* 106 (1998): 22–40.

182. D. Whitehouse, *Excavations at ed-Dur (Umm al-Qaiwain, United Arab Emirates)*, vol. 1, *The Glass Vessels* (Leuven, Belgium: Peeters, 1998); D. Whitehouse, "Ancient Glass from ed-Dur (Umm al-Qaiwain, UAE) 2. Glass Excavated by the Danish Expedition," *AAE* 11 (2000): 87–128.
183. K. Rutten, "The Roman Fine Wares of ed-Dur (Umm al-Qaiwain, UAE) and Their Distribution in the Persian Gulf and Indian Ocean," *AAE* 18 (2007): 8–24.
184. J. K. Papadopoulos, "A Western Mediterranean Amphora Fragment from ed-Dur," *AAE* 5 (1994): 276–79.
185. D. T. Potts, "Namord Ware in Southeastern Arabia," in *Arabia and Its Neighbours*, 207–20.
186. R. Boucharlat and M. Drieux, "A Note on Coins and a Coin Mold from Mleiha, Emirate of Sharjah, UAE," in *The Pre-Islamic Coinage of Eastern Arabia,* D. T. Potts (CNIP 14, 1991), 110–17.
187. For the names and readings, see M. Maraqten, "Notes on the Aramaic Script of Some Coins from East Arabia," *AAE* 7 (1996): 304–15.
188. For the sources see V. F. Piacentini, "La presa di potere sassanide sul Golfo Persico tra leggenda e realtà," *Clio* 20 (1984): 173–210; V. F. Piacentini, "Ardashir i Papakan and the Wars against the Arabs: Working Hypothesis on the Sasanian Hold of the Gulf," *PSAS* 15 (1985): 57–77.
189. G. Widengren, "The Establishment of the Sasanian Dynasty in the Light of New Evidence" in *La Persia nel Medioevo* (Rome: Accademia Nazionale dei Lincei, 1971), 755.
190. D. T. Potts, "The Roman relationship with the *Persicus sinus* from the rise of Spasinou Charax (127 B.C.) to the reign of Shapur II (A.D. 309–379)," in *The Early Roman Empire in the East,* ed. S. E. Alcock (Oxford: Oxbow Monograph 95, 1997), 103.
191. C. E. Bosworth, *The History of al-Tabari,* vol. 5, *The Sasanids, the Byzantines, the Lakmids, and Yemen* (Albany: State University of New York Press, 1999), 54ff.
192. D. T. Potts, "From Qadê to Mazûn: Four notes on Oman, c. 700 B.C. to 700 A.D.," *JOS* 8 (1985): 81–95.
193. For a recent analysis of the economic and social condition of eastern Arabia in this period, see D. Kennet, "The Decline of Eastern Arabia in the Sasanian Period," *AAE* 18 (2007): 86–122.

Chapter 2

The Persian Gulf in Late Antiquity: The Sasanian Era (200–700 C.E.)*

Touraj Daryaee

The evidence of the history of the Persian Gulf in the pre-Islamic period is steadily growing. This is important because in comparison with the Mediterranean[1] and the Black Sea,[2] information on the Gulf is rather meager.[3] This chapter does not attempt to provide a complete history of events, but rather focuses on the region's slow cyclical rhythms with a four-hundred-year perspective. The Parthian Empire (247 B.C.E.–224 C.E.), which ruled the Near East in antiquity, had benefited from the Silk Road trade, which was not only land-based but also a sea trading route. The Parthians ruled in what may be called a feudal system, in which the local kingdoms along the Persian Gulf, in both the northern and southern region, were semi-independent. We know, for example, of a king or local ruler named Sanatruq who ruled over Bahrain.[4] His name suggests that the ruler was Parthian, so we may surmise that he was installed by the Parthian king of kings. We also come across the title of *Arabarch*. The Arabarch was a high official in the Parthian period who appears to have patrolled the desert area where the Arabs lived.[5] Thus, the Parthians were certainly aware of the importance of their southern provinces and concerned with their control.

Sanatruq would lose his life, along with many other petty kings, to an upstart from the province of Fars/Persis at the beginning of the third century. With the ascension of Ardashir I (224–40 C.E.), the Sasanian Empire (224–651 C.E.) was established, and it appears that the Persians now made a more concerted effort to control the Persian Gulf. I believe that there is sufficient evidence to demonstrate that the Sasanians brought changes and a new rhythm to the Gulf, and as the Romans saw the Mediterranean as mare nostrum, the Sasanians saw the Persian Gulf as their mare nostrum and part of *Iranshahr,* or the "Domain of the Iranians."

To understand the changing nature of Persian rule in the pre-Islamic period one needs to consider both the material and the literary evidence. The archaeological work being done around the Persian Gulf in recent years has given us much more information about the region and its integration into the Sasanian Empire. The literary sources used for the pre-Islamic period are usually the Perso-Arabic histories that view the past retrospectively, as they were written in Islamic times. Consequently, only Middle Persian inscriptions, some texts of historio-geographical nature, and Greek and Latin sources give us a contemporary view of the Gulf. By utilizing these sources, which touch on the political, economic, social, and religious (Zoroastrian) aspects of Persian Gulf history during the Sasanian period, one can discern an economic system created by the Persians in Late Antiquity that was passed on to the Arab Muslims and benefited the caliphs in Mecca, Kufa, and Damascus.

The Land and the Sea: Religio-Political Perspective

To grasp the Sasanian view of the Persian Gulf, one needs to be aware of how the religious conception of the lands, climes, bodies of water, and the place of *Iranshahr*, that is, the imperium, influenced their political views. After all, the official religion of the Persians in the third century was Zoroastrianism. The Zoroastrian scriptures saw the world divided into seven climes or regions, where the central clime, *Khwanirah*, is where all humans lived.[6] We are told that *Khwanirah* had a sea encircling and protecting it called Farakhkart. This central clime is the most important of the seven climes, because it was here that the Zoroastrian religion was established and where the sacred history of the Persians takes place.

What is significant is that by Late Antiquity Khwanirah as a clime was identified with Iranshahr, that is, the Sasanian Empire. This development was brought about by the imperial ideology of the Sasanian kings, who saw Iranshahr as a specific territory where the Iranian people lived. On the one hand, the Zoroastrian Middle Persian texts stated that people had migrated to the other six climes and humans now resided in all seven climes.[7] The Avestan view, on the other hand, held that all humanity lived in this clime and the other six climes were uninhabited. Now, Khwanirah was where the Persians had been living and ruling since the Achaemenid period. This change is evident by looking at the boundary of Iranshahr as established by Shahpur I (240–70 C.E.), the second Sasanian ruler, in his inscription at Ka'ba-yi Zardusht:

> I am the ruler of Eranshahr and hold these *shahrs*: Persia, Parthia, Khuzistan, Meshan, Assyria, Adiabene, Arabia (*Arbayestan*), Azerbaijan, Armenia, Georgia, Segan, Albania, Balaskan, up to the Caucasus mountains and the Gates of Albania, and all of the mountain chain of Pareshwar, Media, Gurgan, Merv, Herat and all of Abarshahr, Kerman, Sistan, Turan, Makran, Paradene, India, Kushanshahr up to Peshawar and up to Kashgar, Sogdiana and to the mountains of Tashkent, and on the other side of the sea (*dray*), Oman (*Mazunshahr*).[8]

The last line of the inscription mentions the sea, which, based on the inclusion of Oman,[9] makes it clear that it is the Persian Gulf littoral along with the opposite shore that is mentioned as belonging to Shahpur's domain. This mare nostrum attitude toward the Persian Gulf becomes ever more apparent when we consider that Arabia is also included in the domain. Persian control of the Arabian side is also corroborated by the material culture and Arab sources which state that during the Sasanian period the Persians controlled the shores of the sea, while the Arabs lived in the mountains and deserts.[10] Sasanian material remains exist on both sides of the Persian Gulf to support this literary evidence.

This geographical boundary of Iranshahr, including the Persian Gulf, thus reflects the imperial territory of the Sasanians in the third century C.E. The Sasanian Empire was firmly entrenched in a Zoroastrian worldview and gave special credence to the sevenpartite division of the world. As a result of the political and geographical realities of the

Late Antique world, innovations were made so that the mythical view fit geopolitical realities.

Now we can turn to the Persian Gulf and see how its waters were co-opted into this religious framework. The Middle Persian encyclopedic text, *Bundahishn* (Primal Creation), discusses seven seas and two rivers, which are given historical substance. They are Puidig, Farakhkart, Sadwes, Kamrod, Siyahbun, and two other unnamed seas that act as outlets for the Farakhkart Sea. In the Sasanian period, Puidig was identified with the Persian Gulf, while Kamrod was identified with the Caspian Sea, and Siyahbun clearly refers to the Black Sea, which is next to Rome. The Persian Gulf was seen as the greatest of the three major seas. This would be the image of the world according to the Sasanian commentators on the *Avesta*.

ARDASHIR I, HIS SUCCESSORS, AND THE PERSIAN GULF REGION

After Ardashir defeated the last Parthian king, Ardavan, in 224 C.E., he proceeded to conquer Mesopotamia and Babylonia. This had to be done because another Parthian noble named Valakhsh was still alive somewhere in the west and was promoting resistance in those areas. Ardashir left his son Shahpur in Mesopotamia and headed south to face the Arab tribes. There, Ardashir defeated the Arabs and probably the Parthians still holding out in Oman, Bahrain, and Hajar (on the western coast of the Persian Gulf, including present-day Kuwait, Qatar, and eastern Saudi Arabia). Ardashir had to make sure that the land along the Persian Gulf would be safe from the Arab Bedouins, pirates, and also any Parthian force. His campaign was successful and Sasanian control was established.[11]

In the Sasanian administrative division the Persian Gulf fell under one of the four *kusts*, "sides" or "quarters."[12] This *kust* was called *kust-i khavarwaran* or "southwestern quarter," and a Middle Persian text describes the area as protected at two locations: "The city of Hira was built by Shabuhr, the son of Ardashir, and he appointed Mihrzad the margrave of Hira over the wall of the Arabs."[13] Also, "the city of Asur and the city of Weh-Ardaxshir were built by Ardaxshir, the son of Spandyad. And he appointed Oshag, of Hagar, as the margrave (over the) Do-sar and Bor-gil by the wall of the Arabs."[14]

These two passages suggest that from the early third century up to the Arab Muslim conquest in the seventh century C.E., the Sasanians had a special interest in the Persian Gulf region, where margraves and troops were stationed. In the first passage we have the name of the margrave, Mihrzad, who ruled the region in the third century, but the second passage may refer to the sixth century C.E. This is because Oshag is mentioned as being from Hajar (Syriac, *Hagar*). As for Do-sar and Bor-gil, we now know that these were the names of two armies sent by the Sasanians that were known as Dausar and Shahba'.[15] These two forces along with a third were the elite warriors dispatched by the Sasanians to control the region.[16] The other important issue has to do with the mention of a defensive system built by the Sasanians to keep the Arabs from raiding the empire that is called *war i tazigan,* or "wall of the Arabs." This wall appears to have been close to the city of Hira (on the Euphrates River) and came to be known as Khandaq-i Shahpur.[17] This defensive mechanism was to be implemented at several places in the empire, such as in the Caucasus and Central Asia, to keep nomadic people in check.

Oman, where Ardashir I campaigned in 240 C.E., had also been placed under Persian rule.[18] This event is recalled in the *Karnamak i Ardashir i Papakan* (The Book of Deeds of Ardashir, the son of Pabak), where the battle is recounted in the following manner: "At that time, a son (of the Kirm-Xwaday) who was at Erhestan, with a large number of forces from the Arabs and Omanis who were on the coast of the sea came and fought with Ardaxshir."[19]

Thus, based on the early Sasanian inscriptions (Shahpur I) and an important Middle Persian text, *Shahrestaniha-i Iranshahr* (The Provincial Capitals of Iran), we can see that the Persian Gulf and Arabian Peninsula were regarded as part of the Sasanian Empire. This view, based on the imperial ideology of the Sasanian kings, had consequences for the way in which they dealt with the Gulf and hence brought a new rhythm to its history. The most immediate consequence was the economic interest of the Sasanians. The Persian Gulf was not only important in itself, but it also connected their empire to the larger world. When major empires around them made passage, contact, and trade difficult, the Gulf connected the Persians to the waters, lands, and people beyond their immediate neighbors.

Although in the third century the Sasanians had a firm hold on the Persian Gulf region, in the fourth century Arab Bedouins began to raid the area. According to the historian Tabari, Arab tribes from Bahrain raided areas in and around the province of Fars. Early in his reign the great Sasanian king, Shahpur II (303–79), crossed the Persian Gulf reaching Khatt, the coastal district of Arabia including the towns of Qatif and Uqair, then marched through Bahrain and reached Hajar.[20] We may gather that the Arabs were encroaching on the shore of the Persian Gulf and were attempting to remain there. Consequently this move had upset the balance of power and forced the Sasanians into action. We have the names of some of the Arab tribes at Hajar which Shahpur II dealt with harshly, and consequently was known in Arabic as *Dhu al-Aktaf*—"he who pierces shoulders." As a result of this campaign the Arabs were pushed into the heartland of Arabia,[21] and the Persian Gulf region remained in the hands of the Sasanians.

The recent archaeological work in the Persian Gulf has provided some interesting results and can lead to new conclusions. So far most of the information regarding Sasanian control of the Gulf has come from the southern side. This may simply be due to the fact that more work has been done there than on the coast of modern Iran. However, it may also be that there was a larger Sasanian presence on the southern coast because there was a need to protect it from Arab tribes who raided it from inland areas. Ardashir may have been attempting to bring order to a region made chaotic by Arab pillaging. By this act, he was perhaps attempting to bring security to the Persian Gulf region from the beginning of the Sasanian dynasty.[22] He may also have conquered the Arab shore of the Persian Gulf in order to secure the southern flank of his empire from attacks.[23] This move may additionally have been part of an economic strategy to dominate the Persian Gulf as an access point to the trade routes of the Indian Ocean.

Tabari informs us that, after laying siege to Bahrain in 240 C.E., Ardashir founded the new city of Peroz-Ardashir in Khatt.[24] Archaeological research in recent decades has furnished some information on the Sasanian presence in Bahrain. The Tylos fortress appears to have been built by the Sasanians (most probably Ardashir) to protect navigation of the Persian Gulf from Arab Bedouins and pirates attacking from Bahrain.[25] Pottery from Tylos has parallels with that from Qasr-i Abu Nasr and Hormuz. Also, some architectural features of the Tylos fortress, such as the round towers, are most probably Sasanian in origin.[26] The region was further controlled by Shahpur II's building of the "Wall of the Arabs" to defend the region after his expedition against the Arab tribes.

In the Sasanian geographical treatise, *Shahrestaniha-i Iranshahr*, Yemen and the Arabian Peninsula are mentioned as the southernmost part of the empire. If this is based on historical realities, it would point to the late fifth and early sixth centuries C.E. An Arabic source suggests that even in the late fifth century the Persians were involved in Mecca, where Kawad I is said to have imposed the religious ideas of Mazdak on the Arabs of Najd and Tihama. It is stated that when some of the population of Mecca refused to convert, he ordered one of his Arab commanders to destroy the Ka'ba, but the commander did not comply.[27] Still, Kawud I, through the influence of his Arab agent Harith b. 'Amr, the leader of the Kinda tribe, imposed the Mazdakite faith in Najd and the Hijaz. Later Islamic sources state that even as of the late sixth century there were Arabs in Mecca who were known as Mazdakite (Arabic, *zanadiqa*).[28] We should not forget that while the Prophet Muhammad was preaching his message, there were Arabs challenging his "tales of the men of old," and telling the stories of the Persian epic, that of Rustam and Isfandiyar, in Mecca.[29] The tradition has it that it was then that the "Sura of *al-Tatfif*" (Defrauding) was revealed, stating "When Our Signs are rehearsed, to him, he says: Tales of old (*asatiru al-awwalin*), Nay, but on their hearts is the stain of the (ill) which they do."[30] Thus Persian propaganda and influence were felt in the Arabian Peninsula, both militarily and culturally.

The Quraish who supported the Sasanians were overjoyed when Khusrau II (590–628 C.E.) went on the offensive and conquered Anatolia, Syria, Palestine, and Egypt. It is under such circumstances that the "Sura of Rum" was supposedly made manifest about 615–16 C.E., some six years before the Hijra of the Prophet Muhammad. In the beginning of the sura it is stated that the Roman Empire has been defeated in a land close by, but that they, after their defeat, will be victorious.[31] Yathrib/Medina in the fifth century seems to have also been under Persian influence as the Jewish tribes, notably the al-Nadr and Quraiza, were ruling over it and supported the Sasanians.[32] This fact suggests the far-reaching influence of the Sasanian Persians in Mecca and the Arabian Peninsula.

In the sixth century, Yemen became a major scene of competition. Ethiopian troops had invaded Yemen in 524/25 C.E. and provoked an uprising by the Yemenis under the leadership of Saif b. Dhi Yazan in 570 C.E. He asked the Sasanian ruler, Khusrau I, for help and received it in the form of some eight hundred men under the command of Wahriz. Wahriz was able to kill and defeat the invaders, finally taking San'a'.[33] It is interesting that the forces were Dailamites, which, according to Z. Rubin, suggests a "barbarization" of the Sasanian armed forces.[34] It may also be that the Dailamite forces were the type that could have been most effective in the Yemeni region. First Saif b. Dhi Yazan was placed in charge, but soon Wahriz came to power and became the governor of Yemen. This process began a hereditary rule by his family who were known as Marzban ("margrave," or literally, "defender of the border.")[35] Thus, in the sixth century, Yemen may be seen as the southernmost border of the Sasanian Empire. Wahriz's son Binejan then ruled, followed by Khurra-Khusrau, whose rule coincided with that of Khusrau II.[36] The latter, who had become worried about the "arabization" of the family of Wahriz, put an end to their rule and sent a new governor named Badan, ruling from San'a'. The reason for this may be that the Persian force sent to Yemen had acclimated themselves to the culture, and their interests may have coincided more with those of the local population than with the king of kings in Ctesiphon. From Yemen envoys were sent to Medina by a Persian governor to collect taxes from the people[37] and also to inquire about the rising power of the Prophet Muhammad.

Thus, there was a two-pronged approach to controlling Arabia. The motive for this control may very well have been economic. As we will see below, the importance of Arabia was not only due to its natural resources, but also the rivalry with the Byzantines for influence in Mecca, Yathrib, and the Hira-Mecca route.[38] The Persians who remained in Yemen came to be known as "Sons" (Arabic, *Abna'*), were converted to Islam in the seventh century, and were responsible for some of the early Islamic conquests in the region.

THE ECONOMIC PERSPECTIVE

The reason that the Sasanians attempted to control the Persian Gulf and treated it as mare nostrum was based on not only political considerations, but also economic aspirations. In their competition with the Roman Empire, the Sasanians took to the seas and established outposts and trading communities. This was necessitated by the continuous warfare between the Persians and the Romans, which reduced the amount of traffic on the Silk Road. The seas became ever more important as wars that had raged in the third century intensified again in 502–06, 527–61, and 602–29 C.E.[39] Because of this, the Persian Gulf became an important alternative to the land route.[40]

The province of Fars now became an economic engine that was invigorated by trade and stimulated to mint a large number of silver *drahms* to maintain this trade. The Sasanians also took an interest in city building, which is attested in the Middle Persian and Perso-Arabic sources.[41] For example, Hamza al-Isfahani, in describing the building activity of Ardashir I, supplies the following list of new cities: Wahisht-Ardeshir, Ram-Ardeshir, Ram-Mehrz-Ardeshir, Bud-Ardashir, Batn-Ardashir, Ansha-Ardashir, Bahman-Ardashir, Ardashir-Khwarra, Meli-Ardashir, Harmshir, Hujastan-Wajar, and Beh-Ardashir.[42] As mentioned above, Ardashir also founded a new city in Khatt that was known as Peroz-Ardashir.[43] Daniel Potts has suggested that the king wanted to secure his southern flank from attacks.[44] While this may be partly true, it should be noted that economic considerations may have played a role. The existence of natural resources such as copper in Oman, and silver mines and textile and leather industries in Yemen, must also have prompted Sasanian interest in the region.[45] The Persians also controlled the agricultural lands of Bahrain and Oman.[46] Another example of the Persian Gulf's importance would be its pearls. The tenth-century geographer Istakhri, in his *Kitab al-masalik wa'l mamalik* (Book of Roads and Provinces), states that pearls were found off the coast of the Persian Gulf and nowhere else.[47] It is because of such products and the Gulf's key location that major investment by either individuals, joint ventures, or the state took place.

As at the beginning of the Sasanian dynasty, trade with Rome declined in the sixth and seventh centuries as the Sasanians deliberately increased export tariffs.[48] In the sixth century the Romans forbade the sale of copper and iron to the Persians,[49] and the Sasanians inflated the price of silk during the reign of Roman Emperor Justinian (527–65). These measures forced the Romans to search for new avenues for trade. These new avenues would no longer go through Mesopotamia, but via the sea routes from Clysma (Suez) to the Axumite kingdom (Eritrea) to Yemen and Hadhramawt.[50] Justinian had decided to no longer buy silk from the Persians and instead had resorted to trade with Christian monks in India who had learned the art of silk making.[51] This tactic of Justinian's, however, eventually failed and the Persians kept the monopoly over the silk trade somewhat longer.

It is under these circumstances that Arabia became an important trading center in the late Sasanian period, since trade in Mesopotamia was prevented from going further west. The desert route[52] was a way to stimulate trade in Arabia, not only from western Arabia by the Romans, but also from eastern Arabia by the Persians. It is not certain how conducive this Arabian route was to a large volume of trade in Late Antiquity, but it was certainly a factor in the increased trade in cities such as Mecca.

The New Rhythm of the Persian Gulf Economy

The failure of the traditional routes elevated the significance of the Persian Gulf ports and cities. Already in the fourth century C.E., the Roman historian Ammianus Marcellinus tells us that "all along the coast (of the Persian Gulf) is a throng of cities and villages, and many ships sail to and fro."[53] This rare contemporary view attests to the vitality of the sea trade in the Persian Gulf at the time. The ports were linked to inland cities, where imported commodities from the east were brought or kept to be sold to other merchants. The Sasanian hold on the Gulf was apparent from the beginning. From the start of the dynasty in the third century C.E., ports/forts were established on its northern and southern coasts.[54] Caravans left Fars for the east, making their way to Kirman and beyond. Sources also mention that many traders and businessmen lived in the province of Fars along the Persian Gulf,[55] as well as on the coast of Kirman, all the way to Daibul in Sind, and as far as the coasts of India and China.[56] In regard to port cities along the Gulf, one needs to mention another founded by Ardashir I. According to the Middle Persian text *Karnamak i Ardashir i Papakan,* "when he (Ardashir) saw the sea with his eyes, he gave homage to the Gods and named that rasta, Boxt-Ardaxshir (Bushehr)."[57] The archaeological evidence suggests that the port of Bushehr was linked to Kazirun and Shiraz by a road utilized for the export of commodities to other regions, and that its closeness to the center of Fars (i.e., Shiraz) must have made it an important port.[58]

The other important port was Siraf which dates from the time of Shahpur II.[59] Siraf was linked by road to Firuzabad and Shiraz. There we find the remains of a Sasanian fort under an Islamic city. The presence of Sasanian coins[60] and pottery fragments also attest to the existence of a Sasanian site.[61] There were, additionally, chamber tombs, typical of Zoroastrian *astodan,*[62] found in the hillsides behind the city.[63] In the Sasanian period, Siraf appears to have been a military outpost, while in Islamic times it was transformed into a trading port. It was first mentioned in about 850 A.D. as a flourishing port, and Istakhri states that in the tenth century it was a prosperous city only rivaled by Shiraz in the province of Fars. The city plan shows it was laid out with drainage and sewage pipes. It is claimed that this early Islamic type of town still shows Sasanian stylistic influence. The city also reveals its importance in trade. There are thousands of fragments of Chinese porcelain, together with coins from Spain, Russia, and Syria, and the earliest legible, dated Islamic coins. Glass, lapis lazuli, and much Sasanian-Islamic ware were also found.[64] Coins were found on the site which attest to its occupation as early as 699–700.[65] In fact the ninth-century historian Baladuri refers to the capture of the Sasanian castle of Siraf during the Muslim conquest.[66]

Istakhri states that the houses in Siraf were built with teak (*saj*) that was brought from India and Zanzibar,[67] which again points to the city's trade relations. In fact the inhabitants of Siraf were known for their maritime travel, and the people of Siraf made their living through seaborne trade. To make this point, Istakhri relates the following story:

> And I have heard that a man from Siraf went for trade to the sea and stayed in the boat for forty years and did not come to land. And when he came to the coast, he did not desire to leave the sea. He sent his workers to conduct trade and make profit and come back to him. And when the ship was in ruins, he moved to another one.[68]

Although it is not clear whether Siraf was a port already at the end of the Sasanian period, even if we assume it was only a military outpost it may have functioned as a place where sea traffic was monitored and was used as a base for securing the Persian Gulf. By the thirteenth century, however, the city was in ruins.[69]

Thus, the occupation of this site by the Arab Muslim conquerors may have been due to its economic advantages and its position, which may have allowed the control of trade in the Persian Gulf. Further to the east, there were other cities or ports that had a role in trade. These included the site of (Old) Hormuz near the Strait of Hormuz, which was connected to the northeast. Also, the port of Guzeran or Kujaran Ardeshir was located near Bandar Lingeh, which again had a role in trade and met the needs of the city of Darab in Fars[70]; and finally, the island of Kharg, which appears to have been a late Sasanian settlement thirty-seven miles northwest of Bushehr.[71] There is also the presence of Persian Nestorians on Kharg.

These ports made Fars important as a trade center not only for commodities that were brought there and taken to the inland cities but also as a stopping place for the cargo going from Iraq to Asia or Africa and back.[72] The amount of trade from the ports to the inland area is unclear and the difficult terrain makes the likely volume relatively low. However, not only was it important to control the trade in the Persian Gulf , but these sites were also places the Sasanians aspired to control politically.

Let us now look at the southern side of the Persian Gulf, where we have evidence of occupation from several locations. At Qatif there is the existence of *qanats*, or underground water channels, which point to Persian involvement.[73] The importance of Qatif is that it was an entry port for silk in the late Sasanian period.[74] At Tarut, Sasanian material culture, notably stucco fragments and stamp seals, suggests some sort of presence.[75] Other places that indicate a continuous Sasanian presence include Dammam, with evidence of Sasanian material culture[76]; Khobar, where the Persian qanat system and Sasanian coins from the sixth and seventh centuries have been found[77]; and Jabal Kenzan, where Sasanian coins from the fourth and seventh centuries were found.[78] In northeastern Arabia along the Gulf, the Persian presence is better known. Christian Persian communities had settled there and Persian was known to be spoken as the language of the population.[79]

In southeastern Arabia, Suhar, on the Gulf of Oman near the mouth of the Persian Gulf, provides evidence of Sasanian contact. At Suhar there appears to have been a Sasanian fort, that may have participated in trade, as well as forts at Dama and Jurrafar.[80] More importantly, there seem to have been Sasanian settlements at Jazirat al-Ghanam, an island off the Musandam peninsula, and Ghubb Ali.[81] The Persian outpost at Ghanam, in the Strait of Hormuz, may have overseen shipping.[82] The same scenario appears to be true for Banbhore in Sind and Kilwa in East Africa, where a few Sasanian-Islamic wares have been found.[83] These wares were produced in Iraq and exported to Siraf on a massive scale in the Islamic period.[84] There is evidence of Sasanian contact in the Umm al-Ma region on the west coast of Qatar, where green-glazed pots from Iraq were found.[85] There is also evidence of Sasanian material at Salihiyah near Khawran in Ras al-Khaimah.[86] Fars could have acted as the logistical center to control the shipping close to these outposts.

This is also true of Dubai where excavations by D. C. Baramki in the 1970s brought to light several buildings, including a caravan station, governors' residence, marketplace, and hunting lodge from the late Sasanian period.[87] Other places controlled by the Sasanians during the time of Khusrau I included Muscat in Oman.[88] The importance of Muscat for Persian traders continued into the Islamic period, as ships sailing from India to Aden stopped at this port.[89] Economic considerations went beyond the coastal areas. Sources describe silver and copper mining at Shamam in the Najd, where it is said some one thousand Zoroastrians lived and worshipped at their two fire temples.[90]

There is very little evidence of a Sasanian navy, and indeed there was no need for a robust naval presence on the seas as the Persians or their vassals already controlled the coasts of the Persian Gulf.[91] I would suggest that the Persian maritime presence was mainly established in light of economic considerations. With this presence it is no wonder the Romans were not able to do much via the sea route. This is evident from a statement by the ancient historian Procopius regarding long-distance trade. As mentioned before, Justinian wanted to compete with the Sasanians by becoming allies with the Ethiopians. Until then the Romans had had to buy silk from the Sasanians, and by allying themselves with the Ethiopians who would buy the product for them, they hoped to discontinue this practice. Procopius states, however, that it was "impossible for the Ethiopians to buy silk from the Indians, for the Persian merchants always locate themselves at the very harbors where the Indian ships first put in (since they inhabit the adjoining country) and are accustomed to buy the whole cargoes."[92]

This success of the Persians was such that they established themselves further east as far as Ceylon (Sri Lanka).[93] Persian horses were shipped there,[94] and a Persian colony was established by ships coming from Persia.[95] It appears that there was even a Sasanian colony in Malaysia, but again this does not appear to be military in nature.[96] On the basis of this evidence it is suggested that while the state promoted security for the waterway and more importantly maintained forts in the area, it was the merchants themselves who actively controlled trade in the Persian Gulf.

The province of Fars had a tremendous and steady output of *drahms* from its main centers in the late Sasanian period. The large amount of *drahms* minted in Fars at this time were from five major mints:[97] (1) ART=Ardashir-Khwarra; (2) BYŠ=Beshabuhr; (3) DA=Darabgird; (4) ST=Istakhr; and, in the late Sasanian period, (5) WYHC=Weh-az-Amid-Kawad.[98] It appears, however, that gold and silver mines were scarce there; hence the control of silver and copper mines in Yemen and Oman was imperative. Istakhri confirms that Fars had little silver.[99] Neither his *Masalik wa'l Mamalik* nor the *Farsnama* of Ibn Balkhi mentions any significant silver mines in Fars. The *Hudud al-Alam* mentions only a mine at Istakhr[100] and one in eastern Persis at Na'in.[101] Although it is usually thought that the reason for such a great output of coinage in Fars was the military campaigns of Khusrau I and those of Khusrau II, I would like to suggest that the volume of trade was partially responsible for this amount of output, and Oman and Yemen made this output possible. In this regard a metalurgical analysis of the Sasanian coinage would be most welcome.

CONCLUSION

From the third century C.E., the Sasanians began a campaign of dominating the Persian Gulf and the lands around it. This concerted effort appears to have been much more intense than that of the Parthian period. The evidence not only comes from textual sources, both Middle Persian and Arabic and Persian, but also the archaeological remains. This includes fortifications such as the Khandaq-i Shahpur, most probably built by Shahpur II, and the Tylos fort in Bahrain, probably constructed by Ardashir I. The qanat system on the southern side of the Persian Gulf also hints at the Persian presence in the area, demonstrating their intention to hold on to the coast for strategic reasons.

Their military action translated into economic control and success against the Romans at sea. The issue of trade and controlling the trade routes appears to have been important in Late Antiquity. Both the Persians and the Romans used their clients to purchase and transport commodities, but the proximity of the Persians to Central Asia, India, and China gave them a better position than the Romans. In this scheme, the Persian Gulf came to be dominated by the Sasanians as springboard for further economic activity in the Indian Ocean and the Arabian Sea. This led, by the fifth and sixth century, to Sasanian control of Yemen and incursions into Arabia. We should not forget that the natural resources of Arabia had also become essential to the Persians' survival and competition with the Romans.

The control over the Persian Gulf by the Persians should not be seen as only a state-sponsored program. One must be mindful of the military and naval technology that hindered Sasanian control of the seas. We should not confuse the modern use of naval tactics as those employed by the British in the eighteenth century with premodern traditions of seamanship. The state only went so far as to facilitate trade and provide as much security as it was capable of, which on the seas was not much. It was really the merchants alone who took it upon themselves to control the markets. It is they who organized themselves, most probably based on religious affiliation, in joint ventures to control trade from the Persian Gulf to the Indian Ocean and beyond.

Thus, the textual and archaeological remains from the Sasanian period suggest a new chapter in the history of the Persian Gulf. The expanded Iranian presence appears to have been unprecedented prior to Late Antiquity. The Arabs were integrated and used in this economic and political system and were able to gain the upper hand in the seventh century C.E., after both the Persians and the Romans had exhausted themselves. By this time, the Sasanians had created a network and structure through which the Muslims were able to establish themselves on the Persian Gulf, in its coastal areas, and on the Arabian Sea and Indian Ocean. There was much structural continuity, but the masters had changed, and the Arab Muslims were able to compete with the Romans by utilizing the existing patterns established in Late Antiquity.

NOTES

*The usual diacritics for Avestan, Middle Persian and names have been omitted or simplified for the general reader. I would like to thank H. M. Al-Naboodah for comments, M. Kervran for her kindness in providing me with her latest unpublished manuscript on Bahrain and W. Soward for reading the manuscript.

1. F. Braudel, *The Mediterranean and the Mediterranean World in the Age of Philip II* (New York: Harper and Row, 1972); and also his *Memory and the Mediterranean* (New York: Vintage Books, 2001).
2. Neal Ascherson, *Black Sea* (New York: Hill and Wang, 1995); and more recently Charles King, *The Black Sea: A History* (New York: Oxford University Press, 2004).
3. Still, Daniel Potts has provided a *longue durée* view of the Persian Gulf, which is to be commended. See his *The Arabian Gulf in Antiquity*, 2 vols. (Oxford: Clarendon Press, 1990).
4. C. E. Bosworth, trans., *The History of al-Tabari*, vol. 5, *The Sasanids, the Byzantines, the Lakmids, and Yemen* (Albany: State University of New York Press, 1999), 15.
5. M. A. R. Colledge, *The Parthians*, Ancient Peoples and Places (New York: Frederick A. Praeger, 1967), 63.
6. I. Gershevitch, *The Avestan Hymn to Mithra* (Cambridge: Cambridge University Press, 1959), 80–81; See also *Rashn Yasht*, 15–19; *Vendidad*, XIX.39; *Vispered*, X.1. We know that this division is as old as the time of Zoroaster. In *Yasna*, 32.3 Zoroaster accuses the Daevas of such a crime:

   > But all you Daevas are seed of evil thought, as is the "great" person worshipping you, as well as the actions of deceit and contempt, for which again and again you have become notorious in the seventh clime of the earth.

   (H. Humbach, *The Gathas of Zarathushtra and the Other Old Avestan Texts*, Part I, Introduction: Text and Translation, Heidelberg 1991, 132.) Thus in a hymn to Mithra we find an old reference to the division of the world, confirmed by the *Gathas* of Zoroaster. In India as well we come across such a division where the world is divided into seven regions (Sanskrit *dvipa*) which should convince us that the seven-partite division of the world is of Indo-Iranian origin (See M. Boyce, *A History of Zoroastrianism*, vol. 1 (Leiden, The Netherlands: Brill, 1989), 134). See also M. Schwartz, "The Old Eastern Iranian World View According to the Avesta," in *The Cambridge History of Iran*, vol. 2, *The Median and Achaemenian Periods*, ed. Ilya Gershevitch (Cambridge: Cambridge University Press, 1985), 643.
7. M. Bahar, trans., *Bundahishn*, chapter IX (Tehran, 1369/1991), 71; *Menog-i Xrad* states that in the six tracts people drink milk as a primary source of nourishment (trans. A. Tafazzoli, Tehran, 1364/1986), 15.10.
8. Shahpur, Ka'ba-yi Zardusht (*ŠKZ*) 1–3. Ph. Huyse, *Die dreisprachige Inschrift shabuhrs I. an der Ka'ba-i Zardusht*, vol. 1, Corpus Inscriptionum Iranicarum (London, 1999), 22–24. An identical list is supplied at Naqsh-i Rustam; see M. Back, *Die Sassanidischen Staatsinschriften*, Acta Iranica 18 (Leiden, The Netherlands: Brill, 1978), 285–88; Richard N. Frye, *The History of Ancient Iran* (Munich, Germany: C. H. Beck, 1984), Appendix 4, 371.

9. For the evidence of Sasanian presence see B. de Cardi, "A Sasanian Outpost in Northern Oman," *Antiquity* 46, no. 184 (December 1972): 308; also D. T. Potts, "A Sasanian Lead Horse from North Eastern Arabia," *Iranica Antiqua* 28 (1993): 197.
10. S. M. Awtab, *Kitab ansab al-ʿarab*, Bibliothèque Nationale, Ms. Arabe 5019, 271r., after R. Hoyland, *Arabia and the Arabs from the Bronze Age to the Coming of Islam* (New York and London: Routledge, 2001), 28.
11. Th. Nöldeke, *Die von Guidi herausgegeben Syrische Chronik* (Wien, 1893), 47.
12. The administrative reforms have been associated with Khusrau I in the sixth century. The reforms probably began during the reign of Kawad as a result of the Hephthalite victories during his father's rule and as a result of Sasanian attempts to contend with several fronts at the same time. The Middle Persian and Islamic texts as well as the numismatic evidence suggest this fact. (T. Daryaee, "The Effect of the Arab Muslim Conquest on the Administrative Division of Sasanian Persis/Fars," *Iran* 41 (2003): 1–12; also see the comments of G. Gnoli, "The Quadripartition of the Sassanian Empire," *East and West* 35 (1985): 270.) For the numismatic evidence, see F. Gerent, "Deux notes à propos du monnayage du Xusro II," *Revue belge de Numismatique* 140 (1994): 37. The same ordering is also found in the Armenian Geography of Xorenatsi; see J. Marquart, *Eranshahr nach der Geographie des Ps. Moses Xorenacʿi* (Berlin, 1901).
13. T. Daryaee, *Shahrestaniha-i Eranshahr, A Middle Persian Text on Late Antique Geography, Epic and History* (Costa Mesa, CA: Mazda Publishers, 2002), 18–19, no. 25.
14. Ibid., 20, no. 52.
15. G. Rothstein, *Die Dynastie de Lahmiden in al-Hira. Ein Persischen Geschichte zur Zeit der Sasaniden* (Berlin, 1899), 134–38.
16. M. J. Kister, "Al-Hira, Some Notes on its Relations with Arabia," *Arabica* 11(1968): 167–68.
17. R. N. Frye, *History of Ancient Iran*; H. Mahamedi, "Walls as a System of Frontier Defense During the Sasanian Period," *Menog-i Xrad: The Spirit of Wisdom, Essays in Memory of Ahmad Tafazzoli*, ed. T. Daryaee and M. Omidsalar (Costa Mesa, CA: Mazda Publishers, 2004), 157.
18. J. C. Wilkinson, "The Julanda of Oman," *The Journal of Oman Studies* 1 (1975): 98 and Potts, *Arabian Gulf in Antiquity*, vol. 2, 329.
19. *Karnamak i Ardashir i Papakan* (KAP) VII.12.
20. Bosworth, *The History of al-Tabari*, 54.
21. Ibid., 55.
22. Monique Kervran, Fredrik Hiebert, and Axelle Rougeulle, *Qalʿat al-Bahrain: A Trading and Military Outpost 3rd millennium* B.C.*–17th century* A.D. (Turnhout, Belgium: Brepols, 2005), 211.
23. Potts, *Arabian Gulf in Antiquity*, vol. 2, 233.
24. Ibid., 233–34.
25. Kervran, Hiebert, and Rougeulle, *Qalʿat al-Bahrain*, 211.
26. Ibid., 210–11.
27. For other sources for Arabia see Frye, *History of Ancient Iran*, 324–28.
28. C. E. Bosworth, "Iran and the Arabs Before Islam," in *The Cambridge History of Iran*, vol. 3(1), *The Seleucid, Parthian and Sasanian Periods*, ed. Ehsan Yarshater (Cambridge: Cambridge University Press, 1983), 600.
29. This is told by Nadr of Abd ad-Dar in Martin Lings, *Muhammad: His Life Based on the Earliest Sources* (New York: Inner Traditions International, 1983), 89.
30. Qur'an 83: 13, Trans. A. Yusuf Ali (New York, 1988, 1704); see also Lings, *Muhammad*, 89.
31. Qur'an 30: 2–3, 1051.
32. Bosworth, "Iran and the Arabs Before Islam," 601.
33. Ibid., 606–07.
34. Z. Rubin, "The Reforms of Khusro Anushirwan," in *The Byzantine and Early Islamic Near East: States, Resources and Armies*, vol. 3, ed. A. Cameron (Princeton, NJ: The Darwin Press, 1995), 285.
35. The name for the son of Wahriz is given to be Marzban or Marzwan.

36. Rubin, "The Reforms of Khusro Anushirwan," 286.
37. Kister, "Al-Hira, Some Notes on its Relations with Arabia," 145.
38. Bosworth, "Iran and the Arabs Before Islam," 600.
39. A. H. M. Jones, "Asian Trade in Antiquity," in *Islam and the Trade of Asia*, ed. D. S. Richards (Philadelphia: University of Pennsylvania Press, 1970), 9.
40. For the different routes which the Sasanians used, see A. Mustaufi, *Rah-ha-yi sasani* [Sasanian Roads], Geographical Publication of the University of Tehran, no. 1 (Tehran, n.d.); for the roads in Fars and Kirman, see Christopher Brunner, "Geographical and Administrative Divisions: Settlements and Economy," in *The Cambridge History of Iran*, vol. 3 (2), *The Seleucid, Parthian and Sasanian Periods*, ed. Ehsan Yarshater (Cambridge: Cambridge University Press, 1983), 750–54.
41. For a good discussion of this building activity during this period see N. V. Pigulevskaïa, *Les villes de l'état iranien aux époques parthe et sassanide* (Paris, 1963).
42. H. al-Isfahani, *Kitab-i tarikh-i sini-yi muluk al-arz wa'l-anbiya'*, ed. S. H. Taqizadeh (Berlin, Germany, 1921), 44.
43. Potts, *Arabian Gulf in Antiquity*, vol. 2, 233. Also see R. N. Frye, "Bahrain under the Sasanians" in *Mesopotamien und seine Nachbarn*, vol. 2, ed. H. J. Nissen and J. Renger (Berlin, Germany: Berliner Beiträge zur Vordern Orient, 1983).
44. Potts, *Arabian Gulf in Antiquity*, vol. 2, 233.
45. M. G. Morony, "The Late Sasanian Economic Impact on the Arabian Peninsula," *Name-ye Iran-e Bastan, The International Journal of Ancient Iranian Studies*, vol. 1, no. 2 (2002): 37.
46. Ibid., 30.
47. Abu Ishaq Ibrahim al-Istakhri, *Kitab al-Masalik wa'l Mamalik*, trans. (Persian) as *Masalik va Mamalik*, Iraj Afshar (Tehran: Bungah-i Tarjuma va Nashr-i Kitab, 1340/1961), 34; of course this is untrue, but the statement may mean that the pearls of Fars were valued over other pearls; for a complete list of products of Fars see Paul Schwarz, *Iran im Mittelalter nach den arabischen Geographen*, Teil II (Leipzig, Germany: Otto Wigand, 1910).
48. Jones, "Asian Trade in Antiquity," 8.
49. V. Lukonin, "Administrative Institutions during the Parthian and the Sasanian Period," in *The Cambridge History of Iran*, vol. 3(2), 744.
50. Jones, "Asian Trade in Antiquity," 9.
51. *Procopii Caesariensis Historiarum Temporis Sui Tetras Altera*, De Bello Gothico, Lib. IV, cap. XVII, 212, translated from the Greek into Latin by Claudius Maltretus (Venice, 1729), in *A Source Book for Medieval Economic History*, Roy C. Cave and Herbert H. Coulson (New York: Biblo and Tannen, 1965), 244–45.
52. Jones, "Asian Trade in Antiquity," 9.
53. Ammianus Marcellinus, XXIII, 6, 11.
54. A. Williamson, "Persian Gulf Commerce in the Sassanian Period and the First Two Centuries of Islam," *Bastanshinasi va Honar-i Iran* 9–10 (1972): 97–109; M. Kervran, "Forteresses, entrepôts et commerce: une histoire à suivre depuis les rois sassanides jusqu' aux princes d'ormuz," *Itinéraires d'orient, hommages à Claude Cahen*, Res Orientales 6, eds. R. Curiel and R. Gyselen (Bures-sur-Yvette: Groupe pour l'étude de la civilisation du Moyen-Orient, 1994): 325–50.
55. M. Sutuda, ed., *Hudud al-'Alam*, Zaban va Farhang-i Iran 98 (Tehran, Iran: Tahuri Press, 1362/1983), 130, 131, 132, 135.
56. Istakhri, *Masalik wa'l Mamalik*, 37; E. H. Schafer, *The Golden Peaches of Samarkand, A Study in T'ang Exotics* (Berkeley: University of California Press, 1963), 12–13.
57. B. Farahvashi, ed., *Karnamak i Ardashir i Papakan* (Tehran, Iran: University of Tehran Press, 1354/1976), 46; Kervran, "Forteresses, entrepôts et commerce," 325–50. Also I. Ra'in, *Darya navardi-yi iranian* [The Seamanship of Iranians], vol. 1 (Tehran, 1350/1972), 251–55; and F. Fiorani Piacentini, "Ardashir I Papakan and the Wars against the Arabs: Working Hypothesis on the Sasanian Hold of the Gulf," *Proceedings of the Seminar for Arabian Studies* 15 (1985): 57–77.
58. R. Boucharlat and J. F. Salles, "The History and Archaeology of the Gulf from the 5th Century B.C. to the 7th Century A.D.: A review of the Evidence," *Proceedings of the*

Seminar for Arab Studies 11 (1981): 66; the authors identify Rew-Ardaxshir with Bushehr, 69. Bushehr was a diocesan center for a Christian archbishop created in Fars in 415/420 A.D. under Shahpur II, 69–70.

59. D. Huff, "Archeology IV. Sasanian," *Encyclopædia Iranica* 2 (1987): 303.
60. N. M. Lowick, *The Coins and Monumental Inscriptions*, Siraf XV (London: British Institute of Persian Studies, 1985), 11–16.
61. Valeria Fiorani Piacentini, *Merchants, Merchandise, and Military Power in the Persian Gulf: (Suriyan/Shahriyaj-Siraf)*, Atti Della Accademia Nazionale Dei Lincei (Rome: Accademia Nazionale Dei Lincei, 1992), 117.
62. *Astodon*: a receptacle for bones; see L. Trümpelmann, "Sasanian Graves and Burial Customs," *Arabie orientale, Mésopotamie et Iran méridional: de l'âge du fer au début de la période islamique*, Histoire du Golfe (Paris: Editions Recherche sur les Civilisations, 1984), 317; L. Trümpelmann, *Zwischen Persepolis und Firuzabad, Gräber, Paläste und Felsreliefs im alten Persien* (Mainz, Germany: Verlag Philipp Von Zabern, 1992), 19–20; the cemetery at Siraf also contained chambers, measuring 2 meters across by 1.5 meters high which contained bones. See D. Whitehouse, "Excavations at Siraf: Fifth Interim Report," *Iran* X (1972): 65.
63. D. Whitehouse and A. Williamson, "Sasanian Maritime Trade," *Iran* XI (1973): 35.
64. Ibid., 249.
65. D. Whitehouse, "Excavations at Siraf: Fourth Interim Report," *Iran* IX (1971): 3. There is a Sasanian copper coin in Siraf; see D. Whitehouse, "Excavations at Siraf, Sixth Interim Report," *Iran* XII (1974), 7.
66. In Ibid., 5.
67. Istakhri, *Masalik wa'l Mamalik*, 113.
68. Ibid., 121.
69. Sylvia A. Matheson, *Persia: An Archaeological Guide,* 2nd ed. (London: Faber and Faber, 1976), 247; see now 3rd edition (Tehran, Iran: Yassavoli, 2000), 135–37.
70. B. de Cardi, "A Sasanian Outpost in Northern Oman," 306.
71. Boucharlat and Salles, "The History and Archaeology of the Gulf," 71.
72. For the existence of Sasanian-Islamic ware produced in Iraq and found in Eastern Africa, see "Kilwa: A Preliminary Report," *Azania*, The Journal of the British Institute of History and Archaeology in East Africa 1 (1966): 7.
73. H. St. J. B. Philby, "Southern Najd," *The Geographical Journal* 55 (1920): 168; Potts, *Arabian Gulf in Antiquity,* vol. 2, 208.
74. Mahmood Ibrahim, *Merchant Capital and Islam* (Austin: University of Texas Press, 1990), 48.
75. Potts, *Arabian Gulf in Antiquity,* vol. 2, 215–16.
76. Ibid., 216.
77. Ibid., 216–17.
78. Ibid., 218.
79. Ibid., 245.
80. J. C. Wilkinson, "Suhar in the Early Islamic Period: The Written Evidence," *South Asian Archaeology,* vol. 2, ed. E. Taeddi (1973), 888.
81. Potts, *Arabian Gulf in Antiquity,* vol. 2, 296–97.
82. B. de Cardi, "A Sasanian Outpost in Northern Oman," 308; Besides this evidence, A. A. Ezzah believes that the Sasanians had little presence in Oman other than commercial interest, but later goes on to state that the Arabs in the region wanted to free themselves from the yoke of the Persians. How much the Sasanians were involved in Oman is difficult to say until more archaeological evidence becomes manifest. See *Proceedings of the Seminar for Arabian Studies* 9 (1979): 56 and 61. There was probably more interaction than is known; see Potts, "A Sasanian Lead Horse from North Eastern Arabia," 197.
83. D. Whitehouse, "Maritime Trade in the Arabian Sea: The 9th and 10th Centuries A.D.," *South Asian Archaeology* vol. 2, ed. M. Taddei (1977), 874–79.
84. Ibid., 881.
85. B. de Cardi, "The British Archaeological Expedition to Qatar 1973–1974," *Antiquity* (Rome, Italy) 48, no. 191 (September 1974): 199.

86. B. de Cardi, "Archaeological Survey in N. Trucial States," *East and West* (Rome, Italy) 21, no. 3–4 (September–December 1971): 260 and 268.
87. D. C. Baramki, "An Ancient Caravan Station in Dubai," *Illustrated London News* 2903 (1975); Potts, *Arabian Gulf in Antiquity,* vol. 2, 298.
88. H. M. al-Naboodah, "The Commercial Activity of Bahrain and Oman in the Early Middle Ages," *Proceedings of the Seminar for Arabian Studies* 22 (1992): 81.
89. B. Spuler, "Trade in the Eastern Islamic Countries in the Early Centuries," in *Islam and the Trade of Asia*, 14.
90. Morony, "The Late Sasanian Economic Impact on the Arabian Peninsula," 29.
91. A Sasanian navy is mentioned in Ra'in, *Darya navardi-yi iranian* [The Seamanship of Iranians], 251–55.
92. Procopius I, *History of the Wars,* Books 1–2 (Persian War), trans. H. B. Dewing, Loeb Classical Library (Cambridge: Harvard University Press, 1914; repr. London: W. Heinemann, 1953–62), 12.
93. D. Whitehouse, "Maritime Trade in the Arabian Sea," 868.
94. J. Kröger, "Sasanian Iran and India: Questions of Interaction," *South Asian Archaeology* 5 (1979): 441–48.
95. *Kosma aigyptiou monachou Christianike topographia* [The Christian Topography of Cosmas, an Egyptian Monk], trans. and ed. J. W. McCrindle (London: Hakluyt Society, 1897; repr. New York: Burt Franklin, 1973), 365.
96. Whitehouse, "Maritime Trade in the Arabian Sea."
97. For the identification of the following mints, see R. Gyselen, "Ateliers monétaires et cachets sasanides," *Studia Iranica* 8, fasc. 2 (1979): 210.
98. The location of this mint is controversial and has been attributed to several places. Mitchiner has identified that mint as NIHC for Ctesiphon in the province of Asurestan, in "Mint Organization in the Sassanian Empire," *The Numismatic Circular* 86, no. 9 (September 1978): 473. Gyselen has identified it as Weh-az-Amid-Kawad or Arrajan known in the Islamic period. Gyselen, "Ateliers monétaires et cachets sasanides," 210. Her reading is based on a seal with three cities mentioned: Staxr, Beshabuhr, and Veh-az-Amid-Kavad, thus located in Fars, *La géographie administrative de l'empire Sassanide*, Res orientales 1 (Leuven, Belgium: Peeters, 1993), for the discussion see p. 62, for the seal see p. 112.
99. Istakhri, *Masalik wa'l Mamalik*, 135.
100. Sutuda, *Hudud al-ʿAlam*, 131.
101. Ibid., 136.

CHAPTER 3

THE GULF IN THE EARLY ISLAMIC PERIOD: THE CONTRIBUTION OF ARCHAEOLOGY TO REGIONAL HISTORY

Donald Whitcomb

> *Recent archaeological finds along the whole length of the southern and eastern Arabian coasts bear witness to the intensity of these contacts between the two sides of the Gulf and with the Mesopotamian area . . . But this material, though interesting, is still insufficient for one to be able to advance more precise and detailed theories on the historical level.*
>
> —*Fiorani Piacentini*[1]

> *Geographical evidence has a clear advantage over historical information in that it is not so susceptible to dispute.*
>
> —*M. Lecker*[2]

The latter quotation, shamelessly taken out of context from Lecker's innovative study of the social organization of Madina, forcefully drives home an important point: detailed knowledge of toponyms can verify and explicate otherwise obscure reports. He combines this geographical information with genealogical details to formulate reliable beginnings toward regional history.[3] The approach of Fiorani Piacentini relies on limited and late historical sources that have probably reached the limit of interpretative possibilities, not unlike the utilization of historical sources for the early Islamic Levant. More problematic is her understanding, not atypical for historians, of the role of archaeological evidence and its interpretation for constructing regional history.

New understandings of economic history in the Sasanian period, as exemplified in the previous chapter by Touraj Daryaee, may serve to amplify the still sketchy outlines of the beginnings of the Islamic state. The conquests and the Umayyad period (661–750 C.E.) are characterized above all by the massive movement of Arab populations, settled in the *amsar* or garrison cities of Basra, Kufa, and Shiraz. The last settlement is particularly interesting in its location, as it is equidistant from Bishapur, Jur (Firuzabad), and Istakhr, Sasanian foci of resistance and periodic revolts. In less urbanized areas, a new population seems to have brought a new religion and government while adopting Persian cultural features, an apparently successful mixture that still begs satisfactory description.

The putative Sasanian/Umayyad transitions become a recognizable new pattern with the rise of the Abbasid dynasty (750–1258 C.E.). The economic weight of the capital in Baghdad and its prosperity was due in great part to the organization of the Indian Ocean trade. There exists documentation of families such as the Muhallabi, who combined commerce with governmental authority, and groups such as the Ibadis, who combined mercantilism with a religious movement.[4] Above all, the entrepôt of Siraf, located on the southern coast of Iran and connected with Basra and Oman as well as Shiraz, accounted for shipping extending as far as China and East Africa. Sulaiman and Abu Zaid are names of merchants who correspond to the fictitious Sinbad as personifications of sudden wealth and success attendant on travels beginning in the Persian Gulf.

The Buyid period (932–1062 C.E.) brought a Persian dynasty to power in northern, western, and southern Iran and Iraq that introduced more direct and militaristic governmental control of commercial networks. While prosperity continued, the seeds of socioeconomic change led to the decline and abandonment of Siraf by the twelfth century. This phase of the history of the Persian Gulf may represent the last of an interactive economic system of the early Islamic period. The Buyids endeavored to prolong the prosperity of the Persian Gulf under their political hegemony. Under their rule, the great geographer Muhammad b. Ahmad al-Muqaddasi wrote his *Ahsan al-Taqasim fi Maʿrifat al-Aqalim* (The Best Divisions for Knowledge of the Regions) in the late tenth century.[5]

Among the regions of the Islamic world, Muqaddasi acknowledged the Persian Gulf as a discrete region, as was the habit of the Arab geographers before him.[6] The descriptions of these geographers and the maps that accompanied their books may now be contextualized as historical evidence along with increasing archaeological research on the early Islamic period. The modern historical geographer and urbanologist Paul Wheatley utilizes these resources and stresses the very modern hierarchical organization of space in Muqaddasi.[7] Hadithi, in his discussion of the bureaucratic tradition of the medieval geographers in organizing the world of Islam, notes that Muqaddasi is different: "We do not know where al-Maqdisi [*sic*] got his system of administrative divisions from; perhaps he worked it out for himself."[8] Both Wheatley and Muqaddasi describe urban settlements with their structures, resources, products, and relationships to other places and regions. This is an essentially synchronic organization with only occasional notes on change and former conditions; considerations of historical background are limited and the power of archaeological ruins usually ignored.[9] This critical mass of description may be balanced with an increasing body of archaeological information, essentially diachronic in orientation, to achieve a broader, more reliable level of description.

The detailed geographical presentation in Muqaddasi's book about the Islamic realms covered half the world as we now know it. While much was based on the geographical tradition that preceded him, he based his original analytic abstraction on personal observation and reasoning by analogy. His sequencing of subjects is an important key to this philosophy and went beyond being a mere mnemonic device. For example, the order of presentation of gates of a city is important. Thus the gates of Jerusalem begin with the southwest Sihyun (Sion) gate and move counterclockwise around the city to the Bab Mihrab Daud (Jaffa gate). The districts around the city of Shiraz follow the same pattern, allowing a reconstruction of its immediate region.[10] This method is utilized for provinces, as well as city gates, and the process is demonstrated in his exposition of the entire Muslim world. He adopts the very old *kulturkreise* of the Arab and

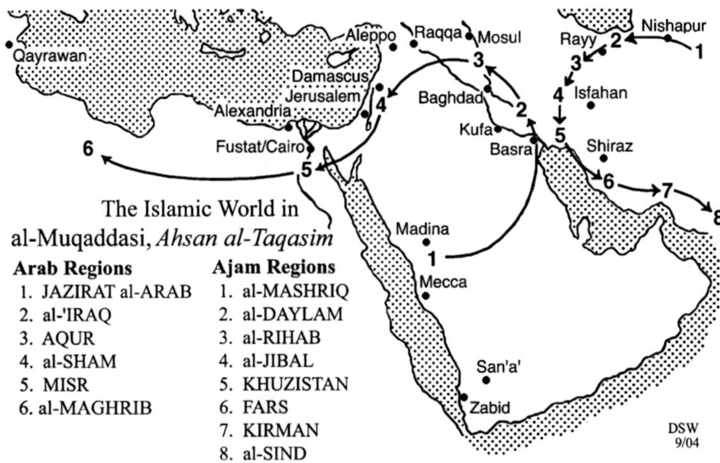

Map 3.1 The Islamic World in al-Muqaddasi, *Ahsan al-Taqasim*.

Ajam spheres (map 3.1). Thus the Arab region begins, as it should, with the Arabian Peninsula (Jazirat al-Arab), then moves counterclockwise to Iraq, Aqur (Jazirah), Sham, and then on to Misr and the Maghrib. The region of Ajam begins with the Mashriq of Central Asia and extends to Dailam, Rihab and Jibal of northern Iran, Khuzistan, Fars, and Kirman, ending this circuit with Sind in the southeast.

One may note that, even more than Iraq and the Jazirah, the Gulf forms the longest intersection of these two regions, the Arab and the Ajam. Muqaddasi takes pains to accurately describe the sea, often called the China Sea, as having an arm with two tongues (reaching Qulzum and Ayla)[11] and "flowing three quarters around the Peninsula of the Arabs (*Jazirat al-Arab*) . . . This sea is most vast and forbidding between Aden and 'Uman . . . thence a tongue stretches to 'Abbadan."[12] The shores of this gulf have their urban centers, the ports, which are entrepôts connected with each other, as well as to interior cities. Consideration of commercial structures needs to take into account both the hinterland and foreland of a port, the latter being the ultimate destination of its shipping. Patterns of this long-distance commerce, the source of great prosperity, have often been studied. On the other hand, the intermediate trade and sociopolitical relations among nearby ports need to be considered. Interpretation of the Persian Gulf as a Sasanian mare nostrum provides an important antecedent to the early Islamic patterns (map 3.2), but with Daryaee's important caveat that these relations are among peoples and not nation-states.[13] As a point of departure, this chapter will consider the Gulf as one interactive system of economic patterns, reflected in narrative descriptions and archaeological evidence.[14]

BASRA AND THE PROVINCE OF IRAQ

Discussion of the settlement structure of the Persian Gulf in the early Islamic period must begin with Iraq in deference to its political and economic dominance (map 3.3). The caliphal capitals of Baghdad and Samarra encapsulate the widening ripples of influence to Basra and the ports of the Indian Ocean, the entire direction known to the Abbasids as the *Ard al-Hind*, to the far reaches of China. The influence of Iraq on the Persian Gulf region finds its focus in the city of Basra, the *misr* or metropolitan center

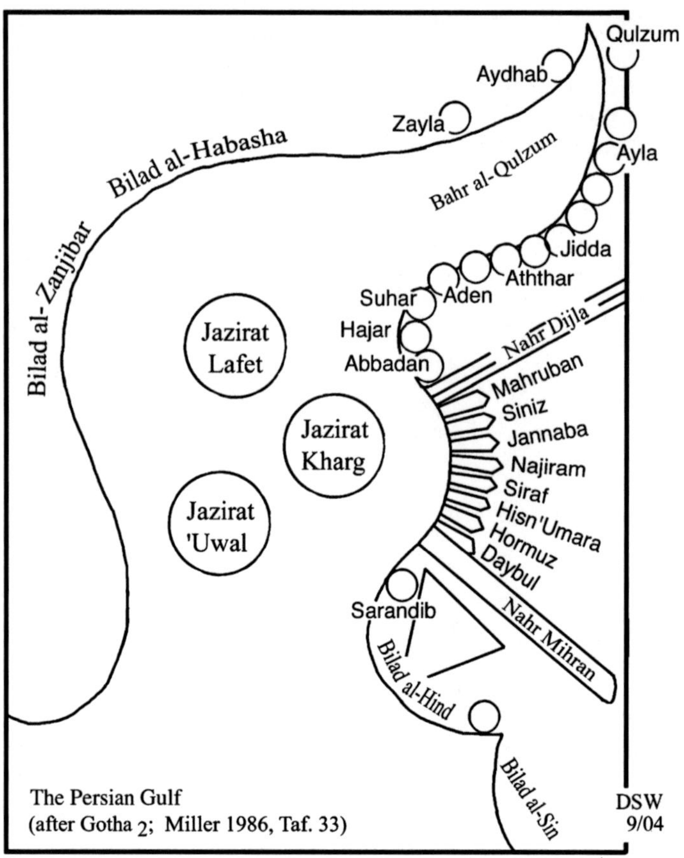

Map 3.2 The Persian Gulf in an Early Islamic Map.

of southern Iraq and indeed possibly the oldest of the *amsar* (founded in 637 or 638).[15] The site was placed near the port of Ubulla and a fortified village called Khuraiba. The city had a port to the east, connected to the Shatt al-Arab by two canals, and an open area (the *mirbad*) to the west. Subsequent expansion of the town was to the west, infilling the *mirbad;* by the late tenth century, Basra is described by Muqaddasi as having the form of a *tailasan* (headcloth), assumed to be a very large rectangle, measuring one-by-two farsakhs, or six-by-twelve kilometers.[16] While hypotheses have been advanced concerning this urban planning,[17] little is known archaeologically from the site, which is generally known as Zubair. Likewise, modern Basra seems to cover much of the actual port of Ubulla, an earlier Sasanian town. Promising investigations by the University of Basra and excavations by al-Janabi in the 1970s remain available only in preliminary sketches[18]; such information served Abd al-Jabbar Naji and Y. N. Ali in their reconstruction of Basra's markets.[19]

Muqaddasi epitomizes Basra as "a port on the sea, and an emporium of the land," as well as a place of manufacture.[20] The first industry here, as in most towns of importance, was textile manufacture. The ceramics industry of Basra was certainly no less important. These products have been studied by Mason and Keall, who have identified a Basran petrofabric, a scientific description of special ceramics such as lusterwares produced in this town or its region.[21] Most of the ceramics studied are white glazed

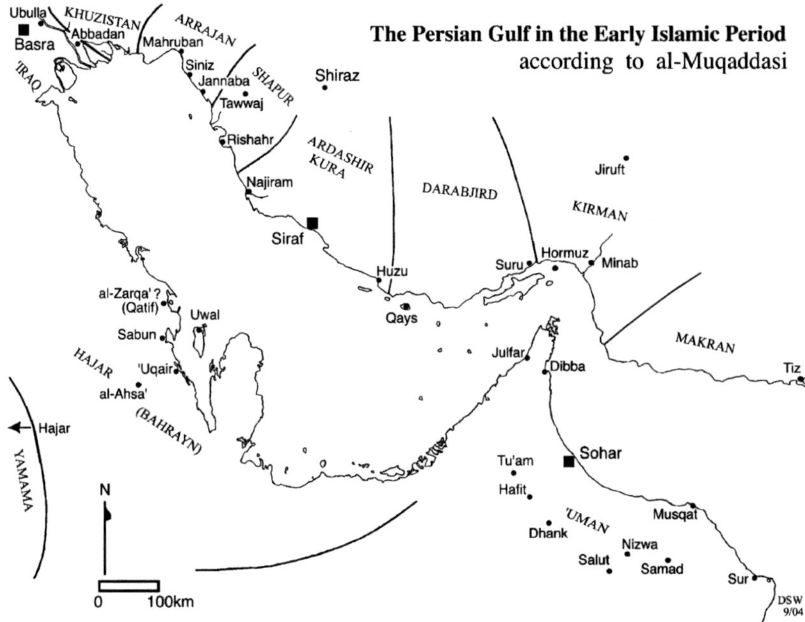

Map 3.3 The Persian Gulf according to al-Muqaddasi.

wares with various decorative embellishments, a widely distributed semiluxury tableware. Another product of Basran kilns seems to have been jars of various sizes with a characteristic blue-green glaze, often with incised and barbotine decorations on the exterior. These jars may have held a specific product of Basra, *dibs,* or date honey; this prized commodity may have been distributed throughout the region and especially in the Arabian Peninsula (*Jazirat al-Arab*) in this distinctive container. Though related to the much earlier blue-green (often called turquoise) glazed wares, the Partho-Sasanian wares are distinguished by their recognizable forms. Ceramic products of Basra have an archaeological importance, in that they are often clear diagnostics for early Islamic occupation in the entire Gulf region and signal a larger commercial interaction among find locations.

The emphasis on manufacturing[22] should not obscure the development of agriculture, from the Sawad or cultivated area of Basra and beyond, and control of food marketing and exports. Basra was supported by the port of Ubulla, which seems to have functioned as a customs post opposite the regional center of Furat (Shiqq 'Uthman?).[23] The narrative section of Muqaddasi mentions only these settlements and Abadan on an island between the Tigris and "river of Khuzistan" (probably the Karun or Bahmanshir river).[24] In another section on Wayla, Muqaddasi implies that there was a controversy about Abadan, that this town might be claimed by three provinces—Iraq, Khuzistan, and the Jazirat al-Arab.[25] Certainly the town seems to have held a symbolic importance, strangely anticipating its modern revival.

SIRAF AND THE PROVINCE OF FARS

Most of southern Iran lies in the province of Fars, the synonym of ancient Parsa and derivation for Persepolis, Persia, and the Persian Gulf (map 3.3). Fars province was divided into five districts in Sasanian times: Istakhr to the north, Arrajan, Shahpur,

Ardashir-Khwarra, and Darabjird. The latter four ranged from the coast into the high mountains and plateau; that is, each district encompassed an ecological diversity symbolized in the *sardsir/garmsir* (cold highland / warm lowland) zones of transhumance. The capital of each district was situated near the division of these zones and thus functioned as an economic center and redistribution point. The most important Sasanian cities in Fars were Istakhr, Bishapur, and Jur (Firuzabad). The foundation of Shiraz in 684 provided a Muslim camp in exactly the center of these three rebellion-prone cities, as mentioned earlier. More importantly, Shiraz signaled a reorientation of Fars as a unified province in direct relationship with the Caliphate in Baghdad. All roads would lead to Shiraz, but a trunk road connected this metropolis with the primacy of Iraq.[26]

Each district along the coastline of the Gulf had a distinctive character, with a complex of urban settlements (not to mention historical background) as is reflected in Muqaddasi's descriptions. The westernmost district was Arrajan, described by Muqaddasi as "plains, mountains and coast, with an abundance of date palms, figs, olives, much revenue and agricultural products;"[27] this is a description which might be extended over most of Fars province.[28] Three ports were found on this coast. Mahruban, which was described as "the port of Arrajan and storehouse of al-Basra,"[29] has been mapped by Iqtidari as containing a mosque and three large caravanserais.[30] The next port was Siniz, said to have been larger with many "palaces" and famed for its linen, which was compared to the finest of Egypt. The third port was Jannaba, again large and noted for textiles, and now an extensive series of tells (mounded ruins) around the modern town of Ganava.[31] Jannaba is noted by Muqaddasi and many others as the origin of Abu Sa'id and Abu Tahir al-Qarmati, who moved their political activities to Bahrain.

The district of Shahpur held the town of Tawwaj, in the extensive palm groves of Borazjan, which was on the site of the pre-Islamic settlement (Taoke) associated with Rishahr or Rev Ardashir on the Bushehr peninsula. The town figured in early battles between Arab raiders and the *marzban* (margrave) Shahruk[32] and was soon colonized by the Arabs, thus boasting one of the earliest mosques in Iran.[33] Tawwaj was noted for its textiles, particularly a multicolored linen shot with gold threads called "tawwazi"; later the Buyid Adud al-Dawla (r. 949–83) transported a group of Syrian Arabs to engage in this industry. Tawwaj was associated with the port of Khur Sif (Khurshid?), which may now be located near the head of the Bushehr peninsula.[34] The study of Rev Ardashir, long plagued with indecision as to location, may be firmly associated with the extensive Sasanian occupation of Rishahr south of Bushehr.[35] Thus, survey materials indicate that the Sasanian development along the Angali canal, connecting Rishahr to Tawwaj, continued through the early Islamic period and Rishahr functioned as the port of Shahpur (as Muqaddasi indicates).

It is tempting to see primacy in the ports of the coast of Fars as shifting from Rishahr to Siraf after the Umayyad period (i.e., before 800, the founding of Siraf's Congregational Mosque). The subsequent fame of the great entrepôt of Siraf is reflected in numerous references by geographers and historians to this port and to the activities of its citizens. These testimonies are now enhanced by the extensive excavations of David Whitehouse from 1966 to 1973.[36] Both of these sources indicate that this port played a pivotal role in control of long-distance shipment and perhaps, cargo transfer within the network of Persian Gulf trade. Excavations and narratives reflect this prosperity in a large, planned urban complex of embellished residences around a large, well-appointed mosque (map 3.4, site B). Some of these structures on the slopes overlooking the city have been interpreted as palaces or official residences. Other features of the city, such as hammams, bazaars, ceramic workshops, and cemeteries, have been uncovered and add to one's appreciation of this metropolis.

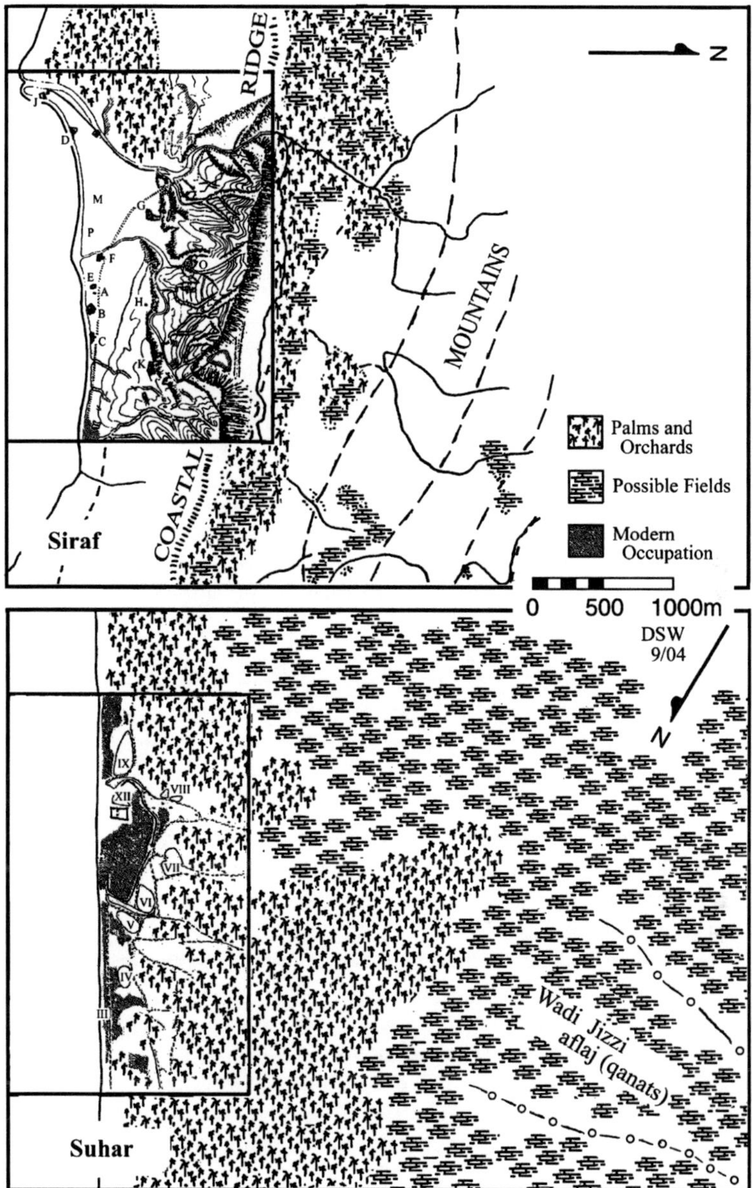

Map 3.4 Land Use and Settlement at Siraf and Suhar.

On the other hand, except for a curtain wall and a gate to the west, there seem to be no indications of a defensive nature. Indeed, one may note that, in the Gulf region, archaeological evidence indicates that there are no early Islamic fortifications. The cessation of occupation at Qal'at Bahrain is one example, but the case of Siraf, where the Sasanian fort was leveled for the Congregational Mosque, is symbolically appropriate. This avoidance of static defense systems may be part of a widespread characteristic of early Islamic communities; it is found in the Levant where citadels were ignored and walls were apparently symbolic.[37]

When Muqaddasi wrote about Siraf he was aware of a change in its fortunes, not only from the earthquake of 977 but from Buyid policy, which seems to have favored Oman.[38] While there were smaller subsidiary ports in the region of Siraf, such as Najiram and Naband, the focus of political activity seems to have shifted to the east, to the area of Suru, Hisn Ibn Umara, Huzu, and the island of Qais. This island, whose Persian name was Kish, succeeded Siraf in the eleventh century as the Gulf's main emporium and flourished in the twelfth and thirteenth centuries. Located about 120 miles southeast of Siraf, Kish contained a large walled city and qanat-based agriculture, despite its torrid climate. It was ruled by Arab amirs of the Bani Qaisar tribe.

Part of this pattern may be explained in the shifting fortunes of the occupants of the coastal region. This eastern coast of Fars province was the territory of the Bani Umara, north and around Siraf was that of the Bani Zuhair, and the area from Najiram north belonged to the Bani Muzaffar. These three *sifs* (or coastal zones) were said to have been occupied by three Arab tribes who had crossed the Gulf.[39] The coastal survey by Williamson includes distinctions in ceramic assemblages that seem to conform to the territories of these tribes.[40] As described by Istakhri, these Arab tribes belonged to either the Julanda (Azd) or the Quraish and the territories of these two supratribal groupings alternated, suggesting a "leap-frog" system of alliance and competition.[41]

HORMUZ AND THE PROVINCES OF KIRMAN, MAKRAN, AND SIND

In the early fourteenth century the port of Hormuz shifted to the island of Jarun and enjoyed a primacy that lasted for more than two centuries and encompassed virtually the whole Gulf.[42] The southernmost district of Kirman was Jiruft, which had connections to the capital of Sirjan or to Bardasir (later called Kirman). Jiruft, or the archaeological site of Shahr-i Daqianus, has revealed an elegant city of the tenth through thirteenth centuries, as Muqaddasi had described.[43] At least part of its wealth derived from the old port of Hormuz, located "a farsakh from the sea"[44] on the Minab river. Archaeological evidence of its early Islamic importance was revealed in the survey by Williamson.[45] The long coast of the Makran is broken by the port of Tiz; according to Muqaddasi, this entrepôt was well developed though one may wonder whether it ever could have posed serious competition to Suhar.

Finally, the port of Daibul, located near the mouth of the Indus (Mihran) River and thus connected to the capital at Mansura, marks the beginning of Sind. The connection of Daibul with the site of Banbhore seems to have been confirmed through the investigation of a large fort on the coast called Ratto Kot.[46] Like the port of Basra and the inland city of Kufa, both Daibul and Mansura were *amsar* established after the Muslim conquest for settlement of the Islamic community. Even more than the organization of early Islamic Iraq, study of this urban phenomenon is tainted by the dominating model of the cantonments of the British Raj.[47]

SUHAR AND THE PROVINCE OF OMAN

When Muqaddasi reached what we would now refer to as the Arabian coast of the Persian Gulf, he divided the region into three provinces: Oman, Hajar, and Yamama. His summary list of the Jazirat al-Arab is even more interesting.[48] After Yemen and the Hijaz, the remainder of the region holds (1) Suhar, (2) Mahra (Shihir), (3) Hadhramawt (al-Ahqaf), (4) Saba, (5) Yamama, and (6) Ahsa. He thus describes southern and eastern

Arabia in terms of a circle, beginning with the city (*qasaba*) of Suhar.[49] The primacy of Suhar in this region seems likely to have originated at least from the Sasanian period, as J. C. Wilkinson has demonstrated through texts[50] and Kervran has shown archaeologically.[51] The port seems to have been associated with the citadel or stronghold of Damsetjird,[52] though this has not been located.[53]

The archaeology of Suhar is illuminated by the work of Williamson and later Kervran.[54] In 1973, Williamson outlined the history of Suhar from his archaeological surveys, heavily influenced by his vast experience in southern Iran and Siraf. He was one of the first to examine the advantages of this site, particularly the plentiful waters in the Wadi Jizzi system, which "produce a considerable surplus of agricultural produce."[55] Study of these agricultural resources, and particularly the *aflaj* (or qanat) system, which drew water onto its extensive fields, led T. J. Wilkinson to speculate on the implications of this surplus. He drew from his study of the field system in the hinterland of Siraf (map 3.4) to note the extreme deficit of food resources at Siraf and the constant need to import supplies.[56] While products from the interior of Iran might be presumed, Wilkinson posits that the surplus of Suhar would be more than ample and transport by sea economically feasible.[57]

Kervran's archaeological study of Suhar makes clear that the period since the work of Williamson has made a significant difference in preservation and opportunities for discoveries, especially for comparison with the excavations at Siraf. While Siraf remained relatively undeveloped, the potential for utilization of Suhar has precluded intensive archaeological excavations. Nevertheless, Kervran was able to discern the prosperity of the ninth to tenth century city, as well as the clear implications for subsequent occupation in the twelfth and thirteenth centuries.[58] Further, her work in Bahrain indicates that the apparent complementary roles of Siraf and Suhar mask a much more complex set of geopolitical relationships in the early Islamic period.

JULFAR, NORTHERN OMAN, AND THE EMIRATES

Muqaddasi mentions that the town of Hafit lies in the direction of Hajar (Bahrain); he uses this same phrase for Dibba and Julfar, suggesting a differentiation from the settlements of central Oman (map 3.3). J. C. Wilkinson discusses the history of the alienation of northern Oman and its orientation toward Bahrain.[59] He also attempts to sort out the role of the Qaramita (Carmathians) in Suhar and Nizwa from at least 930, and the complex relationships with the Buyid ascendancy.

While archaeological research has not illuminated the situation of Dibba, the intensive, international surveys in the Emirates have produced a revolution in our understanding of this region and its role in early Islamic history, as well as for periods both antecedent and subsequent.[60] The first archaeological research at Ras al-Khaimah focused on the mounded settlement called Mataf and Nudud, occupied during the period of Hormuzi ascendancy and later, that is, the fourteenth to seventeenth century.[61] This was a period marked by ubiquitous "Julfar ware," a common unglazed, painted pottery, and extensive imports of porcelain and celadon.[62] Following the detailed analyses of Kennet, one sees the earlier periods as dispersed among several known sites, particularly Jazirat al-Hulailah, Kush, and Khatt, and not one nucleated urban settlement.[63] Perhaps most interesting, from an archaeological point of view, is the Tell of Kush with its apparently long occupation.[64] Unlike the disappointing treatment of ceramics at Siraf, Kush/Mataf provides an artifactual sequence based on imported wares: the Samarra horizon, Indian wares, south Iranian products, and especially Chinese and southeast Asia ceramics. This compilation of archaeological information, based on stratigraphic ceramic studies,[65] leads Kennet to suggest cultural phases, each of which lasted approximately three hundred years, that mark a clear improvement over previous information and suggest cultural patterns that balance details of dynasties and political events and personalities.[66]

But to return to Dibba (or Daba?), there are archaeological discoveries that have been generally disregarded, though they are probably relevant. As Muqaddasi notes this town, perhaps the same noted for its pre-Islamic and Islamic trade fair and major battle of the Ridda wars, lies with Julfar in the direction of Hajar (Bahrain). There is the site of Jumairah, first excavated by Baramki over four campaigns in the 1970s and described by him as a caravan station "situated between Oman and Ctesiphon in Iraq."[67] The principal structure, founded in the Sasanian period (5th–6th century), has been likened to Syrian "desert castles" and the fort at Siraf.[68] The building is now considered a palatial governor's palace which continued in use in the Umayyad period. More important are numerous large residences, a suq, and mosque forming an urban complex from the ninth to the tenth century and later.[69]

Ahsa and the Province of Hajar (Bahrain)

The province of Hajar included the island now known as Bahrain (Uwal), the settlements along the coast (Qatif, Tarut, Uqair), and the capital of Hufuf in the inland oasis of Ahsa (or Hasa; map 3.3). For instance, Insoll's recent initiative at Bilad al-Qadim[70] is one aspect of sites on northern Bahrain island, which would include Khamis and its famed mosque,[71] Barbar-sud,[72] A'Ali,[73] and Qal'at al-Bahrain. Qal'at al-Bahrain was first explored by the Danish expeditions, which discovered an earlier qal'at below the Portuguese fort and upon its ancient mound.[74] This fort, with round towers and a single entrance on the western side, measures 52.5 meters on each side and was initially identified as an early Islamic *qasr,* just as Siraf fort below the mosque.[75] Most recently, Kervran has concluded that the fort has a Hellenistic/Parthian original foundation, occupied into the fifth century and then abandoned until the thirteenth century.[76] The cumulative evidence suggests that Qal'at al-Bahrain[77] did not form an urbanized port as seen at Siraf and Suhar and that early Islamic occupation was rather similar to that seen at Julfar. The situation on the Qatar Peninsula is very similar. The most famous site, Murwab,[78] may be typical of numerous other Islamic settlements with little evidence of towns in the region.[79]

Ahsa is reputed to be the largest oasis in Saudi Arabia, with over thirty thousand acres in cultivation fed by artesian springs and elaborate canalization systems (placing it on a scale comparable to the Suhar field system). The archaeology of Ahsa is represented by surveys isolating the ancient and medieval settlements; a seriation of the latter evidence has yielded Early and Middle Islamic patterns.[80] The early Islamic phase is defined by Samarran Abbasid ceramics as well as local ceramics of the ninth and tenth centuries; these artifacts may serve as a basis for Carmathian archaeology.[81]

One of the most notable movements arising in the Persian Gulf in the late Abbasid period was that of the Qarmatis or Carmathians, who were based in Bahrain and eastern Arabia in the tenth and eleventh centuries.[82] This little-understood movement arose out of a milieu of radical Shiism and Isma'ilism. The Carmathian state was evidently organized on a communal basis, although its economy was based on black slave labor. Madelung clearly indicates the sources and extent of Qarmathian economic power, from the customs on shipping collected at Uwal and at Basra, to tribute from Oman and protection fees on pilgrims, in addition to agricultural production of the oasis and land holdings in southern Iraq.[83]

Having split with the Fatimids, they raided Syria and Palestine, provoked an uprising in Basra in 900, and pillaged it in 924. They also attacked caravans of pilgrims enroute to Mecca. Most notoriously, they removed the Black Stone from the Ka'ba in 930 and took it to Bahrain, where it was kept until 951. The site of Jawatha, reputed to be one of the earliest mosques in eastern Arabia and temporary location of the Black Stone, is an extensive ruinfield and a possible urban center.[84] Their habitual aggression evolved into peaceful protection of eastern trade, which is perhaps the irony indicated by Kervran, who refers to the Carmathians as a violent state providing stability for commerce throughout the Gulf.[85] A joint Saljuq-Abbasid army finally put an end to it in 1078. According to Bosworth, "Isma'ilism has long disappeared from eastern Arabia, but it may have left a distant legacy in the present existence there, within modern Saudi Arabia, Qatar and Bahrayn Island, of significant Twelver Shi'i communities."[86]

For the sake of a complete account, one must mention the inclusion by Muqaddasi of Yamama as the third of the eastern provinces of Arabia.[87] He confines his report only to Hajar, the capital and apparently now known as Riyadh,[88] and Falaj, one of the surrounding forts and towns.[89] While the mining resources (both gold and silver)[90] may have been significant, Hajar lay upon the main pass through the Arid mountains and might be visualized as a port leading toward western Arabia.[91]

SOCIAL ARCHAEOLOGY AND MUQADDASI

> The peoples of the Gulf were animals who did not seek to better themselves and Uman, Siraf and Ubulla were the three sinks of the world.
>
> A Hijazi opinion[92]

> 'Uman belongs to al-Daylam, and Hajar to the Qaramita'
>
> Muqaddasi[93]

This interpretation of the perspective of Sham or the Hijaz suggests an antipathy to the sociopolitical system, if not the commercial prosperity, of the Gulf region during the early Islamic period. Discussion of the role of the Carmathians in the Gulf, operating out of Bahrain, leads to the broader consideration of social geography in the early Islamic period. J. C. Wilkinson suggests a common factor in the Kharijite concepts of the first Islamic century, particularly "the idea that the Arab and non-Arab populations formed a common social structure," one rooted in the perception of discrimination under the Sasanian political system.[94] Of these social movements, the organization most pertinent to the Gulf was the Ibadi, which developed among the Basra merchant community. This was a "polyglot mercantile society whose trading organization inherited from the Sasanids stretched from the Gulf to India (the *Ard al-Hind*)."[95] One might extend this Ibadi initiative even as far as China.[96] Aside from ideologies and force of personalities, the Ibadi mercantile foundation is reflected in a quietist approach (working within the system), avoidance of government interference, wide communication and interchange of information, and the accumulation and utilization of wealth toward facilitating these factors. Ibadi history seems constantly associated with Oman in special ways, particularly in tribal politics of the Azd, who were involved with control of the Persian coast, in alliances with the Abd al-Qais of Bahrain, and in the early settlement within the *misr* of Basra.[97] Tribal organization of the coast of Fars was ignored by Muqaddasi;[98] happily Istakhri provides details of these Omani tribes.[99] The dichotomy introduced by Muqaddasi is revealing in that it regards the Buyids as Persian inheritors of the urban settlements of Fars, while on the other hand, the Carmathians hold or influence settlements on southern and western coasts.

Archaeological evidence has amassed data sufficient to portray a commercial history of the Persian Gulf, a pattern of interactive cities and ports uniting these shores. Excavations at Siraf, Sohar, and even Jumeirah add, in addition to interesting material, a cultural contextualization for the often-fragmentary textual sources. As is too often the case, the pattern is clearest when it breaks down, or at least changes; this is the reason that Muqaddasi's text forms a most useful analytic epitome. He wrote when the early Islamic world was fragmenting (if it was ever really whole) and, within a half century, the Persian Gulf would develop new patterns of interaction based on entrepôts farther to the east. Siraf and Kish in turn were supplanted in the early fourteenth century by Hormuz, which for the next three hundred years was the most famous commercial center in the Gulf and of international renown (see the next chapter). One might argue that what may be defined archaeologically as the middle Islamic period is beginning to be delineated at Julfar and Bahrain.[100] Improved analyses of archaeological evidence is allowing new descriptions of these continuations and innovations in economic patterns, clarifying what has been a "dark age" in the history of the Persian Gulf.

NOTES

1. V. Fiorani Piacentini, "Ardashir I Papakan and the Wars against the Arabs: Working Hypothesis on the Sasanian Hold of the Gulf," *Proceedings of the Seminar for Arabian Studies* 15 (1985): 73.
2. M. Lecker, *Muslims, Jews and Pagans: Studies on Early Islamic Medina* (Leiden, The Netherlands: Brill, 1995), 147.
3. In a similar way, Azd social structure may yield relevant and important information on the eastern Gulf region, as noted by J. C. Wilkinson, "Arab-Persian Land Relationships in Late Sasanid Oman," *Proceedings of the Seminar for Arabian Studies* 3 (1973): 44.
4. J. C. Wilkinson, "The Early Development of the Ibadi Movement in Basra," in *Studies on the First Century of Islamic Society*, ed. G. H. A. Juynboll (Carbondale: Southern Illinois University, 1982), 137–43.
5. Muhammad ibn Ahmad Muqaddasi, *Kitab Ahsan al-Taqasim fi Maʿrifat al-Aqalim*, 2nd. ed., Bibliotheca Geographorum Arabicorum 3, ed. M. de Goeje (Leiden, The Netherlands: Brill, 1906). Also, *The Best Divisions for Knowledge of the Regions: A Translation of* Ahsan al-Taqasim fi Maʿrifat al-Aqalim, trans. B. A. Collins and M. H. al-Tai (Reading, UK: Garnet Publishing, 1994).
6. A useful summary of this literature is found in G. Le Strange, *The Lands of the Eastern Caliphate* (Cambridge: University Press, 1905).
7. This has resulted in a second compendium, *The Places Where Men Pray Together: Cities in Islamic Lands, Seventh through Tenth Centuries* (Chicago: University of Chicago Press, 2001), an essential resource for early Islamic urbanism.
8. Q. A. S. al-Hadithi, "The Bahrain of the Geographers: An Administrative and Economic Study," in *Bahrain through the Ages: The History*, ed. Abdullah bin Khalid al-Khalifa and Michael Rice (London: Kegan Paul, 1993), 267.
9. The exception being certain unavoidable *mirabilia*, such as Persepolis, described by Muqaddasi (*Kitab Ahsan al-Taqasim*, 444) as the prayer house of Sulaiman.
10. This exposition gives a clear example of the *tassuj* as an organizing principle (D. Whitcomb, *Before the Roses and Nightingales: Excavations at Qasr-i Abu Nasr, Iran* (New York: Metropolitan Museum of Art, 1985), 228–31.)
11. That is, the separate gulfs of Suez and Aqaba, not recognized by Western cartographers until the seventeenth century.
12. Muqaddasi, *Kitab Ahsan al-Taqasim*, 11.
13. T. Daryaee, "The Persian Gulf Trade in Late Antiquity," *Journal of World History* 14 (2003): 8.
14. D. Whitcomb, "Trade and Tradition in Medieval Southern Iran" (PhD diss., University of Chicago, 1979).

15. Salih al-Ali, "Khittat of al-Basra," *Sumer* (1952): 72–83, 281–303; and Salih al-'Ali, *Social and Economic Organization of Al-Basra* (Baghdad, Iraq: Matba'a al-Ma'arif, 1953). The meaning of *misr* follows the description adopted in Muqaddasi.
16. Muqaddasi, *Kitab Ahsan al-Taqasim,* 117; F. Sarre and E. Herzfeld, *Archäologische Reise im Euphrat- und Tigris- Gebiet* (Berlin, Germany: D. Reimer, 1911); also 1920, 209, where the urban plan is compared to that of Mosul, itself a very early *misr.* See also M. G. Morony, *Iraq After the Muslim Conquest* (Princeton, NJ: Princeton University Press, 1984). On the later construction of *qusur* and *suqs,* see A. J. Naji and Y. N. Ali, "The Suqs of Basra: Commercial Organization and Activity in a Medieval Islamic City," *Journal of the Economic and Social History of the Orient* 24 (1981): 298–309.
17. L. Massignon, "Explication du plan de Basra (Irak)," in *Westöstliche Abhandlungen; Rudolf Tschudi,* ed. F. Meier (Wiesbaden, Germany: Harrassowitz, 1954); D. Whitcomb, "The *Misr* of Ayla: Settlement at al-'Aqaba in the Early Islamic Period," in *The Byzantine and Early Islamic Near East, II: Land Use and Settlement Patterns,* ed. G. King and A. Cameron (Princeton, NJ: Darwin Press, 1994), 161–62.
18. See "Excavations in Iraq: Basra (Old City)," *Iraq* 35 (1973): 189–204 and "Excavations in Iraq: Basra (Old City)," *Iraq* 41 (1979): 141–81.
19. Naji and Ali, "The Suqs of Basra."
20. Muqaddasi, *Kitab Ahsan al-Taqasim,* 128.
21. Comments on Basra and its ceramics have benefited from a reading of the unpublished thesis by Jessica Hallett, "Trade and Innovation: The Rise of a Pottery Industry in Abbasid Basra" (Oxford University, 1994). R. Mason and E. J. Keall, "The 'Abbasid Glazed Wares of Siraf and the Basra Connection: Petrographic Analysis," *Iran* 29 (1991); R. Mason, "Early Medieval Iraqi Lustre-Painted and Associated Wares: Typology in a Multidisciplinary Study," *Iraq* 59 (1997): 15–61.
22. Muqaddasi, *Kitab Ahsan al-Taqasim,* 33.
23. M. G. Morony, "Continuity and Change in the Administrative Geography of Late Sasanian and Early Islamic al-'Iraq," *Iran* 20 (1982): 35.
24. Muqaddasi, *Kitab Ahsan al-Taqasim,* 118.
25. Ibid., 179.
26. The subject of the economic and archaeological history of Fars province is explored in the author's doctoral dissertation, "Trade and Tradition in Medieval Southern Iran."
27. Muqaddasi, *Kitab Ahsan al-Taqasim,* 421.
28. Muqaddasi reserved for Fars the highest praise for its climate and productivity, "blessings the like of which I have never seen outside of al-Sham" (Ibid., 421).
29. Ibid., 416.
30. This paper relies heavily on a pioneering and detailed study by A. Iqtidari, *Athar-i shahrha-yi bastani, savahil va jazayir-i Khalij-i Fars va Bahr-i Umun* (Tehran, Iran: Organization of National Antiquities, 1348/1969–70). There is no reason to believe that such studies have not been continued in recent times by Iranian scholars, but, if so, access to such research has been severely limited.
31. Ibid., 29.
32. M. Hinds, "The First Arab Conquests in Fars," *Iran* 22 (1984): 39–53.
33. Iqtidari, *Athar-i shahrha-yi bastani,* 93.
34. D. Whitcomb, "Bushire and the Angali Canal," *Mesopotamia* 22 (1987): 315.
35. D. Whitehouse and A. Williamson, "Sasanian Maritime Trade," *Iran* 11 (1973): 29–49.
36. The utility of these excavations is due to the detailed preliminary reports in the journal *Iran,* usually appearing the following year; final publication has been less successful, though fascicules on inscriptions, coins, and mosques appeared in 1983.
37. D. Whitcomb, "The Walls of Early Islamic Ayla: Defence or Symbol?," in *Muslim Military Architecture in Greater Syria, from the Coming of Islam to the Ottoman Period,* ed. H. Kennedy (Leiden, The Netherlands: Brill, 2006), 61–74.
38. Muqaddasi, *Kitab Ahsan al-Taqasim,* 426.
39. Abu Ishaq al-Istakhri, *Kitab Masalik wa'l Mamalik,* Bibliotheca Geographorum Arabicorum 1, ed. M. de Goeje (Leiden, The Netherlands: Brill, 1927), 140–41.

40. A. Williamson, "Persian Gulf Commerce in the Sassanian Period and the First Two Centuries of Islam," *Bastanshinasi va Hunar-i Iran* 9–10 (1972): 104.
41. Whitcomb, "Trade and Tradition," 62–63.
42. The archaeology and history of Hormuz, with Bahrain and Julfar, fall outside the parameters of this paper and must belong to a separate discussion. For Iranian excavations see H. H. Bakhtiari, "Hormuz Island," *Iran* 17 (1979): 150–52.
43. Muqaddasi, *Kitab Ahsan al-Taqasim,* 466. Dr. Hamideh Choobak has excavated much of the remains of Shahr-i Daqianus (Jiroft). She has found the mosque and minaret, large baths, and streets and residences of the Seljuq period.
44. Muqaddasi, *Kitab Ahsan al-Taqasim,* 466.
45. Williamson, "Persian Gulf Commerce in the Sassanian Period" and Peter Morgan, "New Thoughts on Old Hormuz: Chinese Ceramics in the Hormuz Region in the Thirteenth and Fourteenth Centuries," *Iran* 29 (1991): 67–83.
46. M. Kervran, "Forteresses, entrepôts et commerce: une histoire à suivre depuis les rois sassanides jusqu'aux princes d'Ormuz," *Itinéraires d'Orient, hommages à Claude Cahen,* Res Orientales 6, eds. R. Curiel and R. Gyselen (Paris: Groupe pour l'étude de la civilisation du Moyen-Orient, 1994): 335–38.
47. J. J. Bede, "The Arabs in Sind, 712–1026" (PhD diss., University of Utah, 1973), 135–38.
48. Muqaddasi, *Kitab Ahsan al-Taqasim,* 53.
49. This counterclockwise direction is typical of his system of locational analysis. The term *misr* is used here in his sense of the metropolitan center of a region. Arabia had the rare case of more than one *misr* (Mecca in Hijaz and Zabid in Yemen) and Suhar, a second-ranking *qasaba,* though very large (Wheatley, *Places Where Men Pray Together*, 77 and 82, fig. 6).
50. J. C. Wilkinson, "Suhar (Sohar) in the Early Islamic Period: The written Evidence," *South Asian Archaeology 1977*, ed. M. Taddei (Naples, Italy: Istituto universitario orientale, 1979), vol. 2, 887–907.
51. M. Kervran and F. Hiebert, "Sohar pré-Islamique, note stratigraphique," *Golf-Archäologie: Mesopotamien, Iran, Kuwait, Bahrain, Vereinigte Arabische Emirate und Oman,* ed. K. Schippmann, Anja Herling, and Jean-François Salles (Buch am Erlbach, Germany: M. L. Leidorf, 1991), 337–48.
52. Wilkinson believes that this was a fortified quarter called Dastajird; see Kervran, "Forteresses, entrepôts et commerce," 334, for full historical references. On the other hand, one may suggest a corruption of Jamshidgird, with the possibility that a separate Sasanian city may have existed nearby, perhaps even circular in form. Indeed, Jamshidgird is the name of an island in the Indian Ocean associated with Yamakoti, the castle of Jam (=Kangdiz?) (V. Minorsky, trans., *Hudud al-'Alam, 'the Regions of the World': A Persian Geography, 372 A.H.–982 A.D.* (Oxford: Oxford University Press, 1937), 189.
53. These factors have been clearly elucidated by Wilkinson, in "Suhar (Sohar) in the Early Islamic Period," 903–05.
54. M. Kervran, "A la recherche de Sohar: état de la question," in *Arabie orientale, Mésopotamie et Iran meridional: de l'âge du fer au début de la période islamique,* eds. R. Boucharlat and J.-F. Salles (Paris: Ed. Recherche sur les civilisations, 1984), 285–98.
55. A. Williamson, *Sohar and Omani Seafaring in the Indian Ocean* (Muscat: Petroleum Development (Oman) Ltd., 1973), 7.
56. G. F. Hourani has pointed to this factor: "this town was on a hot and barren shore . . . and lived on supplies brought by sea." See his *Arab Seafaring in the Indian Ocean in Ancient and Early Medieval Times,* revised and expanded edition by John Carswell (Princeton, NJ: Princeton University Press, 1995), 69.
57. T. J. Wilkinson, "Feeding Medieval Siraf and Sohar," *al-'Usur al-Wusta: The Bulletin of Middle East Medievalists* 4 (1992): 8–9, 16.
58. Kervran, "A la recherche de Sohar."
59. J. C. Wilkinson, "Frontier Relationships between Bahrain and Oman" in *Bahrain through the Ages: The History,* 554–55.

60. "Julfar has become one of the most extensively surveyed and excavated archaeological sites in the Gulf," according to D. Kennet, "Jazirat al-Hulayla: Early Julfār," *Journal of the Royal Asiatic Society* 4 (1994): 175. He has documented this archaeological history in "Julfar and the Urbanization of Southeastern Arabia," *Arabian Archaeology and Epigraphy* 14 (2003): 103–25.
61. J. Hansman, *Julfār, an Arabian Port: Its Settlement and Far Eastern Ceramic Trade from the 14th to the 18th Centuries* (London: Royal Asiatic Society, 1985).
62. T. Sasaki and H. Sasaki, "Southeast Asian Ceramic Trade to the Arabian Gulf in the Islamic Period," in *Archaeology of the United Arab Emirates: Proceedings of the First International Conference on the Archaeology of the UAE*, ed. D. Potts, Hasan Al Naboodah, and Peter Hellyer (London: Trident Press, 2003), 254–62. Also Hansman, *Julfār, an Arabian Port.*
63. Kush has a mud-brick tower (Period II, ca. 800) and an enigmatic large, mud-brick structure (Period V, ca. 1100); Mataf has an imposed orthogonal street plan with residences (phase 2, ca. 1400); T. Sasaki and H. Sasaki, "Japanese Excavations at Julfar—1988, 1989, 1990, and 1991 seasons," *Proceedings of the Seminar for Arabian Studies* 22 (1992): 105–20.
64. D. Kennet, "Kush: A Sasanian and Islamic-Period Archaeological Tell in Ras al-Khaimah (UAE)," *Arabian Archaeology and Epigraphy* 8 (1997): 284–302.
65. A comprehensive publication of this ceramic evidence is now available in D. Kennet, *Sasanian and Islamic Pottery from Ras al-Khaimah: Classification, Chronology and Analysis of Trade in the Western Indian Ocean*, BAR International Series 1248 (Oxford, 2004). One has in his analysis the first detailed exposition of evidence that will allow vastly more precise evaluation of regional archaeological research.
66. Kennet suggests the following periodization: Late Sasanian/early Islamic, 400–800 C.E.; Samarran Abbasid, 800–1000 C.E.; "Dark Ages," 1000–1300 C.E.; al-Mataf, 1300–1600; and post Mataf, 1600–1900 C.E.
67. D. C. Baramki, "An Ancient Caravan Station in Dubai," *Illustrated London News* 2903, March 29, 1975, 66.
68. As discussed in D. T. Potts, *The Arabian Gulf in Antiquity*, vol. 2 (Oxford: Clarendon Press, 1990), 299–300, fig. 24 and D. Whitehouse, "Excavations at Siraf, Interim Reports," *Iran* 12 (1974): 5–7n9, fig. 3, pl. 1a, b.
69. H. Qandil, "Recent Discoveries at Jumeirah," in *Archaeology of the United Arab Emirates.* The author is grateful to Dr. Hussain Qandil for discussing this site and his excavations.
70. T. Insoll, "Early Islamic Bahrain," *Antiquity* 75 (2002): 495–96.
71. This small mosque of phase 2 may be compared to that at Julfar, phase 1 (Kennet, "Julfar and the Urbanization of Southeast Arabia," 113), as well as the numerous small mosques at Siraf (D. Whitehouse, *The Congregational Mosque, and Other Mosques from the Ninth to the Twelfth Centuries,* Siraf III (London: British Institute of Persian Studies, [1980]). The discrepancy in dating suggests either an early phase at Julfar or a more likely continuation at Khamis. See M. Kervran, "La mosquée al-Khamis à Bahrain: son historie et ses inscriptions: I. Le monument," *Archéologique islamique* 1 (1990): 7–51; L. Kalus, "La mosquée al-Khamis à Bahrain: son historie et ses inscriptions: I. Les inscriptions," *Archéologique islamique* 1 (1990): 53–73; D. Whitehouse, "The al-Khamis Mosque on Bahrain: A Note on the First and Second Phases," *Arabian Archaeology and Epigraphy* 14 (2003): 95–102.
72. J.-F. Salles, Beatrice Andre-Leickam, Geneviève Renisio, and Marie-Anne Vaillant, *Barbar-sud, 1982 (Bahrain): Rapport préliminaire sur une 1 ère campagne de fouilles archéologiques* (Lyon, France: Maison de l'Orient, 1983).
73. T. Sasaki, "Excavations at A'Ali – 1988/89," *Proceedings of the Seminar for Arabian Studies* 20 (1990): 111–29.
74. K. Frifelt, *Islamic Remains in Bahrain,* Jutland Archaeological Society publications, v. 37 (Højbjerg, Denmark: Jutland Archaeological Society, in association with Moesgaard Museum and Ministry of Information, State of Bahrain, 2001)
75. M. Kervran, *Excavation of Qal'at al-Bahrein, 1st Part (1977–1979)* (Bahrain: Ministry of Information, 1982).

76. The evidence of the architecture remains inconclusive and there is the possibility of a late Sasanian or very early Islamic reuse. (S. Gregory, "Was there an Eastern Origin for the Design of Late Roman Fortifications? Some Problems for Research on Forts of Rome's Eastern Frontier," in *The Roman Army in the East*, Journal of Roman Archaeology, Supp. Ser. 18, ed. D. Kennedy (1996): 169–210.)
77. Kervran, *Excavation of Qal'at al-Bahrein*, fig. 2.
78. C. Hardy-Guilbert, "Recherches sur la période islamique au Qatar," *Mission archéologique française à Qatar*, ed. J. Tixier (Paris: Recherches anthropologiques du Proche et Moyen Orient, 1980), 111–28; C. Hardy-Guilbert, "Recherches sur la période islamique au Qatar – 4ème campagne," *Mission archéologique française à Qatar*, ed. J. Tixier (Paris: Recherches anthropologiques du Proche et Moyen Orient, 1982), 35–72.
79. B. de Cardi, ed., *Qatar Archaeological Report: Excavations 1973* (Oxford: Oxford University Press, 1978).
80. D. Whitcomb, "The Archaeology of al-Hasa Oasis in the Islamic Period," *Atlal, Journal of Saudi Arabia Studies* 2 (1978): 95–113; F. S. Vidal, *The Oasis of al-Hasa* (Dhahran, Saudi Arabia: Arabian American Oil Co., 1955).
81. Earlier late Sasanian/early Islamic is not necessarily absent but not isolated from the survey collections (D. Whitcomb, "The Archaeology of al-Hasa Oasis in the Islamic Period," 99). The subsequent period of the Uyunids, from 1067 to the 14th century, is considered a continuation of the Middle Islamic period.
82. For references to this dynasty see W. Madelung, "Karmati," *Encyclopedia of Islam* 4 (1976). Also Clifford Edmund Bosworth, *The New Islamic Dynasties: A Chronological and Genealogical Manual* (New York: Columbia University Press, 1996), 94–95.
83. Madelung, "Karmati," 664.
84. Vidal, *The Oasis of al-Hasa*, 67–69. Refer here to site numbers 208–15 used by the Saudi survey.
85. Kervran, *Excavation of Qal'at al-Bahrein*, 5. Certainly Muqaddasi and other geographers evoked an admiration for Carmathian order and justice (Madelung, "Karmati," 664).
86. Bosworth, *New Islamic Dynasties*, 95.
87. Tabari describes Yamama as "a place in the desert embracing a great number of towns, one called Hajar, another Lahsa, and seven or eight others which to-day are occupied by the Carmathians" (in A. T. Wilson, *The Persian Gulf* (London: George Allen and Unwin, 1928), 84).
88. The capital of the central region of Yamama in the Arid mountains, also known as Jaw al-Khadharim. A. Al-Askar, *al-Yamama in the Early Islamic Period* (Reading, UK: Ithaca, 2002), mentions the need for archaeological work (21, 30n45).
89. Al-Askar, *al-Yamama in the Early Islamic Period*, 16–27.
90. The Yamama was apparently a mint for dirhams in the late 9th century (R. W. Morris, "An Eighth Century Hoard from Eastern Saudi Arabia," *Arabian Archaeology and Epigraphy* 5 (1994): 70–79.)
91. Likewise, Muqaddasi fails to mention the island of Failaka, off the coast of modern Kuwait. Numerous remains of the early Islamic settlements, particularly Qusur, have been found among earlier occupations. S. Patitucci and G. Uggeri, *Failakah: Insediamenti medievali islamici: Richerche e scavi nel Kuwait* (Rome: "l'Erma" di Bretschneider, 1984). Also D. Kennet, "Excavations at the Site of al-Qusur, Failaka, Kuwait," *Proceedings of the Seminar for Arabian Studies* 21 (1991): 97–111.
92. This is reflected in the writing of Tabari and Ibn Faqih; see J. C. Wilkinson, "The Early Development of the Ibadi Movement in Basra," *Studies on the First Century of Islamic Society*, ed. G. H. A. Juynboll (Carbondale: Southern Illinois University Press, 1982), 130 and 243n15.
93. Muqaddasi, *Kitab Ahsan al-Taqasim*, 104.
94. Wilkinson, "The Early Development of the Ibadi Movement in Basra," 129.
95. Ibid., 137; Wilkinson, "Suhar (Sohar) in the Early Islamic Period," 893.
96. T. Lewicki, "Les premiers commerçant arabes en Chine," *Rocznik Orientalistyczny* 9 (1935): 173–86.

97. This association is also picked up by D. Whitehouse, "The al-Khamis Mosque on Bahrain: A Note on the First and Second Phases," *Arabian Archaeology and Epigraphy* 14 (2003): 101. See Wilkinson, "The Early Development of the Ibadi Movement in Basra," 140–43.
98. Istakhri provides a similar analysis of the Zamm al-Akrad ("Kurdish" tribes) of Fars province, including nomads defined as those who wander between summer and winter quarters "in the manner of the Arabs" (Istakhri, *Kitab Masalik wa'l Mamalik,* 113).
99. Whitcomb, *Trade and Tradition in Medieval Southern Iran*, 54–55, 62–63.
100. Recent excavations by Iranian archaeologists on Kish Island should soon amplify this view.

Chapter 4

The Kings of Hormuz: From the Beginning until the Arrival of the Portuguese

Mohammad Bagher Vosoughi

The history of the kings of Hormuz[1] (*muluk-i Hurmuz*) is closely related to the history of Iranian maritime trade. For five hundred years, from the twelfth to the seventeenth century C.E., the island of Hormuz played an important role as the major base and focal center of economic exchanges and marine trade in the Persian Gulf and Indian Ocean. Its history is one of seafaring and marine transportation. Shedding light on the political and economic life of the Hormuz region during the reign of its local amirs will greatly help to assess the Iranian role in the region's marine trade. In addition, it will present a better picture of the extent of the economic exchanges and of the operational mechanism of the merchants of the Persian Gulf region.

The history of the kings of Hormuz can be divided into three distinct periods. The first period begins with the emigration of Muhammad Diramku from Oman to the coast of Iran in the eleventh century and continues up to the transfer of the capital to the island of Hormuz at the beginning of the fourteenth century. The most important features of this period are the power struggles between the amirs of Hormuz and their neighbors, the adoption of a realistic policy of acknowledging the important powers of Kirman and Fars, and the sustaining of Hormuz's economic status.

The second period begins with the transfer of the capital to the island of Hormuz (formerly Jarun) in the fourteenth century, during which time Hormuz replaced Kish as the major emporium in the Persian Gulf. This period, which continues to the early sixteenth century, can be considered the age of efforts to achieve superiority in maritime trade. During the fifteenth century, the island of Hormuz became the focal point of economic transactions in the Indian Ocean and Persian Gulf regions and achieved worldwide acclaim, thanks to the prudent policies of its amirs.

The third period began with the arrival of Afonso de Albuquerque, the Portuguese admiral, in the Persian Gulf in the early sixteenth century and continued until the conquest of Hormuz by Shah Abbas's forces in 1622. During this time, the native economy of Hormuz was heavily damaged. By applying their overwhelmingly militaristic policies, the Portuguese disrupted the trade of the region and created conditions under which the merchants and traders of Hormuz were not able to continue their activities and, as a result, gradually left the region's economic scene.

* * *

In studying the process of the formation of the early Hormuz kings' power and their relationship to other parties, we face numerous problems. What we know of the early history of these kings is scanty. The first Iranian historian who has mentioned the founder of the Hormuz government is Shabankara'i,[2] writing in the 1330s. Next is the book *Shahnama-yi Turanshahi* (The Shahnama of Turan Shah), composed in the late fourteenth century, parts of which have reached us via an intermediary. It contains the most detailed account of the formation of the government of the kings of Hormuz.[3] Shabankara'i briefly mentions that "their leader and the first among them was a king (*malik*) called Diramku and the details of the names of the old kings are listed name by name."[4] Mu'in al-Din Natanzi, writing in the early 1400s, has only mentioned the founder of the kings of Hormuz, that is, Muhammad Diramku.[5] The most detailed account of the establishment of the old amirs of Hormuz is presented in the *Shahnama-yi Turanshahi*.[6] To determine the approximate date of the reign of Muhammad Diramku, and assess the approximate period of his rule, we have to study the different accounts and compare them with historical events.[7] Based on the available evidence, his emigration and the beginning of the reign of the amirs of Hormuz can be estimated at between 1050 and 1100.

During the second half of the eleventh century there were developments that had a deep impact on the commercial and economic status of the Persian Gulf, especially the ports of Siraf in southern Iran and Suhar on the northern coast of Oman. The division of power in the Islamic world between the two caliphs of Cairo and Baghdad resulted in the separation of important economic regions around the Nile and Euphrates rivers. This also divided Muslim naval forces between two hostile poles that were concentrated in the Persian Gulf and the Red Sea. The ever-increasing power of Egypt's Fatimid caliphs and the growing weakness of Baghdad's Abbasid caliphs, finally overthrown by the Mongols in 1258, led to the revival of the commercial sea route through the Red Sea. For some time, the seaports of the Persian Gulf and the Omani coast lost their previous importance. From the beginning of the eleventh century, the flow of merchandise from the West to India shifted from the Persian Gulf to the Red Sea. This happened because of the problems that the Buyids in Iraq had with Bahrain's Carmathians (Qarmatis) and also because of the troubles they faced with the influence of the Fatimids in Damascus.[8] Sauvaget has described the Persian Gulf trade during the eleventh century as a commerce in decline and explains the cause to be the spread of insecurity in the hinterland regions.[9]

In the early eleventh century, these circumstances resulted in the decline of the two famous seaports of Suhar and Siraf. The disputes and the never-ending hostilities between the Ibadiyya Kharijites, residing in the interior of Oman, and the Sunnis, residing in the coastal regions, intensified. Due to civil wars and religious and tribal conflicts, the long period of insecurity in Oman continued from the reign of Muhammad b. Nur to the fall of the Buyids in 1050. The extensive offensive of Bahrain's Carmathians had the most severe impact on the economy of the Omani coast.[10] The port of Suhar bore the greatest damage. Ibn al-Mujawir has briefly described the movement of commerce in different regions of the Persian Gulf and the Oman coast as follows: "After Raysut [near Salala] fell into ruin, Suhar was developed. After Suhar fell into ruin, Tiz and Hormuz were founded. When they fell into ruin, Aden was founded."[11] The decline of commerce in Siraf and Suhar was the reason for the migration of their merchants and their residents, including in the latter case Muhammad Diramku and his followers, from the seaports of Oman to the Iranian coast.[12]

The eleventh century can indeed be considered a period of population movement in the Persian Gulf and the coast of Oman. These migrations occurred along different routes: the people of Siraf migrated to Kish,[13] residents of Suhar moved to Hormuz and the Shirazi emigrants went to the coast of Zanzibar.[14] The suitable geographical conditions of Hormuz and the adjacent regions attracted emigrants, and during the second half of the eleventh century, a large number of merchants and traders of the Omani coast migrated to the coast of Iran. Diramku's successors relocated the seat of government from the inland city of Hormuz to the island of Jarun, which now assumed the same name, and for a century and a half maintained a powerful and prosperous government.

Political Framework

The political history of Hormuz during the twelfth century is not very clear. This period is contemporaneous with the rule of nine amirs known as the "old kings of Hormuz," a term first used by Shabankara'i[15] and later employed by Natanzi at the beginning of the fifteenth century.[16] The development of Hormuz during this period was strongly influenced by events in the inland provinces of Kirman and Fars and the domains of the Shabankara Kurds; for almost one century, Hormuz was the subject of disputes between the rulers of the aforementioned regions. Historians have named Muhammad Diramku, Sulaiman b. Muhammad, Isa b. Sulaiman, Lashkari b. Isa, Kaiqubad b. Lashkari, Isa b. Kaiqubad, Mahmud b. Isa, Shahanshah b. Mahmud, and Mir Shahab al-Din Mahmud (or Malang) as the rulers of old Hormuz but the details of their actions remain obscure.[17] In the thirteen-year period between 1189 and 1201, five persons — Lashkari, Kaiqubad, Isa, Mahmud, and Shahanshah—became amir successively; this can be an indication of internal power struggles or the neighbors' effective intervention in the political affairs of Hormuz.

The first definite historical evidence of the political life of the kings of Hormuz dates back to the reign of Lashkari. His rule was contemporaneous with the power struggles and disputes between the claimants of government in Kirman, which led to the settlement of the migrant Ghuzz tribes in this province.[18] The breakdown of political power paved the way for the intervention of the Fars and Yazd atabaks, the amirs of Shabankara, and the Khwarazm Shahs.

Taking advantage of these circumstances, the amir of Hormuz stabilized his power. At the same time, the Salghurid atabaks of Fars were at war with the successors of the Saljuks and did not have the power to directly intervene in the affairs of Hormuz.[19] On the one hand, since the roads leading to the seaport of Tiz (located at the beginning of the Indian coast near modern Chahbahar) had become insecure owing to the encroachments of the Ghuzz, the merchants had to frequent Hormuz to export and import their merchandise. Because of this, the Hormuz seaport acquired a favorable position. On the other hand, in dealing with the offensives of the Ghuzz leader Malik Dinar, Amir Lashkari adopted an attitude of appeasement,[20] regularly offering taxes and presents to the representatives of the ruler of Kirman. The prudent behavior of the amir of Hormuz demonstrates his acumen and circumspection, and this policy was maintained until the reign of Shahab al-Din Mahmud.[21]

The old kings of Hormuz, who ruled from the first half of the 1100s to 1243, were able to sustain their political life by following a realistic policy on the basis of the circumstances of the day. The peaceful attitude and total submission of the amirs to the demands of their powerful neighbors was the key to their success and the main factor that helped them survive different crises. The cooperation of Isa Jashu[22] with the amir of Kish in 1150, the reconciliation between Amir Lashkari and Malik Dinar in 1189,[23] and the paying of taxes by Amir Shahanshah to the Ghuzz in 1193[24] are historical examples of the application of a policy of patience and perseverance. To this can be added the alliance between Amir Shahab al-Din Malang and Khwaja Qavam al-Din, the ruler of Kirman in 1206[25] and the treaty between Amir Saif al-Din Nusrat and the atabak of Fars in 1228.

The twelfth and thirteenth centuries can be considered a time when Hormuz was holding its own while submitting to the regional powers. During this period, southern Iran was witness to violent transitions of power accompanied by long and wearisome wars with the objective of gaining control over regional commercial transportation routes. Meanwhile, the conflicts among the Saljuks of Kirman, the Shabankara, and the atabaks of Fars had created a triangle of crisis in the regions adjacent to Hormuz.

Rule of Rukn al-Din and the New Kings of Hormuz

With the death of Shahab al-Din Mahmud, the era of the old kings of Hormuz came to an end. The reign of Rukn al-Din Mahmud Qalhati,[26] the first amir of the new kings of Hormuz, was the beginning of a new period in its history. (Qalhat, or Qalat, was the name of a city on the Omani coast and was considered the gateway to the Strait of Hormuz.)[27] The most important characteristic of this period was the attempt to cut all dependence on Fars and Kirman and to project power in the direction of Oman and Bahrain.

Mahmud Qalhati's rule over Hormuz from 1249 to 1286 was contemporaneous with the Mongol attack on Iran. Hulagu Khan destroyed the power of the Isma'ilis in 1256 and established the dynasty of the Ilkhans that ruled Iran until 1336. This naturally led to weakness of the local governments of Fars and Kirman. Taking advantage of this opportunity, Mahmud Qalhati was able to stabilize his power. Internal conflicts in Kirman and Fars also allowed the amir of Hormuz to extend his power throughout the Persian Gulf. In a military expedition, Mahmud Qalhati was able to conquer the prosperous coastal cities of Oman in 1261.[28] Later, he expanded his power up to the Dhofar region.[29]

The domination of the amir of Hormuz over Qalhat had great significance. By forming a powerful navy, he gained control of the important areas of the region. Shabankara'i claims that he "seized Qais, Bahrain, Dhofar of the land of Aden, Qatif and Nizwa to the country of Hormuz."[30] Natanzi has added the names of some of the Indian coastal cities to this list.[31] Aubin regards this historian's statement as evidence that the domination of the amir of Hormuz extended over maritime Sind and the East Makran regions.[32] It seems that he had been able to play an important role in the economic affairs of these regions by encouraging groups of Iranians to immigrate to India.

The real independence of Hormuz, therefore, was achieved during the reign of Rukn al-Din Mahmud. He brought all the marine routes of the region under the control and administration of Hormuz, and because of this, historians have considered him the first of the new kings (*muluk*) of Hormuz. He left a valuable legacy, the most important aspect of which is the experience of an independent and self-sufficient government and the expansion of power to the southern coasts of the Persian Gulf. His successors, benefiting from this new economic and social might, were able to deal with crises successfully; so, by the beginning of the fourteenth century, this region was renowned as the main center of marine trade in the Persian Gulf and Indian Ocean.[33]

Move to Jarun Island: The New Hormuz

The most important event at the beginning of the fourteenth century, during the reign of Baha al-Din Ayaz, was the transfer of the capital from the coast to the island of Jarun. It is worth mentioning that until the beginning of the fourteenth century, "Hormuz" designated the present coastal region of Minab.[34] Natanzi writes about the transfer of the seat of government: "Because of his extreme prudence, Ayaz left the capital and the coasts and went to the island of Jarun and ascended the throne."[35] This event happened in 1296 C.E.[36]

The transfer of the capital to the island of Jarun, henceforth known as Hormuz, had two immediate advantages: the first was security from the constant and extensive attacks of the Nikudaris (Mongols) and the other was the increased capacity to control the movements of ships in the Strait of Hormuz. This transfer resulted in the inauguration of a new era in the economic life of the amirs of Hormuz. From then on, in order to benefit from the enormous transit profits, the amirs used their merchant navy to steer the passage of ships toward Jarun. The establishment of the amirs at the port of Qalhat was thus a great advantage. The first European traveler who visited the island in 1318 describes it thus: "[It is] a city with strong walls and markets full of valuable and plentiful merchandise in which meat and fish can be found abundantly and is five miles away from mainland Iran."[37]

With the fall of the amirs of Kish, the last powerful maritime rival of Hormuz disappeared.[38] Kish had dominated the trade of the Persian Gulf for three hundred years following the decline of Siraf in the eleventh century. This important development took place during the rule of Qutb al-Din Tahamtan, who played an important role in these events. Historians have considered the twenty-six-year period of his rule as Hormuz's brightest economic epoch. At its beginning, the amir of Hormuz conquered Bahrain, which was one of the major exporters of pearls.[39] Despite all his power and wealth, however, Qutb al-Din Tahamtan followed his predecessors' policies and still paid taxes to the Ilkhan, Abu Sa'id (r. 1317–35). These taxes are mentioned in the accounts of the province of Kirman.[40] Ibn Battuta, the famous Moroccan traveler, visited Hormuz during this time and writes: "Jarun is a nice city with good markets and is a seaport of Hind and Sind and Indian merchandise is transported from this city to Arabian and Persian Iraq and Khurasan."[41] After ruling for a long period, Amir Qutb al-Din Tahamtan died in 747/1364.[42] Qazi Abd al-Aziz Nimdihi has fully described the situation of Hormuz and its economic conditions. He writes,

> After having secured his country on land and sea and among Arabs and non-Arabs against his opponents, Sultan Qutb al-Din formed good relations with the sultan of sultans of Gujarat, lands of the kings (*muluks*) of India, Sind, Basra, Kufa, Oman, Kirman, Shiraz and so on until he stabilized his rule and dominance and spread his justice. He prepared ships and sent them everywhere. From all seaports such as Mecca, Jidda, Aden, Sofala, Yemen, China, Europe, Calicut, and Bengal they came by sea and brought superior merchandise from everywhere to there and they brought valuable goods from the cities of Fars, Iraq and Khurasan to that place. From whatever that came by sea they took one tenth, and from whatever was brought to Khurasan from [surrounding areas], they took half of one tenth, and it has remained the same way and order until now and in this year (747/1346) after ruling honorably for twenty-two years, his soul ascended to holy land.[43]

With the death of Amir Qutb al-Din Tahamtan in 1346, his son Turan Shah[44] came to power and ruled over Hormuz and the dependent regions for thirty-two years until 1377. He is the composer of the *Shahnama-yi Turanshahi*, the translation of which a part has survived.

Ethnic and Religious Composition

The urban population of Hormuz at the beginning of the sixteenth century was around 50,000.[45] Barros mentions the figure of 10,000 to 12,000 households in 1554[46]; Figueroa cites a population of 40,000,[47] of which 500 households were Portuguese, 300 Indian Christians, 800 Indian pagans (*kafir*), 200 Jewish, and 1,200 Muslim.[48] Indians were present in the Persian Gulf and its urban areas before the arrival of the Portuguese. For example, in 1507 there were large groups of Gujarati merchants in Khur Fakkan, one of the coastal cities of Oman. The Jews also had a history of settlement in the urban regions of the Persian Gulf coast. In Hormuz, they made wine and participated in trade.[49]

In addition, large numbers of seasonal migrants lived in Hormuz since much of the population left during the hot months. The Mughistan region, in the old Hormuz area, which had running water and large gardens, was the summer residence of the king of Hormuz and its wealthy inhabitants. There had been precedents for the collective emigration of people. When King Saif al-Din Nusrat was faced with an internal rebellion in 1437, about 4,000–5,000 people emigrated with him to the coastal region.[50] In 1522, when a huge rebellion took place against the domination of the Portuguese, almost all the population of Hormuz escaped to the island of Qishm and temporarily established a new government there.[51]

The religious make-up of Hormuz consisted of Shi'i and Sunni Muslims, Christians, Jews, and Hindus. In 1442 Samarqandi mentions that there were pagans in Hormuz.[52] Religious tolerance and complete freedom in performing religious ceremonies was a fundamental principle of internal policy. The king of Hormuz was a Sunni, but the Shi'is were present on the island in relatively large numbers.[53] The famous family of the chiefs of Fali, who were some of the most powerful nobility in Hormuz, were Shi'i and were not afraid of publicly professing their religion. Nur al-Din Fali, the minister of Salghur Shah, even inscribed this verse on his seal: "Whoever follows the Prophet's religion and the king of Najaf/will find honor in Ali's love and will become Nur al-Din Sharaf (the noble light of religion)."[54] The freedom of the Shi'is in performing their religious ceremonies existed from the beginning of the reign of the amirs of Hormuz and had nothing to do with pressure from the Safavid kings.

The amirs of Hormuz did not have any prejudice in favor of their own religion and in many instances personally participated in the ceremonies of other religions. Their interest in the clerics and sayyids of different sects has been mentioned in various sources.[55] Around a minaret that was built in 1387 at the behest of the king of Hormuz at the shrine of Shaikh Rukh al-Din Danial, one of the thirteenth-century scholars, the names of the Orthodox (Rashidun) Caliphs and the twelve Shi'i Imams are written side by side.[56]

The Hindus on the island enjoyed complete religious freedom in performing their rituals. One hundred Jewish families also lived there, but in the seventeenth century only one of them knew Hebrew. Different sects and nationalities of Christians such as the Nestorians, the Jacobeans, the Georgians, and the Armenians enjoyed complete freedom.[57] Upon taking up residence on the island, the Portuguese were so impressed with the current freedoms that, even in their official agreements with the king of Hormuz, they did not deem it necessary to mention religious freedom for the Christians. Religious freedom provided the opportunity for an increasingly better life for all individuals and led to the increasing attraction of capital to this island.

Eating and Drinking

The inhabitants of Hormuz had to get their water from other areas, since the island is barren and salty. For this they depended upon small boats called *terrada* that carried water from Qishm to Hormuz. The water from the Turan Bagh wells, located on the east side of the island, was primarily used to irrigate the royal gardens, but in times of dire need, people used to drink it.[58] The main drinking water reserves were kept in reservoirs, which, after being filled, were closed with a special ceremony and gradually drawn down during the year. The water in these reservoirs was considered vital and was resorted to especially in times of crisis or when the island was besieged. In 1846, three hundred water reservoirs have been mentioned.[59]

Since all of the provisions of the people were obtained from off the island, the Europeans found living there very expensive.[60] Dates and fish were the staples. Those who enjoyed higher incomes could purchase any type of food in the market. The city's inhabitants usually ate in public kitchens and public stores. Barbosa writes, "Many people did not eat home-made food but ate the food sold by street peddlars."[61] A Portuguese inhabitant of Hormuz adds, "Ten thousand of the people eat at public restaurants. In twelve streets and at twenty shops around the city, rice and lamb kebab is sold."[62] Because of the city's extreme climate, people's activities, especially in the streets, continued until midnight. The people of Hormuz were perfumed and sweet smelling; even porters put on perfume when they finished with their work. When rich aristocrats walked about the streets, they had servants that accompanied them and carried cool beverages.[63] Drinking water was sold everywhere. In all the streets there were houses on the sides of which jugs and large jars of water were sold.[64]

Commercial Florescence

The supremacy of Hormuz over the region's commercial affairs became complete during the fourteenth century. This happened after the fall of the dynasty of Malik al-Islam Tibi in Kish, and, as a result, Hormuz established its unrivaled domination over the Persian Gulf for more than a century. The unstable political conditions in southern Iran at the end of Ilkhanid rule were another factor from which the kings of Hormuz profited. Hormuz Island became a commercial city and a secure marine station. The policy of demilitarizing the island encouraged the merchants and provided the necessary security for more investment. The foreign policy of the kings of Hormuz during the fourteenth century can be considered a logical continuation of the policy of caution and compromise adopted toward the neighboring powers in Fars and Kirman, which had been an important strategy for many years. Following such a policy prevented this economic zone from being harmed by the extreme political upheavals of the period. Refraining from intervention in the conflicts of Kirman and Fars, including the disputes between Inju'ids and Muzaffarids, and the power struggles between Muzaffarid princes and Timur and his successors are clear examples of the application of this policy of not aggravating their neighbors. This policy ensured the economic success of Hormuz.

In internal affairs, too, the policy of the amirs of Hormuz was based on giving priority to two important issues: the first was establishing trade security in dependent regions and the second was laying stress on maritime trade and its revenues. The increasing focus of the rulers of Hormuz on the sea-lanes to places such as Bahrain, Qatif, and Qalhat followed from the same policy. Controlling these passageways and gaining enormous profits from transit taxes increased the power of Hormuz. And at the beginning of the fifteenth century, this island was known as the most important commercial marine stopover in the Indian Ocean and the Persian Gulf region. Although during the fifteenth century this island suffered from many internal crises, these events were not able to seriously damage its economy.

A European traveler who visited Hormuz before the arrival of the Portuguese describes that city thus:

> At the time of the arrival of the foreign merchants, it afforded a more splendid and agreeable scene than any city in the East. Persons from all parts of the globe exchanged their commodities and transacted their business with an air of politeness and attention, which are seldom seen in other places of trade. The streets were covered with mats and in some places

with carpets, and the linen awnings which were suspended from the tops of the houses, prevented any inconvenience from the heat of the sun. Indian cabinets inlaid with gilded vases or china filled with flowering shrubs, or aromatic plants, adorned their apartments. Camels laden with water were stationed in the public squares. Persian wines, perfumes, and all the delicacies of the table were furnished in the greatest abundance, and they had the music of the East in its highest perfection. In short, universal opulence, and extensive commerce, politeness in the men and gallantry in the women, united all their attentions to make this city the seat of pleasure.[65]

MERCHANTS OF HORMUZ

The reign of Turan Shah III (1437–60), who favored scholars and mystics, is considered the period of scientific and scholarly growth in Hormuz. Shaikh Safi al-Din Abd-al Rahman Iji,[66] Muhammad b. Abdullah Basikandi Hurmuzi Shafi'i[67] and Qazi Abd al-Aziz Nimdihi[68] are some of his court scholars who historians have mentioned. The commercial and scholarly splendor of Hormuz made it renowned as one of Asia's major trade centers. Abd al-Razzaq Samarqandi, who visited the island during this period, writes,

The merchants of the seven realms from Egypt, Damascus, Rome, Azerbaijan, Arab and non-Arab Iraq, the land of Fars and Khurasan, Transoxania, Turkistan, the Qipchaq plateau region, the Qalmaq area, all the eastern countries, China and Machin and Khan-baligh go to that island, and the sea and coastal people from Arabia to Aden and Jidda bring precious and valuable goods which the moon and the sun and the generosity of the clouds have embellished which have survived the sea transportation to that land. The travellers of the world from everywhere come and whatever they bring they can exchange for whatever they want without much search in that town and do trade both in cash and by bartering and the administrators take one tenth of everything except gold and silver. There are adherents of different religions, and even infidels in that city are plenty, and they do not deal and trade with anyone except fairly and because of this that city is called the abode of safety (Dar al-Aman) and the people of that city have the compliments of the Iraqis and the profound thoughts of the Indians.[69]

Historical documents portray the economic prosperity and splendor of Hormuz during the fifteenth century. Tomé Pires, one of the first Portuguese who visited Hormuz at the beginning of the sixteenth century, writes, "This city has beautiful walls and houses with terraces and beautiful towers and citadel and is one of the four largest cities of Asia. The trade revenues of its neighbors are not comparable with its revenues. If something is needed for eating, be it bought in France or Flanders, it is bought to this island."[70]

Hormuz was the only city in the East in which economic activity was accompanied by political independence. The king, the merchants, and the administrative system, in mutual cooperation, facilitated commerce. In all policy making the first priority was commercial and trade affairs. In reality, the history of Hormuz from the fourteenth century on is nothing but the story of exchange of merchandise and maritime trade. Marco Polo writes, "Merchants come thither from India, with ships loaded with spicery and precious stones, pearls, cloths of silk and gold, elephants' teeth, and many other wares, which they sell to the merchants of Hormos, and which these in turn carry all over the world to dispose of again."[71] The exchange of goods with India took place via two routes. The first traversed the coastal shoreline and the other crossed the Indian Ocean, that is, it extended from Hormuz to Qalhat and from there in a straight line to the western coast of India. Ma'bar is the name that was ascribed to the western Indian coast during the fourteenth century,[72] and trading horses on this route was one of the most profitable businesses.

The influence of Iranian merchants in India during this period is the most prominent social feature of those regions and it continued for several centuries. Portuguese historians have mentioned the active presence of Iranian merchants in Cambay, Calicut, Bengal, and Malacca.[73] In these seaports, they had economic independence, and, using this power, they encouraged the local Indian rulers to give them special trade privileges.[74] Gradually, they acquired important administrative posts in India and some of them played effective political and economic roles.[75]

The merchants of Hormuz were also active in the inland regions of Iran, at the two areas leading to the markets of the Kirman and Shiraz regions. From the fourteenth century on, the traditional route from Hormuz to Shiraz went through the Laristan region.[76] In the struggle to control the commercial routes, the rulers of Hormuz and Laristan sometimes had friendly relations and sometimes hostile ones.[77] Undoubtedly, both regions profited from the enormous economic benefits of sea and land commerce. The amirs of Laristan were in charge of maintaining the security of the land route from Lar to the Hormuz coasts,[78] and this was very important. During the Safavid era, this route was considered the main artery for exchange of goods from southern Iran.[79]

The products of all of Iran and the Persian Gulf region were transported from Hormuz to India and the Atlantic Ocean to be sold. In this city the necessary prerequisites for international trade were provided. Hormuz had a customs house that was called *bangsar,* a word of Hindi origin that was used from Basra to Indonesia in the general sense of storehouse and reservoir.[80] From Fars, all sorts of jams, dried fruit,[81] dyeing materials, and luxury items[82] were brought to Hormuz. From Yazd, silk, carpets, and weapons,[83] and from the Persian Gulf coast wheat, barley, dates,[84] and horses[85] were imported. From Bahrain and Julfar, all sorts of pearls, and Arab and Iranian horses, from Lar horses and weapons,[86] from China and Khotan goods such as silk, musk, and rhubarb,[87] from the Mediterranean coast mercury and silver,[88] and from India pepper, cinnamon, ginger, garlic, herbal medicines, rice, and gold were brought to Hormuz.

Gaspar da Cruz, who stayed in Hormuz for three years after returning from China in 1565, writes of the commerce in Hormuz: "And Hormuz . . . is, among all the wealthy countries of India, one of the wealthiest, through the many and rich goods that come thither from all parts of India, and from the whole of Arabia and of Persia, as far as the territories of the [Mongols], and even from Russia in Europe I saw merchants there, and from Venice. And thus the inhabitants of Ormuz say that the whole world is a ring and Hormuz is the stone thereof."[89]

THE INDIAN TRADE

Among overseas markets, the Deccan (which supplied sugar, rice, and iron) and Gujarat, on the eastern shore of India, were among the most important trade partners of Hormuz. The goods imported from India included spices and herbal medicines.[90] The products that were transported between Iran and India via Hormuz included foodstuffs, aromatic and medical drugs, mineral water, different metals, textiles, and jewelry. The surplus of Indian goods was sent to the Red Sea via Aden and then on to Europe.[91] In addition, the importation of African and Indian slaves to Hormuz[92] and, most important of all, the export of horses to India should be mentioned. Since the climate of southern India was not suitable for raising horses, the (Muslim) Bahmanid kings in the northern Deccan and the Hindu kings of the Vijayanagara region were regular customers.The port of Goa had a special pier for unloading horses from ships. Pires writes about their value, "Iranian horses had very high prices in Goa and the Deccan and other regions of India and because of this, the merchants of Hormuz went there with their horses every year. A horse could have a price of up to three hundred *ashrafis,* equal to three hundred and twenty *réis.*"[93] In 1506 three thousand horses were exported to India and this amount reached ten thousand head in 1567.[94]

The merchants of Hormuz had considerable power and influence in this region, so much so that during the ambassadorship of ‘Abd al-Razzaq Samarqandi, the envoy of the Timurid ruler Shah Rukh to the Vijayanagara court in 1441–42, they were able to arouse the suspicions of the king against his intentions and aims.[95] The head of the Muslim community in Bhatkal, called Nakhuda (Captain) Qaisar, was under the political patronage of one of the ministers (*vazirs*) of Hormuz.[96]

Gujarat, whose location on the northwest coast of India made it a suitable trade partner for Hormuz, was one of the areas that imported horses from Hormuz. Through Gujarat, goods imported from Hormuz were sent to the Deccan and Malabar. The high customs revenues of Hormuz came from the merchandise imported from Gujarat, and a two year trade embargo led to the deterioration of economic conditions in Hormuz.[97] According to the figures that a Portuguese trade representative in Hormuz has provided, the duties on the exports of Gujarat were equal to the duties on the imports of Fars and three to four times more than the duties on the exports of Basra. In 1514, the customs revenues were 100,000 *ashrafis* and Hormuz's other revenues can be estimated at up to 40,000 *ashrafis*.[98]

To balance the expenditure, the amir of Hormuz had to send large amounts of Lari coins to India every year.[99] The gold *ashrafi* coins and the silver Lari coins that were in circulation in all Indian economic circles were among the strongest currencies.[100] When the property of Khwaja Mahmud Gawan (one of the famous ministers of the Bahmanid kings in the Deccan) was confiscated after his death in 1481, there were 1,300 Lari coins among his assets.[101]

Trading slaves, who were used in the military forces or as servants, also formed part of the commerce of these two regions. In search of better jobs and better economic conditions, Iranian youths departed for India from different regions. Pires writes, "There are around ten to twelve thousand Iranian warriors in the Deccan."[102] Some of these warriors were from Iran's Turkish tribes who left Iran after intense insecurity during the fifteenth and sixteenth centuries and immediately after entering India joined the military forces. In a letter, Khwaja Mahmud Gavan asked the amir of Laristan to dispatch young warriors to the Deccan.[103] Amir Yusuf ‘Adil Shah, the founder of the dynasty of the ‘Adil Shahis of Bijapur in the southern region of India, was, according to legend, the son of an Iranian fruit seller who had gone to the Deccan from Hormuz in his youth to sell his master's horses. There he was noticed, achieved high military rank, and eventually founded a new dynasty in 1489.[104] One of the famous military commanders of Hormuz, who was called Faramarz, was responsible for recruiting mercenaries for service in India.[105]

Iranian weapons, warriors, and merchants dominated the whole Indian Ocean region. In addition to human resources, instruments and equipment were used in India's military affairs that were imported from Hormuz. The bows made in Lar were one of these items. Tenreiro writes about this: "In Lar, a type of bow called the Turkish bow is masterfully made which because of its beauty is exported to different places. This bow is as famous as the Milanese helmet is famous among us."[106] Duarte Barbosa says the weapon of the warriors of Hormuz was the Turkish bow, which was made of buffalo horns and fine silk ropes.[107]

CONCLUSION

As a result of the realistic policies of its amirs in the fourteenth and fifteenth centuries, the island of Hormuz became one of the most famous and prosperous trade centers in Asia. During the fifteenth century, on the eve of the arrival of the Portuguese in the East, it enjoyed such a high status that the reputation of its wealth enticed the Portuguese fleet like a powerful magnetic force.

This island's main role was in logical and effective connections between the human and natural resources of the region. Following balanced economic policies, giving commercial elements the opportunity to freely show their potential and talents, following the rules and regulations of free seaports, and applying the policy of religious tolerance and leniency together with the special position of this island were the main factors for its success. Under these circumstances, Hormuz became the biggest seaport and stopover in the Middle East and the Indian Ocean and was rightly regarded as "the golden centerstone in the ring of world trade."[108]

The merchants and traders of the different areas of the region, whether Iranian, Arab, Indian, or African, engaged in commercial transactions in a peaceful environment. Above all, the economy and society of Hormuz during the fifteenth century had a multinational character. The most important principle that was scrupulously observed in the social relations of the people of Hormuz was respecting others' rights and complete observance of the laws and security, which is a good model of a civil society that is created from the peaceful coexistence of different nationalities.

With the arrival of the Portuguese in the Indian Ocean and Persian Gulf, the existence of this society was severely threatened. Hormuz's politicians and especially its distinguished minister, Khwaja Ata,[109] perceived the dangers of the Portuguese presence very well and decided to confront them with all their might. Their confrontation with the new situation was inevitable and everything depended on resisting or surrendering to the invaders. Hormuz was no match for the Portuguese and had no choice but to resist and to finally surrender. With the presence of the Portuguese in Hormuz, a new era in its political life began, a period that started with the arrival of Albuquerque and ended with the conquest of the island by the military forces of Shah Abbas.

This new era can be regarded as a period of gradual and ultimate decline. The conquest by Shah Abbas's forces in 1622 led to the complete fall of Hormuz and its disappearance from the Persian Gulf's economic scene. Along with the fall of the city's towers and ramparts, the splendor of its economy and trade collapsed as well, and to this day, this island has not been able to revive its economic life. According to one scholar, however, "the structure Hormuz represented was already in a state of collapse before the fortress fell."[110] In light of this interpretation, the reason for the complete collapse of Hormuz should be sought in the erroneous political and economic methods used by the Portuguese during their presence in the Persian Gulf, a topic that deserves further investigation.

NOTES

1. The earliest inscription found about the kings of Hormuz belongs to the fourteenth century and is located in Khunj, one of the hinterland cities of the Persian Gulf. The correct spelling of the name has been recorded here as well as in the official correspondence of the kings of Hormuz. For more information about this inscription, see Muhammad Baqir Vusuqi, *Khunj: Guzargah-i Bastani* [Khunj: The Ancient Passageway] (Qom, Iran: Khurram, 1374/1995), 51–52. Also, Allah-Quli Islami, "Khunj," *Majalla-yi Hunar va Mardum* 128 (1352/1973): 77–83. For information regarding the text of the administrative letters of the kings of Hormuz, refer to: Jahangir Qa'im Maghami, "Asnad-i Arabi, Farsi va Turki dar arshiv-i milli-yi Purtighal" [Arabic, Persian, and Turkish Documents in the Portuguese National Archive], in *Maqalat-i Khalij-i Fars* [Persian Gulf Articles] (Tehran: Center for Persian Gulf Studies, 1369/1990), 633–907. Also, Jean Aubin, "Letters of Cojeatar," *Mare Luso-Indicum* 2 (1973): 192–201. In the manuscript of *Tabaqat-i Mahmud Shahi,* it has also been recorded as "Hormuz": Ghazi Abd al-Aziz Nimdihi, *Tabaqat-i Mahmud Shahi*, manuscript, Windsor Library, vol. 160, no. 271.
2. Muhammad Shabankara'i, *Majma' al-ansab*, ed. Mir Hashim Muhaddis (Tehran: Amir Kabir, 1363/1985), 215. Aubin has published extracts concerning Hormuz from the

Majma' al-ansab which have some differences with the text published by Mr. Muhaddis. See Jean Aubin, "Les Princes d'Ormuz du XIIIe au XVe siècle," *Journal Asiatique* 241 (1953): 129–37.

3. William F. Sinclair, trans. and annotated, *The Travels of Pedro Teixeira: With His* Kings of Harmuz, *and Extracts from His* Kings of Persia (London: Hakluyt Society, 1902; repr. Liechtenstein: Kraus Reprint, 1991). This partial translation of the *Shahnama-yi Turanshahi* was done during the seventeenth century by two Portuguese travellers, Pedro Teixeira and Gaspar da Cruz, and is our only source of information about its contents. Other historical sources that offer trivial information, just mentioning the names of the early amirs of Hormuz, include: *Muntakhab al-tavarikh,* written by Mu'in al-Din Natanzi in 1413 C.E. (*Extraits du Muntakhab al-Tavarikh-i Mu'ini (Anonyme d'Iskandar),* ed. Jean Aubin (Tehran: Khayyam, 1957); *Haft Iqlim* [The Seven Realms], written by Amin Ahmad Razi in 1602 (*Haft Iqlim*, ed. Javad Fazil (Tehran: Ilmi, n.d.) and *Jarun Nama* composed by Qadri in 1632 (Manuscript, British Museum no. 7801). For more information about the life of the poet refer to: Muhammad Baqir Vusuqi, "Mu'arrifi-yi dastan-i Jarun" [Introducing the Story of Jarun], *Fars Shenakht* nos. 2 and 3 (Shiraz, 1378/2000), 114–24). See now Muhammad Baqir Vusuqi and Abd al-Rasul Khairandish, eds., *Jangnama-yi Kishm by Anonymous and Jirun-nama by Qadri (d.1043 A.H.)* (Tehran: Miras-i Maktub, 1384/2005).
4. Shabankara'i, *Majma' al-ansab*, 215.
5. Natanzi, *Muntakhab al-tavarikh,* 10.
6. Sinclair, *Travels of Pedro Teixeira*, 153–59. Teixeira has translated two different accounts of the start of Muhammad Diramku's rule, which are contradictory in some of the events and need further investigation and criticism. For a comparison of the two accounts see: Muhammad Baqir Vusuqi, *Tarikh-i muhajirat-i aqvam dar Khalij-i Fars* [The History of the Emigration of Peoples in the Persian Gulf] (Shiraz, Iran: Intisharat-i Danishnama-yi Fars, 1380/2002), 53–56. The date of the composition of the *Shahnama* is between 1346 and 1377, during the reign of Turan Shah b. Qutb al-Din Tahamtan. This text has been used by Teixeira and da Cruz and both of them have translated a summary of it.
7. Teixeira has mentioned eleven early amirs of Hormuz by name without indicating the date of their reign. In describing the rule of the twelfth amir, Rukn al-Din Mahmud b. Ahmad, he has mentioned 676/1277 as the date of his death (page 159). He has named Muhammad Diramku, Sulaiman, Isa, Lashkari, Kaiqubad b. Isa, Isa b. Kaiqubad, Mahmud, Shahanshah b. Mahmud, Mir Shahab al-Din Malang, Amir Saif al-Din Nusrat, Shahab al-Din Mahmud Isa, Amir Rukn al-Din Mahmud b. Ahmad respectively. Rukn al-Din Mahmud b. Ahmad surnamed Qalhati or Qalati is one of the most famous amirs of Hormuz. Teixeira has mentioned his death in 1277 while Natanzi (page 12) and Shabankara'i (page 216) have said it was in 1286. Besides the difference of opinion among the historians, it can be estimated that he ruled between 641 and 685/1243–86. He was the twelfth amir of Hormuz, and if we consider the reign of three amirs in one century as likely, it can be reckoned that the reign of Muhammad Diramku was during the eleventh century between 1058 and 1107. Sinclair and Wilson have mentioned 494/1101 as the beginning of Muhammad Diramku's rule. (Also Sinclair, *Travels of Pedro Teixeira*, 155; Arnold Wilson, *The Persian Gulf* (London: George Allen and Unwin, 1928; repr. 1959), 104. Henry Yule has mentioned 1060 as the beginning of the reign of Muhammad Diramku. (Henry Yule, trans. and ed., *The Book of Ser Marco Polo, the Venetian, Concerning the Kingdoms and Marvels of the East,* 3rd ed., rev. by Henri Cordier (London: Murray, 1903; repr. St. Helier, Jersey, Channel Islands: Armorica, 1975), vol. 1, 121. Based on the account of Afzal al-Din Kirmani, the fourth amir of Hormuz was in power in 585/1189 (Afzal al-Din Abu Hamid Kirmani, *Saljuqian va Ghuzz dar Kirman* [Saljuqs and Ghuzz in Kirman], ed. Muhammad Bastani-Parizi (Tehran: Kurush, 1373/1995), 586–88. On the other hand, based on an account by Ibn al-Mujawir, the reign of Isa Jashu, the third amir of Hormuz, was 545 A.H./1151 A.D. (Ibn al-Mujawir, *Sifat Bilad al-Yaman wa Makkah wa ba'd al-Hijaz al-musamma, Ta'rikh al-Mustabsir*, vol. 1, ed. Oscar Löfgren (Leiden, The Netherlands: Brill, 1951), 124–26.

8. C. Cahen, "Buayhids or Boyid", *Encyclopedia of Islam*, new ed., vol. 1 (1977), 1350–57.
9. J. Sauvaget, "Sur d'Anciennes Instructions Nautiques Arabs pour les Mers de l'Inde," *Journal Asiatique* 236 (1948): 19.
10. For more information about the events of Oman and its commerce during this period see: Abd-Allah b. Humayyid al-Salimi, *Tuhfat al-a'yan bi sirat ahl 'Uman* (Delhi, India: Maktab Insha'at al-Islam, 1330 A.H./1912), 181–203. Also refer to: Sarhan ibn Sa'id Izkiwi, *Tarikh 'Uman al-muqtabas min Kitab kashf al-ghummah al-jami' al-akhbar al-ummah,* ed. Abd al-Majid Hasib Qaisi ([Muscat,] Oman: Wizarat al-Turath al-Qawmi wa-al-Thaqafah, 1980). Also S. B. Miles, *Countries and Tribes of the Persian Gulf* (London, 1963), 80.
11. Ibn al-Mujawir, *Sifat Bilad al-Yaman wa Makkah*, vol. 2 (1954), 287.
12. Teixeira has mentioned Kuhistak as the first stop of the migrants (Sinclair, *Travels of Pedro Teixeira*, 155), while da Cruz has considered Jask, Mughistan, and Ibrahimi to be their first stop (Ibid., 257). The area under discussion included the coastal regions between the port of Jask and present-day Minab. Because of the existence of the perennial Minab River, this region has good alluvial lands and is considered as a tropical region which is bordered by low mountains in the north. Sir Aurel Stein has described some of the natural and historical features of this region in *Archaeological Reconnaissances in North–Western India and South–Eastern Iran* (London: Macmillan, 1937), 128–30.
13. Refer to: Shihab al-Din Vassaf, *Kitab-i Vassaf al-Hazrat* [*Tajziyat al-amsar wa tazjiyat al-a'sar* or *Tarikh-i Vassaf*) (Tehran: Ibn Sina (Avicenna), 1338/1960), 147–49. For more information about the decline of Siraf and the prosperity of Kish, see: Muhammad Baqir Vusuqi, "Iranian va tijarat-i darya'i-yi Khalij-i Fars" [The Iranians and the Marine Trade in the Persian Gulf], *Nama-yi Anjuman* no. 4 (Tehran, 1380/2002), 175–96. See also: Jean Aubin, "La ruine de Sirâf et les routes du Golfe Persique aux Xle et Xlle siècles," *Cahiers de Civilisation Médiévale* 2 (Université de Poitiers, 1959), 295–301.
14. For more information about the emigration of the Iranians to the Zanzibar coast, refer to: S. A. Strong, ed., "The History of Kilwa," *Journal of the Royal Asiatic Society* 20 (1895): 385–430 (from an Arabic MS).
15. Shabankara'i, *Majma' al-ansab* (edited by Aubin), 129.
16. Natanzi, *Muntakhab al-tavarikh,* 10.
17. Among the old amirs of Hormuz and the history of their rule, information is available only about four of them: Isa Jashu (545/1150), Lashkari b. Isa (585/1189), Shahanshah b. Muhammad (598/1202), and Shahab al-Din Malang (599–607/1203–10).
18. For more information regarding the situation of Kirman during this period see: Afzal al-Din Kirmani, *Aqd al-ola lil muqaf al-a'la,* ed. Ali Muhammad Amiri (Tehran: Ruzbihan, 1356/1978), 65–69. Also refer to: Ahmad-Ali Khan Vaziri, *Tarikh-i Kirman*, vol. 2, ed. Muhammad Bastani-Parizi (Tehran: Ilmi, 1364/1986), 417–20.
19. For more information on Fars during this period, see: Ibn Balkhi, *Farsnama*, E. J. W. Gibb Memorial Series, ed. Guy Le Strange and R. A. Nicholson (London: Luzac, 1921; repr. Tehran: Dunya-yi Kitab, 1363/1985), 141–43. Also see: Zarkub Shirazi, *Shiraznama*, ed. Isma'il Va'iz Javadi (Tehran: Bunyad-i Farhang-i Iran, n.d.), 64–66.
20. Kirmani, *Saljuqian va Ghuzz*, 522.
21. To improve relations with the amirs of Kish, Amir Shahab al-Din Mahmud accepted a political marriage (Sinclair, *Travels of Pedro Teixeira*, 158) and befriended the rulers of Kirman. (Afzal al-Din Kirmani, *Al-muzaf ila badayi' al-zaman,* ed. Abbas Iqbal (Tehran: Chapkhana-yi Majlis, 1331/1953), 49.
22. Ibn al-Mujawir, *Sifat Bilad al-Yaman wa Makka,* 215.
23. Kirmani, *Saljuqian va Ghuzz,* 522.
24. Ibid., 598.
25. Kirmani, *Al-muzaf ila badayi' al-zaman,* 52.
26. Historians, including Shabankara'i (*Majma' al-ansab,* 156) and Natanzi (*Muntakhab al-tavarikh,* 11) consider Rukn al-Din Qalhati as the first amir of the new kings of Hormuz. See Vassaf, *Tarikh-i Vassaf,* 177; also Shirazi, *Shiraznama*, 80. The full name of this amir has been mentioned in different sources in different forms. More recent historians have called him Mahmud Qalhati. Shabankara'i writes: "Malik Muhammad was called Qalhati because he was from the island of Qalatou" (Shahbankara'i, ed. by Aubin, 129).

27. Yaqut describes it this way: "Qalhat is a city in Oman on the seashore, where most of India's ships cast anchor and at present it is that land's harbor and is very prosperous and thriving and belongs to the amir of Hormuz." (Ya'qub b. 'Abd-Allah Yaqut al-Hamawi, *Mu'jam al-buldan,* vol. 4 (Beirut, Lebanon: Dar Sadir, n.d.), 393.) Ibn al-Mujawir considered Qalhat to be the seaport from which Arab horses were exported to Khwarazm (Ibn al-Mujawir, *Sifat Bilad al-Yaman wa Makkah,* 281).
28. Izkiwi, *Kashf al-ghummah,* 71. Also see: Salimi, *Tohfat al-a'yan,* vol. 1, 247.
29. Sinclair, *Travels of Pedro Teixeira,* 159.
30. Shabankara'i, *Majma' al-ansab* (edited by Aubin), 130.
31. Natanzi, *Muntakhab al-tavarikh,* 12.
32. Aubin, "Les princes d'Ormuz," 84.
33. For more information see Vassaf, *Tarikh-i Vassaf,* 189.
34. For information about the original location of Hormuz on the Persian Gulf coast, see Peter Morgan, "New thoughts on old Hormuz," *Iran* 29 (1991): 67–83.
35. Natanzi, *Muntakhab al-tavarikh,* 14.
36. For more information about the transfer of the seat of government from the coast to Jarun Island see Aubin, "Les princes d'Ormuz," 94–95. Also Vusuqi, *Tarikh-i muhajirat-i aqvam dar Khalij-i Fars,* 169–82.
37. Henry Yule, *Cathay and the Way Thither: Being a Collection of Medieval Notices of China,* vol. 2 (London: Hakluyt Society, 1913–16; repr. 1966), 112.
38. There is not much information concerning the Bani Qaisar kings that ruled Kish from the second half of the eleventh century until 1229. The island's economic situation improved as a result of the policy of Malik Turan Shah I of Kirman (r. 1085–97), according to Vassaf (*Tarikh-i Vassaf,* 170) and Ibn al-Mujawir (*Sifat-i Bilad al-Yaman wa Makka,* 287). The military power of the Bani Qaisar was also notable; for example, they mounted an expedition against Oman (S. D. Gotein, "Two eyewitness reports on an expedition of the king of Kish (Qais) against Aden," *Bulletin of the School of Oriental and African Studies* 16, no 2 (1954): 247–57). The nature of the contention between the amirs of Hormuz and Kish has been described in the following sources: Shabankara'i, *Majma' al-ansab,* 134–35; Natanzi, *Muntakhab al-tavarikh,* 17; and Sinclair, *Travels of Pedro Teixeira,* 172. Newly found sources indicate that the Sufi clerics of the Qattali sect in southern Iran supported the amir of Hormuz. For the first time, this issue has been discussed in Vusughi, *Tarikh-i muhajirat-i aqvam dar Khalij-i Fars,* 191.
39. Sinclair, *Travels of Pedro Teixeira,* 181.
40. Hamd-Allah Mustawfi, *The Geographical Part of the* Nuzhat al-qulub, E. J. W. Gibb Memorial Series, 23, trans. G. Le Strange (Leiden, The Netherlands: Brill and London: Luzac, 1919; repr. Tehran, 1362/1984), 140.
41. Ibn Battuta, *Rihla,* ed. and intro. 'Abd Al-Hadi al-Tazi (Rabat, Morocco: Matbu'at Academia Al-mamlikat al-gharbia, 1997), vol. 2, 140.
42. The author of *Afzal al-Tavarikh* has mentioned his burial place to be at the shrine of Khizr on Jarun Island. (Khuzani, *Afzal al-tavarikh,* manuscript).
43. Nimdihi, *Tabaqat-i Mahmud Shahi,* manuscript.
44. Natanzi has called him "Yusuf Shah b. Qutb al-Din." See Natanzi, *Muntakhab al-tavarikh,* 17. Qazi Abd al-Aziz Nimdihi mentions him as "Turan-Shah". See Nimdihi, *Tabaqat-i Mahmud Shahi,* manuscript.
45. Jean Aubin, "Le royaume d'Ormuz au début du XVIe siècle," *Mare Luso-Indicum* 2 (1973): 150.
46. Ibid.
47. Muhammad Sa'idi, trans., *The Travelogue of Silva Figuera* (Tehran: Nashre Now, 1363/1985), 59.
48. *A Chronicle of the Carmelites in Persia and the Papal Mission of the XVIIth and XVIIIth Centuries,* vol. 2 (London: Eyre and Spottiswoode, 1939), 1041.
49. W. J. Fischel, "The Region of the Persian Gulf and Its Jewish Settlements in Islamic Times," in *Alexander Marx Jubilee Volume* (New York: The Jewish Theological Seminary of America, 1950), 203–30.

50. Nimdihi, *Tabaqat-i Mahmud Shahi*, manuscript.
51. Aubin, "Le royaume d'Ormuz," 151.
52. Samarqandi, *Safarnama*, 7.
53. Sinclair, *Travels of Pedro Teixeira*, 168.
54. Maghami, "Asnad-i Arabi, Farsi va Turki," Letter no. 46.
55. Ibn Battuta, *Rihla*, vol. 2, 140.
56. For information about the text of the inscription of the Danial minaret, see Islami, "Khunj," 77–83.
57. Sinclair, *Travels of Pedro Teixeira*, 163.
58. Walter de Gray Birch, trans., *The Commentaries of the Great Afonso D'Alboquerque*, vol. 1 (New York: B. Franklin, 1970), 138–40. Also Sinclair, *Travels of Pedro Teixeira*, 166.
59. Muhammad Ibrahim Kaziruni, *Tarikh-i Banadir va Jazayir-i Khalij-i Fars* [The History of the Ports and Islands of the Persian Gulf], ed. Dr. Sutuda (Tehran: Mu'assisa-yi farhangi-yi Jahangiri, 1367/1989), 128.
60. Aubin, "Le royaume d'Ormuz," 156.
61. Duarte Barbosa, *A Description of the Coasts of East Africa and Malabar: In the Beginning of the Sixteenth Century*, trans. Henry E. J. Stanley (London: Hakluyt Society, 1866), 43.
62. Gaspar Correia, *Lendas da India*, vol. 1 (Lisbon, Portugal: Academia Real das Sciencas de Lisboa, 1858), 815.
63. Barbosa, *Description of the Coasts of East Africa and Malabar*, 43.
64. Correia, *Lendas da India*, 815.
65. A quotation from Abbé Raynal, in Wilson, *The Persian Gulf*, 105–6.
66. Shams al-Din Muhammad Sakhawi, *al-Daw al-lami' li-ahl al-qarn al-tasi'* (Beirut, Lebanon: Dar al-Jil, 1992), vol. 3, 150.
67. Ibid, vol. 8, 118.
68. Nimdihi, *Tabaqat-i Mahmud Shahi*, manuscript. He writes about this:

    Sultan Turan Shah was the ruler (*vali*) of Hormuz. In the garden of his [good] fortune the tree of justice and beneficence had grown and the robe of his kingship was adorned with the *tiraz* [decoration] of the love of the descendants of the Prophet and the clerics and the shaikhs . . . In the beginning of [his] reign when I became noble by the miracle [*karamat*] of kissing his feet, to encourage me in my education he assigned two thousand dinars per year as an annuity.

69. Abd al-Razzaq Samarqandi, *Safarnama* (Tashkent: Uzbekistan Science Academy, 1906), 7.
70. Tomé Pires, *The Suma Oriental of Tomé Pires*, trans. Armando Cortesao (London: Hakluyt Society, 1944), 19–20.
71. Yule, *Book of Ser Marco Polo*, I, 107.
72. Vassaf, *Tarikh-i Vassaf*, 301. He has mentioned that Ma'bar extended from Koulem to the area of Nilavar, a distance of three hundred *farsangs* (1800 kilometers) along the coast.
73. Barbosa, *Description of the Coasts of East Africa and Malabar*, 42.
74. For more information regarding the degree of influence of the merchants of Hormuz in India, see Samarqandi, *Safarnama*, 67–68.
75. Also, Khwaja Mahmud Gavani, who was one of the famous ministers of the Bahmanid kings, can be mentioned. For more information, see Mahmud Gawan, *Riaz al-insha'*, ed. by Chand b. Husain (Haidarabad [Deccan]: Sarkar-i Ali, 1948).
76. For more information about the general condition of Laristan during this period, see Jean Aubin, "Références Pour Lar Médievale," *Journal Asiatique* 243 (1955): 501, 507. See now Muhammad Baqir Vusuqi et al., *Tarikh-i mufassal-i Laristan*, 2 vols. [Comprehensive History of Laristan] (Tehran: Hamsaya, 1385/2006).
77. Khwaja Mahmud Gavani has mentioned one of the military confrontations between the amirs of Lar and Hormuz. See Gavani, *Riaz al-Insha'*, 205. (His letter entitled "Fi tahniat Amir al-Kabir Jahan Shah al-Lari fi fath Jarun" has been presented there.)
78. Dorit Schön, *Laristan: eine südpersische Küstenprovinz* (Vienna, Austria: Verlag der Osterreichische der Wissenschten, 1990), 15.

79. For information about the trade routes between Bandar Abbas-Lar and Shiraz, see: Heinz Gaube, "Im Hinterland von Siraf: Das Tal von Galledar/Fal und seine Nachbargebiete," *Archaeologische Mitteilungen aus Iran* 13 (1980): 149–66; Willem Floor, "The Bandar Abbas-Isfahan Route in the Late Safavid Era (1617–1717)," *Iran* 37 (1999): 67–94.
80. In Ibn Battuta's travelogue, this word has been recorded as "Banjsar" and Qadri, the poet of the *Jarun Nameh,* has called it "Bangsar" (he informs us of the events of the war that occurred at the head of the *bangsar*). Refer to: Ibn Battuta, *Rihla,* vol. 4, 59.
81. Sinclair, *Travels of Pedro Teixeira,* 265–66.
82. Pires, *The Suma Oriental of Tomé Pires,* 28.
83. Aubin, "Le royaume d'Ormuz," 165.
84. Pires, *The Suma Oriental of Tomé Pires,* 28.
85. Samarqandi, *Safarnama,* 29. Also see: Gawani, *Riyaz al-Insha',* 207.
86. Gawani, *Riyaz al-Insha',* 207.
87. Barbosa, *Description of the Coasts of East Africa and Malabar,* 42.
88. Pires, *The Suma Oriental of Tomé Pires,* 27.
89. Sinclair, *Travels of Pedro Teixeira,* 265–66.
90. Samarqandi, *Safarnama,* 29.
91. Pires, *The Suma Oriental of Tomé Pires,* 21.
92. Ibn Majid, *Fawa'id fi usul ilm al-bahr wa al-qawa'id,* trans. Ahmad Iqtidari (Tehran: Anjuman-i mafakhir va athar-i milli-yi Iran, 1380/2002), 41.
93. Samarqandi, *Safarnama,* 67.
94. Aubin, "Le royaume d'Ormuz," 169.
95. Ibid., 21.
96. Aubin, "Le royaume d'Ormuz," 174.
97. See the document presented in *Majmu'[a-yi] maqalat-i Khalij-i Fars* [Collection of Persian Gulf Articles] (Tehran: Vizarat-i Kharija-yi Iran, 1369/1991), 660.
98. Aubin, "Le royaume d'Ormuz," 174.
99. C. R. Boxer, *The Portuguese Seaborne Empire, 1415–1825* (London: Hutchinson, 1969), 41.
100. For more information regarding Larin coins, see J. Allan, "Larin," *Encyclopedia of Islam,* new ed.
101. Firishta [Muhammad Qasim Hindu Shah Astarabadi], *Gulshan-i Ibrahimi,* ed. as *Tarikh-i Firishta,* vol. 1 (Delhi, India, 1926), 359.
102. Pires, *The Suma Oriental of Tomé Pires,* 36.
103. Gawani, *Riyaz al-Insha',* 205.
104. Firishta, *Tarikh-i Firishta,* vol. 2, 2.
105. Aubin, "Le royaume d'Ormuz," 177.
106. A. Tenreiro, *Itinerários da Índia a Portugal por terra,* ed. António Baião (Coimbra, Portugal: Impr. da Universidade, 1923), 36.
107. Barbosa, *Description of the Coasts of East Africa and Malabar,* 43.
108. Sinclair, *The Travels of Pedro Teixiera,* 267.
109. For more information about the measures taken by Khwaja Ata against the arrival of the Portuguese in Hormuz, see Jean Aubin, "Cojeatar et Albuquerque," *Mare Luso-Indicum* 1 (1971): 99–134.
110. Niels Steensgaard, *The Asian Trade Revolution of the Seventeenth Century: The East India Companies and the Decline of the Caravan Trade* (Chicago: University of Chicago Press, 1975), 208.

Chapter 5

Boom and Bust: The Port of Basra in the Sixteenth and Seventeenth Centuries

Rudi Matthee

From at least the early sixteenth century, Basra has been one of the principal port cities of the Persian Gulf. It was connected through overland trade with the main centers of the Ottoman Empire via Baghdad and Damascus, with Shiraz and Isfahan in Safavid Iran, and by way of maritime trade with commercial emporia throughout the western Indian Ocean basin, from Surat and Coromandel to Mukha. Besides being a sizeable urban center of some 50,000 inhabitants—the largest city on the Persian Gulf littoral in the seventeenth century—Basra was above all a commercial hub.[1] The trade flow going through Basra included the region's most significant export product, dates, as well as horses, most of which were shipped to India, and some other commodities such as nutgalls, buffalo skins, henna, pearls, camels, and madder dye (used in the textile industry in Gujarat).[2] But the volume of exports was far outstripped by the import of such commodities as spices and bulk goods such as sugar and coffee and, more importantly, enormous amounts of Indian textiles in myriad varieties. To make up for its structural trade imbalance with India, the Ottoman Empire exported large amounts of bullion and specie to the subcontinent. Basra served as a major way station for this precious metal trade.

Until recently, Basra has been a poorly examined topic.[3] This chapter explores the nature and record of Basra's status as a port city between the early sixteenth century—the beginning of the availability of documentary material that enables one to say anything meaningful about the subject—and ca. 1720, the time when, after a long period of intermittent presence, the European maritime companies made the port a centerpiece of their activities. It will do so by considering the various forces that influenced Basra's fluctuating commercial fortunes. Until quite recently, scholars almost reflexively viewed the nature and quality of governance as the single most important determinant of the (economic) health of Middle Eastern cities, wider regions, or countries. In studying non-Western societies, and especially Muslim ones, it was also customary to assume that the often anemic commercial performance of these societies, marked by low investment and poor organization, was mostly due to a tendency of rapacious states to terrorize and fleece supine and hapless merchants.

Of late, the tide has turned and it is now common for scholars to downplay or even disregard the effect of the treatment of merchants by political officials in the early modern period, to follow a "non-statist" approach to the study of economic process by making a more or less explicit case against the inhibiting effects of state organization and behavior on commercial activity.[4] Not surprisingly, the advocates of this approach primarily focus on maritime trade and port cities, the area and sphere where (central) governments are least visible, where commerce is most unregulated, and where cosmopolitan "ecumenical trade zones" appear to prevail. The absence of a central government does not mean the absence of government, however, and the beneficial or even neutral effect of local government needs to be demonstrated rather than assumed. This proposition will serve as a starting point for an attempt to chart the fortunes of Basra in the seventeenth century on the basis of two main variables, local and regional conditions, and their conjuncture with larger transregional economic and political forces. In what follows, it will be seen that, while external forces—ranging from the safety of the Persian Gulf shipping lanes to conditions in rival ports and changes in commercial flows—naturally were a significant factor in Basra's commercial health, the quality of government did matter too, either as a hindrance or as a facilitator. The frequent shift in control over Basra allows one to substantiate this to some extent: in 1546 southern Iraq was nominally incorporated into the Ottoman Empire, while from 1596 to 1669 Basra was effectively ruled by a local dynasty, the Afrasiyab pashas. In the latter year, the Ottomans reestablished full control over the city. But first we must give an outline of the ambient setting, the magnetic field within which the city functioned and the larger, structural forces, including physical and climatological features, that affected and influenced Basra's viability as a port city.

Context and Conditions

Following the approach taken by Hala Fattah and Thabit Abdullah in their respective books on Basra in the early modern period, it is important to view Basra not just as a town in its own right but also as the center of a capacious universe—not only as a commercial and political center interacting with its immediate hinterland but also as a port in a larger regional and transregional setting.[5] In its commercial and political ambit, the town straddled various jurisdictions that did not necessarily coincide with Ottoman borders. To be sure, even before Istanbul extended its influence to Mesopotamia, two main routes connected Basra with the Ottoman port cities of the Mediterranean. The longer one of the two, going to Tripoli via Baghdad and Aleppo, took almost sixty days traveling from north to south (some forty for the leg between Aleppo and Baghdad and fifteen to sixteen days using the river between Baghdad and Basra) and about one hundred going north, with the upstream journey taking anywhere between fifty and sixty days.[6] The second one, the desert route to Damascus, was shorter but also more dangerous, infested as it often was with Bedouin highway robbers—which is why the Ottomans typically ordered all caravans to go through Baghdad.[7] Caravans traveling these routes could be large. A missionary writing in 1680 noted that the caravan he had joined going to Baghdad (and presumably coming from Aleppo) consisted of "almost 1,500 or 1,600 men," who were well armed, as a result of which the roving Arabs "didn't dare attack them."[8]

Situated at the extremity of Ottoman jurisdiction, however, even after its incorporation into the Ottoman realm, Basra was an imperial outpost on which the metropole was unable to impose effective and lasting control. The Ottomans, faced with a scarcity of timber and poor communications in the area, were not even able to build up a permanent naval base in Basra.[9] As such, Basra found itself sandwiched between the Porte in its desire to bring the town under its authority and the recalcitrant resident Arab population, as well as the centrifugal forces of the ambient tribal confederations of the Muntafiq and the Al Ilayan, in addition to myriad other tribes, such as the Banu Ka'b, the Banu Khalid, the Al Kathir, and the Al Fudul.

In keeping with a long history of adjacent major powers wielding influence over the region—Rome and later Byzantium in the west, and successive Iranian dynasties in the east—Basra in this period especially felt the pull of neighboring Safavid Iran. Located just a short distance from what was formally Iranian territory and approximately 500 kilometers from Isfahan, Iran's seventeenth-century capital, the city was within striking distance of the Safavid military. About the same distance separated Basra from the regional Ottoman center, Baghdad, from which expeditions were typically dispatched. Ottoman control over Baghdad itself was often tenuous at best, though, since the Turkish chain of command ultimately began and ended in Istanbul, which was separated from Basra by 2,500 kilometers of inhospitable terrain that ranged from mountainous to desert to marshy. The Safavids were not just close but they also considered Basra to be within their sphere of influence. Their claim on Mesopotamia, or Iraq-i Arab, as they called it, was based on a compelling premise—the area was home to some of the holiest shrines of Shi'i Islam—and rhetorically they viewed the entire region as part of their ancestral homeland.[10] Basra and lower Iraq were an extension of this, although the town's real allure lay in its strategic importance as well as its commercial and transit function. Basra was situated in the orbit of Arabistan (modern Khuzistan), the region that the Safavids had subjugated in the early sixteenth century, when they reduced its principal tribal formation, the radical Twelver-Shi'i Musha'sha', to vassal status. Huwaiza, the capital of the Musha'sha', was but a short distance from Basra, so the power that controlled one of these two cities automatically posed a threat to the other.

Iranian territory frequently served as a refuge for Basra's rulers and even the local population in times of turmoil. Since Basra was the only direct Ottoman outlet to the Gulf and Indian Ocean, for the Safavids capturing it meant impeding the trade of the enemy. The Safavids attacked the city on several occasions. At various times they used the Musha'sha' and the Muntafiq as their proxies to extend their control over the region. For brief periods of time, under Shah Isma'il (r. 1501–24), and again almost two hundred years later, under Shah Sultan Husain at the turn of the eighteenth century, Basra was under direct Safavid control. It is, in sum, hardly surprising that, in the seventeenth century, the governor of Basra sent ten to twelve horses every year to the Ottoman sultan *and* the Safavid shah.[11]

Basra also served as an important relay station for the hajj. Indian pilgrims traveling by sea arrived in Basra before continuing overland to the holy cities in Arabia. Basra similarly was a transit point on the hajj trail between Iran and Mecca. Thousands of Iranian pilgrims accompanied by even greater numbers of camels annually converged upon the city before setting out on the hazardous last leg of the pilgrimage through Najd. In the late seventeenth and early eighteenth century, when religious fervor strengthened its hold on the Safavid court elite, ten thousand or more Iranians habitually made the trip to Mecca, traveling via Basra.[12] Since the hajj was a lucrative business for the authorities of transit cities, one understands why the governors of Basra and Baghdad were engaged in fierce competition over which town would serve as the point of departure for pilgrims coming from Iran.[13]

Beyond the permanent reach of Ottomans and Safavids alike, Basra finally was part of a maritime world that spanned the entire Persian Gulf and extended to the western shores of the Indian subcontinent. Inasmuch as the Gulf and its coastal areas constituted a distinct unit separate from surrounding regions, including the land-based empires of the interior, Basra's interaction with rival ports of the Gulf, among them Bahrain, Bandar Abbas, Kung, and Muscat, was at least as intensive as with its immediate Iraqi hinterland.

This outward orientation included provisioning. Some of the town's food, other than fruit, fish, and the dates that grew so abundantly nearby, came from other parts of the Persian Gulf. A substantial part of the cereals consumed in Basra, for instance, was imported from the nearby coastal areas in Iran, around Bandar Dailam and Bandar Rig, where wheat and barley were cultivated.[14] The city's dependence for victuals on outside sources naturally was a crucial issue and one that may have contributed to the openness of its rulers to trade and to their efforts to keep the port free and tolls relatively low. As Della Valle explained in 1625:

> They told me also that free trade was granted to all the Inhabitants of this Persian coast between Chang [sic, Kung] and Bassora, both by the Portugals and the People of Bassora, so that they were not molested by any party; the ground of which I take to be, because Bassora hath not sufficient Victuals, the greatest part being brought thither from these lands of Persia; and on the other side the Portugals need Provision for their Fleet which they keep at Bassora.[15]

Basra was open to the Persian Gulf and was in close interaction with the other port cities that dotted its shores, but the strongest commercial pull came from India. Scholars whose purview extends to the Indo-Muslim world have long recognized that India was Basra's most important trading partner (as it was the primary trading partner of all the Gulf ports), but this fact easily eludes those who work from an Ottoman-centered perspective, which is likely to focus more on the empire's European and Mediterranean domains than on its interaction with the Indian Ocean basin. As Aubin noted, the very terminology used for Basra's entrepôt, *bangsar* (warehouse), denotes an Indian orientation. Next to the bangsar, which handled maritime trade, was the *sif*, another entrepôt that handled riverine trade, the market in cereals and that in other local products.[16] Basra's trade directly connected it to a variety of regions in the western half of the subcontinent, from Sind to Gujarat to Malabar and the rest of Kerala. The goods brought from India included pepper and other spices, indigo, gumlac, and above all cloth and textiles in a multitude of varieties. Ottoman *qanun-namas* of 1551 and 1575 list a great volume of imports consisting of Iranian products and various kinds of Indian fabrics, ranging from precious muslins, calicoes, and women's cloth, which was dyed black in Basra itself. Raw cotton, prepared and washed in town, counted among the imports as well.[17] Dutch sources from a century later still list a wide variety of Indian textiles in addition to indigo and pepper as the main import goods from India. Dates–Basra is said to have provided India with all the dates it needed—horses, pearls, and large quantities of precious metal, in the form of minted coins as well as bullion, comprised the bulk of the flow going in the other direction.[18]

Since Basra was the only Ottoman outlet to the Indian Ocean via the Persian Gulf, it is easy to overstate the port's importance and significance in terms of shipping movements and the volume of long-distance goods handled. We need to remember in this regard that Basra was an unlikely location for a port, situated as it was at the treacherous confluence of the Tigris and the Euphrates, a poorly charted estuary full of shifting shoals and sand banks. Its harbor was hard to access, and not just because it was located some 120 kilometers from the open sea. Although the Euphrates emptied its water into the Gulf via four or five outlets, none of them was navigable by large ships, and freight ships did not go through the Shatt al-Arab, today the dividing waterway between Iran and Iraq, but could only make use of the Bahmanshir channel that led to Basra across what today is Iranian territory. (At the time, the Ottoman-Safavid border ran farther to the east than it currently does, and the Khur Musa, today in Iranian territory, formed the border between the Safavids and the Ottomans. This means that Qubban and the island of Khizr (modern Abadan) were Ottoman territory.)[19]

Even the entrance via the Bahmanshir channel was extremely difficult to navigate and required experienced and expensive pilots, who typically came from the isle of Kharg off the Iranian coast, but sometimes had to be recruited from as far as the port of Kung, also in Iran, some 800 kilometers away.[20] So treacherous were these waters and so confusing the entrance to the estuary that even professional pilots at times lost their way and, therefore ships often used more than one.[21] There was also a limit to the size and tonnage of ships that could sail as far up the Euphrates as Basra. According to an English report, only vessels of no more than six to eight tons might make it up that far fully loaded.[22] A last obstacle to easy accessibility was the fact that Basra was situated about 3 kilometers from the Euphrates, with which it was connected by a man-made canal only navigable by rowboats; in Hamilton's words, "a small Rivulet that washes its walls on the West side, and discharges its Waters into the Euphrates."[23]

These were not the only obstacles to trade conducted with a modicum of security and predictability. Basra's hinterland was vast, stretching all the way to Baghdad and, in commercial terms, reaching from the Levant and Azerbaijan to the Iranian cities of Shiraz and Isfahan and beyond the Persian Gulf as far as the western shores of the Indian subcontinent. Its immediate surroundings were hardly conducive to easy commercial exchange, however, inhabited as they were by Arab Bedouin tribes whose habit of extracting protection money from passing caravans often descended into outright plunder, thus complicating and occasionally severing communication between lower Iraq and the cities of the north such as Baghdad and Aleppo. Their concentration in the Jaza'ir, the marshy lands of the estuary formed by the confluence of the Euphrates and the Tigris that consisted of hundreds of islands and creeks, made them particularly intractable. From their impenetrable redoubt, these tribes posed a continual threat to the riverine and overland commercial traffic between Basra and Baghdad. Their presence and activities, in addition to Basra's torrid climate and a lack of local timber, was one of the reasons why Ottoman attempts to establish a shipyard in Basra ultimately failed, so that they were forced to move their shipbuilding activities to the town of Birecik on the upper Euphrates, in modern Turkey.[24] The formation of an effective administrative apparatus was thus constrained by what M. B. Rowton has called a dimorphic structure, a situation in which the autonomous chiefdom, centered in a town, "exerts a varying blend of rule and influence over nomadic and sedentary tribes in the countryside."[25] All this made Basra a commercial center fraught with the chronic risk of instability.

There were yet other factors that set limits on Basra's commercial potential. The city was prone to flooding. A combination of abundant water, hot and humid weather, and poor sanitary conditions made Mesopotamia particularly susceptible to the outbreak of epidemics.[26] Jean de Thevenot, talking about the hellish climate, claims that during his stay in Basra in July 1665, 4,000 people died in a span of three weeks during a period when the notorious *shamal* winds were blowing.[27] As will be seen in the last part of this chapter, the pestilence of the early 1690s decimated the city's population.

Not only did Basra's trading season coincide with the brutal summer months, it was also short, circumscribed as it was by the rhythm of the Indian monsoon. Caravans from Aleppo arrived in April, while the more frequent ones coming from Baghdad tended to reach the city in late July.[28] Ships, taking advantage of the prevailing monsoon winds, would arrive in July as well and had to depart again for India by October, after which they could no longer sail toward open sea because of contrary winds. The Portuguese so-called Muscat fleet, which annually sailed between India and the Persian Gulf, is a case in point. Leaving from Goa, Diu, Daibul and Muscat, it would depart in May and June with its merchandise, consisting of black cloth in a multitude of varieties, spices, and other goods, stop off in Kung, and arrive in Basra in July. On the return journey the ships, laden with specie, dates, and pearls, would set sail in late August and September, calling at Muscat before returning to India.[29] All this made for a narrow window of opportunity for synchronizing exchange. If any group of merchants was delayed due to natural disaster or military conflict, the entire trading season might be ruined.

Conducting trade in Basra was risky for merchants for other reasons as well. René Barendse submits that the attractiveness of any Persian Gulf port was less related to the prevailing price structure—the cheaper the prices the more popular the port—than to the services it provided and the information that could be garnered on the spot. Therefore trade tended to concentrate where merchants, money, and reliable news were to be found, rather than where goods could be obtained cheaply.[30] Arguably, the two were intertwined, and if, with regard to prices and information, Basra had some advantages, these were largely offset by the drawbacks attached to its other market conditions. Basra was well positioned for a quick transmission of news, situated as it was at one end of the shortest land corridor between the Indian Ocean and the Mediterranean. As such, the maritime companies used it as a relay station for their homeward-bound mail. Indeed, one of the reasons why the Dutch set up and (intermittently) maintained a presence in Basra was the opportunity to dispatch messages to Europe overland.[31]

Prices in Basra fluctuated from year to year and the market had little transparency. This was of course characteristic of port cities around the Persian Gulf or for that matter most anywhere in the early modern world, but the phenomenon was particularly pronounced in Basra with its brief trading season. Since the trade was seasonal and not even visitors from the region stayed all year round, it was imperative for merchants to sell all merchandise that they had brought to town before the end of the season. Being left with any meant either being forced to dump it at below-cost prices at the end of the season or having to transport it back, which meant having to pay entreposage dues. Either way the losses were considerable.

This lack of predictability was exacerbated by the serious disconnect between supply from maritime channels and demand from those coming overland. Goods that were in short supply one year would be brought in abundant quantity the next. Time and again, reports note that, while the harbor was choked with ships arriving from India, the number of merchants coming down from Aleppo and Baghdad had been disappointingly low due to political turmoil or pestilence. It is therefore not surprising that the merchants frequenting Basra, and especially the ones who came down from Baghdad and beyond, can almost all be categorized as peddlers, that much-maligned epithet that no serious scholar would use lightly anymore. Those coming from Baghdad and Aleppo in the mid-seventeenth century were truly men of rather modest means, in contrast to the ones who frequented Bandar Abbas in Iran. A rich merchant from Aleppo or Baghdad, the Dutch noted, carried no more than 4,000 to 5,000 *reals* (of eight) with which to trade, and the average ones disposed of no more than 600 to 700 *reals*.[32] Fluctuations might have been mitigated by the formation of rings of merchants banding together and negotiating en bloc, as they often did in Bandar Abbas and elsewhere in the Gulf basin. While there are indications that merchants pooled their merchandise for the duration of the trip along the Euphrates, there is no evidence that this type of cooperation existed in the market place of Basra itself.[33]

All this obviously circumscribed the degree to which Basra was able to attract and sustain business and set an upper ceiling on its potential. The frequent outbreaks of unrest and violence that gripped the town and its surroundings, caused by tribal strife and the continued struggle over political control between the Ottomans and local forces as well as between the Ottomans and the Safavids, further contributed to the wild fluctuations in Basra's fortunes. It made Basra something of a "back-up port," at least for nonindigenous, Western maritime merchants, an outlet to which they could resort to sell their merchandise at times when adverse trading conditions in Bandar Abbas or political problems with the Safavid government made Iran a poor choice. Basra retained this function for the duration of the seventeenth century. The city's bashas and toll masters seem to have been keenly aware of the port's status as one among a number of competing ones, for time and again they used the prospect and promise of low tolls and fees—typically 7 percent for all goods except for cloth, which at 5 percent was even cheaper—as an incentive for merchants to gain comparative advantage by relocating to Basra.[34]

Basra between Ottomans, Safavids, and Portuguese

During the period in the early sixteenth century when Iraq was nominally under Safavid jurisdiction, the region languished commercially, and trade between Basra and the Levant was almost exclusively conducted via the dangerous overland desert route to Damascus rather than via the safer fluvial route through Iraq. Because the overland route connecting Basra to Damascus was in decline, too, in this period, the Red Sea took the bulk of the goods carried between India and the Levant.

Increased Portuguese influence in the Persian Gulf—where they seized control of Hormuz in 1515—proved to be a turning point for Basra. With Hormuz, the Portuguese acquired a stronghold that would become the linchpin of their operations in the western Indian Ocean, especially after they were forced to cede the Red Sea to Ottoman control after the latter took Egypt in 1517. Of the more than one hundred and fifty ships that visited Hormuz in 1514, over sixty had been diverted from the Red Sea by the Portuguese. Over time, Basra benefited from this development as well, with many of the vessels arriving at Hormuz going on to unload their merchandise at its port.[35] Soon Basra received drugs and spices from India, transshipped from Hormuz. These were in part destined for the internal Ottoman market, in part carried via Baghdad and Aleppo to Tripoli or Damascus for transshipment to European markets. The Portuguese, who had become acquainted with Basra through the voyage of João de Meira in 1517, referred to the trade in spices, indigo and cloth between India and Basra and, speaking about the overland trade with Syria, noted that "many days were not wanting until a caravan came from [the] land of Xama [Syria] consisting of seven hundred camels, and they did not carry another thing save gold in bars, coined money, a great number of fine *contas*-beads, many velvets and veils, an infinite quantity of camlet and saffron . . . and writing paper . . . and an infinite quantity of mercury."[36] Still under Safavid vassalage although effectively controlled by the Al Mughamis tribe as of 1524, Basra by this time had become, in the words of Ramusio, a "city of great trade in specie and spices, which come from Hormuz."[37] In 1529, an observer commented on the numerous vessels arriving from Calicut, laden with spices destined for Syria. Three years later the same observer spoke of three hundred ships carrying spices ready to be taken to Syria.[38]

The subsequent Ottoman thrust into lower Iraq further reinforced this expansion. In 1534–35, Rashid b. Mughamis of Basra and several tribal chieftains from the surrounding area submitted to the sultan, thus enabling the latter to extend his control over Iraq at the expense of the Safavids. Although the Ottoman hold over the region remained tenuous at best, traffic shifted as a result, and merchants, preferring the fluvial route to the more dangerous desert road, now began to use the waterways of Mesopotamia. This led to the rise of Aleppo and its ascendance over Damascus as the terminus for goods moving between the Persian Gulf and the Mediterranean.[39] In the 1540s, Istanbul ordered caravans of spice merchants leaving Basra to take the route to Aleppo via Baghdad rather than the shorter desert route via Damascus, in part because the desert route was more dangerous and in part out of a desire to tax the merchandise.[40] Following a series of tribal challenges to their control, the Ottomans in 1546 once again subdued Basra, and this time more thoroughly. Strengthening their grip on the city, they incorporated its customs administration into the imperial framework. This was part of a series of initiatives designed to increase the Ottoman presence in the Persian Gulf basin and around the Arabian Peninsula into the Indian Ocean, which also included military campaigns against Yemen in 1538 and Qatif and Hasa in 1550–51 and several naval expeditions against the Portuguese launched from Basra. Historians ascribe different motives to this intervention, with some seeing a vigorous and well-planned attempt to extend strategic and commercial control over the Persian Gulf and the Arabian Sea as an alternative to the Red Sea. Yet, given the rather meager resources devoted to these initiatives, it is doubtful that imperial expansion was the objective.[41] The single most important Ottoman concern seems to have been to open supply routes through both the Red Sea and the Persian Gulf to maximize commercial revenue.[42]

There is some recent evidence that the Ottomans followed a concerted commercial strategy in the region, and they clearly made efforts to maximize the profits derived from the trade coming through Basra, if only to allow the city's revenue to pay for the costly campaign undertaken to subdue the city and for the maintenance of a military garrison afterwards.[43] Basra's first Ottoman governor, Bilal Mehmet Beg, soon after being appointed sent a letter to Hormuz in which he explained to its Portuguese chief that the reason why Ayas Pasha—the commander in chief of the 1546 campaign—had been dispatched to subdue Basra was precisely the oppression the city's merchants had suffered under its previous governor, Yahya Pasha. (Never mind that two years later, Bilal Mehmet Beg himself was deposed for fleecing Basra's merchants for personal gain.) To attract merchants, Bilal Mehmet Beg, within months after taking up his post, sent letters on behalf of Basra's Muslim merchants to the Portuguese commander of Hormuz, explaining that stability had returned to the city and guaranteeing safety for any merchant who would visit the port. The Portuguese reaction to such conciliatory gestures was mixed, with some officials arguing that Basra ought to be boycotted since it was the gateway to Ottoman-held Baghdad, but they did not stand in the way of improved commercial traffic.[44]

Dejanirah Potache (Couto), relying on Portuguese sources, has argued that Basra's trade was severely disrupted as a result of the Ottoman takeover.[45] However, any decline in the city's commerce seems to have been confined to the period immediately following the occupation. In spite of the political and ideological differences that remained, the Ottomans and the Portuguese came to some sort of agreement whereby the Portuguese would leave the Red Sea in peace and the Ottomans would no longer challenge Portugal's commercial preeminence in the Persian Gulf, so that in the second half of the sixteenth century little stood in the way of further commercial growth.

Other impediments did exist, though. One was the effect of the periodic outbreaks of unrest among Arab tribes inhabiting the hinterland. Already in 1547, shortly after the Ottoman capture of the city, the combined forces of the Musha'sha' and local Arab tribes managed to cut off Basra's food supply.[46] Two years later we hear of a tribal revolt that blocked passage in lower Mesopotamia and made caravan trade impossible between Baghdad and Basra. Not until 1553 did the Ottomans manage to pacify the city again; it is only in that year that Ramazan Ughli Kubab, who by then had been *basha* for four years, was called the grand ruler of Basra, Cevazir (al-Jaza'ir), and Medeyne (Mada'in).[47] And it was only in 1562 that the *beylerbey* or Ottoman governor of Basra sent an envoy to Hormuz to engage in negotiations about a resumption of commercial relations through the Persian Gulf.[48] The Ottomans were also hit by a financial crisis in the final quarter of the century, so that toll levies in Basra went up. By 1575 these had become so onerous that merchants ended up bypassing Basra in favor of other ports. It remains unclear if the subsequent decision to lower customs dues was implemented and what the effect may have been.[49] Still, fluctuations aside, trade in and out of Basra appears to have done quite well in this period, and the port continued to thrive into the 1600s, its trade protected by Portuguese naval power.[50] At the turn of the seventeenth century, the annual flow of silver exported from Basra toward India is said to have exceeded 2 million Spanish *reals*.[51] In 1609, several ships arrived in Basra each month.[52]

Basra additionally benefited from developments at Hormuz, which in turn occurred in the context of the period's most momentous political change, the rise of Iran as a state with strategic and commercial designs on the Persian Gulf. Lacking a navy, the Safavids never posed a direct military threat to any maritime power in the Gulf, but Shah Abbas's conquest of Bahrain in 1602 exemplified Iran's rising influence and imperial ambitions in the region. In response, the Portuguese drew closer to the Ottomans or at least to the regional authorities of Basra, to the point where, for the next few decades, the Portuguese became the chief defenders of Basra's territorial integrity—mostly against Iran. Portuguese behavior in Hormuz—where they are said to have insulted Shah Abbas, treated his decrees with contempt, and behaved arrogantly toward Iranian merchants, obstructing them and forcing them to buy merchandise at highly inflated prices—benefited Basra's trade as well, for in reaction, numerous Muslim merchants shunned Hormuz, choosing instead to wait for ships to arrive in Basra or to make purchases, at higher prices, in Shiraz.[53]

This development culminated with the fall of Hormuz to the Iranians in 1622. On the face of it, this event was something of a double-edged sword for Basra in that it entailed the rise of Bandar Abbas as a rival, Iranian-controlled port at the east end of the Persian Gulf. It also complicated Portuguese access to Basra.[54] Ali Basha, the town's ruler since 1624, in a complaint he directed against the English for having assisted the Iranians in dislodging the Portuguese from Hormuz, contended that the fall of Hormuz had been detrimental to Basra's trade.[55] However Della Valle, writing in 1625, insisted that trade at Basra had actually picked up since 1622, at least for the Portuguese, and that, while he was in Basra, five of their ships "rode continually in."[56] In 1628, twenty Portuguese ships were in the harbor, and in August 1630 twenty-five Portuguese merchant vessels arrived in the port—a record as the observer in question pointed out.[57]

Changing power constellation in the Gulf

On balance, Basra indeed seems to have profited from the changing of the guard at Hormuz, and not just because the Portuguese decamped. Especially from the moment in the late 1620s when the Basrenes managed to subdue the Al Ilayan, the main tribal formation in the Jaza'ir region, its trade increased.[58] The Portuguese, having moved their operations to Muscat, now set out to redirect their Persian Gulf trade to that port. The Iranians tried to thwart this development, making efforts to take Muscat from the Portuguese by naval power, but they were unsuccessful in doing so, in part because of an English and Dutch refusal to participate in the venture, in part because of vigorous Portuguese resistance.[59] Although the Portuguese lost a naval battle against a joint English-Dutch fleet in 1625, their presence and power in the Persian Gulf hardly diminished at this point. As mentioned, they strengthened their link to the ruling house of Basra and soon would assist the Afrasiyab regime against Iranian attack. Trade out of Basra and other Gulf ports continued to move under their protection, although it now used Muscat rather than Hormuz as a way station.

All in all, therefore, Basra seems to have been a net beneficiary of the changing power constellation in the Persian Gulf, even if the Portuguese as of 1630 forced all ships destined for the upper part of the Gulf, including Basra, to first pass by Kung—which they had just made into their base—and pay dues there.[60] The attendant period of prosperity coincided with, and clearly benefited from, the long rule of Ali Basha, the son of

Afrasiyab who in 1596 had purchased the right to govern the town from the Ottomans. In the early part of Ali Basha's governance, which lasted from 1624 until 1650, Basra repeatedly came under Iranian attack, and it was only because of its continuing alliance with the Portuguese that the city was spared defeat and possibly occupation.[61] Despite the challenges this produced, Basra thrived in this period, growing in commercial significance, to the point where Fath Allah al-Ka'bi, a local historian, likened Ali Basha's reign to that of Harun al-Rashid, the caliph who presided over the Abbasid caliphate at its height, in terms of prosperity, intellectual curiosity, quality of poetry, and safety.[62] Judging by the verdict of two outside observers, the transformation indeed appears to have been remarkable. In 1608, the Portuguese De Orta Rebelo had called Basra "the most miserable place" he had yet seen.[63] A generation later, in 1635, a resident missionary insisted—evidently not without hyperbole—that "this town has grown so greatly in riches, merchandise and for the numbers of people resorting to it, that it can be compared to Constantinople."[64] Textiles from India played an important part in the florescence. Especially the coarse black variety, used for the *abayas* worn by women, was extremely popular and could always find a market.[65]

Advent of the Maritime Companies

In the 1640s, new merchants entered the market in Basra. The Dutch and the English had settled in the Persian Gulf decades earlier, but initially they had focused on Iran and its commercial potential. It was only when they were faced with problems in Bandar Abbas that they cast an eye on Basra. The Dutch were keen to explore the trade of Basra as early as 1627, but these initial plans came to nothing.[66] Nine years later, the English decided to expand their influence in the Persian Gulf to Basra as well. Their first foray failed, though, because the vessel they sent was so unseaworthy that it was forced to return after getting no farther than Damman.[67] Still, the English East India Company (EIC) was the first of the European maritime companies to enter the trade of Basra. Unable to compete with the Dutch in Bandar Abbas, the English in 1639 dispatched a mission to Basra, and shortly thereafter they decided to establish a trading post in the port.[68] In 1643, the EIC sent two ships.[69] Initial returns were good, with cloth netting 45 to 50 percent in profits.[70]

In 1644, the Dutch extended their operations to Basra as well. The context of this venture was a conflict between the Dutch East Indies Company (VOC) and the Iranian authorities that had been simmering for years. This conflict culminated in the Dutch imposing a naval blockade around Bandar Abbas and attacking Qishm, the island across from Bandar Abbas. Having made Bandar Abbas inaccessible, they decided to explore the market in Basra with goods that had remained unsold in Iran from the previous season, hoping to take advantage of low customs to lure private Iranian and Turkish merchants to this Ottoman port.[71] The VOC agent in Bandar Abbas noted Basra's central location in relation to Aleppo and Damascus, and also drew attention to the fact that it would be easier for merchants from Isfahan and Shiraz to travel to Basra than to come down to Bandar Abbas.[72]

The advent of the maritime companies greatly enhances our insight into the fluctuations of Basra's trade. Especially the reporting from Basra by the Dutch agents who were sent there intermittently allows one to follow subsequent developments with some regularity. Both the English and the Dutch soon discovered that Basra was not the El Dorado it was made out to be, despite welcoming gestures on the part of its basha (pasha) and the promise of toll fees of 6 percent on imports (7% on dry goods).[73] Some of this had to do with disappointing results following unrealistically high expectations. A VOC attempt to sell tea in Basra, for instance, met with little success. (Tea was never to make a splash in the region.) In 1645, VOC resident Sarcerius reported that the Chinese tea that had been imported had found few buyers since the drink was hardly known among the people.[74] Similarly, the maritime companies, faced with a declining silk supply from Iran, learned that silk might be obtained through Basra. The English for a while managed to deal in small amounts of Iranian silk.[75] As for the Dutch, although it seemed that good-quality silk was available in Basra at 45 tumans per load (two bales), the VOC failed to buy any.[76] Friendly treatment by the authorities and the port's location promised long-term profitability provided one could be patient. Yet short-term profits remained low.

Most importantly, the very attention the port received soon led to fierce competition between merchants of different nationalities. Basra quickly became oversupplied with goods, few of which could be sold at decent prices. In 1644, for instance, the Dutch reported that the English had made good money in Basra the previous year.[77] But in 1646, barely two years later, conditions had changed dramatically. "Never was trade worse in these parts," lamented the EIC factor in reference to a glut of textiles, pointing to the fact that since February more than 2,000 bales of Indian cloth had arrived in port and that more was expected, so that "these merchants will find but little benefit."[78] Later that year the English noted that a saturated market resulting from large Dutch supplies had caused the price of pepper to fall precipitously as well. To make matters worse, far fewer merchants than anticipated actually came down from Baghdad.[79] This was due in part to an outbreak of a fresh round of warfare over Crete between the Ottomans and the Venetians. The other reason was the eruption of armed conflict between the basha of Baghdad and the Basrenes, which impeded commercial traffic up and down the Euphrates. Nevertheless, the English continued to conduct a modest operation in Basra.[80] The turmoil had wider repercussions as well: as trade was at a standstill in Basra, a number of Thatta (in Sind, near Karachi) merchants dealing in textiles were ruined in 1646.[81]

As conditions in Iran did not improve, Basra remained an alternative option for the European merchants for some time to come. In 1648, the Dutch even reported that the English were about to abandon their factory in Bandar Abbas and set up one at Basra.[82] This renewed attention and activity had predictable consequences. In 1651, the town's inhabitants estimated that in one season more had been brought ashore than in the three preceding years. On August 18, 1651, the Dutch agent Elias Boudaen wrote that since his arrival in Basra on May 14, when only one English ship had been present in port, two large Portuguese ships, and eleven "Moorish" ones, aside from a large number of smaller vessels, had made a call at the port, bringing a staggering amount of merchandise. Ironically, many merchants who normally would come down to Basra had gone to Isfahan, Bandar Abbas, and Mukha on the Arabian Red Sea coast that same season because the year before they had been unable to find enough merchandise for their money so that they had been forced to carry more than 500,000 reals back with them.[83]

As recounted, worsening political and commercial conditions in neighboring Iran helped to boost Basra's commercial fortunes in this period. Abusive treatment by the authorities and uncompetitive fees in Bandar Abbas in the 1660s caused many merchants to call on the smaller ports that dotted the Iranian coast, several of which were poorly patrolled and lacked an official tollhouse. Kung, located approximately 150 kilometers west of Bandar Abbas, is a case in point. As early as 1638, the Dutch referred to Kung as the place that was preferred over Bandar Abbas by Banyan (Indian) merchants. And with a very reasonable toll tariff of 7 percent (as opposed to 10 percent in Bandar Abbas), and, more importantly, better treatment by the governor of Lar, it was to be a popular alternative for many merchants for decades to come. Bandar Rig, even farther west, benefited from this trend as well. In 1664, the Dutch claimed, more ships than ever had docked at Bandar Rig, where they not only had delivered many goods but had also taken on much of Iran's export products for India. Although it evidently did not escape official scrutiny, Basra, too, profited from this westward movement. In 1663, Godinho called Basra "the richest port of call in that sea" and claimed that forty ships from India berthed at its port each year.[84] De Thevenot claims to have seen fifteen ships—Dutch as well as Muslim ones—docked in Basra when he visited in 1665.[85] In the late 1660s, the English claimed that of late Basra had become the "flourishingst [sic] port in India," receiving many goods that hitherto had been taken to Bandar Abbas.[86]

An additional boon for Basra in this period was that it began to attract a large percentage of the silver bullion and specie that usually moved from the Ottoman Empire to Iran. This was a paradoxical development, for it occurred at a time when Iran was experiencing a severe silver shortage and many Safavid mints had to close for lack of mintable silver. To counter these problems, the Iranian authorities imposed restrictions on exporting bullion through Safavid ports and tightened inspections on silver transports to the Persian Gulf littoral. They thus slapped a 5 percent fee on the export of all silver and banned the export of gold ducats.[87] In response, merchants coming from the ports of the Levant began to take much of their bullion and specie to freewheeling Basra, where merchants eager to export specie to India paid better prices for ducats and several silver currencies than these monies fetched in Europe and the Levant.[88] This phenomenon also explains the frenzied activity of the mint of Huwaiza in neighboring Arabistan. Even as Basra and its environs were wracked by disease and war in the early 1690s, large quantities of silver continued to be taken there.[89]

The Late Seventeenth Century: Trade And Turmoil

As problems in Iran offered multiple opportunities for growth, the recurrent turmoil and disaster that befell Basra between 1654 and 1669 severely hampered the port's ascendance as a serious competitor to Bandar Abbas. Following the death of Ali Basha and the accession of his son, Husain Basha, in 1650, Basra entered a period marked by tyrannical rule, internecine war among its local authorities, and protracted conflict between the Ottomans and the region's Arab population. It is true that Husain Basha did not lack in concern for trade, so that even under this ruler, merchants continued to visit Basra in search of making a profit. Yet war and a lack of security caused by marauding Arab tribesmen across Basra's hinterland evidently did little to foster a hospitable commercial climate in this period. In some years, chaos in and around the city made it impossible for trade to be conducted at all. Not all seasons were bad for trade, though. Even years of considerable political turmoil might not dampen commercial activity, for the moment that stability returned, merchants demonstrated their proverbial resilience by traveling down the Euphrates again, just as ships once again started arriving from Surat.[90]

The years 1654 and 1665 to 1668 were ones of especially great political and military turmoil. In the former year, popular discontent with local rule triggered an Ottoman campaign against Basra, as a result of which strife broke out in the surrounding countryside and the city itself filled up with refugees. A new period of chaos marked by invasion and occupation began in 1665 with the refusal of Husain Basha to acknowledge the (nominal) suzerainty of Istanbul over the city. He sent his brother-in-law, Yahya Aqa, to the Ottoman court, but was betrayed by him and saw himself faced with an Ottoman campaign. This initially produced a protracted stalemate between Turks and Arabs that in late 1667 led to Basra's evacuation and torching by Husain Basha, and in the following spring resulted in the Ottomans taking the city.[91] A year later, an Arab fighting force assembled by Yahya Aqa invaded the city and put some 5,000 of its inhabitants to the sword. Only in late 1669 did the Turks manage to retake Basra.[92]

The brutality of their methods notwithstanding, the successive rulers who took control of the city in this tumultuous era all showed a concern to revive trade. Thus, Yahya Aqa, who after betraying his in-law was installed as Basra's new governor by the Ottomans, upon his accession invited all inhabitants who had fled the city to move back and the foreign merchants to return and resume their trade as well. To facilitate the revival of trade he extended a temporary tax reprieve to all merchants.[93] As a result, trade quickly picked up again and the Dutch reported that by the summer of 1668—mere months after its occupation by the Turks—indigenous merchants had begun to ply their trade in Basra again and that some fifteen to sixteen ships had already arrived from Surat.[94] Yahya Aqa's success in reviving trade, however, in addition to his increasingly autonomous tendencies, soon prompted the Ottomans to start intervening in his governance. They applied various forms of harassment, such as appointing a Turkish *shahbandar* (toll master) who deprived him of his customs receipts, and accusing him of making common cause with the Iranians, so that in 1669 he fled to Iran.

Expectations that full Ottoman control would spell the end of Basra's problems proved illusory. Barthélemy Carré found Basra much changed in the summer of 1672, compared with the last time he had been there, in 1669 and 1670. As he put it, "There was less trade than formerly, the town having been abandoned by the majority of its inhabitants as a result of the extortion and pillaging by the Turks. This has also caused seditious revolts by the Arabs, who were no longer quiet."[95] This latter observation is a reference to the fact that, while the Ottomans had finally established control and were actively soliciting trade, they also imposed a harsh fiscal regime on the city. Faced with costly wars in Europe and the need to maintain a large and expensive military force in and around Basra, they raised taxes and forced the local merchants to come up with substantial sums of money.[96]

It stands to reason that the various cycles of turmoil did little to promote trade in Basra, although it is difficult to assess the effect of the political regimes. The notion that the rule of the Afrasiyab was automatically beneficial to Basra and that, conversely, the end of Basra's prosperity was a function of Ottoman domination and the rapaciousness of Turkish authorities, is patently false. In 1646, a time when Basra was virtually autonomous and under local Arab control, the Dutch bitterly complained about the shahbandar who extracted money from each and everyone in town and who had the basha under his thumb.[97] In 1681, by contrast, the VOC agent noted that the Ottoman-appointed basha did his best to lure merchants to his port and for that purpose had not farmed out the position of shahbandar that year, but appointed a Turkish administrator to ensure that nothing over and above the regular tolls would be levied so that merchants would not bear any excessive burden.[98] Yet there was nothing inherently benevolent about Turkish overlordship. Indeed, it seems that, in spite of good intentions, Ottoman control did have a negative effect on Basra's commercial viability and that their dire need for money, having to do with a new outbreak of warfare in Europe and its effect, a growing scarcity of silver, was mostly responsible for this. Throughout the 1680s, the cash-starved Ottoman treasury imposed a heavy tax burden on Basra, increasing regular remittances and at various times adding incidental imposts.[99]

Because of these recurrent crises and the attendant insecurity, Basra never reached a "take-off" point. In 1680, the VOC directors in Batavia called the trade of Basra "unimportant," in a statement that appears to have reflected overall trade and not just the part played by the Dutch or the Europeans in general.[100] In July 1681, the Dutch managed to get the local basha to agree to an arrangement whereby VOC goods would only have to pay 6 percent for weighable goods and 5 percent for piece goods, and only goods that were sold would be taxed. They closed the books at the end of the next trading season with mixed results. Tin had fetched low prices, Indian merchants having brought 90,000 pounds of it. The sale of pepper they deemed satisfactory, despite the fact that, in the absence of the Portuguese, the Arabs of Muscat were busy dealing in the same commodity. Only four ships arrived from Surat that year, but they all were so richly laden with mostly fine textiles and indigo that their cargo was worth at least twice the usual amount. Aside from the vessels from Surat, a number of small ones had arrived from Jidda, Mukha, Sind, and Muscat.[101]

In 1684, the Dutch became embroiled in a conflict in Iran that resembled the one of 1645 in that it entailed the blockage of Bandar Abbas. And once again, they cast an eye toward Basra for its potential as an alternative port. Yet even Basra's rise as a principal center for the sale of the pearls collected at various places in the Upper Gulf was not enough to cause a return of the city's commercial luster.[102] Thus, in 1687, when memories of the latest conflict with the Safavid shah were still fresh enough to make the Dutch look for alternatives to Bandar Abbas, the VOC directors in Holland, the Heren XVII, decided not to relocate trade from Iran to Basra, because its commerce was not picking up and the money circulating that year was of questionable alloy.[103] Once again, the verdict was that the trade in Basra did not meet expectations and that, since no reduction of tolls could be expected, it would be unwise to transfer the entire Iranian operation thither.[104] The Dutch indeed suffered losses in Basra in this period.[105]

Matters further deteriorated when the plague visited the region. In 1690, sixteen or seventeen ships still arrived in Basra from India alone[106]; a short while later the plague struck, emptying Basra's bazaars and causing all foreigners to flee the city.[107] The epidemic afflicted a large swath of the Middle East, in an arc stretching from Izmir in western Anatolia to Baku in the Caucasus to Surat in western India.[108] Lower Iraq, which may have been the origin of the disease, and especially Basra, suffered in particular. One report claimed that as many as 80,000 people perished in the city. Given a population of perhaps 50,000, this is clearly an exaggeration, unless the entire region with its estimated population of 250,000 is meant. Regardless of the exact numbers, the horror portrayed is unmistakable.[109] Trade naturally came to a halt. The French missionary Gaudereau reports how he was forced to stay in Baghdad for two and half months in 1690, not just on account of the plague but also in the face of tribal unrest, with Bedouins raiding all the way up to the city gates.[110]

Nor was this the end of the troubles. In 1692, a new conflict between the Turks and the Muntafiq tribal confederation led by Shaikh Mani‘ b. Mughamis erupted, threatening Ottoman control over the city. Turkish troops were sent and arrived in Baghdad, and in response, the Arabs blocked all routes between Baghdad and Basra. This was kept secret from the populace, however; the official news was that relief was on the way in the form of Turkish soldiers who would rout the Arabs. Refugees from Basra arriving in Kung, however, told of a city in turmoil that was about to be taken over by the Arabs, so that many tried to flee the city, with the Turks doing all they could to prevent this. The city was left "mostly desolate and without commerce."[111] In early 1693, the tide seemed to turn with the arrival of a new Ottoman basha accompanied by 14,000 soldiers.[112] But the euphoria this caused did not last: soon unrest broke out again. The Dutch reacted to this by abandoning the port surreptitiously, only leaving a small consignment of merchandise that they could not carry with them.[113]

A year later, a prominent Turkish merchant arrived in Bandar Abbas as an envoy from the new basha, carrying a mandate to conclude a contract with the Dutch involving tolls and immunities if only they would send a ship to Basra. He spoke of the desire of the basha to encourage trade and how the road to Baghdad was no longer infested with Bedouin marauders. As the VOC representative put it, the local authorities petitioned them to return, not so much because of the considerable profits this would engender but more since a return of the VOC would attract other merchants as well. The Dutch reacted cautiously, promising to send a ship as soon as one was available from India and on condition that the basha would grant them all old rights and privileges. Using the old rule of thumb, they considered Basra an alternative option, a port to seek recourse to in case they faced trouble in Iran.[114] Concerns about Portuguese resentment and apprehensions about instability following the death of Shah Sulaiman in 1694 made them hesitant to reopen their trade connection with Basra. Yet, a year later, they changed their mind as it transpired that peace and quiet had indeed returned to the city after the bashas of Basra and Baghdad had pacified the region. As Banyan merchants were said to be coming back to Basra from Kung, they considered returning with a consignment of merchandise as well.[115]

The next few years reveal a mixed picture. When in late 1695 Shaikh Mani‘ retook the city, its trade plummeted. As the Turks sent an army and Shaikh Mani‘ seemed ready to leave, many of Basra's inhabitants, fearful that his soldiers might first wreak havoc on the population, fled the town.[116] On March 26, 1697, the Iranians entered Basra after defeating the troops of Shaikh Mani‘. Although they initially showed a willingness to hand the keys of the city back to the Ottomans, they would hold on to Basra until early 1701. In the intervening period, trade seems to have picked up, even though Shaikh Mani‘ continued to threaten the city and even managed to lay siege to it again.[117] The resident Carmelite fathers were in fact rather upbeat about Basra's fate during the Iranian occupation. According to them, the town had prospered under their benevolent rule, and decline, manifested by famine and misery, had only set in with the Arab siege in 1701.[118] Hamilton, too, praised what he called the Iranian encouragement of trade and contrasted their rule to that of the Turks, which, according to him, was "insolent to strange merchants."[119] Whatever measures were taken, however, it was not enough to induce either the Dutch or the English to return to Basra.

In 1701, the Iranians returned control over Basra to the Ottomans. Having reestablished themselves in the city, they quickly sent letters to Surat and other quarters inviting merchants to resume their commercial activities in Basra.[120] Jacobus Hoogcamer, VOC envoy to Isfahan, thus received a note from the new Ottoman basha requesting the Dutch Company as the "oldest and the one with a house" to return and engage in trade in Basra. His request was accompanied by an offer of reduced customs dues. The Dutch accepted, mostly because of expected profitability, but also because trade in Basra meant leverage in Iran, both with the Safavid authorities and with Iranian merchants who might thus be "brought to reason."[121] The English soon followed, and English private merchants were spotted in Basra in 1701. The immediate results were meager, though: for the time being, the road to Baghdad remained infested with bandits.[122]

In 1702, the EIC returned to Basra. Agent Goodshaw had been instructed to pursue trade with the following main conditions: that the EIC should have the liberty to hire a convenient house and warehouse at a rent that, once agreed on, would not be subject to more exactions, and that the EIC would be free from paying any customs either for what they carried and imported or bought and exported. This would not only encourage the English to expand their trade but also serve to enrich the basha and thus enhance the glory of the sultan.[123] Arriving in the latter port on September 2, Goodshaw was told by the basha that granting privileges as requested by the English was not within his power. Looking through his customs books, he had discovered that the EIC had previously paid 5 percent, which, with some additional impositions, would come to 7 or 8 percent. He therefore was willing to show his goodwill by reducing the impost to 3 percent without additional impositions, adding that if the company would contemplate settling in Basra, he would "make the home and other conveniences encouraging to them." This made Goodshaw quite optimistic about future prospects, which would consist of exchange of Indian woolens for merchandise Basra received from Aleppo, such as lead, iron, sword blades, and small ordnance. The freight in Basra was also 40 percent better than in Iran, he noted.[124]

Basra seemed poised for recovery. The Ottomans were firmly in power, with 2,000 soldiers garrisoned in the city, enough to keep the unruly Arabs at bay. But all was not well. As before, the Ottoman presence proved to be no safeguard against fiscal oppression. Trade also continued to be badly affected by the unrest that periodically plagued the roads connecting Basra to the north, even if merchants would immediately set out from Baghdad as soon as such unrest subsided.[125] Decades of instability and turmoil had taken their toll. By 1705, Basra was a shadow of its former self, its housing stock reduced to only 5,000, its population shrunk to a mere 20,000.[126] And this was on the eve of yet another Arab assault on the city, which caused further ruination.[127] Formerly some twenty or twenty-one ships annually would deliver their goods at Basra, including textiles from Surat, coffee and indigo, as well as pepper, and even at times when the merchants from Baghdad and Aleppo were not in a position to come down, the inhabitants were able to buy these goods and consume them in part.[128] The Ottoman records confirm the trend: whereas before 1697, some sixteen to seventeen ships would dock at Basra each year, in 1707 only six arrived.[129] Only with the fall of the Safavids and the onset of protracted chaos in Iran did Basra have another chance of finally becoming a serious contender for the position of premier port city in the entire Persian Gulf basin.

Conclusion

Basra was far from being an ideal port to serve as the main entrepôt for commercial interaction between the Levant and the Indian Ocean. Situated at a considerable distance from the open water of the Persian Gulf, it was only accessible via a treacherous estuary filled with shifting shoals and sand banks. Its hinterland was vast, but here too, access was difficult, hindered by impenetrable marshes and their inhabitants, fiercely independent Bedouin tribes who were given to raiding and plunder. The area was hot and humid and prone to flooding and outbreaks of devastating epidemics. The trading season, coinciding as it did with the height of summer, was brief and uncomfortable, complicating a smooth coordination between supply and demand, especially since few merchants stayed all year round.

Despite all these obstacles, throughout the sixteenth and seventeenth century Basra was without a serious contender in the upper part of the Persian Gulf. Kuwait, although endowed with superior access to the sea, was too remote to be of any use to the Ottomans and would only begin to challenge Basra after it had been settled in the mid-eighteenth century. The same is true for Bushehr, which would take over from Bandar Abbas as the principal Iranian port in the same period. Muhammara (present-day Khurramshahr) was as yet an insignificant town. Its turn would only come in the nineteenth century.

In the early 1500s, coinciding with the onset of Safavid control, Basra seems to have been a backwater. Trade was conducted mostly overland, besides which the bulk of commercial traffic between the Indian Ocean and the Levant used the Red Sea route. Its fortunes changed with the Portuguese seizure of Hormuz in 1515. It is difficult to chart fluctuations throughout the sixteenth century, but overall, it seems that the fall of Hormuz entailed greater activity for Basra and that under Portuguese protection, the port did rather well. It seems to have continued its commercial ascendance under the local Afrasiyab dynasty, turning into the largest and busiest of the Gulf ports.

From the 1640s onward, the arrival of the European maritime companies and their reporting vastly increases our knowledge of Basra. It is not always easy to distill information about the port's commercial status and performance on the basis of the documents produced by these companies, especially not if we heed Rhoads Murphey's reminder about early modern port cities that "domestic trade, including transit and entrepot trade, was greater at all periods than external trade."[130] After all, what was good for the

Europeans did not necessarily benefit their competitors, that is, domestic and regional merchants. Yet there was enough symbiosis involved in the relationship between the two groups for a careful reading of the maritime documents to reveal a picture that covers both.

On the basis of the information provided, especially by the Dutch, it becomes clear that beyond the ceiling set by its inherent limitations, Basra's commercial fortunes were a function of a great many variables. Of these, the intuitive ones of good governance and security and stability—inside the city as well as along its access routes—stand out. Political leaders keen to foster trade and political stability had a beneficial effect on the port's commercial fortunes, whereas turmoil in the form of tribal raiding, warfare between the Ottomans and local forces, and rapacious authorities tended to be harmful to trade—even if merchants were extraordinarily resilient, resuming their operations at the slightest sign that chaos and unrest were abating.

The dynamic between politics and commerce has been explored here with a particular eye to the widespread notion—often presented as an unstated assumption—that in their greater concern about their own subjects and realm, local rulers tended to be better for a port's prosperity than the more anonymous administrators representing the central, imperial government. It appears that Basra prospered under the Afrasiyabs, or at least under the rule of the dynasty's founder, Afrasiyab, and his son, Ali, covering the first half of the seventeenth century. In later times, the picture becomes more mixed. Local authorities, whether they acted as agents for the Ottomans or represented a local dynasty, had a keen eye for trade and often solicited merchants and facilitated the operations, holding out low customs rates and other preferential treatment. But it is also clear that, as elsewhere, mercantile interests in Basra as a rule were generally subordinate to political imperatives, so that maximizing toll revenue at times defeated the desire to expand commercial activity. Local authorities were not necessarily more benevolent in this respect than the representatives of outside rulers.

The second half of the seventeenth century saw the city and its environs engulfed in waves of turmoil and destruction. Much of this had to do with the inherently fragile balance of power in and around the city, with local forces and Ottoman troops engaged in a protracted struggle for control and domination. When the Ottomans finally gained control over the city, it had suffered terribly. They began their administration intent on reviving trade, but their good intentions were soon overshadowed by a pressing need for money. The oppressive fiscal regime this gave rise to, in addition to the continuing and recurrent unrest in the access routes to the north, prevented the much-needed regeneration of the city from taking place. Basra's death knell came in the form of a series of devastating epidemics in the 1690s, which were followed by yet another round of warfare. By the early eighteenth century, Basra was a shadow of its former self, devastated and depopulated. In the absence of an alternative port at the upper part of the Persian Gulf, merchants had no choice but to continue to visit Basra, but decades would pass before the port could again aspire to the status of being the most prosperous of the Gulf.

Notes

Author's note: The research for this study was made possible in part with a joint research travel grant from the University of Leiden and the University of Delaware.

1. With some 50,000 inhabitants in the seventeenth century, Basra matched the estimated number of people in Hormuz in its heyday in the early 1500s. See Jean Aubin, "Le royaume d'Ormuz au début du XVIe siècle," *Mare Luso-Indicum* 2 (1973): 150.
2. National Dutch Archives (NA), The Hague, Verenigde Oostindische Compagnie (VOC) 1135, Geleynssen de Jongh, Gamron to Batavia, 30 March 1641, fol. 663; VOC 1188,

Elias Boudaen, Report on Basra, 29 November 1651, fol. 541v. Dates were exported in large quantities, to places all around the Persian Gulf. See Pedro Teixeira, *The Travels of Pedro Teixeira*, trans. and ed. William Sinclair and Donald Ferguson (London, 1902), 29. Hamilton in the early eighteenth century claimed that Basra annually exported some 10,000 tons of dates. See Alexander Hamilton, *A New Account of the East Indies*, 2 vols., ed. Sir William Foster (London, 1930), 1:52. Pearls from the upper part of the Persian Gulf, collected near the island of Kharg, were especially coveted in India for being heavier and denser than the ones from Tuticorin in India. See NA, VOC 1251, Van Wijck, Gamron to Heren XVII, 6 April 1666, fol. 1232. Horses were more expensive in Basra than in Iran, but at least Muslim merchants were allowed to export them freely. For the authorities of Basra, access to horses was an important aspect of successful campaigns against neighboring tribal formations. See Dina Rizk Khoury, "Merchants and Trade in Early Modern Iraq," *New Perspectives on Turkey* 5–6 (1991): 67.

3. The recent publication of Willem Floor's comprehensive study on the Persian Gulf in the sixteenth and seventeenth centuries includes two major chapters on Basra. See his *The Persian Gulf: A Political and Economic History of Five Port Cities 1500–1730* (Washington D. C., 2006). This came out too late to be fully incorporated into the present study. Aside from the classic study by Stephen Hemsley Longrigg, *Four Centuries of Modern Iraq* (Oxford, 1925), which remains the standard history for the period and the region, there is Dina Rizk Khoury's excellent article, cited in the previous note, which considers Basra as well as Mosul, and now Rudi Matthee, "Between Arabs, Turks and Iranians: The Town of Basra, 1600–1700," *Bulletin of the School of Oriental and African Studies* 69 (2006): 53–78.
4. This trend has become prominent in the study of Mughal India. See, for instance, Sinnapah Arasaratnam, *Merchants, Companies and Commerce on the Coromandel Coast 1650–1740* (Delhi, India, 1986) and Sanjay Subrahmanyam, *The Political Economy of Commerce: Southern India, 1500–1650* (Cambridge, 1990). For Safavid Iran, see Rüdiger Klein, "Trade in the Safavid Port City of Bandar Abbas and the Persian Gulf Area (ca. 1600–1680): A Study of Selected Aspects" (PhD diss., University of London, 1994); and, for a more implied example, Stephen Dale, *Indian Merchants and Eurasian Trade, 1600–1750* (Cambridge, 1994).
5. Hala Fattah, *The Politics of Regional Trade in Iraq, Arabia, and the Gulf 1745–1900* (Albany, New York, 1997); and Thabit A. J. Abdullah, *Merchants, Mamluks, and Murder: The Political Economy of Trade in Eighteenth-Century Basra* (Albany, New York, 2001).
6. See K. Heeringa, ed., *Bronnen tot de geschiedenis van de Levantsche handel*, 2 vols. (The Hague, Netherlands: 1910–17), 2:163; and Jean de Thevenot, *Voyages de Mr. de Thevenot en Europe, Asie et Afrique*, 3rd ed., 5 vols. (Amsterdam, Netherlands, 1727), 4:557–58.
7. Sanjay Subrahmanyam, *The Portuguese Empire in India 1500–1700* (London, 1993), 76.
8. Archives des Missions Etrangères (AME), Paris, 350, letter Pierregrosse, Baghdad to Paris, 29 May 1680, fols. 469–76 (471). In the next letter, from Basra, he mentions a hostile confrontation halfway to Basra. See ibid., letter from Basra, 15 July 1680, fols. 481–83.
9. Colin Imber, "The Navy of Sülayman the Magnificent," in *Studies in Ottoman History and Law*, Colin Imber (Istanbul, Turkey, 1996).
10. See Rudi Matthee, "The Safavid–Ottoman Frontier: Iraq-i 'Arab as Seen by the Safavids," *International Journal of Turkish Studies* 9 (2003): 157–74; reprinted in Kemal H. Karpat and Robert W. Zens, eds., *Ottoman Borderlands: Issues, Personalities, and Political Changes* (Madison, WI, 2004).
11. Le Gouz de la Boullaye, *Les voyages et observations du Sieur Boullaye-de la–Gouz* (Paris, 1657; repr. 1994), 163–64.
12. The number of 10,000 Iranian pilgrims for some years is given by Jean Chardin, *Voyages du chevalier Chardin en Perse et en autres lieux de l'Orient*, ed. L. Langlès, 10 vols. and atlas (Paris, 1810–11), 3:135.
13. Jean de Thevenot, *Relation d'un voyage fait au Levant*, vol. 2, *Suite du voyage* (Paris, 1674), 321–22.

14. De Thevenot, *Voyages*, 3:536 and Hamilton, *New Account*, 1:89. Teixeira, *Travels*, 29, makes it clear that cereals and rice were grown around Basra as well, but he also mentions imports. Duarte Barbosa in the early sixteenth century claimed that "plenty of wheat" was exported from Basra. (See Duarte Barbosa, *The Book of Duarte Barbosa*, ed. Mansel Longworth Dames, 2 vols. (London, 1918), 1:89.) The first Portuguese foray into the port of Basra was also designed to purchase wheat and ship it back to Hormuz. See Ronald Bishop Smith, *The First Age of Portuguese Embassies, Navigations and Peregrinations in Persia (1507–1524)* (Bethesda, MD, 1971), 59. All of this may have been wheat that had been brought to Basra from the coastal area in Iran. See for this question Khoury, "Merchants and Trade," 64–65.
15. Pietro della Valle, *The Travels of Sig. Pietro della Valle, a Noble Roman, into East India and Arabia Deserta* (London, 1665), letter x, 20 May 1625, 243.
16. Aubin, "Le royaume d'Ormuz," 165.
17. See Gilles Veinstein, "Commercial Relations between India and the Ottoman Empire (Late Fifteenth to Late Eighteenth Century): A Few Notes and Hypotheses," in *Merchants, Companies and Trade: Europe and Asia in the Early Modern Era*, ed. Sushil Chaudhury and Michel Morineau (Cambridge, 1999), 97–98.
18. De Thevenot, *Voyages*, 4:561–62.
19. For a discussion of the changes, see A. Hotz, "Cornelis Roobacker's scheepsjournaal Gamron-Basra (1645); de eerste reis der Nederlanders door de Perzische Golf," *Tijdschrift van het Koninklijk Aardrijkskundig Genootschap*, 2nd ser., 24 (1907): 370–71; and introduction by A. Hotz, 344–46. André Wink, "From the Mediterranean to the Indian Ocean: Medieval History in Geographic Perspective," *Comparative Studies in Society and History* 44 (2002): 427, draws attention to the instability of rivers and coastlines along the Indian Ocean and the resulting lack of durability of ports and cities in the region. See also Richard Schofield, "Position, Function, and Symbol: The Shatt al-Arab Dispute in Perspective," in *Iran, Iraq, and the Legacies of War*, ed. Lawrence G. Potter and Gary G. Sick (New York: Palgrave Macmillan, 2004), 29–70.
20. Elias Boudaen, traveling from Surat to Basra in 1651, engaged five pilots in Kharg and paid them each 2 tumans with the promise of another tuman upon arrival in Basra. See NA, VOC 1180, Basra Daghregister (Diary), 14 March–14 May 1651, fol. 854v.
21. NA, VOC 1135, Geleynssen De Jongh, Gamron to Batavia, 30 March 1641, fol. 663; and VOC 1088, Boudaen, Report on Basra, 29 November 1651, fol. 538v. Manuel Godinho, *Intrepid Merchant: Manuel Godinho and His Journey from India to Portugal in 1663*, ed. John Correia-Afonso, trans. Vitalio Lobo and John Correia-Afonso (Bombay, India, 1990), 124. Pietro della Valle, traveling from Kharg to Basra in 1625, relates how the pilot of his ship couldn't find the "mouth of the river of Bassora." See Della Valle, *The Travels*, 243.
22. India Office Records (IOR), London, G/40/2, Surat to London, 2 November 1668, fol. 36.
23. Hamilton, *A New Account*, 1:51.
24. Imber, "The Navy of Sülayman the Magnificent," 60.
25. M. B. Rowton, "Urban Autonomy in a Nomadic Environment," *Journal of Near Eastern Studies* 32 (1973): 201–15.
26. For the outbreak of 1044–45/1634–35, see Muhammad Ma'sum b. Khajigi Isfahani, *Khulasat al-siyar: Tarikh-i ruzgar-i Shah Safi-yi Safavi* (Tehran, Iran: 1368/1989), 195. The epidemics in the late seventeenth century are discussed at the end of this essay.
27. Jean de Thevenot, *Travels*, 157.
28. William Thurston and Edward Pearce, Basra to Company, London, 22 June 1640, in *Armenian Merchants of the Seventeenth and Early Eighteenth Centuries: English East India Company Sources*, ed. Vahé Baladouni and Margaret Makepeace (Philadelphia, PA: 1998), 39.
29. NA, VOC 1135, Geleynssen de Jongh, Gamron to Batavia, 30 March 1641, fol. 663; William Thurston and Edward Pearce, Basra to Company, London, 22 June 1640, in *Armenian Merchants*, 39.
30. René Barendse, "Reflections on the Arabian Seas in the Eighteenth Century," *Itinerario* 25 (2001): 37.

31. Barthélemy Carré, *Le courrier du roi en Orient. Relations de deux voyages en Perse et en Inde 1668–1674*, ed. Dirk Van der Cruysse (Paris, 2005), 473. See also René J. Barendse, "The Long Road to Livorno: The Overland Messenger Services of the Dutch East India Company in the Seventeenth Century," *Itinerario* 12, no. 2 (1988): 34.
32. NA, Coll. Geleynssen de Jongh 283, Sarcerius, Basra to Geleynssen de Jongh, Bandar Abbas, 25 September 1645, fol. 159.
33. See R. J. Barendse, *The Arabian Seas: The Indian Ocean World of the Seventeenth Century* (Armonk, NY, 2002), 170.
34. For these fees in 1581, see the report by John Newbury in Samuel Purchas, *Hakluytus Posthumus or Purchas His Pilgrimes*, 12 vols. (Glasgow, UK, 1905), 8:455.
35. Dejanirah Silva-Couto, "L'expédition portugaise à Bassora en 1551," *Comptes rendus des séances de l'année 2002*, [France] Académie des Inscriptions et Belles Lettres, 479.
36. Letter of João de Meira to the King D. Manuel," in Smith, *The First Age of Portuguese Embassies*, 60.
37. Vitorino Magelhães-Godinho, *L'Economie de l'empire portugais aux XVe et XVIe siècles* (Paris, 1969), 772.
38. Ibid., 769.
39. Ibid., 769–71. That not just Aleppo but the entire region surrounding it underwent an economic upswing is reflected in the fact that the city of Aintab (modern Gaziantep) witnessed an economic recovery and saw its tax revenue increase dramatically as of the mid-1530s. See Leslie Peirce, *Morality Tales: Law and Gender in the Ottoman Court of Aintab* (Berkeley, CA, 2003), 28–30.
40. Magelhães-Godinho, *L'Economie de l'empire portugais*, 769–71.
41. In this context Rhoads Murphey draws attention to the relatively modest size of the Ottoman fleet deployed in the Indian Ocean. See his review of Palmira Brummett, *Ottoman Sea Power and Levantine Diplomacy in the Age of Discovery*, in *Bulletin of the School of Oriental and African Studies* 58 (1998): 561–63.
42. Veinstein, "Commercial Relations between India and the Ottoman Empire," 97.
43. Giancarlo Casale has recently made a strong argument for the proposition that the Ottomans did follow a concerted commercial strategy in the Red Sea, the Persian Gulf and the Arabian Sea. See his "The Ottoman Administration of the Spice Trade in the Sixteenth-Century Red Sea and Persian Gulf," *Journal of the Economic and Social History of the Orient* 49 (2006): 170–98.
44. Walter Posch, *Der Fall Alkâs Mîrzâ und der Persienfeldzug von 1548–1549* (Würzburg, Germany, 2000), 87, 350.
45. Dejanirah Potache, "The Commercial Relations between Basrah and Goa in the Sixteenth Century," *Studia* [Centro de Estudos Históricos Ultramarinos, Portugal] no. 48 (1989): 145–61.
46. G. Schurhammer, *Zeitgenössischen Quellen zur Geschichte Portugiesisch-Asien und seiner Nachbarländer zur Zeit des Hl. Franz Xaver (1538–1552)*, 2nd ed. (Rome, 1962), 230 [2524].
47. Posch, *Der Fall Alkâs Mîrzâ*, 352.
48. Salih Özbaran, "The Ottoman Turks and the Portuguese in the Persian Gulf, 1534–1581," *Journal of Asian History* 6 (1972): 68.
49. In Khoury, "Merchants and Trade," 59.
50. Nicolau de Orta Rebelo, *Un voyageur portugais en Perse au début du XVIIe siècle*, ed. Joaquim Veríssimo Serrão (Lisbon, Portugal: 1972), 142–43.
51. In João Teles e Cunha, "Armenian Merchants in Portuguese Trade Networks in the Western Indian Ocean in the early Modern Age," in *Les Arméniens dans le commerce asiatique au début de l'ère moderne/Armenians in Asian Trade in the Early Modern Era*, ed. Sushil Chaudhury and Kéram Kévonian (Paris: Éditions de la Maison des Sciences de l'homme, 2007), 197–252.
52. Salbanke, "Travels," in Purchas, *Purchas his Pilgrimages*, 1:237.
53. Anon., ed., *A Chronicle of the Carmelites in Persia and the Papal Mission of the XVIIth and XVIIIth Centuries*, 2 vols. paginated as one (London, 1939), 102–04.

54. B. J. Slot, *The Arabs of the Gulf 1602–1784* (Leidschendam, Netherlands: 1993), 99.
55. In W. Noel Sainsbury, ed., *Calendar of State Papers, Colonial Series, East Indies, China and Persia, 1625–1629* (London, 1884), 661–62; and Sir William Foster, ed., *The English Factories in India, 1624–29* (London, 1909), 324; 'Ali Pasha of Basra, to the English and Dutch Chiefs at Surat, ca. March 1629.
56. Della Valle, *Travels*, 246
57. Filippo della S. Trinita, *Viaggi Orientali* (Venice, 1670), 56.
58. For this, see Tarik Nafi Hamid, "The Political, Administrative and Economic History of Basra Province 1534–1638" (PhD diss., University of Manchester, 1980), 77–83.
59. H. Dunlop, ed., *Bronnen tot de geschiedenis der Oostindische Compagnie in Perzië, 1611–1638* (The Hague, The Netherlands: 1930), 16, 142, 158; Foster, ed., *English Factories, 1622–23*, 181, 186–87. The Dutch were explicitly enjoined by their superiors not to get involved in Safavid-Ottoman disputes. See Dunlop, ed., *Bronnen*, 158–59.
60. Merchants who wished to take their goods from Kung or Basra also had to allow the Portuguese to have a 50 percent share in the cargo. According to De Thevenot (*Suite de voyage*, 354), they collected vast sums of tribute from many places throughout the Gulf, including Bahrain, Qatif, Kung and Qishm. In Basra itself, the Portuguese agent received a daily payment from the basha. See also Dunlop, ed., *Bronnen*, 683–86.
61. For details about this episode, see Matthee, "Between Arabs, Turks and Iranians"; and Floor, *The Persian Gulf*, 545ff.
62. al-Shaikh Fath Allah b. Alwan al-Ka'bi, *Zad al-musafir wa lahnat al-muqim wa al-hadir*, ed. Ala' al-Din Fu'ad, 2nd ed. (Baghdad, 1377/1958), 18–19.
63. N. de Orta Rebelo, "Relacao da jornada que fez . . . .," in *Un voyageur portugais en Perse au début du XVIIe siècle*, ed. J. Veríssimo Serrão (Lisbon, Portugal: 1972), 143.
64. Anonymous, ed., *A Chronicle of the Carmelites*, 1135.
65. Klein, "Trade in the Safavid Port City of Bandar 'Abbas," 303–06.
66. Dunlop, ed., *Bronnen*, 786.
67. Sir William Foster, *England's Quest for Eastern Trade* (London, 1933), 313.
68. Frederick Charles Danvers, *List of Factory Records of the Late East India Company* (London, 1897), introduction, xxii.
69. NA, VOC 1141, Constant, Isfahan to Heren XVII, 16 October 1643, fol. 518.
70. Foster, ed., *English Factories 1646–50*, 44, Cranmer, Basra to London, 3 August 1646; NA, VOC 1168, Verburgh, Gamron to Batavia, 19 December 1647, fol. 775.
71. NA, VOC 1146, Constant, Gamron to Batavia, 12 February 1644, fols. 908b, 913b. Also see Willem Floor and Mohammad H. Faghfoory, *The First Dutch-Persian Commercial Conflict: The Attack on Qeshm Island, 1645* (Costa Mesa, CA, 2004).
72. NA, VOC 1146, Constant, Gamron to Batavia, 12 February 1644, fols. 902–07.
73. NA, VOC 1152, Sarcerius, Basra to Heren XVII, 6 August 1645, fols. 64–66; ibid., Sarcerius, Basra to Heren XVII, 9 January 1646, fols. 254b–55.
74. NA, Coll. Geleynssen de Jongh 286c, Sarcerius, Basra to Geleynssen de Jongh, Gamron, 25 September 1645.
75. Foster, ed., *English Factories 1646–50*, 44, Cranmer, Basra to Company, 3 August 1646; NA, VOC 1168, Verburgh, Gamron to Batavia, 19 December 1647, fol. 775.
76. NA, VOC 1188, Boudaen, Basra to Heren XVII, 16 June 1651, fol. 824.
77. NA, VOC 1146, Constant, Gamron to Batavia, 12 February 1644, fol. 908v.
78. Foster, ed., *English Factories 1646–50*, 40, Factors at Basra to Company, 13 April 1646.
79. NA, VOC 1152, Geleynssen de Jongh, Gamron to Heren XVII, 23 November 1645, fol. 212.
80. Foster, ed., *English Factories 1646–50*, 44, Cranmer, Basra to Company, 3 Aug. 1646; NA, VOC 1168, Verburgh, Gamron to Batavia, 19 December 1647, fol. 775.
81. Foster, ed., *English Factories 1646–1650*, 44, Cranmer, Basra to Company, 3 August 1646.
82. NA, VOC 1168, Verburgh, Gamron to Batavia, 28 August 1648, fol. 665.
83. NA, VOC 1180, Boudaen, Basra to Batavia, 18 August 1651, fols. 824v; ibid., Boudaen, Basra to Heren XVII, 5 October 1651, fol. 824r; and VOC 1188, Boudaen, Report on Basra, 29 November 1651, fol. 540.

84. Godinho, *Intrepid Merchant*, 124.
85. De Thevenot, *Voyages*, 4:561–62.
86. IOR, G/40/2, Surat to London, 2 November 1668, fol. 36.
87. NA, VOC 1251, Van Wyck, Gamron to Heren XVII, 6 April 1666, fol. 1330.
88. M. de Bourge, *Relation du voyage de monsigneur l'éveque de Beryte . . . par la Turquie, la Perse . . .* (Paris, 1683), 62.
89. NA, VOC 1476, Gamron, Van Leene, to Batavia, 29 April 1690, fols. 405–14.
90. The events of 1654–56 provide a good example of the sudden swings in the fortunes of merchants operating in Basra. In 1653, the resident Carmelite fathers noted how the Dutch had become dominant traders in shipping with India and Iran, so that in that year not a single English or Portuguese ship had docked in Basra. (See Anon., ed., *Chronicle of the Carmelites*, 1027, 1034, 1140.) The Dutch at this time were making serious attempts to penetrate the lucrative Basra market for textiles from Sind. Lacking sufficient shipping capacity of their own, they even made use of local vessels to transport a sizeable volume of these. Between 1654 and 1656 they thus imported 46,000 pieces. They also brought a great deal of pepper. But a combination of forces turned the venture into a disaster, with part of the merchandise lost to piracy in the Persian Gulf. (See Klein, "Trade in the Safavid Port City Bandar 'Abbas," 306–07). Although the English did not have a representative in Basra at this point, their private merchants continued to frequent its port. These were responsible for bringing in some 400,000 lbs. of pepper in 1656, as a result of which prices and profits fell dramatically. Enormous quantities of goods at competitive prices had also been supplied by indigenous merchants from Muscat, Kung, and Bandar Abbas. In addition, more than 700 packs of textiles had arrived from Sind, while twelve fully laden ships had come in from Surat. (See Foster, ed., *English Factories 1655–60*, 28; NA, VOC 1210, Basra to Heren XVII, 19 July 1656, fol. 924v; and VOC 1210, Barra, Basra to Van Gent, Surat, 11 September 1656, fol. 929; and ibid., 20 October 1656, fol. 937.)
91. This entire episode is recounted in great detail in Longrigg, *Four Centuries*, 115–17 and, more recently, in Matthee, "Between Arabs, Turks and Iranians," 68–69; and Floor, *The Persian Gulf*, 566ff.
92. Carré, *Le courrier du Roi*, 127–31; NA, VOC 1270, Goske, Gamron to Batavia, 18 June 1669, fol. 967v.; Anon., ed., *A Chronicle of the Carmelites*, 1154. For a detailed examination of this episode, see Matthee, "Between Arabs, Turks and Iranians," 70–71; and Floor, *The Persian Gulf*, 570ff.
93. Carré, *Le courrier du Roi*, 130.
94. NA, VOC 1270, Goske, Gamron to Batavia, 18 June 1669, fol. 967v.
95. Carré, *Le courrier du Roi*, 473; English trans. in Abbé Carré, *The Travels of the Abbé Carré in India and the Near East 1672 to 1674*, 3 vols. paginated as one (London, 1948), 1:90.
96. See Matthee, "Between Arabs, Turks and Iranians."
97. NA, Coll. Geleynssen de Jongh 283, Van Reythoven, Basra to Geleynssen de Jongh, Gamron, 29 October 1646, fol. 449–50.
98. NA, VOC 1379, Casembroot, Gamron to Batavia, 2 October 1681, fol. 2634.
99. NA, VOC 1425, Van Bullestraeten, Basra to Heren XVII. 26 September 1687, fol. 460v.; Ahmet Tabakoğlu, "The Economic Importance of the Gulf in the Ottoman Era," *Studies on Turkish-Arab Relations* 3 (1988): 161.
100. Coolhaas, ed., *Generale Missiven* 4, 13 March 1680, 398. One should be cautious not to extrapolate from meager trade results for the Dutch in a given season and to conclude that, therefore, overall trade was bad in Basra in the same period. There is also the issue of unreported private trade of factors. Yet, in many cases it is clear that the two coincided. Thus in 1683, the level of trade in Basra dropped again and was called "very bad" as a result of unrest by the Arabs. Dutch sales that season were minimal. They only sold 1,100 *man* of lead, 38 *bahar* of coffee, 112 sword blades, and 40 coarse pieces of cloth. See NA, VOC 1373, Van Heuvel, Gamron to Batavia, 19 April 1683, fol. 882v.
101. NA, VOC 1364, Verdonck, Basra to Heren XVII, 26 September 1681, fol. 438.
102. Coolhaas, ed., *Generale Missiven*, 4:822; 5:143.

103. NA, VOC 322, Heren XVII to Batavia, 16 November 1687, fol. 455.
104. NA, VOC 322, 16 November 1687, fol. 455b.
105. NA, VOC 1459, Van Leene, Isfahan to Heren XVII, 20 December 1690, fol. 1016r. From March 1688 to February 1689 they booked a net profit of Dfl 46,610. But the following year, March 1689–February 1690, their meager net profit of Dfl 21,287 had to be entered as a loss of Dfl 3,603 after subtracting losses in the amount of Dfl 24,194 suffered on the conversion of gold and silver currency in Malabar.
106. Abdullah, *Merchants*, 61–62.
107. François Valentyn, *Oud en nieuw Oost-Indien*, 8 books in 5 volumes (Dordrecht, The Netherlands: 1727), 5:255.
108. The occurrence of the plague in Izmir is mentioned in NA, Smyrna I, letter to States General, 12 June 1689, fol. 78. For the plague in Kirman, see IOR, G/40/4, Gladman, Gombroon to London, 25 July 1692. The Surat reference is found in AN, Coll. Colonies C2, 64, Le Sr. Roques, Suratte, 28 January 1692, fol. 26a. See also Ovington, *Voyage to Suratt*, 347.
109. This figure is given by Hamilton, *A New Account*, 1:82–3. Abbas al-Azzawi, *Tarikh al-ʿIraq bayn al-ihtilalain*, 7 vols. (Baghdad, 1954), 5:129, 131, speaks of 100,000 deaths in Baghdad in 1689 and up to 1,000 casualties a day for 1690. Other references to the plague in Basra and Khuzistan in 1691 are found in Carmelite Archives, O. C. D. 184a, *Annales de la mission de Bassorah*, 1691, fols. 54–5; NA, VOC 1476, Renshagen, Kung to Heren XVII, 19 May 1691, fol. 633a; VOC 1493, Van Leene, Isfahan to Batavia, 13 October 1691, fol. 283b; and in Rasul Ja'farian, *Ilal-i bar uftadan-i Safavian* (Tehran, 1372/1993), 331. For other cities, see [Vachet], "Journal," fols. 561–2, 574, 578.
110. MEA, vol. 348, fol. 468, report Gaudereau.
111. NA, VOC 1507, Verdonck, Gamron to Heren XVII, 16 August1692, fol. 443v.
112. NA, VOC 1507, Bout, Basra to Verdonck, Gamron, 24 February 1693, fol. 344; idem to idem, 8 March 1693, fol. 344.
113. NA, VOC 1507, Verdonck, Gamron to Batavia, 2 August 1693, fol. 466v.
114. NA, VOC 1549, Verdonck, Gamron to Batavia, 24 October 1694, fol. 609r–v.
115. NA, VOC 1571, Verdonck, Gamron to Batavia, 26 June 1695, fol. 167–68.
116. NA, VOC 1582, Verdonck, Gamron to Batavia, 15 May 1696, fol. 140–41.
117. Anon., ed., *A Chronicle of the Carmelites*, 2:1170ff.; NA, VOC 1614, Hoogcamer, Gamron to Batavia, 31 May 1700, fol. 1131vo.
118. Ibid., 1170ff. The Dutch, by contrast, in 1700 insisted that Basra's trade had declined under Iranian rule. See NA, VOC 1614, Hoogcamer, Gamron, to Batavia, 31 May 1700, fol. 1131v.
119. Hamilton, *A New Account*, 1:82–84.
120. Ashin das Gupta, *Indian Merchants and the Decline of Surat c. 1700–1750* (Wiesbaden, Germany, 1979; repr. Delhi, 1994), 136.
121. Valentijn, *Oud en nieuw Oost-Indien*, 5:277–78.
122. NA, VOC 1667, Wichelman, Gamron to Hoogcamer, Isfahan, 6 December 1701, fol. 128.
123. IOR E/3/64/7933, Surat, Instructions for W. Beavis and Joseph Goodshaw, 1 May 1702.
124. IOR E/3/64/7982, Goodshaw, Basra to Company, 27 Oct. 1702, unfol.
125. NA, VOC 1694, Wichelman, Gamron to Batavia, 20 August 1703, fol. 20; VOC 1714, Macare, Basra to Wichelman, Gamron, 28 August 1704, fol. 104; Coolhaas, ed., *Generale Missiven*, vol. 6, 1698–1713, 409; VOC 1714, Macare, Basra to Wichelman, Gamron, 10 December 1704, fol. 280.
126. NA, VOC 1714, Macare, Basra to Wichelman, Gamron, 25 January 1705, fol. 300. Macare implausibly claimed that, in former times, the city used to have a population of 250,000.
127. NA, VOC 1732, Macare, Basra to Casteleyn, Gamron, 9 November 1705, fols. 417–18.
128. NA, VOC 1714, Macare, Basra to Gamron, 25 January 1705, fols. 302–03
129. Abdullah, *Merchants*, 50, 61–62.
130. Rhoads Murphey, "On the Evolution of the Port City," in Frank Broeze, ed., *Brides of the Sea: Port Cities of Asia from the 16th–20th Centuries* (Honolulu, HI: 1989), 227.

Chapter 6

The Arab Presence on the Iranian Coast of the Persian Gulf

Shahnaz Razieh Nadjmabadi

The close relationship between the Iranian and Arab populations in coastal areas of the Persian Gulf is not a recent development or a consequence of the economic boom due to oil production in the Arab countries. Rather, it is the result of a long and partly conflict-laden history. To illustrate the forms of exchange relations between these populations, it is necessary to explore the background of the current interconnections and conditions that preceded them. This will be achieved by an analysis of the local history, as far as written sources are available and the historical memory of the population can be interrogated. History here means, in particular, settlement history: the coexistence of Iranian and Arab settlements in the Iranian coastal region, their entwinement, and their relationship with the Arab world.

A comprehensive history of settlement along the Iranian coast has not been compiled so far. The present study of the formation of the settlements in Hormuzgan, one of the three Iranian provinces on the Persian Gulf,[1] does not claim to replace this missing historiography or to give the Arab element a meaning to which it is not entitled in reality. Rather, as I conducted anthropological field research in Hormuzgan, time and again I observed references to Arab life and forms of behavior that made the closer study of Arab influences appear necessary.

The aim of the following study is to augment and offer explanations of this area's settlement history by using ethnographic data and to show that a local history of the Iranian coastal region cannot be constructed without considering its interaction with the Arab countries on the Persian Gulf. At the same time, a position is taken that opposes a hegemonic Iranian or Arab historiography, which for ideological/political reasons grants a meaning either to the Iranian or to the Arab element that is not appropriate and "arabizes" or "iranizes" the population and culture. This paper aims to demonstrate that in a multiethnic state such as Iran, despite a dominant national culture and language, there cannot exist only one homogeneous historiography.

As far as the relationship between history and anthropology is concerned, I agree with the Comaroffs that "there ought to be no 'relationship' between history and anthropology, since there should be no division to begin with. A theory of society which is not also a theory of history, or *vice versa,* is hardly a theory at all."[2] Dealing with historiography, anthropologists are concerned with the process of construction (reconstruction) of reality. For them, the smallest community has got its own historicity, and their efforts are oriented to understanding the different forms of historical consciousness in this context. Since written documents are missing in most cases where anthropologists conduct research, they construct their own archives. "They work both in and outside the official record, both with and beyond the guardians of memory in the societies they study."[3]

The area of research, Gavbandi, is administratively one of the subprovinces *(shahristan)* of the province of Hormuzgan. Gavbandi encompasses fifty-four settlements, with a majority Sunni population (in 2006) of 37,400 persons in 8,000 households. About twelve villages are inhabited by a purely Arabic-speaking population. Among them, as well as in Persian-speaking areas, one can observe in everyday life (food, clothes, festivities, birth, marriage, and funeral ceremonies, etc.) events and practices that are designated as "Arab" but not as "alien." Interaction with neighbors in the Arab countries is mainly through work migration (80%) and local trade (approximately 10%), with the remainder involved in agriculture and other activities. The Iranian coastal dwellers always emphasize their togetherness and solidarity—*"Anha ham az khodemanand"* (they also belong to us)—and loyalty to their neighbors on the other side of the Persian Gulf.

In the depiction below, I first analyze whether and in what way the presence of the Arab population in Hormuzgan and their integration into existing social systems is recognized in written sources, and what information about the nature of this presence we can infer from these records. In order to sketch the historical account of the events as completely as possible, interviews were conducted with women and men who volunteered their knowledge about the settlement history of the region. Documents in written and oral form—such as essays and texts written by young people, teachers, or people with an interest in their own local history, as well as poems, spoken verses, and songs with reference to the past—were collected and evaluated.[4]

In the Western as well as in the Persian written sources, questions concerning the population and way of life in the coastal area of the Persian Gulf are to a large extent neglected, while ethnographical/historical records are completely missing. The information about single regions and their populations differ greatly: we have, for instance, rich material about the Banu Ka'b, who settled in Khuzistan, and the Qawasim, who had their domain primarily in Bandar Lingeh,[5] while, on the other hand, data about smaller tribally organized groups in the coastal region are lacking.[6]

The European sources concentrate on geopolitical and economic aspects and their own political-military role in the Persian Gulf. They examine to what extent local and state measures and changes in the respective countries endanger Western interests. In these sources the population receives little attention. Regarding the Persian sources, we have to point out the ambivalence with which the topic of the Arab presence on the Iranian coast is addressed. While older Persian sources mention the coexistence of Arab and Persian villages and populations,[7] newer publications—if the population in the Gulf region is mentioned at all—try to represent any Arab influence as minimal.[8] Hegemony in this sense is part of a dominant ideology. The modern Persian sources about the history of the Persian Gulf primarily deal with the presence and the influence of foreign powers, the Portuguese, Dutch, and English, while they pay little attention to local Iranian developments.

On the whole the written sources do not contain concrete information about the form, structure and organization of the Arab communities in the Iranian coastal region. Here only that literature in which the presence of the Arab population is noted (if at all) was considered, from the rich and various material about the historical development of the Persian Gulf. Beyond that, the search was guided by the aim of evaluating, aside from the well-known and established classical European writers, such as Carsten Niebuhr, George Curzon, John Lorimer, and Arnold Wilson[9], appropriate literature in Persian. I assume that further documents and archival material exist that still elude my knowledge. In this respect, the sources on the subject are not yet complete and this study represents a first attempt to present the problem coherently.

The sources mentioned were examined to illuminate the following aspects:

- Proof of the presence of Arab populations in the Iranian coastal province of Hormuzgan
- Reasons and motives that led to the settlement of the Arab groups in the Iranian coastal region
- Form and process of the settlement
- Completion of the inflow of Arab populations into the Iranian coastal region

THE PRESENCE OF ARAB POPULATIONS IN THE IRANIAN COASTAL PROVINCE OF HORMUZGAN

As documented in numerous written sources, we can assume that, in the pre-Islamic period, intensive exchange relations existed between the populations on both sides of the Persian Gulf[10] and the Iranian coast was already inhabited by Arab groups in Sasanian times (224–651 A.D.). However, only from the early to the middle of the eighteenth century is it possible to recognize a systematic settlement of Arab tribes on the Iranian coast between Kangan and Bandar Lingeh, which was terminated with the assumption of power by Reza Shah in the 1920s. I will, therefore, start my historical analysis in the mid-eighteenth century.

As one of the first travelers to the Persian Gulf and one who drew maps of the area on the basis of his own observations, Niebuhr states that the eastern bank (by which he means the Iranian coast) was the most densely populated, and that it was on this side where the most islands were located, which *belonged to* Arab groups that had lived there for centuries.[11] F. Warden offers a complete list of the Iranian ports, which shows that the tribal chiefs (*shaikh,* pl. *shuyukh*) reigning at the ports were of Arab descent and that the ports carried Arab names.[12] In the second half of the nineteenth century, Lewis Pelly and Curzon confirmed the presence of an Arab population in Bandar Lingeh. Besides the Africans living there, Pelly observed that the wealth of Bandar Lingeh was in the hands of the group that he designates as "Persianised Arabs."[13] Curzon also seems impressed by the ethnic variety there, regarding this however as a typical feature of maritime towns east of Port Sa'id (Egypt).[14] In the *Persian Gulf Historical Summaries* it is even doubted whether there were Iranian populations at all in the coastal region, and the authority of the Iranian government vis-à-vis the Arab population seemed questionable.[15] At the beginning of the nineteenth century, Morier visited the Iranian coast and stresses likewise the independence and sovereignty of the Arab tribal chiefs.[16] Finally Thomas Miller Ricks, who investigated trade relations in southern Iran in the eighteenth century, concludes that at the end of that century the trade in the south lay in the hands of Arabs. He also includes a listing of the ports and the influential and dominant Arab *shuyukh* there.[17]

Among the Persian sources that refer to the Arab presence, the work of Ahmad Iqtidari has to be mentioned above all.[18] As a historian and archaeologist he is concerned with the history of the Persian Gulf in detail. In general, he criticizes Western and Arab sources in which, he maintains, the history of this area was time and again manipulated to the disadvantage of Iran. For example, he refers to the Arabization of geographical names (thus Gavbandi becomes Qavbandi)[19] and to the changes in the genealogies of Iranian families in order to prove their Arab descent. Arab historians and chroniclers did not even flinch from translating the title of a work as well known as Lord Curzon's *Persia and the Persian Question* into *"al-Khalij al-'Arabi"* (The Arab Gulf). He accuses Western sources of a lack of neutrality and finds their self-interest responsible for misrepresentations. Like Ricks, he especially criticizes the data of Lorimer.[20] Finally, Iqtidari insists on the view that for 3,000 years and up to the arrival of European powers in the Persian Gulf, Iranians and their inventiveness were decisive. It was they who founded the first cities there and established the basis for the social order. Only because the language of the groups living there was Arabic were they also called *arab* in written sources. However, all of them, including Banu Ka'b, Hamadi, Nasuri, Bani Abasian, Ubaidili, Al-i Ali, Mubarak, and Ra'isi were Iranians or had been "persianized." Their descendants were Iranians, and their language, songs, music, and customs were always Persian. Finally, he argues that even if we assume that Arab families from Najd (eastern Arabia) sought refuge in Iran, they came at the earliest 500 years ago, which means since the Safavid period, and thus were no longer *Arab*, but had become *Irani*.[21]

Other Persian sources, however, speak of Arab populations in the coastal region whose settlement is also dated from the beginning to the middle of the eighteenth century. Anjum-Ruz dates the beginning of systematic Arab immigration to the time of Sultan Husain Safavi (1694–1722) and Nadir Shah (1736–1747).[22] Husain Nurbakhsh assumes that the Arab tribes came here at the time of the Qajars (1796–1925) from Ras al-Khaimah, Sharjah, Abu Dhabi, Bahrain and Qatar at the request of the shuyukh of the Qawasim that had already settled in Lingeh. From here, they and their descendants spread in different directions, and until 1315/1936, they held hegemony over the Iranian coast.[23] M. A. Muvahhid also refers to the Qawasim, who had, after the death of Nadir Shah in 1747, time and again tried to settle on the Iranian coast.[24] Only in 1779 did they succeed in coming to terms with the Iranian state and assume supremacy over the city of Lingeh. The Iranian government installed one shaikh of the Qawasim as *farmandar* (commander) of Bandar Lingeh, so that starting from this time and for the following hundred years, that is, until 1887, the governance of Lingeh lay in the hands of Arab shuyukh. The islands of Abu Musa, the Tunbs, and Sirri belonged likewise to their domain.[25]

The origin of the Arab population is attributed to completely different regions in the written sources. Indeed, here we are not dealing with a finite group that reached the Iranian coast together at a certain time. It has to be assumed that immigration to the Iranian coastal region took place from different areas, at different times, and under various conditions. Pelly and Curzon, who agree about the origin of the Arab tribes, refer however only to the Qawasim.[26] Gustave Demorgny attributes the origin of all Arab groups living on the coast to Najd, Oman and Yemen.[27] Likewise, Henry Field assumes that the Arab groups in Khuzistan were brought there by Shah Isma'il (1501–24) from Najd.[28] Roger Savory attributes the regional destabilization in southwestern Iran in the seventeenth and eighteenth century to the large-scale movement of the Arab tribes to this area, which he also identifies as coming from Najd.[29]

Reasons and Motivations for the Arab Settlement

The majority of the sources mention the weakness of the Iranian government in general, particularly during the reign of the Zand dynasty (1750–1797) as a cause for the systematic and continuous settlement of the Arab tribes on the Iranian coast. On the one hand, the political turbulence in the region, caused by the presence of foreign powers, raids and attacks by "pirates" of different origins on the Iranian coast and internal conflicts, led to an unstable situation in the coastal cities and villages. The Iranian central government, unable to provide the local population the necessary protection, was dependent on support from Arab tribes. On the other hand, the favorable situation of the Iranian commercial ports and the possibility of collecting duties, and thus obtaining high income, lured the Arab tribes to settle there.

Ricks points to the internal conflicts at the time of the Zand dynasty and interprets the lack of interest of the Iranian central government as "leaving the Gulf to its own devices."[30] Hawley is of the opinion that the Qawasim had already come to the Iranian coast in 1717.[31] However, they only gained a foothold there after the assassination of Nadir Shah in 1747, a time of chaotic conditions that persisted until 1757. Karim Khan, who, contrary to Nadir Shah, was very Arab friendly, supported the settlement of the Qawasim on the Iranian coast in the second half of the eighteenth century and fought with their assistance for the preservation of his power.

Persian sources differentiate more strongly between the areas of origin of the different tribes. Thus, it is said that in 1154/1775 a raid from Suhar and Muscat occurred on Qishm and Bandar Abbas. A number of Arab Bedouins, coming from Arabia, had established themselves in Oman and from there had attacked merchant vessels and also Qishm and Lingeh.[32] Sadid al-Saltana calls all inhabitants of the coastal region Arab, meaning that they came from Oman.[33] Nurbakhsh refers only to the Qawasim living in Lingeh and attributes their place of origin to today's UAE. They immigrated first to the island of Qishm and then to the Iranian coastal region.[34] Only Muvahhid states that the origin of the Qawasim cannot be resolved definitely.[35] Some assume that they migrated in the first century after the Hijra of the Prophet (i.e., in the eighth century) from Najd to Oman, while others hold the opinion that they originally resided on the Iranian side in Siraf (Tahiri) and after its destruction resettled in Muscat and Ras al-Khaimah. In this fact they see the reason that these tribes were still called Bani Siraf for a long time. The Qawasim themselves maintain that they came from the Iranian coast.

In the Persian sources the weakness of the central government is likewise seen as decisive for Arab settlement.[36] Ahmad Faramarzi stresses the Arab-friendly attitude of Karim Khan and believes that he was preoccupied with internal conflicts and thus lost control of the area.[37] Abbas Anjum-Ruz holds the view that the first Arab settlers came here at the time of internal political chaos under Sultan Husain Safavi and Nadir Shah to settle in the region only temporarily, to use the pasture land and engage in agriculture. Owing to the weak central government at the time of the Qajars (1796–1925), local Arab centers of power came into existence. They won more and more influence in relation to the Iranian state, and their leaders called themselves shaikh and amir.[38]

FORM AND PROCESS OF SETTLEMENT

From written documents it can be concluded that the Iranian central government and the Arab chiefs, the shuyukh, had a contractual relationship. For the payment of a lease, the shuyukh received the right to collect duties from the population on all sources of income (such as pearl fishery, agriculture, cattle breeding, and fishery), to determine the amount of taxes, and to freely dispose of the tax revenue. In return they committed themselves to protecting the population of the coastal region against attacks from outside and regularly paid taxes *(maliat)* to the Iranian state. To be able to contract this tenancy, the shuyukh had to become Iranian citizens.[39] With the conclusion of the contract, the shuyukh were declared the avowed "subjects" of the Iranian state and defined themselves as *"nowkar-e dowlat-e Iran"* (*standing* in the service of the Iranian state). After the termination of the contract, the *shuyukh* were permitted to remain in Iran.

With smaller tribal federations, no firm contracts were entered into. Numerous sources describe the lease system between the shuyukh and the Iranian government.[40] Detailed data about the amount and form of the taxes that had to be paid by the coastal dwellers to the Arab shuyukh are offered by Curzon, Pelly, and Warden.[41] Pelly presents a very exact list of the different leases and classifies them depending on the allocation of the estates and the payment of duties.[42]

Even more precise data about the lease system are given in the Persian sources.[43] They inform us comprehensively about the amount and form of tribute in the whole region, including the common fiscal system. The term that is normally used for this form of lease in the Persian language is *mal al-ijara* or *ijara*.[44] The *Farsnama-yi Nasiri* and *Tarikh-i Jahangiriya* state the conditions for the leases with the Qawasim.[45]

From the above, it can be concluded that the Arab shuyukh settled on the Iranian coast with the agreement of the Iranian government. The resident local population had no choice other than to accept their presence. The Iranian government used the Arab population as a kind of protective barrier against attacks by Arab groups from the other side of the Persian Gulf as well as against other encroachments on its coastal region. The fact that the Arab shuyukh became Iranian citizens can be regarded as a reason why Persian sources rarely speak explicitly about Arabs. In the same way one has to understand Iqtidari who— as mentioned above—speaks about the originally Arab population as "Irani" and holds the view that only owing to their language were they designated as "Arab." We may surely assume a mutual interdependence between the Iranian state administrative machinery and the Arab shuyukh. The Iranian authorities *(vali, hakim)* kept the shuyukh under control by binding them through the system of duties. Resistance and breach of contract could lead to withdrawal from power. This nevertheless did not prevent the Arab shuyukh from overstepping their limits or competence, time and again, to claim more land, collect more taxes, and thus gain influence and even declare their independence and autonomy in relation to the central government. The fact that the interdependence between the Iranian state and the Arab tribes is reflected in the bestowal of land in fief, honors, and titles in exchange for military protection is documented by Ricks.[46]

Questions important from an anthropological point of view—such as form, content, and quality of the exercise of power by the shuyukh, the organization and structure of their power hierarchy and their disposal and the structure of the coexistence of the Iranian/Arab groups—are not treated in the written sources. From the limited data, we may assume that power was passed on by patrilineal descent. Kelly, however, refers to the possibility of being elected as a shaikh by the tribe members.[47] In any case, the cooperation and consent of the tribe members were needed to exercise power.[48]

About the position and sphere of influence of the shuyukh, Muvahhid says that they sometimes were *hakim* and *nayib al-hukama* (their deputies), and occasionally they paid *maliat* (taxes) directly to the vali (governor) of Fars or to the hakim of Bushehr.[49] Local military conflicts, in which Arab tribal chiefs as well as Iranian local governors tried time and again to gain economic and political power, find a central place in most of the European records.[50]

The Persian sources create the impression that the history of the Iranian southern provinces is a history of military conflicts. They address these conflicts at length and provide detailed information, such as when and where assaults occurred and which groups challenged one another. However, these sources contain neither the exact information about the goal and strategy nor the details about the consequences of these conflicts. Aside from providing a listing of the heroic deeds of individual rulers, they are unsystematic and not very enlightening. It can be gleaned that the population was repeatedly forced to leave their villages and settlements to find peace and refuge in other regions, at least temporarily.[51]

End of the Arab Settlement Process

Curzon mentions that already in 1887 the supremacy of the shaikh of Bandar Lingeh was brought to an end.[52] Although Jinab recognizes the banishment of the Arab shuyukh from Lingeh and explains that they were replaced with Iranian civil servants, he points out that this victory was only relative and that the Arab influence was not completely eliminated.[53] As to the end of the Qawasim, Muvahhid, like Curzon, reports that a certain Shaikh Katib reigned until 1887 in Lingeh, at which time he had to undergo an interrogation by Iranian officials and thereupon was sent to Tehran.[54] About his fate we do not get any further information. None of the sources that I consulted offer a satisfactory explanation of the process of the end of the Arab supremacy in the coastal province of Hormuzgan or deal with the alterations that this change of power had for the population in the economic and social sphere.

The end of Arab settlement in the Iranian coastal region has to be seen in the larger context of the reforms implemented under Reza Shah (1925–1941). His efforts to strengthen the central power required administrative and political restructuring, which led to the weakening and reduction of local political rulers throughout the country. Starting with the years 1936–37, a mass emigration of an Arab as well as an Iranian population from the Iranian coastal region to the Arab countries on the other side of the Persian Gulf occurred, which was surely due to the nationalization of commerce under Reza Shah (*inhisar-i tijarat,* 1933–35). The new restrictions, as well as the obligation to replace the traditional clothes of men and women for European ones and for women to unveil (*kashf-i hijab*, 1936), was a retrenchment in everyday life of the local population that led many to decide to abandon the Iranian coast and shift their commercial activities to the Arab countries. [55]

Overview

In summary, the few written sources give us the following picture: the arrival of foreign powers (Portuguese, Dutch, and English) in the Persian Gulf promoted, on the one hand, the development of international trade, while on the other hand the Iranian coastline was exposed to threatening assaults, raids, and spreading piracy. The central government, weakened by internal conflicts, was unable to protect the population of the southern provinces against attacks from outside during the reign of the Zand dynasty. In an effort to strengthen its power and not lose its influence completely in the region, the Iranian government agreed to a contractual relationship with the Arab chiefs of tribes that originated in today's Saudi Arabia, Oman, and UAE. Starting from the middle of the eighteenth century, we can speak of a continuous, systematic Arab settlement in the Iranian coastal provinces of the Persian Gulf.

For the annual payment of a tax lease to the local Iranian administration (mostly to the responsible provincial governors), land was relinquished to the shuyukh for settlement. They received the right to levy taxes on all sources of income of the population and to collect duties on trade. A certain portion of these taxes (maliat) had to be paid annually to the Iranian state. The form of the contractual relationship and the amount of the taxes differed from region to region. To be able to conclude this contractual relationship, the shuyukh were obliged to accept Iranian nationality and serve the Iranian central government. In this way they took over the power and control of a limited region within a restricted time frame and under conditions prescribed by the Iranian government. The Iranian state needed military/strategic support to secure its power and the Arab chiefs of tribes and their followers benefited from the income of the Iranian coastal towns. As long as the shuyukh abided by the agreements with national and local Iranian administrative organs and showed no resistance, no limits were set to their arbitrariness in relation to the population. In each case with the retreat from the Iranian coastal region of the Arab shuyukh, who were particularly influential in commerce, capital also moved away from the region. Once flourishing cities, such as Bushehr, Bandar Lingeh, and Kung lost their importance and became completely impoverished.

Arab Settlement in Gavbandi

We do not learn from the written sources what precisely the relationship between the Arab shuyukh and their followers and the Iranian rulers was like, to what extent the Arab settlers partook in the existing local social organization and dominant structures, and which power hierarchies developed. How did they deal with the existing traditional political structures they found? Was there permanent cooperation between Iranian and Arab groups, or were there separate tasks and responsibilities for each group?

Questions that remain unresolved in the written sources can be partly answered by the case study of Gavbandi, a subprovince of the province of Hormuzgan. As sources I use on the one hand an Arabic chronicle, which is available to me in Persian translation, Abd al-Razzaq Muhammad Siddiq's *Sahwa al-faris: fi tarikh al-Arab al-Fars*,[56] and the results of my empirical inquiry. Gavbandi belonged until 1945 variously to the provinces of Laristan, Bastak, and Shibkuh. All three regions were considered during a search of the literature. Gavbandi is mentioned time and again in Western sources, yet they do not offer any detailed references that could shed light on the form of leadership of the Arab shuyukh and the characteristics of the population.[57] The chronicle of Sadiq, specified above, first deals with the conditions of the exercise of power by the Arab shuyukh, followed by a description of their relationship with the Iranian administrative authorities and provincial governors. Referring to the leading position of the shuyukh, it is said that they must dispose of the following characteristics to take over the leadership of a tribe *(qabila*, pl. *qaba'il): nisbat-i khuni* (blood relationship, genealogy, descent), *maqam* (esteem, prestige) or some "Arabic" attributes such as *shaja'at* (courage), and *bakhshandagi* (generosity). Every *farmanrava* (commander) lived in a region with his own and a friendly *qabila*. The leaders were subordinate to the constant control of the Iranian central government; their claim to power was limited and not meant to contradict the representatives of the central government. The relationship among the tribes was defined by contracts and agreements that the leaders concluded with one another and in which they pledged mutual assistance and support in case of war and other disputes.[58] At the same time, they competed with one another for supremacy in their respective regions. Frequent causes for martial conflicts were the disposition of land and villages and disagreement about the amount and form of payment of taxes and duties. Not only were these disputes over land and taxes reasons for military conflicts, but also there were old, longtime enmities reaching back to the time when the tribes still lived in their Arab places of origin. Occasionally their conflicts became so violent that even the Iranian central government had to intervene.

Regarding the Arab tribes that settled in Gavbandi, the chronicle further says that the southern region, known as Shibkuh, was inhabited by different Arab qaba'il that had their own *ru'asa* (leaders) and shuyukh.[59]

Group 1: Bani Hamad, Al-i Haram, al-Maraziq, and bin Beshr
Group 2: Ubaidal, Bani Khalid, Al-i Nasurin, and Al-i Ali

Between these groups, a fundamental competition existed for leadership of the region, which was expressed in the form of military conflicts. Due to alliances and mutual obligations, however, every qabila had to come to the aid of an allied qabila in case of an attack by an enemy. Since the line of the Nasuri is the most influential among the four Arab tribes mentioned in Group 2, in the following paragraphs, the history of this family will be recounted in an abbreviated form, as it is set down in the chronicle of Sadiq.

Around the beginning of the eighteenth century (the time cannot be specified exactly), the al-Nasuri came from Najd (Arabia) and settled first in Kalatu, east of Bushehr. After the death of their first leader, Bin Khalid bin Muhanna, it was Banu Khalid Khawl bin Mansur, called Yasir, who took over the leadership. Since in this region there were not sufficient pasturelands for their camel and sheep herds and the rainfall was low, the qabila demanded that their leader find another place of settlement.[60] Bin Mansur led his people from Kalatu to the interior of the region, to a place called Bambariya, approximately 5 kilometers south of today's Gavbandi. There the qabila split: one group went to the region and city of Tahiri and the other one remained in Gavbandi and the neighboring territory, Shibkuh.

At that time, Gavbandi was under the leadership of the Al-i Haram and Bani Tamim. When Yasir settled in this region, the number of his herds and followers increased.[61] All subordinates of Shaikh Yasir bin Mansur were known as the *Al-i Nasurin*. Yasir died in 1132/1719–20 and his son Shaikh Jabbara took over the leadership. He became so powerful that in 1136/1723–24 he even occupied Bahrain. However, in 1150/1737–38 Bahrain was taken by the Iranian government and Shaikh Jabbara was sent back to the village of Bambariya where he lived till his death in 1187/1773–74. The leadership was passed on to his son Hatam, who selected Gavbandi as his central seat of government. He and his eldest son, Jabbara, time and again opposed the demands of the Iranian central government and its officials. Jabbara supported above all the efforts of the Arab tribes that demanded their autonomy from the Iranian central government. During his reign, prosperity prevailed in Gavbandi *("ne'mat ziyad bud")*, security was ensured, and all inhabitants lived in peace.[62] Shaikh Jabbara ruled until 1266/1849–50, when he died and was buried in Gavbandi.

After his death his son Mazkur decided together with his allies to detach the region of Shibkuh from the supremacy of the Iranian central government and declare its autonomy and independence. They coined their own money, refused to pay taxes, opposed the orders of the khans of Bastak, and in 1297/1879–80 proclaimed the independence of the region. After this declaration, the commander in chief of Shiraz issued the order to arrest Shaikh Mazkur and bring him to Shiraz. When Shaikh Mazkur heard about this, he immediately fled and entrenched himself on a mountain, Shahin Kuh, known as Kalat-i Surkh (7 kilometers south of today's city of Gavbandi). The soldiers lay siege to Kalat-i Surkh, which lasted six months; many soldiers and men on the side of the state were killed. Finally Shaikh Mazkur and his followers were deceived, imprisoned, and brought to Shiraz. There the shaikh was hanged in the year 1297/1879–80.[63] Following the execution of Mazkur, his three sons disappeared. However three years later Shaikh Hasan, the eldest son, secretly returned from Bahrain, and through the intermediation of the khans of Bastak, was again made commander. After he was killed in 1335/1916–17 by one of his closest collaborators his son Mazkur became the last hakim of Gavbandi.

In 1349/1930–31 (after the seizure of power by Reza Shah), the khan of Bastak received the order from the Iranian central government to bring all shuyukh of the Arab qaba'il to Tehran. Upon his arrival, Shaikh Mazkur b Hasan was sent to prison, where he died in 1350/1931–32 after drinking either poisoned water or wine.[64]

DISTRIBUTION OF POWER BETWEEN NASURI AND RA'ISI

In the chronicle of Sadiq, the relationship between the house of Nasuri and the local political leadership already present in Gavbandi before them is not mentioned. However, the data collected in the field showed that at the same time and parallel to the exercise of power by the Nasuri, local political leadership existed, namely the house of the Ra'isi. In the following, I will attempt to represent and distinguish the spheres of control of the Nasuri and Ra'isi, as it was revealed in interviews with members of the Nasuri and Ra'isi families and individuals from Gavbandi versed in its history. [65]

According to those accounts, before the settlement of the Arab tribes, the Iranian coastal region was neglected and insignificant. The lack of habitat, the poor quality of life on the small islands and conflicts between the tribes are mentioned as motives for the Arab groups to settle on the Iranian coastline. Here they found uninhabited areas and sufficient pasturelands for their herds. After the settlement of the Arab tribes, the coastal region experienced a remarkable development, so that inland groups from Lamird, Minab, and Rudbar looked here for refuge due to years of drought in those areas. These immigrant Iranian groups accepted the language, way of life, and habits of the Arab settlers and were arabized in this way. Before the Arab tribes settled in Gavbandi, the local political leadership lay in the hands of the Ra'isi family. (*Ra'is* (pl. *ru'asa*)) was a title, which designated political leaders in Iran.) The line of the Ra'isi came from the village of Fumistan, 3 kilometers from the central place of this region, Bardul, which later became the city of Gavbandi.

The Ra'isi owned large estates, and until the arrival of the Nasuri in Gavbandi they held the position of *kadkhuda* (village chief) and were responsible for the collection of the taxes in natural produce. In return for the levied duties, the ru'asa like the kadkhuda in all other regions of Iran were obliged to mediate between the population and the civil authorities.

When the Nasuri settled in Gavbandi, they divided power with the Ra'isi. The Nasuri concentrated on the collection of taxes on imported goods and duties that were paid in different forms. The population was obligated to pay one-tenth duty on all agricultural products and animals (cattle, goats, cows, and chickens and their products, such as animal fat) as well as pearl fishery. A member of the Ra'isi family, Muhammad Salih, was assigned by the Nasuri to levy taxes from the population and send them to the governors in Bastak or Lar, to which Gavbandi belonged administratively until around 1930.[66] The Nasuri, like other local leaders, were obliged to provide military troops as requested by the Iranian government, in which case the Arab settlers as well as the Iranians were called upon equally.

For their services the Ra'isi were released from taxes, and during the absence of the Nasuri they acted as their deputies. The relationship between Nasuri and Ra'isi was not only occasionally conflict-laden but also shaped by close cooperation. At times of distress, however, they always held together. Time and again it was confirmed that the Ra'isi family was never under the control of the Nasuri: they were not their subordinates, but nearly equal. Some members of the Ra'isi family were especially popular and respected among the population, since they stood up for their interests and protected them against exploitation. The last politically influential leader from the line of the Ra'isi was Ra'is Mubarak (d.1980). He lost his life in an accident, but lives on in the memory of the population as a broad-minded, generous and courageous political leader.

According to the accounts of the population, the supremacy of the Arab shuyukh ended with the seizure of power by Reza Shah (around 1925), when about 2,000 soldiers were sent to Gavbandi in order to arrest all shuyukh of the region and bring them to Tehran. The last shaikh in power, Mazkur, was captured in 1930 and brought to Tehran, where he died in prison. Some years later, a law was enacted according to which a *shawra-yi namayandagi-yi bakhsh* (district council) was founded in rural areas. All inhabitants of the district and villages were called to elect a representative. Both the son of the last executed Nasuri, Yasir, as well as Ra'is Mubarak took part in the elections. Ra'is Mubarak received the majority of votes, and remained kadkhuda (mayor).

In oral representation, the presence of the Arab shuyukh is judged and recounted differently. There was no control, and the population was exposed to the arbitrariness of the rulers. They did not possess legal means to defend themselves against exploitation and violence; their only option was to migrate from one place to another with the hope of being exposed to less exploitation elsewhere. There are, however, other voices that hold the opinion that the Arab shuyukh advanced social and economic development by pleading for the establishment of a school and educational system. All agree that with the seizure of power by Reza Shah, law and order returned to this region.

Up to the Islamic revolution in 1979, many descendants and families of the shuyukh still lived in Gavbandi. However, the restriction on the flow of trade, the closure of customs facilities and a decline of other possibilities to earn income as well as the outbreak of the Iran-Iraq War, compulsory military service for young men, the loss of many rights for the Sunni majority living in this region,[67] and last but not least the efforts of the UAE to recruit the Iranian coast dwellers for thinly settled regions in that country[68] again gave rise to a massive migration to the Arab Gulf states. There they immigrated as qabila (tribes) and were accepted as natives, although most of them had broken off their relationship with the Arab world. The descendants of the Nasuri decided to stay in Gavbandi. In order to strengthen and maintain their power, they had taken women from the *khavanin-i galladar* (a rich and powerful Iranian group in the area) and a number of them even converted to the Shiite faith. Their children received their education in Iran, spoke the Persian language fluently, and were thus more integrated into Iranian society and culture than many of their neighboring Arab tribes. Today some of their descendants live in Gavbandi and are respected as members of the Nasuri family, without any political claim or influence.

Summary and Conclusion

Drawing from the written sources on Arab settlement in the province of Hormuzgan, I have tried to point out that the Arab tribes, under the guidance of their political leaders, the shuyukh, settled in the Iranian coastal region with the approval of the local Iranian authorities. The oral recollections in Gavbandi and the written chronicle of Sadiq show that the shuyukh arranged a treaty with the local administration and settled there peacefully, acknowledging their dependence on the Iranian central government. Those that had attendants and loyal followers were often tempted to declare their autonomy and independence from the Iranian state. But as soon as one of the shuyukh became too powerful, the extension of the lease was refused or the entire administrative machinery was mobilized against him.

Empirical questioning has shown that, as far back as the memory of the population goes, Arab groups have lived in this area and are regarded as an integral component of the population. Regarding the power, influence, and effects of the Arabs on the Iranian coast, the people referred with enthusiasm to the military conflicts between the various tribes and recounted the heroic acts of individual leaders. Concerning the relationship of the shuyukh with the population, usually the people were exposed to their exploitative suppression, and the only way to avoid their arbitrariness was to leave and look for refuge in another place in the region. However, in another place and under the rule of another shaikh, they could not be sure of having a kinder fate. Incidentally, this repellent view of the Arab supremacy is held by the Iranian as well as Arab groups. The latter were not privileged because of their Arab descent and were exposed to the same mechanisms of suppression as the Iranian groups. There are only a few voices in Gavbandi that connect a positive memory with the exercise of power by individual shaikhs.

The ending of the rule of the shuyukh around 1930 by Reza Shah, who deprived the local rulers (khan, shaikh, hakim) of their power and had many of the influential chiefs executed, meant salvation from the yoke of suppression and exploitation for most inhabitants of Gavbandi. However, particularly due to the nationalization of trade, which lay in the hands of wealthy Arab shuyukh, the latter were induced to leave the Iranian coast and shift their commercial centers to Arab countries, including Kuwait and the UAE. With their departure, capital was also removed from this region and some once-flourishing cities, such as Bushehr, Bandar Lingeh, and Kung, were exposed to a process of impoverishment that still continues today. The partly forced emigration from Iran toward the Arab countries, particularly after the Islamic revolution in 1979, resulted in the enlargement of the Iranian community in the Arab countries and the intensification of the interaction between the Iranian/Arab populations on both sides of the Persian Gulf. The recording of the settlement history also proves that Arabic-speaking populations living today in Gavbandi are descendants of those Arab tribes that settled in the Iranian coastal region during the eighteenth century and decided to stay in Iran. They are Iranian citizens, their language is Arabic yet they still maintain intensive relations with their relatives, who in part migrated back to the Arab countries of the Persian Gulf. The human as well as material network of relations that developed in this way should be taken as the basis and starting point for all future research that deals with processes of social change and cultural and material transformations in this region.

Despite a past full of conflict and numerous migrations, neither the Arab nor the Iranian population of Gavbandi feels the pressure for legitimation to justify their right to be present in this region. While we are not offered a homogeneous settlement history, we are confronted neither with a double voice nor with a contradictory representation by different groups. Disagreement exists only in the question of whether the first settlers in the region, the "first comers," were of Arab or Iranian origin. The ambiguity stems from the fact that, as pointed out earlier, individual groups that immigrated to this area did not stay in one place, but changed their locality again and again and occasionally returned to the first place of their settlement after a long absence. For example, Arab groups in Gavbandi, when asked about their place of origin, always named the first station of their immigration in Iran. Only in a second step was the answer *"asl-e asl-e ma az . . . hast"* ("our origin is . . . ") and the Arab place was designated so far as it was known.

The question of whether the population was "Iranized" or "Arabized" is only asked by an observer coming from outside, in my case as an anthropologist. Not without self-confidence, the answer is—and this is only understandable in light of the settlement history—"When we are there [in the Arab countries], we are Arabs, when we are here [Iran], then we are Iranians."[69] With this statement, they describe their behavior as adapted to the respective locality. It does not escape their notice that the view from outside is the opposite: in Iran, seen from the interior, the Iranian coast dwellers in everyday usage are called Arab, on the one hand, because the Arabic language is still widely used among them, while the affiliation of the majority to Sunni Islam brings them closer to Arab culture and identity. Conversely, the coastal population refers to the inland people as "Ajam," a term used mainly by Sunnis to denote Shiite affiliation.

In the Arab countries, according to my interviewees, they are considered as *hawli* (lit. those moving back and forth, travellers) or "Irani." These variational self and external attributions are lived as a life experience without conflict, as long as no pressure is exerted on them from outside to decide on one identity. This happened for example after the Islamic revolution: to avow oneself a Sunni or Shi'i potentially means to accept disadvantages or to benefit from certain privileges respectively. Elsewhere, I have written about the distinction between "Arab" and "Ajam" in Gavbandi.[70]

It is useful to outline the various axes of differentiation among Iranians resident in the Arab states. According to my interviewees, the Arab population in Qatar and the UAE have their own way of differentiating between Iranians coming from the coastal regions (between Bandar Lingeh and Bandar Abbas) and those coming from other areas of Iran such as Isfahan and Shiraz. The migrants from the coastal regions, whether they are Arabic or Persian speakers, are referred to as "Faris" or "Hawli" by the Arabs. The usage of "Hawli" in the Arab countries designates mainly those groups of Arab origin who once had left their home countries to settle in Iran and now have returned to the Arab countries.[71]

The others from the interior of Iran are simply called "Irani." My informants feel that the use of the term "Faris" sets them apart as somehow closer or even "preferred" by the Gulf Arabs. They explain that their coastal affiliation can be useful in employment and administrative processes, and the "Faris" are privileged compared to others looking for employment. Clearly, the geographical proximity is understood, or at least argued, to suggest a greater degree of shared culture. And, of course, coastal Iranians are more likely to speak Arabic than are Iranians from the interior. This sense of cultural and linguistic affinity combined with the family networks and support available to migrants staves off some of the feelings of alienation among the Iranian migrant workers.[72]

In regard to the relationship of the population to its local and settlement history it can finally be concluded that the interest of the population in the events of the past is not very pronounced. Local history is not even part of the curriculum in the schools, and daily life experience requires no reference to history.[73] The population only rarely and reluctantly turns back to the past; the memories of the local population do not orient themselves by using years and a marked chronology, but rather by using events and breaches that caused a change in everyday life, shifts within the political/economic sphere, or ecological changes, such as natural catastrophes. History means: the time of the *qahti*/dry period (in the fifties, around 1952); when the *zilzila*/earthquake happened (around 1915); when the *vaba*/epidemic took place (around 1930); and when the mobilization for the military happened (around 1935). Questions about origins are never posed. Their attention and concern in times of uncertainty are directed toward the future in the sense of James Clifford[74]: they do not ask themselves "where we are from?" but "where are we between?"

Notes

1. The other two are Khuzistan and Bushehr.
2. John and Jean Comaroff, "Dialectical Systems, History, and Anthropology: Units of Study and Questions of Theory," *Journal of Southern African Studies* 8: 143–72.
3. John and Jean Comaroff, *Ethnography and the Historical Imagination* (Boulder, CO: Westview Press, 1992), 34.
4. These documents are all in my personal possession.
5. For further literature see "Banu Ka'b" by A. M. Abu-Hakima and "Al-Kawasim" by G. Rentz in *Encyclopedia of Islam*, New Edition; Willem Floor, "The Rise and Fall of the Banu Ka'b: A Borderer State in Southern Khuzistan," *Iran* 44 (2006): 277–315; H. Field, *Contributions to the Anthropology of Iran* (Chicago: Field Museum of Natural History, 1939); D. Hawley, *The Trucial States* (London: Allen & Unwin, 1970), 90–125; J. G. Lorimer, *Gazetteer of the Persian Gulf, Oman and Central Arabia* (Calcutta, India: 1908 and 1915; reprint Farnham Common, England: Archive Editions, 1986), 2095ff.; S. B. Miles, *The Countries and Tribes of the Persian Gulf* (London: Harrison and Sons, 1919), 430; L. Pelly, "Remarks on the Tribes, Trade and Resources around the Shore Line of the Persian Gulf," in *Transactions of the Bombay Geographical Society* 17 (1865): 32–103; J. R. Perry, "The Banu Ka'b: An Amphibious Brigand State in Khuzestan," *in Le Monde Iranien et l'Islam* 1 (1971), 133; Thomas Miller Ricks, "Politics and Trade in Southern Iran and the Gulf,

1745–1765" (PhD diss., Indiana University, 1975), 270; Sultan Muhammad Al Qasemi, *The Myth of Arab Piracy in the Gulf* (London: Croom Helm, 1986); A. Iqtidari, *Kishta-yi Khish: Majmu'a-yi panjah maqala* (Tehran: Intisharat-i Tus, 1357/1978); A. Faramarzi, *Karim Khan-i Zand va Khalij-i Fars* (Tehran, 1346/1967); H. Nurbakhsh, *Bandar Linga dar sahil-e khalij-i Fars* (Tehran, 1358/1979), 29.

6. For the definition of "tribe" I refer to James Peoples and G. Bailey, *Humanity* (St. Paul, MN: West Publishing, 1994), 237, "Tribes . . . have' formally organized institutions that unite scattered residential communities, give the society greater cohesiveness, and make possible a more united response to external threats."
7. [Daryadar] Ghulam-Ali Bayandur, *Khalij-i Fars* (Khurramshahr, 1938); Mirza Hasan Husaini Fasa'i, *Farsnama-yi Nasiri* (Tehran: Amir Kabir, 1367/1988); Muhammad Ali Janab [Jinab], *Khalij-i Fars: Nufuz-i Biganigan va Ravidad-ha-yi Siasi* (Intisharat-i pazhuhishgah-i ulum-i insani, 2536/1977); A. Mas'udi, *Khalij-i Fars dar dawran-i sar bulandi va shukuh* (Tehran: Mu'asisa-yi Ittala'at, 1357/1978); M. M. Sadiq Musavi, *Tarikh-i giti gusha dar tarikh-i khandan-i Zand* (Tehran: Kitabfurushi-yi Iqbal, 1317/1938); M. A. Sadid al-Saltana, *Bandar Abbas va Khalij-i Fars*, ed. Ahmad Iqtidari (Dunya-yi Kitab, 1363/1984); S. Sirjani, *Vaqayi'-i ittifaqiya* (Tehran: Nashr-i Paikan, 1376/1986).
8. Abbas Anjum-Ruz, *Burqa pushan-i Khalij-i Fars va Darya-yi Uman* (Tehran: Homa, 1371/1992); E. Dildam, *Khalij-i Fars* (Tehran: Navin, 1363/1984); H. Ilahi, *Khalij-i Fars va masa'il-i an*, 2nd ed. (Tehran, 1375/1996); Iqtidari, *Kishta-yi Khish*, 1357; Muhammad Ali Khan Sadid al-Saltana, *Tarikh-i Masqat va Uman, Bahrain va Qatar va ravabit-i anha ba Iran*, ed. A. Iqtidari (1933) (repr. Tehran: Dunya-yi kitab, 1370/1991); A. Faramarzi, *Karim Khan-i Zand va Khalij-i Fars* (Tehran, 1346/1967); M. H. Ruknzada Adamiyat, *Awza'-i ijtima'i-yi Khalij-i Fars* (Tehran: Idara-yi kull-i intisharat va radio, 1342/1963), 101–44; E. Yaghma'i, *Khalij-i Fars* (Tehran, 1352/1973).
9. C. Niebuhr, *Beschreibung von Arabien, aus eigenen Beobachtungen und im Lands selbst gesammelten Nachrichten* (Copenhagen, Denmark: 1772); George N. Curzon, *Persia and the Persian Question*, vol. 2 (London: Longmans, Green, 1892; repr. Frank Cass, 1966); J. G. Lorimer, *Gazetteer of the Persian Gulf, Oman and Central Arabia* (Calcutta, India: 1908 and 1915; reprint Farnham Common, England: Archive Editions, 1986); A. T. Wilson, *Persia* (London: Benn, 1932).
10. J. C. Wilkinson, "Arab-Persian Land Relationships in Late Sasanid Oman," *Proceedings of the Seminar for Arabian Studies* 3 (1973); Wilson, *Persia* (London: E. Benn, 1932); Ilahi, *Khalij-i Fars va Masa'il-i an* (Tehran, 1375/1996).
11. Niebuhr, *Beschreibung von Arabien*, 310.
12. F. Warden, "Extracts from Brief Notes Relative to the Rise of the Arab Tribes of the Persian Gulf," in *Selections from the Records of the Bombay Government*, New Series no. 24 (Bombay, India, 1856), 286.
13. L. Pelly, "Visit to Lingah, Kishm, and Bundar Abbass," *Journal of the Royal Geographical Society* 34 (1864): 252.
14. Curzon, *Persia and the Persian Question*, 409.
15. "There is not a single really Persian village or town from Mohammerah, on the Shat-el-Arab, to Gwadur, on the Baluchistan border. Excepting Bushire, every town, village, and island is inhabited by Arabs, with a very small sprinkling of Persian blood among them, over whom the Persian Government would be incapable of asserting authority should any concerted rising take place." (Foreign Office, "Memorandum respecting British Interests in the Persian Gulf," 12 February 1908, FO 881/9161, 67, included in *The Persian Gulf Historical Summaries, 1907–1953*, vol. 1, *Historical Summary of Events in Territories of the Ottoman Empire, Persia and Arabia affecting the British Position in the Persian Gulf, 1907–1928* (Gerrards Cross, UK: Archive Editions, 1987).
16. J. J. Morier, *Reisen durch Persien in den Jahren 1808 bis 1816*, ed. K. K. Walther (1918 repr., Berlin, Germany: Rütten and Loening, 1985), 32.
17. Ricks, "Politics and Trade in Southern Iran and the Gulf," 74–75.
18. Iqtidari, *Kishta-yi Khish* and *Tarikh-i Masqat va Uman, Bahrain va Qatar.*

19. Iqtidari, *Tarikh-i Masqat va Uman, Bahrain va Qatar*, 545.
20. Iqtidari proves misinterpretations in the work of Lorimer (Iqtidari, *Tarikh-i Masqat va Uman, Bahrain va Qatar*, 527).
21. As we will demonstrate later, this statement refers to the fact that the shuyukh had to accept Iranian nationality in order to receive land, titles, and privileges from the Iranian government. Therefore Iqtidari regards all these groups as "Iranized" or "Persianized." This opinion of Iqtidari has to be rejected with reference to anthropological literature and research that supposes that ethnic affiliation of a group does not orient itself by linguistic, religious, or territorial criteria but is processual and renegotiated and redefined anew depending on the respective context. F. Barth, *Ethnic Groups and Boundaries: The Social Organization of Culture Difference* (Boston: Little, Brown, 1969); Abner Cohen, ed., *Urban Ethnicity* (London: Tavistock Publications, 1974); S. Hall and P. du Gay, eds., *Questions of Cultural Identity* (London: Sage, 1996).
22. Anjum-Ruz, *Burqa pushan-i khalij-i Fars.*
23. Nurbakhsh, *Bandar Linga dar sahil-i khalij-i Fars,* 34.
24. M. A. Muvahhid, *Mubaligha-yi musta'ar. Barrasi-yi madarek murid-i istinad-i Shuyukh dar iddi'a bar jazayir-i Tunb-i kuchak, Tunb-i buzurg, Abu Musa* (Tehran: Nashr-i Karnama, 1380/2001), 22.
25. For further Persian literature about the Arab settlement see P. Mojtahidzada, *Jughrafiya-yi tarikh-i Khalij-i Fars* (Tehran: Danishgah-i Tehran, 1354/1975); E. Ra'in, *Darya-navardi-yi Iranian* (Tehran, 1356/1977); P. Varjavand, *Safarnama-yi junub: sayr va safari dar kinara-ha va jazayir-i darya-yi Uman* (Tehran, 1313/1934; repr. 1351/1972); and M. B. Vusuqi, *Tarikh-i muhajarat-i aqvam dar khalij-i Fars* (Shiraz, Iran: Danishnama-yi Fars, 1380/2001).
26. Pelly, "Visit to Lingah, Kishm, and Bundar Abbass," 252 and Curzon, *Persia and the Persian Question*, 409.
27. G. Demorgny, "Les reforms administratives en Perse," *Revue du Monde Musulman* 22 (1913): 103–04.
28. Field, *Contributions to the Anthropology of Iran*, 604n7.
29. Roger M. Savory, "A.D. 600–1800," in *The Persian Gulf States: A General Survey*, ed. Alvin J. Cottrell (Baltimore: Johns Hopkins University Press, 1980), 37.
30. Ricks, "Politics and Trade in Southern Iran and the Gulf," 391–92.
31. Hawley, *The Trucial States*, 92.
32. Muhammad Abbasian-Bastaki with Abbas Anjum-Ruz, *Tarikh-i jahangiriya va Bani Abasiyan-i Bastak* (Bandar Lingeh: n.p., 1339/1960), 110.
33. Sadid al-Saltana, *Bandar Abbas va Khalij-i Fars,* 1342/1963.
34. Nurbakhsh, *Bandar Linga dar sahil-i khalij-i Fars,* 29.
35. Muvahhid, *Mubaligha-yi musta'ar,* 24.
36. Anjum-Ruz, *Burqa pushan-i khalij-i Fars;* Faramarzi, *Karim Khan-i Zand va Khalij-i Fars;* Jinab, *Khalij-i Fars;* Nurbakhsh, *Bandar Linga dar sahel-i khalij-i Fars* and *Khalij-i Fars va jazayir-i Iran* (Tehran: Kitabkhana-yi sana'i, 1362/1983); Muvahhid, *Mubaligha-yi musta'ar.*
37. Faramarzi, *Karim Khan-i Zand va Khalij-i Fars,* 7, 9.
38. Anjum-Ruz, *Burqa pushan-i khalij-i Fars,* 91.
39. Iqtidari, *Tarikh-i Musqat va Uman;* Muvahhid, *Mubaligha-yi musta'ar.*
40. C. U. Aitchinson, *A Collection of Treaties, Engagements and Sanads Relating to India and the Neighbouring Countries* (Calcutta, India; 1933); Curzon, *Persia and the Persian Question*; Warden, "Extracts from Brief Notes." Curzon and Savory use the term "lease" in order to describe the relationship. Badger speaks about "rental of these places" (G. P. Badger, *The History of the Imams and Seyyids of Oman* [London: Hakluyt Society, 1871]); von Oppenheim applies the term "Erbpacht" (long lease) (M. Freiherr Von Oppenheim, *Vom Mittelmeer zum Persischen Golf* [Berlin, Germany: Dietrich Reimer, 1900]).
41. Curzon, *Persia and the Persian Question*; Pelly, "Visit to Lingah, Kishm, and Bundar Abbass"; and Warden, "Extracts from Brief Notes."
42. Pelly, "Remarks on the Tribes, Trade and Resources," 32–33.

43. Bastaki, *Tarikh-i jahangiriya*, 238; Iqtidari, *Kishta-yi Khish* and *Tarikh-i Masqat va Uman*; Fasa'i, *Farsnama-yi Nasiri*; Qa'im-Maqami, *Mas'ala-yi Hurmuz dar Ravabit-i Iran va Purtughal* (Tehran, 1354/1971) and M. A. Sadid al-Saltana, *Tarikh-i Masqat va Uman, Bahrain va Qatar va ravabet-i anha ba Iran* (Dunya-yi Kitab, 1370/1991).
44. A. A. Bina, *Tarikh-i duhazar-va pansad sala-yi Khalij-i Fars* (Tehran, 1964), 222; Muvahhid, *Mubaligha-yi musta'ar.*
45. Fasa'i, *Farsnama-yi Nasiri* (1367/1988) and Bastaki, *Tarikh-i jahangiriya,* 131. In Iqtidari, who adopts much information from Sadid al-Saltana, *Bandar Abbas va Khalij-i Fars* we find contracts about the lease system (Iqtidari, *Tarikh-i Masqat va Uman,* 120, 154). Muvahhid, *Mubaligha-yi musta'ar*, 158 and Jinab, *Khalij-i Fars* also give a listing of these contracts. For further literature about tributes and customs refer to: Curzon, *Persia and the Persian Question,* 470, 521, 554; Miles, *The Countries and Tribes of the Persian Gulf*; Von Oppenheim, *Vom Mittelmeer zum Persischen Golf* ; Lorimer, *Gazetteer of the Persian Gulf*; and Al Qasemi, *The Myth of Arab Piracy.*
46. Ricks, "Politics and Trade in Southern Iran and the Gulf," 9ff.
47. J. B. Kelly, *Britain and the Persian Gulf 1795–1880* (Oxford: Clarendon Press, 1968), 40.
48. Willem Floor, "A Description of the Persian Gulf and Its Inhabitants in 1756," *Persica* 8 (1979): 169–70.
49. Muvahhid, *Mubaligha-yi musta'ar*, 57.
50. Curzon, *Persia and the Persian Question;* Willem Floor, "The Revolt of Shaikh Ahmad Madani in Laristan and the Garmsirat 1730–33," *Studia Iranica* 12 (1983); Hawley, *The Trucial States;* Lorimer, *Gazetteer of the Persian Gulf*, 2065; J. A. Saldanha, *The Persian Gulf Précis 1903–1908* (repr. Archive Editions, 1986); *The Persian Gulf Administration Reports, 1873-1947,* vol. 8 (Gerrards Cross, UK: Archive Editions, 1986)*;* Warden, "Extracts from Brief Notes"; and Von Oppenheim, *Vom Mittelmeer zum Persischen Golf.*
51. Bastaki, *Tarikh-i jahangiriya;* Faramarzi, *Karim Khan-i Zand va Khalij-i Fars;* Fasa'i, *Farsnama-yi Naseri;* M. H. Haj-Kiramati, *Tarikh-i dilgusha-yi ivaz* (Shiraz: Intisharat-i Navid, 1380/2001), 128–29ff; Saidi-Sirjani, *Vaqayi'-i ittifaqiya* (Tehran: Nashr-i Paykan, 1376/1997); and M. A. Sadid al-Saltana, *Bandar Abbas va Khalij-i Fars* (Tehran: Dunya-yi kitab, 1363/1984).
52. Curzon, *Persia and the Persian Question*, 409–10.
53. Jinab, *Khalij-i Fars,* 52.
54. Muvahhid, *Mubaligha-yi musta'ar*, 59 and Curzon, *Persia and the Persian Question*, 409–10.
55. It was not possible to find a summary work about the effects of the *kashf-i hijab*. The investigations of Ustad al-Mulk and Murtaza deal more generally with the meaning of clothing and hijab. (See F. Ustad al-Mulk, *Hijab va kashf-i hijab dar Iran* (Tehran, 1367/1988) and J. Mortaza, *Vaqi'a-yi kashf-i hijab* (Tehran, 1371/1992).)
56. Abd al-Razzaq Muhammad Siddiq, *Sahwa al-faris: fi tarikh al-Arab al-Fars,* comp. Arash Nasuri (1373/1994, unpublished). This is a local unpublished chronicle in Arabic, made available to me by an informant in Gavbandi.
57. About the Arab population particularly in Laristan and Shibkuh we find references in Field, *Contributions to the Anthropology of Iran*, 228.
58. Siddiq, *Sahwa al-faris: fi tarikh al-Arab al-Fars,* 8.
59. Some of these tribes are mentioned in European written sources, such as Niebuhr, *Beschreibung von Arabien;* Warden, "Extracts from Brief Notes"; Ricks, "Politics and Trade in Southern Iran and the Gulf"; and the works of Floor.
60. Siddiq, *Sahwa al-faris: fi tarikh al-Arab al-Fars,* 47.
61. It cannot be extracted from the chronicle to what extent the settlement of the Nasuri was connected to military conflicts with Arab groups that already lived here and whether the Iranian state was in any way involved in the redistribution of power.
62. Siddiq, *Sahwa al-faris: fi tarikh al-Arab al-Fars,* 54.
63. The story of Kalat-e Surkh is very popular and those who experienced the events were pleased to recount the episode. An account is also given in Lorimer, *Gazetteer of the Persian Gulf*, 2063; Fasa'i, *Farsnama-yi Naseri* 1367/1988; and Sirjani, *Vaqayi'-i ittifaqiya,* 108.

64. Siddiq, *Sahwa al-faris: fi tarikh al-Arab al-Fars,* 74–75.
65. As far as possible I have compared the statements with records in written sources, such as *Farsnama-yi Naseri* and accounts of local historians like Anjum-Ruz, *Burqa pushan-i khalij-i Fars* and Nurbakhsh, *Bandar Linga dar sahil-i khalij-i Fars.*
66. In *Tarikh-i Jahangiriya* we read that Ra'is Muhammad Salih-i Fumistani, a member of the Ra'isi clan, was "*ma'mur,*" that is, he had the right to collect taxes.
67. For example, before the revolution people in important administrative positions (province governor, director of schools, and other institutions) were all Sunni. After the revolution all of them were dismissed and replaced by Shiites.
68. Shaikh Zayid Al Nahayyan (d. 2004), the ruler of Abu Dhabi and president of the UAE, personally promoted the immigration of Iranian coastal inhabitants to the UAE. He invited them to settle on the island of Dalma, and assured the potential migrants that they would be integrated as "natives" into the social heirarchy of the UAE since their language as well as their identity was Arabic. He personally and publically assumed responsibility for their well-being.
69. For questions concerning identity, such as *ʿarab/ʿajam, Sunni/Shiʿi,* see S. R. Nadjmabadi, "Identité éthnique contre nationalité: Le cas de l'île de Larak (Golf Persique)," in *Le fait éthnique en Iran et en Afghanistan,* ed. J. P. Digard (Paris, France: CNRS, 1988), 65–74; also S. R. Nadjmabadi, "'Anha ham az khodemanand': Ravabit-i faramahalli va faramarzi dar kinara-yi Khalij-i Fars" ("They are one of us": Transregional and Transnational Relations among Persian Gulf Coast Dwellers), *Anthropology (Insan shinasi)* 1, no. 2 (2001) (Tehran University Publication).
70. Nadjmabadi, "Identité éthnique contre nationalité"; Nadjmabadi, "'Arabzadeh' (Born Arab): The Arab-speaking Population among the Iranian Shoreliners on the Persian Gulf," in *The Anthropology of Ethnicity: A Critical Review* (Amsterdam, The Netherlands: "The Anthropology of Ethnicity" Workshop, December 15–19, 1993).
71. Anie Montigny, "Les Arabes de l'autre Rive," *Cahiers d'études sur la Méditerranée orientale et le monde turco-iranien* 22 (1996).
72. Ibid. Also: S. R. Nadjmabadi,"'Arabisiert' oder 'Iranisiert'? Siedlungsgeschichte in der iranischen Provinz Hormozgan am Persischen Golf," *Welt des Islam* 45 (2005): 108–50; Nadjmabadi, "'Anha ham az khodemanand'."
73. The situation differs with that of Bushehr, where there are more written sources about its history and there was more outside interest in the area. In the region between Bandar Lingeh and Bandar Abbas the local history is more one of migration.
74. J. Clifford, *Routes, Travel and Translation in the Late Twentieth* Century (Cambridge: Harvard University Press, 1997).

Chapter 7

Gulf Society: An Anthropological View of the *Khalijis*—Their Evolution and Way of Life

William O. Beeman

One of the longest running toponymic battles in the world revolves around the nomenclature of "The Gulf." I even received an e-mail admonishing me to only use the term "Persian Gulf" when referring to the body of water between Iran and the Arabian Peninsula. I explained to the writer that although as a rule I do use "Persian Gulf" in my writing, my purpose in this paper was to call into question the nature of the ethnic identity of the denizens of this region.[1] Rather than identifying them as either Persian or Arab, I want to make the case for these individuals as Gulf residents, independent of an exclusive Arab or Persian identity. I very much like a term that the people of the region use themselves on occasion: *Khaliji,* from the word for Gulf, *khalij,* which has the virtue of working in Arabic, Persian, and South Asian languages, and is very expressive.

This essay is partially a thought exercise, but I believe that considering the population of the region to have more *internal* cultural communality than explicit ties with either the Arab or the Persian cultural world not only makes sense ethnographically, but it also partially explains why there has been so much controversy over the nomenclature of the region, and so much hostility over such matters as the possession of some of the islands that lie between Iran and the United Arab Emirates.

It is my contention that this community would have greater self-recognition if it had not been enmeshed in an arena of territorial competition early in the colonial period. The imposition of state structures in the region, which had been blissfully absent, caused an overlay of state identity that has served to obscure the basic communalities between the members of the populations of the region.[2]

A New Kind of Community

Social scientists have been actively pursuing questions of "community" and "identity" in recent years. The work of Benedict R. Anderson and Eric J. Hobsbawm, and renewed interest in the work of Maurice Halbwachs in determining ethnic identity, has frequently placed the locus of identity on the individual or group.[3] Thus communities become "imagined" when enough people believe they belong and develop symbols and institutions that unite them. The Gulf community is the opposite. It is an "unimagined" community—a community in fact, but not in name and not in its social identification. The roots of its existence as a community are centuries old and are now so commonplace that few of the people of the region bother to think about it.

Linguistically, the denizens of the Gulf form a "Sprachbund," an area of overlapping languages that mutually influence one another.[4] Most of the residents are fully bilingual, and frequently tri- and quadri-lingual. The heavy borrowed vocabulary between Arabic and Persian sometimes makes this difficult to detect, but it is a fact nonetheless, as Persian intonations affect the Arabic spoken on both coasts.

As befitting an "unimagined community," the boundaries of the region are very fluid, as are the conditions that bind the residents together. In fact, in its social makeup, the Gulf region may most resemble the Caribbean, with a distinct culture and feel to it that is neither Arab nor Persian but a creolized mixture of both.

MIXTURES, MÉLANGES, CREOLES

Just as David Decamp noted about the people of Jamaica,[5] in a creolized population one finds people at the extreme antipodes of the two or more dominant cultural influences that affect the population, and many more people in the middle, exhibiting various mixtures of cultural influence in their speech, customs and behavior. In DeCamp's Jamaica, a certain small proportion of the population was, for all intents and purposes, completely Anglicized. Another small group was completely Afro-Caribbean. The rest of the population fell somewhere in between. He developed a form of the Guttman scale[6] that showed a combination of linguistic and cultural markers that would allow people to be ranked and compared according to the degree to which they were influenced by one tendency or the other. By carrying out this kind of exercise, one is able to create a "spectrum" of mutual cultural influence, much like a color spectrum.

Such communities come about as the result of historical factors: migration, trade, shifting colonial boundaries, and the resulting intermarriage and cultural borrowing that take place naturally when populations come into contact. The Caribbean links an enormously diverse set of populations of indigenous origin with European migrants and colonists. One symbolic culmination of this is the language Papiamento (from the Spanish/Brazilian word *papear*, "to chat, to talk"), which derives from at least seven linguistic roots.[7]

The Gulf concentrates an equally rich mélange of cultural influences: Arabic, Persian, South Asian, East African, Portuguese, French, and English, to name just a few. Wave after wave of travelers have, from ancient times, contributed to this mix. The impenetrability of the geography separating the Gulf from interior regions added to the concentration of this mélange, as people living on the Gulf littoral found it far easier to communicate with one another than with those inland. Before modern air transportation, a trip from the Iranian coast to the inland city of Shiraz might take a week, but a boat could reach Dubai in two days with a good wind. Moreover, boats could transport much more with far less physical effort than humans or pack animals.

Thus, one might do the same for the Gulf population on the analogy of DeCamp's Guttman scales for Jamaica. A scaling could be constructed that would include linguistic habits, habits of cuisine, dress patterns, marriage patterns, religious ritual, and discourse structures. One would find some individuals who speak Arabic all the time, wear Arab clothing exclusively, drink Arab coffee, and have families with polygynous members. At the opposite antipode would be individuals who speak Persian exclusively, wear a shirt and trousers if a male and a dress and chador or *mantu*[8] if a woman, drink tea, and come from families that are predominantly monogamous. This is a rough-and-ready list whose items and characteristics one could analyze with great profit to obtain a snapshot of the cultural elements that characterize Khaliji society.

The East African and South Asian populations who have migrated into the region add additional flavor to the cultural mix. When I was living on Lavan Island (historical name: Shaikh Shu'aib) off the coast of Iran in 1963, one village there consisted entirely of people of African descent. The Hindu temple at Hormuz in Iran is testimony to the long-standing cultural influence of the Indian community, which increased as British influence in the Gulf strengthened.

The Interconnections

As suggested in the previous section, I speculate that the Gulf community is largely held together by patterns of trade and commerce, replicating historical patterns that have existed for more than a millennium and probably since ancient times. Although sea trade has been the principal interconnection, as water transport has waned, air and even land connections have increased. The result is that the Khaliji community has actually grown in scope and size, with outposts outside of the Gulf region. Modern electronic communication has also increased the interconnection between people separated by the waters of the Gulf. As recently as thirty years ago, it was impossible to telephone from the Iranian coast to the Arabian coast of the Gulf. Now such communication is commonplace. I will mention some of the historical movements below, but note that the specific historical events of migration and settlement are not as important as the fact that they have constituted a pattern for millennia.[9] Therefore, each specific case that we can cite in modern times is only a manifestation and reinforcement of this pattern, rather than being attributable as a causal impetus for the formation of the Khaliji social and cultural pattern.

The original trade patterns were of course those of the so-called dhow trade (somewhat ironically named, because dhow is an African or South Arabian term rarely if ever heard in the Gulf). The dhows plied the entire East African coast to the Comoros Islands bringing not only goods but also people in the form of able-bodied sailors, as well as slaves.[10] The African influence also may have brought one of the most characteristic ritual forms of the Gulf, the Zar, a curing ritual involving shaman-like practitioners going into a trance to control the *jinn* that inhabit individuals, making them disordered physically and mentally.[11]

An Autobiographical Note

I should mention here that my introduction to the Middle East came in the early 1960s when I was a college student working for an oil company based on Lavan Island off the Iranian coast. I came to the end of my employment and spent six months in the village of Laz, the main settlement on the island, and additional time sailing with tradesmen and fishermen throughout the Gulf. This was before the British had left the region, and I was able to visit virtually every major port and every significant island in the Gulf. I wrote an undergraduate thesis about the village of Laz,[12] and have great affection for the entire region. I have not been able to replicate this youthful maritime adventure, but have spent time in Bahrain, the UAE, Kuwait and on the Iranian coast on many occasions since then.

The thesis I am articulating in this chapter was initially formulated during this first period of my contact with the Gulf region. I was struck by the mixed nature of the populations and the fluidity of travel and residency throughout the region that continues to this day. During this earlier period no visas or even passports were required by the governments of the region with the exception of Saudi Arabia; or if they were required, no one ever checked. I was only confronted once during my travels. The official, amazed at discovering an American at a small port, just told me to be quiet and not tell anyone I was there.

During this time I was able to make friends with many extended families, who had brothers, sisters, and cousins living all over the Gulf on both sides. There were households everywhere and widespread intermarriage. Even as a very young anthropologist, I noticed that this community was vastly different than either the general non-tribal Iranian population or the other Arab populations of the Arabian Peninsula.

ORIGINS

The trade connections in the Gulf have been well documented from antiquity, and others have dealt with them extensively. There are several events in modern times that have shaped and reinforced the patterns of interconnection that have bound members of Gulf society. In the modern historical period, Iranians migrated to the Arabian Peninsula and Arabs migrated to the Iranian mainland. In particular, following the demise of the Safavids in the early eighteenth century, there was weakness in both the central Iranian regimes (Zand, Afshar, Qajar) and on the Arabian Peninsula, still under nominal Ottoman rule but with no central organization. This left the Gulf region more or less to its own devices, allowing the rise of individual shaikhs and shaikhdoms. Concomitantly during this period, the British, adamant to protect their Indian empire, were able to establish their political influence throughout the region.

In a remarkable paper, the anthropologist Louise Sweet makes the strong case for an integrated post-Safavid Gulf society based on the unique combination of political organization, control of the pearling industry, and seafaring skills. She points out that this enabled this society to "seek to control all merchant shipping moving through the Persian Gulf, including European."[13] This is nowhere more in evidence than in the rise and dominance of the Qawasim in the Gulf region.[14] James Onley and Sulayman Khalaf[15] go so far as to call the Qawasim a "state" alongside the Wahhabi and Omani regimes from the same period (roughly 1750–1860). Whatever label one places on these familial political organizations, their organization and economic activity was uniform throughout the region, forming what most modern anthropologists would recognize as an integrated culture—which, as I have stated above, persists to the present day, though eroded and compromised by political processes starting during the Qajar period in Iran.

The following events had a profound effect on the Gulf community:

1. The ouster of the Qasimi shaikh of Bander Lingeh by the British in 1887, combined with increased tariffs in Gulf ports in 1903.
2. The accession of Reza Shah Pahlavi to power and the consolidation of Saudi Arabia under Ibn Sa'ud.
3. The abandonment of the Gulf region by the British in late 1971 at the height of the power of Mohammad Reza Shah Pahlavi.
4. The Iranian Revolution in 1978–79.

Each of these events altered migration and trade in the Gulf in fundamental ways and had profound effects on the integrated culture of the Khalijis.

THE OUSTER OF THE QASIMI SHAIKHS OF BANDAR LINGEH[16] AND INCREASED TARIFFS IN THE GULF

The British began to exert their influence in the Gulf region at the beginning of the nineteenth century. The Qawasim were recalcitrant and were labeled as "pirates" in much of the literature of the day. This piracy appellation has been resisted in recent times by contemporary historians, most notably Shaikh Sultan b. Muhammad al-Qasimi (the ruler of Sharjah), who disputes the idea that the Qawasim were anything more than a polity engaged in territorial and trade protection.[17] The British led expeditions against the Qawasim in 1806, 1809–10, and 1819, and in 1820 they established a general treaty with many of the smaller shaikhdoms on the Arab side of the Gulf. The final ouster of the Qasimi shaikhs from Bandar Lingeh in 1887,[18] combined with the imposition of high customs duties in 1903,[19] ended the preeminence of this city as a de facto free port, to the eventual benefit of Dubai. As William Floor notes, Lingeh (Lengeh) was primarily an entrepôt.[20] Goods were deposited here for transshipment to other ports on the Gulf. The Qasimi shaikhs were the aristocracy of the lower Gulf, having been situated there by their own account since the Abbasid Empire, and having branches on both sides of the Gulf, notably in Sharjah and Ras al-Khaimah as well as Bandar Lingeh. Colonel Lewis Pelly, writing in 1864 about a visit to the area in the previous year, describes the nature of the commercial enterprise at Bandar Lingeh as well as the clear Qasimi involvement with it.

> The Sheikh of Lingah is an Arab, and claims to be a descendant of a family that emigrated to the Persian Gulf at the period when the Arabs were at the height of their power in Baghdad. He is, I believe, related to the Rasulkhymah Chief on the opposite coast. No import or export duty is due in Lingah, and it is probably to this fact, and to that of geographical position having preserved the port from governmental interference, that its hitherto prosperity is due. At present the township, with its adjacent suburbs, may contain from 8,000 to 10,000 inhabitants, of whom the bulk are evidently Africans. The wealthier class are Persianised Arabs, and some Persians also have been attracted from the upper country for labour on the spot, or as carriers into the interior. There are also some twenty Hindoos residing in the place as agents for firms in Bombay or Kurrachee. It appears from this statement, as well as from the conversation of the merchants themselves, that the little commercial importance of this place is due to its being conveniently situated as a point of agency for trade coming from India and seeking a market along the Arabian coast of the Gulf, and to the Persian territory in the immediate neighbourhood of Lingah and towards Lar. Goods are landed, and, if prices pay, are sold on the spot and are sent towards the interior at the risk of the purchaser. Lingah merchants consider the road through the Eliant haunts [*sic*] too insecure to permit of their trading themselves with the interior. It is, however, I think, obvious that, unless owing to accidental circumstances, Lingah, from its geographical position and from its dangerous anchorage, would be quite unable to compete with the inland trade of Bushire or Bunder Abbass; and its statistics show that the bulk of its trade is with the maritime Arab ports, goods being reshipped thither in small coasting craft, according to demand and opportunity. Specie and pearls, and perhaps a little salt-fish, are, I believe, the only returns from the Arab ports.[21]

Nevertheless in that commercial role it was a major trading port for pearls and other goods. The Qasimi shaikhs, who operated throughout the eastern Gulf, but primarily in Ras al-Khaimah and Bandar Lingeh, were seen as troublesome pirates who interfered with British naval operations. However, they were likewise major merchants in the sea trade. Their removal from the Iranian coast shifted commercial activity to the Arab side. The Qawasim shifted their base of operations to Sharjah, but more significantly to the better port of Dubai as their principal port of transshipment.

Lingeh was a major port for the importation and transportation of tea, which had been gaining steadily as a replacement for coffee as the beverage of choice in the Iranian interior.[22] Floor attributes a great deal of the economic shifts in trade in the Gulf both to the rise of tea consumption and to changes occurring in import routes for tea during the nineteenth century. Tea was imported to Iran from China, India, and Java. Russia provided one import route, and whenever this was too expensive or inconvenient, the Gulf ports served; Floor also notes that coffee continued to be consumed on the Gulf coast even after tea became dominant in the interior.[23] In 1910 coffee consumption at Bandar Lingeh was reported to be two to three times the consumption of tea,[24] and even today in the Gulf, Arab-style coffee is served alongside tea in everyday hospitality.[25]

The traders on the Iranian coast moved the focus of their activity gradually to the Arabian coast starting in 1877, culminating after the general tariff imposition on Iranian ports in 1903, eventually making Dubai the dominant center of trade for the entire Gulf. Trade and family connections with Iran never ceased, however. In fact, trade at Bandar Lingeh continued to grow for two years after the ouster of the shaikhs there before it went into decline. This shift was the basis for regular sea trade and personal travel between the Iranian and Arabian coasts. Families became spread out, with members on both coasts. The Iranian settlers in Dubai still recalled their origins in the area northwest of Bandar Lingeh, called Bastak. They established a district of Dubai named after their former home, called Bastakiya.

The decline in trade in Bandar Lingeh eventually also affected trade in Bushehr and Bandar Abbas. With the entrepôt at Lingeh moved to Dubai, it became much more reasonable to import goods into Iran from Dubai through nearby Bandar Abbas. By the beginning of the twentieth century, Bandar Abbas had outstripped Bandar Lingeh entirely in Iran,[26] but largely because all Iranian ports had been supplanted by the Arabian ports as primary trading centers.

Dubai continued to flourish under British-protected status after its ruler, along with other Trucial shaikhs, signed an "Exclusive Agreement" in 1892. It had a reputation as a free port, especially for the trading of gold. The mix of inland Arab families and émigrés from Iran, India, and Pakistan added to the international flavor of the community.

The Accession of Reza Shah to Power and the Consolidation of Saudi Arabia under ibn Sa'ud

Although the Qajar shahs had an interest in the Gulf region largely as a route for importing foreign goods, they barely exercised political control or sovereignty there. The exception was Bandar Abbas, which was under the control of the Sultan of Muscat until it was brought under Qajar control in 1868.[27] The Qawasim continued to have de facto control over the shipping lanes between the Persian and Arabian coast, leading to some ambiguity in later years over the sovereignty of many of the islands in the lower Gulf, such as Greater and Lesser Tunb, Sirri, and Abu Musa—a controversy that continues today. Reza Shah Pahlavi's reign reestablished Iranian control over the Gulf through road building and the establishment of a strong Iranian navy. Until Reza Shah, Iran had been somewhat indifferent toward naval operations.

The consolidation of Saudi Arabia forced the British to protect their territories, drawing boundaries, some of which have still not been resolved, for the first time.[28] The development of the oil industry made the region suddenly essential for the Iranian economy, causing a shift of Iran's economic life from agriculture to oil and industry. This had a profound effect on life in the Gulf. Gradually a shift in the symbiotic relationship between the Persian coast, from where agricultural goods were exported to the Arabian Peninsula, changed to a relationship of competition, where the Gulf became a territory to be fought over for its resources and strategic advantage. This political and economic change served to divide the Khaliji community.

In short, the events of this period brought the Gulf region into the modern nation-state system for the first time. Residents of the Gulf region now had to choose a nationality and carry documents identifying themselves as citizens of a specific state. Families slowly became divided and parceled out among states. During this period, however, travel between nations was allowed for many Gulf residents upon producing a simple identity card.

THE ABANDONMENT OF THE GULF BY THE BRITISH IN 1971

The British pullback from the Gulf was announced well in advance in 1968. The withdrawal was attributed by the British government to the high cost (£12 million per annum) of maintaining a military presence in the region. The shaikhdoms there, however, did not want this. Indeed, the rulers of Abu Dhabi and Dubai offered to pay the costs of maintaining the British fleet and expected the other Gulf rulers to contribute. The British refused, however, despite this offer of local support and the estimation of many that this was a relatively small expenditure. They removed themselves from the region in December of 1971.[29]

The British departure resulted in the near-forcible creation of the modern states of Bahrain, Qatar, the UAE and Oman. More significantly, it impelled an anxious United States to play a more active role in the region. At the height of the Cold War, America feared that the Soviet Union would use this vacuum to make incursions into the Gulf—gaining its historically coveted "warm water port" as well as access to the petroleum supplies of the region. The Soviet Union had briefly sponsored autonomy movements in (Iranian) Azerbaijan and Kurdistan following World War II, and this was still fresh in the memory of Washington. Therefore, the British departure ushered in the beginning of United States influence in the region. The most significant political development was the establishment of the so-called Twin Pillars policy, with Iran and Saudi Arabia serving as U.S. surrogates to obstruct Soviet influence in the Gulf and protect Gulf oil supplies.

As a result of these new political realities, travel between nations became more difficult for Gulf residents. Increased focus on security in the Gulf resulted in more scrutiny and documentation for the inhabitants of the region. Suddenly, people had to have passports and work permits. Citizenship became an issue throughout the region. A Kuwaiti "citizen," for example, would have extensive rights to medical care, education, and other social guarantees that a noncitizen would not enjoy. Many people became, by happenstance, citizens of the new nations where they happened to be living when the new states were formed, despite the fact that their immediate families might be spread out all over the Gulf.

One of the great casualties of this period was the pearling industry. The combination of new political and economic realities throughout the region, with the rise in artificial pearl cultivation in East Asia and a general decline in the popularity of pearls as jewelry and as tokens of economic value, has completely eliminated the industry. It now lives only in memory and as an echo of a distant past.

THE IRANIAN REVOLUTION OF 1978–79

The Iranian Revolution removed one of the Twin Pillars—Iran—from U.S. influence, and ushered in regional competition over the Gulf, including renewed claims by Iran to Bahrain, and the dispute with the UAE over the islands of Abu Musa, Greater Tunb, and Lesser Tunb. Many Iranians left Iran, with large numbers going to Gulf states on the Arabian Peninsula. A large colony of Iranians settled in the UAE, particularly in Dubai.

Nevertheless, the revolution also introduced a new dynamic into the region as Iran began to assert its political authority. The Iranian navy became a major military force in the Gulf, and as the United States engaged in military attacks against Iraq in the early 1990s and again in 2003, a confrontational dynamic was established between the Iranians and Americans that continues today.[30]

At present, the underlying unified ethnic composition of the Gulf is masked by international economic and travel processes. One very interesting development during the reign of Mohammad Reza Shah Pahlavi was the development of Kish (Qais) Island off the Iranian coast as a luxury resort. This took place late in his reign, shortly before the revolution of 1978–79. Although it has become more available to the middle classes, Kish remains a bastion of upper-class privilege to the present day. Kish continues the mercantile culture of the Gulf region of old, only with European and American luxury goods available for purchase for the fortunate individuals wealthy enough to enjoy travel there.

Dubai has likewise become an astonishingly successful tourist destination with extravagant amenities such as golf courses, artificial islands, and what is expected to be the tallest building in the world. American entrepreneurs, such as Donald Trump, have invested millions in resort development in Dubai, and it is rapidly becoming an even more astonishing center for international business as its Westernized amenities proliferate.

As a result, the Khalijis have become a hidden population. They are still very much present in the region, but major governmental and economic forces have overshadowed this presence. One can go to Dubai and barely ever see a native Khaliji, though the hardy Qasimi family still remains prominent in local political and economic life.

Air Routes Replace Sea Routes

Although the former sea routes have not been completely replaced, they have largely been supplemented by air transport throughout the Gulf region. The routes between the Arabian Peninsula and Iran form an air bridge that replaces or replicates much of the former ship traffic.

One of the most interesting aspects of this traffic is the continued role played by the city of Shiraz as an important cultural capital for the Gulf region. For many years, residents of the Gulf have used Shiraz as a summer residence. Even today, citizens from throughout the Arabian Peninsula and the Iranian Gulf littoral own land and houses in Shiraz and maintain parts of their family there. It has been a long-standing pattern for a second or third wife to live in Shiraz with her children while the first wife lives in Dubai or Bahrain.

Khaliji Music

In recent years a new phenomenon has begun to appear in the Gulf region, the emergence of "Khaliji" music. This popular music form combines Arabic, Persian, African, and Indian influences in a perfect melding of cultural influences. One of the principal figures in this modern pop phenomenon is Saudi Arabian singer Muhammad Abdu, who has gained unprecedented popularity in the Arab and Persian world through albums such as *Masa' al-khair* (Good Night) and *Al-amakin* (The Places). Singers from other regions, such as Lebanon, have started singing with a "Khaliji" accent. Many websites now have sections devoted exclusively to Khaliji music and its stars.[31]

Three Gulf Families

Shahnaz Nadjmabadi provides in this volume an excellent sketch of families and residents now living in the region around Bandar Lingeh. It is noteworthy how much of the traditional Khaliji culture is preserved in their everyday way of life. The communities she describes exhibit the same creolized culture noted by Pelly, and analyzed by Sweet as mentioned earlier in the chapter.

I would like to contribute to this discussion by presenting material on several families whom I have encountered in my own research on the Gulf region. Below I provide a sketch of how they live and something of their background, emphasizing the characteristics that remain alive in Khaliji culture today.

The Karmati Family

The Karmatis come from a village around Shiraz. Assad-Allah, the father, is the son of a settled Qashqa'i chief. His wife comes from Bushehr. His two sons have moved to the Gulf coast to work in the petrochemical industry. One is living in Bushehr, and the other near Ahwaz. One of his daughters has married an Iranian citizen who resettled in Dubai after the revolution. Two of his other daughters are married locally around Shiraz.

The son living in Bushehr married a woman whose mother came from Bahrain, and whose father's family was from Bandar-i Ganava north of Bushehr. Earlier in the twentieth century, his family had boats and traveled back and forth between Bushehr and Bahrain. The Karmatis in Shiraz live in a traditional modern Iranian house, steel framed with mud brick and plaster walls. They have a sitting room for guests, a courtyard with a pool and garden, and other rooms used for both sleeping and eating. All the married members of the family are monogamous.

The Hamadi (Khamadi) Family

The Hamadis come originally from Rustaq, a large inland town north of the island of Kish. I first met one of the young brothers of the family, Sulaiman, on Lavan Island, where he had set up shop as a merchant. He had four other brothers: one living in Dubai, one in Rustaq, one in Kuwait, where he was working in the oil industry, and one in Bandar Abbas. Some of his uncles called themselves Khamadi, since family names only became required by the government during the reign of Reza Shah. Sulaiman had a wife on Lavan Island, and a temporary contractual wife (*sigha*) in Shiraz.[32] However, he was Sunni. I asked him how he was able to contract a *sigha* relationship if he was Sunni, and he was quite matter-of-fact: "Nobody ever asked," he said. His brother in Bandar Abbas had two wives—one in Bandar Abbas, and one in Rustaq. The brother in Rustaq was monogamous and the brother in Kuwait was unmarried, but planning to marry his cousin. Over the years Sulaiman had children by both his *aqdi*, or "official," wife under Islamic law and his *sigha* wife, to whom he remained surprisingly faithful. Sulaiman was a regular traveler to Sharjah and Dubai by boat. His everyday dress on Lavan Island was Western, but he sometimes wore a dishdasha within his household. However, when traveling to Dubai or Sharjah, he would adopt full and rather elegant Arab dress. In recent years he has stopped traveling himself, and is sending his twenty- and twenty-two-year-old sons, who still take wheat and other agricultural produce from Bandar-i Maqam, Bandar-i Chiru, and Bandar-i Lingeh to the UAE. Sulaiman lives in a compound with a separate *madhaf*. He is fully bilingual in Arabic and Persian. He speaks to his wife most often in Arabic, and to his sons most often in Persian, since they were educated in Iranian schools. However, his sons are also fluent Arabic speakers, but they confess that they don't read or write Arabic very well.

The Khalifa Family

The Khalifa family lives in Dubai. The patriarch of the family, Musa, claims to be "pure Arab," but traces his ancestry to the area around Bandar Lingeh and Bandar Abbas. His sons are predominantly Arabic speakers, but also know enough Persian to carry out a social conversation. His three sons all live in Dubai in the large family compound. Each son with his family has a quarter to themselves. The oldest, who is now over forty, has two wives, each of whom has her own rooms at opposite ends of the compound. They appear friendly and are distantly related both to each other and to their husband. The middle son married late, in his thirties, to a maternal cousin, and the youngest married a girl who was the sister of a close male school friend. Three of Musa's four daughters are married to men from the UAE, but the fourth is married to an Iranian shopkeeper in Shiraz, who saw her when she was there on vacation. There was some discomfort in allowing the marriage, but the family now commutes freely between Shiraz and Dubai. The Khalifa men all eat together for the main meal of the day, though they take breakfast with their wives and children, and switch between eating something in the evening with their father in the central *madhaf* and with their wives and children. The children—all cousins—are everywhere. It is unclear merely from observing the family's overt social behavior who their biological parents are. They are as likely to be hugged and petted by their uncles and aunts as by their parents. The Khalifas maintain a family residence in Shiraz in Qasr al-Dasht, the garden area on the west side of the city. They travel there regularly throughout the summer and fall, and with so many flights from Dubai, it is very easy. Although the men wear the dishdasha in Dubai, they switch to trousers and shirts in Shiraz. Two of the sons and the father somehow have Iranian passports as well as their UAE passports. The family are all merchants. They have retail enterprises throughout the UAE and they import a variety of things—largely building and construction materials from around the Gulf and even from India and Europe. The middle son carried the burden of the business for many years, traveling extensively, which may explain why he married so late.

Comparing these three families, we see that they all have a presence that encompasses the entire Gulf region, but their patterns of living are slightly different. The Karmatis live in a typical Iranian fashion. They have married outside of their family. They are monogamous, and they speak Persian. Still, they live partly on the Gulf littoral and have connections throughout the region. The Hamadis are a mix of Arabic and Persian cultural patterns. They are not only bilingual but also heavily bicultural. In some ways, they are the most Khaliji of the three families. The Khalifa family is the most Arabized of the three familes. They speak Arabic and have more Arabian family interaction and marriage patterns than the other families, but they still maintain important cultural ties with Iran and retain the ability to communicate in Persian.

The Meaning of Khaliji Identity

It is my belief that much of our understanding of the history of the Gulf region has revolved around the study of governmental conflict. At the same time, the population of the region is comfortable with a mixed culture, which allows them a seamless flow between the Arabian and Persian cultural spheres. By contrast, both Iranians and Arabs who live in inland areas have very strong feelings about the other populations that border on prejudice. Most Riyadhi citizens don't speak Persian and would not allow their daughters to marry Iranians; and most Tehrani citizens would feel likewise about Arabs.

The fluidity of identity in the Gulf was probably always present. And understanding that this is the nature of the ordinary people who live in the region helps explain why the battle to control and shape their identities can be so fierce. The Shi'i-Sunni division of the population makes the matter yet more complicated. This religious division has been long-standing, as shown by the earlier account in this paper by Lewis Pelly and in the chapter by Nadjmabadi. Nevertheless, historically the Shi'i and Sunni communities have lived side by side with little strife. In today's heated political climate, where increasing Shi'i power in the region is causing consternation at the state level, this peaceful coexistence may come under additional duress.

It would certainly be damaging to the patterns of interaction, trade, and family structure to enforce any kind of strict border or trade controls. In many ways the strength of the economy and social fabric of the region depends on this freedom of interchange. The Khaliji identity and way of life is also a source of strength for both Iran and the Arab nations of the peninsula. Recognition of this will be an important tool in improving regional relationships and insuring peace in the region.

NOTES

1. Louise Sweet had the same problem in describing the people of the Gulf. She footnotes her article as follows: "Initially I have called the region the Persian or Arabian Gulf to accommodate the present claims issuing from the states concerned today. Thereafter, I use simply 'the Gulf'." (L. E. Sweet, "Pirates or Polities? Arab Societies of the Persian or Arabian Gulf, 18th Century," *Ethnohistory* 11 (1964): 276). Many Iranians regard the use of "The Gulf" in referring to the Persian Gulf as a sophistry, and object to it. Since I am describing an Arabic-Persian mixed population indigenous to the Gulf, and belonging to neither the Arabic nor Persian cultural spheres exclusively, I see no other alternative for this discussion. I acknowledge that the body of water itself is properly called the Persian Gulf.
2. There are a few similar regions in the world where the same mechanism has taken over. The split ethnic groups of Africa, or the Moldovians (who are virtually indistinguishable from Romanians), and the distinct, yet unified nations of Latin America might be considered analogous to the Khalijis.
3. See here Benedict R. Anderson, *Imagined Communities: Reflections on the Origin and Spread of Nationalism* (London and New York: Verso, 1991); E. J. Hobsbawm and T. O. Ranger, *The Invention of Tradition* (Cambridge: Cambridge University Press, 1983); E. J. Hobsbawm, *Nations and Nationalism Since 1780: Programme, Myth, Reality* (Cambridge: Cambridge University Press, 1990); and Maurice Halbwachs and Lewis A. Coser, *On Collective Memory* (Chicago: University of Chicago Press, 1992).
4. Henrik Becker, *Der Sprachbund* (Leipzig, Germany: Humboldt Bücherei, 1948). The Sprachbund has been used widely to describe linguistic situations where there is heavy vocabulary and grammatical influence between different languages, particularly when they come from different "families." Good examples are the languages of the Caucasus, and Northern China, where Sino-Tibetan and Altaic languages converge.
5. David DeCamp, "Toward a Generative Analysis of a Post-Creole Speech Continuum," in *Pidginization and Creolization of Languages*, ed. Dell Hymes (Cambridge: Cambridge University Press, 1971).
6. A Guttman Scale is an implicational scale of items that indicate the strength of the presence or absence of a particular characteristic. Developed by Louis Guttman in 1944, the process of scaling is based on Guttman's insight that those who agree with a more extreme test item will also agree with all less extreme items that preceded it; however, it has many other uses besides measuring opinion. It may also measure behavioral or cultural tendencies in a population. The scale may be thought of as an array with items placed horizontally from left to right. If the extreme left side of the scale indicates a 100 percent existence of a characteristic, and the extreme right side a 100 percent absence of that characteristic, the presence of an item in the middle of the scale implies the presence of all items to its left, and the absence of all items to its right. The scale can be set up with two mutually exclusive characteristics on either end of the scale. DeCamp's scale for Jamaica (see note 5)

contrasts "Creole" with "English" characteristics for the Jamaican population. Individuals can be ranked along the scale as being "more Creole" or "more English" depending on their clothing, speech, and cultural preferences. Cf. Louis Guttman, "The Basis for Scalogram Analysis," in *Measurement and Prediction,* Samuel A. Stouffer, et al. (Princeton, NJ: Princeton University Press, 1950).

7. Spanish, Portuguese, Dutch, Arawak, perhaps Ladino, and several West African languages.
8. Modern all-encompassing tailored frock worn widely by fashionable women in Iran following the revolution of 1978–79. The word derives from the French *manteau* or "overcoat."
9. D. T. Potts, *The Arabian Gulf in Antiquity,* 2 vols. (Oxford: Clarendon Press, 1990).
10. Thomas Ricks, "Slaves and Slave Trading in Shi'i Iran, A.D. 1500–1900," *Journal of Asian and African Studies* 36 (2001): 407–18.
11. The Zar resembles the Hamadsha of Morocco and other places in North Africa documented so well by Vincent Crapanzano and others. (See his *The Hamadsha: A Study in Moroccan Ethnopsychiatry* (Berkeley: University of California Press, 1973). There is very little written about the *zar* in the Gulf—the exception being the study by Ghulam-Husain Sa'idi, *Ahl-i Hava* [People of the Wind] (Tehran: Danishgah-i Tehran, Mu'assisa-yi Mutala'at va Tahqiqat-i ijtima'i, Intisharat 36, Munugrafi 8, Chapkhana-yi Danishgah, 1345/1966).
12. William O. Beeman, "The Village of Laz: An Anthropological Investigation of a Village Community in the Persian Gulf" (BA thesis, Wesleyan University, Middletown, CT, 1964).
13. L. E. Sweet, "Pirates or Polities? Arab Societies of the Persian or Arabian Gulf, 18th Century," *Ethnohistory* 11 (1964): 264.
14. The a Qasimi are referred to in literature variously as Qasimi, or in the Arabic plural as Qawasim, or Qawasemi, or in Sweet and other studies by the corrupted British appellation Jowasim.
15. James Onley and Sulayman Khalaf, "Shaikhly Authority in the Pre-oil Gulf: An Historical-Anthropological Study," *History and Anthropology* 17 (2006): 189–208.
16. Transliterated orthography for Iranian and Arabian place names is notoriously variable. This book uses Lingeh, but historical sources also spell the name of the town as Lengah. Similary Ras al-Kheima may be written as Rasulkhymah or Ras al-Khayma; Bandar Abbas as Bunder Abbass, etc. Other similar variations will be seen throughout this discussion reflecting the idiosyncrasies of different authors and commentators.
17. Sultan Muhammad Al-Qasimi, *The Myth of Arab Piracy in the Gulf,* 2nd ed. (London: Routledge, 1988); also Patricia Risso, "Qasimi Piracy and the General Treaty of Peace," *Arabian Studies* 4 (1978): 47–57, and Charles E. Davies, *The Blood-Red Arab Flag: An Investigation into Qasimi Piracy, 1797–1820* (Exeter, UK: University of Exeter Press, 1997).
18. George N. Curzon, *Persia and the Persian Question,* vol. 2 (London: Longmans, Green, 1892; repr. London: Frank Cass, 1966), 409–10.
19. This appears to have been a reflex to the increased import duties being imposed by Russia on Iran's northern borders at this time. The Iranians, cognizant that most shipping in the Gulf involved British goods, wanted to make up for the increased Russan duties by imposing the higher tariffs on the Gulf ports. For Bandar Lingeh, this made its entrepôt even less tenable. (Cf. Willem Floor, "Tea Consumption and Imports in Qajar Iran," *Studia Iranica* 33 (2004): 47–111, see here 72–73). Floor notes that Russian dominance in the tea trade—one of the most important imports—came to an end in 1917 at the end of World War I, and the Gulf again became the main source for tea imports, but it was too late for Bandar Lingeh at this point. The trade had already moved to Dubai.
20. Floor, "Tea Consumption and Imports in Qajar Iran."
21. Lewis Pelly, "Visit to Lingah, Kishm, and Bunder Abbas," *Journal of the Royal Geographical Society of London,* 34 (1864): 252.
22. Floor, "Tea Consumption and Imports in Qajar Iran," 77–79; Rudi Matthee, "From Coffee to Tea: Shifting Patterns of Consumption in Qajar Iran," in *The Pursuit of Pleasure: Drugs and Stimulants in Iranian History, 1500-1900* (Princeton, NJ: Princeton University Press, 2005), 237–66.

23. Floor, "Tea Consumption and Imports in Qajar Iran," 98.
24. Ibid., 63.
25. The coffee served is brewed from macerated crushed coffee beans. This is not "Turkish" coffee, in which finely ground coffee is simmered with sugar. It is unsugared and served in small handleless cups from a specially shaped coffee ewer. Typically each cup is refilled three times, at which point the receiver wiggles the cup back and forth to indicate he has had enough.
26. Floor, "Tea Consumption and Imports in Qajar Iran," 79.
27. See further Lawrence Potter, "The Consolidation of Iran's Frontier on the Persian Gulf in the 19th Century," in *War and Peace in Qajar Persia: Implications Past and Present,* ed. Roxane Farmanfarmaian (London: Routledge, 2008), 125–48.
28. The boundary disputes and negotiations were a continual feature of British occupation, as the twenty-nine volumes of documents solely on this topic attest. See Richard Schofield and Gerald Blake, eds., *Arabian Boundaries: Primary Documents* (Farnham Common, UK: Archive Editions, 1988). For a narrative study see John C. Wilkenson, *Arabia's Frontiers: The Story of Britain's Boundary Drawing in the Desert* (London: I. B. Tauris, 1991).
29. James Onley, "The Politics of Protection in the Gulf: The Arab Rulers and the British Resident in the Nineteenth Century," *New Arabian Studies* 6 (2004): 30–92.
30. William O. Beeman, *The "Great Satan" vs. the "Mad Mullahs": How the United States and Iran Demonize Each Other* (Westport, CT: Praeger/Greenwood, 2005).
31. For more on khaliji music, see "Africans in the Arabian Gulf," interview with Joseph Braude, in *Afropop* e-Newsletter (produced by World Music Productions, Brooklyn, NY), located at www.afropop.org.
32. Contractual wives, called *sigha* or *mut'a* wives are exclusively a Shi'i phenomenon. The institution is decried by Sunnis. The contract can be as short as one minute, and as long as 99 years, and is outside of the four wives allowed under Islamic law. The institution has been described by Shahla Haeri in *Law of Desire: Temporary Marriage in Shi'i Iran* (Syracuse, NY: Syracuse University Press, 1989).

Part II

The Gulf and the Indian Ocean

Chapter 8

The Cultural Unity of the Gulf and the Indian Ocean: A *Longue Durée* Historical Perspective

M. Redha Bhacker

The oceans and the seas unite, rather than divide, the peoples of the world.[1]

Visitors to the Middle East, and the Gulf region in particular, are often surprised by the ethnic diversity of its people. It is tempting to offer as an explanation for this the recent oil boom and resulting inflow of expatriate workers. Yet, the genetic imprint of East Africa, Southeast Asia, and the Indian subcontinent on the people of the Gulf long predates the oil era. The diversity of the Gulf and Indian Ocean populations reflects millennia of migrations between seafaring communities strung out along the shores of the region as far as Africa and the South China Sea. The more recent influx of expatriates primarily from the Asian subcontinent during the oil era serves only to underscore the continuity of links between the Gulf and Indian Ocean rim countries since ancient times. Overland trade routes fed into Indian Ocean trading ports and sea trade routes stretching, at certain periods of history, from China down through the Strait of Malacca to Ceylon, India, Arabia, and as far as the east coast of Africa, south of Zanzibar, to the gold mines inland of Sofala, in present-day Mozambique. Valuable merchandise such as gold, silks, precious stones, fine porcelain, and thoroughbred Arabian horses as well as commodities such as rice and cotton was transported along these routes.

For thousands of years, seafarers, merchants, artisans, missionaries, and adventurers traded their goods, technologies, ideas, and faiths from one side of the ocean to the other. No wonder then, that when we travel from the farthest corner of southeast Arabia to other parts of the Indian Ocean, much of what we experience seems more than a little familiar. From Penang (in modern Malaysia) to Pemba island (near Zanzibar), we can observe in a boat, a door, a window, headgear, jewellery, a face, or a song, traces of a shared history that resonate to the present day. This paper aims to show that despite the ethnic diversity of the people of the Indian Ocean, there existed among them a sense of belonging to a common Indian Ocean culture.

Cultural Identity of the Indian Ocean

If we consider cultural spheres of influence, and view oceans as continents, we are able to make sense of the empirical observations across millennia that the coastal peoples of the Indian Ocean shared a greater cultural identity with one another than they did with the hinterland inhabitants of their own landmasses. The *Ichthyophagi,* or "Fish-Eaters," of the *Periplus* in the first century A.D. inhabited thousands of kilometers, from the Egyptian and Arabian shoreline and islands in the Red Sea, to southern Arabia and the island of Masirah (Oman) and beyond.[2] They survived in narrow inlets gathering shellfish, catching fish, grinding it into meal for animals and living in shelters constructed of whalebone in the same way as their cousins did in ancient Gedrosia, on the Makran coast, as observed by Nearchos in 325 B.C.[3] The degree of cultural diversity of coastal communities is striking even at this early period. The classical sources describe different tribes speaking languages (some more than one) each partly or wholly different from the other. They describe not only the Ichthyophagi, but also nomads, agriculturalists, pastoralists, villages of Arabs and Persians, and trading ports peopled by royal slaves, the king's officers, Indian traders, and Arab shipmasters and sailors.[4] From these early times, we are dealing then not with one but with a number of distinct cultural identities that are wholly or partly replicated along the different shores of the Indian Ocean. The commonality of cultures among coastal inhabitants, whether at the beginning of the historical period, the early Islamic period or later times, is easier to comprehend if we view the Indian Ocean basin as a continent in itself navigated with comparative ease on regular, alternating monsoon winds from the coast of Africa to the Gulf, west India, and beyond.

Although the Indian Ocean region has been characterized as including culturally distinct entities—Persian, Arab, Indian, or Chinese; Islamic, Hindu, or Muslim; Asian or Near or Middle Eastern—there is always the underlying impression that the Indian Ocean has its own distinct identity and sphere of influence. Parallels to the Braudelian concept of the Mediterranean Sea here are obvious.[5] From a *longue durée* Braudelian perspective, this sense of identity has been further shaped by climatic conditions, most notably the powerful effects of the monsoon wind system. The word "monsoon" comes from the Arabic *mawsim* (season), and ever since sailors had dared to venture on voyages across the open seas, the seasonal monsoon winds bore their ships between the Gulf and its near and, with time, distant neighbors. Invaders to the Gulf area came and went, but the lives of the ordinary people were ruled more by nature, by the perpetual monsoons rather than ephemeral rulers. People of the Gulf and the great ocean beyond knew that for six months the winds blew one way, then in the reverse direction during the other half of the year. The sailing pattern and consequently the trading seasons of the region were fixed to coincide with the prevailing winds. These could be gauged with remarkable accuracy by sailors and navigators. The sea captains of old might not have understood why the monsoons blew—how colder air was being sucked northwards over the ocean in summer toward the hot lands of Asia, then southwards from the Himalayas and the Indian plains in winter. For them it was sufficient that the winds came on time, year in and year out, to fill their sails.

Medieval Arab navigators, such as the fifteenth-century Ahmad b. Majid al-Najdi and Sulaiman al-Mahri, in their formidably detailed navigational treatises reveal an intimate knowledge of the monsoons and sailing routes and how these varied according to the configuration of the coast at any given point.[6] These treatises calculate down to the last day the periods during which it was possible for a vessel to leave a given port to cross the ocean before the onset of bad weather. They were almost certainly compiled from existing charts and pilot guides in circulation among the Indian Ocean pilots handed down from father to son. As early as the tenth century A.D., Baghdad-born geographer and historian Abd al-Husain al-Mas'udi (ca. A.D. 893–956) wrote: "All the sailors who sail in these waters [the sea of Oman] are familiar with the monsoons, the timing of which they are able to gauge perfectly. This science is the fruit of observation and long experience and they pass it on by theory and practice. They are guided by certain signs and specific phenomena in recognising an approaching storm, high winds or calm periods."[7] The amount of navigational detail in the *Periplus* itself suggests that the author had access to a written pilot guide even at that early date.[8] In any event, it is clear that knowledge of the monsoons was clearly rooted in the accumulated sea-lore of millennia, passed from generation to generation.

We now have archaeological evidence that suggests that the Gulf region is one of the oldest continuously inhabited places in the world and that puts back the origins of the impact of maritime trade on the Gulf to as early as the sixth millennium B.C.[9] For thousands of years, even before classical writers described the Ichthyophagi, their prehistoric ancestors flourished on rocky platforms along the littoral of the Gulf between coastal lagoons, mangroves, and open sea. The shell middens of these ancient fishing communities dating back as early as mid-sixth millennium B.C. have been excavated at Ras al-Hamra in Muscat and observed all the way along the southeastern shores of Oman from Quriyyat to Sur and Ra's al-Jinz. Excavations at Ras al-Hadd and Ras al-Jinz at the southeasternmost tip of the Arabian Peninsula, an area rich in fish stocks and pelagic mammals, have revealed two important facts: (1) the economy of these fishermen of the Omani seaboard was based almost exclusively on their fish catch, shrimp, and mollusks gathered from rocks and among the roots of mangroves as well as marine mammals; and (2) by the fourth millennium B.C. these prehistoric fishing communities were hunting large fish in offshore waters, indicated by excavated shellfish hooks used for fishing from boats. These people were long-distance seafarers who built both wooden and reed boats.[10]

The Longue Durée Historical Perspective

Neville Chittick's observation that the Indian Ocean has constituted "the largest cultural continuum in the world," which continued "during the first millennium and a half A.D.,"[11] is a perfect example of the Braudelian concept of longue durée that Braudel defines as "a history whose passage is almost imperceptible, that of man in his relationship to the environment, a history in which all change is slow, a history of constant repetition, ever-recurring cycles."[12]

The longue durée historical perspective applied to the Indian Ocean draws us back to the early origins of human civilization and seafaring as outlined above. More than one thousand years after the *Periplus*, Ibn Battuta sailing north from Dhofar landed at Hasik (about a hundred miles north of Salalah) and noted that like their forefathers, the only livelihood of the inhabitants was fishing, and that their huts were built of fish bone and roofed with camel hides. Sea transport by *qirba* (inflated skins or rafts supported by inflated skins) is depicted on Assyrian bas-reliefs from the ninth century B.C., and referred to in the *Periplus* (as offshore fishing in the Arabian Sea on "locally-made rafts of skin floated on inflated hides") and by Pliny (Arab pirates sailing on rafts made of inflated skins on islands at the mouth of the Red Sea).[13] Qirba have been used with extraordinary ingenuity and skill by fishermen in the Arabian Sea, Bahrain (a geographical region that includes present-day Bahrain Island, formerly known as Uwal, and some territories of Hasa on the opposite mainland) and Iraq until modern times. Nineteenth-century European writers described qirba fishing by the poorest tribesmen of the Omani seaboard from Ja'lan to Ras al Madrakah, remarking upon the dexterity and courage of the Janaba fishermen as they balanced on inflated skins wrestling with large sharks. Reluctant to lose their prey, the fishermen were often towed by the shark out "a great distance to sea."[14] Samuel Miles describes how the fishermen netted sharks or caught them with a hook attached to an iron chain before clubbing them over the head.[15] The Janaba were still fishing using qirba as late as the 1950s.[16]

The coastal peoples of the western Indian Ocean, Arabia, Iran, and India have been united, since prehistory, by the Indian Ocean basin and seasonal monsoon winds in a culture and economy entirely dominated by the sea and a lifestyle still observable today in many coastal fishing communities. In Oman, from the Batina coast in the north to remote settlements beyond Ras al-Hadd in the south as far as Dhofar, livestock are still fed on dried sardines. Women scavenge the shoreline for shellfish and in Dhofar, dive fully clothed to winkle abalone out of rock crevices. As in unchanging millennia past, rock oysters and chiton rock slugs (mollusks) are still an important staple food for coastal and island communities in these parts.[17]

Links between Persia, Arabia, India, and East Africa

Maritime trade in the Indian Ocean and the history of people involved in it was shaped however not only by the monsoons but by the location of natural harbors, islands, and reefs, and by accessibility to hinterland production. An incomplete picture would be obtained if the maritime world was considered in isolation, for it cannot be separated from rivers and overland caravan routes that both competed with, and supplied, the sea routes. Points of contact between land and sea were provided by several urban centers at the coast. For example, Basra in southern Iraq, Zanzibar in East Africa, Gujarati ports in western India, or Palembang on the island of Sumatra gave access to important inland centers connected by rivers to their respective hinterlands. The maritime world also cannot be separated from land-based political units. Cooperation between political elites and merchants, military imperatives such as naval campaigns, the choice of import and export commodities, and investment decisions all contributed in establishing links between land and sea. From a cultural perspective, trade expansion on both land and sea gave rise to migratory waves of people from all shores and to all parts of the Indian Ocean. Movement of people by definition involves the exchange of ideas, economic systems, social usage, political institutions and artistic traditions. All these have played and continue to play an important part in the cultural evolution, in its widest sense (social, economic, political, religious, and spiritual), of the people of the Gulf, East Africa, and the wider Indian Ocean sphere.

Maritime Trade: India and the Gulf

It is clear from the *Periplus* that, at the beginning of the historical period, the Indian Ocean was the preserve of Arab and Indian navigators who discovered how to sail across the ocean instead of coasting around it. This knowledge was a closely guarded secret until supposedly uncovered in the first century B.C. by an enterprising Greek trader, Hippalus. Knowledge of the monsoons by Indian Ocean peoples was clearly rooted in the accumulated sea-lore of millennia and gives the lie to the claim that the Greeks were the first to discover sailing using the monsoons. As Colonel Samuel Miles caustically observes, the Arabs had been familiar with the monsoons thousands of years "before the modest Grecian Hippalus took the credit of their discovery to himself."[18]

Recent archaeological excavations in Oman and elsewhere in the Gulf suggest that Arabia is not only one of the oldest continuously inhabited places in the world but also provides the earliest evidence of long-distance seafaring. In 1994, an important discovery for our knowledge of pre-historic seafaring and boat building in the Indian Ocean was made at Ras al- Jinz, a headland about 10 kilometers south of Ras al-Hadd, the southeastern promontory of the Oman peninsula. Excavations by a Franco-Italian team (Joint Hadd Project) brought to light the "first direct evidence of ancient Arabian ship building."[19] Buildings excavated at Ras al-Jinz contained a total of 295 bitumen slabs in a mid-third millennium B.C. context. These slabs have been identified as caulking material that had evidently been stripped from boats and stored for reuse. A number of slabs bear the imprint of lashed reed bundles and twill-patterned woven mats and provided archaeologists with a virtual construction template of the boats that sailed the waters of the Gulf and Arabian Sea 4,500 years ago. Other bitumen fragments recovered at Ras al-Jinz bear the impress of sewn or lashed wooden planks. The technique used by Omani shipbuilders to bind the wooden planks of their vessels with twisted coconut twine is attested in historical times, and the practice was widespread in the Indian Ocean up to the modern era. The evidence preserved in these slabs was used 4,500 years later by Professors Serge Cleuziou and Maurizio Tosi and marine archaeologist Tom Vosmer in an experimental reconstruction of a boat from lashed bundles of reeds gathered in Sur. The boat, *La Nave di Magan,* was successfully sailed in the waters of the Arabian Sea in February 2002.

Mesopotamian ceramic sherds containing bitumen traces of Iraqi origin indicate that as well as stripping and reusing bitumen from boats, the shipbuilders of Ras al-Jinz imported the raw material in storage jars from Mesopotamia. Large engraved Indus ware, possibly cargo containers, and stamp seals inscribed in Indus script dated to 2300–2100 B.C. are the earliest evidence so far of direct trade relations between Oman and India.[20] The discoveries at Ras al- Jinz provide important evidence about the role of ancient seafaring communities inhabiting this stretch of the Omani seaboard. They indicate that thousands of years ago these coastal inhabitants were engaged in long-distance sailing, trade, and exchange. They had developed sophisticated boat-building skills and had imported the raw materials they required to build both reed and sewn-plank boats capable of sailing in the rough waters of the Arabian Sea.

This archaeological evidence ties in with ancient cuneiform texts that describe seaborne trade between the lands of Dilmun, Melukhkha, and Magan. Magan is widely identified with Oman as the major source of copper for Mesopotamian civilization. Mesopotamia's other main trading partners were the seafaring lands of Dilmun and Melukhkha. Dilmun is identified as Bahrain; Melukhkha is otherwise known as the Harappan civilization of the Indus Valley in western India that encompassed Sind, Rajasthan, Baluchistan, and the western Punjab. The cuneiform texts tell us that in the late third millennium the boats and shipbuilders of Magan were already docking at the quay of Agade, the new capital and head harbor established by Sargon of Akkad after his victory over Ur and other cities of southern Mesopotamia (ca. 2350 B.C.). A few centuries later the Magan ships were bringing cargoes of timber and copper from the Lower (Arabian) Sea. A later text of around 2000 B.C., referring to "the shipwrights of Magan," suggests that by that time, the Omanis of Magan were active shipbuilders as well as traders and copper miners.[21] Other excavations in Oman also suggest similar direct links between Oman and India in Harappan times. The earliest settlement so far excavated in Oman is that of Maysar, which is thought to have been a prosperous mining settlement located in Wadi Samad. Maysar has yielded the find of a triangular seal depicting a dog and another quadruped (possibly a goat) on one side, a zebu bull and a scorpion on another side and an ibex and sheep on the third, which are characteristic of the Indus Valley.[22]

The demonstrable skills of the Ras al-Jinz communities surely pre-date the evidence in both the monumental inscriptions of Mesopotamia and the available archaeological record. These accomplishments of building wooden and reed boats capable of navigating the Arabian Sea were not achieved overnight. Arguably, the seafarers of Oman would have been a vital component and catalyst in the rise of the ancient civilizations of the Near East with whom they traded in the third millennium. A persuasive case has been made that since the civilizations of the Near East were riverine societies with short seaboards they would have had little opportunity to themselves develop the navigational and technological skills for long-distance voyages and trade.[23] Viewed in this light we can conjecture that, far from being peripheral to developments of international trade in ancient times, the accumulated seafaring skills and vessels of Omani seafarers would have been pivotal.

Links between Persia, the Gulf, and East Africa

At the narrowest point in the Strait of Hormuz, the two landmasses of Arabia and Persia are separated by a distance of less than 60 kilometers. At this bottleneck, the Gulf waters are dotted with islands and craft are able to hop from one to another. At the entrance to the Gulf, where maritime and caravan routes from all corners converged, the overwhelming impression is one of geographical, political, and economic unity of Arabia and Persia. By the eighth century A.D., the Gulf was referred to as "Bahr al-Arab" (Sea of the Arabs), and the impression of unity is reinforced by medieval maps that depict the two coastlines as opposing shores of a lake studded with islands. The discovery of greyware pottery of Persian origin in the graves of the prehistoric fishermen of Ras al-Hamra dates the connections between the Oman Peninsula and the Persian mainland to at least the mid-fourth millennium. In antiquity, the two landmasses were connected by land bridge and communities of hunter-gatherers would have ranged freely between them until waters started to enter the Gulf ca. 11,000 B.C.[24] It seems reasonable to assume that movement of people traveling on primitive rafts, canoes, and qirba would have continued across a gradually expanding lake. As seafaring developed, maritime and fishing communities striking out from the shores of the Gulf would have been carried by the monsoon winds from the tip of Musandam toward Jask on the Makran coast of Iran.

With these developments, transitory or permanent movements of people continued throughout millennia. Both the Omani and Persian chronicles relate traditions of major migrations from South Arabia to the Persian mainland after the dawn of the historical period. These chronicles relate the epic journeys of the Azd and Hormuzi tribal migrations. Separated in time by a thousand years or more, these two migratory movements came out of southern Arabia to Oman. Qalhat on the southeast coast near Ras al-Hadd was used as a major staging post from which splinter groups embarked upon further migrations to coastal Kirman and its hinterland, intermarrying with the local aristocracies and establishing independent kingdoms. Qalhat remained a stronghold, anchoring dynasties to the Arabian mainland while rooted in Persia, as well as serving as a refuge in times of conflict. Striking similarities between the trajectories and destinies of these two migrations can be interpreted as reflecting an enduring, long-standing pattern of exchange and settlement between the Arabian and Persian shores of the Gulf.[25]

From the other direction, the coast of Arabia was also invaded and ruled by dynasties from the Persian side of the Gulf throughout history from the time of the Achaemenids (sixth century B.C.) to the Sasanians (third to seventh century A.D.) and to Nadir Shah in the 1730s A.D. This is compelling evidence of the need to eschew a rigid compartmentalization of scholarship, which limits Africa for Africanists, Arabia for Arabists, Persia for the Persianists, and so on. We need to develop an integrated approach in space and time to arrive at a more complete understanding of cultural dynamics free of distortion and bias.

The credit for the development of an integrated maritime trading system in the Gulf, with land routes snaking into eastern Arabia, Iraq, and Iran goes to the Sasanians (A.D. 224–651). From its early days this Persian dynasty subjugated the coastal peoples of the Arabian Peninsula from the geographical region known as Bahrain to the borderlands of Yemen, so much so that the name of certain Arab tribes (notably the Azd) became synonymous with seafaring.[26] Sasanian naval power expanded in the course of the dynasty's wars against Byzantium, and they established Persian control along the length of the Arabian shoreline to the entrance of the Red Sea and possibly even to East African territory. Given the dominant far-reaching role of the Sasanians in the pre-Islamic trade of the western Indian Ocean region, it is not surprising that the Swahili language has been heavily influenced by Persian. As for Arabic, its influence on the Swahili language is almost as prominent as it is on Malabari and Bahasa (the Malay language) on the other side of the Indian Ocean. All of these tantalizing fragments of evidence point to the need for scholars on both sides of the Arab/Persian studies divide to pursue complementary fields of research to determine the linkages between communities in Arabia and Persia throughout history and to build a more complete picture of migratory patterns and the origin of cross-cultural influences.

From China to East Africa: Trade and Civilization

In the first half of the seventh century, two major historical forces combined to surprising effect. In 618 Emperor Li Yüan came to power in China and established the Tang Dynasty (618–907), one of the greatest in the long history of China. Four years later, on July 16, 622, Muhammad b. Abd-Allah (the Prophet Muhammad) abandoned Mecca, his birthplace, and carried out his hijra (migration) to Medina. The administrative unification and economic achievement of Tang China were responsible for the creation of new consumer demands and social tastes for luxuries within the empire and for the spread of Chinese cultural influence throughout the east. This expansion of Chinese culture in the East was accompanied in the West by the rise of Islam and its phenomenal journey of conquest and conversion across the fertile lands of the Near East and beyond to the west, to India and South Asia in the east. Despite the dissimilarity of social and political values, these two separate and unconnected events combined to link the eastern and western halves of the Indian Ocean for more than eight hundred years in a long chain of transoceanic trade from South China to the eastern Mediterranean.

Inheriting the pre-Islamic Sasanid mercantile organization in the early Islamic period, the people of the Gulf, prominent among them the Omanis, the original "boat people," were dominant in the early expansion of commercial activity eastward to China. The earliest references to the Islamic transoceanic trade are dated to the late seventh century when we have descriptions of Gulf ships sailing to Canton to buy Chinese silks. The ninth-century anonymous work *Relations of China and India* details the sailing routes to China followed by the seafarers and merchants of prominent Gulf ports such as Siraf as they set forth on their annual voyages to China, to Daibul and Calicut in India, and to the city-states of East Africa.[27] The first port of call on the outward journey was Muscat or Suhar. The ships carried incense, thoroughbred horses, gemstones, pearls, sandalwood, and spices, returning with silk and porcelain. The battle for control of this highly profitable maritime trade with the East played a key role in determining the early Islamic avenues of conquest, in particular the conquest of Sind in western India by Omani merchants from the seventh century.[28] The supremacy of Arab and Persian seafarers as universal carriers of cargo and passengers at this early period may have been due to their navigational abilities that allowed them to strike out across the ocean and sail out of sight of land. On the other hand, heavy Chinese junks did not begin to sail to the Malabar Coast until the end of the tenth century under the Sung dynasty (960–1126). However, by 916, long distance voyages from the Gulf to China had come to an end and instead ships from Siraf and Oman met with those from the Far East at Kalah Bar (probably present-day Kedah) on mainland Malaysia. A north-south axis of seaborne trade between the Gulf and East Africa intersected the main east-west axis along the shores of Arabia. Among the luxury goods originating in East Africa prized by successive Chinese dynasties were ivory and gold. There was a brief revival of long-distance voyages in the fifteenth century. This time the Ming Dynasty (1368–1644) launched a series of seaborne expeditions under the legendary Chinese eunuch Admiral Zheng Ho between 1404 and 1433 to Hormuz, the Gulf, and East Africa before they were abandoned. China, threatened by Japanese piracy, decided to close its coasts to foreigners and banned Chinese overseas commerce.[29]

From the seventeenth century onwards, the tremendous trade expansion and the intensification of cultural unity in the western Indian Ocean under the Omani Ya'rubid and Al Bu Sa'id dynasties, are now well known and documented.[30] During this period, traders of different "nationalities," ethnic identities, and a multitude of religious persuasions in Zanzibar, Muscat, and Mandvi (in Gujarat) maintained commercial links via their family networks and related merchant communities on distant shores in Calicut (India), Kedah (Malaysia), and further east. This further encouraged the longue durée historical trend of the spread of common cultural values from dress to music to furniture to the style of buildings and even to similarity of food preferences all the way from Kilwa to Canton.

The relatively recent arrival of the imperial powers in the Indian Ocean introduced new ideas such as the conduct of trade by warfare, the crusader mentality of the Portuguese, the implantation of flags, and the drawing of boundaries by European nations to safeguard their own interests, as well as the propagation of alien cultural values with which the people of the Gulf and the wider Indian Ocean are still struggling to reconcile. But despite the upheavals provoked by the European powers, the ties uniting the peoples of the Indian Ocean continue to endure. Even today there are still Omanis who live according to age-old traditions and rhythms, with one house and wife in Oman and another house and wife in Zanzibar, spending part of the year here and the other part there. There are also Yemenis and Hadhramis who have similar arrangements in Malaysia, Borneo, Hyderabad, or the Indonesian islands and back home in Hadhramawt. Only now, the great old dhows, which for centuries carried their forefathers, have been relegated to museums, as curiosities or remnants of a bygone age. Today the modern Indian Ocean nations, and particularly the Gulf nations with their palm-fringed beaches, seek in earnest to attract tourists to their shores in their search to diversify their economies before the oil runs out as *inshallah,* God willing, it one day surely must.

Notes

1. N. Chittick, "East Africa and the Orient: Ports and Trade before the Arrival of the Portuguese," in *Historical Relations across the Indian Ocean: Report and Papers of the Meeting of Experts Organized by Unesco at Port Louis, Mauritius, from 15 to 19 July 1974* (Paris: UNESCO, 1980), 13.
2. G. W. B. Huntingford, trans. and ed., *The Periplus of the Erythraean Sea* (London: Hakluyt Society, 1980), 19, 31.
3. Ibid., 196–97.
4. Arrian, Herodotus, Strabo, Ptolemy, Agartharkhides, and Pliny, quoted in A. T. Wilson, *The Persian Gulf: An Historical Sketch from the Earliest Times to the Beginning of the*

Twentieth Century (London: George Allen and Unwin, 1928), 36–55 and Huntingford, Periplus, 166–97.

5. Fernand Braudel, *The Mediterranean and the Mediterranean World in the Age of Philip II,* 2 vols., trans. Siân Reynolds (New York: Harper and Row, 1972–73).
6. G. R. Tibbets, *Arab Navigation in the Indian Ocean before the Coming of the Portuguese, Being a Translation of* Kitab al-Fawa'id fi usul al-bahr wa'l-qawa'id *of Ahmad b. Majid al-Najdi, Together with an Introduction on the History of Arab Navigation* (London: The Royal Asiatic Society of Great Britain and Ireland, 1971).
7. Al-Masudi quoted in Xavier Beguin Billecocq, ed., *Oman: vingt-cinq siècles de récits de voyage=Twenty-five Centuries of Travel Writing* (Paris: Relations Internationales and Culture, 1994), 31.
8. Tibbets, *Arab Navigation in the Indian Ocean,* 1–2.
9. S. Cleuziou and M. Tosi, "Ra's al-Jinz and the Prehistoric Coastal Cultures of the Ja'alan," *Journal of Oman Studies* 11 (2000): 19–73.
10. M. Beech, "Fishing in the 'Ubaid: A Review of Fish-Bone Assemblages from Early Prehistoric Coastal Settlements in the Arabian Gulf," *Journal of Oman Studies* 12 (2002): 36.
11. Chittick, "East Africa and the Orient," 13.
12. Braudel, *The Mediterranean and the Mediterranean World,* vol. 1, 20.
13. Huntingford, *Periplus,* 61.
14. J. R. Wellsted, *Travels in Arabia,* vol. 1 (London: J. Murray, 1838), 79–80.
15. S. B. Miles, *The Countries and Tribes of the Persian Gulf,* 2nd ed. (London: Cass, 1966), 491–92.
16. D. A. Agius, *In the Wake of the Dhow: The Arabian Gulf and Oman* (Reading, UK: Ithaca Press, 2002), 131.
17. Tim Mackintosh-Smith, *Travels with a Tangerine: A Journey in the Footnotes of Ibn Battutah* (London: John Murray, 2001), 263–64.
18. Miles, *Countries and Tribes of the Persian Gulf,* 15.
19. T. Vosmer, "Model of a Third Millennium B.C. Reed Boat Based on Evidence from Ra's al Jinz," *Journal of Oman Studies* 11 (2000): 149–52.
20. Cleuziou and Tosi, "Ra's al-Jinz and the Prehistoric Coastal Cultures of the Ja'alan."
21. For an analysis of Sumerian/Babylonian texts see D. T. Potts, *The Arabian Gulf in Antiquity,* vol.1, *From Prehistory to the Fall of the Achaemenid Empire* (Oxford: Clarendon Press, 1990), 135–50.
22. S. Cleuziou, "Magan through the Ages," International Symposium, Muscat, 24–25 May 2004.
23. S. Cleuziou, "Early Bronze Age Trade in the Gulf and the Arabian Sea: The Society behind the Boats" in *Archaeology of the United Arab Emirates,* ed. D. T. Potts, H. Al Naboodah, and P. Hellyer (London: Trident Press, 2003).
24. S. Cleuziou, personal communication, Muscat, May 26, 2003.
25. For details of these migrations and ties between Arabia and Persia, see M. R. Bhacker and B. Bhacker, "Qalhat in Arabian History: Context and Chronicles," *Journal of Oman Studies* 13 (2004): 11–55.
26. Yaqut and Mas'udi, quoted in J. Wilkinson, *The Imamate Tradition of Oman* (New York: Cambridge University Press, 1987), 41.
27. Z. Jun-Yan, "Relations between China and the Arabs in Early Times," *Journal of Oman Studies* 6 (1983), part 1, 91–109.
28. Abd-Allah b. Humayyid al-Salimi, *Tuhfat al-a'yan bi sirat ahl Uman,* vol. 1 ([Oman]: Maktabat al-Istiqamah, 1997), 263–64; Al-Mas'udi, *Muruj al-dhahab wa ma'adin al-jawhar,* vol. 1 (Beirut, Lebanon: Dar al-Andalus, 1965), 198; see also A. Esmail and A. Nanji, "The Ismailis in History", in *Ismaili Contributions to Islamic Culture,* ed. S. H. Nasr (Tehran: Imperial Iranian Academy of Philosophy, 1977), 233.
29. K. N. Chaudhuri, *Trade and Civilisation in the Indian Ocean: An Economic History from the Rise of Islam to 1750* (New York: Cambridge University Press, 1985), 60–62.
30. See M. R. Bhacker, *Trade and Empire in Muscat and Zanzibar: Roots of British Domination* (London and New York: Routledge, 1992).

CHAPTER 9

The Persian Gulf and the Swahili Coast: A History of Acculturation over the *Longue Durée*

Abdul Sheriff

The sea is not the end of the world. It is the beginning of a whole new world of resources and opportunities.[1]

The Swahili Coast and the Persian Gulf are only a monsoon apart, and the dhow provided a dependable vehicle for perennial two-way economic and sociocultural interaction across the Indian Ocean for hundreds of years, creating the "largest cultural continuum in the world."[2] Whatever colors one may use to paint the various continents around the Indian Ocean, only a multicolored ribbon can begin to characterize the historical and cultural complexity of its long littoral. On the one hand it represents an interface between the continental and marine environments; and on the other, for hundreds of years the littoral people have been interacting with each other across the ocean economically, socially, and culturally. These littoral peoples are strategically located at the confluence of continental and maritime environments, able to exploit both economically, and to be fashioned by them socially and culturally. In this chapter, I propose to review social interaction in the two littoral societies over the *longue durée* to highlight the social processes that produced cosmopolitan maritime communities.

The Trade Connection

One of the primary processes of interaction across the Indian Ocean was trade, which was the raison d'être for much of the communication, and it was the monsoon that probably had the greatest impact on sociocultural relations between these two areas over the longue durée. The first glimpse of such external connection of the East African coast occurs right at the beginning of the Christian era. It was then said to be under the suzerainty of a south Yemeni kingdom. The *Periplus of the Erythraean*

Sea, a Greek commercial guide to the Indian Ocean written in the first century A.D., says:

> They send out to it merchant craft that they staff mostly with Arab skippers and agents who, through continual intercourse and intermarriage, are familiar with the area and its language.[3]

The quote expresses, in a nutshell, the predominant tendency of transoceanic interactions throughout subsequent centuries down to the middle of the twentieth century, based largely on mundane and uncelebrated peaceful trade, intermarriage, and sociocultural interpenetration.

The earliest extant Arabic and Persian sources for the Swahili coast are probably derived from such commercial relations when the fulcrum of the trade had shifted to the Persian Gulf after the rise of the Abbasid dynasty at Baghdad. The conquest of Iran[4] by the Muslims during the seventh century apparently did not lead to the disappearance of the Iranians from the seaways, which they continued to dominate during the early Islamic period. A Chinese scholar of the ninth century specifically mentions large Iranian trading expeditions to the Horn of Africa, and they dominated the sea-routes as late as the tenth century.[5] The medieval geographer Mas'udi says the people of Siraf, the famous port on the Iranian coast close to Shiraz, made voyages to the land of the Zanj, and in 916 A.D. he sailed in one of their vessels. The term "Zanj," which predated the rise of Islam and is used by the Arabs and Iranians alike, referred to the black people from the East African coast and forms the root of the modern name of Zanzibar.[6] In the middle of the tenth century, the geographer Abu Ishaq al-Istakhri says:

> The most important town . . . after Shiraz, is Siraf, which is almost as large as Shiraz; its houses are of teak wood, or of other wood from [the country of the Zanj]. . . . The inhabitants take such great pride in the elegance of their houses that some spend 30,000 dinars in constructing it and surrounding it with gardens.[7]

'Aja'ib al-Hind (Wonders of India) is a collection of numerous sailors' stories by Buzurg b. Shahriyar, a former Iranian sailor, about the adventures of many famous captains and merchants from Siraf who were of Iranian extraction. In one of the longest stories he recounts a slaving adventure in 922 A.D. to Sofala (on the Mozambique coast), where a captain traded for two hundred slaves. He then tried to maximize his profit by kidnapping the local ruler who was sold into slavery in Oman. Eventually, the ruler escaped and returned to his home country where he converted his followers to Islam.[8]

Abu Uthman Amr b. Bahr al-Jahiz (ca.767–868), whose learning was encyclopaedic in almost every branch of knowledge, was one of the most illustrious writers and philosophers in ninth-century Iraq. His family may have been a product of the slave trade from the African coast, and he derived a lot of his information about the coast from the large Zanj slave population that inhabited the country around Basra at that time. He mentions the eloquence of Zanj preachers who could discourse before their rulers continuously from sunrise to sunset.[9] Mas'udi says Qanbalu, the most famous place on the coast at that time (thought to refer to a site on the island of Pemba in the Zanzibar archipelago), traded in ambergris and leopard skins, in gold from the land of Sofala, and in ivory that was exported to India and China via Oman. He wrote at great length on the political and military organization of the Zanj and on their "elegant" language. He also made references to their religious practices, including ancestor worship, although by then Qanbalu had "a mixed population of Muslims and Zanj idolaters." By the twelfth century Idrisi, the noted Arab geographer, remarks the population of Zanzibar was mostly Muslim, but he says it was mixed, and Yaqut in the following century says that one of the two towns on Jazirat al-Khadra (the Green Isle or Pemba) was ruled by an Arab from Kufa in Iraq, apparently the only direct reference to the assumption of power by the immigrants in these external sources.[10]

THE PEOPLE OF THE DHOW

These anecdotal references in the earlier sources acquire greater resonance when read in conjunction with Alan Villiers' *Sons of Sinbad,* the most incisive account of an actual voyage on an Indian Ocean dhow in the twentieth century. This probably gives an indication not of an unchanging oriental trade but of the *longue durée* commercial relations between the two regions.[11] Trade is not merely an economic activity. The commodities exchanged have considerable social and cultural as well as economic significance for the societies among which they are being exchanged. It was bound to exercise considerable influence on the social tastes and even architecture of the communities involved in the exchange. One of the main items of export on these dhows from East Africa was timber, especially mangrove poles, which are the cheapest and strongest wood for house construction. Mangrove poles, however, were not merely a trade good. As Villiers put it, "the dimensions of many an Arab room are fixed on the beach at Lamu" on the coast of Kenya, since the normal length of these poles determined the width of the rooms of many historical towns along the Swahili coast as well as in the Persian Gulf, such as Siraf and on the nearby island of Qishm.[12] The dhow in which Villiers sailed from the Swahili coast to the Persian Gulf in 1938–39 picked up 6,000 poles which were sold at Bahrain to an agent of King Abd al-Aziz b. Sa'ud of Arabia who was then building a palace in Riyadh. Apart from these articles of mass consumption, sailors and private merchants on the dhows also carried a great variety of commodities for which they could find a market: colorful sarongs (loincloths) from Indonesia that have become part of the dress of people all around the Indian Ocean; small straw fans from Mukalla in south Yemen for hot and humid Mombasa and Zanzibar; and Indian harem veils that were popular with Somali women.

Another highly consequential characteristic of the dhow trade was that it was typically a peddler trade, which the Dutch economic historian J. C. Van Leur had dismissed as archaic in his 1955 classic, *Indonesian Trade and Society.* Trade routes, he said, ran from port to port, exchanging luxuries and raw materials rather than items of mass consumption, and involving a large number of traders.[13] Some historians have undertaken an economic refutation of this conception of "oriental trade," but what is important is to understand the long-term social consequences of this type of trading. In 1945–46 more than three hundred monsoon dhows entered Zanzibar. Tracing the origin and routes of these ancient crafts on a map describes a very dense web of intercommunication over the western Indian Ocean, with substantial ramifications on the societies and cultures of the region. Of these, less than a fifth sailed directly from their port of origin to their destination. The rest made more than four hundred landfalls at intermediate ports along the coasts of south Arabia, Somalia, and East Africa before arriving finally at Zanzibar, and some went beyond to Mozambique, the Comoro islands, and Madagascar.

The Omani ports of Muscat and Sur, which were more favorably located directly on the Arabian Sea, played an entrepôt role for the Gulf as a whole. When the decline in the Arab dhow trade set in after the discovery of oil, dhows from the Iranian ports of Bushehr, Lingeh, and Kung emerged during the 1970s as the more prominent dhow traders at Mombasa on the Kenya coast.[14] A century earlier, if the passage of slaves through the Persian Gulf island of Kharg is any indication, it seems that although Muscat and Sur still handled 50 percent of the traffic, Lingeh on the Iranian side of the Gulf and the Qasimi ports on the Arab side handled nearly 40 percent of the trade, and they may have had direct dhow connection with the Swahili coast. In the early centuries of Islam the migration of the main port from the head of the Gulf at Ubulla successively to Siraf, Qais, and Hormuz at its mouth forms an interesting chapter in the history of the Persian Gulf.[15]

In the mid-1940s more than two-fifths of the dhows arriving at Zanzibar came from Oman, especially from the famous port of Sur. Many of them first sailed to Basra at the head of the Gulf to pick up cargoes of dates, sometimes returning to their home ports to collect dried fish and salt. They then sailed to India or Aden to unload part of their cargoes and take on other commodities for the Swahili coast. About an eighth of the dhows originated from the Indian subcontinent, bringing foodstuffs, timber, spices, and textiles, influencing both the cuisine and dress. The red clay tiles from Mangalore (India) have transformed the roofscape of many colonial towns in East Africa. Finally, about a tenth of the dhows came from the Somali coast, bringing dried fish, livestock, and the famous Kismayu *ghee* (clarified butter), an essential ingredient of many Indian Ocean dishes.

The monsoons imposed a regime that not only facilitated regular seasonal movement but also restricted it in one important way, requiring dhows to spend a long time between the monsoons in their ports of destination. Again, this may be considered uneconomic, but it provided great potential for social interaction between visiting sailors and local people. Although movement of goods was the primary reason for much of the transoceanic connections, it was the movement of people that probably had a more long-lasting impact on the social and cultural history of the Indian Ocean. We can talk of three groups of people who moved in these dhows across the ocean, but women in general did not do so to the same degree, with important consequences.

Dhows were commanded and manned by men who, through long experience of life on the common sea, had developed a sense of community not only among themselves but also with the various maritime communities they visited on their annual voyages. Villiers was impressed by what he called a "brotherhood of the sea":

> The friendship of these nakhodas [captains] . . . was a very real thing and they formed a united band. They were prepared at any time to assist another's vessel in any circumstances . . . Theirs was a real brotherhood of the sea.[16]

On board the dhow the crew belonged to different sects of Islam, and many were of slave origin, but this seemed to make little difference. They all ate the same food and in the same quantities.

The dhow traffic involved a very large floating population. The more than three hundred foreign dhows that put in at Zanzibar in 1945–46 carried more than 6,000 sailors, which economists may consider uneconomic. But what is important for the history of the Indian Ocean is the social impact of this substantial movement of people to and fro, year in and year out. For the sake of comparison, many large steamers, each with a tonnage of several tens of dhows, put into East African ports these days with small crews of Koreans, Taiwanese, or Greeks, and they spend a couple of days on shore while the cargo is being unloaded by cranes. They may scatter a few wild oats, but their social impact on the local people, or of the local people on them, is minimal.

The dhow sailors were no mere flotsam. Racial intermingling and integration reached quite high levels in these maritime communities. Some of the *nakhudas* in the famous dhow port of Kuwait were of very dark complexion, but Villiers was told nonchalantly that they were all Arabs. After the long voyage, sailors on Villiers' dhow often talked of *bebes* (ladies) and *bints* (girls) for which Lamu and Zanzibar were said to be famous. As a result of polygamy, captains and sailors had established liaisons with local women at many places they regularly visited. The legendary Sindbad seemed to find a wife in nearly every port, and the North African globetrotter Ibn Battuta married one at almost every landfall in the Indian Ocean.[17]

Thus, family bonds were forged that stretched across the ocean. Evidence from the beginning of the twentieth century shows that at least a quarter of the population of Sur had such transoceanic connections. Many nakhudas had established second and third homes along the Somali and Swahili coasts, in the Comoro Islands and northern Madagascar. One who had been trading between Arabia and East Africa had established a home in Mombasa, where one son was born and settled, and another at Lamu, where another son was born by a Swahili woman. The son later married a Lamu woman, and from his inheritance he bought a dhow, two houses and a piece of land there. Europeans, bound by ideas of monogamy and the nation-state, were thoroughly bewildered by the sailors of the Indian Ocean, who appeared to them to have a "plurality of domiciles" and to "divide their favours, connubial and commercial, between their ports of origin and their ports of adoption."[18] By trying to box them into neat nationalities, the British were trying to impose their conceptions in place of the global unity of the Indian Ocean world.

Interviews conducted at the dhow port of Sur in Oman in 1997 showed that this pattern of social interaction persisted into the late twentieth century, leaving a rich residue of social and cultural relations several decades after the dhow trade itself had almost come to an end. My host family during a visit there was probably typical. The old captain, Sa'id b. Muhammad b. Mubarak al-Mu'allim al-Mukhaini, had an Arab wife in Sur, another in Zanzibar, and a third, who was an African, in the interior of Tanzania. When I went for lunch I witnessed a rainbow family with all shades of brown and black, but I could sense no social distinctions between them. Others were apparently of slave origin; but they were all Arabic speaking and had adopted the local tribal surnames. As Salih b. Yusuf, another resident of Sur, said, four generations of his family were born in Sur, but the fifth was from Africa. "All the people here were from Africa," he said with some exaggeration. "After two or three generations they were considered Omani; even half the government was African—the mother was African and the father was Omani. But all are Arabs."[19]

Almost all of them retain a very nostalgic image of Zanzibar as "the island of dreams."[20] They remember it as a peaceful place where one could sleep anywhere in safety and where food was cheap. Some of them still like to visit East Africa, although these days they fly. The ninety-year-old Jum'a b. Khamis, belonging to the Bani Bu Ali tribe of Aija across the creek from Sur, was a nakhuda as his father had been. He said they were like fish, spending nearly ten months of the year at sea. He had spent seven years as a boy at Zanzibar, where his uncle had a house, and he had almost forgotten Arabic when he returned. He was referred to by his nephew with the Swahili honorific title *Mzee*. He himself told me with a twinkle in his ancient eyes that he had learned all his Swahili from the women of Zanzibar. His brother, Subait b. Khamis, who still builds dhows, is a famous drummer playing the Swahili *msondo* drum. Another carpenter now builds large models of dhows, which are very popular in all Suri homes. He had earlier married a woman from Sur by whom he had several grown-up children. Although the dhow traffic with the Swahili coast has now ended, the social link between Sur and Zanzibar has not been severed. Seventeen years earlier he flew all the way to Zanzibar via Gulf Air to marry one of the famed *banat* (daughters) of Zanzibar by whom he already had a whole string of children.

Apart from the sailors who were typically birds of passage (although many also settled down), dhows also carried passengers who included seasonal traders as well as longer-term migrants. Every northeast monsoon, a very mixed population boarded dhows from Arabia for the East African coast or the west coast of India, including merchants, hawkers, migrants, porters, women, children, and even musicians and beggars, and apparently only a small number returned. The private merchants from Hadhramawt in south Yemen and Sur in Oman were on a trading venture much as their ancestors had been for centuries, those who Villiers called "Sons of Sinbad." A certain Sa'id from Sur used to go to East Africa with his father who, Villiers says, had been a slave trader. At the age of six he had gone to Bagamoyo (Tanzania) and then into the Congo. Majid had been a captain and knew his way around the East African coast, including the Rufiji River, Comoro Islands, and Madagascar, as well as the Gulf of Kutch in western India. He spoke Swahili, Persian, Hindustani and several Indian dialects, Somali, and Arabic, and could curse well in English.

Hadhramis had been coming down to Mombasa and Zanzibar from time immemorial. They sought work as porters, water carriers, coffee sellers, night watchmen, petty hawkers, and minor shopkeepers, which was an envied profession. As soon as Villers landed in Lamu and Mombasa, he saw some of the passengers hawking through the streets, carrying small bundles of sarongs, singlets, shawls, and turbans. Other cases show the intricate web of trade and settlement that encompassed the whole Indian Ocean from the interior of Hadhramawt to Southeast Asia in one direction and inner Africa in the other. A sixty-five-year-old blind Yemeni *sayyid* from somewhere in the interior of Hadhramawt came on board at Mukalla to go to Africa to wind up the affairs of a brother who had died somewhere in the Congo. He himself had spent eight years on ocean steamers, and had been an automobile worker in Detroit where he had lived in the Polish quarter and spoke the language. There were several others who were born in Indonesia or Malaysia, were half-Malay and half-Hadhrami, speaking Malay and Dutch, reading newspapers written in Arabic and Dutch, and playing an ancient gramophone with records from Cairo and Damascus.

There was also a large number of children on the dhow, traveling on their own or accompanying other passengers. A young boy of eight born somewhere on the Gulf of Oman had been a beachcomber since he was three years old. He had already been to Zanzibar, and was now going there to stay because he thought it was better than Arabia. A blind beggar brought on two boys whom he passed off as his sons. He was supposed to feed them, but when he failed to do so, they were prepared to choose another patron. As soon as he landed at Mombasa he started begging with his two boys.

As in the case of many other cultures, sea life was predominantly the sphere of men into which women were allowed to intrude only grudgingly. The captain of the dhow did not want women on board because they had to be sheltered and segregated, and "they often made trouble." He charged them one-third more fare than men, and they had to pay it in advance, although other captains denied there was a difference in the fare. He envied his fellow nakhuda who had only three women among his 150 passengers whereas he had taken on fifteen at Shihr in the Hadhramawt. Women formed only 1 percent of the 2,654 passengers who landed at Mombasa in 1945.[21] The very small number of females among the passengers was bound to have an important implication for social and cultural as well as racial integration in the western Indian Ocean. Arab women were always scarce overseas, and many of the Arab men married local women, giving rise to a rainbow population and a very cosmopolitan culture. In a description that could have been repeated almost verbatim for many other Indian Ocean ports, Villiers says of Mukalla on the Hadhramawt coast:

> The streets of Mukalla teemed with strange human beings dressed in all the colourful costumes of the East—Banyan merchants in their flappy diaphanous trousers and little black hats, Yemenites in sarongs and turbans, Beduin in black and indigo, . . . Persian,

> Somali, Kuwaiti, Suri, Batini sailors and nakhodas, wandering half-castes with blood from all the East in them, half-Malays, half-Turks, half-Africans, half-Egyptians, half-Baluchi, half-Balinese. The Hadhrami wanders far and takes his women where he finds them, bringing back the male offspring to his native land, and the blood of the whole East pulses in those busy Mukalla streets.[22]

At Zanzibar Villiers' dhow took on three schoolteachers, the only passengers for the return journey. He initially described them as Swahili, who he said were more "Negroid" in appearance than any of the sailors. On closer acquaintance he found that in fact two of them were Baluchi brothers, progeny of an ivory trader from Baluchistan on the border between Iran and Pakistan and a woman from the Congo. The other was a distant relation of an Arab prince born in Zanzibar who was, according to Villiers, a quarter Negro. They all had relatives in Muscat. They had been boy scouts and were well educated, speaking English well. They wore trousers and did not say their prayers regularly, to the chagrin of the captain. Most of the time, they kept to themselves and spoke Swahili, apparently discussing politics, much as their modern compatriots. They wanted to join the British Navy or some steamer in the Persian Gulf to see the world, or hire a car at Kuwait to take them to Mecca. As soon as they approached Muscat, they changed to Arab gowns and began to say their prayers more regularly in preparation for their adjustment to life in Arabia.

The Swahili Coast as a Refuge: The Ibadi and Shirazi Traditions

While trade was the bedrock on which the perennial social relations between the Persian Gulf and the East African coast were built, at certain times and in some circumstances there may have been more purposive migration and settlement of larger groups of people, either to escape religious persecution or to conquer and colonize an area. Strangely enough, contemporary Arabic sources referred to above rarely mention such events. On the other hand, local chronicles from the East African coast and Oman, often written long after the events by local literati, tended to place migrations of religious refugees from the Islamic heartland at center stage.

These chronicles dwell on the migration of a series of religious refugees from the Islamic heartland as dynastic rule was entrenched and the Sunni orthodox schools emerged as the established religion under the Umayyads and Abbasids. One of the earliest migrations is recorded in the Omani chronicle that speaks of the migration in ca. 705 A.D. of Sa'id and Sulaiman of the Julanda dynasty of Oman to the land of the Zanj after the defeat of the Ibadi Imamate by the Umayyad governor Hajjaj b. Yusuf. John Wilkinson argues that these traditions are confirmed by contemporary *fiqh* (jurisprudence) materials called the *Kilwa Sira* (Tradition of Kilwa) dating to the twelfth century. They relate to two brothers who were propagating Ibadism on the Swahili coast. They also talk of a missionary from southern Iraq who had been successfully converting the masses to Ithna Ashari ("Twelver") Shi'ism by a disgruntled faction of the Ibadi creed at Kilwa,[23] a city that had emerged as the pre-eminent port there.[24]

From the other end of the monsoon, the Chronicle of Kilwa speaks of a series of migrations of religious refugees from the troubled Persian Gulf in the early centuries of Islam. The earliest version of this story was recorded by the Portuguese chronicler João de Barros in the middle of the sixteenth century. According to it, the first foreign people who came to settle on the East African coast from overseas were followers of Zaid, a Shi'i rebel against the Umayyads who died in 740. His followers spread along the coast and intermarried with the indigenous people.

More widespread is the tradition of the Shirazi migrations. The famous Iranian city of poets and saints may appear to be a very distant place, but all along the East African coast there are echoes of an ancient connection between that city and the land of the Zanj, with populations or families claiming origin from Shiraz. While this folk memory may not be the whole historical truth, there is much archaeological, linguistic, and cultural evidence for migration to the Swahili coast from Iran, which was no less probable than that from the Arabian side of a unified historical entity, although some historians seem to be reluctant to accept this.[25]

After the final downfall of the Iranian Buyid dynasty of Fars in 1062, many Sirafis migrated to the island of Qais on the Iranian side of the Gulf, and to many other parts of the Indian Ocean, and some went even as far as China. The Arab geographer Maqdisi says "Most of the shipbuilders and seafaring men are Persians." The greater part of the inhabitants of Aden and Jidda were Iranians, although the language was Arabic, while at Jidda, "the Persians are the ruling class and live in splendid palaces." At Suhar in Oman, "the Persians are masters of it," and "they speak and call out to each other in Persian."[26] It is remarkable that there are many Persian references in the writings of Ibn Battuta in his travels across the Indian Ocean in the fourteenth century, and the famous Chinese admiral Zheng He in 1410 left a stele in Ceylon to record his stupendous transoceanic voyages in three languages: Chinese, Tamil, and Persian.[27] It is within this historical context that the Shirazi tradition along the East African coast has to be viewed.

According to the de Barros version (written in 1552) of the Kilwa chronicle, a prince from "Shiraz, which is in Persia," Ali b. Hasan, escaping from the stigma of an Abyssinian slave mother, embarked in about A.H. 400/1010 A.D. for the East African coast.

> Having come to the settlement of Mogadishu and Barawa, *as he was of Persian origin and belonged to the sect of Mahamed which . . . was different from that of the Arabs,* . . . he sailed down the coast until he came to the port of Kilwa . . . he bought it from [the Kafirs] at the price of some cloth.[28] [Emphasis added]

It is clear from the quotation above that the immigrants belonged to one of the minority sects, possibly Shi'i.[29] He bought the island of Kilwa from its African chief, paying for it in cloth, which may betray the commercial background of this merchant prince.

Three centuries later an abstract of an Arabic history of Kilwa, belonging to Shaikh Muhiyy al-Din b. Abd-Allah al-Qahtani, then the Shafi'i Qadi of Zanzibar (1837–70), came into the hands of the British Consul, John Kirk. However, the sectarian aspect of the Shirazi immigrant appears to have been suppressed since the original dynasty had been replaced by the Sunni Mahdali dynasty from the Yemen in the fourteenth century. Rizvi, though, has presented a very persuasive argument that the preface to the Arabic chronicle contains a lengthy discussion on the role of reason that could only have been inspired by the Mu'tazilite school, and specifically Shi'i Ithna Ashari (Twelvers), rather than the Shafi'i Sunni who are Ash'arites on this question, an argument that Wilkinson finds convincing.[30]

The Shirazi tradition is widespread along the Swahili coast from the Benadir in Somalia to northern Mozambique, the Comoros, and northern Madagascar. It was recorded at Kilwa at the end of the eighteenth century by the French slave trader Morice who signed a commercial agreement with Sultan Hasan b. Ibrahim b. Yusuf al-Shirazi. It held that the Shirazi came to Kilwa "with a fleet of forty sail 963 years ago" counting from the Islamic *Hijri* calendar, which would take us back to 842 A.D. At the beginning of the twentieth century Carl Velten recorded an oral tradition at Kilwa Kisiwani that Sultan Ali b. Selaimani, "the Shirazi, that is the Persian," bought the island with enough cloth to cover the whole distance from the island to the mainland.

He married a daughter of the local African chief. The son inherited and combined the island and the mainland into a single kingdom.[31]

These traditions seem to receive confirmation from a number of inscriptions on the Swahili coast. The earliest dated inscription so far found there is that on the *mihrab* of the Kizimkazi mosque in Zanzibar. It commemorates the erection of the mosque by Sayyid Abi Imran Mfahamu al-Hasan b. Muhammad in A.H. 500/1107 A.D., the middle title Mfahamu probably being among the earliest evidence for a Swahili word for ruler, *mfaume*, although Mas'udi had already mentioned some Swahili words in the tenth century. Of more immediate relevance is the floreate Kufic script that Whitehouse has identified as coming from a calligraphic school at Siraf, and he is convinced that the Kizimkazi inscription could only have been carved by a Sirafi sculptor or was imported from Siraf. Recently an apparently contemporaneous inscription has been unearthed at Tumbatu off the northwest coast of the same island, now in the Zanzibar Museum, although it has not as yet been deciphered.[32] At the northern end of the Swahili coast there are two inscriptions at Mogadishu that specifically recall Iranian settlers there. An epitaph in Arabic on a tomb mentions Abu Abd-Allah b. Raya b. Muhammad b. Ahmad al-Naisaburi al-Khurasani, of obvious Iranian descent, dated to A.H. 614/1217 A.D. The other is an inscription in the *mihrab* of the mosque of Arba'a Rukn that commemorates its erection in A.H. 667/1269 A.D. It names Khusrau b. Muhammad al-Shirazi, which is an unequivocal Iranian name and traced directly to Shiraz itself. During his exploration of East Africa in the middle of the nineteenth century, Richard Burton found a tile inlaid on a pillar tomb at Tongoni on the coast of Tanzania that contained the Persian legend "Shid-i-raushan" (the bright sun), which he clearly illustrated in the frontispiece of his book on Zanzibar.[33]

These inscriptions point to close sociocultural connections with the Persian Gulf, which are confirmed by large quantities of "Sasanian-Islamic" pottery that are thought to have been mostly manufactured in southern Iraq during the late Sasanian and early Islamic period. They have been found at many places along the Swahili coast, including Unguja Ukuu on Zanzibar, and at Kilwa, almost replicating the assemblage found at Siraf in the Gulf. At Manda in the Lamu archipelago, they have been found from the earliest strata (mid-ninth to early eleventh centuries) and constituted 23 percent, while unglazed "Siraf" ware formed nearly half of the total imported pottery.[34] More recently a new coin hoard has been found at Mtambwe in Pemba in which there are many coins bearing the name of Ali b. al-Hasan, mentioned in the Kilwa chronicle. It also included forty-two coins bearing the name of Bahram which is unmistakably an Iranian name.[35]

The tradition receives further support from a seam of Persian words contained within Swahili, the language of the coast. They were first identified in the nineteenth century by the German missionary Krapf who compiled the first Swahili dictionary. The first systematic analysis of words of oriental origin was by Bernhard Krumm, who enumerated seventy-eight Persian words that he says probably entered the Swahili language directly, and an additional twenty-six which may have entered through Arabic. Jan Knappert has extended the list to over three hundred words. Some loanwords, mostly relating to textiles, are found even in the oldest extant Swahili poetry, such as *Herekali* which dates to the early eighteenth century. Many of these words relate to navigation, traveling, shipping and commerce, vegetables and spices, chemicals and minerals, tools, textiles, and beads of different colors. Some of the words appear to have come directly from Persian while others came through other mediating languages, especially Arabic and Indian languages. Abdulaziz Lodhi has identified at least six words which he says came from an "older layer," and Derek Nurse and Tom Hinnebusch confirm that at least some of this loan material "is likely to antedate much of that from Arabic," and they associate it with Iranian power and influence along the south Arabian and East African coast in the late first and early second millennium A.D.[36]

The Zanj Connection

One of the important aspects in the relations between the East African coast and the Persian Gulf is the slave trade, and while it was not the continuous hemorrhage that colonial and post-colonial historians have tended to make it out to be, there were nevertheless two main periods when it was historically significant: the century leading up to the Zanj Rebellion in the ninth century, and during the eighteenth and nineteenth centuries. However, it would be a mistake to impose the paradigm about slavery derived from the Atlantic experience on a region where the phenomenon was more complex.

Slavery had existed in Arabia before the coming of Islam, but a majority of the African slaves were probably Ethiopians from across the narrow Red Sea. It was then largely domestic slavery, and while Islam did not abolish slavery, it sought to humanize it. It emphasized the human dignity of slaves, banned prostitution of female slaves, and urged legal marriage. Strangely enough for a religion often associated with slavery, a majority of the references in the Quran concerning slavery relate to manumission, which was considered an act of charity and piety. This inbuilt program for manumission thus provided for the gradual exit of slaves from servitude to freedom, and the integration of slaves into society. One of the most important reforms related to the inevitable intercourse between owners and their female slaves: whereas the Christian concept of marriage found this difficult to accommodate, Islam recognized it as a legal relationship, with the offspring of those unions being free children of their free fathers, with full rights as children by free mothers. Their mother, *umm walad*, could not be resold, but was automatically freed on the death of her master. Thus both the slave mother and her children were drained out of the slave pool and were integrated into the mainstream of free society. Islam thus provided a window of upward social mobility, what Ali A. Mazrui called "ascending miscegenation," in contrast to the American system where both remained slaves, what Mazrui terms "descending miscegenation." However, as Bernard Lewis points out, "in one of the sad paradoxes of human history, it was the humanitarian reforms brought by Islam that resulted in a vast development of the slave trade inside, and still more outside, the Islamic empire" since Islam forbade the enslavement of Muslims to continuously replenish the slave pool.[37]

The reforms, however, did not necessarily eliminate social oppression and discrimination, since there was often a gap between religious exhortation and the practice of some Muslims. This led Jahiz, apparently of slave descent, to complain bitterly in his impassioned treatise *Kitab fakhr al-Sudan ala al-Bidan* [The pride of the Blacks vis-à-vis the Whites]. Perhaps with stories like that of Antar, the dark-skinned hero in Arabian legends, in his mind he taunted the vainglorious Arabs:

> In the time of heathendom you regarded us as good enough to marry your women, yet when the justice of Islam came, you considered this no longer valid, and you found us distasteful, though the desert is full of our people who married your women, who were rulers and leaders, who defended your honor and saved you from your enemies.[38]

Jahiz in fact died on the very eve of a powerful rebellion which shook the Abbasid empire, led by the Zanj slaves and others who controlled southern Iraq for fourteen years. With the shift of power from Umayyad Syria to Abbasid Iraq in the middle of the eighth century, there had been a concerted attempt to rehabilitate irrigated agricultural lands in the southern marshes. Wealthy proprietors and merchants received extensive grants *(iqta)* of tidal land on condition that they desalinate it and make it arable. Slaves from many parts of Africa, including the Swahili coast, were recruited for the task, and the story of a slaving venture recorded by Buzurg b. Shahriyar and quoted above relates to this period. Although the rebellion was ultimately crushed, the slaves did not have to go back to the salt pans but were absorbed into society as domestics and in the army, and slave trade appears to have diminished.[39]

The next upswing in the slave trade with the Persian Gulf region occurred nearly a thousand years later. The expulsion of the Portuguese from their coastal forts in the middle of the seventeenth century had reinvigorated the Omani economy with the expansion of Omani commerce in the Indian Ocean. The profits accrued were invested in the expansion of irrigated date plantations on the Batina plains using slave labor. Imam Saif b. Sultan (1692–1711) is said to have owned 1,700 slaves and one-third of the date palms in Oman, and planted 30,000 date palms and renovated or constructed seventeen irrigation channels (*aflaj*). With increasing prosperity there was also a growing demand for domestic slaves as well as dhow sailors and soldiers, and especially for divers in the Persian Gulf, due to the growing world demand for its famous pearls. The slave trade from the Swahili coast was therefore revived, although it never attained the fantastic proportions claimed by some anti-slavery colonial authors such as Reginald Coupland.[40]

There was plenty of evidence of the legacy of past slave trade in the dhows of the Indian Ocean into the twentieth century. A high proportion of Kuwaiti and Suri sailors had African blood, and on the dhow on which Villiers sailed, the captain's mate and the muezzin (caller to prayers) were of slave origin. Racial intermingling and integration had reached quite high levels in the society, which seemed to surprise Villiers. Many of the captains were very dark, and at a feast in Kuwait many guests were "almost pure Negro," but Villiers was told that they were all Arab.[41]

The contrasting attitude to slavery and race by Villiers and his Arab hosts can be explained by the fact that the system of slavery operating here was quite different from that in the Atlantic region, especially in its social consequences. A majority of slaves taken across the Indian Ocean to the Middle East were absorbed as domestics, as concubines, or as pearl divers. Secondly, before the discovery of oil, the society around the Persian Gulf was very poor, and many of those who acquired slaves did so to get an extra hand to work on the farm or the boat. Relations between the master and the slave in such situations were diametrically different from those on plantations, such as in Zanzibar or in the Americas, where the owner may have been an absentee landlord living in a mansion in the town. In the home of a former dhow captain in Sur, I was struck by the fact that on the wall in the *majlis* (sitting room) the photographs of the owner, his dhows, and his *khadim* (servant, freedman or slave) were placed in exactly the same line.[42]

The system had a significant influence on social integration in Muslim societies. Throughout the nineteenth century there are indications of substantial populations of African origin all around the Persian Gulf, of whom about a third were free long before the coming of the British, according to Lorimer at the beginning of the twentieth century. The African population did not remain a separate entity, but African (and for that matter Indian) blood was flowing in Arab veins due to miscegenation. At Muscat in Oman, according to an Indian physician who carried out a medical survey at the end of the nineteenth century, nearly a quarter of the population was African, and the "mixed race, composed principally of the different degrees of admixture between the Arab and the Negro, and the Arab and the Abyssinians," formed more than a third of the total population, but they were not considered by the Arabs as essentially distinct from themselves. "The pure Arab element," he reported, was "remarkably small . . . being gradually absorbed by the mixed race, owing to the easy means of slave concubinage and the legitimacy of its product." At Sharjah there was "a large negro community" many of whom still spoke Swahili.[43]

On the Iranian coast a similar "hybrid race" is described at Bandar Abbas that included a mixture of Iranians, Baluchis, and Arabs as well as Africans, collectively called Abbasis, and the lower classes spoke a local dialect or pidgin which was a compound of Persian, Baluchi, Arabic and Swahili ingredients. In Baluchistan, George Curzon noted "a considerable admixture of the African element, due to the large importation of slaves from Muscat and Zanzibar." M. R. Izady states that the Omani Sultan of Zanzibar, Sayyid Sa'id (1804–56), tried to extend spice plantations to the Gulf by settling African farmers and slaves in the Minab-Jask region of Iran, and Behnaz Mirzai has traced the survival of a considerable amount of African cultural practices, such as the *zar* spirit possession, in the population of southern Iran.[44]

The Longue Durée of the Dhow Culture

A similar mélange of peoples and cultures has developed all around the Indian Ocean. If we may amplify Villiers' memorable sentence, the blood of Africa and the whole East pulses in those busy ports of the Indian Ocean. It refers not merely to the rainbow colors of its mixed populations but, more importantly, to their cosmopolitan cultures. As Anirudha Gupta has put it, "where boats ply, commerce generally follows." In the Indian Ocean before the coming of the Europeans, and in some cases long afterwards, "cooperation, not conquest was at the root of maritime prosperity of the coast."[45] Seafaring commerce demands exchange necessarily between peoples of different ecologies and cultures, and calls for a continuous expansion of intercommunity relations between the native and the foreigner. It has given rise to a "maritime ethos," a distinctive maritime culture.[46]

It was only from the 1950s that significant changes began to undermine long-distance dhow traffic in the western Indian Ocean. The most important single factor was the discovery of oil in the Persian Gulf that began to transform the economies of these states that had previously played such a central role in the dhow culture. By the 1950s, dhow captains were facing great difficulty making up their crews when there were easier means of livelihood in the oil industry at their doorsteps. The last Kuwaiti long-distance trade dhow is said to have sailed in the mid-1950s, although others from the western shores of the Persian Gulf and from Iran continued to trade into the 1970s.[47]

The death knell was sounded by the Zanzibar Revolution of 1964 when many people of mixed Arab origin were massacred, others were reportedly packed onto dhows then in the harbor and driven out to sea where some may have perished, and dhows were prohibited from entering Zanzibar harbor. Traumatic though the revolution was for the society engendered by the dhow, the age-old dhow traffic had already left a rich social residue all around the rim of the Indian Ocean that has proved to be a resilient plant that was not snuffed out by these political and economic changes. The return of people of Arab origin to Oman and the Persian Gulf, rather than sundering the age-old connection between the two sides of the rim of the Indian Ocean, has ironically revived and strengthened it. After several generations on the Swahili coast these people had to all intents and purposes become Swahili. Most of them had long forgotten Arabic, and the Swahili language had become their mother tongue. During that long period of interaction, they had enriched it through Arabic loanwords, motifs, and poetry in which some of them excelled to become major Swahili literary figures.[48] When they went back to Oman, they carried their new language, which has become the unofficial second language in Oman, widely spoken from the international airport at Muscat to the most remote village in the interior. Over a few generations they may well revert to Arabic, but it is bound to be influenced by their Swahili experience; it is equally possible that the Swahili language will grow roots in Oman and survive as a second language there.

Similar tendencies are discernible in other aspects of culture of the two peoples who had been brought together by the dhow. The older influence of Arabic music in the *Taarab* of the Swahili coast has been studied in great depth, while the impact of Swahili and other African musical cultures on that of the maritime peoples of Oman and Persian Gulf has begun to be explored.[49] The return of people of Arab origin from eastern Africa to Oman has given a new impetus to artistic exchange between them. While several Taarab groups have been formed in Oman and Dubai and one of the popular singers in Oman is a returnee, Omani marriage songs have become popular in Zanzibar, in some cases displacing old Swahili ones. The same can be said about dress. Swahili *khangas* (rectangular colorful cotton wraps for women) are widely worn in the households of the returnees in Oman, and their tastes and aspirations have already begun to influence the design and sayings printed on them. On the other hand, Arab attire has begun to influence the way people dress along the East African coast. Omani caps and Gulf designs of the long *khanzu* male dress have become commonplace in Zanzibar and other coastal cities, and the female black gown and scarf or veil has all but displaced the traditional Swahili *buibui* (black overall veil) in the towns.

All these are not merely aspects of a fossilized or unchanging dhow culture. Rather, they illustrate the longue durée character of a culture that gives new forms and meaning to changing relations between peoples brought together by the sea over several millennia whose potential for social and cultural as well as economic interaction has not been exhausted. For two decades following the revolution, Zanzibar tried to turn its back on the sea and develop an autarkic pseudo-socialist economy. When that experiment was shown to have failed by the mid-1980s and Zanzibar instituted a "trade liberalization policy," it was hardly surprising that many Zanzibari businessmen turned to the vibrant entrepôt of Dubai to obtain their supplies of trade goods to revive Zanzibar's commercial economy. There they found acquaintances and relatives, earlier returnees, as business partners and friends.

With the normalization of relations between Zanzibar and the Gulf countries and the restoration of business confidence, richer relatives in Oman and the Gulf could remit money to their poorer relatives in Zanzibar to help them set up shops along the main Mbuyuni-Mchangani shopping area there or elsewhere on the mainland. People began to visit each other more regularly, Zanzibaris seeking business and employment opportunities in the Gulf, while the returnees sought to get away from the insufferably hot summers in Arabia and to indulge in nostalgia about the old days in Zanzibar and elsewhere in East Africa. At least three airlines have tried to capitalize on this traffic with an almost daily flight. In the days of the dhow, Arab sailors used to talk excitedly about the beautiful damsels of Lamu and Zanzibar, many of whom they had married to give birth to the cosmopolitan society around the rim of the Indian Ocean. The virtual stoppage of the monsoon-regulated dhow traffic has by no means put an end to that long tradition of intermarriage. In the old dhow port of Sur, I met at least two people who had flown since the 1980s by Gulf Air to the Swahili coast to marry the famed banat of Zanzibar.

NOTES

1. A. Sheriff, "Between Two Worlds: The Littoral Peoples of the Indian Ocean," in *The Global Worlds of the Swahili: Interfaces of Islam, Identity and Space in 19th and 20th Century East Africa,* ed. Roman Loimeier and Rudiger Seesemann (Berlin, Germany: Lit, 2006), 15.
2. As described by Chittick in H. Gerbeau, "The Slave Trade in the Indian Ocean," in *The General History of Africa: Studies & Documents* 2: *The African Slave Trade* (Paris: UNESCO, 1979).
3. L. Casson, *The Periplus Maris Erythraeai* (Princeton, NJ: Princeton University Press, 1989), 61.
4. Iran was known abroad as Persia until 1935. I use Iran and Iranians generally except in direct quotes; Persian to refer to the language (Farsi); and to the Persian Gulf which is an ancient name even in the old Arabic geographical works, although there is an attempt by Arab authors to change it to the Arab Gulf.
5. Thomas M. Ricks, "Persian Gulf Seafaring and East Africa: Ninth–Twelfth Centuries," *African Historical Studies* 3 (1970): 342–43; J. J. L. Duyvendak, *China's Discovery of Africa* (London: Probsthain, 1949), 12–14.
6. G. S. P. Freeman-Grenville, "Zandj," in *Encyclopedia of Islam,* 2nd ed., vol. 11, 445.
7. A. T. Wilson, *The Persian Gulf* (London: George Allen and Unwin, 1928), 94. Wilson mentions Zanzibar, but the Arabic original says *Bilad al-Zanj,* Lands of the Zanj. See Abu Ishaq al-Istakhri, *Kitab Masalik wa'l-Mamalik,* ed. M. J. de Goeje (Leiden, The Netherlands: Brill, 1870), 127.
8. G. S. P. Freeman-Grenville, *East African Coast: Select Documents* (Oxford: Oxford University Press, 1962), 14; G. S. P. Freeman-Grenville, *Captain Buzurg Ibn Shahriyar of Ramhormuz, The Book of the Wonders of India* (London and The Hague: East-West Publications, 1982), 67; L. M. Devic, tr., *The Book of the Marvels of India* (London: George Routledge, 1928), 13, 42, 56; H. Hasan, *A History of Persian Navigation* (London: Methuen, 1928), 126n; Ricks, "Persian Gulf seafaring and East Africa," 339–57.
9. G. van Vloten, *Tria Opuscula Auctore Abu Othman Amr Ibn Bahr al-Djahiz Basrensi* (Leiden, The Netherlands: Brill, 1903), 57–85; V. V. Matveyev, *The Zindjs of E. Africa in the Accounts Left by Al-Dhakhiz* (Moscow, USSR: International Congress of Africanists, 1967), 7; B. Lewis, *Islam* (New York: Harper and Row, 1974), vol. 2, 210–16; G. H. Talhami, "The Zanj Rebellion Reconsidered," *International Journal of African Historical Studies* 10 (1977): 451; G. S. P. Freeman-Grenville, "Mtambwe Mkuu," *Encyclopedia of Islam,* 2nd ed., vol. 7, 249; C. Pellat, *The Life and Works of Jahiz* (Berkeley: University of California Press, 1969), 195–96.
10. Macoudi, *Les Prairies D'Or,* trans. C. Barbier de Meynard and Pavet de Courteille (Paris: Imprimerie Impériale, 1861), vol. 1, 205–06, 230–34; vol. 3, 2–3, 6–8, 29–30; Freeman-Grenville, *East African Coast,* 14–17; E. Renaudot, *Ancient Accounts of India and China* (London: Harding, 1733), 90; Tadeusz Lewicki, *Arabic External Sources for the History of Africa to the South of the Sahara,* Polska Akademia Nauk. Komisja Orientalistyczna. Prace, no. 9 (Wroclaw, Poland: Zaklad Narodowy Imienia Ossolinskich, 1969), 41; H. N. Chittick, "The Peopling of the East African Coast," in *East Africa and the Orient,* ed. H. N. Chittick and R. I. Rotberg (New York and London: Africana, 1975), 32; J. Gray, *History of Zanzibar* (London: Oxford University Press, 1962), 18.
11. Alan Villiers, *Sons of Sinbad* (New York: Charles Scribner's Sons, 1940; reprint, London: Arabian Publishing, 2006). Much of the description of travel on a dhow in the following pages, unless otherwise indicated, comes from this important source.
12. D. Whitehouse, "Excavations at Siraf," *Iran* 7 (1968): 51–52; Behnaz A. Mirzai, "African Presence in Iran," in *Traites et Esclavages: Vieux Problemes, Nouvelles Perspectives?,* ed. O. Petre-Grenouilleau (Paris: Société française d'Histoire d'Outre-mer, 2002), 233.
13. J. C. van Leur, *Indonesian Trade & Society: Essays in Asian Social and Economic History,* trans. James S. Holmes and A. van Marle (The Hague, The Netherlands: W. van Hoeve, 1955), 219.
14. Koji Kamioka and Hikoichi Yajima, *The Inter-Regional Trade in the Western Indian Ocean* (Tokyo, Japan: Institute for the Study of Languages and Cultures of Asia and Africa,

1979). See also Hikoichi Yajima, *The Arab Dhow Trade in the Indian Ocean* (Tokyo, Japan: Institute for the Study of Languages and Cultures of Asia and Africa, 1976).

15. Wilson, *The Persian Gulf,* 10. A. Sheriff, *Slaves, Spices & Ivory in Zanzibar* (London: Currey, 1987), 39.
16. Villiers, *Sons of Sinbad,* 284.
17. Ibid., 165. Ibn Battuta, *The Travels of Ibn Battuta,* vol. 2, trans. H. A. R. Gibb (Cambridge: Hakluyt Society, 1962).
18. Political Agent, Muscat to Resident, Persian Gulf, 3.5.1897, in the Case on behalf of His Majesty's Government. British Library: India Office Records: R/15/1/406.
19. Salih b. Yusuf b. Sulayim al-Ghailani, interviewed at Sur, Oman, December 9, 1997.
20. M. R. al-Jarwan, *Risalat ila Waladi* (Sharjah: Al-Khaleej, 1985), 201.
21. E. B. Martin and C. P. Martin, *Cargoes of the East* (London: Elm, 1978), 70.
22. Villiers, *Sons of Sinbad,* 57–59.
23. J. C. Wilkinson, "Oman and E. Africa: New Light on Early Kilwan History from the Omani Sources," *International Journal of African Historical Studies* 14 (1981): 275; Freeman-Grenville, *The Medieval History of the Coast of Tanganyika* (London: Oxford University Press, 1962), 31–32.
24. Wilkinson, "Oman and E. Africa," 272–305.
25. J. de V. Allen, "The 'Shirazi' Problem in East African Coastal History," *Paideuma* 28 (1982): 9, quoting James Kirkman approvingly as an authority.
26. Hasan, *History of Persian Navigation,* 123–25; K. Yajima, "Yemen and the Indian Ocean: On the Sirafi Migrants in South Arabia," *Journal of Asian and African Studies* (Tokyo), 5 (1972): 144. K. Yajima, "Maritime Activities of the Arab Gulf People and the Indian Ocean World in the 11th and 12th Centuries," *Journal of Asian and African Studies* (Tokyo) 14 (1977): 207, quoting Maqdisi.
27. Ibn Battuta, *Travels,* passim. F. Viviano, "China's Great Armada," *National Geographic* (July 2005): 41.
28. Freeman-Grenville, *Medieval History of the Coast of Tanganyika,* 75–76.
29. Ibid., 31–32.
30. S. A. Rizvi, "Some Evidence of Shi'ite Connection with Early History of East Africa," *The Light* 6 (1972): 3–6, 23–27. Rizvi also refers to the Swahili epic poem *Utenzi wa Seyyidna Huseni Bin Ali* by the nineteenth century Swahili poet Shaikh Hemed Abd-Allah al-Buhri, narrating events following the death of the Prophet's grandson Husain. It led to the formation of the Kaisaniyya sect that withered away before the middle of the eighth century. The tradition may have reached the coast before then. (Wilkinson, "Oman and East Africa," 295.)
31. G. S. P. Freeman-Grenville, *The French at Kilwa Island* (Oxford: Clarendon Press, 1965), 29, 42, 164, 182. Freeman-Grenville, *East African Coast: Select Documents,* 221. For a fuller discussion see A. Sheriff, "The Historicity of the Shirazi Tradition along the East African Coast," in *Historical Role of Iranians (Shirazis) in the East African Coast* (Nairobi, Kenya: Cultural Council of the Embassy of I. R. Iran, 2001).
32. S. Flury, "The Kufic Inscriptions of the Kizimkazi Mosque," *Journal of the Royal Asiatic Society* 21 (1922): 257–64. Flury, who apparently did not know the Swahili language, incorrectly rendered the word Mfahamu to read "Musa bin". See H. N. Chittick, "The 'Shirazi' Colonization of East Africa," *Journal of African History* 6 (1965): 288. Freeman-Grenville, *Medieval History of the Coast of Tanganyika,* 40n44 and *Captain Buzurg Ibn Shahriyar of Ramhormuz,* 68. D. Whitehouse, "Excavations at Siraf," *Iran* 6 (1968): 20.
33. E. Cerulli, *Somalia* (Rome: A Cura Dell'Amministrazione Fiduciaria Italiana, 1957), 2, 9. G. S. P. Freeman-Grenville and B. G. Martin, "A Preliminary Handlist of Arabic Inscriptions of the Eastern Coast of Africa," *Journal of the Royal Asiatic Society* 2 (1973): 102–03. R. F. Burton, *Zanzibar: City, Island and Coast* (London: Tinsley, 1872), vol. 2, frontispiece and 132–34.
34. Chittick, "The 'Shirazi' Colonization of East Africa," 283. Abdurahman Juma, *Unguja Ukuu on Zanzibar: An Archaeological Study of Early Urbanism* (Uppsala, Sweden: Uppsala University, 2004), 109. Whitehouse, "Excavations at Siraf," 14.

35. Freeman-Grenville, *East African Coast: Select Documents*, 67, 84, 148. S. A. Strong, "The History of Kilwa," *Journal of the Royal Asiatic Society* 20 (1895): 414. M. Horton, H. M. Brown, and W. A. Oddy, "The Mtambwe Hoard," *Azania* 21 (1986): 118, 120.
36. B. Krumm, *Words of Oriental Origin in Swahili* (London: The Sheldon Press, 1940), 26, 31 and Glossary. J. Knappert, "Persian and Turkish Loanwords in Swahili," *Sprache und Geschichte in Afrika* 5 (1983): 111–17. A. Lodhi, "Oriental Influences in Swahili: A Study in Language and Culture Change" (PhD diss., University of Gothenburg [Sweden], 2000), 62, 228, 230. D. Nurse and T. J. Hinnebusch, *Swahili and Sabaki: A Linguistic History* (Berkeley: University of California Press, 1993), 313, 328–29.
37. Ali A. Mazrui, "Comparative Slavery in Islam, Africa and the West," (Paper at the Second International Conference on Islamic Thought, Istanbul, 1997), 2–3, 9. B. Lewis, *Race and Slavery in the Middle East: An Historical Inquiry* (Oxford: Oxford University Press, 1990), 5–6, 10.
38. B. Lewis, *Islam from the Prophet Muhammad to the Capture of Constantinople,* vol. 2, *Religion and Society* (New York: Harper and Row, 1974), 211–12.
39. T. Noldeke, *Sketches from Eastern History* (London: Adam and Charles Black, 1892; repr. Beirut, Lebanon: Khayats, 1963), 146–75. A. Popovic, *The Revolt of the African Slaves in Iraq in the 3rd/9th Century* (Princeton, NJ: Markus Wiener, 1999), 22. G. H. Talhami, "The Zanj Rebellion Reconsidered," *International Journal of African Historical Studies* 10 (1977): 451.
40. Sheriff, *Slaves, Spices & Ivory in Zanzibar*, 19, 35–40. R. Coupland, *East Africa and its Invaders* (Oxford: Clarendon Press, 1938), 500.
41. Villiers, *Sons of Sinbad,* 338.
42. Interview with Abd-Allah b. Muhammad b. Khalfan b. Rashid al-Alawi, owner of a house with a large cement model of a dhow, Aija, Oman, 1997.
43. J. G. Lorimer, *Gazetteer of the Persian Gulf, Oman and Central Arabia,* 9 vols. (Calcutta, India 1908 and 1915; repr. Gerrards Cross, UK: Archive Editions, 1986), 241, 490, 1762. On the racial composition of Muscat, see Surgeon A. S. G. Jayakar, "Medical Topography of Muscat," in *The Persian Gulf Administration Reports, 1873—1947,* vol. 3 (Gerrards Cross, UK: Archive Editions, 1986), 101
44. Lorimer, *Gazetteer of the Persian Gulf,* 10, 589. He refers to only ten families of servile origin at Gwadar and the Makran coast, "some with Baluchi blood." G. N. Curzon, *Persia and the Persian Question* (London: Longmans, Green, 1892; repr. London: Cass, 1966), 259. M. R. Izady, "The Gulf's Ethnic Diversity: An Evolutionary History," in *Security in the Persian Gulf: Origins, Obstacles, and the Search for Consensus,* ed. L. G. Potter and G. G. Sick (New York: Palgrave Macmillan, 2002), 61. Behnaz A. Mirzai, "Slavery, the Abolition of Slave Trade, and the Emancipation of Slaves in Iran (1828–1928)," (PhD diss., York University, Canada, 2004).
45. A. Gupta, ed., *Minorities on India's West Coast* (Delhi, India: Kalinga, 1991), ix, xii–xiii.
46. A. H. J. Prins, *Sailing from Lamu* (Assen, Netherlands: Van Gorcum, 1965), 263–75.
47. Y. Y. al-Hijji, *The Art of Dhow-building in Kuwait* (Kuwait: Centre for Research and Studies on Kuwait, 2001), 4.
48. L. Harries, *Swahili Poetry* (Oxford: Clarendon Press, 1962), 4.
49. K. M. Askew, *Performing the Nation* (Chicago: University of Chicago Press, 2002); J. T. Fargion, "The Role of Women in *Taarab* in Zanzibar: An Historical Examination of a Process of 'Africanisation'," *The World of Music* 35 (1993): 109–25. Issam el-Mallah, *The Complete Documents of the International Symposium on the Traditional Music in Oman,* 3 vols. (Wilhelmshaven, Germany: Florian Noetzel, 1995).

Chapter 10

India and the Gulf: Encounters from the Mid-Sixteenth to the Mid-Twentieth Centuries

Patricia Risso

In 1573, the famous Mughal emperor Akbar visited the west-central Indian coastal area around the Gulf of Cambay that his forces had recently conquered. The area included the ports of Cambay and Surat. Reportedly, Akbar had never before seen the ocean, and one could only wonder what he might have thought of its possibilities or limitations.[1] Akbar's familial heritage was Central Asian, and in India his experience was land-based power. Although Akbar extended his rule from coast to coast across India, from the Arabian Sea to the Bay of Bengal, his focus was on interior concerns. He built a good roadway system, bridges, and caravanserais for interior trade, just as his near contemporary Shah Abbas did in Safavid Persia.[2] Yet India was already well connected by land and sea to the wider world, including the Persian Gulf. As we will see, Akbar's successors would become more involved in maritime concerns.

This chapter explores the varied relationships between the Gulf region and South Asia[3] from the Mughal period (1526–1858) into the twentieth century. It encompasses social, cultural, economic, and political interaction. This broad scope demands a high degree of selectivity, reflected in the first section of this chapter, "Early Modern Politics and Economy", that attempts to give some insight into major patterns of this contact. The second section of the chapter discusses highly interconnected labor, business, and oil wealth. At the outset, it is important to provide a context and to introduce the types of available source material.

The broad political context for the long time period under consideration underwent substantial changes. The Mughals of India were strong from the mid-sixteenth century through the early eighteenth, but then lost territory and power first to a Hindu tribal confederation known as the Marathas and then to British India. By the early nineteenth century, the Mughal ruler controlled not much more than the city of Delhi, and the British pensioned off the last Mughal shah in 1858.

Iran was unified and economically powerful during the reign of the Safavid Shah Abbas (1588–1629), but for much of the period covered here, there was civil war and political fragmentation. The Qajar dynasty imposed some degree of control during the nineteenth century. The Qajars moved the capital city from Isfahan north to Tehran and turned some of their commercial interests away from the Gulf and toward Russia, although the value of independent Persian trade with India remained high.[4] The Qajars bequeathed many serious structural and financial problems to the Pahlavi regime that took power away from them in the 1920s.

Throughout nearly all of the period in question, the Ottoman Empire controlled an area centered in what is now Turkey and stretching well into Europe and North Africa, passing from great strength during Sultan Suleyman's time (r. 1520—1566) to decline and dismemberment after World War I. In 1517, the empire conquered Egypt and Syria, and Ottoman Egypt plays a limited role in this chapter. From the late 1530s, the Ottomans ruled southern Mesopotamia and its port of Basra. They also at times laid claim to Yemen and parts of eastern Arabia and were players in the history of the Gulf.[5] It should be noted that in 1775, Karim Khan Zand, a ruler of Iran, ordered a siege of Ottoman Basra, by land and sea. Both the Ottomans and the Zands drew upon assistance from Gulf and Indian allies. Basra fell the following year and remained under Zand control for three years. The conflict disrupted—but did not stop—regional commerce.[6] This is a particularly good example to illustrate the resiliency of trade even in the face of extended hostilities.

In fact, commerce provides a continuous link between the Gulf and India over the centuries. Ports along the entire Indian coastline conducted commerce with ports of the Gulf, and overland routes into and through Iran provided caravan links, such as the route from Indian Lahore to Persian Isfahan where there was a small Indian community. The Red Sea competed for India's attention at ports that served Mecca and Cairo, while the eastern coast of Africa was essential to the larger commercial patterns that evolved over time. The Gulf region had an ongoing, significant demand for certain Indian commodities: timber for shipbuilding, cotton cloth for clothing, and rice as a dietary staple. Some Indian crops, such as grains and fruits, were introduced into places in the Gulf region where irrigation was possible. India was a market for both Central Asian and Arabian horses, Iranian silk, and palm dates that grow particularly well in the Gulf region. Pepper from Southeast Asia was an attractive commodity in both Indian and Gulf ports, and the transshipment of pepper forged further commercial links between the two.

Cultural patterns also evolved. A significant number of Indian merchants and commercial agents, Hindu and Muslim, chose to live in the Gulf. Arab and Persian merchants and agents from the Gulf region also settled in Indian ports. Migrant laborers who were dockworkers, seamen, unskilled builders, or agricultural workers all contributed to the demographic flux. India added to Arabian and Persian influences on Gulf architecture, design motifs, and cuisine.

There is a vast, complex, and uneven body of sources for the history of the relationship between India and the Gulf over the long period of time covered here. Among them are biographical materials for the Mughal rulers, shipping and legal records, and chronicles. There are also European trading company records, most notably Portuguese, Dutch, English, and French. For the later part of our time period, there are also documents from the United States, for example, commercial records of U.S. importation of Gulf palm dates.[7]

A few examples of the available material can illustrate their variety. In the 1780s, a Persian-speaking agent of the ruler of an Indian state kept a record of the travels and tribulations of an official delegation of which he was a part. The delegation sailed from

India through the Gulf on its way to the Ottoman sultanate, in search of recognition and alliance.[8] The agent provides fairly detailed political and commercial information. From the nineteenth century, we have an Arabic-language chronicle by Ibn Ruzaiq that was sponsored by the ruler of coastal Oman and Zanzibar. Ibn Ruzaiq's work is particularly valuable because it describes some of the same events that are covered in European records.[9] Also of interest are sources for the maritime history of Ottoman Egypt, because that history frequently intersects both the Gulf and India at the same time. An example of such a source is Katib Chelebi's seventeenth century *History of the Maritime Wars of the Turks*.[10] Another Ottoman Turkish seventeenth-century source describes Egyptian merchants at Istanbul: "There are a great number of rich merchants [here] who [also] have commercial establishments in India, Arabia, Persia, Yemen, and Frengistan [Europe]. They all walk clad in sable pelisses, followed by from forty to fifty servants."[11]

This chapter focuses on the history of various peoples of India and the Gulf, while the impact of Europeans is covered more extensively in other parts of this book. However, European records are important for information about local situations for the period covered in this chapter. Some agents of trading and shipping companies wrote political and commercial reports that form a framework for the European representation of the region.[12] The European sources dominate in terms of sheer volume, but they must be placed in a context of European imperialism and be used in conjunction with local sources.[13]

EARLY MODERN POLITICS AND ECONOMY

This central section provides examples of specific historical situations that illustrate the relationships between the Gulf and traditional India during the period under consideration. The first example attempts to explain the growing involvement of Mughal rulers in maritime affairs in the seventeenth century, particularly though not exclusively in the direction of the Gulf. The second example is the eighteenth-century history of a Muslim ruler in south-central India who extended his commercial reach to Muslim Oman. The third example focuses on a significantly large Indian expatriate community at the entrance to the Gulf.

Mughals and the Sea

The term Mughal is a corruption of Mongol, from whom the royal family claimed descent through Tamerlane back to Genghis Khan. The family established their rule over northern India between 1526 and 1556, when Akbar officially began his reign. His administration consolidated a large portion of traditional India. Diverse topography and climate, multiple languages and cultures, and regional economies usually generated small, competitive states in traditional India, and unity was problematic. In addition to the usual decentralizing tendencies, there was also the fact that the Mughals used the Persian language and patronized Persianized Muslim culture, while the overwhelming majority of their subjects were Hindus who spoke numerous languages derived from either Sanskrit or Dravidian.

As mentioned at the outset, Akbar's forces conquered territory around the Gulf of Cambay (modern Gulf of Khambhat), an inlet of the Arabian Sea along the west coast of India, in 1573–74. This included the formerly independent kingdom of Gujarat, which extended from the Kathiawar peninsula into the mainland coast, southward. By 1576, Akbar's army had also conquered all of Bengal, so that the new empire stretched from coast to coast. In the Gujarat region, Cambay was the most prominent port, but silt was beginning to collect in the harbor, making it less accessible and navigable. A port to the south, Surat, grew as Cambay declined.[14] Merchants from East Africa, the Red Sea and the Gulf all gravitated toward Surat. When Europeans set up their trading enterprises in western India, they chose the growing Surat and contributed to the size of the port and the volume of its trade. On the eastern coast, the Mughal port of note was Hugli, upriver in the Ganges delta in Bengal, not far from where the English would build their Fort William in Calcutta. Like Surat, Hugli attracted considerable trade. While the Mughal administration benefited from customs duties, the overall development of these ports and trade during Akbar's reign was largely independent of government sponsorship or policy.

Trade between India and geographically neighboring Iran focused on Indian cotton, indigo, and sugar in exchange for Central Asian horses, Persian silk, and carpets. This trade could be maritime, for example, between Surat and Bandar Abbas, or could involve caravan and riverine routes as well.[15] Purely overland routes beg the rhetorical question: how far inland does the Gulf region extend? The very designation "Gulf region" denotes a body of water, so the emphasis here is on contact via the Arabian Sea and the Gulf.

In the seventeenth century, Shah Jahan (r. 1628–1658) and Aurangzeb (also known as Alamgir, r. 1658–1707), showed somewhat more interest in maritime affairs than had Akbar. The rulers demonstrated an interest in subduing maritime violence that was disruptive to both trade and maritime transportation to Mecca for the pilgrimage.[16] Aurangzeb conquered part of the eastern Coromandel coast, including its port of Masulipatnam, that had become important due to its exchange of locally woven cloth for Southeast Asian pepper.[17] However, Mughal attention to the Indian Ocean still did not represent a consistent, long-term policy.

At Surat, the Mughals experienced maritime competition from a powerful Hindu tribal confederation called the Marathas, which dominated much of central India. While Cambay was within traditional Gujarat territory, Surat was far enough south to be in territory contested by the Maratha rulers who used maritime trade revenues to fund wars with the Mughals. The Marathas hired a mercenary navy, a fleet belonging to an independent mariner, Kanhoji Angre. The Maratha ruler gave Kanhoji the Persian title *sarkhil*, signifying a commander or admiral, in 1690. Kanhoji maintained a varying relationship with the Maratha regime—ranging from full alliance to territorial competition—until his death in 1729. He was paid indirectly, by having rights to one-quarter of the ships and cargo he seized. Kanhoji did not confine himself to Mughal shipping, however, and often targeted other local or European vessels as well, notably Omani and British.[18] The latter dubbed him a "pyrate." His presence was a clear challenge to the Mughals at Surat, and drew their attention to the coast.

Another problem lay still further south at the port of Goa, the last bastion of the Portuguese trading company in the region. The Portuguese presence in western India ironically brought about tensions between the Mughals and a Gulf regional power, Oman. The Portuguese had earlier wielded considerable influence in the western Indian Ocean (see Chapter 11). They had built fortified trading establishments along Africa's eastern coast, in western India, and in the Gulf. Beginning in the early sixteenth century, the Portuguese had tried to monopolize control over trade into and out of the Gulf by commanding the ports of Hormuz Island and of coastal Oman. A glance at a map clearly indicates the geographic bottleneck at the opening of the Gulf. The Safavid ruler of Iran, with some English assistance, expelled the Portuguese from Hormuz in 1622. The Omanis retook their own coastal strip by 1649, and asserted control over Gulf trade themselves. Not satisfied simply to remove the Portuguese, Omanis proceeded to chase and engage Portuguese ships everywhere in the Arabian Sea, including at Goa and other ports along the west coast of India where Portuguese interests were represented. In the context of recent occupation of Oman by the Portuguese, this maritime campaign can be recognized as warfare between two enemies. However, the Omanis quickly earned a reputation for indiscriminate maritime violence, perpetrated against European, Mughal, and Marathi ships, acts that Europeans regarded as piracy.[19]

By the second half of the seventeenth century, the combined threats from the Marathi navy and the Omani fleet convinced the Mughals that they needed to strengthen their maritime force. They engaged and maintained the services of a distinct group of seafarers, called Sidis, to protect commerce at Surat and at a then-smaller port to the south, Bombay (now Mumbai). The Muslim Sidis were originally slaves from Africa who started arriving in the twelfth century or before and who established communities in western India, particularly Gujarat. The group of Sidis referred to here harbored on a small island just south of Bombay. This Mughal decision to hire a mercenary navy generates two points that are relevant here. One is that maritime relations with Oman—and, by extension, with the Gulf—were not always smooth. The second is that the Mughal administration was now closer than ever before to having a maritime *policy*. European presence and regional resistance to it, along with the direct threat from the Marathas, drew Mughal India further into maritime concerns.

As it turned out, the Sidis were effective until they came up against the larger, faster ships used by European marauders. A series of failures to protect Mughal shipping occurred between 1691 and 1697. In 1691, European mariners seized a ship belonging to an Indian Muslim merchant, Abd al-Ghafur, who had a high profile in Surat.[20] He complained directly to his sovereign, the Mughal shah Aurangzeb. Abd al-Ghafur at first thought the culprits were English, but investigation indicated they were Danish. Nonetheless, Abd al-Ghafur made the argument that since most European marauders were in fact English, the English should be held accountable for all of them.[21] Soon after, an Englishman called Henry Avery took a Mughal ship carrying cargo and pilgrims returning to Surat from Mecca. The ship belonged to Aurangzeb himself. The well-known Englishman Captain William Kidd, who spent his maritime career first in the Caribbean, and then in the western Indian Ocean, was responsible for an incident in 1697. He seized a Mughal ship, the *Quedah*, which belonged to a member of the royal family. Clearly, the Sidi mercenaries were not able to protect Mughal shipping. Aurangzeb then put pressure on the English and Dutch companies to provide naval convoys, particularly for ships sailing to the port of Jidda in western Arabia for the annual Muslim pilgrimage and its concomitant trade. The pressure that Aurangzeb applied involved restrictions on European commerce at Surat. He also put employees of the English East India Company under house arrest until he got the promise of a convoy that he wanted. In Chapter 14, J. E. Peterson covers the very different balance of power in the nineteenth century, when the British were able to dictate terms for policing maritime violence, particularly in the Gulf.

Mysore

The second example to illustrate India-Gulf relations is from the last quarter of the eighteenth century when an Indian state ruled by a Muslim sought connections with the wider Islamic world. Mysore was a traditional province of southern India where the population was predominantly Hindu. In the late 1750s, a Muslim named Haidar Ali seized the province from a Hindu governor loosely associated with the Mughals. Haidar Ali wished to build a powerful state but with limited reference to the declining Mughal regime. In his efforts to strengthen and enlarge his own state, Haidar Ali found it necessary to resist both the Maratha tribal confederation and British influence in his part of India. His son and heir, Tipu Sultan, who ruled from 1782 until his death in 1799, continued this pattern of resistance.

Tipu appealed to his majority Hindu and his minority Muslim subjects alike, using the rhetoric and symbols of power familiar to all and patronizing both temples and mosques.[22] At the same time, however, he wanted to build Islamic power and continued to fight territorially competitive Hindu neighbors and the Christian British, sometimes encouraging interreligious conflict only *outside* Mysore.[23]

It was important for Tipu to establish his legitimacy since he could be viewed as the son of a usurper. An understood, even expected, means of doing so was to obtain a formal document of recognition from a larger power.[24] Such a document, or *sanad*, was a well understood gesture of approval and support. It made sense for Tipu to seek a sanad from the Ottoman sultan in Istanbul. The sultan was also the caliph, meaning "successor" to or "deputy" of the Prophet Muhammad and, theoretically, the paramount Sunni Islamic authority.

In planning his diplomacy with the sultan/caliph, Tipu had other considerations. He wanted some promise of military assistance in his ongoing conflict with his neighbors in India. Tipu instructed his representatives to solicit such assistance from the Ottoman administration. Past Ottoman policy had demonstrated a willingness to confront Europeans, particularly the Portuguese, in both India and the Gulf. In the 1530s, as the Mughals were establishing themselves in northern India, Ottoman Egypt launched a naval expedition to western India in an unsuccessful effort to unseat the Portuguese at Goa. Over the next several decades the Ottomans made other attempts against the Portuguese at Hormuz in the Gulf and at Goa.[25] Tipu hoped that the Ottomans of his era would still be interested in the fate of Muslim India.

Tipu also wanted to negotiate trade agreements with regional Muslim states, because he saw a correspondence between economic vigor and political success.[26] He instructed his agents to ask the Ottoman administration for a very specific exchange of resources: Tipu would give his trade revenues at Mangalore, in farm, to the Ottomans, in exchange for the trade revenues at Ottoman Basra. This was an improbable suggestion because it clearly favored Mysore, but it is indicative of Tipu's growing commercial ambitions.

With plans in place and instructions given, in late 1785 Tipu sent out a large entourage from his capital city, on its way to Istanbul by way of the Gulf. There were four representatives, two secretaries, and several hundred servants and soldiers. They carried with them large quantities of cloth and other commercial items, as well as impressive gifts—including four elephants that did not survive the trip—for the Ottoman sultan and other rulers met along the way. The entourage set sail from India in March 1786, in four large ships. Before entering the Gulf, the group spent about three months at Muscat in Oman, from early April to late June, 1786.[27] This visit would prove to be the most fruitful part of the entire expedition.

When he first came to power, Tipu Sultan had sent a commercial agent to Muscat, a man named Maoji Seth. The ruler of Oman at the time was Sa'id b. Ahmad Al Bu Sa'id[28] (r. 1783–1789), who divided his time between coastal Muscat and the tribal interior capital of Rustaq. The newly arrived Mysori agents were able to learn details about Muscati trade from Maoji Seth. What he described was very promising. For example, merchants from the Mysori port of Mangalore paid only four percent customs duties at Muscat while merchants from other Indian ports paid eight. Clearly, Sa'id wanted to attract Mangalori merchants, primarily because they brought to Oman a crucial commodity, rice. Upon learning this information, Tipu's administration began to remit half of all duties levied on Omani merchants at Mangalore, achieving something close to a mutual most-favored-nation situation. Tipu also sent word to Sa'id, inviting him to delegate a permanent commercial agent at Mysore. Trade between the two states flourished. From Mysore came rice, cardamom, timber, cloth, sandalwood, and pepper. Oman exported in return palm dates, Arabian horses, and mules.[29]

After long delays, the entourage of Tipu finally reached Istanbul and obtained the sanction of the Ottoman sultan, a sanad that recognized the legitimacy of Tipu Sultan as a rightful Muslim ruler. With this decree in hand, Tipu then referred to himself by the illustrious title of *Padshah* (lord-king or protector-king), equating himself with the greatest of the Mughal shahs. However, it is not clear who took notice, since Tipu had already separated himself from Mughal authority.[30] From Istanbul, the Mysore delegation received only vague and ultimately empty promises of military assistance in India. The now declining Ottomans were not willing or perhaps not able to muster a naval force for the sake of a distant and relatively small Muslim state.

Trade negotiations were only successful with Oman. From Tipu Sultan's point of view, the relationship with coastal Oman had a dual purpose. The obvious one was to encourage trade between two states for their mutual economic benefit. The other was to form a commercial alliance between two growing Muslim states, for Islam was the key to Tipu's rhetoric of resistance to Hindus and Christians in his bid to replace the nearly defunct Mughals.

Tipu also sent envoys to Iran in March 1798. They sailed first to Muscat, where they spent a month. They sailed on to Bushehr on the Persian coast, and then went into the interior to Shiraz and Tehran, the latter being the capital of the new Qajar regime. The Mysoris asked for military assistance in India against the British, and the Qajar shah sent a few of his own envoys back to Tipu's capital city, Seringapatam, but they arrived after the fall of the city and the death of Tipu himself. Thus, the effort to enlist Iran's military assistance failed.

The relationship between Mysore and Oman came to the attention of the revolutionary French government that, like the royal government before it, wanted to reestablish its position in India, a position lost as a result of the Seven Years' War (1756–63). The last major French outpost in the region was Île de France (modern Mauritius), an island in the Indian Ocean that they controlled from 1722 to 1810 and that had a strong commercial relationship with Muscat.

In 1798, Napoleon Bonaparte invaded and occupied Egypt, an event that made the broad India scheme more plausible. From Cairo, Bonaparte wrote a letter to the ruler of Oman, who was by then Sultan b. Ahmad Al Bu Sa'id, informing him of the French presence in Egypt and asking him to forward an enclosed letter to Tipu Sultan.[31] The enclosure expressed a vague desire to liberate Tipu from the British in India and also asked Tipu to send an agent to Paris.[32] The British intercepted both letters, the contents of which only confirmed their worst fears about an alliance between the French, Oman, and Mysore, fears that motivated the British to launch a concerted campaign against Mysore in 1799. The British took the capital, Seringapatam, and Tipu died in battle. The British governor at Bombay wrote a warning letter to the Omani ruler, Sultan b. Ahmad, announcing the death of Tipu, "thus completing his own ruin, having allied with the French."[33]

Expatriates

The third example of India-Gulf relations focuses on the Indian communities in the Gulf region as well as Gulf migrants to India. In the sixteenth century, when the Mughals came to power, we have good evidence that small Indian communities already existed at Gulf ports. These communities included import/export merchants, commercial agents, and bankers who chose to live abroad for the sake of their businesses. Often their families accompanied them to what would be a permanent home. In eighteenth-century

Ottoman Basra, Indians constituted a small but prominent community, working mainly as moneylenders (*sarrafs*) rather than as merchants or brokers.[34] At one of the most important Persian ports, Bandar Abbas, Hindus formed about one third of the population and had an important temple there and in the nearby town of Isin. European observers remarked on their rituals and ceremonies.[35] In the early twentieth century, Lorimer mentions a small population of Khojas (56) and Hindus (26) out of a population in Bandar Lingeh of some 12,000[36]; at Bandar Abbas he counts sixty-seven Khojas and sixty-six Hindus out of a population of about 10,000.[37] At the present day, there is an ornate Hindu temple in the center of Bandar Abbas that was built by Indian merchants in 1893.[38]

On the other side of the Gulf, there is clear indication of Indian communities at Bahrain, Qatif, and Doha at least as early as the nineteenth century and probably earlier.[39] The ports where expatriates became most numerous were Mutrah and Muscat in Oman. Possibly by the late fifteenth century, Banyans or Hindu merchants mainly from Gujarat had relocated at Muscat.[40] The Omanis, who were Arab Muslims of the Ibadi sect, welcomed Indians and accommodated them, exempting the Hindu Banyans from the poll-tax on non-Muslims (*jizya*) and allowing Hindu temples to be constructed. Oral tradition says that in the late seventeenth century, the Banyans brought in a representation of the deity Govindaraj for a temple at Muscat. Ironically, Govindaraj did not come directly from India but from the Ottoman and predominantly Muslim port of Basra, where the Hindu community had built an earlier temple.[41] The German explorer Carsten Niebuhr spent two weeks in Muscat in 1765 and described the Banyans: "[T]heir number in this city amounts to no fewer than twelve hundred. They are permitted to live agreeably to their own laws, to bring their wives hither, to set up idols in their chambers, and to burn their dead."[42] The latter two practices were, in fact, repugnant in Islam, so these concessions to Hindus were significant.

In the eighteenth century, Khojas (Khwajas), locally referred to as Lutis, who were probably from Sind, also migrated to Oman and settled in Mutrah. These new migrants were Muslim, from a sect of Shi'i Islam. Another wave of Khojas arrived at Mutrah in the late nineteenth century. Some of the new arrivals had British Indian citizenship, raising the contentious possibility of extending British protection beyond India.[43] During the nineteenth century, the British employed a large number of "native agents" throughout the Gulf—some Indians, who enjoyed British protection.[44]

By the nineteenth century, the Indian communities at Mutrah and Muscat numbered in the several thousands. Banyans dominated Omani trade. The Indians tended to live clustered together in distinctive quarters of town, and retained their customs and manner of dress. Over the course of the nineteenth and twentieth centuries, the Omani government allowed Hindu Indians to build several more temples in Muscat. In 1970, however, there was a political sea change in Oman and the new government defined citizenship. All but a few favored Indians were denied citizenship in the new Oman, business laws now favored citizens, and most Indians chose to move elsewhere.[45]

People from the Gulf region also migrated to India. A prominent example is a clan of Turkish Muslim merchants from Ottoman Mosul and Baghdad, the Chelebis (or Çelebis), who came to western India in the seventeenth century and became wealthy and influential figures especially at the port of Surat.[46] There were other Muslim merchants at Surat as well—Arabs, Persians, and of course Mughals. One Persian merchant who made his fortune there was Mirza Muhammad Taki. At the opening of the eighteenth century, he enjoyed influence at both the courts of the Safavids and Mughals, and became leader of the Mughal merchants at Surat.[47] He retired to the country of his birth in 1705 with enormous wealth and a large extended family.

MIGRANT WORKERS, MERCENARY SOLDIERS, EMPIRE, AND THE LEVERAGE OF OIL WEALTH

Elites exemplify the early modern examples of migration for purposes of trade. The subject of mobile labor in the western Indian Ocean region broadens the scope of this study to include ordinary and often poor people. Expanding, contracting, and geographically shifting labor needs necessitated a brokered labor market for crews, dockworkers, porters, construction workers, and soldiers. The men came from all over the Arabian Sea region, including the interior. Some were slaves or debtors while others were free laborers.[48] This exchange of labor was another interconnection between the Gulf and India, embedded in the wider context of the Arabian Sea. Migrant labor patterns were well developed by the eighteenth century.

An area that blurs the geographic distinction between the Gulf region and South Asia is the coast of traditional Baluchistan, known as Makran, which is now divided between Iran and Pakistan, countries of the Gulf and traditional India, respectively. Baluchis were part of the migrant labor phenomenon described above. They had a long-standing reputation as effective warriors that made them sought-after mercenaries.[49] From as early as the sixteenth century and through the nineteenth, the successive rulers of Oman and later Zanzibar employed Baluchi mercenary soldiers, entrusting some with high rank and responsibility.[50]

In the late nineteenth and early twentieth centuries, as British policies to end the slave trade went into effect, the Omanis found it more difficult to acquire African slaves, and Makran became an alternate source. These Baluchis served in a variety of capacities, for example, as agricultural laborers in Oman's palm date groves and in Zanzibar's clove plantations, or as domestic servants.[51]

India and the Gulf during the British Raj

Throughout the nineteenth century and into the twentieth, the British administration in India considered the Gulf to be the key communication link between the governments in India and London. The British feared French, German, and especially Russian imperial expansion in the region, which would endanger that communication route. In the 1890s, Germany negotiated with the Ottoman government to build a railway to the port town of Kuwait. Rumor had it that Russia supported this railhead on the Gulf. The British viceroy in India, George Nathaniel Curzon, pushed for and achieved a treaty relationship with Kuwait's local ruling family, the Al Sabah, a relationship that would prevent any foreign power except Britain to have influence in and around the port town in exchange for British protection of the family's interests.[52] In the early twentieth century, the discovery of commercially viable oil in the Gulf area provided an additional British imperial interest in the region.

When the Middle East theater of World War I opened, British India sent two million Indian soldiers to fight the Germans in Flanders and the Ottomans at both Gallipoli and in Mesopotamia. The British Indian Army seized Faw and Basra in what would soon become southern Iraq. Indians living under British rule saw the war as an opportunity to take advantage of U.S. President Wilson's idea of self-determination, and they were deeply disappointed when Britain maintained martial law in India after the war. The British Indian government's desire to control the Gulf, even to view it as a British lake as Curzon did, brought South Asians and peoples of the Gulf together into political and military contact that was not of their own making. A consistent British fear was that appeals to Islam would be carried from the Gulf to threaten their rule in India.

An interesting business venture illustrates interaction between the Gulf and India and also segues nicely into the modern period when oil wealth created more such opportunities for regionally initiated commerce. In 1861, the British India Steam Navigation Company (BI) began operating in the Gulf.[53] By 1866, the company had a regular schedule of stops along the west coast of India and in the Gulf. The British Indian government subsidized the company in exchange for the transportation of official mail through the Gulf, on its way to Basra, then to Aleppo, and on to London, as well as the reverse, thus satisfying the need for imperial communication. The BI inspired competition from a new business venture, the Arab Steamer Company (ASC), which was launched in 1911.[54] Arab and Indian Muslim merchants in Bombay amassed the start-up funding for the ASC and the company was registered at that port. The managing director was a Gulf merchant with connections to both the Persian and Arabian sides of the Gulf. The larger, well-connected BI was able to shut out the challenger within just a few years, but the significant point here about the ASC is that an essentially Arab Gulf business venture built itself on the infrastructure of a large, established commercial center in India.

Modern Times

The introduction of oil wealth in the twentieth century is a salient characteristic of modern Gulf-India relations, since wealth drove the building of infrastructure and the need for cheap construction and service labor. The number of foreign laborers burgeoned after World War II, as oil revenues increased and paid for new development. The high oil prices of the 1970s produced another sharp rise in the number of foreigners attracted to jobs in oil states. Male workers often migrated temporarily and alone, in order to send money home. Sometimes they brought their families with them for longer or permanent stays. In the mid-1980s, however, oil states saw the large number of foreign workers as a cultural intrusion and began to "indigenize" their labor forces, attempting deliberately to reduce dependence on foreign labor, with mixed results. The modern Gulf states that had the highest percentages of foreign labor, including Indians, Pakistanis, and Bangladeshis, are those with a combination of small indigenous populations and oil wealth: Saudi Arabia, Kuwait, Qatar, the UAE, and Oman. (The numbers of foreign workers in well-populated Iraq and Iran were relatively small.)[55]

Various international organizations estimated the Saudi kingdom's population in 1997 at about nineteen and a half million, including roughly six million foreigners, most of whom were workers. Before 1980, the majority of foreign workers were from Arabic-speaking countries, with a growing number from South Asia. The Kuwaiti government calculated its own state's population in 1997 at just over two million, with more than sixty percent foreign. Most foreign workers were males without their families who stayed only a few years. Since about 1980, the Kuwaiti government has indicated a preference for Asian workers due to both their lower wage costs and a language barrier that rendered Asians less likely to interact with Arabic-speaking citizens. In 1997, the UAE had a population approaching three million, citizens constituting only about 22 percent, while approximately three quarters of the population were migrant workers from South Asia. Qatar had a population of just over one hundred thousand in 1970 but that grew to 522,000 by 1997. Of that number, only about 157,000 were Qatari nationals. South Asians and Arabs from other states made up the bulk of the population.

In Oman, the population in 1997 was about two and one third million. Although Arabs were in the majority, about 614,000 foreigners, most of them South Asian, lived there. It should be repeated here that in 1970, the government offered citizenship to very few South Asians, and many of those without citizenship chose to leave. The current number includes those who chose to stay as well as subsequent arrivals, particularly in the northern half of the state.[56] As in other Gulf region states, Oman is currently trying to reduce dependence on foreign labor. The increase both in education and contact beyond the region contribute to an ongoing change in the work culture of all these states, so that young nationals aspire to work and even to take jobs formerly held by foreigners.[57]

Migrant workers in the oil states often put up with less than ideal working and living conditions. Human Rights Watch issued a report in 2006 when half a million migrant construction workers were employed in the UAE. The report cited "wage exploitation, indebtedness to unscrupulous recruiters" and hazardous working conditions; the organization recommended that the UAE federal government address these issues and that the United States, the European Union, and Australia exert pressure on the Emirates to do so.[58] In all the oil states, the presence of foreign workers generates dichotomies that have yet to be resolved, dichotomies between citizenship and guest worker status, between inclusion and exclusion.

Another way in which oil has changed the relationship between traditional India and the Gulf region has to do with consumption patterns. Oman is a good example. Traditional India was for a long time Oman's major trade partner. Now it is Japan. Japan has need of Gulf oil and manufactures the vehicles and high technology that are in demand in Oman and all the oil states.

The twentieth century, in comparison to the sixteenth through nineteenth centuries, represents a reversal of fortunes. Traditional India supplied the Gulf region with crucial rice and cotton cloth and also provided a sophisticated business infrastructure and a market for Gulf dates and pearls. After World War II, the Gulf oil states were in a position to dominate regional economics. However, the depletion of oil and the development of alternative fuels, or both, may alter the situation yet again, as may India's major role in high technology, which may increase the gap between rich and poor in that country but that also improves India's position in the global economy.[59] India has recently entered into an economic relationship with the Gulf Cooperation Council and with the Oman Chamber of Commerce and Industry. In contrast to India, less-developed Pakistan accepts aid from Gulf oil states. Pakistan also has seconded troops to Saudi Arabia for decades, a practice that, at its height in the 1980s, comprised perhaps ten thousand men. Today, Saudi Arabia aims to use its own manpower. [60]

In regard to aid, it is Saudi Arabia's investment in Pakistan that draws most attention. Lack of access to documents and the still fluid nature of the phenomenon limit the ability of historians to analyze the situation, but Barbara Metcalf offers historical analysis of Pakistan from the 1940s into the 1970s that is very helpful here. She is concerned with tracing changes in Islamic identity in Pakistan over those decades. Her argument begins with the establishment of the state, including its West and East portions, in 1947, in which Islamic identity offered a basis of unity between Urdu- and Bengali-speaking South Asians who populated the new Pakistan. The Muslims who formed the backbone of the economy were well-to-do merchants and professionals who were concentrated in the West, particularly in Punjab, and whose interests were protected by the state. After the 1971 civil war that rendered East Pakistan the new state of Bangladesh, the remaining western portion of Pakistan found a new identity as a bordering "fortress" (*qal'a*) of the Islamic heartland, the Middle East—and, more especially, Arabia.[61] One of the country's most ardent Islamic movements, Jama'at-i Islami (the Islamic Society), endorsed explicit policies of Islamization, and found support for this from Saudi Arabia.[62] This shift in Pakistani identity toward the Islamic Middle East and away from

South Asia provided the opportunity for Wahhabi Saudi Arabia to influence politics and the educational system through oil money and ideology.

About two decades after the beginning of this shift in Pakistan's identity, the Taliban arose in Afghanistan. The Taliban has its roots in a politicized segment of a specific educational movement that originated in colonial India. This movement began in the nineteenth century at a town called Deoband, north of Delhi, at a religious school (*madrasa*) dedicated to preserving a particular, traditional understanding of Sunni Islam. The Deobandi school was popular and branches multiplied quickly in northern India, Pakistan, and Afghanistan. In the environment of Afghanistan occupied by Soviet troops, a highly politicized Deobandi offshoot, the Taliban ("students"), attracted the volunteer military participation of Arab and other Muslim men, including Osama bin Laden from Saudi Arabia.[63]

Conclusion

The first section of this chapter selectively illustrates situations that prompted contact between the Gulf and South Asia. Due to local and European maritime threats, the Mughal government became involved in protection of its commercial and hajj-related shipping. Tipu Sultan of Mysore, as part of his state-building strategy, sought to extend a maritime commercial network, successfully to Muscat, unsuccessfully to Ottoman Basra. His outreach to coreligionists is an example also of religious identity directed toward the reinstatement of Islamic power in India. Beginning at least as early as the fifteenth century, South Asians from Sind and Gujarat migrated to the Gulf area as merchants, commercial agents, and moneylenders. In the ports of Oman, they became a significant part of the population and the economy. Migrant workers and mercenary soldiers were also part of the early modern scenario, and they continued to be significant in the modern period as well.

The second section focused on such mobile labor, the intrusive agenda of British India, and oil wealth, all features of the modern period. British India imposed linkages between the Gulf and India that neither sought. One was the imperial need to keep other Europeans away from the Gulf, an important British communications route. This was accomplished through shows-of-force and treaty restrictions. Another was the use of mercenary Indian soldiers in Mesopotamia during the Great War. Oil money has changed many aspects of the Gulf-India exchange. The migrant labor situation has undergone change in two phases. First, when oil wealth seemed endless, Saudi Arabia and the smaller Arab oil states brought in large numbers of foreign workers and soldiers. As the size of these communities grew, they seemed to threaten the identities of nationals, and the treatment of foreigners became more problematic. As Arab Gulf states better understood the limits of both oil and undiversified economies, there was a policy shift in favor of national labor. Finally, Saudi Arabia in particular has used oil wealth to encourage Wahhabi Islam, and the success of that endeavor in Pakistan has established an ideological link.

Saudi influence in Pakistan tends to overshadow more mundane and less newsworthy aspects of South Asia-Gulf ties in the late twentieth and early twenty-first centuries, such as the continuation of both maritime and overland trade and migrant labor. In the history of the relationship between the two regions during the long period under consideration, changes in relative wealth stand out in sharp relief, most obviously in the case of oil revenues. Changes over time also include issues of identity, and Saudi Arabia and Pakistan in recent decades have perhaps trumped geographical identity with ideology.

Notes

1. M. N. Pearson, "The Sixteenth Century," in *India and the Indian Ocean, 1500–1800,* Ashin Das Gupta and M. N. Pearson (Calcutta, India: Oxford University Press, 1987), 79.
2. Stephen Frederic Dale, *Indian Merchants and Eurasian Trade 1600–1750* (Cambridge: Cambridge University Press, 1994), 37–42.
3. By "Gulf region," I refer not only to the wide littoral of the Gulf proper but also to Oman in southeastern Arabia. "South Asia" indicates traditional India, including what are now the modern nation states of India, Pakistan, and Bangladesh.
4. John R. Perry, *Karim Khan Zand: A History of Iran 1747–1779* (Chicago: University of Chicago Press, 1979), 249.
5. A good source of information on Ottoman interests and policies in the Gulf region is Frederick F. Anscombe, *The Ottoman Gulf: The Creation of Kuwait, Saudi Arabia, and Qatar* (New York: Columbia University Press, 1997). See also Anscombe's chapter in this book.
6. Perry, *Karim Khan Zand*, chaps. 11 and 15.
7. Calvin H. Allen, Jr., "Sayyids, Shets and Sultans: Politics and Trade in Masqat under the Al Bu Sa'id, 1789–1914" (PhD diss., University of Washington, 1978), 142–56.
8. The major source for this delegation and its journey is Abdul Qadir, *Waqa'i-i mananzil-i Rum: A Diary of a Journey to Constantinople*, ed. Mohibbul Hasan (Aligarh, India: Aligarh Muslim University, 1968).
9. Hamid b. Muhammad ibn Ruzayq, *Al-fath al-mubin al-mubarhim sirat al-sadat Al bu Sa'idiyin* (Cambridge University Library, Add. MS. 2892). There is also an English translation by G. P. Badger, under the title *History of the Imams and Seyyids of Oman* (London: Hakluyt Society, 1871).
10. Katib Chelebi, *The History of the Maritime Wars of the Turks*, Oriental Translation Fund 17, trans. James Mitchell (London, 1831; repr. New York: Johnson Reprint Corporation, 1968). "Katib Chelebi" was a sobriquet meaning, "esteemed scribe." The author's name was Mustafa ibn Abdullah.
11. Evliya Efendi, *Narrative of Travels in Europe, Asia, and Africa in the Seventeenth Century*, trans. Joseph Hammer-Purgstall (London: Oriental Translation Fund, 1834; repr. New York: Johnson Reprint Corporation, 1968), 138.
12. A famous example of a study of the British East India Company records from inside the company is J. G. Lorimer, *Gazetteer of the Persian Gulf, 'Oman, and Central Arabia*, 2 vols. in 5 parts (Calcutta, India: Superintendent of Government Printing, 1908–1915; repr. Farnsborough, UK: Gregg, 1970).
13. A highly detailed study based largely on Dutch, Portuguese, and English archives is R. J. Barendse, *The Arabian Seas: The Indian Ocean World of the Seventeenth Century* (Armonk, NY: M. E. Sharpe, 2002).
14. Ashin Das Gupta, *Indian Merchants and the Decline of Surat c. 1700–1750* (Wiesbaden, Germany: Franz Steiner, 1979).
15. Dale, *Indian Merchants and Eurasian Trade*, chaps. 2–3.
16. Patricia Risso, *Merchants and Faith: Muslim Commerce and Culture in the Indian Ocean* (Boulder, CO: Westview Press, 1995), 65.
17. Ibid.
18. Patricia Risso, "Cross-Cultural Perceptions of Piracy: Maritime Violence in the Western Indian Ocean and Persian Gulf Region during a Long Eighteenth Century," *Journal of World History* 12 (2001): 304–05.
19. Ibid., 305–06.
20. Das Gupta, *India and the Indian Ocean*, 77–79.
21. Robert C. Ritchie, *Captain Kidd and the War against the Pirates* (Cambridge: Harvard University Press, 1986), 131.
22. Kate Brittlebank, *Tipu Sultan's Search for Legitimacy: Islam and Kingship in a Hindu Domain* (Delhi, India: Oxford University Press, 1997).
23. Brittlebank, *Tipu Sultan's Search for Legitimacy*, 35–36.

24. Ibid., 65, referring to Stewart Gordon, "Legitimacy and Loyalty in Some Successor States of the Eighteenth Century," in *Kingship and Authority in South Asia*, 2nd ed., J. F. Richards, ed. (Madison, WI: Department of South Asian Studies, University of Wisconsin, 1981).
25. Katib Chelebi, *Maritime Wars of the Turks*, 65–66, 71–77.
26. Mohibbul Hasan, *History of Tipu Sultan* (Calcutta, India: The World Press Private Ltd, 1971), 129–30.
27. Ibid., 128–31. One of the four ships caught fire and sank in the Gulf.
28. "Al Bu Sa'id" is the clan name. The "Al" indicates "family of" (not the definite article "al-") and the "Bu" is short for "Abu," "father of".
29. Hasan, *History of Tipu Sultan*, 345–46.
30. Brittlebank, *Tipu Sultan's Search for Legitimacy*, 67–72.
31. The French administration was apparently unaware of the identity of the ruler of Oman, as the letter is not addressed to Sultan ibn Ahmad by name. The text of Bonaparte's letter to Tipu Sultan, addressed to him by name, can be found in *Correspondence inedite officielle et confidentielle de Napoleon Bonaparte*, vol. 6, book 4 (Paris, 1809–20), 192.
32. Originally, Tipu had instructed the Abd al-Qadir entourage to proceed from Istanbul to Paris, to ask Louis XVI for a military alliance in India, but he recalled the group from Istanbul. Later, in 1787, Tipu sent a new embassy to Paris. These representatives sailed on a French ship from Pondicherry to France via the Cape of Good Hope, and arrived in Paris in July of 1788. The request they made, for 10,000 French soldiers, was met with the news that the French government had decided to withdraw all their troops from India and regroup on the Île de France, in hopes of making a comeback in India at a later date. See Hasan, *History of Tipu Sultan*, chapter 7.
33. Patricia Risso, *Oman and Muscat: An Early Modern History* (London: Croom Helm and New York: St. Martin's Press, 1986), 151.
34. Thabit A. J. Abdullah, *Merchants, Mamluks, and Murder: The Political Economy of Trade in Eighteenth Century Basra* (Albany: State University of New York Press, 2001), 27. Tipu employed a Jewish broker at Basra, perhaps confirming that Indian expatriates were not in that line of work at that particular port. (Hasan, *History of Tipu Sultan*, 346.)
35. Willem Floor, *The Persian Gulf: A Political and Economic History of Five Port Cities 1500–1730* (Washington, D. C.: Mage Publishers, 2006), 271.
36. Lorimer, *Gazetteer*, vol. 2, 1097.
37. Ibid., vol. 2, 10.
38. Ali-Akbar Aghajiri, photographer and Ali-Reza Pakdaman, text, *Hormozgan* ([Abadan?]: Government of Hormuzgan, 1383/2004), photo on page 52.
39. Anscombe, *Ottoman Gulf*, 10.
40. Calvin H. Allen, Jr., "The Indian Merchant Community of Masqat," *Bulletin of the School of Oriental and African Studies* 44 (1981): 39–40.
41. Ibid., p. 41.
42. Ibid.
43. Ibid., 48–50.
44. James Onley, "Britain's Native Agents in Arabia and Persia in the Nineteenth Century," *Comparative Studies of South Asia, Africa and the Middle East* 24, no. 1 (2004): 21–23.
45. Allen, *Oman*, 12.
46. The origin of the Turkish term *çelebi* is unclear, but it first came into use in Asia Minor as a title of respect for a writer, poet, sage, or head of a Sufi order. Later, it became a family name (similar to the transformation of *khan*) and is most closely associated with the merchant clan in question. (Das Gupta, *India and the Indian Ocean*, 76–79.) Also see note 10 on Katib Chelebi.
47. Das Gupta, *India and the Indian Ocean*, 75 and 132.
48. Anh Nga Longva, *Walls Built on Sand: Migration, Exclusion, and Society in Kuwait* (Boulder, CO: Westview Press, 1997), 19–22.
49. As an example of the basis for the military reputation in 1698–99, Baluchi tribesmen raided Kirman, in southeastern Iran, that was then under the weak control of the Safavid dynasty. The Baluchis posed a threat both to the city of Yazd and to the port of Bandar Abbas, over three hundred miles away. (Roger Savory, *Iran under the Safavids* [Cambridge:

Cambridge University Press, 1980], 241.) The depth and breadth of the Baluchi incursion foreshadowed an Afghani assault in 1722 that would bring an end to Safavid power.

50. Beatrice Nicolini, *Makran, Oman and Zanzibar: Three-Terminal Cultural Corridor in the Western Indian Ocean (1799–1856)*, trans. Penelope-Jane Watson (Leiden, The Netherlands: Brill, 2004), 4–23.
51. Nicolini, *Makran, Oman and Zanzibar*, 118–22.
52. Anscombe, *The Ottoman Gulf*, 109–12.
53. Robert Geran Landen, *Oman Since 1856: Disruptive Modernization in a Traditional Arab Society* (Princeton, NJ: Princeton University Press, 1967), 89–91. Michael Pearson, *The Indian Ocean* (London and New York: Routledge, 2003), 204–05.
54. For this fascinating business example, I am indebted to Brian Begy, who has given me permission to use the information from his unpublished paper, "Trade and Technology in the Gulf, 1880–1930: British Steamers and the Local Response," Middle East Studies Association 31st Annual Meeting, San Francisco, November 22–24, 1997.
55. Unless otherwise noted, the statistics in the following two paragraphs come from Andrzej Kapiszewski, *Nationals and Expatriates: Population and Labour Dilemmas of the Gulf Cooperation Council States* (Reading, UK: Ithaca Press, 2001), 39, Table 1.4; 65, Table 3.3 and Figure 3.1.
56. For a detailed account of minorities in Oman, see J. E. Peterson's two articles: "Oman's Diverse Society: Northern Oman," *The Middle East Journal* 58, no. 1 (Winter 2004), 32–51 and "Oman's Diverse Society: Southern Oman," *The Middle East Journal* 58, no. 2 (Spring 2004), 254–69.
57. Kapiszewski, *Nationals and Expatriates,* 80.
58. Human Rights Watch, http://hrw.org/reports/2006/uae1106/1.htm
59. An example of an Indian enterprise of global consequence is the famous Tata Group. It started with entrepreneur Jamsheed Tata's cotton mills in the nineteenth century, then diversified to steel, and now is the umbrella organization for ninety-one companies, including several producing information technologies.
60. Anthony H. Cordesman, *Saudi Arabia Enters the Twenty-First Century: The Military and International Security Dimensions*, vol. 1 (Westport CT: Praeger, 2003), 52.
61. Barbara D. Metcalf, "Islamic Arguments in Contemporary Pakistan," in *Islamic Contestations: Essays on Muslims in India and Pakistan,* Barbara D. Metcalf (Delhi, India: Oxford University Press, 2004), 237. Metcalf's chapter originally appeared in William R. Roff, ed., *Islam and the Politics of Meaning* (London: Croom Helm and Berkeley CA: University of California Press, 1987).
62. Metcalf, "Islamic Arguments in Contemporary Pakistan," 240.
63. Barbara D. Metcalf, "'Traditionalist' Islamic Activism: Deoband, Tablighis, and Talibs," in *Islamic Contestations*, 277. This chapter originally appeared in Craig Calhoun, Paul Price, and Ashley Timmer, eds., *Understanding September 11* (New York: The New Press, 2002).

Part III

The Role of Outsiders

Chapter 11

The Portuguese Presence in the Persian Gulf

João Teles e Cunha

The history of the Kingdom of Hormuz, as French historian Jean Aubin put it in his classic article, is similar to that of other city-states like Calicut, Cochin, Cannanore, Kilwa, and Qais (Kish): a type of metropolis, capital of a small autonomous state whose survival depended on maritime commerce, whose merchant groups influenced its fate, and whose cultural framework was characterized by an ethnic cosmopolitanism and religious diversity.[1] According to Aubin, what made the difference in Hormuz, and thus its specificity, was its geographical position between three major worlds (Persian, Arab, and Indian). Socially and materially speaking Hormuz was more an Indo-Muslim urban center than an Islamic Middle Eastern one. Even so, its history was closely connected with the wider region of which Hormuz was a part, and thus suffered from the attention of all political powers with hegemonic designs on the Persian Gulf.[2]

Starting in the early sixteenth century, one of these powers was Portugal. Much of what has been said about the Portuguese presence in the Gulf echoes the words of the traveler Pedro Teixeira, written four centuries ago: after thriving for two hundred years, Hormuz declined thanks to the oppression and violence exercised by Portuguese captains and officials.[3] Though his assessment reflected only one century of interaction, it was widely used to characterize the remaining period and still weighs on present-day historiography.[4] Teixeira was partly right and partly wrong in his judgment. His words can be included in the "literature of reform" so typical of Portuguese history after 1565, which sought to reflect on contemporary "decay" and present a cure that ultimately would restore Portugal's lost grandeur. This opinion reflected somewhat the old opposition between the "imperialists," who favored a more militaristic approach, and the "liberals," whose concern was mainly economic.[5]

The Portuguese presence must be studied and understood taking into consideration a multiform local and regional reality, and its evolution placed in a wider historical context, not forgetting that Portugal chose to occupy areas of influence in the Persian Gulf according to her interests and imperial designs. On the one hand, influence in the Gulf projects itself into the Indian Ocean, Central Asia, India, the Near and Middle East, and the Eastern Mediterranean basin. On the other hand, the Portuguese presence there cannot be studied in isolation from her own Asian empire, whose character evolved over time. By Portuguese I mean here an open, fluid, and very differentiated category and not a closed set of characteristics.

Portugal and the Gulf: An Overview, 1507–1750

Portugal interacted with the Persian Gulf for more than two centuries, but little changed in the nature of their relationship over this time. The Gulf was and remained on the periphery of Portugal's Asian Empire, whose center was in India's west coast, and the Gulf only mattered if Indian security was menaced by a naval power emerging from the Strait of Hormuz, or if the economic viability of the Cape route was threatened.[6] Despite being peripheral, though, the Gulf had a substantial economic importance in the context of Portuguese Asia, and Hormuz was always a profitable fortress, perhaps more so than all the others in Estado da Índia (State of India, the string of Portuguese coastal settlements and fortifications in the Indian Ocean area).[7] The Gulf, aside from Muscat, continued to be a regular source of income to Portuguese India after 1622.

The official Portuguese presence was far from being effective throughout the Gulf. Even at the height of their power, the Portuguese had chosen to focus on Hormuz, the axis at the intersection of three major trade routes: to India, to Basra, and to the Iranian market.[8] They had preferred to maintain the pre-Portuguese status quo as long as there was no direct menace to Hormuz and as long as goods and navigation could flow freely. Hormuzi officials and the local aristocracy kept their position, thus maintaining the pre-Portuguese institutional framework, and its formal allegiance to an increasingly feeble political center, which in time made them independent. To ensure the continuation of naval protection, there was a permanent naval force stationed in the Gulf after 1515.[9] The Portuguese only acted militarily in the periphery when there was a threat to the axis, or to the free course of trade. This was true when the center was in Hormuz (1515–1622), in Muscat (1622–50), and later in Kung (1650–1725), though the political and economic background differed from place to place.

Despite having conquered the center of the thalassocracy (Hormuz), the Portuguese never felt compelled to occupy all their possessions in the Gulf with garrisons, even at a few strategic points, as they preferred to exercise their dominion through a naval presence. This trend only changed in the second half of the sixteenth century, after the Ottoman threat had become more pronounced. Portuguese military and naval power was not always effective in enforcing vassals' formal allegiance to Hormuz, as proved in the fiasco of the Bahrain expedition of 1529, or in the collapse of Hormuzi authority in Mughistan around 1538.[10]

Portuguese guns and sails could only exert a temporary influence that lasted for the expedition's duration, and the cannon's range. In any case, the economic burden of maintaining a large number of garrisons would have been forbidding. The number of soldiers and sailors stationed in Hormuz increased from 410 in 1581 to 534 in 1610,[11] but this was nothing compared with Oman, where it grew from 727 men enrolled in 1623 to 1739 in 1633.[12] This increase was gradual. It began with the mounting Ottoman pressure from the 1540s to the 1580s,[13] and because of a local phenomenon, the Nakhilu pirates, which became a constant nuisance after the 1550s.[14] By the late sixteenth century, the consolidation of the Safavid presence along the Gulf littoral and their conquest of Bahrain in 1602, along with the emergence of an Omani naval power in the 1640s, later projected into the western Indian Ocean,[15] contributed further to this state of affairs. The appearance of new exogenous powers, the English first and then the Dutch in the early seventeenth century, aggravated even further the violence in the Gulf, which was a symptom of a widespread occurrence in Asian seas.[16]

It seems that Portuguese perceptions of some Gulf realities, such as local political organization and social ties, remained superficial, inaccurate, and full of prejudice. The defining element of the "other" side was religion, and it represented, at least at the official level, a gap that was never overcome, though private individuals did so. Strangely, the Gulf and the adjacent areas, especially Iran, were never fruitful for missionaries, despite several attempts made during two centuries. The Jesuits, perhaps the best endowed Catholic religious order for missionary work, gave up their activity in the Gulf in 1568.[17] The Augustinians had no greater success than their predecessors. They stuck to the Portuguese enclaves in the Gulf and opened three houses in Iran, where their convent, in Isfahan, became the informal Portuguese embassy to the shah's court.[18] In time things changed, though a certain crusader spirit never waned completely. This was a reminder of Portugal's own past forged in the *Reconquista,* the Christian reconquest of the Iberian Peninsula that ended in the fifteenth century.[19]

It was not surprising that in the Gulf the Portuguese made use of the same method employed by them elsewhere in Asia: divide and rule. At first they used it in Hormuz, to pit king against vizier and Persian against Arab, in a process to internally weaken the kingdom and gradually take over the reins of power.[20] The same principle was employed later against the Ya'rubi rulers of Oman, whom the Portuguese sought to overturn by supporting local uprisings, as in 1652 when the ruler of Khasab asked for Portuguese military aid to free himself from his overlord. This type of military adventure ended without any concrete outcome, except to incite both sides to war and lead the Portuguese to spurn Omani truce offers in exchange for illusions of conquest.[21]

On a regional scale, the Portuguese sought allies among other Gulf states, to obtain a balance of power favorable to them and to prevent the emergence of any serious contender. It might even use them as auxiliaries against more threatening adversaries, particularly in the moving border between contending empires. At an international level, the Portuguese followed the traditional European policy applied since Mongol times. They sought an alliance based on the dominating power in Iraq and Iran to weaken the menacing enemy in the Mediterranean basin—the Mamluks—that in the early sixteenth century was also the threat in the Indian Ocean. For that reason the Portuguese sought Safavid assistance against the Mamluks first, and the Ottomans afterwards. The Gulf became instrumental for Portuguese strategy when the Ottomans gained easy access through their conquest of Basra in 1546. However, the system of alliances changed when a peaceful modus vivendi was established with the Porte in the late sixteenth century, and Iran became the enemy (1614–30), though later the old alliance was reestablished.

Portuguese Policy: International Dimensions

The first period of Portuguese interaction with the Persian Gulf began with the exploratory voyage of Pêro da Covilhã in the late fifteenth century. Even before the Portuguese arrived in 1507, the Gulf had been entangled in a wider international conjuncture involving Portuguese interests in the Indian Ocean, particularly on India's west coast, Egyptian commercial aims (given their ascendancy in the Red Sea) to control the intermediary Asian spice market, and the economic and political situation in the Mediterranean. Here, the Ottomans were already the key player, especially due to their thrust into the Balkans and Central Europe. A fourth player appeared in 1501, when in Iran the first Safavid shah, Isma'il, seized Tabriz and proclaimed Shiism as the state religion.

Only at a late stage, after having established a bridgehead in India and a permanent naval presence in the Indian Ocean, did the Persian Gulf attract Portuguese attention. This was understandable since the Gulf had closer economic and political ties with Gujarat and Kanara than with Malabar, then the center of Portuguese India. It was more pressing for them to consolidate their Malabar bridgehead, secure the supply of spices and drugs for the newly built factories, fight local and international opposition to their presence in Asia, and guarantee the economic viability of the recently established Cape route.

From 1502 to 1509 the Portuguese blockaded the Red Sea to obstruct the spice trade and damage Mamluk economic interests, while strengthening their position in India and eliminating the Egyptian menace. It was Afonso de Albuquerque, India's second governor (1509–15), who in 1507 finally turned their full attention to the Gulf, only to meet opposition from his men and from the Kingdom of Hormuz.[22] Later, due to his failed expedition in the Gulf, Albuquerque had to confront Dom Francisco de Almeida, the first Portuguese viceroy of their possessions in India (1503–09). Their struggle surpassed the personal antagonism that arose between them, and was deeply rooted in a wider fight between two distinct approaches guiding Portuguese expansion in Asia.[23] One was more "liberal" and commercially orientated, with its center of interest laying mainly in Malabar and adjoining areas. Exporting spices to Europe via the Cape route was their principal concern, and as such they only acted politically, military, and economically in southern maritime India, freely opening other parts of Asia to Portuguese "private" enterprise. Their imperialism was primary a commercial one, and D. Francisco was their chief representative in India. However, they had wide political influence in governmental bodies in Portugal, such as the Royal Council.[24] D. Francisco's plan for the Gulf was very simple: make the Kingdom of Hormuz a vassal state whose sovereigns would pay annual *páreas* (tribute) to King D. Manuel (r. 1495–1521). His plan attracted Khwaja Ata, the vizier of Hormuz (1505–11), as it enabled him to consolidate his power over Hormuz's periphery, besides giving him a valuable ally to face Safavid expansionism. And traditionally, Hormuz had always preferred an absent and distant overlord to one close by.

A countervailing idea was championed by D. Manuel, and Albuquerque was one of its supporters. He was also the principal implementer of the king's plans in Asia. D. Manuel's imperialism was more political than economic, and the king's ultimate goal was to deliver Jerusalem from Muslim hands and crown himself as paramount emperor of Christianity. Therefore, its major objective was to weaken the declining Mamluk sultanate in Egypt (1250–1517) through a commercial blockade. This was to be complemented with the conquest of key places at choke points of the main Indian Ocean trade routes. Almeida did his best to deter this policy while he remained in India as viceroy. And he succeeded almost completely.[25]

With Albuquerque in charge, however, from 1509 to 1515, D. Manuel's plan began to be executed. Albuquerque conquered Goa (1510) and Malacca (1511), but he failed in the face of Aden's resistance in 1512, and only in 1515 did he conquer Hormuz. His general design was to control all strategic points where the main maritime trade routes met and irradiated.[26] It was Albuquerque who gave birth to what would be the backbone of the Portuguese presence in Asia until 1663: the control of key emporia situated at strategic points of confluence.[27] This was to master major trade routes of important products (spices, medicinal drugs and aromatics, textiles, precious metals, pearls, ivory, and horses), not only to obtain them for the Crown's monopolistic commerce, but also to influence their flow to other markets and finally to tax some of them to finance their own political and economic enterprise in Asia. To implement these measures, in 1502 Portuguese authorities began issuing safe conducts known as *cartazes* to allied

Asian shipping to prevent them from being attacked and robbed by Portuguese vessels policing the seas near strategic points like the Malabar coast or Bab al-Mandab. Their prime objective was to prevent key products, especially pepper and other prized spices, from supplying rival markets, rather than to tax indiscriminately all maritime traffic. This strategic conception changed during the sixteenth century, when Portuguese authorities started to issue *cartazes* to control profitable trade in certain products, such as horses from the Gulf after 1510, and to tax trade on certain routes, such as the richly laden Mughal ship sent annually to Mecca after the 1570s, which was obliged to pass through Diu's customs.[28]

THE OTTOMAN CHALLENGE

After the Mamluks had disappeared from the scene in 1517, the Ottomans inherited their newly built fleet in the Red Sea, but it took Constantinople a decade to launch a new offensive against the Portuguese. However, every single Ottoman naval offensive against the Portuguese in the Indian Ocean failed, including those of Selman Re'is (1527–28), Hadim Süleyman Pasha (1538), Piri Re'is (1552), Murad Re'is (1553), and Seydi Ali Re'is (1554). No major Ottoman action was attempted after 1560, though they backed all uprisings against the Portuguese in Asia from 1565 to 1575 with technical expertise and money.[29] They took Muscat briefly in 1581.[30] Mir Ali Beg commanded the last Ottoman incursions in the Indian Ocean between 1588–91 to Africa's east coast, where he was ultimately defeated in Mombassa, with the providential and involuntary help of the Zimbas (a warrior people from the Zambezi valley), who cannibalized his men.[31]

More than the domain of the Indian Ocean, the Ottomans hoped to gain control of two "windows" that would enable them to have direct access to the Asian commercial world.[32] The first was obtained in 1538, with the conquest of Yemen; the second, Hormuz, always eluded them despite their having a naval base in Basra since 1546–47. The real Ottoman objective was, however, to keep open the traditional supply routes to the Red Sea and the Persian Gulf rather than to compete with Portugal's distributive role in Europe.[33] Despite having been included under the Porte's suzerainty in 1536, Basra was only occupied in December 1546, and nearby Qatif became part of Lahsa (Hasa) *beylerbeylik* in 1550–55. After that, the Gulf, and Hormuz, became the bone of contention between Ottomans and Portuguese, and violence between them achieved a peak unknown until then.

Despite the truce obtained in 1563, there were some quarters in India where Hormuz and the Gulf were still seen as a sensible border zone with the Ottomans. As the Ottoman Empire focused its attention in Central Europe, the periphery grew more autonomous, and Basra was no exception.[34] Basra's pashas cultivated commercial links with the Portuguese authorities in the Gulf, who were also acting increasingly independent from Goa after 1622. Local Portuguese and Ottoman authorities as early as 1547 had always found a way to establish a status quo favoring the peaceful flow of trade between Hormuz and Basra[35] and tried to maintain it even during the height of confrontation in the 1550s.[36]

Bahrain managed to keep its autonomy within the Hormuzian thalassocracy and was governed by someone connected with the Hormuz vizier's family between its conquest in 1521 and its fall to Safavid hands in 1602. But fear of a possible Ottoman presence in Bahrain posed a serious threat to the Gulf's balance of power. It was Bahrain that prompted the first large Portuguese intervention there, under the pretext of collecting the tribute due to Turan Shah IV (king of Hormuz), but in reality it was sent to eliminate a possible Ottoman bridgehead.[37] The Portuguese only intervened quickly in case of danger, particularly during the war-torn 1550s,[38] and again in the siege of 1560,[39] until a peaceful status quo was attained after 1563. Bahrain continued to receive close attention until the eighteenth century, as the island was the best source for horses and pearls, and several plans were made to recover it after 1602.[40]

Until 1545 the use of Portuguese naval power in the Gulf was seen as enough to establish a favorable balance of power, and keep the trade routes open. In 1528–29 a small expeditionary force intervened for the first time in the Shatt al-Arab to broker the conflict between Ali Megamis of Basra and chieftains of Jaza'ir (the area at the confluence of the Tigris and Euphrates rivers).[41] Around 1530 the growing militarization of the Gulf was noticeable, particularly the naval forces belonging to Hasa, Basra, and Rishahr, which posed the most formidable menace.[42] Though Rishahr was a Safavid port, its governor had acted independently since the days of Mir Abu Ishaq (ca.1503–ca.1528), and his son and successor Shah Ali Beg (ca.1528–40) followed in his father's footsteps, much to the distress of Shah Tahmasp who asked for Portuguese assistance to oust Shah Ali Beg in 1534.[43] The expedition commanded by D. Jorge de Castro ended in disaster, and the Rishahr menace continued until 1540, when a joint Portuguese-Iranian operation finally achieved Shah Ali Beg's capitulation.[44]

After a decade of confrontation (1550–60), a period of truces followed by direct negotiations between Lisbon, Constantinople, and Goa lasted from 1565–66 to 1622, which reinforced Portugal's status as the Gulf's paramount power. During the hostilities, and even before, both sides had made use of local forces against each other to undermine the opposite side, only to discover that their allies also used them. The Gulf's militarization had made their emergence possible and sustainable, particularly in areas where the contending empires negotiated with a third party to have nominal control. The paradigm of this unstable ally were the Musha'sha', who, after being a nuisance to Portuguese interests in the 1520s, successfully won their support during Sayyid Mubarak b. Muttalib b. Badran's reign (1587–1616).[45]

The Mediterranean Dimension

There was also a Mediterranean dimension to Portuguese policy in the Gulf, and in the Red Sea it connected with economic and political interests in India. D. Manuel envisaged the destruction of the Mamluks and the subsequent division of the spoils with Shah Isma'il of Iran (Jerusalem to him and Mecca to his ally). Albuquerque put into practice his master's plan after 1510,[46] and during his governorship he sent three embassies to Isma'il.[47] Surprisingly, Isma'il shared the same ideal of world conquest,[48] and he wanted Portuguese assistance in an alliance against Egypt and the Porte, a goal he maintained even after his defeat at Ottoman hands in Chaldiran in 1514.[49] This alliance proved to be short-lived in effective terms. When a Safavid army of 6,000–7,000 men appeared opposite Hormuz in 1516 demanding assistance and boats to transport them to conquer Bahrain and Hasa, the Iranian request was dismissed with a vague promise of future help after consultation with Goa and Lisbon.[50]

There was a shift in the core of the traditional alliances as the Gulf slipped more into the periphery of the Ottoman, Safavid, and Portuguese empires during the seventeenth century. The Ottomans ceased to be a menace to Portuguese India after 1595, if not before, and Iran's threat to the Arab side of the Gulf ended after 1624. Portugal was then left to face the mounting Ya'rubi danger in Oman. Goa's diplomacy for the Gulf from 1650 to 1750 was to find allies to attack Muscat's seaborne empire, either locally by unsatisfied Arab shaikhs or by Iran, whose imperial designs over the Gulf's Arab shore never disappeared. Both never came to fruition.[51]

The Indian Ocean Dimension

The Gulf's international influence was also projected over India and the Indian Ocean. Part of it was economic, as the Gulf had served as a trade route between India and the Middle East for millennia, and another part was politico-military, as Iran served as a recruiting zone for the Indian sultanates, especially in the Deccan. Albuquerque wanted to stop the arrival in India of this flow of *gente branca* (Persian, Turkish, and Arab mercenaries) via the Gulf, since they were recruited as soldiers and bureaucrats[52] by the Deccan's sultanates, thus swelling the ranks of Portuguese enemies in India.[53] This was to no avail, as Iranians continued to be a regular presence in Indian armies and bureaucracies.[54] Albuquerque also wanted to eradicate Isma'il's growing influence in India; his fear, and that of his successors, was that a coalition of Shiite sultans would attack Portuguese settlements there.

The Gulf also supplied horses to India, where, due to the hot weather and lack of a thorough equine knowledge, there was steady demand.[55] India's awesome equine mortality, indeed, made it necessary to import large quantities annually. Albuquerque estimated it at about 700 to 1,000 horses per year,[56] whereas around 2,000 were exported to India ca.1550.[57] The horse trade also represented a source of gold currency to Hormuz, with which the kingdom paid the deficit of its trade balance with India and acquired essential victuals.[58]

Safavid Iran never had a naval force in the Indian Ocean, despite the presence of active Iranian merchant communities scattered on its shores,[59] and as such it never represented a real danger for Portuguese power outside the Gulf. During Shah Abbas's reign, however, Iran developed imperial ambitions in the Gulf, which led it to oppose Portuguese interests and power. Bahrain was conquered in 1602, and the remaining Hormuzian possessions in Mughistan were taken in 1614, before a final assault was launched to take Jarun Island in 1622 with English assistance.[60] But Abbas's plans in Oman failed for lack of European naval help, and because of a resolute counteroffensive in 1622–23.[61]

Unlike their Iranian neighbor, Ya'rubi Muscat became a seaborne power after 1650, and its navy turned out to be a regular nuisance to Portuguese maritime routes and, above all, to her dominions in India and in East Africa.[62] While Oman succeeded in carving out an overseas empire on the Swahili coast,[63] the Ya'rubi were less successful in India, despite attacks on cities on its western coast, including Bombay (1661–62), Diu (1668 and 1676), and Bassein (1674).[64] Goan authorities were able to prevent their expansion to Kanarese ports, vital to Goa's supply of rice, until 1750.[65] That was why a Portuguese fleet was sent almost yearly to the Gulf after 1650, not only to protect shipping and collect dues for Kung's customs, but also as a show of force.

The Portuguese in the Gulf

By 1514 the Gulf had become a pressing problem that the Portuguese Crown had to solve, as it had become a major political, strategic, and economic risk. The policy to stanch Shiism in its cradle had failed, and Hormuz was seen as more than ever in the orbit of Safavid Iran. Turan Shah IV (1513–21) gave orders that the Friday *khutba* be said in the name of the Twelve Imams, and even accepted Isma'il's red cap.[66] This could be seen as the traditional Hormuzian subterfuge to avoid greater dependence, but it triggered a hostile reaction in Albuquerque. He sent his nephew Pêro de Albuquerque to Hormuz in 1514, with orders to finish the fortress begun in 1507, to collect the tribute in arrears since 1512, and to explore the Gulf, probably to get a better picture of its political situation.[67] As his nephew's expedition did not accomplish the objectives set by him, Albuquerque had to proceed personally to Jarun Island in 1515, where he took advantage of the current political situation (the Hormuz elite was more divided than ever) to sign a new treaty recognizing Portugal's suzerainty, to eliminate the vizier Ra'is Ahmad Fali (1514–15) and to construct the long-desired fortress.[68]

In 1515, the peripheral areas of Hormuz's thalassocrassy (Basra, Bahrain, and Rishahr) sent envoys to Jarun Island to discover Albuquerque's intentions and how they would fit into the Gulf's new status quo.[69] Iran's reaction, however, was less moderate, as Isma'il had an outburst of wrath when he discovered that Hormuz had been taken, and a fortress had been built in a kingdom he viewed as vassal by a man he considered an ally.[70] But his outburst was in fact meaningless, as Isma'il was eager to secure D. Manuel's alliance.[71]

Albuquerque seemed happy to gain naval control over the Strait of Hormuz, and to build a fortress on Jarun, leaving the rest of the Gulf free of Portuguese interference. His only offensive action was taken against the "Nautaque" pirates on the Makran coast, part of a joint Portuguese-Iranian operation, but his aim was to secure trade routes, which were plundered more often since Hormuz had fallen into political turmoil after 1505.[72] For precaution's sake Albuquerque demilitarized the kingdom[73] and put its sovereign Turan Shah IV under the supervision of a bodyguard commanded by a trusted man. Official Portuguese involvement in the Gulf had only begun, and its evolution until 1750 occurred in parallel with local crises that triggered changes in its shape and structure.

During two and half centuries, the Portuguese never showed any interest in controlling the entire Persian Gulf, or even directly most of its major ports (Bahrain, Qatif, Basra, Rishahr), though they tried to keep them in their orbit of influence. They manifested, though, an interest in Bahrain, India's source for horses and pearls. In Lisbon and in India it was thought that the hold over Hormuz, then the paramount local power, would lead local "vassals" to transfer their loyalties to the new suzerain. That showed how little they had understood the nature of Hormuzian thalassocracy. It was an error under which Portugal labored until the seventeenth century, because Hormuzi sovereigns were used to legally control the kingdom and its dependencies, even if these gradually grew more autonomous and eventually became independent. That Portuguese conception of power and of political relationships was applied automatically,[74] and even after Hormuz was lost plans were made in the 1630s to restore its last monarch, Muhammad Shah IV (r. 1609–22).[75] A similar attempt was made in Oman immediately after Hormuz fell in 1622,[76] which also failed, as the Ya'rubi united Oman's interior and succeeded in ousting the Portuguese in 1650.[77]

Until 1650 the Portuguese presence in the Gulf was structured around a fortress: Hormuz until 1622 and then Muscat until 1650. From 1650 to the 1720s, it was centered in Bandar Kung, a small Iranian town situated near the Strait of Hormuz. Kung had been thriving since around 1628, when Rui Freire de Andrade managed to erect a factory and collect half of its customs,[78] but the shadow of Bandar Abbas always made it a secondary player.[79] The Safavid downfall in 1722, with the subsequent chaos felt in Iran, led the Goan government to revive old projects to recover Hormuz and Bahrain in the 1730s,[80] after Kung's factory had been lost.[81] By then Portugal's presence in the Gulf was marginal, and it ended when the Augustinian Fr. José de Santa Teresa abandoned Isfahan in 1748 against royal orders.[82]

After 1650 the character of Portugal's presence changed when she lost all her territorial possessions in the Gulf with Muscat's fall, as Kung was a factory on Iranian soil like those kept by the Dutch and the English East India companies in Bandar Abbas.[83] Goa's government, however, managed to maintain a naval presence through a small fleet sent almost every year to escort shipping from Gujarat and Sind to Kung and Basra and back, and to harass Ya'rubi shipping and raid Oman's coast. The economic effort made to equip ships and men was enormous, given Estado da Índia's difficult financial situation after 1660,[84] and there were people who criticized the Strait Fleet as a useless squandering of money.[85] Goa however profited with half of Kung's customs revenues, even if the Iranian side seldom paid it.[86] Political relations were also modified after 1650, as links with India were reduced to the annual call of the Strait Fleet, which gave the factor a wide margin of autonomy vis-à-vis Goa, and some amassed small fortunes out of their position.[87] No other European power had such a political presence in the Gulf up to the nineteenth century, when Britain began gradually to gain a foothold due to its growing Indian Empire, which the British, like their Portuguese forerunners of the sixteenth and seventeenth centuries, wanted badly to protect from possible enemies coming out from the Strait.

Type of Rule

To rule in the Gulf, the Portuguese made use of Hormuz political structures, with their web of familial ties, particularly between the royal and the Fali families (who often served as viziers). The conquest in 1515 and the subsequent treaty had made Turan Shah IV not only a vassal of D. Manuel but also someone who had surrendered his kingdom to the Portuguese monarch and received it back in exchange for a yearly tribute, on the express condition to return it whenever asked to do so.[88] Each new king received his right to rule from the Portuguese captain of Hormuz in the name of the ruling sovereign in Portugal under these conditions. The process was crippling to the kingdom's autonomy, as each new monarch saw his power thwarted by the collusion he had to enter into with the Portuguese captain, or even with Crown officials to secure his accession.

In exchange, the Hormuzian political order and administrative structure was maintained,[89] though changes were visible after the demilitarization of the kingdom and the mounting Portuguese interference in the customs management, culminating in their complete takeover in 1543.[90] The direct administration of the thalassocracy and the appointments to its cities, ports, and fortresses were kept in local hands, though Portuguese officials tried to foster conflicts between the vizier and the king over them. For example, there was a crisis in 1529 regarding the appointment of a new vizier for Bahrain, which resulted in a serious blunder for Portuguese prestige with the disastrous expedition of Simão da Cunha.[91]

In nearby Mughistan, Portuguese involvement became necessary to secure the Hormuz maritime front from the onslaughts of the princes of Lar, like Ibrahim Khan (r. 1541–1602). Furthermore, Mughistan had always been a troublesome part of the kingdom, a focus of rebellion against royal power,[92] and it also suffered from the incursions of Safavid armies, which threatened to interrupt caravan trade. Around 1538 the authority of Salghur Shah II had collapsed almost entirely in Mughistan,[93] and it was only reinstated in 1545 after Portuguese intervention. The demilitarization of Jarun Island did not mean the loss of military initiative and capability to recruit men by the king or the vizier, as proved by the expedition against Bahrain in 1521.[94] Despite the limitations imposed by the treaty of 1523,[95] the kings and viziers of Hormuz were still able to recruit soldiers in Mughistan, where the monarch kept fortresses up to the seventeenth century.

The most important military action in the Gulf, however, rested on Portuguese shoulders. They lacked the means to control everything, and so opted to master the Strait of Hormuz, which enabled them to interfere with all major maritime routes.[96] They only intervened in the Gulf itself when there was a direct challenge to their naval primacy by local powers supported by larger powers, or when vital commercial links became imperiled. Since 1515 there had been a flotilla roaming in the Strait and along Oman's littoral with a few ships (only two galleys and foists around 1582[97]). The Gulf became more and more militarized, which led to the reinforcement of naval forces. Around 1607 Hormuz had ten ships, 550 soldiers, and 440 sailors, as commercial shipping was usually convoyed by armed foists, and the expenses were paid by taxes (1% charged to all merchants).[98] Numbers kept growing, and reached a maximum between 1623–33, with a growth of 239 percent in a decade, of which, 1,249 men (72%) were Asian soldiers and sailors in 1633.[99] In case of danger, the naval forces were reinforced with big ships sent from India, as in the 1550s during the height of Portuguese-Ottoman confrontation. Large men-of-war, however, were regularly absent from Gulf fleets, replaced by the more maneuverable *terradas* or galleys, which put Portuguese ships on a par with those of their local opponents, namely the Nakhilu.[100] As long as they maintained fortresses in the Gulf, the Portuguese opted to employ galleys, which were particularly useful, for instance, in the jagged fjords of the Musandam peninsula. After 1650 frigates and other ships of line progressively replaced the galleys.[101]

It was mainly the growing Ya'rubi naval presence in both gulfs (Persian and Omani) following their conquest of Muscat in 1650, however, which increased the level of violence. As Portuguese-Omani maritime warfare intensified, waged from the Swahili coast to India and touching Bab al-Mandab, so did the size of ships on both sides.[102] Since Oman lacked timber to build large ships, its sultans resorted to Indian shipyards (in Surat and Bombay) whose expertise, cheapness, and closeness made them attractive.[103] Even if Goan authorities tried to prevent their construction in India, or attempted to intercept them en route to Muscat, some large ships arrived unhindered because Estado da Índia periodically had no ships, nor sailors to man them.[104] Although they had checkmated the Ottomans, defeating them at sea and confining them on land to Hasa and Basra,[105] the Portuguese did not have the same success with the Ya'rubi; in fact they were beaten on land (in Oman and Africa), and at best achieved some victories at sea, while they also suffered some naval defeats.

Naval hegemony with a local balance of power continued to be Portugal's aim for the Gulf after 1564, even if conditions had changed, namely with the appearance of the Nakhilus. They had migrated to the Iranian littoral through Larak Island from the Gulf's Arab side following a rift with neighbors, and the possible exhaustion of a pearl bank.[106] They divided their activity between pearl fishing in Bahrain (July–August) and off Oman's coast (September),[107] along with robbing ships on the Hormuz-Basra route. More than ever shipping was sent in convoys escorted by warships, as the Nakhilu proved to be resilient opponents despite three successive Portuguese punitive expeditions in the 1580s.[108] These setbacks harmed Portuguese prestige in the Gulf, and partly led to the recrudescence of illicit "Pimenteiro" traffic (see below, p. 220),[109] evincing how weak their policing activity had become, notwithstanding the increase in expenses for ships and defense since the 1580s.[110]

The Safavid conquest of Bahrain in 1602 initiated a period of transition, which ended in 1623, characterized by the appearance of new protagonists—the English and the Dutch—on the Gulf's periphery. The Dutch notion of "Persian Gulf" corresponded to Bandar Abbas and little else, something they shared with the English, and even the French. From 1623 until the nineteenth century, there was no real hegemonic power in the Gulf until the British slowly intruded into its affairs. During the second half of the seventeenth century up to ca.1720 Portuguese objectives in the Gulf were subsidiary to those connected with Estado da Índia's security vis-à-vis Oman, along with economic interests in the Kung-Basra route. Besides escorting the annual *qafila* from India to Kung and Basra, Portuguese fleets intervened in the Gulf from time to time.

THE "OUTER GULF"

Whereas Portuguese sovereignty within the Gulf proper remained nominal, and their presence felt only in case of challenge to their naval hegemony, they had an effective presence in the "outer Gulf," along Oman's littoral. They simply followed a Hormuzian tradition of controlling a vital zone traversed by shipping entering or leaving the Gulf.[111] For a long time, it was exclusively a naval presence of roaming between Hormuz and Oman, whose numbers were quite modest.[112] Oman's shaikhs, particularly the ruler of Muscat, preserved their autonomy, and Portuguese forces were not stationed permanently there until the last quarter of the sixteenth century.

To have greater control, the Portuguese played Arabs against Persians, taking advantage of the twofold ethnicity of the Hormuzian elite, as part of a similar policy carried out in other parts of their Asian empire. That policy failed as long as the Persian elite appointed governors for port cities in Oman. There were parts of Oman, though, where Hormuzian and Portuguese authority eventually lapsed, namely Suhar, whose shaikh by 1610 was offering his port as an effective alternative to Hormuz, particularly to those merchants who traded with Shiraz.[113] The Safavid offensive against the last remnant of Hormuzian presence in Mughistan in 1614 led to the strengthening of the Portuguese presence along Oman's littoral, to guarantee the safety of the commercial shipping using Hormuz.[114]

Portugal created a string of forts from Quryat, south of Muscat, to Liwa, north of Suhar, which constituted her line of defense after Hormuz had been taken in 1622. That presence was complemented with a series of agreements made during Rui Freire de Andrade's captainship (1623–33) with the petty rulers of the Gulf's Arab coast.[115] Despite attempts made to establish political ties with Oman's shaikhs and clans, though, Portuguese authority eroded and it never had a truly deep impact outside some coastal oases and ports until it disappeared in 1650. The Portuguese never gave up trying to gain a foothold in Oman and on the Gulf's Arab coast after 1650, but all their attempts failed.

The "outer Gulf," in reality the Gulf of Oman, had an impact on the affairs of the "real" Gulf, and its weight increased over time as its influence was felt as far as Sind. Sind was perhaps the great new protagonist, even if it already had economic links with Hormuz and the Gulf prior to the Portuguese arrival. In 1549 its trade had a share of 7.7 percent–8.2 percent in Hormuz's revenues,[116] but Sind's importance grew with the commerce carried by Hormuz's captains over the years, particularly after 1550. That importance grew with Sind's integration into the Mughal Empire (1592), as its ports served as entrepôts for the hinterland (going as far as Punjab and the Doab), and traded with the Red Sea and the Gulf, to which its traffic increased whenever the Kandahar Pass was closed. In spite of occasional problems with local authorities in Thatta, especially during periods of confrontation between Estado da Índia and the Mughal Empire, Portuguese ascendancy grew in Sind.[117] Things changed after 1650 when Portuguese merchants disappeared from this route,[118] but up to the beginning of the eighteenth century, Goa sent almost annually a fleet to escort Sind's merchant ships to Kung and Basra, and back.

ECONOMY, SOCIETY, AND POLITICAL STRUCTURE

Economy

Teixeira was wrong about Hormuz's prosperity prior to its conquest by Albuquerque in 1515, as the kingdom's economy had been declining for the previous decade for internal political reasons, and also thanks to the rivals emerging on its periphery. Albuquerque's incursion in 1507–08 might have worsened the situation, as some merchant communities began searching for more peaceful havens to trade,[119] but he was not the cause of its decline. In reality, the bases of Hormuz's economy were more frail than depicted in Portuguese sources, as it was too dependent on long-distance trade, which amounted to more than half of its total revenue in 1515. Any problem along trade routes had an immediate impact on the overall commercial activity and revenues of Hormuz. The kingdom had profited from the economic boom felt in the Indian Ocean during the fifteenth century, despite the fact that "the duties are high, one tenth of everything," according to Nikitin.[120] It is noteworthy that some commercial products paid more tax than others, especially those westward bound.

During the fifteenth century Hormuz had become increasingly more integrated into the Gujarati networks operating in the Indian Ocean.[121] Tomé Pires admired their commercial technique so much that he compared them to the best merchants of his age, the Italians.[122] Hormuz trade remained closely attached with Gujarat after 1515, so that the new agreement reached in 1523 stipulated that the annual tribute, which was raised from 25,000 to 60,000 *xerafins* (seraphins) would not be paid in case of war with Gujarat.[123] An estimate made around 1549 showed that trade with Gujarat amounted to 36 percent–38.5 percent of the total revenues, which made it the island's greatest trading partner.[124] This partnership was translated in the settlement of Gujarati communities at several points of the Hormuzian thalassocracy in the Gulf, such as Khur Fakkan. In Jarun Island they paid an annual rent of 700 *pardaus* to the king to allow the practice of their religion.[125]

Hormuz acted as a great transhipment center, and the transactions made there were on a large scale. To cover possible losses, an additional allowance (*picotá*)[126] existed, which varied according to the merchandise quality. Everything was sold by weight, and despite its complexity no one dared to violate the regulations enforced by clerks.[127] Despite the island's barrenness "it is exceeding rich and well furnished with victual of every kind, is yet very dear, for the reason that everything comes to it from outside."[128] Its visitors had always praised its bazaars full of provisions, which were packed with people even by night.[129] Political instability since the fifteenth century was translated into the episodic disruption of supply lines that reached as far as Honavar and Bhatkal in India. This only led to the inflation of prices and to the threat of famine hovering over an island populated by some 50,000 people, not counting the seasonal trading population.

Despite the mounting problems, trade remained Hormuz's main source of revenue and its merchant community was a cosmopolitan and complex group.[130] If some of the foreign merchants who visited Hormuz did so seasonally, there was a local trading community of mixed Arab and Persian origin,[131] of whom some were great traders.[132] Furthermore, trade was a transversal activity and it touched all strata of Hormuzian society one way or another. The royal family was no exception, participating in trade either through taxation or by direct investment. Some members of Hormuz's elite even had privileged trade, such as Muscat's shaikh, who was the only one in that port entitled to sell fresh water and cordage to passing ships. This was part of a larger set of privileges, which included the customhouse income, the official weighing brokerage (*qapan*), and the position of customs judge, which the Muscati family held until 1591.[133]

The pattern was not different elsewhere in the kingdom and at its center the Fali family, which held the post of vizier, managed to receive 1 percent of all Indian textiles passing through the customhouse. This grant of a royal rent was a sign of the king's political feebleness in an age of turmoil, and of the Fali ascendancy in the kingdom's politics. The pattern repeated itself during Portuguese rule. From the early sixteenth century,[134] the vizier acted as the market's chief broker, which gave him great profits even during the Portuguese period.

Hormuz's market was extremely sophisticated, and by 1515 there were 21 different urban rents in the capital alone, some of which were probably farmed.[135] One of these was to the renter who received emoluments from certain bulk products (indigo, sugar, rice, butter, raw cotton)[136] traded through the *bangsar.*[137] He was the man who oversaw the weighing of all merchandise in Hormuz's official *qapan*, and calculated the picotá for each trader.[138] Farming royal rents seemed to be a widespread phenomenon by 1515, like the pearl fishery—a royal privilege in Ibn Battuta's time[139]—but now farmed for 120 *lakh* (6,000 *ashrafi*).[140] Pearl brokerage however was a separate rent in Jarun Island with an annual income of 3,750 pardaus.[141] Farming royal rents seems to have been the solution found by the sovereigns to have cash in advance in order to pay their increasing expenditure. Jarun Island was exclusively responsible for more than two thirds of the known royal revenue, and customs alone accounted for more than half of it. This was, however, an incomplete picture of the total revenues. Expenses in 1515 amounted to 49,364 seraphins, spent mainly on the royal household, the royal family, and a few officials. There is no data available for other expenses, particularly those connected with defense and the bureaucracy, which should double the sum known.[142] Even so, the king could hoard, at least theoretically, about half of his revenues.

After 1515 things changed, particularly for the king, whose revenue depended greatly on the customs. As feared by Turan Shah IV, the Portuguese took over the custom-house little by little, until they gained complete control in 1543.[143] From that date on, Hormuz's monarchs became pensioners of the Portuguese Crown, regularly receiving a pension of 40 lakh, equivalent to 564,140 *réis* in 1554, which was later reduced by inflation. Dynastic struggles and troubled successions between rival branches of the royal family only contributed to the sovereign's impoverishment, and concomitantly to their loss of political ties with their old vassals. Unlike their masters, the Falis retained much of their economic power after 1515—though the family was removed from office for almost two decades (1528–46)—as they managed to preserve their role in the local market until Hormuz's fall in 1622. Both were under the protection of Portugal's sovereign, to whom they frequently (and usually successfully) appealed in case the captain and other Portuguese officials violated any of their prerogatives.

Settlement and Trade in the Gulf

The Portuguese preferred to settle in the core areas of their presence, especially in Hormuz, and only a few lived in urban centers at its periphery. Most of them were obliged to do so because of official appointments, while others acted privately as factors for officers and merchants alike. Still the Portuguese impact was small in this, the greatest city of the region, whose population was estimated at around 50,000 during the sixteenth century, and about 40,000 in the seventeenth century.[144] Fr. António de Herédia referred to 150 "Casados"(literally, "married"), that is, Portuguese married to local Christian women or their descendants, who were obliged to serve as soldiers and bureaucrats at a given place, among Portuguese and Asian Christians in 1554,[145] and there were 200 Portuguese Casados around 1600, not counting other Christians.[146] Apart from the Casados,[147] most of the Portuguese living in the Gulf until 1650 were soldiers. In Hormuz alone, where they constituted a rowdy group always prone to create havoc among the Casados, they ranged normally from four hundred to five hundred, depending on the political situation.[148] Later in Muscat from 1623 to 1650, besides Portuguese and "Descendants" (Descendentes), that is, those descended from a Portuguese Casado and a local woman who professed Catholicism, there existed an important number of Asian auxiliary forces.[149] Thus, most of the Portuguese living in the Gulf depended on or were dependants of the Crown to which they had to account for their actions.

Muscat never had a sizeable Portuguese community, particularly until 1622, and they did not distinguish themselves from local inhabitants, as some Casados even lived with Muslim women.[150] In 1552 the city had sixty Casados.[151] Kung had even fewer, as the superintendent and the factor were probably the only Portuguese residents. There was, however, a floating population made up of Portuguese merchants resident in India who traveled through the Gulf in the trading season. In 1635 Bocarro counted two hundred in Sind alone,[152] but after 1650 they disappear slowly, as Estado da Índia ceased to have strongholds in the Gulf.

The Gulf never attracted Portuguese settlement partly due to its weather conditions—too hot—which were remarked on by all who visited it. According to Fr. Barzeus in 1549, "is this land [Hormuz] so hot that the Portuguese go naked [from the waist up] and they are almost always inside water [tanks]."[153] His description is nicely illustrated by the drawing made by the contemporary anonymous author of the *Codex Casanatense*, who pictured two Portuguese couples being lavishly entertained inside a pool by servants.[154]

As it had limited resources, the Gulf could not attract the same kind of settlement developed in the Northern Province of India, in Ceylon, and in Mozambique, nor the economy associated with it. So trade, especially long-distance commerce, became their main activity, even for those who depended on Crown salaries and stipends, which included the majority of the Portuguese living in the Gulf. Local trade, apart from those goods that interested outside markets (like horses, pearls, and sulfur) did not traditionally attract Portuguese capital, as the risk was too great and the benefit too little. However, farming urban rents in Hormuz did attract Portuguese investment, particularly the customs if it was farmed. That happened whenever there was need for money. Muscat never took off as a finance center, though it served as a hub for regional and international trade routes in the Gulf,[155] a role that Kung managed to maintain from 1650 to ca.1725.

Most of the traffic was carried out to and from India, thus continuing a pre-Portuguese pattern, and was controlled mainly by Gujarati merchants. Around 1548 India represented about 44 percent–47 percent of Hormuz's total trade revenue, followed by Safavid Iran (34%–37%), with Portuguese traders in third place (10%–11%), and the commerce conducted with Basra (about 9%) in fourth place.[156] The overall weight of India's trade might have risen or diminished a little with time, but it continued to drain precious metals and currency from the Mediterranean basin.

There were changes in the goods traded through the Gulf under Portuguese domination, partly as a result of the changes occurring at their sources (India, Ceylon, and Southeast Asia). Spices, particularly pepper, which constituted the bulk cargo of Carreira da Índia ships and remained a Crown monopoly, were the most important product affected.[157] The Crown always privileged the exportation of spices to Europe, even if their sale in Asia through their factories was considered from time to time. As a result of the Portuguese influence in spice-producing areas, and in its distributive ports, along with the Red Sea blockade, the Gulf had emerged by 1513 as the principal route to supply Levantine ports with pepper.[158]

"Illicit" trade called "Pimenteiro" was the answer to a growing Asian demand. In Hormuz there were networks of Portuguese smugglers, who frequently escaped imprisonment thanks to the protection given by its captain.[159] The Pimenteiro phenomenon never disappeared, though its character changed radically after the 1590s.[160] By 1550 other modifications were taking place, namely in India with the war ravaging Gujarat that had diminished Hormuz's revenues during the 1540s,[161] but especially thanks to the changes that had affected the exploration for luxury spices in the Moluccas.[162] Pepper was replaced by cinnamon, cloves, nutmeg, and mace as the most-traded spices through the Gulf.

The Portuguese-Ottoman truce obtained in 1564 only helped to increase the volume of trade carried through the Gulf, strengthening the shift to luxury spices and Indian textiles already noticeable in the late 1540s.[163] In the last quarter of the sixteenth century, the volume of Indian textiles traded through the Gulf equalled that of the spices, and their importance grew during the seventeenth century.[164]

Cosmopolitan Society

The Portuguese settlements in the Gulf only partially benefited from this trade during this period (1515–1750), which explains why it retained much of its cosmopolitan character. The numerous nations enumerated by Fr. Barzeus in 1549 (Jews, Turks, Persians, Armenians, Russians, Poles, "and other barbarous nations") were the same registered by the informer of Diogo do Couto ca.1600.[165] This cosmopolitan air survived the Portuguese conquest, much to the abhorrence of missionaries who fought against it. A scandalized Fr. Barzeus wrote that: "[in Hormuz] the Christians live so mixed with Moors, Turks, Jews, and Gentoos, that you can not notice the difference."[166] Worse still, conversion meant that the same family shared different creeds, "and there are other [houses] where the daughter is Christian, and the mother Moor, like the sisters,"[167] not to mention sexual promiscuity, also visible in the periphery, as in Muscat.[168] The religious orders were powerless to destroy this coexistence, even if temporarily there was greater pressure to set communities apart.[169] Political realism, however, prevailed in Goa and Lisbon over missionary zeal, even if Fr. Barzeus occupied one mosque and transformed it into a church in 1550, and managed to prohibit the muezzin from calling the faithful from Hormuz's main mosque.[170] The Jesuits knew how to compose a picture to suit their missionary work, and claim victory, though they achieved none in the Gulf and eventually left for good in 1568.

That cosmopolitanism was reflected in religious tolerance, and the same Fr. Barzeus reported in 1549 that in Hormuz, God was celebrated four times in a week, "the Hindus on Monday, the Moors on Friday, the Jews on Saturday, and the Christians on Sunday."[171] And despite the anti-Semitism latent in Portuguese society, Jews continued to dwell in Hormuz, and were used as interpreters, spies, or more often as commercial partners. Outbursts of intolerance targeted these trading nations, particularly after 1580, as the Crown did not extend its protection to the synagogue and to the Hindu temples in Hormuz, which it did continuously to Islam.[172] Some communities were temporarily forbidden to reside there for security and economic reasons, like the Venetians and the Armenians in 1563, and again in 1598;[173] others, like the Banyans, given their local importance were allowed to trade, even if other regions of the Portuguese Empire in Asia were barred to them.[174] Despite these prohibitions they kept coming and living in Hormuz, but the economic crisis felt locally from 1600 onwards took its toll in the trading communities, as they were rich enough to be harvested by Crown officials. Portuguese Muscat (1622–1650) did not have this cosmopolitan look, though it maintained a diversified seasonal trading community, like the factory in Kung.[175]

Political Structure

The king appointed people in Asia as a reward for services rendered to the Crown, taking into account the recipient's status and family connections, as well as the post itself. Hormuz captainship, possibly the most coveted in Asia, was usually granted to "fidalgos" or noblemen coming from Portugal.[176] Some captains, like D. Antão de Noronha (1553–56) and Matias de Albuquerque (1584–87), later became viceroys of India.

Women also received grants to marry fidalgos, who in turn would go to Asia and serve the Crown.[177] The remaining offices were given in the same fashion for a three-year period, according to the appointee's social background, court connections, and services rendered. As there were more appointees than posts, it became natural to wait several years before enjoying them, and if he was a well-connected "fidalgo" an appointee could even receive another post while waiting.[178] Other appointees never enjoyed their grants, because they died before they could enter into office, while others simply sold it to someone else. The offices covered four areas: defense, commanded by the captain; judicial, with one magistrate (*ouvidor*) in charge; fiscal, under the supervision of the factor and the customs judge; and then came the church, including priests and auxiliaries.

In Hormuz, as elsewhere in Asia, there was a clear trend to have more and more people paid by the yearly budget of Estado da Índia, which ultimately depleted its financial resources. The medieval character of the appointment still survived in another institution, as some officials were entitled to bring family and clientele to help them discharge the office, particularly the captain who was entitled to have fifty dependents, later augmented to sixty, paid by the Crown.[179] Other officials, especially those connected with the fiscal area, like the factor, had servants paid to deal with the transactions carried out locally, some of whom knew Persian and Arabic.[180] It was in the customs that the Hormuzian officials, some appointed by the monarch, survived and were integrated in the Portuguese structure, as their language skills and know-how were useful for their Portuguese colleagues.[181]

Besides their pay, the officials made money from commerce, which was viewed as natural by their contemporaries. During the last quarter of the sixteenth century, with the changes occurring in the Crown monopolies, a new ethos emerged, that of the gentleman-merchant, who dominated socially, politically, and economically. The system supported and consolidated these as a social group at the expense of the middle bourgeoisie.[182] Pressure always existed from top officials to get their men into key positions, or simply to appoint them to profitable offices. Some conflicts arose from jurisdictional disputes between officials, as there were gray areas, though the captains tended to regard everything as under their authority.

Conflicts and violence were natural, but they did not characterize solely the Portuguese society of that age, and they did not prevent institutions from working regularly. Some complaints distorted reality to suit the interests of the author, who frequently portrayed himself as unjustly suffering from the wrongdoings of the powerful in the hope of receiving a reward from his king. Complaints worked, even if they took time to reach their destination. If not resolved locally, people appealed to a higher jurisdiction in Goa (the viceroy or the governor), or in Lisbon (the king). Power in the early Modern Age, however, dwindled as soon as it left the center, and became feebler the further it went, which meant that negotiation and compromise were necessary between the center and the periphery. Distance and transport also meant that an intervention from outside took six to eight months to reach the Gulf if it came from Goa, and a year and a half to three years if it came from Lisbon. And it worked. João da Fonseca, Estado da Índia's superintendent of the exchequer in the late 1560s, named three captains of Hormuz that were removed from office and imprisoned.[183] In the late 1580s each captain was obliged by law to give an account of his captaincy when he left it.

Another explanation for this behavior in the Gulf was its fabled wealth, partly true and partly fabricated by the Portuguese, who made it a topic in every description of Hormuz. Afonso de Albuquerque was one of the first who contributed to this idea, stating that the Crown could collect annually 200,000 seraphins in 1515,[184] though contemporary documents presented a more moderate estimate, around 145,000 pardaus.[185] Curiously, it was in the middle of the sixteenth century that despite evidence to

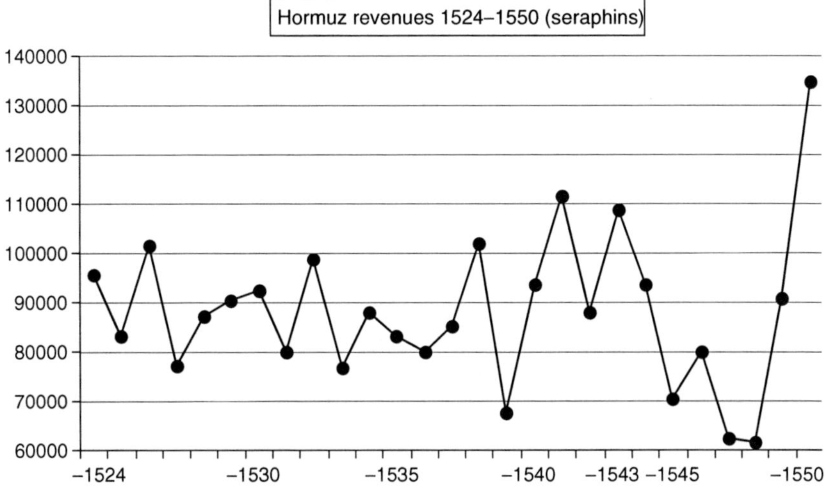

Figure 11.1 Hormuz Revenues 1524–50 (Seraphins)

the contrary this idea was present more than ever. When Portugal took over the customs in 1543, the official who received the account books suspected that the treasurer of King Salghur Shah II concealed some documents, and suspicion persisted that Hormuz revenues were greater in the past.[186] The crude reality of numbers showed a different picture, but the image transmitted in the 1550s was that "the world is a ring, and Hormuz is the precious stone set on it,"[187] and was still alive when the city lay in ruins in 1663 (see figure 11.1).[188]

The known figures, however, evince a different evolution over more than a quarter century (1524–50), with very irregular revenues and with an average annual income of 88,330 seraphins, clearly less than the 145,000 seraphins collected ca. 1515. Only in 1550 did the collected revenue (135,000 seraphins) approach that of pre-Portuguese times.[189]

Although the Hormuzian officials were not concealing revenues nor withholding registers from Portuguese officials, the suspicion remained present in their minds until 1550. These had even accused vizier Ra'is Nur al-Din Fali of having introduced new taxes in Hormuz's customs to pay the annual tribute to D. Manuel.[190] The tribute demanded by Portugal progressively became an unbearable burden to the kingdom's finances, and from 1529 to 1543 the sovereign accumulated a debt of 518,537 seraphins, which was settled by the cession of the customhouse to the Portuguese Crown.[191]

The Portuguese were responsible for part of the revenue decline, though the commercial traffic through the Gulf did increase from 1515 to the 1530s. The problem lay in the change occurring in the Indian Ocean trade structure and routes since the arrival of the Portuguese in 1498, which had affected the distributive centers in the Mediterranean and in the Middle East. Hormuz and the Gulf lay in the middle of those changes, and its traditional role was under pressure. The new tribute agreement of 1523 had underlined Hormuz's excessive dependence vis-à-vis Gujarat, introducing a safeguard clause to protect the kingdom in case of war in that sultanate.[192]

The takeover of Hormuz's customs by the Portuguese Crown did not immediately increase the revenues as expected, but after the 1550s it made the Gulf the second greatest source of income in Estado da Índia after Goa, a place kept until the beginning of the seventeenth century when Diu took that position. Hormuz's contribution to Goa's exchequer remains enshrouded in mystery, as only part of the surplus was sent by the factor. Around 1600 the Gulf had lost its pre-eminent place, a trend accentuated after 1622, as Muscat failed to attract merchants to its port and, unlike Hormuz, its balance was always negative.

From the 1590s onward, small changes were occurring in the Gulf that altered everything, especially with Abbas's expansion after 1602, and the existence of alternative routes to the official ones, where even private Portuguese merchants invested. Goa's intervention by sending superintendents of the exchequer only aggravated the economic situation, as they ended up in open confrontation with the captains. By then the customs revenue share in the total income was higher than in pre-Portugueses times, 53 percent–56 percent in 1515 to 98 percent (1607) and 82 percent (1609), which suggests that some old urban rents were still in the hands of the local elite (king and vizier), though the captain did his best to obtain them. In Muscat, the percentage was similar, as the customs represented 89 percent of the total revenue in 1634.[193]

Kung, on the other hand, had a positive balance, but the Safavid officials seldom paid the moiety from 1650 to 1680,[194] and when they did it was only a small sum. Kung continued to be an additional source of income to Estado da Índia. It was debatable whether it was really profitable, but the gentry and the minor nobility were always interested in serving in the Gulf for the sake of plundering merchant vessels.

Conclusion: The "Key" of India—Image and Reality

For more than two hundred years (1515–1750) the Persian Gulf acted as one of Estado da Índia's keys, but not as *the* key. Its primordial role was always that of an outpost in a border zone that served as India's first line of defense, and at the same time functioned as the tap to control the traffic of goods monopolized by the Crown.

If Estado da Índia succeeded in the first objective, with some mishaps over the long run, in the second it failed completely, as its agents and other private merchants engaged in the lucrative "illegal" trade carried on through the Gulf. This had less to do with the effectiveness of the political structure than the way the Crown's objectives were carried out by its representative in Asia (governor or viceroy), which seldom coincided with local interests. For one thing, the Crown always privileged the Cape route over Asian consumption. Since Albuquerque's time, though, it had become clear that, to survive, their embryonic Asian empire should have local revenues collected from commerce, thus taking advantage of the way the Indian Ocean trading world worked.[195]

Though always on the periphery of Estado da Índia, the capture of Hormuz in 1515 had a deep historical significance in the Gulf's history, as it became part of a wider arena for political and economic control between contending empires. Portuguese suzerainty over the Gulf proved to be crucial to Estado da Índia's survival, since the outcome would have differed if the Ottomans had managed to gain control of it in the 1550s. Even after 1622, and again after 1650, the Gulf continued to play an important role in the Portuguese line of defense in Asia, as the rising Omani power made painfully aware almost everywhere in the western Indian Ocean. Its importance only vanished in the 1740s when the Omanis had ceased to be a menace to Estado's fortresses in the region. In that sense, the Gulf was the western key to secure Portuguese India.

That reality was perceived and conveyed differently according to the author's intention. In official quarters, the Gulf was seen as the economic key of Estado da Índia, mostly due to Hormuz revenues. (That, however, corresponded only to the second half of the sixteenth century, even if during the seventeenth century the Gulf was still profitable for the Portuguese Empire, excepting Muscat from 1623 to 1650.) According to others, the Gulf was already in economic decay in the sixteenth century due to the oppression exercised by Portuguese captains. However, trade volume did increase during that century, which explains the continuous growth of Hormuz's revenues, discarding the simple increase of customs taxes as the main motor behind it. The way the Portuguese presence was established, and the nature of the Gulf's economy, made it virtually impossible to have different economic relations. The captain tried to control everything, but there were other private merchants (Portuguese, Descendents, Asians, and Europeans) who continued to trade independently or were associated with the captain. The profit margin from international commerce was considerable for everyone, including for those who traded with the enemy (whether Turk, Safavid, or Omani).

In a sense the Gulf's economy was always too official, even the "illegal" one, as it depended too much on the authorities' ubiquitous role in the market. As the Gulf was in the western Indian Ocean, the core area of Estado da Índia, the official presence constrained everything, including the social structure. The Portuguese settlements in the Gulf were official, under the Crown's authority, even if there were some Portuguese who lived and traveled outside its jurisdiction. That explains why they disappeared after having lost the last official stronghold (Muscat in 1650), given that Kung was a simple factory, and economically their capital was reinvested elsewhere in India.

Contemporary accounts portray a society that lived on the periphery and in a natural border zone, and some of them also convey the idea of decay or malaise long before Teixeira did in 1604. Others, especially the Crown officials connected with the exchequer, also conveyed a picture of abuse, particularly those made by the captains. To them, it was necessary to have greater control over such a sensible zone for defense objectives, and, above all, to plug any breach in the spice monopoly. Their goal was to give the Crown, and its representatives, more power to intervene in the market to protect everyone from the "abuses" committed by Hormuz's captain.

The idea of decay, corruption, incompetence, and oppression was a constructed image, though reflecting a reality tinted with darker tones by its authors to achieve their goals. It also reflected the way the Portuguese Empire in Asia had been built socially and economically since 1500, as a long and discontinuous political entity, by a small far-flung homeland in Renaissance Europe still imbued with medieval principles.[196]

Despite the contradictory data, by the middle of the sixteenth century the Gulf, that is, Hormuz, had established its prestige among the Portuguese as a place to defend the empire from the Turk, and mainly as a source of incredible wealth for those fortunate officials who had received an office there. The Gulf became a metaphor for riches and a magnet for the fidalgos serving in India. Officially its well-being reflected that of Estado da Índia as a whole, which explains why Fr. Diogo de Sant'Ana singled out the loss of Hormuz in 1622 as the leading cause of the collapse of Portuguese trade and power in Asia. He was wrong—it was just another symptom—but that was the image that survived for posterity.

Notes

1. For an overview of Hormuz see Jean Aubin, "Le royaume d'Ormuz au début du XVIe siècle," *Mare Luso-Indicum* 2 (1973): 77–179, along with Aubin's other classic article, "Les princes d'Ormuz du XIIIe au XVe siècle," *Journal Asiatique* 241 (1953): 77–137. See also Valeria Fiorani Piacentini, "L'emporio e il regno di Hormoz (VIII-fine XV secolo d. Cr.)—Vicende storiche, problemi e aspetti di una civiltà costiera del Golfo Persico," *Memorie dell'Istituto Lombardo – Accademia di Scienze e Lettere* 35 "Memorie," no. 1

(Milan, 1975), which covers a wider span of time. This work was not consulted due to its unavailability. Recently, Willem Floor has presented a more comprehensive view of the Early Modern Age in *The Persian Gulf: A Political and Economic History of Five Port Cities 1500–1730* (Washington, D. C.: Mage Publishers, 2006).

2. Jean Aubin, "Le royaume d'Ormuz," 77–78, 162–63.
3. Pedro Teixeira, *The Travels of Pedro Teixeira; with his* "Kings of Harmuz," *and Extracts from his* "Kings of Persia," ed. William F. Sinclair and Donald Ferguson (Hakluyt Society, 1902; repr. Nendeln/Liechtenstein: Kraus Reprint, 1967), 168–69.
4. The best example of which remains Niels Steensgaard's work, *The Asian Trade Revolution of the Seventeenth Century: The East India Companies and the Decline of the Caravan Trade* (Chicago: The University of Chicago Press, 1974).
5. See the lengthy and scholarly introduction by António Coimbra Martins to Diogo do Couto's *O Primeiro Soldado Prático* (Lisbon, Portugal: CNCDP, 2001), 13–356.
6. For an overview of the Portuguese presence in the Gulf over these two centuries see Jean Aubin, "La politique iranienne d'Ormuz, 1515–1540," *Studia* 53 (1994): 27–51; Luís de Matos' synthesis of all available documentation in *Das relações entre Portugal e a Pérsia 1500–1758: Catálogo bibliográfico da exposição comemorativa do XXV centenário da monarquia no Irão* (Lisbon, Portugal: Fundação Calouste Gulbenkian, 1972); and Floor, *The Persian Gulf*, especially chapters 1 to 4 and 6 to 7.
7. Vitorino Magalhães Godinho, *Les finances de l'État Portugais des Indes Orientales (1517–1635) (Matériaux pour une étude structurale et conjoncturelle)* (Paris: Fundação Calouste Gulbenkian/Centro Cultural Português, 1982), 44–50.
8. Adelino de Almeida Calado, ed., *Livro que trata das cousas da India e do Japão: Edição crítica do códice quinhentista 5/381 da Biblioteca Municipal de Elvas* (Coimbra, Portugal: Imprensa da Universidade, 1957), 128–29.
9. On the frailty of its forces in 1515–18 see Jean Aubin, "Ormuz au jour le jour à travers un registre de Luís Figueira, 1516–1518," *Arquivos do Centro Cultural Português* 32 (1993): 27–30.
10. António Dias Farinha, "Letter of Pêro Fernandes to D. João III," Goa, 20.10.1538, in "Os portugueses no golfo Pérsico (1507–1538): Contribuição documental e crítica para a sua história," *Mare Liberum* 3 (1991): 103–5.
11. João Teles e Cunha, "Economia de um Império: Economia política do Estado da Índia em torno do mar Arábico e golfo Pérsico. Elementos conjunturais: 1595–1635" (MA thesis, Faculdade de Ciências Sociais e Humanas, Universidade Nova de Lisboa, 1995), 147–48.
12. "Letter of Rui Freire de Andrade to King Filipe III," Muscat, 20.06.1623, in *Instituto dos Arquivos Nacionais/Torre do Tombo* (henceforth IAN/TT), *Miscelâneas manuscritas de São Vicente* (henceforth S. V.), cod. 19, ff. 266–67and following; also "Budget of *Estado da Índia* in 1634", in Biblioteca Nacional de Portugal, *Fundo Geral* (henceforth BNL, *FG*), cod. 1783, 5v–10ff.
13. See Salih Özbaran, *The Ottoman Response to European Expansion: Studies on Ottoman-Portuguese Relations in the Indian Ocean and Ottoman Administration in the Arab Lands during the Sixteenth Century* (Istanbul, Turkey: Isis Press, 1994).
14. Francisco Rodrigues Silveira, *Reformação da milícia e governo do Estado da Índia Oriental*, ed. Luís Filipe Barreto, Benjamim N. Teensma, and George D. Winius (Lisbon, Portugal: Fundação Oriente, 1996), 41.
15. Patricia Risso, *Oman and Muscat: An Early Modern History* (London: Croom Helm, 1986), 13.
16. Auguste Toussaint, *Histoire de l'Océan Indien* (Paris: Presses Universitaires de France, 1961), especially chaps. 8 to 10; Kenneth McPherson, *The Indian Ocean: A History of People and Sea* (Delhi, India: Oxford University Press, 1998), 137–97.
17. Luís Filipe F. R. Thomaz, "Descobrimentos e Evangelização: Da Cruzada à missão pacífica," in *Congresso Internacional de História: Missionação Portuguesa e encontro de culturas*, vol. 1, *Cristandade Portuguesa até ao século XV: Evangelização interna, ilhas atlânticas, e África Ocidental* (Braga, Portugal: Universidade Católica Portuguesa/CNCDP, Fundação Evangelização e Culturas, 1993), 118–25.

18. "Memórias da Congregação Agostiniana na Índia Oriental," in *Documentação para a História das Missões do Padroado Portiguês do Oriente–India* (henceforth *DHMPPOI*), vol. 12, ed. A. da Silva Rego (Lisbon, Portugal: Agência Geral do Ultramar, 1958), 69–71.
19. Still visible ca. 1673, cf. "Project of Aires de Sá Sotomaior for the Gulf," undated [ca.1673], in Arquivo Histórico Ultramarino [AHU], *Documentos avulsos da Índia* (henceforth AHU, *Índia*), caixa (henceforth cx.) [29A] 53, doc. 171.
20. Aubin, "Le royaume d'Ormuz," 144–45.
21. "Letter of João Correia de Sá to the Prince Regent D. Pedro, Kung, 06.07.1673," in AHU, *Índia*, cx. [29A] 53, doc. 171.
22. On this matter see Jean Aubin, "Cojeatar et Albuquerque," in *Le Latin et l'Astrolabe*, vol. 2 (Lisbon/Paris: CNCDP/Centre Culturel Calouste Gulbenkian, 2000), 149–96.
23. For an overview see Luís Filipe F. R. Thomaz, "L'idée impériale Manuéline," in *La découverte, le Portugal et l'Europe: Actes du colloque Paris le 26, 27 et 28 mai 1988*, ed. Jean Aubin (Paris: Centre Culturel Calouste Gulbenkian, 1990), 35–100; Sanjay Subrahmanyam, *The Portuguese Empire in Asia 1500–1700: A Political and Economic History* (London: Longman, 1993), 62–69.
24. Luís Filipe F. R. Thomaz, *De Ceuta a Timor* (Lisbon, Portugal: Difel, 1994), 196–206.
25. Thomaz, "L'idée impériale Manuéline," 35–100.
26. Thomaz, *De Ceuta a Timor*, 207–15.
27. Ibid., 211.
28. For an overview see Luís Filipe F. R. Thomaz, "Portuguese Control over the Arabian Sea and the Bay of Bengal: A Comparative Study," in *Commerce and Culture in the Bay of Bengal, 1500–1800*, ed. Om Prakash and Denys Lombard (New Delhi: Manohar for Indian Council of Historical Research, 1999), 128–29.
29. Luís Filipe F. R. Thomaz, "A crise de 1565–1575 na história do Estado da Índia," *Mare Liberum* 9 (July 1995): 481–519.
30. Diogo do Couto, *Década* 10ª, I-xi (reprint of Régia Oficina Tipográfica's edition of 1777–88) (Lisbon, Portugal: Livraria Sam Carlos, 1973–74), 84–92. (Note: Couto and Barros are cited in this fashion, with the title first [*Da Ásia* in Barros' case and *Década* in Couto's], then the decade [first to fourth in Barros and fourth to twelfth in Couto], after which follows the book number in capital Roman numbers, and finally the chapter number in small Roman numbers. There are some variants in Couto, because not all of his chronicles survived in their definitive version, but only in an abridged one, as in *Décadas* 8.ª, 9.ª, and 11.ª).
31. Couto, *Década* 11ª, chaps. V–XI, 26–59.
32. Sanjay Subrahmanyam, "The Trading World of the Western Indian Ocean, 1546–1565: A Political Interpretation," in *A Carreira da Índia e as rotas dos Estreitos Actas do VIII seminário internacional de história Indo-Portuguesa*, ed. Artur Teodoro de Matos and Luís Filipe F. R. Thomaz (Angra do Heroísmo, Portugal: CNCDP/Fundação Oriente/ Secretaria Regional de Saúde e Segurança Social, 1998), 210–11, 219–20.
33. Giles Veinstein, "Commercial Relations between India and the Ottoman Empire (Late Fifteenth to Late Eighteenth Centuries): A Few Notes and Hypothesis," in *Merchants, Companies and Trade: Europe and Asia in the Early Modern Age*, ed. Michel Morineau and Sushil Chaudhuri (Cambridge: Cambridge University Press, Paris: Maison des Sciences de l'Homme, 1999), 97.
34. André Raymond, "Les provinces arabes (xvie–xviiie siècle)," in *Histoire de l'Empire Ottoman*, ed. Robert Mantran (Paris: Fayard, 1989), 378–91.
35. "Letter of Sebastião Lopes Lobato to governor D. João de Castro," Hormuz, 03.02.1546 and "Letter of D. Manuel de Lima to governor D. João de Castro," Hormuz, 23.06.1546, in *Obras Completas de D. João de Castro* (henceforth *Obras*), ed. Armando Cortesão and Luís de Albuquerque (Coimbra: Academia Internacional de Cultura Portuguesa, 1976), vol. 3, respectively, 357, 413–16.
36. Couto, *Década* 7ª, VII-xi, 145–54.
37. João de Barros, *Da Ásia*, 3ª, VI-iii (reprint of Régia Oficina Tipográfica's edition of 1777–88) (Lisbon, Portugal: Livraria Sam Carlos, 1973–74), 25–28.

38. See Özbaran, *The Ottoman Response to European Expansion*, 119–40.
39. Couto, *Década*, 7ª, VII-vii–xi, 109–52.
40. The plans were drawn up in 1623–27 by Rui Freire de Andrade, who counted on the support of Qatif's shaikh. See "Proceeding of the State Council," Goa, 20.03.1626, 13.02.1627 and 05.04.1627, in *Assentos do Conselho do Estado (Proceedings of the State Council at Goa), Supplementary Series (1624–1627)*, vol. 1–2, ed. V. T. Gune (Panaji, India: Tipografia Rangel, 1972), respectively 93, 119–20, 129.
41. Barros, *Da Ásia*, 4ª, III-xiii–xv, 331–50.
42. See Aubin, "La politique iranienne d'Ormuz," 36–37.
43. Gaspar Correia, *Lendas da Índia* (henceforth Correia, *Lendas*), ed. Rodrigo José da Lima Felner (reprint of Academia Real das Ciência's edition of 1858–64) (Coimbra, Portugal: Imprensa da Universidade, 1922–69), tome III, 557.
44. Fernão Lopes de Castanheda, *História do Descobrimento e Conquista da Índia pelos Portugueses* (henceforth Castanheda, *História*), ed. Pedro de Azevedo (Coimbra, Portugal: Imprensa da Universidade, 1924–33), Book IX, chap. 28, 571–72.
45. P. Luft, "Musha'sha'," in *Encyclopédie de l'Islam*, vol. VII (Leiden: E. J. Brill, Paris: G. P. Maisonneuve and Larose, 1993), 672–75.
46. "Letter of Afonso de Albuquerque to Esma'il Shah I" [Goa], nondated [after December 1510], in *Cartas de Afonso de Albuquerque, seguidas de documentos que as elucidam* (henceforth *CAA*), ed. Raimundo António de Bulhão Pato and Henrique Lopes de Mendonça (Lisbon, Portugal: Academia Real das Ciências, 1884–1935) , vol. 1, 387–90.
47. See Ronald Bishop Smith, *The First Age of the Portuguese Embassies, Navigations and Peregrinations in Persia (1507–1524)* (Bethesda, MD: Decatur Press, 1970), 13–56.
48. See Jean Aubin, "L'avènement des Safavides reconsidéré (Études safavides III)," *Moyen Orient et Océan Indien* V (1988): 1–130.
49. Smith, *The First Age of the Portuguese Embassies*, 49–50.
50. "Letter of Pêro de Albuquerque to King D. Manuel," Hormuz, 05.08.1516, in *CAA*, vol. 7, 166–67.
51. See Jean Aubin, *L'ambassade de Gregório Pereira Fidalgo à la cour de Châh Soltân-Hosseyn, 1696–1697* (Lisbon, Portugal: Fundação Calouste Gulbenkian, 1971).
52. Functions not necessarily separated; see Masashi Haneda, "Emigration of Iranian Elites to India during the 16–18th centuries," in *Cahiers d'Asie Centrale* 34, *L'Héritage Timouride: Iran-Asie centrale-Inde XVe-XVIIIe siècles*, ed. Maria Szuppe (Tachkent, Urbekistan, Aix-en-Provence, France: Édisud, 1997), 129–35. Though the author only studies Mughal India, the same principle can be applied elsewhere in the Indian subcontinent.
53. "Letter of Afonso de Albuquerque to D. Manuel," Cochin, 01.01.1514, in *CAA*, vol. 1, 260–61. Another Albuquerque concern was to halt the recruitment of Ottoman experts in casting artillery, much in demand in India.
54. Luís Filipe F. R. Thomaz, "La présence iranienne autour de l'océan Indien au XVIe siècle d'après les sources portugaises de l'époque," *Archipel* 68 (2004): 59–158.
55. Geneviève Bouchon and Denys Lombard, "The Indian Ocean in the Fifteenth Century," in *India and the Indian Ocean 1500–1800*, ed. Ashin Das Gupta and Michael N. Pearson (Calcutta, India: Oxford University Press, 1987), 52, 57; André Wink, *Al-Hind: The Making of the Indo-Islamic World*, vol. 2, *The Slave Kings and the Islamic Conquest 11th–13th Centuries* (Leiden, The Netherlands: Brill, 1997), 282.
56. "Letter of Afonso de Albuquerque to D. Manuel," Hormuz, 22.09.1515, in *CAA*, vol. 1, 372, 374–75.
57. "Estado da Índia e aonde tem o seu princípio," in *Documentação Ultramarina Portuguesa* (henceforth *DUP*), vol. 1 (Lisbon, Portugal: Centro de Estudos Históricos Ultramarinos, 1960), 231; Jean Aubin, "Le royaume d'Ormuz," 168–70.
58. Duarte Barbosa, *The Book of Duarte Barbosa*, ed. Mansel Longworth Dames (London: Hakluyt Society, 1918–21; repr. New Delhi: Asian Educational Services, 1989), vol. 1, 185–94; Tomé Pires, *The Suma Oriental*, ed. Armando Cortesão (London: Hakluyt Society, 1944; repr. Nendelyn/Liechtenstein: Kraus Reprint, 1967), 61–62.

59. As in Masulipatnam, where the shah kept a factor to trade with Iran. In 1666 the Portuguese man-of-war *São Pedro* captured a ship bound for Bandar Abbas in the Strait of Hormuz and towed it to Goa, thus starting a diplomatic conflict with Golconda and Iran over the liberation of the ship, the merchants, and restitution for the cargo. See "Proceeding of the State Council," Goa, 22.09.1666, 02.10.1666, 04.12.1666, and 08.01.1667, in *Assentos do Conselho do Estado* (henceforth *ACE*), ed. P. S. S. Pissurlencar (Bastorá, India: Tipografia Rangel, 1953–57) , vol. 4, 163–67, 175, 177.
60. For an overview see Steensgaard, *The Asian Trade Revolution,* 209–343.
61. José Gervásio Leite, ed., *Comentários do grande capitão Rui Freire de Andrada* (Lisbon, Portugal: Agência Geral das Colónias, 1940), chaps. 43–44, 239–45.
62. Patricia Risso, *Oman and Muscat,* 13–15.
63. Justus Strandes, *The Portuguese Period in East Africa* (Nairobi, Kenya: East African Literature Bureau, 1968), 195–259; Eric Axelson, *Portuguese in South-East Africa 1600–1700* (Johannesburg, South Africa: Witwatersrand University Press, 1960), 155–75; A. I. Salim, "East Africa: The Coast," in *UNESCO General History of Africa*, vol. 5, *Africa from the Sixteenth to the Eighteenth Century,* ed. B. A. Ogot (Paris: UNESCO, Oxford: Heinemann International, Berkeley: University of California Press, 1992), 767–75.
64. Patricia Risso, *Oman and Muscat,* 13.
65. B. S. Shastry, *Goa-Kanara Portuguese Relations 1498–1763,* Xavier Centre for Historical Research studies, no. 8 (New Delhi, India: Concept Publishing, 2000), chaps. 7–9.
66. Brás de Albuquerque, *Comentários de Afonso de Albuquerque* (henceforth Brás, *Comentários*), ed. Joaquim Veríssimo Serrão (Lisbon, Portugal: Imprensa Nacional-Casa da Moeda, 1973), vol. 2, Book IV, chap. 26, 136–37; Castanheda, *História,* Book III, chap. 128, 311.
67. Castanheda, *História,* Book III, chap. 128, 311–12; Barros, *Da Ásia,* 2ª, X-i, 400–02; Brás, *Comentários,* vol. 2, Book IV, chaps. 24–25, 124–33.
68. Ibid., chaps. 31–37, 157–94; Correia, *Lendas,* tome 2, 408–10, 417–42.
69. "Letter of Basra's sheikh to Afonso de Albuquerque," [Basra], undated [post-August 1515], in *CAA,* vol. 1, 255; "Mandate of Afonso de Albuquerque," Hormuz, 02.10.1515, "Mandate of Afonso de Albuquerque," Hormuz, 04.10.1515, in *CAA,* vol. 6, respectively 350, 354.
70. "Account of the embassy of Fernão Gomes de Lemos to Esma'il Shah," 1515–1516, in *CAA,* vol. 2, 240; Correia, *Lendas,* tome 2, 444.
71. "Letter of Esma'il Shah I to Afonso de Albuquerque," undated [ca.1515], in *CAA,* vol. 3, 252.
72. Ibid.
73. "Letter of Afonso de Albuquerque to King D. Manuel," Hormuz, 22.09.1515, in *CAA,* vol. 1, 379; "Letter of Pêro de Alpoím to King D. Manuel," Hormuz, 11.10.1515, in António Dias Farinha, "A dupla conquista de Ormuz por Afonso de Albuquerque," *Studia* 48 (1989): 468–69; Correia, *Lendas,* tome 2, 433–36, 450–51; Castanheda, *História,* Book III, chap. 148, 354–55.
74. For an overview see António Manuel Hespanha, *História das instituições: Épocas medieval e moderna* (Coimbra, Portugal: Almedina, 1982); António Vasconcelos de Saldanha, *Iustum Imperium: Dos tratados como fundamento do império dos portugueses no Oriente. Estudo de história do direito internacional e do direito português* (Lisbon: Fundação Oriente/Instituto Português do Oriente, 1997).
75. "Letter of King Filipe III to viceroy Pedro da Silva," Lisbon, 30.01.1636, in IAN/TT, *Livros das Monções,* codex 36, fol. 97.
76. "Letter of Constantino de Sá de Noronha to King Filipe III," Goa, undated [1623], in IAN/TT, *Miscelâneas Manuscritas,* codex 1116, 682–90ff.
77. Patricia Risso, *Oman and Muscat,* 12–13.
78. *Comentários do grande capitão Rui Freire de Andrada,* Book II, chap. 48, 261; Fr. Manuel Godinho, *Relação do novo caminho da Índia para Portugal,* ed. A. Machado Guerreiro (Lisbon, Portugal: Imprensa Nacional-Casa da Moeda, 1974), chap. 14, 121–24.

79. Jean-Baptiste Tavernier, *Voyage en Perse et description de ce royaume par [. . .] marchand français*, ed. Pascal Pia (Paris: Éditions du Carrefour, 1930), 337–39.
80. See the documents cited by Luís de Matos, *Das relações entre Portugal e a Pérsia*, 354–60.
81. The last known record of the collection of Kung's annual tribute dates from the 1720s. See "Letter of King D. João V to viceroy João Saldanha da Gama," Lisbon, 18.03.1729, in Luís de Matos, *Das relações entre Portugal e a Pérsia*, 355.
82. "Manual Eremítico da congregação da Índia oriental dos Eremitas do N. P. S. Agostinho", in *DHMPPOI*, vol. 11 (Lisbon, Portugal: Agência Geral do Ultramar, 1955), 204–05; "Letter of Fr. José de Santa Teresa to the Augustinian Provincial," Esfahan, 26.05.1748, in Luís de Matos, *Das relações entre Portugal e a Pérsia*, 362.
83. For the VOC see Willem Floor and Mohammad H. Faghfoory, *The First Dutch-Persian Commercial Conflict: The Attack on Qeshm Island, 1645* (Costa Mesa, CA: Mazda Publishers, 2004); for the French attempts to penetrate Safavid Iran see Ann Kroell, *Louis XIV, la Perse et Mascate* (Paris: Société d'Histoire de l'Orient, 1977).
84. For an overview of this period see Glenn J. Ames, *Renascent Empire? The House of Braganza and the Quest for Stability in Portuguese Monsoon Asia, ca.1640–1683* (Amsterdam, The Netherlands: Amsterdam University Press, 2000); and R. J. Barendse, *The Arabian Seas: The Indian Ocean World of the Seventeenth Century* (Armonk, NY: M. E. Sharpe, 2002), 299–380.
85. "Letter of unknown to the regent D. Pedro" [Goa], undated [1676], in AHU, *Índia*, cx. [30] 54, doc. 146.
86. Jean Aubin, *L'ambassade de Gregório Pereira Fidalgo*, 12–13, 26.
87. He acted as Kung's factor in the 1660s and 1670s. See "Consultation of the Ultramarine Council," Lisbon, 29.10.1680, in AHU, *Índia*, cx [31] 56, doc. 73.
88. See "Title of the Contracts Made by the Governors with the King of Hormuz and Its Viziers," in Simão Botelho, "Tombo do Estado da Índia," in *Subsídios para a História da Índia Portuguesa*, ed. Rodrigo José da Lima Felner (Lisbon, Portugal: Academia Real das Ciências, 1868), 78–79.
89. See Luís Filipe F. R. Thomaz, *De Ceuta a Timor*, 224–25; António Vasconcelos de Saldanha, *Iustum Imperium*, 611, 627–30.
90. Botelho, "Tombo do Estado da Índia," 90.
91. "Letter of António Lopes to D. Jaime Duke of Bragança (?)," [Hormuz], 18.11.1529, in António Dias Farinha, "Os portugueses no golfo Pérsico (1507–1538)", 98–99.
92. Like the one faced by Khwaja Ata in 1508, cf. Brás, *Comentários*, vol. 1, Book 1, chap. 59, 300.
93. "Letter of Pêro Fernandes to D. João III," Goa, 20.10.1538, in António Dias Farinha, "Os portugueses no golfo Pérsico," 103–05.
94. Barros, *Da Ásia*, 3ª, VI-iii, 28–29; Castanheda, *História*, Book V, chap. 59, 94.
95. "Treaty between D. Duarte de Meneses and King Muhammad Shah," Hormuz, 15.06.1523, in Júlio Firmino Júdice Biker, *Colecção de Tratados e concertos de pazes que o Estado da India Portugueza fez com os reis e senhores com quem teve relações nas partes da Asia e Africa Oriental desde o princípio da conquista até ao fim do século XVIII* (Lisbon, 1881–87; repr. New Delhi, India: Asian Educational Services, 1995), vol. I, 43–44.
96. See "Livro das cidades e fortalezas, que a Coroa de Portugal tem nas partes da Índia, e das capitanias, e mais cargos que nelas há, e da importância deles," ed. Francisco Paulo Mendes da Luz, *Studia* 6 (July 1960), fol. 32v.
97. Ibid., ff. 36v–37.
98. "Letter of King Filipe I to viceroy D. Duarte de Meneses, Lisbon, 06.02.1587," in *Arquivo Português Oriental* (henceforth *APO*), ed. J. H. da Cunha Rivara (Goa, 1857–77; repr. New Delhi, India: Asian Educational Services, 1992), fasc. 3, 89–90.
99. Teles e Cunha, "Economia de um Império," 138–47.
100. Francisco Rodrigues da Silveira, *Reformação da milícia e governo do Estado da Índia Oriental*, 42–45.
101. "'Certificate of Domingos Barreto da Silva,'" aboard a galley, 13.10.1673, in AHU, *Índia*, cx. [29] 52, doc. 154.

102. Sultan Saif b. Sultan (1692–1711), for instance, owned 28 ships, one of which had 80 guns. See Patricia Risso, *Oman and Muscat,* 13–14.
103. Ibid., 82–83.
104. "Letter of Francisco de Abreu Castelo Branco to the governors of *Estado da Índia,*" Kung, 08.05.1693, in AHU, *Índia,* cx. [37] 67, doc. 76.
105. That is why Giles Veinstein called it a half-success for the Ottomans; see Veinstein, "Commercial Relations between India and the Ottoman Empire," 97.
106. Francisco Rodrigues da Silveira, *Reformação da milícia e governo do Estado da Índia Oriental,* 41–42.
107. Pedro Teixeira, *The Book of Pedro Teixeira,* 175–77.
108. In 1581 (Couto, *Década,* 10ª, II-x, 215–19); in 1583 (Couto, *Década,* 10ª, VI-x, 68–71), and in 1586 (Couto, *Década,* 10ª, VII-xviii, 250–59).
109. Anthony Disney, "Smugglers and Smuggling in the Western Half of the *Estado da Índia* in the late Sixteenth Century and early Seventeenth Centuries," *Indica* 26 (1989): 57–75.
110. Artur Teodoro de Matos, *O Estado da Índia nos anos de 1581–1588. Estrutura administrativa e económica. Alguns elementos para o seu estudo* (Ponta Delgada, Portugal: Universidade dos Açores, 1982), table 1.
111. Aubin, "Le royaume d'Ormuz," 120.
112. Aubin, "Ormuz au jour le jour," 27–30.
113. António Bocarro, *Década 13ª da História da Índia,* ed. Rodrigo José de Lima Felner (Lisbon, Portugal: Academia Real das Ciências, 1876), chap. 157, 641–48; "Letter of viceroy D. Jerónimo de Azevedo to King Filipe II," Goa, 29.12.1616, in *Boletim da Filmoteca Ultramarina Portuguesa* (henceforth *BFUP*), no. 4 (Lisbon, Portugal: Centro de Estudos Históricos Ultramarinos, 1955), 851.
114. Bocarro, *Década 13ª*, chap. 79, 347.
115. *Comentários do grande capitão Rui Freire de Andrade,* Book II, chaps. 44–45, 240–49.
116. *Livro que trata das cousas da Índia e do Japão,* 128–29.
117. Teles e Cunha, "Economia de um Império," 38–41.
118. Willem Floor, "The Dutch East India Company's Trade with Sind in the 17th and 18th Centuries," *Moyen Orient & Océan Indien* 3 (1986): 113.
119. Brás, *Comentários,* vol. 1, book I, chap. 27, 134; Correia, *Lendas,* tome I, 875.
120. "The Travels of Athanasius Nikitin," in *India in the Fifteenth Century: Being a Collection of Narratives of Voyages to India,* ed. R. H. Major (London: Hakluyt Society, 1857; repr. New Delhi, India: Deep Publications, 1974), 19.
121. Jean Aubin, "Marchands de la Mer Rouge et du Golfe Persique au tournant des 15e et 16e siècles," in *Marchands et hommes d'affaires de l'Océan Indien et de la Mer de Chine, XIIIe-XIXe s.,* ed. D. Lombard and J. Aubin (Paris, 1988), 85–86. The Gujarati trading communities were diversified, and included Muslims, Hindus, and Banyans: see Tomé Pires, *Suma Oriental,* 41 and Irfan Habib, "Merchant Communities in Pre-Colonial India," in *The Rise of Merchant Empires: Long Distance Trade in the Early Modern World, 1350–1750,* ed. James D. Tracy (Cambridge: Cambridge University Press, 1990), 380.
122. Tomé Pires, *Suma Oriental,* 41. The Lisbon manuscript of Tomé Pires' work declares them to be even superior to the Italians.
123. Botelho, "Tombo do Estado da Índia," in *Subsídios para a História da Índia Portuguesa,* 82.
124. *Livro que trata das cousas da Índia e do Japão,* 128–30.
125. "Revenue of the kingdom of Hormuz," undated [1515], in António Dias Farinha, "Os portugueses no golfo Pérsico," 38.
126. There is no trace of its origin, or of its use outside Hormuz; see Henry Yule and A.C. Burnell, *Hobson-Jobson: The Anglo-Indian Dictionary* (Ware, UK: Wordsworth Editions, 1996).
127. Castanheda, *História,* Book II, chap. 58, 338; *The Book of Duarte Barbosa,* vol. 1, 97; Jean Aubin, "Le royaume d'Ormuz," 149.
128. Barbosa, *The Book of Duarte Barbosa,* vol. 1, 96.
129. Castanheda, *História,* Book II, chap. 58, 338; Barbosa, *The Book of Duarte Barbosa,* 1, 94–97.

130. Aubin, "Le royaume d'Ormuz," 149.
131. Barbosa, *The Book of Duarte Barbosa*, vol. 1, 91.
132. Castanheda, *História*, Book II, chap. 58, 338.
133. "Donation of Muscat's Customs House," Hormuz, 22.05.1591, in Rivara, *APO*, fasc. 5III, 1247–51.
134. Aubin, "Le royaume d'Ormuz," 148.
135. Farinha, "Os portugueses no golfo Pérsico," 38–39.
136. "Letter of Afonso de Albuquerque to D. Manuel," Hormuz, 22.09.1515, in *CAA*, vol. 6, 377.
137. A warehouse, and also office of the harbormaster or port authority (this latter form is only acknowledged in English India after the seventeenth century).
138. António Nunes, "Livro dos pesos da Índia," in *Subsídios para a História da Índia Portuguesa*, 23.
139. Ibn Battuta, *The Travels of Ibn Battuta A.D. 1325–1354*, vol. 2, ed. H. A. R. Gibb (London: Hakluyt Society, 1959; repr. Banham, Norfolk: Archival Facsimiles , 1995), 430.
140. "Letter of Afonso de Albuquerque to D. Manuel," Hormuz, 22.09.1515, in *CAA*, vol. 6, 378.
141. Farinha, "Os portugueses no golfo Pérsico," 38.
142. Barros, *Ásia*, 2ª, X-vii, 480–83.
143. Godinho, *Les finances de l'État Portugais des Indes Orientales*, 44–50.
144. Aubin, "Le royaume d'Ormuz," 150–51.
145. "Letter of Fr. António de Herédia to Fr. Ignatius of Loyola," Hormuz, 20.10.1554, in *Documenta Indica* (henceforth *DI)*, vol. 3, ed. Joseph Wicki (Rome: Institutum Historicum Societatis Iesu, 1954), 101.
146. "Estado da Índia e aonde tem o seu princípio," in *DUP*, vol. 1, 213.
147. On this social category that included Portuguese born in Portugal and also their descendants born in Asia, see Subrahmanyam, *The Portuguese Empire in Asia*, 220–21.
148. "Letter of Fr. Gaspar Barzeus to his Jesuit brothers," Hormuz, 01.12.1549, in *DI*, vol. 1 (Rome: Institutum Historicum Societatis Iesu, 1948), 611–12.
149. Teles e Cunha, "Economia de um império," 125, 139.
150. "Letter of Fr. Gaspar Barzeus to his Jesuit brothers," Hormuz, 01.12.1549, in *DI*, vol. 1, 604.
151. Diogo do Couto, *Décadas*, 6ª, X-i, 408.
152. António Bocarro, *O livro das plantas de todas as fortalezas, cidades e povoações do Estado do Índia Oriental*, ed. Isabel Cid (Lisbon, Portugal: Imprensa Nacional-Casa da Moeda, 1992), vol. 2, 66.
153. "Excerpt of letter written by Fr. Gaspar Barzeus," Hormuz, September 1549, in *DI*, vol. 1, 502–03.
154. Luís de Matos, *Imagens do Oriente no século XVI: Reprodução do códice português da Biblioteca Casanatense* (Lisbon, Portugal: Imprensa Nacional-Casa da Moeda, 1985), print XVIII.
155. Teles e Cunha, "Economia de um Império," 137–47.
156. Calado, *Livro que trata das cousas da India e do Japão*, 128–29.
157. Vitorino Magalhães Godinho, *Os descobrimentos e a economia mundial*, vol. 3 (Lisbon, Portugal: Editorial Presença, 1987), 57–69; Luís Filipe F. R. Thomaz, *A questão da pimenta em meados do século XVI: Um debate político do governo de D. João de Castro* (Lisbon, Portugal: CEPCEP, 1998), 48–80.
158. "Letter of Afonso de Albuquerque to King D. Manuel," Goa, 25.10.1514, in *CAA*, vol. 1, 346.
159. "Letter of Simão Botelho to King D. João III," Cochin, 30.01.1552, in *Subsídios para a História da Índia Portuguesa*, 30–31.
160. Disney, "Smugglers and Smuggling in the Western Half of the *Estado da India*," 57–75.
161. Botelho, "Tombo do Estado da Índia," in *Subsídios para a História da Índia Portuguesa*, 90–91.
162. See Manuel Lobato, *Política e comércio dos portugueses na Insulíndia: Malaca e as Molucas de 1575 a 1605* (Macao: Instituto Português do Oriente, 1999), 91–121.

163. "Report sent from Venice," Venice, 20.07.1566, in *Gavetas da Torre do Tombo,* ed. A. da Silva Rego (Lisbon, Portugal: Centro de Estudos Históricos Ultramarinos, 1964), vol. 4, 97.
164. Veinstein, "Commercial Relations between India and the Ottoman Empire," 101–02, 110.
165. "Letter of Fr. Gaspar Barzeus to his Jesuit brothers," Hormuz, 10.10.1549, in *DI*, vol. 1, 647; "Estado da Índia e aonde tem o seu princípio", in *DUP*, vol. 1, 213–15.
166. "Letter of Fr. Gaspar Barzeu to his Jesuit brothers," Hormuz, 01.12.1549, in *DI*, vol. 1, 250.
167. "Letter of Fr. António de Herédia to Fr. Ignatius of Loyola," Hormuz, 20.10.1554, in *DI*, vol. 3 *(1553–1557)* (Rome, 1954), 104.
168. "Letter of Fr. Gaspar Barzeus to his Jesuit brothers," Hormuz, 01.12.1549, in *DI*, vol. 1, 604–10.
169. See Aubin, "Le royaume d'Ormuz,"162–63.
170. "Letter of Fr. Gaspar Barzeus to his brothers of the Jesuit college in Coimbra," Hormuz, 24.11.1550, in *DI*, vol. 2 *(1550–1553)* (Rome: Institutum Historicum Societatis Iesu, 1950), 87–88.
171. "Letter of Fr. Gaspar Barzeus to his Jesuit brothers," Hormuz, 01.12.1549, in *DI*, vol. 1, 599.
172. "Letter of King Filipe I to viceroy D. Duarte de Meneses," Lisbon, 05.03.1587, in *APO*, fasc. 3, 99.
173. "Law of D. Sebastião," Lisbon, 14.08.1563; "Letter of King Filipe II to viceroy count of Vidigueira," Lisbon, 21.11.1598, in Luís de Matos, *Das relações entre Portugal e a Pérsia,* respectively 224, 241.
174. "Law of King Filipe I," Lisbon, 11.03, 1595, in *APO*, fasc. 3, 540–42.
175. Fr. Manuel Godinho, *Relação do novo caminho da Índia para Portugal,* 122–23.
176. Mendes da Luz, "Livro das cidades e fortalezas," fol. 33.
177. Luciano Ribeiro, ed., *Registo da Casa da Índia* (Lisbon, Portugal: Agência Geral do Ultramar, 1954–55), vol. 1, no. 2098, 492.
178. *Registo da Casa da Índia*, vol. 1, no. 2112, 496.
179. "Regiment of the fortress of Hormuz," Goa, 20.08.1568, in *Regimentos das fortalezas da Índia*, ed. Panduronga S. S. Pissurlencar (Bastorá, India: Governo Geral do Estado da Índia, 1951), 173.
180. Ibid.
181. Ibid., 181–84.
182. Vitorino Magalhães Godinho, "1580 e a Restauração," in *Ensaios*, vol. 2, *Sobre a História de Portugal* (Lisbon, Portugal: Livraria Sá da Costa, 1968), 268.
183. "Enformação das fortalezas e lugares da India," India, 1569, in Joseph Wicki, "Duas relações sobre a situação da Índia portuguesa nos anos de 1568 e 1569," *Studia* 8 (July 1961): 178–79.
184. "Letter of Afonso de Albuquerque's to King D. Manuel," Hormuz, 22.09.1515, in *CAA*, vol. 1, 378.
185. "Revenues of the kingdom of Hormuz," undated [1515], in António Dias Farinha, "Os portugueses no golfo Pérsico (1507–1538)," 38–39.
186. Botelho, "Tombo do Estado da Índia," 1552, in *Subsídios para a História da Índia Portuguesa*, 89.
187. Barros, *Da Ásia*, 2ª, II-ii, 108.
188. Fr. Manuel Godinho, *Relação do novo caminho da Índia para Portugal*, chap. 12, 105.
189. "Letter of Simão Botelho to King D. João III," Cochin, 30.01.1552, in *Subsídios para a História da Índia Portuguesa*, 26.
190. "Letter of Álvaro Pinheiro to King D. Manuel," Cochin, 12.01.1519, in *CAA*, vol. 7, 198–99.
191. Vitorino Magalhães Godinho, *Les finances de l'état portugais des Indes Orientales (1517–1635)*, 45–46.
192. "Contract made between governor D. Duarte de Meneses and King Muhammad Shah II," Hormuz, 15.06.1523, in *Subsídios para a História da Índia Portuguesa*, 79–84.

193. BNL, *FG,* codex 1783, ff. 5v10.
194. See "Consultation of the Ultramarine Council," Lisbon, 11.03.1676, in AHU, *Índia,* cx. [30] 54, doc. 88.
195. Luís Filipe F. R. Thomaz, *De Ceuta a Timor,* 211–13.
196. For an overview see Sanjay Subrahmanyam and Luís Filipe F. R. Thomaz, "Evolution of Empire: The Portuguese in the Indian Ocean During the Sixteenth Century," in *The Political Economy of Merchant Empires: State Power and World Trade 1350–1750,* ed. James B. Tracy (Cambridge: Cambridge University Press, 1991), 298–331.

Chapter 12

Dutch Relations with the Persian Gulf

Willem Floor

Although the Dutch did not arrive in the Persian Gulf until 1623, Dutch interest in that part of the world began much earlier. Prior to that date Dutchmen had come to the Gulf as part of Portuguese operations rather than to advance Dutch interests.[1] Until 1594 direct maritime voyages from Europe to Asia were a Portuguese-enforced monopoly. This monopoly was breached in the same year by Dutch and English commercial voyages. In 1602, the Vereenigde Oostindische Compagnie (VOC) or Dutch East Indies Company, was created to provide financial and political strength and cohesion to Dutch commercial efforts to compete with other Europeans for Asian commodities. Its primary objective was to gain control over the Spice Islands in Southeast Asia. It was only after the Dutch had firmly established themselves there that they began to develop their commercial network in other parts of Asia. The Dutch were well aware of the existence of the integrated Indian Ocean market and its close commercial ties with West and Southeast Asia. This realization meant that their next logical step was to advance into the Indian Ocean. Before the VOC could extend its commercial relations to the Persian Gulf, it first had to establish itself in South Asia, where it faced fierce competition from the Portuguese and the English. Iran and the Gulf, therefore, were not as yet on the horizon of Dutch policy makers.

Although Shah Abbas I's ambassador to the European courts had visited the Netherlands in 1608 to ask for technical and military assistance, the Dutch were not yet ready to start operations in Iran. The VOC directors had further received information in 1608 that the king of Hormuz had risen against the Portuguese. They wrote to their admirals in India that "if this be true, you will try to conclude an alliance with this king so that we may secure the trade of Persia. You will also try to get a substantial cargo of raw silk from Persia, if this is possible, as well as other many goods which may be profitable here."[2] From this report it is clear that the Dutch were interested in Iranian silk, because by that time Amsterdam had become a major center of the European silk industry. Although the VOC decided not to develop trade relations with Iran as yet, several wheeler-dealers, among them Sir Robert Sherley and Dutch competitors, tried to promote Dutch silk trade with Iran in the years thereafter. The VOC, however, did not make a decision based on a single commodity, but rather how this commodity fit into its inter-Asian trading network. All of the Chinese silk that it had bought at Pattani (Thailand) since 1609 was needed for the trade with Japan. The VOC was therefore very much interested in Iranian silk, which it needed for the European market.[3]

The Portuguese, however, were still dominant in the Indian Ocean area and the VOC therefore first had to build up its military and financial strength. Development of trade with Mukha, Ceylon, and Surat were as yet of greater importance than that with Iran. Slowly the Dutch spread their trading stations over South Asia, in strong rivalry with the English and the Portuguese, and from that safe base the VOC moved into the western Indian Ocean and turned its attention to the Persian Gulf. Hormuz was both commercially and strategically the obstacle that had to be overcome if access to Iranian silk was to be obtained. The Dutch and the English, despite their competition elsewhere, decided in 1620 to jointly develop the silk trade with Iran. Neither party felt strong enough, financially and militarily, to do this on its own. A joint fleet would defeat the Portuguese and the silk trade would be jointly financed, with the VOC having a majority share. To that end, an armada of nine ships under Admiral Jacob Dedel sailed from Batavia (now Jakarta in Indonesia) in September 1621 to cooperate with an English fleet against the Portuguese. Dedel also had instructions to explore and develop trade possibilities in Malabar, Surat, Iran, and Mukha. Because he did not have enough capital to buy Iranian silk, Dedel was instructed to buy samples. His fleet came too late to join forces with the English fleet, which, in a joint operation with Iranian land forces, had taken the fortress and town of Hormuz in May 1622. The fall of Hormuz meant the beginning of the end of Portuguese power in the Gulf. At the same time that Dedel left Batavia, the governor-general of the VOC had instructed merchant Huybert Visnich to travel overland from Coromandel, the southeastern coast of India, to Surat to open trade with Iran, and he arrived in Bandar Abbas on June 20, 1623.[4]

VOC Organization

Before continuing with developments in the Persian Gulf and Iran and the Dutch role therein, it is necessary to know how the VOC was managed and the nature of its organization in Iran. The VOC was a joint-stock company managed by a board of seventeen directors, who were known as the *Heeren Zeventien* (the seventeen gentlemen) or, in short, the XVII. This board delegated daily management of its operations in Asia to a governor-general and his council, who were based in Batavia. This body took decisions by majority vote. Operations in Asia were organized along the lines of so-called directorates. The Persian Directorate included not only Iran but also Basra, Bushehr, and Muscat. By 1753, the directorate only included Kharg Island and Bandar Abbas. The head[5] of the Persian Directorate was based in Bandar Abbas. Like the governor-general, he was assisted by a council, which consisted of the leading VOC commercial staff. The military, which was only based there in time of insecurity, had no voice in the management of the directorate. When needed, one or more officers would be invited to voice their opinion. The commanding military officers could only be members of the policy council (*raad van politie*) but never of the trade council (*negotie raad*). When the ships' captains were included in the deliberations the council was referred to as the broad council (*breede raad*). A council could override a director and did so on many occasions. The collegial form of management proved to be both flexible and effective in the absence of rapid means of communications with Batavia or the XVII. The same council system also existed at the trading stations that depended on Bandar Abbas, such as Isfahan and Basra.

The VOC had the following hierarchy for the commercial staff in its directorates: the highest-ranking official (director, *gezaghebber* or *resident*) usually held the rank of chief merchant (*opperkoopman*), the next in rank was a merchant (*koopman*), followed by a junior merchant (*onderkoopman*), a bookkeeper (*boekhouder*), and finally an assistant (*assistent*). The last might be a member of the council in a small factory. Other lower-ranking staff were not members of the council.[6]

The VOC maintained trading stations in Bandar Abbas (1623–1765) and Isfahan (1623–1745) as well as rest houses in Lar and Shiraz. (In Shiraz the VOC also had a winemaker, usually an Armenian, to ensure the necessary supply of wine for export.) It also had trading posts in Kirman (1659–1758) and Bushehr (1734–53). When the Bushehr office was closed, one was opened on Kharg Island that lasted until 1766. The VOC was only intermittently present in Basra between 1645 and 1753.

The total staff of the VOC in the Persian Directorate was limited. Usually, some twenty-five people would stay in Iran, of whom about twenty were in Bandar Abbas. In 1701, the Dutch received permission to build a new factory, or trading station, because the old one had become too small. The VOC factory was well armed with thick walls sufficient to withstand an attack by a foe having artillery, and it could repulse such an attack using its own cannon and mortars as well as muskets with which its military was armed. The new fortress-like Dutch factory built in 1701 was useful because of the growing insecurity after 1710 due to the weakening of Safavid authority, which led to regular incursions by Baluch marauders. In normal times, until 1721, there were no military forces at the factory, but the insecurity in the town and environs as a result of the Afghan occupation of Iran and the Baluch incursions into southern Iran had changed that. Each time Safavid officials fled and left the town's population and the Europeans to fend for themselves. The continued presence of soldiers in the factory after the defeat of the Afghans in 1729 was due to the insecurity created by the misrule under the last Safavid shah and his successor, Nadir Shah. The VOC could not henceforth rely on the authorities to provide protection, because they themselves were the cause of the insecurity. The VOC soldiers would stay in Bandar Abbas, and later in Kharg, until 1766. Although 150 soldiers came initially, there were usually only some forty to fifty due to high mortality and the reduced number of replacements sent to the factory. If need be, the factory would also take sailors from the ships lying in the roads to help protect it.[7]

LIFE IN BANDAR ABBAS

Bandar Abbas was an extremely hot, unhealthy location, and sickness and death were constant companions of those visiting and living there. There was hardly any vegetation, and most food supplies, which were abundantly available, as well as water came from the port's hinterland. The water, however, was infested with guinea worm, thus adding to the poor inhabitants' health problems. The mortality rate among the Europeans was very high. Although no statistics are available, impressionistic data suggest a death rate of at least 25 percent and often higher. When people fell ill, if they did not die quickly they were taken to the mountains in the city's hinterland. Europeans, Indians, and other rich locals had gardens a few kilometers away at Naband and Isin where they stayed during the hot season (April to September). There was vegetation, water, and acrobats and dancing girls to divert those who had fled the heat.

Bandar Abbas in the summer was almost a ghost town. The majority of the population had gone elsewhere and only the poor remained behind, as well as some of the European staff who had to look after the stored merchandise. The Dutch also retired to Lar and Taduvan, where they had a house and garden respectively. Also, there were sulfurous sources, as at Ghinaw, which were used for curative purposes by the VOC staff. According to Fryer, "There was but an Inch-Deal betwixt Gomberoon and Hell."[8]

The dead were buried in the cemetery on the east side of the town. The living engaged with some abandon in drinking bouts and (mostly Sindi) prostitutes, because marriage was forbidden to VOC staff, unless, and that very rarely, permission had been given.

Life in Bandar Abbas was not only unhealthy and uncomfortable but it was also, above all, mind-numbingly boring. For the leading company officers there were routine meetings with Safavid officials, which were formal, polite, and ruled by etiquette. The only diversion was Persian music and dancing girls after dinner had been finished. The drinking parties among Europeans were livelier, and inebriation was rarely avoided. Otherwise, life meant keeping up appearances with Safavid officials and the English. The VOC staff were dressed in costly clothes, despite orders that banned the custom, and the director had a large staff when going about town. For the lower ranks as well as the sailors on shore leave, wine, arak, and other spirits were available; there were coffee- and sherbet-houses that they frequented especially in the evening. Sailors who had been at sea for a few months rode straight to the prostitutes' quarter, which consisted of huts (*kapar*) made of palm tree branches. Otherwise, they diverted themselves with donkey rides (they would be thrown by the donkeys to the delight of the bystanders) as well as by visits to the Banyan tree at Isin, where they also could swim. Although the Muslims had their mosque, the Jews their synagogue, and the Banyans their temple, the Europeans had no church, only an occasional a minister, but they had a cemetery outside the walls, where tombs were the only reminder of their often fleeting presence in Bandar Abbas.

Relations with Safavid Officials

It is important to realize that the European trading companies usually had an adversarial relationship with the Asian rulers of the areas where they tried to establish commercial control. However, in Safavid Iran, the relationship was different, because the Europeans realized that they would be unable to successfully wage a land war against them. Shah Abbas I (r. 1588–1629) signed various treaties with European states such as England, Spain, Venice, the German Empire, Poland, France, and the Dutch Republic that accorded various rights to the citizens of the states concerned. In the case of England and the Netherlands, the latter country had even accorded certain rights of equal treatment to Safavid subjects.[9] However, whereas the Dutch considered these treaties as binding for both parties, the Safavids viewed them as incidental expressions of goodwill and friendship between the parties concerned. The letter of the treaty need not be literally adhered to; there was room for flexibility, all at a price, of course. Whereas in the Netherlands public law regulated life, in Iran it was the shah's will. This did not mean that the Dutch always respected their treaty with Iran to the letter; they did not and were very upset when that was pointed out to them.

The Safavid shahs had set out certain rules that allowed sufficient revenues to be raised to govern their realm and to satisfy their personal need for luxuries and other interests. If the revenues were not enough it was understood that those who had been allowed to benefit from running the state and the economy would do the right thing and offer "presents" to the shah (or to the magnates, all the way down the ladder of bureaucratic power) to correct the market's failure by giving the shah and his elite their due.[10] These "presents" should not be regarded as a form of corruption, but rather as a service fee and a further affirmation of the patron-client relationship that existed between the shah (and by extension his government officials) and the merchants. These same officials may have viewed the Dutch obsession with respect for the letter of the legal documents and their insistence on reliability as to timing of quantity and quality of supplies as exasperating at times. Neither the shah nor his representatives, such as the grand vizier, wanted to be bothered by VOC agents to discuss treaty terms when market conditions had changed. Mirza Taqi, the grand vizier (1634–45), became quite angry with the Dutch agent Willem Bastingh in 1642 when the latter asked that the price of royal silk be lowered by two *tumans*. The grand vizier told him: "Our friendship does not depend on the price of silk. This is a merchant's affair; it has not more value than straw."[11] Of course, if the Dutch were serious about it, then an adequate present needed to be bestowed and things could be sorted out.

This difference in sociopolitical outlook continued to characterize Dutch-Safavid relations until the very end in the mid-eighteenth century. Although the Iranian power elite dealt with merchants and even invested their capital in commercial operations, they were not interested in the details of the functioning of the market, only in its positive results. If these results were negative, they had enough political influence to turn a financial loss into a profit. Also, the power elite had no direct experience with the outside world. At best, they had heard about Europe and the European naval forces in the Persian Gulf, but they had no frame of reference to understand its true import. True, the Safavid court knew very well that the Dutch were the stronger power in the Persian Gulf, when compared with England, despite the latter's efforts to demonstrate otherwise. However, it had no real idea about the strategic political and military situation in the Indian Ocean, or in Europe. The fact that the many European embassies that visited the Safavid court, with one or two exceptions, are not even referred to in contemporary Persian chronicles, is indicative of that lack of interest and understanding. If European documents and travelogues did not exist, one would not even guess that important commercial relations had existed between Europe and Safavid Iran.

Relations with Safavid officials were mainly limited to official meetings; even when these were of a social nature the atmosphere remained formal. It also happened (in 1641 and 1668) that the Safavid governor of Bandar Abbas had his men beat the VOC director when the latter did not give in to certain points of discussion. The Dutch would protest and the grand vizier would send instructions ordering the governor to treat the VOC director with respect. But no apology was given. Although the Dutch twice used military force (in 1645 and 1685), blockading Safavid ports and attacking and occupying Qishm Island, they knew that they would be unable to wage a war with Safavid Iran to settle commercial differences. Elsewhere in Asia, where military might could make the difference, the Dutch had successfully waged such wars (e.g., Malabar and Ceylon), but in the case of Iran other means would be more effective to achieve commercial goals. It is of interest that these two attacks had no negative consequences for Dutch relations with the Safavid court; trade was even resumed after a few months. Invariably an embassy, sometimes a long-lasting one, and many costly presents smoothed the path to the continuation of relations as if nothing had happened.[12]

In addition to relations with government officials the Dutch had, of course, much contact with merchants (Muslim, Jewish, Armenian, Banyan) through their business activities as well as with the local people in their service, ranging from Banyan brokers to Muslim porters. Although they spent much of their time inside the factory they also made outings to the VOC garden, went on business trips to Lar, Shiraz, Kirman, and Isfahan, and in the early years also to Gilan. Through these varied and wide-ranging contacts, the Dutch had a good idea what was going on in the country, and if people did not come forward to inform them what was happening they themselves would send out informants. They did this during the troubled times in the 1720s, when, due to the general insecurity, information was essential to safeguard the factory.

Beginning of Dutch Relations with Iran

For the Dutch, apart from being a supplier of silk Iran formed a link in its Asian trading network. For Abbas I, the Dutch were a welcome additional buyer of raw silk and a source of cash. He had established an export monopoly on silk as of 1619 to maximize his returns on its sale and to get as much cash as possible, which he needed desperately. Like the English East India Company (EIC), the VOC therefore started its trading relationship with Iran based on a royal trading contract. On November 17, 1623, the shah agreed to a treaty that stipulated, inter alia, that the Dutch had complete freedom of trade in Iran as well as exemption from customs duties. Road-duties, or *rahdari,* were to be paid, but not at more than the usual rate. In exchange for these privileges, the Dutch would have to buy silk from the shah at 48 tumans per *carga* (200 kilograms), which was more than the going market price. This treaty had the advantage that the VOC was able to barter much of its imports (75% in goods and 25% in cash) against raw silk, the only major export commodity Safavid Iran had. The Dutch had to supply the shah with a specified quantity of a number of goods at fixed prices and 25 percent of the total amount was due in cash. The manner of payment was organized via a separate contract with the shah's factor, or commercial agent, Mulayim Beg. This arrangement worked fine as long as the shah had silk to barter and its price was right, and as long as the goods that the Dutch provided were also fairly priced and not abundant in the market.[13] This, of course, did not happen and difficulties arose regularly between Visnich and Mulayim Beg about the interpretation of their mutual rights and obligations. Because of these different interpretations of what rights the shah had granted, armed conflicts arose three times between the two parties during the Safavid era (1645, 1685, and 1712).

After 1622, due to the fall of Hormuz and the presence of the Dutch and English, Bandar Abbas became the most important port in the Persian Gulf and it remained so until about 1750. However, in 1623 Bandar Abbas was still a minor fishing village, while the Dutch and English still were not yet securely established in the Gulf. In February 1625 perhaps the largest naval battle ever fought in the Gulf took place near the island of Larak between the Dutch and the English against the Portuguese, which ended in a draw. Because the Portuguese failed to win, it meant that they had lost control of the Gulf. Although they would still hold out until 1650 on the Arab side of the Gulf, Portuguese power had been broken. As a consolation, the Portuguese acquired a toehold at Bandar-i Kung, a small port about a hundred miles west of Bandar Abbas, which gave them a nice, although intermittently paid, income until 1719. Despite continued Dutch enmity toward the Portuguese, the Dutch declined the requests made by Imam-Quli Khan, the governor-general of Fars, to assist the shah with naval forces to attack the Portuguese forces at Muscat. The Dutch feared that military assistance to Iran, the archenemy of the Ottomans, might upset the latter, and thus possibly negatively impact Dutch trade in the Levant. Although the Dutch actively pursued the Portuguese in the Indian Ocean, they did not do so in the Persian Gulf. Whenever they ran into Portuguese shipping in the Gulf, however, they seized and confiscated the vessels. The question became a moot one when, after 1653, the Portuguese were mostly absent from the Gulf apart from intermittent annual visits to Kung. Moreover, a lasting peace was concluded between Portugal and the Netherlands in 1661.

Although Dutch trade had a firm contractual footing in Iran, there were problems with the interpretation of the terms of the commercial treaty from the very beginning. The Dutch usually were not able to pay the shah 25 percent in cash and therefore oversupplied his factor with goods. The latter, who of course complained, had not been able to supply the Dutch with the required quantities of silk and also did not deliver them on time. The initial complaints were resolved by appealing directly to the shah, so despite

Table 12.1 List of Goods to Be Supplied to the Royal Factory by the VOC

Weight	Commodity	Unit cost	Total cost
6,000 *man* (12 lbs.)	Pepper	@ 2 ory*	12,000 tumans
500 *man*	Cloves	2 ory	600
1,200 *soms* (312 lbs.)	Sugar	3.5 ory	4,200
500 bundles	Sarkhei indigo	21 ory	1,050
1,400 to 1,500 *man*	Nutmeg	5 ory	730
500 *man*	Mace	6 ory	325
55,000 *man*	Tin	3.5 ory	1,925
400 *man*	Sandalwood	6 ory	200
500 *man*	Cochineal	11 ory	5,500
3,000 pieces	Indian steel	2 ory	300
12,000 ells	Cloth (ordinary)	2 ory	2,400
2,000 pieces	Kersey	1 ory	200
—	Camphor and Benzoin	At market price	570
Total			30,000 tumans

Source: Willem Floor and Mohammad H. Faghfoory, *The First Dutch-Iranian Commercial Conflict* (Costa Mesa, CA: Mazda, 2004), 32–33.
Note: **Ory* is short for *ducato d'oro* or [the Venetian] gold ducat, which was widely used in trade in the Middle East. The book value of the tuman was Dfl. 40.

all this Dutch trade flourished. In 1626 problems occurred once again, which required a renegotiation of the terms of the royal contract, namely the Dutch payment terms. In 1627, Visnich and Mulayim Beg agreed to a new three-year contract, which listed the goods that Mulayim Beg would accept and specified their prices and quantities, all on the condition that one third of the payment was to be made in cash. The VOC would provide the commodities listed in table 12.1.

In payment for these goods, the VOC would receive Iranian silk; half would be *ardasse* and half would be *legie* silk.[14] Despite these continuing problems with the implementation of the silk contract, in the 1620s the Dutch were quite pleased with their trading results. Silk profits were promising, and later the profits from pepper sales were also excellent.[15]

Under Shah Abbas I's successor, his grandson Shah Safi I (r. 1629–42), serious difficulties arose for the first time about the interpretation of the treaty, which Shah Safi had confirmed upon his accession. Although the new shah had reduced the number of privileges that the Dutch had enjoyed under his predecessor, they nevertheless retained the most important rights, namely freedom of trade with no restrictions on its volume, total exemption from customs, permission to export specie, and the right to transport their goods without examination by royal officials, although road duties had to be paid at the usual rate. In exchange the VOC had to buy silk from the shah at a rate above the market price, that is 50 tumans per carga. In 1632 Shah Safi also granted the Dutch exemption from payment of road duties and similar imposts.

The causes that led to the commercial conflict between the Dutch and the royal court were created by the abolishment of the silk export monopoly, the fall in silk production in the early 1630s, and the nature of the Safavid state. In 1629, Shah Safi I abolished the silk export monopoly and the supply of silk to the royal storehouses was limited to the shah's revenues from the silk-producing provinces, which were paid in kind rather than in cash. However, when silk production in these provinces was severely reduced—first, by a revolt; second, by a lack of labor due to this revolt and a subsequent plague; and third, by the normal agricultural cycle of ups and downs in silk output—the shah was unable to honor his contracts. He did not have enough silk to supply either the Dutch or the English. Because of the general shortage, it was much more profitable for the shah to sell his silk to Armenian merchants in Iran who exported it to the Levant. In addition, these merchants paid in ready cash rather than in kind. The shah eventually paid the VOC and EIC with silk, but late and in insufficient quantities. The factors of the two companies had to feed the monster called the market, which demanded more silk. The Dutch factors therefore approached the Armenian merchants to buy silk from them to satisfy their company's needs. This was a normal business practice and was formally permitted by the shah. Although the contract between the shah and the Dutch Company stated that the latter was free from the payment of customs duties, this only held for silk bought from the shah. The Dutch had become so accustomed to not paying customs duties that they treated this issue rather offhandedly. Although the VOC director, Nicolaas Overschie, told Mirza Taqi, the grand vizier, that he did not mind paying customs duties, he was very upset when his bluff was called later. When Overschie refused to pay customs duties, Mirza Taqi took 4,600 tumans from him by force. The Dutch felt taken advantage of. Granted, the Iranians were right and the VOC owed customs duties, but what about the loss of interest on capital when the Dutch company had supplied its part of the contract with the shah, who had then been unable to do his part? Although an understandable argument, it was not a valid one, and the Dutch, or their staff in Iran, knew it.

At the headquarters of the VOC in Batavia the enforced payment was considered an outrage and the new director, Adam Westerwolt (and when he died in 1639, his successor), was ordered to protest against this transgression of the commercial treaty and demand repayment of the money, which had been "extorted." Mirza Taqi, however, told the Dutch that they only enjoyed freedom of trade and from taxes on condition that they bought silk from the shah. He even went so far as to force the Dutch to buy as much silk as he stipulated and at prices fixed by him. This position was unacceptable to the Dutch. Silk was becoming less important as an export commodity and the VOC wanted to buy as little as possible. In addition, it wanted to get rid of its burden of debt in Iran, which was the result of the silk buying policy of previous years. Now that Mirza Taqi forced them to buy large quantities of silk at high prices, the Dutch had to continue to borrow money at 20 percent interest per annum, which meant that they were losing money. When Mirza Taqi refused to give in to Dutch protests, Batavia finally decided in 1644 to go to war against Iran.

Dutch-Persian War

In May 1645, a fleet of six Dutch ships arrived at Bandar Abbas. These blockaded Iranian ports, seized some Iranian vessels, and on June 10 landed troops on Qishm Island and bombarded the fortress, which they were unable to take. These events caused consternation in Isfahan. The shah offered favorable terms to the VOC, but before these could be granted the Dutch commander of the fleet and plenipotentiary died in Isfahan. Although the Dutch thereafter raised the blockade and withdrew their fleet, the conflict was not resolved. The Dutch were allowed, however, to continue to trade customs-free pending negotiations and without having to buy silk. Abbas II (r. 1642–66), who had succeeded his father, decided to try for better terms by holding up the negotiations. As a result a Dutch mission in 1647 could not get an agreement to their proposal, and therefore in 1649 once again a Dutch fleet arrived at Bandar Abbas. The Iranians had been forewarned by the English and had reinforced the town's defenses. This time no hostilities ensued, and it was agreed to find a peaceful solution. The differences between the VOC and Iran were finally settled in 1652 when ambassador Joan Cunaeus obtained new *farmans* (decrees) from Shah Abbas II. The new privileges stipulated that the Dutch would enjoy freedom of trade in Iran and exemption from customs, while their goods could be transported without inspection by the Iranian authorities. Moreover, in future the Dutch would not have to pay road duties. However, the shah had placed an upper limit on the customs-free import and export, viz. a value of 20,000 tumans per year, and the Dutch were forbidden to export specie. Finally, the Dutch had to buy 300 cargas of silk each year from the shah at a price of 48 tumans per carga in exchange for these privileges.[16] This agreement, with minor changes in subsequent agreements, formed the basis for Dutch trade with Iran until 1696.

It is of interest to note that neither party learned much from the 1645 conflict. The underlying reasons for the conflict were not and could not be resolved by the Cuneaus embassy. In fact, on August 26, 1652, two days after the Dutch embassy had left Iran, Dirck Sarcerius, the VOC director in Iran, was informed by the deputy governor of Bandar Abbas that the Dutch company had to pay 335 tumans and 36 mahmudis in customs duties on the amount of goods imported that year above the 20,000 tumans customs-free limit. Sarcerius refused to pay, referring him to the recently obtained royal decree, which stipulated that the VOC was entitled to import and export goods to the value of 20,000 tumans above the (estimated) amount of 15,000 tumans for the silk trade. The deputy-governor countered that Sarcerius's interpretation of the royal decree was erroneous. He deferred the claim until he had received further instructions from Isfahan and would recommend that the VOC interpretation would be accepted. The issue was finally settled, of course, with a present.[17]

Although neither the VOC directors nor the governor-general were pleased with the outcome of the Cuneaus embassy, the Dutch nevertheless would rule supreme in the Gulf for the rest of the seventeenth century. The VOC may not have been able to obtain all that it wanted from the shah, but its standing in Iran and the Gulf increased significantly. This was because the Dutch had been able to thoroughly defeat the English, their major competitor. After their "defeat" of the Portuguese in 1625, the two former allies, England and the Netherlands, had stopped joint voyages into the Gulf by 1630. Thereafter they started a fierce competition with one another, which reflected the political and commercial rivalry in Europe. When this rivalry led to war between the two nations in Europe (the first Anglo-Dutch War, 1650–52), hostilities also spread to the Gulf and the rest of Asia. In 1652 a major naval battle took place near Bandar Abbas in which the Dutch were victorious. "The repulse of the Portuguese at the beginning was succeeded by collapse against the Dutch at the end. The liberators of Ormus became the scorned at Gombroon."[18] It meant the collapse of the English trade in the Gulf, although it would make its comeback at the end of the seventeenth century.

The conflict with Iran also led to the beginning of Dutch trade relations with Basra, because the Dutch wanted to have a fall-back position in case trade with Iran became impossible. Two ships were sent there in May 1645 and an agreement was concluded with the autonomous governor, Husain b. Ali Padshah, in August 1645. Although direct trade with Basra would continue until 1753, the Dutch only had an intermittent presence there due to various political and commercial problems. After the first voyage, for example, the Dutch only returned in 1651 and remained until 1654 when they temporarily abandoned the Basra trade to resume it later in 1662.[19]

Despite the initial misgivings of the governor-general, the 1652 treaty proved to be an effective basis for Dutch trade until the end of Shah Abbas II's reign. This did not mean that there were no problems. During the period of 1650–61 the function of *shahbandar* of Bandar Abbas was usually held by a familial member of the powerful grand vizier, Muhammad Beg (1655–61). They used their position and family relation to extract additional monies from merchants calling at Bandar Abbas, whose welcome also left much to be desired. As a result, Asian merchants started to avoid Bandar Abbas and increasingly preferred to call on other Gulf ports, in particular Muscat, Bandar-i Kung, and Bandar-i Rig, where the reception was friendlier and customs rates lower. The diversion of trade to other Gulf ports shows that they functioned as alternatives. If customs duties were too high at one port, another offering lower tariffs would attract more trade. The fact that the VOC traded at Bandar Abbas, offering an array of best-selling goods, plus the fact that the roads connecting Bandar Abbas with Isfahan were better than in the case of these other ports, ensured that it maintained a certain baseline of trade.

This resulted in lower revenues for the shah, who in 1664 sent one of his courtiers to assess the situation. The latter asked the Dutch for naval assistance to attack Muscat, which had drawn most of the Malabar trade away from Bandar Abbas. Because the Dutch had been invited to trade in Muscat they decided to reconnoiter the Omani coast and evaluate the pros and cons of moving VOC operations to Muscat and of helping the projected Iranian invasion. The upshot of the voyage was that the Dutch decided neither to help the shah nor to move to Muscat. The shah meanwhile had abandoned the Muscat invasion plan, while the Imam of Muscat had raised his customs duties to placate Iranian feelings, and in general kept a lower profile. This accommodating approach was induced by the fact that the Imam also had trouble with many tribal leaders, who were on the point of revolting. The Safavid government finally decided to close the option of obtaining lower customs rates by calling on ports other than Bandar Abbas. As of 1668, it farmed out the customs administration for all its Gulf ports to one operator.

Under Abbas II's son and successor, Shah Sulaiman (r. 1666–94), new problems arose, however. Under Shah Abbas II, the stipulated 300 cargas of silk had hardly ever been delivered by the court, a situation that was greatly appreciated by the Dutch. Silk from Iran had lost its allure and the VOC, which lost money on it, preferred to obtain as little as possible. It had gained access to an alternative source in Bengal as of 1650. Moreover, the VOC was much more interested in exporting precious metals (gold, silver) from Iran than silk. However, in 1670, the new Iranian government under the dynamic grand vizier, Shaikh Ali Khan (1669–89), insisted that the VOC buy the obligatory 300 cargas of silk per year. This change of policy was caused among other things by the deterioration of the Iranian economy and the court's need for money.

Trade problems once again became acute in the 1670s; it was in fact a kind of repetition of those of the 1630s–40s about silk deliveries and interference with Dutch trade. To explore whether the VOC might abandon its operations in Iran a trading station was established in Muscat in August 1673. However, it was not possible to reach a commercial agreement with the Imam, Sultan b. Saif (r. 1640–80), who was mainly interested in obtaining Dutch naval protection against the Portuguese, and, failing that, the delivery of military supplies, neither of which the Dutch were willing to provide. The station was therefore abandoned in January 1676. In addition, trade prospects were disappointing and the war in Europe with the English had ended (the Dutch had used Muscat as a lookout post to alert their Bandar Abbas office, in case hostile English or French ships were approaching).[20]

The Second Dutch-Iranian Commercial Conflict

In 1678 a conflict arose between the governor of Bandar Abbas and the VOC director over the former's demand for more gifts and thirty-four years of rent arrears for the Dutch factory. The Dutch armed themselves and made ready to withdraw from Iran, but their protest to the shah resulted in orders to the governor not to interfere with Dutch trade or traders and a declaration that the factory was Dutch property. The sale of the contracted amounts of silk to the Dutch continued, although the VOC representatives' request for a reduction in deliveries was refused. In 1679 the Iranian government claimed payment of *rahdari* or road duties from the Dutch, claiming that they had not been exempted from paying this impost. When the Dutch refused to pay, the Iranian authorities took payment by force in 1680. Batavia wanted to take military action, but was occupied elsewhere at the time. It therefore ordered its director to ask for annual silk deliveries of only 150 cargas. When this request was presented to the grand vizier Shaikh Ali Khan in 1680, he became angry and said: "You are dealing with a King, not with a merchant, and that if we did not like it we had better leave." At the same time, he ordered 300 cargas of silk to be delivered to the Dutch factory. The Dutch agent in Isfahan refused to accept it, which led to an exchange of angry words as a result of which the Dutch representative was beaten and forced to receive the silk. He thereupon lodged a complaint with the grand vizier and repeated his request for a reduction in silk deliveries. The grand vizier replied that "he could not understand what kind of rascally people we were, for he had informed us of his wishes in writing. Further, if we were not interested in sticking to the contract in this manner then we could go to hell and were free to leave the country."

The VOC director in Iran advised Batavia to take military action, to which Batavia agreed. It sent a fleet (five men-of-war and a hooker) to blockade the Persian Gulf and seize Iranian vessels or goods or both, while a landing force attacked and seized the island of Qishm and its fortress, which the Dutch held for one year. The shah then invited the Dutch to open negotiations in Isfahan, but the two VOC representatives were confronted with a very hostile government, which refused to negotiate unless the Dutch withdrew from Qishm and ended the blockade of the Gulf. When the Dutch did so, the grand vizier showed even less inclination to negotiate terms. He also did not allow the two negotiators to return to Bandar Abbas, nor the entire Dutch staff who had embarked on the ships. The choice that the grand vizier put to the Dutch was simple: either buy the contractual amount of silk or pay customs duties. He finally allowed the Dutch to return to Bandar Abbas after they had promised that an ambassador would be sent to settle their differences. Trade was resumed again in 1687 under the supervision of two royal inspectors who recorded all VOC imports and exports. Batavia therefore decided to send an ambassador, who arrived in Iran in 1690.[21]

The ambassador, Johan van Leene, managed to get new privileges after lengthy talks and the payment of costly presents. Shah Sulaiman confirmed Dutch rights to freedom of trade in Iran and exemption from payment of customs duties up to a maximum annual import and export value of 20,000 tumans. Moreover, exemption from payment of road duties was granted as well. Finally, Iranian officials were forbidden to open Dutch packages, chests, and bales. In exchange for these privileges the VOC had to buy each year 300 cargas of silk from the shah at 44 tumans per carga. However, these farmans had not yet been sealed by the shah when the ambassador left, and the promise to send them after him was not honored. In 1694 the Dutch sent a special mission from Bandar Abbas to obtain these farmans, but then Shah Sulaiman died.[22]

His eldest son and successor, Shah Sultan Husain (r. 1694–1722), not only confirmed the privileges granted by his father, but also settled a dispute with regard to the wool trade with Kirman to the advantage of the VOC. The improved relations also led to a request to assist the shah with an attack on Muscat, whose growing power hurt Iranian interests. Surprisingly, the VOC agreed to this request, with a view to bolster relations. The fleet arrived in the Gulf in 1697, but by that time Shah Sultan Husain had lost interest in the matter and the fleet returned without having done anything.

When the shah was unable to deliver any silk in 1696, the Iranian government proposed that the obligatory delivery of silk be abolished, and instead the VOC would pay an annual quantity of selected goods to the shah. The VOC declined to accept this change of the treaty, but Batavia nevertheless considered it opportune to send another ambassador, Jacobus Hoogcamer, to Iran in 1701. In a short time, Hoogcamer (who was VOC director in Iran) was able to conclude an agreement with the shah by which the shah would sell the VOC an annual amount of 100 cargas of ***kadkhudapasand*** silk at a price of 44 tumans per carga. In exchange the VOC was entitled to carry on its trade anywhere in Iran and to import and export a volume of goods, which were exempt from the payment of customs and other imposts, to the amount of 20,000 tumans per year. In addition, the VOC had to deliver to the shah an annual amount of so-called *recognitie goederen* or treaty goods of the following composition:

10,000 *man-i Tabriz* or 60,000 (Holland) lbs. granulated sugar
1,120 *man-i Tabriz* or 6,720 lbs. loaf sugar
119 *man-i Tabriz* or 864 lbs. cardamom
119 *man-i Tabriz* or 864 lbs. cloves
289 *man-i Tabriz* or 1,704 lbs. cinnamon
289 *man-i Tabriz* or 1,704 lbs. pepper
1,000 *mithqals* or 111 lbs. nutmeg
130 *mithqals* or 1.3 lbs. mace
650 *mithqals* or 6.5 1bs. of aguilwood
4 *man-i Tabriz* or 24 lbs. benzoin
24 *man-i Tabriz* or 144 lbs. white sandalwood
2,000 *mithqals* or 20 lbs. radix china
8 *man-i Tabriz* or 48 lbs. candied nutmeg
4 *man-i Tabriz* or 24 lbs. candied cloves

The VOC was not obliged to deliver these goods if the shah did not supply the company with the contracted annual amount of silk. However, if the VOC did not want to purchase any silk, it was still obliged to deliver the recognitie goederen. The first difficulty occurred as early as 1703, when the shahbandar (customs master) of Bandar Abbas, Mirza Sadiq, accused the VOC of having carried on trade worth Dfl. 1,053,653 more than the amount of 20,000 tumans during the last five years. He therefore demanded the payment of customs over this amount at a rate of ten per cent or Dfl. 135,753. The farmer of the ducat trade in Isfahan also complained that the VOC bought too many golden ducats. Although neither of these accusations led to any action by the Iranian government, they cast a shadow over Iranian-Dutch relations, for not only did they contribute to the buildup of friction, but these same problems would be pivotal to the conflict between the two parties ten years later and would result in the revocation of the 1701 treaty.

In 1705, new difficulties arose when the shah gave the right to buy all goods that the VOC imported into Iran for him to two brothers. All other merchants now had to buy their goods from the shah through the two royal factors and were excluded from this trade. The governor-general ordered the director in Iran to protest strongly against this new scheme. If need be, the director should make his protest more palatable by giving presents. However, if the Iranian government would not yield, the director was authorized to deal with the royal factors. This system of dealing with a royal factor to whom all imports were sold was not a new phenomenon for the VOC. Under Shah Abbas I, a similar system had existed and the VOC had in those days greatly profited from its dealings with him. In fact, the system that came into being later was a variation on it, for the VOC sold all its goods to a few principal merchants who in turn sold the goods to a great number of smaller merchants. However, a present of 300 tumans to the grand vizier led to the restoration of the customary situation. Nevertheless, in 1707 the royal factor, Mir Murtaza, tried to enforce his rights by demanding that the VOC deliver goods to the value of 4,000 *tumans* to him in exchange for which he would allow all merchants to trade freely without having to buy only from him. The VOC director, Frans Castelijn, complained in Isfahan, but owing to the demise of the grand vizier the whole issue was dropped by Mir Murtaza. The new grand vizier, Shah-Quli Khan, who was appointed in June 1707, would play an important role in the conflict of 1712. In June 1710 the farmer of the ducat trade again complained about excessive exports of golden ducats by the VOC. In response, the shah issued a decree permitting him to control and examine the VOC caravans. However, after a protest from the VOC the decree was revoked. As we have seen, the governor-general was right to be satisfied with the rather undisturbed nature of trade in Iran; after 1712 this picture would be totally changed.[23]

The Third Dutch-Iranian Commercial Conflict

The cause of the last major commercial conflict between Iran and the VOC was a quarrel between Willem Backer Jacobsz, the VOC director at Bandar Abbas, and his deputy and chief of the Isfahan office, Pieter Macaré Jr. This quarrel had to do with both gentlemen's private interests in the export of specie. Moreover, the personal ambitions of Macaré as well as the fact that he probably was not responsible for his actions (being slightly deranged) played a big role in it. In 1710 Macaré had written to the XVII, the directors of the VOC, that Backer Jacobsz had organized a plot against his life. Macaré tried to arrange for Backer Jacobsz to be dismissed and have himself appointed as director in Iran. In his turn, Backer Jacobsz complained about Macaré, but Batavia was not convinced by his accusations and replied that he had to supply proof. In 1711 Backer Jacobsz asked to be allowed to resign; Batavia decided to appoint Macaré in his place and hoped that this would put an end to the troubles. However, by that time Macaré had accused his interpreter of wanting to poison him, and therefore van Biesum, his deputy, took over management of the Isfahan office declaring Macaré mad and incompetent. The latter tried to regain his position by appealing to the grand vizier. To make him more interested in the matter, Macaré informed the grand vizier about the illegal export of specie by the VOC, without having paid the required export duty. The grand vizier demanded to examine the VOC accounts, which van Biesum refused. What followed was an endless tug of war between the two sides, the grand vizier threatening to demand a large amount of money from the VOC, and the VOC threatening to leave Iran. The grand vizier had also been able to obtain a large loan from Macaré, who still held the VOC's money, with the promise of royal protection against the VOC.

To find a solution to the problem the grand vizier sent an envoy (Muhammad Ja'far Beg) to Batavia in 1714. He also took Macaré with him, who, despite the promise of Iranian protection, was handed over to Dutch authorities to stand trial. The envoy returned in 1715 without having achieved anything but a promise of the arrival of an ambassador to discuss the matter. Meanwhile, the new grand vizier was able to get money from the VOC office in Isfahan through threats of immediate action, because he did not want to wait for the ambassador to arrive.

Johan Josua Ketelaar, the VOC ambassador, arrived in Isfahan on May 31, 1717. After several rounds of talks on July 31, the grand vizier offered to grant the VOC the same privileges that Hoogcamer had obtained in 1701 with the exception of the following:

- Free export of ducats would not be allowed, because this had not been granted in the farmans which Hoogkamer had obtained.
- All the VOC caravans would have to be examined and their bales sealed before departure, as in former times.

- The VOC would have to waive the shah's debt to the VOC.
- The recognitie goederen or treaty goods would have to be twice the amount henceforth.

The grand vizier also informed Ketelaar that the shah's claim on the VOC amounted to 68,392 tumans at that time, which would be waived if Ketelaar agreed to his offer. Under pressure Ketelaar accepted, but he received the new decrees only after having paid 1,000 tumans to the grand vizier. A few days later, the grand vizier invited Ketelaar for talks about the Omani threat in the Gulf—the Omanis had once again attacked and seized Bahrain. The shah asked for Dutch military support to retake the island. Ketelaar replied that he had no authority to assist, but that he would inform the governor-general of the request. The grand vizier offered to send an envoy to Batavia and offered advantageous privileges, but Ketelaar told him that it was of no use to do so, because his instructions stated clearly that the VOC was not interested in military ventures. Ketelaar only promised to give passage to an Iranian envoy to Goa to ask the Portuguese for military support. On his return to Bandar Abbas, Ketelaar found that the Omanis also had taken the islands of Qishm and Larak and were besieging the fortress of Hormuz. The governor of Bandar Abbas asked the Dutch for military support, which was refused. He then surrounded the Dutch factory to enforce their compliance. During the blockade Ketelaar, who had been ill since his arrival in Iran, died. The siege was then raised.

In view of the circumstances, Ketelaar's mission had been rather successful. Of the four main points that the VOC wanted, he had been able to get agreement to two favoring the Dutch view, that is, freedom of trade in Iran and exemption from customs and taxes for VOC imports and exports, while the third point, the examination of VOC goods, was settled in an acceptable manner. With regard to the export of ducats, he acted in accordance with his instructions. He could not get an explicit right to exemption from taxes, but obtained a farman containing the same phrasing as the one that Hoogkamer had obtained. He had, moreover, obtained the waiving of the shah's claim on the VOC, while he had refused to do the same for the VOC's claim on the shah. In fact, he had been given a commitment for its payment, although the Iranian Government expected it to be waived in exchange for a de facto right to the tax-free export of ducats.

Although the Ketelaar mission apparently had solved the outstanding issues between the two trading partners, the governor-general insisted that the director, Jan Oets, try to get better terms. This attempt to renegotiate some of the agreed points only led to trouble for the VOC in 1720, for the royal court then raised issues about the interpretation of some of the privileges that had already been granted. Discussions dragged on, which led to no resolution and were ended by the fall of the Safavid dynasty in 1722.[24]

The Afghan Occupation of Iran

A lot of things were rotten in the kingdom of Iran and by the second decade of the eighteenth century much of the country was either in rebellion or insecure due to marauding by the Baluch and other tribal groups. The biggest threat came from the Ghilzai Afghans of Kandahar, who had thrown off Safavid rule in 1704. In 1719 they had devastated much of eastern Iran, and in 1721 they returned to march on Isfahan. After a five-month siege the city was taken and rulership was handed to Mahmud Khan, the Ghilzai chief. The Dutch staff in Isfahan were kept under house arrest until the Afghans fled in December 1729.

A large group of Baluchis attacked Bandar Abbas in 1721. (They had been infesting the littoral and its hinterland for a number of years.) The size and ferocity of this attack combined with the general lack of security in Iran made the VOC decide to send a military force to Bandar Abbas to protect its factory. Afghan forces only reached the coast in 1725 and did not stay long. As a result of the operations by two Safavid pretenders in the Bandar Abbas area, an Afghan force finally arrived in 1727 to take control over the port and its hinterland. The presence of Afghan troops led to strained relations with the Dutch. The latter were now considering moving their base of operations to Hormuz, whose garrison had invited them to do so. These contacts could not remain a secret to the Afghans, who arrested the director and a senior merchant during an official event at which the Dutch senior staff were present. The Dutch tried to negotiate their release and when this failed, they counter-attacked. Unfortunately, while being liberated, the director was shot and the Dutch withdrew to their factory. After a few days of exchange of fire, both sides agreed to maintain peaceful relations and not to pursue the matter. The whole issue became irrelevant when the Afghans were defeated by Safavid forces. When on January 9, 1730 the Afghans left Bandar Abbas, they gave the keys to the citadel to the Dutch.

Needless to say there was no trade to speak of with Iran during this period. The only Dutch trade during that time took place in Basra, where the VOC had reluctantly returned in 1724 at the invitation of the pasha after an absence of seventeen years. The VOC had not bothered to reply to several invitations from Basra in previous years. However, by 1723, it had become clear that the economic situation in Iran would not improve soon. Trade was nonexistent and the VOC had to make money, at least enough to cover the cost of its expensive establishment in the Gulf.[25]

Afsharid Iran

The Afghan occupation heralded the beginning of the changed nature of the relationship between the Dutch and the government of Iran. First, as of 1721 the Dutch had to keep a permanent military garrison at Bandar Abbas to protect their staff and trading operations. Second, the quid (no customs duties) pro quo (purchase of silk) arrangement between the two parties was altered. The formal basis of Dutch trade relations with Iran still rested on the premise of tax-free trade in exchange for the purchase of silk and the supply of the annual present to the court. However, after 1730 neither was silk purchased (or supplied by the court for that matter) nor was the annual present sent. The court therefore felt free to demand services from the Dutch. This started already in 1730, when Shah Tahmasp II's general Tahmasp-Quli Khan (the later Nadir Shah) asked the Dutch to patrol the littoral to prevent Afghan leaders from fleeing. He asked a similar service when he was engaged in suppressing the revolt of the Sunnis in Laristan under Shaikh Ahmad Madani in 1733. The demand to ferry Iranian ambassadors and their goods gratis to Thatta, in the Indus delta, also became a regular item. The demand for these services became especially onerous and expensive when Nadir Shah (r. 1736–47) started his invasion of Oman in 1737. His generals regularly demanded that the Dutch ferry across supplies for the troops and provide equipment to the newly formed fleet. As to the latter the Dutch refused to sell any ships to Nadir Shah, although they temporarily made some craftsmen available for his shipyard at Bushehr. When in 1741 half of the royal fleet mutinied, Iranian authorities insisted that the Dutch supply ships participate in punitive naval operations against the mutineers, all Hula (Hawla, Hawala) Arabs. The Dutch reluctantly gave in and supplied two ships, which were unable to ensure that the Iranian fleet overcame the Arab mutineers. Thereafter, demands to ferry supplies to Oman continued to be made and carried out, although these demands finally stopped when Mirza Taqi Khan rebelled in 1745. During the fights between the rebels and forces loyal to Nadir Shah, the Dutch refused to choose sides and told both parties that they were there to trade not to fight. They would only do so if forced to defend themselves.[26]

The End of Dutch Presence in the Gulf

The death of Nadir Shah in 1747 brought temporary tranquillity to the littoral and trade. However, the succession war that had broken out in Iran spilled over to the Gulf. In 1751, forces of Ali Mardan Khan, the Bakhtiyari leader, took Bandar Abbas. The Dutch had left the city prior to their arrival, leaving a skeleton staff behind to look after their affairs. Although the full staff returned in 1752, the final bell had tolled for the VOC factory there. It was closed down in 1758, and in 1760 temporarily taken over by the governor of Lar, who had established his rule over the littoral. A Dutch caretaker looked after the building from 1761 until 1765.[27]

The decision to abandon the factory at Bandar Abbas was part of a rearrangement of the VOC operations in the Gulf. The VOC had established a factory in Bushehr in 1734 with a view to increase sales. The fortunes of this new factory were varied and not all positive. Apart from disappointing sales, there also was the problem of demands for services by local officials as well as interference in trade by the local chief, Shaikh Naser al-Mazkur. At the same time, sales at Bushehr had a negative impact on those of the VOC factory in Basra. This office had become independent of the Persian Directorate in 1747. When in 1751 Tido von Kniphausen, the VOC chief in Basra, was accused of having relations with a Muslim woman and was forced to pay a large sum to obtain his freedom, he was able to convince the governor-general in Batavia of the advantage of a reform plan for Dutch trade in the Gulf. Von Kniphausen suggested that the VOC close down its factories in Basra and Bushehr, and eventually also in Bandar Abbas, and build a factory on Kharg Island. Here the VOC staff would be free from demands from local officials. When von Kniphausen returned to the Gulf in 1753 with three ships, he blockaded the Shatt al-Arab and forced the Basrene authorities to return the money extorted from the VOC. He further closed the factory of Bushehr much to the chagrin of Shaikh Nasir, the city's ruler, and built a new one on Kharg Island. Von Kniphausen was able to draw most Dutch trade to Kharg, thus rendering the Bandar Abbas factory irrelevant, and it was therefore closed in 1758.

Although trade temporarily increased it soon fell back to the lackluster level where it had been before. To increase revenues von Kniphausen suggested either becoming engaged in pearl fishing or conquering Bahrain, to which end he made a detailed proposal. The governor-general disapproved of the Bahrain proposal, but liked the pearl fishing plan and actually sent a diving bell to Kharg. Because the users' manual had not been included it was not employed. After von Kniphausen's departure in 1759, his successor had to deal with the piratical activities of Mir Muhanna, the chief of Bandar-i Rig. The latter also contested the Dutch claim that his father had given Kharg to them and in 1762 attacked the island, although he was repulsed. By that time Batavia had received orders to close down Kharg, which was losing money, and withdraw from the Gulf, although Batavia sugar interests ensured that this decision was postponed.

When the decision was finally taken in 1765 it was too late, because in late December 1765 Mir Muhanna had attacked Kharg again. This was due to the fact that the Dutch, against their better judgment, had allowed themselves to be persuaded to support a military operation against Mir Muhanna by the new ruler of Iran, Karim Khan Zand. Mir Muhanna of Rig not only preyed on his neighbors on land but also was engaged in piracy at sea. Karim Khan Zand and the chiefs of the neighboring ports, therefore, wanted to mount a combined land and sea operation against Mir Muhanna. His forces had expelled Mir Muhanna from Rig, who then had fled to the small island of Khargu, next to Kharg. The Dutch were supposed to assist Bushehr forces led by Shaikh Sa'dun, who fled when Mir Muhanna attacked them. Dutch forces that had landed on Khargu were no match for Mir Muhanna. They suffered considerable losses and withdrew to Kharg. Mir Muhanna then immediately attacked the Dutch factory, which surrendered on January 3, 1766. Although he kept the goods that he found there as booty, Mir Muhanna allowed the Dutch staff to depart and even gave them a few small boats to reach Bushehr.[28]

Thus ended 143 years of continuous Dutch presence in the Persian Gulf. It did not mean that the Dutch no longer came to the Gulf. Until 1793, each year one ship or sometimes two, usually privately owned, sailed from Batavia directly to Muscat to sell its cargo, mostly consisting of sugar and spices. Although letters were received from local governors (Hormuz, Bandar Abbas, Bushehr, and Basra) inviting the Dutch to come and trade again at those ports, the VOC had decided that trading in the Gulf was too risky and not profitable enough. It could sell the same goods in the market of Surat, whence they would be taken by country traders into the Gulf.[29]

DUTCH TRADE IN THE PERSIAN GULF

As far as exports were concerned, Iran did not have much to offer, apart from silk. This was why the Dutch came to the Gulf, but their interest soon faded. Silk exports fluctuated, and total silk exports from the Gulf may have represented about 25 percent of total production in Iran. In the 1630s the Dutch tried to corner the market, in vain. The VOC even imported about 50 percent less silk than it had done in the 1620s, a consequence of the abolition of the export monopoly and silk crop failures. It was after this failed attempt, which coincided with disappointing profits on the sale of Iranian silk in Europe, that the VOC wanted to be rid of silk altogether. Nevertheless silk exports were very considerable during the first half of the 1640s. However between 1645 and 1651 there was no silk export at all. During the 1652–65 period the Dutch usually exported 250 bales, and from 1670 until 1684 some 420 bales (see table 12.2). After 1696 silk exports tapered off.

Table 12.2 Exported Quantities of Raw Silk during 1624–1714 (in bales)

Years	Exported Quantity/Bales	Average no. Bales Exported Per Year
1624–29	2,553	426
1630–39	2,199	220
1640–45	1,894	379
1645–51	No silk bought	—
1652–59	2,234	280
1660–69	2,417	242
1670–79	4,403	440
1680–83	1,563	391
1683–90	No silk bought	—
1691, 1695–96	1,607	535
1697–1703	No silk bought	—
1704	80	80
1705–12	No silk bought	—
1713–14	327	163

Source: Willem Floor , "The Dutch and the Persian Silk Trade," in *Safavid Persia*, ed. Charles Melville (London: I. B. Tauris, 1996), 341, Table 1.

Deliveries of silk by the royal court experienced difficulties both before and soon after the conclusion of the treaty of 1701. In fact, the first silk delivery did not take place until 1704 and thereafter only eighty bales were delivered instead of the two hundred contracted. No silk was delivered for a number of years after 1704. The Heeren XVII issued instructions in 1705 that the director in Bandar Abbas should not insist on the delivery of the silk because it hardly yielded any profit in Europe. If the shah demanded the supply of recognitie goederen even when no silk was delivered, the director was authorized to comply. In this way the VOC would not be troubled by other problems. No more silk was delivered to the VOC until 1710, and thereafter much reduced silk deliveries were only resumed in 1714. After that year, no more silk was delivered to the VOC at all. Although future discussions with the royal court included the supply of silk neither party was really interested in pursuing the matter. The last time the VOC showed some interest in silk was around 1740, but it was too expensive and too difficult to transport and the matter ended there.[30]

After 1659, apart from silk, the Dutch were interested in Kirman wool or goat hair (*kurk*) for which they had a standing order of 60,000 lbs. They never were able to obtain this quantity, however, while the quality of the wool usually was low. The VOC wanted red wool; the other varieties, especially white wool, had to be declined whenever possible. This gave rise to a lot of complaints from Batavia and the Netherlands, but there was no change in the situation. The VOC stopped exporting goat hair between 1725–31 and 1743–50 and finally stopped its purchase altogether in 1761 (see table 12.3).[31]

Other export goods were mainly small quantities of all kinds of dried fruits and nuts such as pistachios, almonds, hazelnuts, and rhubarb. Goods like garden seeds, medicines, rose water, and Shiraz wine were also regular export items.[32]

The only other commodity that was worth exporting was specie. After 1645, when silk lost its relative importance, gold, or rather golden European ducats, and silver became the VOC's most important export commodity from Iran. The VOC exchanged Iranian money for European gold, for the *Abbasis*, Mahmudis, and Nadiris yielded too much loss when exported to Coromandel and Ceylon, where most of the gold and silver went. This was the result of an increasing debasement of the Iranian currency by the government, especially of the silver Abbasi, due to the deterioration of Iran's economy. In the

Table 12.3 Exported Quantities of *Kurk*

Years	VOC (lbs.)	EIC (bales of 90–100 lbs.)
1658–1670	12,189 lbs.	14,690 lbs
1671–1680	3,830 lbs.	1,457 lbs
1681–1690	13,495 lbs.	628 lbs
1691–1700	104,828 lbs.	2,030 lbs
1701–1710	244,686 lbs.	1,569 lbs
1711–1720	271,440 lbs.	900 lbs
1721–1730	104,870 lbs.	?
1731–1740	259,660 lbs.	379,009 lbs.
1741–1750	1,098 lbs.	111,699 lbs.
1751–1760	69,675 lbs.	297,243 lbs.
1760–1763	4,300 lbs.	40,625 lbs.

Sources: Rudi Matthee, "The East India Company Trade in Kirman Wool, 1658–1730," in *Études safavides,* ed. J. Calmard (Tehran and Paris, 1995), 367–69; Willem Floor, *The Persian Textile Industry, Its Products and Their Use 1500–1925* (Paris: Harmattan, 1999), chap. 5, table 10.

second half of the seventeenth century on average Dfl. 500,000/year in gold and silver was exported, and sometimes more than Dfl. 1 million. From 1700–21, each year on average Dfl. 900,000 in gold was exported by the VOC. In the 1730s and 1740s, gold and silver became so scarce that only small quantities at high prices could be obtained. As a result of the shortage of coinage the Dutch, like other foreign traders, were forced to accept old copper as payment, which was exported to India, at a loss.[33]

Imports by the Dutch were substantial and consisted of spices (pepper, mace, cloves, nutmeg, and cinnamon), textiles (cottons, silks, and broadcloth), sugar (crystal and loaf sugar), metals (copper, tin, iron, zinc, and steel), timber (sappan wood and sandalwood), indigo, radix china, gumlac, benzoin, camphor, and other smaller items.[34]

During the VOC's early years in Iran its imported goods were mostly transported for sale to Isfahan, especially when the merchants in Bandar Abbas did not offer high enough prices. However, as of the 1650s sales increasingly took place in Bandar Abbas, and in 1692 Batavia prohibited the transportation of goods to Isfahan altogether because of problems such as theft, shortages, and obnoxious behavior by internal tax farmers. The sale of VOC goods afterwards took place exclusively in Bandar Abbas in the following manner: after the arrival of the VOC ships, the director in Bandar Abbas informed the principal merchants in Isfahan, Shiraz, and Lar by letter. This held especially for the most important merchants dealing with the VOC. Then negotiations were begun with these merchants or their agents, who usually came in April and May to Bandar Abbas for that purpose. If the director perceived that the principal merchants were trying to agree among one another to form a kind of buyers' cartel to enforce lower prices, he would threaten to transport the goods to Isfahan, which usually had the required result. The VOC staff also had to see to it that Iranian officials did not interfere in the negotiations. These officials wanted to buy only the best-selling items, on credit, and even then payment was only obtained with the greatest difficulty. The shahbandar, who each year bought some goods for the shah, was the only official allowed to bid as well, though he had to pay in cash. The merchants usually got the goods on credit. They paid with drafts drawn on creditors in Isfahan or elsewhere. Despite repeated orders from Batavia to demand cash payments, this was impossible in practice, and implementation of this order would have meant that no trade could have been carried on. The usual credit period around 1715 was three months, but would double after 1722.[35]

The decision to sell had to be cleared with the council of the Bandar Abbas office. The council would take into account such issues as last year's prices, the import of similar goods by other merchants since then, and the prices obtaining in Isfahan. Each month the Isfahan office would therefore send a price list of a specified number of items to Bandar Abbas. "On this basis it was calculated what the merchants could pay after deduction of transportation cost, road-taxes, spillage, etc. in order to provide the Hon. Company with a good profit and on the other hand to enable the merchants to stay in business by means of a modest profit, which would also induce them to trade."[36]

The council also saw to it that merchants bought all the goods and not just the best-selling ones, so that the company would not run the risk of being unable to sell the less desirable goods. If it would help sales, the council sometimes lowered the prices of the best-selling goods in order to animate trade. However, this did not hold for such goods as radix china, aguilwood, and sandalwood of which not much was imported, and could always be sold in small quantities to the shopkeepers in Bandar Abbas.

The sales themselves were concluded through the intermediary of brokers. These formed a kind of buffer between the VOC and the Iranian merchants. The VOC always supported the brokers in difficult situations, if only to prevent disrespect being shown to the company. Goods sold were weighed in the Dutch factory with Dutch weights before delivery to the merchants. The brokers were security for the payment of the drafts with which the merchants paid for the goods. If the drafts were not honored, the brokers had to pay. As recompense for their work and risk they received one percent of the total receipts of sales from the VOC and the Iranian merchants, although for some goods they only got 0.75 percent.

The VOC set great store by good relationships with the Iranian and other merchants, and so the director in Bandar Abbas and the staff in other places maintained friendly ties with them. The gate of the VOC factory was always open to them, to induce them to trade. For the same reason, the principal merchants were given presents of sugar and cloth after the sale had been concluded to confirm their good relations.[37]

This indicates that the nature of the Persian Gulf market had changed after 1622. Prior to the fall of Hormuz, the Portuguese had controlled access to the Gulf market by nonauthorized traders with varying success. Only those having a pass from Portuguese authorities were allowed to sail into the Gulf and engage in trade, although there was a lot of smuggling due to the high profits to be made. The Portuguese also tried to control the trade of certain commodities such as iron and pepper, which were a Portuguese state monopoly. After 1622, access to the Gulf was freer, and there was fierce competition between all comers. Only in times of conflict did Asian merchants obtain passes from the offices of the European companies in India that allowed them to come to the Gulf unhindered. Although the Dutch had the monopoly of spices and tried to have a stranglehold on that of pepper as well, they achieved effective market domination only through competitive pricing. If they sold pepper, for example, at too low a price in Surat or Basra, it might be reexported from there to be sold at Bandar Abbas and vice versa. Although the Dutch were the most important power in the Gulf during the seventeenth century they did not exercise that power except in the case of war. If the Dutch blockaded the coast of Iran, for example, they did not allow other European or Asian ships to call on Iranian ports and disembark their goods. They allowed them, however, to sail to Basra to sell these same goods. The use of force against other Europeans was determined by events in Europe. If there was war between the Netherlands on the one side and England and France on the other, this led to attacks on each other's shipping in the Persian Gulf and elsewhere with Asia.

Although the VOC was financially and militarily a powerful company, it did not mean that it automatically could impose itself on the market. For those commodities where it held a monopoly it had a firm control over the quantities marketed and their prices. For most other commodities the VOC dominated the market, but that did not mean that its position went unchallenged. For example, in the sugar market there was fierce competition from English and Asian merchants, including exports from Oman. After a slow start with imports that were below 100,000 lbs./year, after 1650 the VOC usually exported about 0.6–1.3 million lbs. of granulated sugar and some 200–300 lbs. of candy sugar annually to Iran, though there were years when less was imported. This volume of sugar imports was reduced to next to nothing during the Afghan occupation of Iran. During the 1730s and 1740s sales initially picked up again (456,128 lbs. in 1730). However, soon an intermittent pattern of decreasing imports may be discerned, while in some years (1742–43) no sugar was imported at all. Sales picked up again as of 1747 only to drop after 1760. During the 1750s the Dutch imported an average of 600,000 lbs. of granulated sugar and 200,000 lbs. of candy sugar. This volume increased in the 1760s when, for example, in 1759–60, 1.1 million lbs. of sugar were sold, a level that it more or less remained at until 1764, when sales dropped by 50 percent and continued falling thereafter. Prices during that period remained unchanged and were fixed.[38]

But how different was the situation in the textiles market. Both Asian and European traders imported Indian textiles, but the former held the largest market share. Based on a VOC 1634 estimate of the volume of textile imports into Iran, the VOC, and probably

Table 12.4 Average Annual Gross Profits in the Persian Gulf during 1700–54.

Years	Profits (in Dfl.)
1700–09	402,859
1710–19	363,728
1720–29	175,856
1730–39	72,587
1740–49	73,912
1750–54	137,131
1700–54	218,456

Source: Willem Floor, "The Dutch on Khark Island: A Commercial Mishap," *IJMES* 24 (1992): 444, Table 1.

also the EIC, only held some 15 percent share of the textile market at that time. The market share of the European companies was further reduced in the second half of the seventeenth century by strong competition from Asian traders, who usually did better in this segment of the market.[39]

The VOC had started its trading activities in Iran and the Gulf in 1623. This was the beginning of a very profitable business for it, and throughout the seventeenth century and much of the eighteenth century the VOC was Iran's most important foreign trading partner. Profits during the seventeenth and the two first decades of the eighteenth century were very good. We do not have sufficient data as yet for the seventeenth century to calculate the annual profits obtained during that period, but I estimate they were at least as high as during the first decade of the eighteenth century (see table 12.4).

However, after 1722 profits dropped considerably and in fact the VOC was operating at a loss in the Gulf. The net profits were lower due to the fact that the figures of table 12.1 do not include expenditures such as the cost of the shipping between Batavia and the Gulf, loss of interest on unsold merchandise, amortization of ships, and maritime insurance. But even taking these costs into account the VOC had a profitable operation in Iran until the fall of the Safavid dynasty. This changed after 1722 when expenditures grew considerably due to losses (loans of money and ships), higher personnel cost, lower sales, higher losses on exports, and the like. This was already clear to the VOC in the 1730s, but for various reasons it decided not to do anything about it. Also, the company hoped that the tide would turn and that the situation in Iran would revert to its pre-1722 conditions. This did not happen.[40]

THE NINETEENTH CENTURY

The Dutch presence in the Persian Gulf throughout the nineteenth century was but a pale reflection of its dominant role during the era of the VOC. It was only in 1824 that the first direct voyage from Batavia to Bandar Abbas was made again, for the first time since 1793. Four other voyages followed, and although profitable, the direct voyages were abandoned after 1831 due to lack of security in the Gulf and the arbitrary behavior of the shaikh of Bushehr in trade matters. Private Dutch merchants and Iranian Armenian merchants residing in Batavia continued trade with Bushehr, which increased sixfold between 1855 and 1865, mainly owing to increased consumption of Java sugar in Iran.[41] To counter a declining trade thereafter, the Dutch government appointed a consul at Bushehr in 1868, Richard Keun. He built a large villa just outside Bushehr, which he named "Hollandarabad" and which served as the Dutch consulate. Keun tried to interest Dutch entrepreneurs to invest in Iran. One of them, Hotz, established the Perzische Handels Vereniging (PHV) or Persian Trading Company J. C. P. Hotz and Son and began trading in carpets and opium (export) and textiles, tea and a variety of other products (import). His son, A. Hotz, was the first to start drilling for oil in Iran (at Daliki); he also took an interest in developing Iran's coal reserves, the irrigation potential of Khuzistan, and Iran's banking sector. He was, for example, one of the founders of the Persian Bank Mining Rights Corporation, which was owned by the Imperial Bank of Persia of which he was a board member, while he established the first department store in Iran (the Tehran Toko). Dutch trade meanwhile dropped from Dfl. 1.4 million in 1866 to Dfl. 160,000 in 1884, and the Bushehr consulate was abandoned for a post in Tehran. The Dutch consulate at Bushehr, Hollandarabad, was sold to the French. The Dutch consul general was then able to obtain the right of entrepôt from the government of Iran, a right that no other nation had been able to obtain until then. However, the Dutch parliament was not interested in approving the treaty, indicating that relations with Iran, commercial or otherwise, were of no interest to the Netherlands. The bankruptcy of the long and well-established Hotz & Son Company (which had become a British-protected firm as of 1880) in February 1903 came as a shock to the mercantile community in Iran. The bankruptcy was not due to the lack of profitability of commercial activities in Iran, but to losses the company's manager of the London office had suffered in Basra, which he had kept carefully hidden from management. Hotz, who was a strong believer in the profitability of trade with Iran, in 1896 made a proposal for a direct shipping line between Java and Bushehr, but there was no interest in this plan. The same fate befell the proposal made by A. Graadt van Roggen, a Dutch engineer in Iranian employ, to build a dam at Ahwaz and develop the agricultural potential of Khuzistan. Although Dutch trade became insignificant, one Dutchman, P. ter Meulen, a former Hotz employee, was able to establish a thriving import-export business in Ahwaz in 1900, the so-called Handelsvereniging Holland-Perzië (Dutch-Persian Trading Company), which he continued until the end of the Qajar period.[42]

CONCLUSION

From the above it is clear that during the entire 143 years of relations between the VOC and Safavid and Afsharid Iran, the Iranians and not the Dutch were in the stronger bargaining position. The shah could get all the revenues he needed just by raising the tax level. He also could obtain the goods that the Dutch sold in Bandar Abbas from India via the land route (Lahore-Kandahar) or from other traders via the maritime route. In the final analysis, the VOC needed Safavid Iran more than Safavid Iran needed the VOC. The shah was willing to deal with the Dutch, because, due to their market position, they were able to provide large sums of cash immediately, reliably, and predictably. The same funds might also be obtained from a large number of individual trading merchants, but more slowly, and in fits and starts. The Dutch should have been forewarned by the rather disinterested attitude of the shah toward Dutch trade after the 1645 crisis. After the cessation of hostilities, the Dutch did not export any silk or pay any customs duties for six years. This happened at a time when the shah needed money for his Kandahar campaign. However, nothing was done to make life easy for the Dutch; even when the Dutch embassy arrived in 1651, it was met by a rather matter-of-fact attitude on the part of the grand vizier, who told the Dutch they had no recourse but to accept his terms. They did, which, despite everything, yielded sufficient profits to continue their commercial relationship with Safavid Iran. The same happened in 1690 and 1717 when other ambassadors, raising similar issues, were told to "take it or leave it."

In these cases they also took it, and trade results were still good, despite the governor-general's dissatisfaction about the imposed terms.

The manner in which commercial conflicts between the Dutch and the Safavid court developed and were resolved showed the underlying problem, which was the meeting of two different cultures. The Dutch wanted a clear agreement, based in law, which would be respected by all parties. It was for this reason also that the Dutch asked that all royal decrees be addressed not to current office holders, but rather to functionaries, both current and future. The problem was that the letter of the law was mutable in Iran. Anything was possible, and everything had its price. The system of government in Iran was based on the fact that all power and authority belonged to the shah, who was in theory limited by reason and Islamic law, but in actual practice was almost unfettered in his exercise thereof. The negotiations with the Dutch were viewed not as a deal to benefit both countries, but rather as a deal to benefit the shah. The VOC wanted to trade in the shah's kingdom, fine, but at what price? The entire discussion was focused on that issue, not on whether Dutch trade might be a positive factor in the Iranian economy. The Dutch not only had to pay the ultimate benefactor, the shah, but also those who had made the deal possible and who had provided the access to the shah. This meant that "presents" had to be paid to the grand vizier and other grandees. The text of the actual agreement was of less importance. When disagreement broke out over the ceiling of custom-free trade, the grand vizier maintained that it did not matter. Indeed, during the remainder of Safavid rule it did not matter, unless it was of interest to somebody in government to raise the issue and be recompensed.

Finally, despite their wealth and prowess in the rest of the world, European merchants were tolerated foreigners in Safavid Iran. The shah was willing to deal with them, as he dealt with Iranian and other Asian merchants, but on his terms. Despite all the talk by some European countries about a common front against a common enemy (the Turk), the shah sought his own advantage, not that of the Europeans. Moreover, neither the shah, his ministers or factors nor the Persian (Armenian, Jewish, Muslim) merchants were the financial, commercial, or intellectual inferiors of the Europeans. In fact, the Iranian side (government and private sector) did quite well in its dealings with the Dutch and English as evidenced by the chagrined reaction by the management of both companies to the various negotiations, trade results, and competition experienced during their long relationship.

In the nineteenth century Dutch trade was very limited. Most of it was carried out by Armenian merchants based in Batavia and consisted mainly of sugar, spices, and tea. However, despite the small volume of trade, Dutch representatives were among the most influential merchants in Iran at that time. The Dutch were the only ones to whom the government of Iran granted the right of entrepôt, while the Dutch firm of Hotz & Son played a leading role in foreign trade with Iran as well as the development of its economic resources. However, with the bankruptcy of this company in 1903, Dutch interests were then limited to one import-export firm in Ahwaz.

Notes

1. A case in point is the most famous and influential of them, Jan van Linschoten (1563–1611). However, van Linschoten was in the service of the Portuguese and did not necessarily write about his voyage to help shape Dutch policy. His account of his voyage in 1589 to Asia, and in particular to the Gulf, nevertheless was influential throughout Europe and raised Northwestern European interest in direct trade with Asia and Iran. Van Linschoten had detailed both the riches that could be gained as well as the weakness

of the Portuguese in Asia that could be overcome and thus whetted Dutch and English commercial appetites. See J. H. van Linschoten, *The Voyage of Jan Huygen van Linschoten to the East Indies*, ed. and trans. A. C. Burnell and P. A. Tiele, 2 vols. (London: Hakluyt Society, 1885).

2. National Archives (NA) (The Hague), VOC 478 (Amsterdam, 11 April 1608).
3. Willem Floor, "The Dutch and the Persian Silk Trade," in *Safavid Persia,* ed. Charles Melville (London: I. B. Tauris, 1996), 323–27.
4. Ibid., 327–29, 331–35.
5. Depending on the importance of the trading station it was managed by a governor, director, commander, *gezaghebber*, *resident*, or *opperhoofd* and council.
6. See Femme Gaastra, *The Dutch East India Company: Expansion and Decline* (Zutphen, The Netherlands: Walburg Pers, 2003).
7. Willem Floor, *The Afghan Occupation of Persia, 1722–1730* (Paris: Cahiers Studia Iranica, 1998), 11–13.
8. John Fryer, *A New Account of East India and Persia, Being Nine Years' Travels, 1672–1681*, vol. 2 (London: Hakluyt Society, 1909), 165.
9. Floor, "The Dutch and the Persian Silk Trade", 323–68.
10. For more detail see Willem Floor, *A Fiscal History of Iran in the Safavid and Qajar Period* (New York: Bibliotheca Persica, 1999), chap. 1
11. Algemeen Rijks Archief (ARA), Collectie Geleijnsen 167b (14/10/1642), unfoliated. Similar sentiments were aired by Shaikh Ali Khan Zangana, the grand vizier in the 1670s. See Willem Floor, *Commercial Conflict between Persia and the Netherlands 1712–1718,* Occasional Paper no. 37 (Durham, UK: Centre for Middle Eastern and Islamic Studies, University of Durham, 1988), 2.
12. On this issue see Rudi Matthee, "Negotiating Across Cultures: The Dutch van Leene Mission to the Iranian Court of Shah Sulayman, 1689–92," *Eurasian Studies* III/1 (2004): 35–63 and Willem Floor and Mohammad H. Faghfoory, *The First Dutch-Iranian Commercial Conflict* (Costa Mesa, CA: Mazda, 2004), 3–5.
13. H. Dunlop, ed., *Bronnen tot de Geschiedenis der Oost Indische Compagnie in Perzie*, Rijks Geschiedkundige Publicatiën 72 ('s-Gravenhage, The Netherlands: Nijhoff, 1930), 677–82; M.-A. Meilink-Roelofsz, "The Earliest Relations between Persia and the Netherlands," *Persica* 6 (1975): 18–19; A. Hotz, *Journaal der Reis van den Gezant der O. I. compagnie, Joan Cunaeus naar Perzie in 1651–52* (Amsterdam, The Netherlands: Müller, 1908), 47.
14. For the meaning of these and other terms denoting the various qualities of Persian silk see Floor, "The Dutch and the Persian Silk Trade", 336–37; see also Willem Floor, *The Persian Textile Industry: Its Products and Their Use* (Paris: Harmattan, 1999), 14–15.
15. Floor, "The Dutch and the Persian Silk Trade", 349–51.
16. Floor, *The First Dutch-Iranian Commercial Conflict.*
17. *NA*, VOC 1195, Sarcerius to governor-general (8/9/1652), fol. 885; W. P. Coolhaas, ed., *Generale Missieven der Vereenigde Oostindische Compagnie*, vol. 2 ('s-Gravenhage, The Netherlands: Nijhoff, 1964), 629; R. W. Ferrier, *British-Persian Relations in the 17th Century* (PhD diss., Cambridge University, 1970), 199.
18. Ferrier, *British-Persian Relations,* 97.
19. For more details see Floor, *The First Dutch-Iranian Commercial Conflict*, Annex 3; also Willem Floor, *The Persian Gulf: A Political and Economic History of Five Port Cities 1500–1730* (Washington D.C.: Mage Publishers, 2006), chap. 8.
20. Willem Floor, "A Description of Masqat and Oman in 1673 AD/1084 Q," *Moyen Orient & Ocean Indien* 2 (1985): 1–69.
21. Rudi Matthee, *The Politics of Trade in Safavid Iran: Silk for Silver, 1600–1730* (Cambridge: Cambridge University Press, 1999); Floor, *The First Dutch-Iranian Commercial Conflict.*
22. P. van Dam, *Beschrijvinge van de Oost Indische Compagnie*, ed. F. W. Stapel, Rijks Geschiedkundige Publicatiën 83 ('s-Gravenhage, The Netherlands: Nijhoff, 1939), 318–21; Coolhaas, *Generale Missieven*, vol. 4, 299–300, 358–63, 582–83, 740–43, 826–27; F. Valentijn, *Oud-en Nieuw Oost-Indiën. . . .* vol. 5 (Dordrecht, The Netherlands: van Braam and Onder de Linden, 1726), 250–70; Matthee, *The Politics of Trade in Safavid Iran.*

23. Floor, *The Afghan Occupation of Persia*, chap. 1.
24. Floor, *The First Dutch-Iranian Commercial Conflict.*
25. Floor, *The Afghan Occupation of Persia.*
26. Willem Floor, "Dutch Trade in Afsharid Persia (1730–1753)," *Studia Iranica* 34 (2005): 43–94; Willem Floor, "The Iranian Navy in the Gulf during the Eighteenth Century," *Iranian Studies* 20 (1987): 31–53.
27. Willem Floor, "The Decline of the Dutch East Indies Company in Bandar 'Abbas (1747–1759)," *Moyen Orient & Ocean Indien* 6 (1989): 45–80.
28. Willem Floor, "The Dutch on Kharg–A Commercial Mishap," *International Journal of Middle East Studies (IJMES)* 24/3 (1992): 441–60; Willem Floor, "The Dutch on Kharg Island. The End of an Era. The Baron von Kniphausen's Adventures," in *Europeens en Orient au XVIIIe S., Moyen Orient & Ocean Indien* 11 (1994): 157–202.
29. Willem Floor, "Description of the Persian Gulf and Its Inhabitants in 1756," *Persica* 8 (1979): 163–86; Willem Floor, "Dutch Trade with Masqat in the Second Half of the Eighteenth Century," *Asian and African Studies* 16 (1982): 197–213; Willem Floor, "First Contacts between the Netherlands and Masqat, or A Report on the Discovery of the Coast of 'Oman in 1666. Translation and Introduction," *Zeitschrift der Deutschen Morgenländischen Gesellschaft* 132 (1982): 289–307; Floor, "The Dutch on Kharg: A Commercial Mishap"; John Perry, "Mir Muhanna and the Dutch: Patterns of Piracy in the Persian Gulf," *Studia Iranica* 2 (1973): 79–95.
30. Floor, "The Dutch and the Persian Silk Trade"; Willem Floor, *The Economy of Safavid Persia* (Wiesbaden, Germany: Reichert, 2000).
31. Willem Floor, *A Fiscal History of Iran in the Safavid and Qajar Period* (New York: Bibliotheca Persica, 1999); Floor, *The Economy of Safavid Persia*; Rudi Matthee, "The East India Company Trade in Kerman Wool, 1658–1730," in *Études safavides,* ed. J. Calmard (Tehran and Paris, 1995), 343–83.
32. Floor, *The Economy of Safavid Persia.*
33. William Floor and Patrick Clawson, "Safavid Persia's Search for Gold and Silver," *IJMES* 32 (2000), 345–68; Floor, *The Economy of Safavid Persia.*
34. Floor, *The Economy of Safavid Persia.*
35. Floor, *Commercial Conflict between Persia and the Netherlands*; Floor, *The Economy of Safavid Persia.*
36. Floor, *Commercial Conflict between Persia and the Netherlands*, 6n28.
37. Ibid., 4–6; Floor, *The Economy of Safavid Persia.*
38. Floor, *The Economy of Safavid Persia.*
39. Ibid.; Floor, *The First Dutch-Iranian Commercial Conflict.*
40. Floor, "The Dutch on Khark: A Commercial Mishap"; Floor, "Dutch Trade in Afsharid Persia." Also Willem Floor, *The Persian Gulf: The Rise of the Gulf Arabs—The Politics of Trade on the Persian Littoral 1747–1792* (Washington D.C.: Mage Publishers, 2007).
41. N. J. Den Tex, "Onze Handel in de Perzische Golf en in de Roode Zee," *De Economist* 1 (1871): 23–31.
42. A. Hotz, "Java-Bombay-Perzische Golf. Een nieuwe Stoom-vaartlijn," *De Economist* 2 (1896): 725–26; 739; Hotz, "Onze Handel met Perzie en de Levant," *De Gids* 24 (1906): 376; Floor, "Hotz versus Mohammad Shafi': A Study in Commercial Litigation in Qajar Iran 1888–1894," *IJMES* 15 (1983): 185–209;" Floor, "Le droit d'entreposage dans Qajar Iran," *Studia Iranica* 13 (1988): 59–77 and 179–82; Floor, "Le Karun et l'irrigation de la plaine d'Ahvaz," *Studia Iranica* 29 (1999): 95–122; Floor, "Dutch Retail Shops in Qajar Iran," *Studia Iranica* 36, no. 2 (2007): 185–226.

CHAPTER 13

THE OTTOMAN ROLE IN THE GULF

Frederick Anscombe

Modern histories of Arabia and the Gulf have tended to slight the Ottoman influence on the region's development.[1] The dictum that the victors get to shape the history is quite apt in this case, in which most of the Ottoman involvement in the Gulf was marked by rivalries with foreign powers, particularly Britain, before 1914. Much of the scholarship on modern Gulf history has drawn heavily on the rich, and easily accessible, records in London, reflecting to some degree British attitudes and assumptions as a consequence. Although the Ottomans controlled Hasa (now the Eastern Province of Saudi Arabia) for over a century from 1550, it was their second, briefer period of administration there that brought them into the British records and thus set the tone for their treatment by historians. The sultan's flag may have flown over Hasa, Kuwait, and Qatar from 1870–71 to 1914, but few dramatic events seemed to involve the Ottomans directly. Istanbul sparred with Britain with diplomacy, never with arms. Ottoman administration of Hasa was routine or inefficient—in either case, unspectacular. The Ottoman civil and military presence in the area eventually dwindled as the empire faced crises elsewhere, and Istanbul's final loss of control was almost an anticlimax, overshadowed as it was by the more disastrous contemporary losses of territory in Macedonia, Albania, and Libya. It is thus hardly surprising that, until recently, the Ottomans were written out of Gulf history almost as efficiently as they were pushed out of eastern Arabia.

Such elision of the Ottomans from Gulf history was aided by the limited nature of Istanbul's concerns in the area. The empire had only one important goal in establishing and maintaining control over the Arabian coast: securing its southern borders against the further spread of European influence. It failed to achieve its aim. Its primary interest coming to naught, having invested fairly modest sums in the development of the area, and leaving behind relatively few tangible artifacts (primarily scattered forts and mosques that echo little of the architectural splendor of Istanbul), neither the residents of the area nor the British would have much encouragement to keep alive a vibrant memory of the Ottoman era in the Gulf. The one state with an urge to do so, the Ottoman Empire itself, disintegrated a few years after being expelled from the Gulf. From this comes the tendency to see developments in the region during the nineteenth and twentieth centuries as driven primarily by British action.

Yet such a view overlooks ways in which the Ottoman Empire did exert a significant influence on the course of Gulf history, in spite of its comparatively short-lived control over eastern Arabia. The most significant effect of Ottoman authority was the boost it gave to the political power of shaikhs in Kuwait and Qatar. This meant not only an increase in security of tenure for individual shaikhs but also the strengthening of their ability to dominate specific lands and peoples. This naturally had an effect on the setting of boundaries in eastern Arabia as well. Although Ottoman influence in other spheres was more indirect than in the rise of state authority in traditional shaikhdoms, it can be seen also in religious and socioeconomic developments. By incorporating eastern Arabia into the empire, the Ottomans expanded the area's connections with, and exposure to, regions far beyond its established trade and travel routes. And although the Sufi-oriented, Hanafi religious practices of the empire hardly left a lasting trace upon the more conservative views of the Arabian population, the empire did serve as an important influence upon Wahhabi and Saudi attitudes by being the power against which those linked movements so often campaigned.

The Eras of Ottoman Rule in Eastern Arabia

Istanbul exercised direct control over parts of eastern Arabia in two distinct periods, with the second era beginning some two centuries after the close of the first. In spite of the wide gap in time, the motivation driving the Ottomans into the region and some of the problems they faced in administering the area a second time echoed those of the first period. Istanbul regarded eastern Arabia as a forward base for the defense of the empire's frontier, but the difficulties of communication with a province so remote from the empire's core made maintenance of control expensive and ultimately impractical.

Hasa first came under Ottoman control as a delayed consequence of Sultan Suleyman the Magnificent's conquest of the Iraqi provinces in 1534. Iraq was to achieve notoriety as an often violent frontier between the Sunni Ottomans and Shi'i Iran. By contrast the Ottomans faced no serious resistance to their establishment of control over Hasa, which became the frontier against another hostile religious community, the Catholic Portuguese. Portugal had a base at Hormuz and also threatened Ottoman control of the Hijaz in the Red Sea, as was demonstrated by an attack on Jidda in the 1540s. To support their military deployments in Hasa, the Ottomans brought the area under regular administration, collecting a range of taxes and dispensing justice through the system of religious courts. With most of their attention in the area devoted to Safavid Iran, however, the Ottoman military clashed only rarely with the Portuguese in the Gulf.[2] After the Dutch and the British pushed the Portuguese out of Arabian waters, Istanbul saw little need to maintain a very strong military presence in Hasa, and eventually the Ottomans were expelled from the territory by the Bani Khalid tribe in 1670.

While Istanbul maintained the sultan's theoretical claim to eastern Arabia, the state showed only sporadic interest in turning the notion into reality until 1870–71.[3] Echoing the sixteenth-century threat posed by the Portuguese, the expansion of British political involvement in the Gulf in the late 1860s, particularly in Bahrain and in a simmering conflict along the Hasa and Qatar coasts, excited great suspicion in Istanbul and the province of Baghdad. As viewed from the imperial center, the rise of British activism in the Gulf was part of a worrying trend toward greater European influence around the edges of the empire. In 1870 Russia repudiated the demilitarization of the Black Sea that had been agreed at the end of the Crimean War in 1856, thus reopening a worrisome threat to Istanbul itself. The vulnerability of the Hijaz, an area of tremendous importance to the sultan's legitimacy due to his role as protector of Mecca and Medina, also increased with the opening of the Suez Canal in 1869, which eased access to the Red Sea for the British and French militaries. In response to the heightened sense of weakness in western Arabia, Istanbul began to strengthen its military and civil presence in the area in 1870. This effort culminated in a military expedition to consolidate Ottoman control over Asir and, from 1872, the highlands of Yemen, the frontier facing the British base at Aden, near the southern entrance to the Red Sea.

In line with the vigorous steps taken in the Red Sea, Midhat Pasha, the *vali* (governor) of Baghdad, organized an expedition to eastern Arabia to secure the area against damaging rivalries between tribal groups and shaikhs, and to protect the Gulf coast against British attempts to exploit such rivalries to spread its influence ever closer to Iraq. The Ottomans in the seventeenth century had been cautious about seeking direct conflict with the Portuguese, and the subsequent decline of their military power relative to western Europe put an attack against British forces or protégés out of the question. Instead of seeking to drive the British out by military means, therefore, Istanbul created a defensive bulwark by working with local leaders, except in Sa'udi-dominated Hasa, where direct Ottoman control was established.

Midhat's arrangements remained in effect with little alteration for more than forty years.[4] The shaikhs of Kuwait and Qatar accepted appointments as Ottoman office-holders and agreed to uphold Istanbul's rights of sovereignty or suzerainty in their districts. Kuwait was formally a district (*kaza*) attached to Basra; Hasa and Qatar formed the subprovince of Necd (Najd), subordinate to the vali of first Baghdad and then Basra. While the shaikhs of both Kuwait and Qatar later tried to distance themselves from Ottoman control, they continued to hold their appointed posts. Istanbul sent high officers to govern directly in Hufuf, the main town of Hasa, and they ran an administration generally similar to those found in other Ottoman territories, although no attempt at military conscription was ever essayed.[5]

Throughout the second Ottoman period in eastern Arabia, the state kept a most watchful eye on the Gulf. This priority is suggested by the curious fact that, while the subprovince was named for Najd, the vast center of the Arabian Peninsula, the Ottomans were content to control only the coastal region. Various schemes to counter British influence in the Gulf were considered and occasionally tried, but they resulted in little more than wastage of resources. One of the most alluring prizes sought was Bahrain, not only because of British influence there, but also because it offered a good port that would have eased communication and supply problems between Basra and the Ottoman Gulf outposts. Both the strengths and weaknesses of these Ottoman plans and priorities were demonstrated in the final overthrow of the Ottoman administration in eastern Arabia. In May 1913 Hasa was captured not by the British but by Sa'udi forces from the Najd interior. The Ottoman garrisons in Arabia had been drawn down to just a few hundred men, due to pressing military needs elsewhere during the First and Second Balkan Wars, and reinforcements from Basra could not arrive in time to repel the attack. Although the Sa'udi ruler, Abd al-Aziz b. Sa'ud, reached an agreement with Istanbul in 1914 by which Hasa would continue under the sultan's suzerainty, the Ottoman period in eastern Arabia was effectively at an end by May 1913.[6]

Ottoman-Influenced Political Change

While the Ottoman presence in eastern Arabia was extinguished with barely a struggle, the events of the previous four decades had wrought changes that would outlive Istanbul's authority. Prior to the extension of Ottoman control from Basra down the coast to Doha in 1870–71, the shaikhs of settlements enjoyed influence but little of the power that Europeans expected any "ruler" to have at that time. They had limited security of position and executive authority. By the time of the Ottoman exit from the Gulf, two shaikhs, Mubarak al-Sabah in Kuwait and Qasim al-Thani in Qatar, had established something closer to "rule." Since both men had cultivated good relations with the British and were known to be at odds with the Ottomans, it has usually been assumed that their ability to fend off Istanbul's attentions was a sign of Ottoman weakness, and that the stability of their position was due to British support. Britain's involvement in Gulf affairs was indeed important to this transformation, but it was the reality of Ottoman activity in the region that proved key.

Before the advent of both the Ottomans and the British on the Gulf shores, most settled communities stood in little need of, or could afford, a strong ruler. Generally, a respected family would provide a shaikh who fulfilled the basic security needs of the settlement, mediating or adjudicating disputes within the community to prevent domestic discord, and managing relations with external powers, be they neighboring shaikhs or representatives of more distant states. Most settlements stayed poor, earning enough from trade and the sea to survive but hardly grew rich, except perhaps for the few families who dominated commerce, particularly the pearl industry. An individual shaikh might collect a share of pearling revenue and other customs revenue, as well as *zakat* from tribes acknowledging his authority, but the sums were quite modest in comparison with the expenditures necessary to maintain his standing in the community and among the tribes. Allegiances were revocable, moreover. If a shaikh did not maintain his web of patronage, or if he pressed demands for more revenue, he could lose his position and even, on occasion, his life. Sections of the community, including the wealthiest merchant families, could simply migrate, should they be displeased by the shaikh's actions. If they did not choose to leave, they could promise support to a more sympathetic member of the shaikh's family, which, if typical, suffered its fair share of sibling rivalries. The position of shaikh was that of customary leader rather than formal "ruler."[7]

Crucial to the transformation of modest shaikh to powerful amir was the involvement of outside powers. Britain's intrusion into coastal politics stabilized the position of the shaikhs with whom it established relations, as has been shown in the cases of the Trucial Coast of Oman shaikhdoms and Bahrain.[8] An attack on the Qatari coast in 1867 by Shaikh Muhammad al-Khalifa of Bahrain, for example, led to his ouster at the hands of British Indian forces. When Britain's chosen successor was himself overthrown by family rivals, the British Resident in the Gulf returned with a reinforced flotilla to install yet another candidate, Isa al-Khalifa, and to demonstrate that further infighting among the Al Khalifa would not be tolerated. With British support, Isa al-Khalifa then retained the position of shaikh in Manama for some fifty-four years.[9]

Britain played the new role of foreign arbiter of community leadership, driven by its truly alien views of government, law, and administration. Just as the Ottoman Empire had limited aims in the Gulf, the British Empire confined its serious interest in the region to issues of concern to the safety and well-being of India. In the coastal waters of Oman and Bahrain, that meant essentially the security of shipping. To that end it pressed the trucial system upon the shaikhs of this area, under which they had to agree to maintain the maritime peace. Under the existing system of political practice understood by the shaikhs, relations and agreements were never static. Just as allegiances of tribes and coastal communities were revocable, so the maritime treaties could not be valid in perpetuity without continuous cultivation of the relationship. This was something Britain would not, or could not, always provide. When individual shaikhs strayed from the treaties, however, Britain used force to drive home to them that the European understanding of a treaty governed the agreements. Britain, used to dealing with states, not individuals, demonstrated that it would oust any shaikh who broke the agreed terms—but equally would support any shaikh who demonstrated continuing fidelity to the treaties. Not only did such support put new limits on rivalries within the shaikhs' families, it could also discourage migration between coastal communities, the old weapon of families who objected to their shaikh's actions. There were nevertheless distinct limits to Britain's willingness to become closely involved in political issues outside the maintenance of maritime peace, seeing little to gain from becoming entangled in "the intricate domestic relations of the Arab tribes," which the British could not hope to understand fully.[10] Although active British involvement might not always be forthcoming, shaikhs came to realize the potential advantages in this new political circumstance, and claimants in disputes began to seek British acknowledgement of their cause.[11]

Britain's activism thus began a slow process of political change on the lower Gulf coasts of Oman and Bahrain. The strengthening of the power of shaikhs, a transformation that made them the kind of "rulers" with which a European government was most accustomed to dealing, proceeded haltingly until the mid-twentieth century and the discovery of large petroleum reserves.[12] The income from oil exports loosened the financial constraints that had kept the influence of the rich merchant families (whose fortunes had by then lessened with the collapse of the market for natural pearls) strong enough to rival the shaikhs. British representatives also found a reason at this time to involve themselves much more closely in local affairs, usually in support of shaikhly authority, because of the need for stability to keep petroleum production strong. In areas further up the Gulf for most of the nineteenth century, before the advent of oil, the British by contrast showed very little interest in the politics of areas where there was no serious threat to Indian shipping from maritime conflict. Kuwait and Qatar (leaving aside for now the Hasa coast) thus continued the old style of shaikhly politics until the arrival of the Ottomans in the 1870s.

Qatar

Of the leaders in these two settlements, the Al Thani shaikhs of Qatar (or more properly of Doha and nearby settlements) had the weaker, diplomatically more delicate position. The area beyond the Doha settlements in which their authority was acknowledged was rather limited. In addition to rivalry with other shaikhs of notable tribes in the peninsula, such as the Al Musallam of Huwaila on the north coast, the Al Thani had to struggle against claims to land and people made by more distant leaders, including shaikhs of Abu Dhabi and the Al Sa'ud. The most significant threat to their position came from the Al Khalifa shaikhs of Bahrain, however, who maintained a claim to authority over much of the Qatar Peninsula. The Al Thani sporadically had to send zakat to the shaikhs of Manama. It was indeed one of the periodic tests of strength between the Al Thani and Al Khalifa shaikhs that produced the violent raids and counterraids of 1867–68, the trigger for British intervention in choosing which member of the Al Khalifa should assume responsibility in Manama. At the same time the British Resident in the Gulf concluded an agreement with Shaikh Muhammad al-Thani, binding him to keep the maritime peace and regulating the payment of tribute to Bahrain. Although this step established direct relations with the Al Thani, Britain saw little need to involve itself any further in Qatari politics, regarding the Al Thani as subordinates of the Al Khalifa shaikhs and thus to be controlled, if necessary, through Manama.[13] Therefore the opening of contact with the British did not boost significantly the authority or security of the Doha shaikh.

In 1871 the arrival of the Ottoman expeditionary force in Hasa changed the status of Doha, and with it the standing of its shaikh. Using a member of the Kuwaiti Al Sabah family as an envoy, the Ottoman military commander made overtures to Shaikh Muhammad al-Thani. Muhammad, having seen how the British Gulf Resident dealt with shaikhs who went against his wishes, temporized. Not so his son, Qasim, who could see the advantages in gaining recognition from a great power. Qasim requested aid from the commander of the Ottoman expedition, and the general duly sent Qasim four Ottoman flags with which to mark the establishment of the sultan's sovereignty over Qatari territory—with Qasim appointed to embody it as the representative of the ruler. Midhat Pasha himself confirmed the appointment by issuing a decree naming Qasim the governor (*kaymakam*) of the new district (kaza) of Qatar.[14]

Qasim gained by this in several ways. With Shaikh Muhammad still alive and Qasim's succession to the shaikhdom unsecured, having the region's new overlord grant official recognition of his legitimacy as an administrator was a good step toward succeeding his father. Whoever became shaikh, after all, would have to have diplomatic skill to manage relations with a powerful new neighbor and overlord. Once a garrison of Ottoman troops arrived in Doha, the wisdom of accepting Istanbul's protégé as shaikh became self-evident. Adding further weight to Qasim's case for the succession was the added strength the Ottoman tie gave him to organize resistance to territorial claims advanced by Bahrain, centered on Zubara on the northwest coast, and by Abu Dhabi, focusing on Udaid to the southeast. Qasim immediately sent one of the four Ottoman flags to Udaid, whose shaikh was pleased to fly it whenever visited, or threatened, by outsiders. Qasim also tried to persuade the Ottomans to back him in an attempt to refuse the zakat payment to Bahrain agreed with the British in 1868.

The Ottoman tie fulfilled Qasim's expectations, at least in its early stages. He duly succeeded his father as shaikh and held the position with relative ease until his death in 1913, in spite of a late effort by his brother, Ahmad, to displace him in 1905. By that time there were clear signs of lasting estrangement between Qasim and the sultan's government. Ahmad tried to take advantage of this circumstance. In the same way as Qasim had done in 1871, Ahmad sought a public sign of Ottoman backing as he maneuvered against his brother, hoping to be named kaymakam, but his death by assassination brought his efforts to a dismal end.[15] The Ottoman presence undoubtedly helped to disentangle the knots binding Qatar to Bahrain, because Britain had no wish to have to discuss Gulf policies and protocols with Istanbul, including the difficult issue of agreeing on the limits of Ottoman sovereignty. Qasim also used the cover offered by Istanbul's backing to expel Indian traders from Doha in the 1880s, taking over their part of the pearl trade to boost his own resources. The Ottoman flag was less effective in his struggles to hold Udaid, however, since the British felt little need to restrain the shaikh of Abu Dhabi in his rivalry with a man who used the Ottoman flag to ward off British pressure.[16] Qasim's resentment over the lack of active support from Ottoman forces in the Udaid question was one of the reasons for his eventual alienation from his suzerain.

Qasim's other great source of frustration with allegiance to Istanbul was the gradual growth of Ottoman interference in his affairs, particularly in revenue collection. When Midhat Pasha established the administrative arrangements for eastern Arabia, he mandated no salary for the kaymakam, because Qatar was not expected to remit any revenue. Midhat had made a similar disposition for Kuwait, as we shall see. Unlike in the case of Kuwait, however, Midhat's successors did not abide by his decision. With the permanent stationing of troops in Doha, which entailed a significant expense in spite of the garrison's modest size, the Ottoman authorities became ever more determined that Qasim should help the hard-pressed provincial treasury. Pearls were the great untapped resource for the Ottoman administration in the Gulf, and until such time as they were able to displace the British as protectors in Bahrain, Qatar was their only possible source of significant income from the trade. Qasim's growing position in pearling following the expulsion of the Indians only heightened Ottoman interest. Istanbul paid Qasim a stipend of dates, but this hardly reconciled him to parting with more cash in return.

Tensions built over the 1880s as Qasim balked at paying demanded tax arrears, while the Ottoman authorities heard complaints from Qataris about Qasim's increasingly high-handed ways and reports that he was in touch with the British.

Armed confrontation broke out in 1893. The vali of Basra sailed to Doha with reinforcements for the garrison; evidently he wished to settle all disputes with Qasim, by parley if possible, by force if not. Qasim stayed away from Doha and refused to meet the vali. A column of Ottoman troops ventured into the interior to try to flush Qasim out, but the force was attacked by Qasim's Bedouin supporters and routed.[17]

The results of the clash demonstrated the degree of change in the position of the shaikh of Doha. In 1868 Muhammad al-Thani had been forced by Britain to acknowledge allegiance to Bahrain and to pay an indemnity for damage caused during a reprisal raid on Manama. His very cautious attitude in 1871 when the Ottomans occupied Hasa was the hardheaded result of previous experience: a misstep could bring calamitous retribution. His son Qasim, by contrast, attacked the forces of his great power suzerain. The fact that he won made his action that much more serious, since it could not have any but a weakening effect upon Ottoman standing throughout the Gulf. Yet Qasim survived, unpunished. Here was the clearest lesson ever given to coastal shaikhs: the high levels of suspicion dogging Anglo-Ottoman relations in the Gulf gave tremendous maneuvering room for politically astute leaders. Qasim survived unmolested because he convinced the Ottomans that he was loyal to the sultan, "proving" this by telling the authorities that Britain had offered him protection, which he refused out of his devotion to Istanbul. The government faced a tough choice, if it tried to remove him: fail to accomplish it quickly, and Qasim would turn to Britain for aid, or deal with him without warning, which would dissuade every shaikh in the Gulf from trusting the Ottomans enough to assist in efforts to keep Britain at bay. Istanbul chose to overlook the revolt.

When Qasim died a peaceful death in 1913, he left behind a relatively stable shaikhdom. His son Abd-Allah was recognized as his successor, clearly the most powerful man on the Qatar Peninsula (in spite of residual intrafamily rivalries). With the departure of the remaining Ottoman garrison the same year, Qatar was ready to enter treaty relations with Britain—not as an equal, perhaps, but at least on the same autonomous footing as the erstwhile dominant shaikh of Bahrain, and Qasim's dangerous rival, the shaikh of Abu Dhabi. The means Qasim used to build his authority would be studied, and used, by other leaders.

Kuwait

In comparison with the Al Thani shaikhs before 1870, the Al Sabah in Kuwait enjoyed clearer authority within the community and rather more influence among tribes of surrounding areas. As a family, moreover, they usually suffered less than the Al Thani from internal rivalries. Various reasons have been suggested for this deeper solidity of status: Kuwait's greater age as a community, larger size, and more advanced economy that combined pearling and fishing with entrepôt trade.[18] Kuwait's trade network extended much further than Doha's, both overseas around the Indian Ocean and Red Sea, and overland in Arabia and Iraq. The complicated nature of the economy made recognition of a capable leader necessary, to maintain favorable relations with tribes of the hinterland and to mediate disputes among the sizable population. Kuwait's proximity to the sometime Ottoman administrative center of Basra also doubtless gave the diplomatic skills of the Al Sabah shaikhs even greater value. In spite of several Ottoman suggestions in the 1860s that a customs house should be established in Kuwait, in order to close a very significant hole in the state's customs regime, the Al Sabah managed to dissuade the authorities from pursuing the matter.[19]

Although the Al Sabah enjoyed a higher status than did the Al Thani, the shaikhs of Kuwait also had real limits to their power to "rule." Wealthy merchant families carried great influence in the community. Maintaining the well-being of the settlement and its economy was an expensive business, and the shaikhs had limited sources of income. Perhaps their most valuable assets were date groves on the Faw peninsula near Basra. The groves' location in Ottoman territory was another source of weakness, since it marked a serious vulnerability to pressure from Kuwait's powerful neighbor. The authority of the shaikh thus was relatively fragile, in spite of the veneer of stability.

Midhat Pasha recognized both the strengths and vulnerabilities of the Al Sabah position. He used the latter in order to gain the former for his own political purposes. Already having in mind the need to bolster the empire's control over its southern borders, in 1870 he ordered that the revenues from the Faw lands be withheld from the shaikh, Abd-Allah al-Sabah. Members of the Al Sabah and perhaps other notable families met with Midhat in Basra, to learn what must be done to resume the revenue flow, and with it the network of relationships under Abd-Allah's care. Midhat proposed an arrangement that in all likelihood was similar to the one initially agreed with Qasim al-Thani: the Ottoman flag would fly over Kuwait and on Kuwaiti ships, and the shaikh would uphold all Ottoman rights in the region under his influence. Abd-Allah was appointed kaymakam, but no other Ottoman officials or soldiers were to reside there, and Kuwaitis were otherwise effectively exempted from the normal rules and requirements of Ottoman law. No salary was to be paid to the kaymakam, but no taxes were to be collected for the state, a point of particular concern for the Kuwaiti delegation. All resolution of disputes was left to the shaikh and the Shafi'i *qadi* of the port.[20] Midhat justified this grant of unusual autonomy by noting of the Kuwaiti community, "the incidence of complaints and disputes that would involve the government is rare, the inhabitants really all being like members of a family."[21]

Both sides kept this bargain until the end of the nineteenth century. The only alteration was the addition of a stipend paid from Basra beginning in 1872. Abd-Allah died in 1892, but the relationship continued under his successor as shaikh and kaymakam, his brother Muhammad. Another brother, Mubarak, led Kuwaiti land forces participating in Ottoman military expeditions in 1871, 1878, and 1892–93. For its part, Istanbul resisted occasional suggestions from officials in Basra that closer control over Kuwait would be very beneficial, particularly in curtailing the arms smuggling carried on through the port. The Ottoman status of Kuwait was sufficiently clear to Britain, as well, so that its shaikhs were spared from demands for compensation on the rare occasions when Indian shipping suffered attack near the shaikhs' domains. The status of the Al Sabah shaikhs in the 1890s was much as it had been in 1870.

Mubarak al-Sabah's assassination of Muhammad, and Muhammad's brother and confidant Jarrah, in 1896 and assumption of the title of shaikh seemed to offer little more than a momentary threat to Kuwait's tranquillity and the stability of the Kuwait-Ottoman relationship. Mubarak offered repeated assurances of loyalty to the sultan and requested appointment as the new kaymakam. He might have secured the appointment, were it not for the recent events in Qatar. The Ottoman general commanding forces in Iraq pointed out that the murders were nothing more than the usual order of business among tribesmen in Arabia, that would prove far too costly to try to check—echoing the rationale behind Britain's reluctance to be drawn into the domestic politics of most Arabian communities. The fact that there appeared to be no other suitable member of the Al Sabah alive who could displace Mubarak also was an important consideration, since Istanbul could not countenance so rash a move as pushing aside the Al Sabah, thus breaking all established practice in Arabia.[22]

The general's arguments almost carried the day, but his reference to the impossibility of policing routine tribal violence must have reawakened memories of the Qatar disaster. Qasim and his tribal supporters had escaped punishment for their humiliation of the government, and the Ottoman reputation had suffered lasting damage throughout Arabia. Could Istanbul allow the murder of its lawfully appointed kaymakam to go unpunished without bringing its authority in the entire region to the brink of collapse? Again echoing British imperial thinking, Istanbul recognized the need to support the authority of shaikhs with whom it established formal arrangements. And in a further repetition of considerations familiar from the Qatar episode, Istanbul also felt hamstrung by deep suspicion of some kind of British involvement in the affair. Heirs and supporters of the murdered men clad their calls for retribution in shrouds of cloak-and-dagger mystery, claiming that Muhammad and his brother had been killed because they refused to join a secret "Arab confederation" that included Qasim al-Thani and Isa al-Khalifa and had as its goal the delivery of Arabia into British hands. If Qasim showed that the Ottomans could be kept at bay by letting drop the name "Britain," those interested in gaining Istanbul's help quite reasonably hoped to spur the government to action by whispering the same word.[23]

Unfortunately for them, Mubarak proved to be the undisputed master of the tactic. The Al Sabah had never produced a better example of the family talent for diplomacy. To every insinuation of British plots put forward by his opponents, he countered with claims of Britain's support for the anti-Mubarak camp's effective head, Yusuf al-Ibrahim, a member of a leading merchant family. That Yusuf's wealth derived in part from trade with India, where his family had members residing as their agents, gave Istanbul grounds for taking Mubarak's charges seriously. Mubarak seems seriously to have wanted the relationship with the Ottoman administration to continue unchanged, recognizing both the advantages the kaymakam position could confer, as well as the vulnerabilities to Ottoman pressure that had not changed since 1870. He made overtures to the British Gulf Resident only when Istanbul indicated that the relationship could not immediately resume its former track without the charges of British involvement being fully laid to rest. Mubarak's first message to Britain's Gulf Resident in 1897 came in response to the temporary posting of an Ottoman quarantine inspector to Kuwait harbor, a move that probably served a legitimate purpose, as the European-advised Quarantine Board in Istanbul was pushing for strong measures to control a plague outbreak in India and the Gulf. Mubarak nevertheless feared, probably with reason, that the inspector also would report on whatever happened in the town, particularly if a British ship were to make a port call.

Britain had no interest in becoming involved in the Kuwait dispute due to the diplomatic problems with Istanbul that must ensue, but it did keep the area of Kuwait under observation. If Mubarak and his enemies tried to resolve their dispute by arms, then Indian shipping to the nearby Shatt al-Arab could be at risk. When Yusuf al-Ibrahim did resort to a sea attack on Kuwait, Istanbul reacted quickly, in part due to awareness of British sensitivities concerning maritime warfare. To quiet the troublesome area, the Ottoman government finally appointed Mubarak as kaymakam at the end of 1897.[24]

All interesting events might have ended there, with yet another Al Sabah shaikh continuing unaltered the thirty-year relationship with Ottoman authority, had imperial rivalries not again opened up opportunities for the ambitious shaikh to increase his powers. Rumors of Russian, and subsequently German, schemes to build a railway to the Gulf made Britain reconsider promptly its hands-off attitude toward Kuwait. The Gulf Resident, Colonel M. J. Meade, visited Mubarak in January 1899 to negotiate a non-alienation of territory bond, under which Mubarak essentially agreed to keep

Kuwait closed to foreign nationals and governments, in return for 15,000 rupees and a promise of Britain's "good offices." This last issue was the only object of serious negotiation, since Mubarak wanted British help primarily to safeguard his properties at Faw. The most Meade could offer, however, was this rather vague, cautious promise—which Mubarak was later able to use to push Britain to defend all of his interests from Ottoman pressure.[25]

Mubarak played the British and Ottoman empires off each other most effectively. Whenever Ottoman officials asked him to show his loyalty to the sultan, he declined to give more than such assurances as would preserve his autonomy of action, warning them if they continued to push that Britain had offered him protection. He claimed he had refused the offers out of loyalty, but if he were pressed too hard, he would have no choice but to accept. Whenever he faced such visits from Ottoman representatives, or suffered setbacks in his ventures in Arabia, he declared in turn to his British contacts that he would have to accept Ottoman protection, if British forces did not demonstrate largely symbolic but unmistakable support for his authority. Such demonstrations, of course, only made more credible to Istanbul Mubarak's assertions that the British were pressing him to accept their protection. He hardly lived up to the letter of the 1899 bond, since he received delegations from not only the Ottomans (and if they were not foreigners, then how could Kaymakam Mubarak conclude an agreement with Britain?) but also from the Russians and the Germans. To each he expressed his inclination to their state and his wish to have their help in fending off pressures from troublesome powers—British, Ottoman, French, or Persian, as the circumstances dictated. The result was effective and obvious British protection and a lack of Ottoman pressure for meaningful change in Mubarak's behavior.[26]

Mubarak used his unusual freedom of action to build his authority in Kuwait and his influence in Arabia. His first goal was to settle a growing dispute with Ibn Rashid, the amir of Ha'il in Najd. The conflict seems to have developed from competition for the collection of zakat from tribes of the interior, although other issues, such as Mubarak's purported responsibility for an attack on a Ha'il caravan a few years previously, also were involved. Estrangement between the two was deepened by Ibn Rashid's taking up the cause of Muhammad and Jarrah al-Sabah's heirs, while Mubarak openly supported Ibn Sa'ud, who had sheltered in Kuwait during the years when Ibn Rashid held Riyadh. Ibn Rashid eventually dealt Mubarak's men a military defeat in the Arabian interior, but thereafter the shaikh of Kuwait continued to support the Sa'udi cause in other ways. If Mubarak could not control Najd himself, he at least hoped to play the kingmaker. His control over trade routes into the interior free from Ottoman supervision, and particularly his role in the arms trade, gave him at this tense time continued influence in Najd greater than any previously exercised by the Al Sabah shaikhs.

Mubarak's ambitious schemes for extending his power in the interior depended on his ability to raise revenues. The shaikh continued to receive income from Faw, as well as a modest, sporadic subsidy from the Ottoman treasury in Basra. He petitioned the British for a more substantial subsidy, but received none until 1907. Whereas Qasim al-Thani had used the Ottoman flag to cover his displacement of Indian competitors in Qatar's pearl trade, Mubarak had neither the great-power backing in his first years as shaikh nor such an obvious wealthy alien group to target. Once he had British support on which to rely to quell opposition, however, he started to raise taxes, such as customs charges, and introduce new levies. The most controversial of these was a tax on pilgrims performing the hajj. Extortionate property and excise taxes also aroused opposition, culminating in the temporary emigration of several leading pearl merchants. Although Mubarak relaxed some of the harshest of his new taxes in order to persuade them to return, he nevertheless had created the rudiments of a state revenue system. His expansion of the previously simple tax regime caused him to enlarge his administrative staff, marking the beginnings of a bureaucracy.[27] With these developments, the balance of influence between the shaikh and the wealthy merchants gradually shifted in Mubarak's favor.

The seal of Mubarak's success in developing his own power, as well as the status of Kuwait in Arabian politics and international affairs, came in 1913 in the form of an Anglo-Ottoman convention. The result of several years of negotiations, the accord settled a variety of outstanding issues between the two countries concerning Gulf affairs. Its importance for Kuwait lay in its definition of Mubarak's domain as "an autonomous kaza of the Ottoman Empire" and in setting boundaries for this territory. Although the convention recognized that Kuwait was under some form of the sultan's sovereignty or suzerainty, it also stated explicitly that it was a territorial unit distinct from surrounding territories, and that its shaikh had the ability and right to manage the affairs of the community. In the treatment given it in the accord, Kuwait gained recognition of development as a proto-state beyond the level achieved by any other shaikhdom in Ottoman Arabia. The convention marking this progress was ratified by the Ottomans, but Britain had yet to approve it before the First World War erupted and made the agreement moot. It proved an enduring achievement nevertheless, as Kuwait remained autonomous after Britain established its control over neighboring formerly Ottoman territories following the war. The northern limit of the kaza described in the convention also became the model for the Kuwait-Iraq frontier to this day, in spite of all attempts to change it.[28]

Kuwait's status was the product of Shaikh Mubarak's diplomatic skills, just as the strengthened position of the shaikh of Doha-Qatar was Qasim al-Thani's significant achievement. The role of the Ottoman Empire in this process of turning weak shaikhs into powerful men must be remembered, however. Qasim used Ottoman support to secure his control over territory, and he discovered the real scope of political opportunity made possible by the Ottoman presence in the Gulf. The Ottomans acted as a major power compelling British attention toward parts of the Gulf previously ignored, were effective in separating Bahrain from mainland politics, and competed with the British for the allegiance of the shaikhs. It was the Ottoman foray into the Gulf that set up the Great Power rivalry that Mubarak and Qasim exploited so effectively.

SOCIAL CHANGE

So far little mention has been made of Ottoman influence on what is now Saudi Arabia, or of the empire's interaction with the Al Sa'ud. Nor has anything been said of social change at this time. This may seem rather strange, because Hasa was the part of eastern Arabia most clearly associated with direct Ottoman rule from 1871 to 1913. As in much of the rest of the territory once administered by the empire, however, the successor regime was pleased to be able to wipe away many traces of its predecessor's rule. Indirect influences may nevertheless be discovered in these areas.[29]

One effect of eastern Arabia's inclusion in the Ottoman Empire was a geographic broadening of its socioeconomic contacts. The trade networks of Kuwait, Hasa, and Qatar had long connected them with foreign lands, not only in the Gulf, notably with Iran, but also around the Indian Ocean, from Zanzibar in the west to India in the east. The Ottoman Empire, with its center of balance far to the north and west, extended the zone of active contact. Merchants and goods from the Balkans, Anatolia, and Russia spread through the Ottoman provinces during the nineteenth century, after the old Ottoman system of controlling the movement of merchandise and people fell apart. The opening naturally affected Iraq and Arabia. The projected extension of the Berlin-to-Baghdad railway to Basra is the best-known symbol of this linkage of the Gulf to a wider world to the north. The effects of the easing of north-south movement were likely to be seen most clearly in a place such as Kuwait, which offered an excellent port thriving on low-customs imports and exports. It has been termed the "Marseilles of the Gulf"[30] during this period because of the variety of people drawn by its economic vitality, which reached new peaks of activity during Mubarak's reign.

Inclusion in the Ottoman realm drew an assortment of traders and tradesmen to Hasa and Qatar, as well. In addition to merchants from Iraq who followed well-established trade routes to Hufuf, the Ottoman mission to Hasa also drew more unaccustomed figures to join local society. The military expedition in 1871, for example, reportedly drew camp-followers from Iraq, including a number of prostitutes and liquor salesmen.[31] Alcohol remained much more openly available than under Sa'udi rule before or after the Ottoman era. Jews from Iraq appear to have carried on the trade in alcohol, although there is no sign that they had to restrict their sales to only their own community, which was relatively small but robust.[32] Christians were fewer but not unknown, and probably also came from Iraq; Indian traders included both Hindus and Zoroastrians. The Muslim community also appears to have been quite multifaceted, including adherents of all Sunni *madhhab*s and Jafari Shi'is.[33]

It is likely that the majority of Muslims from distant parts of the Ottoman Empire who came to Hasa arrived in some official capacity. The most numerous of these were probably the large numbers of Kurds who served in the Arabian gendarmerie, the vital force in maintaining Ottoman control over a difficult region. Other officials, both military officers and civilian administrators, originated from all the disparate regions of the empire, including Anatolia and the Balkans. While the influx of people from distant lands may not have affected the Hasawi population to the degree seen in Kuwait, a few Ottoman officials did remain in position after the eviction of the empire's forces in 1913, leaving for a time some living memory of its presence.[34]

The last effect of the Ottoman Empire on the Gulf that remains to be mentioned is its role in the development of Sa'udi and Wahhabi practices and fortunes. Muhammad b. Abd al-Wahhab may have been motivated to speak out against the unorthodox practices of Muslims in the Arabian interior, but his ideas were part of the broader revulsion against the mysticism of the quite esoteric Sufi practices still dominant in the Ottoman lands in the eighteenth century. It was thus hardly accidental that the violent campaigns to eradicate unorthodox practices, motivated by Ibn Abd al-Wahhab's message and prosecuted by the family of his ally, Muhammad b. Sa'ud, should eventually have been carried into the heart of the Arab provinces of the Ottoman empire. In the Hijaz, Syria, and Iraq, the Sa'udi-Wahhabi raids targeted particularly shrines and tombs that were objects of popular veneration (and one of the changes in Hasa created by the Ottoman conquest in 1871 was the lifting of the Sa'udi ban on cemeteries).[35] The violence inflicted, and the strong public reaction against it, ensured a vigorous response, even at a time when the empire's survival seemed at risk from the combined pressures of foreign wars against Europe and internal chaos stirred by local notables and rapacious officials. The most effective Ottoman efforts against Sa'udi power were the extended campaigns launched by Muhammad Ali, the Ottoman vali of Egypt, in 1810 and 1837. They succeeded in destroying Sa'udi power, at least for a time.

Abd al-Aziz al-Sa'ud learned from the political mistakes committed by his uncompromising predecessors. Given his maturation to adulthood in Kuwait, he also benefited from close observation of Shaikh Mubarak's methods of handling the Anglo-Ottoman rivalry. Like his tutor, Ibn Sa'ud used effectively the tactic of sweet diplomacy with both powers, biding his time with Istanbul until he saw the opportunity to expel the forlorn remains of the Ottoman garrisons in eastern Arabia. As Mubarak did, he immediately made overtures to Istanbul to make good the damage done by his violent action. He was able to negotiate his own appointment as vali of Necd (Najd) before the First World War put an end to Ottoman aspirations in the region. When that happened, however, he was already on good terms with British India, due to his assiduous courting of favor at the same time as his negotiations with the Ottomans. The efficacy of his diplomacy could be seen during the war, when he entertained bids from both powers for his active support, yet used none of his resources to aid either of them, concentrating instead on destroying his rivals in Ha'il, the Al Rashid. In practicing this more diplomatic style of politics, Abd al-Aziz was able to create a state that has proven to be more durable than those established by his predecessors.[36]

CONCLUSION

Far from leaving little mark on the modern Gulf, as implied by some previous historians, Ottoman control over eastern Arabia opened the way to the practical establishment of the modern territorial states of Saudi Arabia, Kuwait, Qatar, and Bahrain. By 1914 the present ruling families had achieved practical autonomy, if not outright independence, in the eyes of neighboring powers and, by extension, the international community. The territorial limits of the rulers' authority had also been established in practice, even though the formal agreement of borders was still incomplete.[37] These lasting achievements resulted from Ottoman state policies and from the initiative shown by local leaders in their relations with Ottoman authorities.

Lack of proper consideration of the Arabian shaikhs' political skill is one of the faults to be found in the common assumption that Britain determined the development of Gulf politics, economy, and society in much of the nineteenth and twentieth centuries. Given the tactics of ingratiating words to all ears chosen by notables such as Qasim al-Thani, Mubarak al-Sabah, and Abd al-Aziz al-Sa'ud, the British records give a misleading impression of weak, squabbling leaders in Arabia who could do little more than wait for rescue by a decisive outside power. Comparison of the British with the Ottoman records reveals that, far from being helpless incompetents, these leaders were remarkably astute politicians. They realized the opportunities opened up by great power rivalry in the region, and through it they were able to harness the strength of each to the interests of the weakest parties.

The conditions that rewarded their initiatives with success resulted from Ottoman concerns about European schemes to dominate the region, and from the policies adopted by Istanbul to counter the perceived British threat. Istanbul's attempts to ward off the creep of British influence toward Iraq ultimately failed; in this sense, the old tendency to view the Ottoman era in the Gulf as a period of futility cannot be dismissed blithely. How should Britain's ultimate victory in the imperial competition for influence in the Gulf be seen? Beyond consideration of the different resources available to the empires, it is important to keep in mind the variant strategies pursued by them, and the peculiar challenges posed by Gulf geography.

While populations around the Gulf have long shared common cultural characteristics, the region has no natural political focal point. Mountains in Iran and desert in Arabia separate the few good ports from productive hinterlands and populations large enough to make military and political dominance feasible. The only possible means of exerting even limited control over the Gulf would be clear domination of the shipping channels, the only practicable communications network tying the region together in the pre-jet-engine age. This was precisely the goal that the governments of British India and London consciously decided to focus upon, using India as the only viable base to support the necessary naval forces. They also secured ready access to some of the most important ports in the Gulf (Manama in Bahrain and Bushehr in Iran) to support naval operations, and they effectively barred rival powers from using others, notably Kuwait. With control over shipping lanes established at a sustainable cost (and the British rightly made little effort to patrol closely the broad area of shallow waters off much of the Arabian coast), they were assured of political importance in the communities along the shores of the Gulf. Groups beyond the range of naval guns and relatively less dependent upon the sea for their livelihood, however, remained outside the sphere of British influence. The strategy of the British Empire in the Gulf thus was limited, but sound and sustainable in this period.

In contrast to Britain's approach to the political-security challenges posed by the Gulf region, the Ottoman Empire adopted a strategy that proved much more difficult to sustain. Moving into the region from Basra only after Britain had already established its dominance over much of the Gulf's shipping routes, Istanbul chose—or was forced—to try to build its authority by using control over land to project power over water. This proved impossible to do at sustainable cost. Hasa lacked good ports with a hinterland productive enough to support the naval forces needed to maintain an effective presence in the relatively distant important shipping lanes of the Gulf. The task was only made more difficult by the added requirements of trying to limit security threats from the vast, almost impenetrable expanse of the Arabian interior, a challenge that Britain wholly avoided until the post-1918 period. When Britain did take a more active part in the political affairs of the Arabian Gulf coast with the rise of the oil industry there, it too found it difficult to defend against Sa'udi pressure on the coastal shaikhdoms.[38]

Unable to support the effort needed to maintain its status in the Gulf, Istanbul saw its hold over eastern Arabia broken by the Sa'udi-Wahhabi assault from Najd. While the new Sa'udi regime altered some of the characteristics of Hasawi social and religious life seen in the Ottoman period, it proved unable to roll back the political advances made in the 1870–1913 period. The Ottoman Empire had maintained an effective presence in the Gulf long enough to trigger enduring changes, especially in Kuwait and Qatar, but also in Bahrain and Saudi Arabia. Most obviously, the coastal shaikhs could not have achieved the strengthening of power and position that they achieved before the First World War, had the Ottoman border remained near Basra. The political history of the Arabian coast in the twentieth century thus is the main Ottoman legacy to the Gulf today.

NOTES

1. The magisterial study by John B. Kelly, *Britain and the Persian Gulf, 1795–1880* (Oxford: Clarendon Press, 1968), springs most readily to mind. Briton Busch's standard-setting work for the period following that covered by Kelly, *Britain and the Persian Gulf, 1894–1914* (Berkeley: University of California Press, 1967), is less ready to treat the Ottomans as inert or irrelevant figures in Arabia, but it too is distinctly Anglo-centric in its analysis. Several recent socioeconomic studies of Iraq and the Gulf in the Ottoman period have escaped the Anglo-centrism of the mainstream histories: Hala Fattah, *The Politics of Regional Trade in Iraq, Arabia, and the Gulf, 1745–1900* (Albany: State University of New York Press, 1997), and Thabit Abdullah, *Merchants, Mamluks, and Murder: The Political Economy of Trade in Eighteenth-Century Basra* (Albany: State University of New York Press, 2001). For a detailed study that draws upon Ottoman sources, see Frederick Anscombe, *The Ottoman Gulf: The Creation of Kuwait, Saudi Arabia, and Qatar* (New York: Columbia University Press, 1997).
2. For the first Ottoman period in eastern Arabia, see Jon Mandaville, "The Ottoman Province of al-Hasa in the Sixteenth and Seventeenth Centuries," *Journal of the American Oriental Society* 90 (1970): 486–513.

3. The governor of Egypt, Mehmed Ali (or Muhammad Ali) Pasha, was the only officer to reestablish Ottoman authority over the area in the intervening two hundred years, when forces commanded by his sons reached the Gulf during successful campaigns to destroy the Sa'udi-Wahhabi state in the early nineteenth century.
4. Basbakanlik Osmanli Arsivi, Istanbul (BA), Irade Dahiliye 44930, 3 January 1872 contains a collection of four lengthy reports to Istanbul in which Midhat Pasha detailed the conditions then found in eastern Arabia and the arrangements he made for its future administration. The importance of these documents has been recognized by Yusuf Halacoglu, who has transliterated them into modern Turkish lettering in "Midhat Pasa'nin Necid ve havalisi ile ilgili bir kac layihasi," *IUEF Tarih Enstitusu Dergisi* 3 (1972): 149–76.
5. The Ottomans may be said nevertheless to have applied their modernized administrative practices only where they felt it to be necessary. On this subject see Frederick Anscombe, "Continuities in Ottoman Centre-Periphery Relations, 1787–1915", in *The Frontiers of the Ottoman World,* ed. Andrew Peacock (Oxford: Oxford University Press, 2009).
6. For fuller details of Ottoman concerns and the events in eastern Arabia during this period, see Anscombe, *Ottoman Gulf,* especially 74–85 and chap. 7.
7. For the best descriptions of the position and powers of a shaikh, see Peter Lienhardt, "The Authority of Shaikhs in the Gulf: An Essay in Nineteenth-Century History," *Arabian Studies* 2 (1975): 61–75, and James Onley and Sulayman Khalaf, "Shaikhly Authority in the Pre-oil Gulf: An Historical-Anthropological Study," *History and Anthropology* 17, no. 3 (2006): 189–208. See also Peter Lienhardt, *Shaikhdoms of Eastern Arabia,* ed. Ahmed Al-Shahi (Basingstoke: Palgrave, 2001), especially chaps. 1, 5, and 6.
8. On the Trucial Coast see the works by Lienhardt cited above. For Bahrain, see Talal Farah, *Protection and Politics in Bahrain, 1869–1915* (Beirut, Lebanon: American University of Beirut, 1985).
9. Full details of the story can be found in John G. Lorimer, *Gazetteer of the Persian Gulf, Oman and Central Arabia,* vol. 1: *Historical* (Calcutta, India: Superintendent Government Printing, 1915), 982–89.
10. Foreign Secretary of India Aitchison, cited in J. A. Saldana, *Précis of Turkish Expansion on the Arab Littoral of the Persian Gulf and Hasa and Qatif Affairs* (Calcutta, India: Government of India, 1906), 15.
11. Amir Abd-Allah al-Sa'ud, for example, tried to claim "treaty relations" with Britain during a dispute with the Sultan of Oman in 1866. Kelly, *Britain and the Persian Gulf,* 654–55.
12. See Jill Crystal, *Oil and Politics in the Gulf: Rulers and Merchants in Kuwait and Qatar* (Cambridge: Cambridge University Press, 1995), chap. 1, and Lienhardt, *Shaikhdoms,* chap. 5.
13. For a summary of this early Al Thani history, see Crystal, *Oil and Politics,* 26–30. For a more detailed account, see Kelly, *Britain and the Persian Gulf,* 672–85.
14. Anscombe, *Ottoman Gulf,* 31–33.
15. Ibid., 147–48.
16. Kelly, *Britain and the Persian Gulf,* 755–56.
17. BA, Yildiz Esas Evraki 14/250/126/8, 22 September 1893 is a substantial report on the Qatar problem and the Ottoman position in the Gulf, prepared by Ottoman officers sent on an inspection tour. For these events see also Anscombe, *Ottoman Gulf,* 85–90.
18. Crystal, *Oil and Politics,* 33–34. See also Salwa Alghanim, *The Reign of Mubarak al-Sabah, Shaikh of Kuwait 1896–1915* (London: I. B. Tauris, 1998), 5–31.
19. Anscombe, *Ottoman Gulf,* 21.
20. For a translation of Midhat's report of this meeting (BA, Usul-i Irade Dosya 77, Baghdad Governor to Grand Vezir, 9 February 1870), see Frederick Anscombe, "An Official Report on Efforts to Re-Establish Ottoman Control over Kuwait, 1870" in *The Modern Middle East: A Sourcebook,* ed. Camron Amin, Benjamin Fortna, and Elizabeth Frierson (New York: Oxford University Press, 2005). A slightly abbreviated version of the document and a translation of Midhat's report on his subsequent visit to Kuwait in 1871 (BA, Irade Dahiliye 44930, enclosure 2) appear in Frederick Anscombe, "The Ottoman Empire in Recent International Politics—I: The Case of Kuwait", *The International History Review* 28,

no. 3 (September 2006): 537–59, an article that examines in detail the peculiarities of Kuwait's status among Ottoman lands, the crux of the disputed claim that Kuwait has been historically a part of Iraq.

21. BA, Irade Dahiliye 44930, enclosure 2.
22. Anscombe, *Ottoman Gulf*, chap. 5; Alghanim, *Mubarak*, 31–38.
23. For the frenetic political maneuvering concerning the possibility of punishing Mubarak, see Anscombe, *Ottoman Gulf*, especially 94–99.
24. BA, Bab-i Ali Evrak Odasi Giden-Gelen 78415, 1 December 1897.
25. Busch, *Britain and the Persian Gulf, 1894–1914*, 105–12.
26. Anscombe, *Ottoman Gulf*, chap. 6. On Mubarak's appeals to Russia, see Efim Rezvan, *Russian Ships in the Gulf, 1899–1903* (Reading, UK: Ithaca Press, 1993), 7–8 and Grigori Bondarevsky, "Mubarak's Kuwait in Russian and German Policy" in *Kuwait: The Growth of a Historic Identity*, ed. Ben J. Slot (London: Arabian Publishing, 2004), 49–57. On Mubarak's warm welcome to a German delegation, see Jens Plass, *England zwischen Russland und Deutschland: der Persische Golf in der Britischen Vorkriegspolitik, 1899–1907* (Hamburg, Germany: Institut für Auswärtige Politik, 1966), 266–67.
27. Crystal, *Oil and Politics*, 25. On taxes, see Alghanim, *Mubarak*, 135–41.
28. David Finnie, *Shifting Lines in the Sand: Kuwait's Elusive Frontier with Iraq* (Cambridge: Harvard University Press, 1992), 32–38.
29. For an account of the variegations seen in eastern Arabian society in the Ottoman period, see Frederick Anscombe, "An Anational Society: Eastern Arabia in the Ottoman Period," in *Transnational Connections and the Arab Gulf*, ed. Madawi Al-Rasheed (London: Routledge, 2005), 21–38.
30. Jacob Goldberg, *The Foreign Policy of Saudi Arabia: The Formative Years, 1902–1918* (Cambridge: Harvard University Press, 1986), 31.
31. Saldana, *Turkish Expansion*, 46. For an insight into the legal grounds for the Hanafi Ottoman government's relatively relaxed attitude toward some issues involving alcohol, see Ralph Hattox, *Coffee and Coffeehouses: The Origins of a Social Beverage in the Medieval Near East* (Seattle: University of Washington Press, 1985), 46–57.
32. BA, Sura-yi Devlet 2184/6 is a collection of documents related to an investigation of possible malfeasance by the governor of Hasa, Said Pasha, in 1901. Its hundreds of pages contain references to events involving the local Jewish community.
33. On the religious nature of the population in eastern Arabia, see Anscombe, "An Anational Society," 23–26.
34. Ibid., 21–38.
35. For an example of the practice of veneration and its critics in Ottoman Egypt, see Rudolph Peters, "The Battered Dervishes of Bab Zuwayla," in *Eighteenth-Century Renewal and Revival in Islam,* ed. Nehemia Levtzion and John Voll (Syracuse, NY: Syracuse University Press, 1987), 93–115. For Ibn Abd al-Wahhab's ideas on religious reform, including strictures against any semblance of graveside worship, and the particular dislike of Ottoman religious practice evinced by him and later Wahhabis, see David Commins, *The Wahhabi Mission and Saudi Arabia* (London: I. B. Tauris, 2006), chaps. 1–2.
36. The best analysis of Ibn Sa'ud's political acumen is in Goldberg, *Foreign Policy.*
37. The most significant later alteration of territorial limits came in 1922, when British negotiators awarded to Saudi Arabia some of the land south of Kuwait that had been recognized as under Shaikh Mubarak's influence in the 1913 Anglo-Ottoman convention. While other borders (e.g., Kuwait-Iraq, Qatar-Bahrain, Saudi Arabia-Qatar) have been subject to recurring dispute, they have stubbornly resisted revision.
38. For a recent, detailed study of Anglo-Sa'udi relations in the mid-twentieth century, see Shafi Aldamer, *Saudi Arabia and Britain: Changing Relations, 1939–1953* (Reading, UK: Ithaca Press, 2003).

Chapter 14

Britain and the Gulf: At the Periphery of Empire

J. E. Peterson

In 1876, Queen Victoria was acclaimed by durbar as Empress of India, and the dual designation of British monarch and empress/emperor was maintained by her successors until 1947. This illustration of the role of India as the jewel in the crown of the British Empire was reflected in British policy in and relations with the Gulf. For the three-and-a-half centuries before Indian independence, British activities in the Gulf were dictated largely by their relevance to India—whether those activities were concerned with commerce, diplomacy, imperial defense, or strategic position.

It was only after the Second World War that oil took center stage and, even then, British strategy in the Gulf seemed to be derived largely from broader, lingering, "East of Suez" concerns and a certain lethargy: Britain had responsibilities in the Gulf because it had always had them, or so it seemed. Not until 1968, when the Labour government announced Britain's official withdrawal from the Gulf, were these responsibilities abandoned. If, despite its predominant position during the nineteenth and first half of the twentieth centuries, Britain began its adventure in the Gulf in a minor, tentative way, it certainly left the Gulf in the same manner.[1] In between arrival and withdrawal, Britain based its position on its greatest strength:

> Command of the sea is the prerequisite of power in the Persian Gulf. Only twice since the decline of the Abbasid Caliphate has a single state succeeded in imposing a hegemony upon its waters, and in both instances the state concerned was a maritime power—the kingdom of Portugal in the sixteenth century and the empire of England in the nineteenth. . . . Whereas the Portuguese came to the Gulf as soldiers and conquerors, to impose their will upon the Gulf states, the English came initially as merchant adventurers, seeking trade and fortune. Two centuries were to elapse before the attainment of territorial dominion in India compelled them to obtain and hold command of the Gulf. By the second quarter of the nineteenth century their position there was unassailable, and from that time forward the guardianship of the Gulf rested in British hands.[2]

In very broad strokes, the canvas painted here is a triptych. The early period of British involvement in the Gulf—roughly the seventeenth and eighteenth centuries, before India came to the foreground—was characterized by the circumstances of British interests outweighing capabilities. The heyday of British influence, that is, the nineteenth and first half of the twentieth centuries, was the opposite: power often outweighed interests. After Indian independence, and particularly following official withdrawal, the situation returned to what it was previously: British interests in the Gulf were, and remain, considerably weightier than British power to advance those interests.

It should be noted that there were important differences between the two side panels of the triptych. In the earlier period, the Gulf was of only minor importance to Britain and British India, whereas in the last (and present) period it is of considerable importance. Nor are the entities and peoples of the Gulf the seemingly passive actors they were in the past. Furthermore, earlier Britain was able to make full use of its military and maritime powers to advance its policy goals and commercial interests. Since 1971, Britain has abandoned its role as security guardian for the Gulf and must base its commercial position solely on the quality of its services and products.

This chapter begins by categorizing the nature and types of British interests in the Gulf. For the most part, these are remarkably similar over the long run of three-and-a-half centuries. It then seeks to explain how Britain advanced and protected those interests, and how Indian interests in the Gulf were most often subordinated to broader interests of the empire as seen from London. The chapter ends with an evaluation of the impact of the British experience in the Gulf. Some would judge it to have been a success; others would decry British involvement as simply one more example of unjustified imperialism. But even as the specific events and motivations in the history of Britain's role in the Gulf inexorably fade, it cannot be denied that the impact on both Britain and the Gulf has been considerable and will remain so well into the future.

British Interests in the Gulf

The principal impetus for initial British entry into the Gulf was a combination of a search for markets and an effort to deny European rivals supremacy in the region. Indeed, trade was the reason the English East India Company was founded in 1600, and, with English woolens difficult to sell in hot India, trading links were soon established with Iran and the first English factories in the Gulf were established at Shiraz, Isfahan, and Jask in 1617–18. A few years later, in 1622, after helping to expel the Portuguese from Hormuz, the English established their commercial headquarters at Bandar Abbas. Although Gulf trade remained modest, it was important in bolstering the East India Company's trading sheets, thus fending off the company's critics. By 1763, though, declining Persian trade and political turmoil forced the closure of the Bandar Abbas factory and the transfer of the political agency to Basra where a factory had existed since 1723.[3]

The action against the Portuguese and rivalry with the Dutch and the French illustrate the other motivation for British activity in the Gulf. Still, these seventeenth-century rivalries were of minor significance for British interests in the region. Portuguese power was fading in the first half of the seventeenth century even as British interest was increasing: although the Portuguese retrenched in Muscat after the fall of Hormuz, they were ousted from there by 1650. The low level of British interest in the Gulf meant that the emergent Dutch competition was not an important threat, and by the time Britain began to assert its dominance in India, European developments in the early eighteenth century had forced the Dutch challenge in the western Indian Ocean to subside.

Thus Britain's principal opponent in the conquest of India, just as it was in Europe, turned out to be France. Despite reverses, such as the French capture of Madras, Britain was able to demonstrate its mastery over France in India by the mid-eighteenth century. "[B]y 1765 Britain had become the dominant European power in India, and the East India

Company had transformed itself from a trading company into a territorial power with important possessions in Bengal. The metamorphosis of the company had repercussions on its Gulf operations."[4]

With trade in the Gulf reduced to virtually nothing and political interests absent (and expressly forbidden by the directors of the East India Company), why did the company not simply withdraw from the Gulf? First, the Bombay Marine, the naval force of the company (as well as being that of the Mughal Empire), had assumed responsibilities for protecting shipping of the India country trade (local trade) and these could not be easily abandoned. Second, it was necessary to protect the route for overland mail. Perhaps even more importantly, the French expedition to Egypt in 1798 revived the European threat to a British area of influence.

As Britain began to deepen its mastery of India in the eighteenth century, the Gulf emerged as a peripheral concern of India, rather than as a strategic concern of London. As a consequence, British policy regarding the Gulf up to the Second World War was primarily formulated and conducted by the Government of India and not Whitehall. More often than not, Indian aggressiveness in the Gulf was stymied by London, which saw the Gulf as possessing only minor importance and certainly not worth jeopardizing grander strategy in Europe. Still, the Gulf's role in Indian foreign policy was not entirely negligible.

Imperial Frontiers

In the first place, the Gulf represented one of India's imperial frontiers. It is in the nature of such frontiers to be inherently expansionist. Perceived threats to the British position in India were seen as emanating from various quarters, with one of the principal ones being the direction of the Gulf. If the Gulf was one of India's outer frontiers, it followed that the Gulf must be kept under British influence and control. European challenges to the British position in the Gulf constituted potential threats to India, either because they threatened British predominance in the Gulf or because they were seen as possible encroachments on India itself. As India established itself in and around the Gulf with factories, political representatives, and military outposts, it found it necessary to defend those elements, and that, in turn, deepened the concomitant commitment.

Another source of commitment came with the rooting of British and indigenous Indian commerce in the region. Commercial interests and resident subjects and property had to be protected. This was a primary factor in the campaign waged against "Arab piracy" in the first two decades of the nineteenth century, and it also explained British hostility to shifts in political power in Muscat in 1868–71 and 1895.

Lines of Communication

The second significant role of the Gulf in Indian imperial policy was its importance in providing lines of communication between India and Britain. The particular nature of these communications has changed over time. Perhaps the earliest was that of mail. Originally, dispatches were sent aboard the East Indiamen ships making their way from England to India via the Cape of Good Hope, but the length of the route meant that replies to messages often took two years to be received. Although the Gulf had been used intermittently for the transmission of posts, a more usual route was across Egypt and down the Red Sea. But difficulties in dealing with the Ottoman authorities made this route intermittently problematic and Napoleon's invasion of Egypt exacerbated the situation. By the mid-eighteenth century, the route through Basra, Baghdad, and Syria had become well established and resulted in Basra becoming the East India Company's headquarters in the Gulf. However, the main route was shifted back to the Red Sea in 1833, and its primacy was aided by the acquisition of Aden in 1839, the construction of the Alexandria-to-Suez railroad in 1858, and completion of the Suez Canal in 1869. Reliable mail communications with the Gulf were restored only with the introduction of a Bombay-to-Basra steamer mail service in 1862.[5]

Another advance was the use of steam navigation to speed imperial communications, with interest expressed during the 1830s in the development of a route up the Euphrates River in addition to the main route up the Red Sea. But the use of steam navigation on open waters appeared only in the 1860s and reached its apogee with the establishment of the British India Steam Navigation Company, which served principal ports in the Gulf as well as offering services elsewhere around the Indian subcontinent. Nevertheless, the introduction of a steamship service in the Gulf owed much to European political rivalries, and Gulf services, such as the post that was carried up the Gulf by steamship, served only to improve India's communications with the Gulf and not with London.

The telegraph was a contemporaneous technological advance that greatly improved imperial lines of communication. A submarine and coastal telegraph system was established through the Gulf in 1864, enabling the Indo-European Telegraph Department (later Cable and Wireless) to provide an essential and profitable service until undercut by wireless competition in the 1920s. Another submarine cable was laid between Bombay and Suez in 1869.[6]

The final advance in communications was that of air routes. Proposals for a London-to-India air service had been advanced as early as 1912 and were renewed after the First World War. An air service was finally opened in 1921 between Cairo and Baghdad, reducing the time for mails between London and Baghdad from twenty-eight to nine days. Imperial Airways was born in 1923 from a merger of several earlier airlines and it introduced a passenger service between Cairo and Basra in 1927. Continuation of the route through the Gulf, however, faced political problems. Negotiations for a route through Persia were troubled by competing European schemes and by disagreement over the course of the route. A limited service using Bushehr and Jask aerodromes was introduced in 1928 and this was incorporated into the Cairo-to-Karachi service that operated between 1929 and 1932. By the latter date, Britain had reached agreements with various rulers on the Arabian coast to establish aerodromes in their territories and newer, longer-range, aircraft made traversing the long segment between the Trucial Coast and the Makran Coast feasible.[7]

Aerial lines of communication acquired even greater urgency with the Second World War when they constituted a vital, if vulnerable, link between the European and Far Eastern theaters of war. Air routes continued to be important after the war, with the route through the Gulf, which utilized Habbaniya in Iraq as a staging base, supplementing the main Red Sea route. This added importance to retaining treaty arrangements with Iraq and use rights within the Baghdad Pact. The Kuwait crisis of 1961, when Iraq appeared to threaten the emirate's existence shortly after independence, demonstrated the increasing vulnerability of air routes as Turkey and Sudan refused overflight rights during the crisis and the deployment of Royal Air Force units was successful largely because of existing bases in Bahrain and Sharjah.[8]

Responsibilities as Protector and Administrative Requirements

India's expanding concern with Gulf affairs necessarily brought concomitant responsibilities and administrative requirements in its wake. India's efforts to create tranquillity on the seas prodded the local rulers on the Arab coast to agree to a system of maritime truces. These began in 1835 and were renewed at intervals until the General Treaty of

Maritime Truce was concluded in 1853. Britain's formal influence over much of the Arab littoral was reinforced in the 1890s when treaties of protection were signed with the rulers of Bahrain and the Trucial States. Muscat agreed in 1892 not to cede any territory without British approval, thus bringing the sultanate into a subordinate Indian orbit. Treaties of protection were also forged with Kuwait in 1899 and with Qatar in 1916.

Only Najd, Hasa, and Mesopotamia remained outside the British sphere of influence. The latter's situation changed with Indian occupation during the First World War and establishment of the Iraq Mandate in 1920. India's hesitation to embrace Abd al-Aziz Al Sa'ud after his recapture of Riyadh in 1902 was dictated largely by London, which favored the Hashimi kingdom in Hijaz. It took decades for Abd al-Aziz to prove his power and permanence and extend his authority from Najd over Hasa, Hijaz, and the southern borderlands with Yemen. The British championing of Hashimi states in Transjordan and Iraq, as well as stiff resistance to Saudi expansion into the shaikhdoms, hampered bilateral relations and the oil concession was allowed to slip into American hands.

While Persia remained outside India's control, political weakness there virtually dictated greater British involvement in Persian affairs. In part, concern was prompted by Russian inroads. The weak Qajar shah, Muzaffar al-Din, secured two massive Russian loans in 1900 and 1902 and then found his foreign trade closely tied to Russia. British concern over developments was assuaged by the Anglo-Russian Declaration of 1907, which led to the division of Persia into British and Russian zones of influence apart from a central buffer area. This agreement was made possible by Russia's defeat in its 1905 war with Japan and growing British fears of German penetration through the Ottoman Empire. India's concern for the security of the waters of the Gulf and trade with the immediate hinterland led to the creation of a quasi-sovereign position in south Persia.[9]

Thus, by the 1920s, India's predominant position was quite secure throughout the Gulf. Indian interests were administered by a network of representatives along the littoral. Apart from Iraq, which was given its own government in 1921 and independence in 1932, a political resident in the Persian Gulf, headquartered in Bushehr, supervised the system. The political resident was directly responsible to the External or Foreign Secretary of the Government of India. Under him were political agents resident in Kuwait, Bahrain, Qatar, Sharjah, Muscat, and eventually Dubai and Abu Dhabi. Because of Muscat's formal independence, the political agent there was also styled consul (later consul-general) and thus reported on some matters directly to the Foreign Office in London as well.

With the independence of India, the residency was shifted from Bushehr to Bahrain but the system remained intact until British withdrawal at the end of 1971. Kuwait's independence in 1961 entailed the replacement of the political agent by an ambassador, and the creation of a new regime in Muscat in 1970 led to the redesignation of the political agent/consul-general there as ambassador in 1971. With the demise of the Government of India, the system was incorporated into the Foreign Office (Foreign and Commonwealth Office from 1968).[10]

British Representatives

For the most part, being a British representative in the Gulf was a thankless task. Duty stations were often extremely isolated, living conditions could be exceptionally harsh, and the work frequently ignored by the powers that be. For many, posting to the Gulf was tantamount to a sentence and, for a few, a death sentence (the first four British residents in Muscat at the turn of the nineteenth century all died in short order). The Gulf was a convenient place to send the mediocre and troublesome. For most, toiling in the Gulf meant a career of obscurity.

On the positive side of the ledger, the Gulf Residency could command the resources of men who dedicated their careers to service in the Gulf and were intimately familiar with the people, the ruling families, tribal intricacies, political circumstances, and the languages and culture. Many complemented their official duties by translating cardinal historical and religious texts, by publishing their own histories and observations, and by collecting geological, botanical, and zoological data. This cadre almost constituted a separate Gulf service in practice even if not formally. After Indian independence, when full responsibility for the Gulf devolved upon the Foreign Office, new blood was injected into the Gulf system for a time by old hands from Sudan and Aden.

This chapter would be remiss in not mentioning at least a few of the British officials connected to the Gulf who stood out for both positive and negative reasons. Major-General Sir John Malcolm (1769–1833) first entered the Madras army but turned to civil service as a surer route to advancement, later serving as governor of Bombay and as a member of Parliament. Sent as ambassador to Persia on three occasions, Malcolm sought to advance British interests by making arrangements to freeze out European competitors. Most importantly, he was the first would-be architect of a forward policy in the Gulf, which involved establishing a base there to allow Britain to dominate local politics. Never reticent to advance his own cause with superiors, "Malcolm made a great hero. Judging from his treatment of anybody who stood in his way, he was also the nastiest of [Governor-General] Wellesley's associates; quite as nasty as Harry Flashman."[11]

One of the earliest Residents was Samuel Hennell, to whom fell the responsibility of making the nascent trucial system work.

> In 1826, at the age of 26, he was posted to the Gulf as assistant Resident, at a time when the piratical tribes were still smarting from their defeat by [Major-General Sir William Grant] Keir [in 1819], and a half dozen cruisers were required on the station to protect merchant shipping. When he departed twenty-six years later one cruiser sufficed to watch over the peace of the Gulf. . . . He was, without doubt, the greatest Political Resident Britain has ever had in the Persian Gulf.[12]

Equally influential was a successor as resident (1862–72), Lewis Pelly (1825–92), who stanched Al Sa'ud designs on the Gulf and thwarted the implementation of an Ibadi imamate in Muscat. He also used his position to advance "modernization" in the Gulf: "He developed and asserted Britain's extraterritorial privilege in the Gulf as much to assure freedom of business operations as to advance British political influence."[13]

One of the last of the residents was Sir William Luce (1907–76), a veteran of the Sudan Political Service who subsequently served as governor of Aden (1956–60) and political resident in the Persian Gulf (1961–66). His success in the latter position led to his being recalled from retirement to take on the difficult and thankless task of being the Foreign and Commonwealth Secretary's Personal Representative for Gulf Affairs, that is, to work out the arrangements for British withdrawal from the Gulf and usher the smaller Gulf principalities into full independence. In his role in orchestrating the withdrawal, "Luce had to deal with the vain and arrogant Pahlavi government in Iran, with suspicious Saudis and anxious Gulf Rulers, not to mention his political bosses in London, some of whom were far from committed to the decision to terminate the British protective presence in the Gulf. He charmed everybody, he persuaded everybody, he was patient, good humoured (with occasional explosions) and skilful."[14]

Muscat served as a germinal station for a number of British representatives. Prominent among them was Col. Samuel Barrett Miles (1838–1914), who spent most of 1872–86 serving as political agent in Muscat. He also traversed most of Oman and was one of the first Europeans to venture to many of its remote areas. These journeys were published in exacting detail in various journals of the day and his death interrupted the completion of his lifetime work, *The Countries and Tribes of the Persian Gulf*, which covered only Oman when it appeared in print. "Miles was an accurate observer, a good classical scholar and Arabist, and a keen antiquarian. These qualities are displayed to advantage in the accounts of his travels . . . and in the papers he presented to learned societies in his lifetime."[15]

Sir Percy Cox (1864–1937) was another erstwhile political agent in Muscat (1899–1904) who went on to become political resident in the Persian Gulf (1904–13), foreign secretary of the Government of India (1913–14), chief political officer of the Indian Expeditionary Force in Mesopotamia during the First World War, and acting British minister to Persia (1918–20). But it was his role as the first High Commissioner of Iraq (1920–23) and his forging the foundations of the Iraqi state for which he is best remembered. With policy in Iraq crumbling because of the 1920 revolt, Cox returned to Baghdad where, "possessed of enough Asian experience to outshine even Curzon, [he] was able to force London to take decisions, however unpalatable."[16]

Cox's longtime assistant, Sir Arnold Wilson (1884–1940), served as Civil Commissioner in Iraq (1918–20) and Resident in the Gulf (1920). He later went on to employment with the Anglo-Persian Oil Company, became a member of Parliament, and wrote an early authoritative history of the Gulf before dying in combat during the Second World War while serving as a gunner in the Royal Air Force. But it was on Wilson's watch that the 1920 revolt took place. "[S]omehow, Wilson never fulfilled the promise he displayed as a young political officer in Persia, the Gulf, and Iraq. If Curzon never lived down being Viceroy of India, Wilson never lived down being Civil Commissioner of Iraq."[17]

Twentieth Century Concerns

Britain's responsibilities as protector of the smaller states in the Gulf were significant but not onerous. Formally, it acted as the protecting state in foreign affairs and defense. In practical terms, this meant that all diplomatic relations with these states and visa requests were conducted through the Government of India. A small British military apparatus was at the Resident's call. However, until Indian independence, there were few actual requirements for military assistance and the occasional port call by the cruiser at the Resident's disposal sufficed to either protect a new successor as shaikh or apply pressure against a recalcitrant one. While the Resident and his subordinate agents were not directly involved in rulers' affairs, they were able to exercise considerable persuasive power over the shaikhs and, occasionally they helped push rulers into exile.

When Britain thought it necessary to replace a sitting shaikh, it preferred to work behind the scenes and within the ruling family. In 1923, Britain forced the abdication of Shaikh Isa b. Ali Al Khalifa in Bahrain and his replacement by his son Hamad b. Isa in order to institute what it believed to be long-overdue reforms in the country. In 1965, members of the ruling Qawasim family in Sharjah were encouraged to depose Shaikh Saqr b. Sultan, a thorn in the British side because of his admiration for pan-Arab nationalism and ties to Gamal Abdel Nasser and the Arab League. In 1966, Britain prodded Shaikh Zayid b. Sultan Al Nahyan to remove his long-serving brother Shakhbut, who was clearly unsuitable to govern an oil-era state. In 1970, Britain encouraged young Sayyid Qabus b. Sa'id to overthrow his father as Sultan of Oman.[18]

The advent of oil-producing status in the Gulf states simultaneously increased and decreased British influence. As functioning governments were formed and expanded, the need for advisers in financial, development, and military affairs also grew, and bureaucrats in London generally picked these advisers for rulers. At the same time, however, the residency system held little actual power to force rulers and their families to do their bidding. Newly created government departments generally became the fiefdom of close relatives of the ruler, who used them to create personal fortunes and, in many cases, to gain relative independence from the ruler. Rulers came to rely on long-serving British advisers, sometimes to the advantage of Her Majesty's Government (HMG) who thus gained another channel of persuasion. At other times, however, rulers clung stubbornly to advisers that even HMG wished to see long gone, as was the case of Charles Belgrave in Bahrain.

By the mid-twentieth century, oil clearly had become Britain's predominant interest in the Gulf.[19] The combination of British predominance there, the Gulf's emergence as the world's leading source of oil, and the strong position of British oil companies in the region, all served to increase the Gulf's importance in British perceptions. This interest had been building for some time. Only a few years after the discovery of the first oil in the Gulf at Masjid-i Sulaiman in Iran in 1908, the Anglo-Persian Oil Company (later, Anglo-Iranian Oil Company and later still, British Petroleum [BP]) became a major source of fuel oil for the Royal Navy during the First World War. British oil interests were also responsible for developing the oilfields in Iraq in the 1920s.

During the Second World War, Bahrain was the principal supplier of oil to the Royal Navy. After that war, British oil interests in the Gulf were a major contributor to a positive British balance of payments and Kuwait was a major participant in sterling area accounts. By 1949–50, the Gulf was the source of more than 80 percent of Britain's crude oil imports.[20] The Iranian oil crisis of 1953, when Prime Minister Muhammad Musaddiq nationalized Anglo-Iranian Oil Company assets, threatened to bankrupt the company and devastate the British economy.

The emergence of the Cold War also increased British concern over the Gulf, thus forming another strategic interest, since Britain and the West remained suspicious of Soviet designs for greater influence in the region. While Soviet-backed breakaway republics in postwar Iran were soon suppressed, the Iraqi revolution of 1958 eliminated British bases in that country and introduced a new threat of subversion, with Soviet assistance. The Yemen revolution of 1962 and consequent civil war introduced Egyptian troops and Soviet military equipment and advisers to the Arabian Peninsula. British withdrawal from Aden resulted in the establishment of a quasi-Marxist regime in South Yemen, which then provided active support for the separatist front in southern Oman.

Inescapably, the Gulf became part of Britain's inexorable process of retreat from empire. In part, Britain's retreat from the Gulf was the consequence of changing political circumstances: the ill-advised Suez invasion in 1956 had poisoned Britain's position throughout the Arab world and the accelerating pattern of pan-Arab nationalism made Britain's politico-military position in the region increasingly vulnerable. Rather paradoxically, Britain's abandonment of the Gulf was accelerated by budgetary concerns. The relatively minor expense of maintaining a military presence in the Gulf was judged to be unnecessary and a retrenching Labour government announced withdrawal in 1968.

From 1971 on, Britain's interests in the Gulf had turned full circle: access to markets and the pursuit of local trade were at the top of the list. This became even more of a concern following the 1973–74 oil price revolution when the need to recycle increased payments for oil with a greater volume of trade with the Gulf states was obvious.

The Gulf in Imperial Foreign Policy

It is perhaps easier to divine the importance of the Gulf to Britain and British India in retrospect than at the time, at least to policymakers in Whitehall. Time and time again, India-proposed strategic policy initiatives in the Gulf were subordinated to perceived greater Europe-centered policy considerations in London. This was as true of John Malcolm's grand strategy at the beginning of the nineteenth century to establish a British base in the Gulf to dominate local politics as it was of Curzon's grand strategy at the end of the nineteenth century to pursue a "forward policy" to deny European rivals any influence in the Gulf. Even the early advantages in securing the first oil concessions in the Gulf and in crafting the legal bases for British supremacy were not exhaustively pursued, thereby permitting an American entry into the Gulf arena.

> It is clear that oil was an important issue that demanded agreements between the oil companies and governments concerned, but there is no good evidence that the desire to control supplies of oil played a decisive part in the evolution of British policy toward Iraq during the immediate postwar period. Nor is there convincing evidence that British policy in the Gulf during the interwar period was strongly influenced by the desire to control oil resources. British oil companies had sufficient oil for their needs, and although they evidently wished to reserve possible deposits for the future, they were unwilling to invest the money needed to develop them.[21]

Although Britain exercised considerable command of the Gulf during the Second World War, its activities there were almost always something of an afterthought.

This seeming paradox in British foreign policy deserves closer examination. Prior to the beginning of the nineteenth century, British interests in the Gulf were relatively minor, relating to some trade and European rivalries. The conquest of India and its denial to France and other rivals occupied the focus of British concern and the Gulf received scant attention, left largely to its own internal forces and rivalries.

The first Indian effort to engage the Gulf in a broader strategic view occurred at the turn of the nineteenth century, when Captain John Malcolm, an assistant resident at Hyderabad, was ordered by Governor-General Lord Wellesley to negotiate a treaty with Fath Ali Shah of Persia to prevent further invasions of India by Zaman Shah of Afghanistan, and to oppose any attempts by the French to encroach on the Gulf. In Tehran, Malcolm was struck by the threat posed to the shah's domains by Russian expansionism and recognized its potential for threatening India. In the end, however, the treaty was largely obsolete even as it was being signed in 1801, and its value was soon discounted even as Wellesley was recalled from India.

Resumption of a forward policy in the Gulf began with Wellesley's replacement, Lord Minto, who viewed a new alliance between France, Russia, and Persia with suspicion. His instrument was Malcolm again, by this time Resident at Mysore. Failing in his 1808 mission to convince the shah to sever relations with France, Malcolm proposed his grand scheme for the Gulf: seizure of Kharg Island off the Persian coast and the transfer to it of the Basra and Bushehr Residencies and all commercial activities in the Gulf. Malcolm secured Minto's approval for an expedition to carry out his plan but the expedition was cancelled when London sent another emissary to Fath Ali Shah, who successfully negotiated a treaty of friendship. London had trumped Calcutta and the Gulf receded from Indian awareness.

Strategic interest in the Gulf did not disappear, however, since the problem of "piracy" retained India's attention. In particular, India was concerned by the activities of the Qawasim, based at Lingeh and Ras al-Khaimah. They had attacked British shipping as early as 1778 and, after a pause, their attacks had increased in 1804 and in the following years, at least partly a result of their alliance with the Al Sa'ud of Najd. Some assistance was provided to the ruler of Muscat in his defense against the Qawasim, but Muscat's efforts were also directed at defending the coast from the invading army of the Al Sa'ud, which was assisted by the Qawasim. In 1809, a naval expedition was sent to attack the Qasimi port of Ras al-Khaimah and Malcolm's instructions included a determination of the most suitable island in the vicinity on which to establish a residency and keep an eye on the Qawasim. In late 1809 and early 1810, the combined British-Omani expedition successfully overran Ras al-Khaimah, Lingeh, and then Shinas, but most of the Qasimi fleet escaped destruction. In the end, however, Lord Minto abandoned the idea of a base in the region as the Al Sa'ud, to whom the Qawasim were believed to be subordinate, promised to respect British shipping.[22]

When Qasimi attacks again became prevalent, another expedition was launched to capture Ras al-Khaimah and other Qasimi ports and to destroy ships and raze all fortifications. Having succeeded in this endeavor, a "General Treaty of Peace with the Arab Tribes" was signed in 1820, and it subsequently included non-Qasimi leaders and tribes as well as Bahrain. Renewed treaties were signed at intervals until the permanent General Treaty of Maritime Peace came into force in 1853. The impetus for a base in the Gulf was still alive, however, and a garrison was established on Qishm Island. But the search for an ideal location was interrupted by an ill-advised expedition to punish the Bani Bu Ali tribe of eastern Oman for acts of piracy. When the Omani-British force attacking the Bani Bu Ali headquarters was routed in 1820, a second, larger, expedition had to be mounted in the following year to avenge the loss. The garrison at Qishm was evacuated in early 1823, in part because of its unsuitability and Persian opposition but, even more, because of Calcutta's unwillingness to countenance a military base in the Gulf for fear of involvement in Gulf politics. From then on, British supremacy was to rest upon diplomacy and a maritime presence (including at Basidu on Qishm island).

Although British supremacy in the Gulf was assured, and trade increased marginally due to the advent of steam navigation, the Gulf remained of secondary interest to Britain and India during the second half of the nineteenth century. Even the Persian War of 1856–57, triggered by Persian expansionist activities in Afghanistan, British opposition to a rival claimant in Muscat in 1868–71, and muted reaction to Ottoman expansionism in Hasa and Qatar in the 1870s and 1880s were little more than aberrations.

Indeed, strategic interest in the Gulf was renewed only in the 1890s. A preliminary measure involved formalization of the British position vis-à-vis the Arab states, prompted by increasing Ottoman and French interest. In 1891, the ruler of Muscat signed an agreement never to transfer any of his domains to any foreign power. In 1892, the various shaikhs of the Trucial Coast (including Abu Dhabi, Dubai, Ajman, Sharjah, Ras al-Khaimah, and Umm al-Qaiwain) signed more restrictive agreements foreswearing treaty relations with and the acceptance of agents of any other powers. Also in 1892, the shaikh of Bahrain signed a nearly identical agreement, even though he had signed an agreement in 1880 abjuring relations with foreign powers. Kuwait signed a similar agreement in 1899, and Qatar was eventually brought into line with a similar agreement in 1916.[23]

Although these agreements seemed to be little more than a tidying up of an existing British position—one that rested more on influence, persuasion, and policy, and the efforts of individual residents and agents than it did on legal documents—they did provide the foundations for the attempt at a larger forward strategy for the Gulf during the term of Lord Curzon as Viceroy of India (1898–1905). Curzon's vision of empire, and the requirements to sustain it, extended well beyond the narrow confines of India. The Gulf had been of considerable concern even before his viceroyalty, as shown by the publication of his *Persia and the Persian Question* in 1892.[24]

Furthermore, the Gulf's importance in global geopolitics and the growing interest expressed in the Gulf by Britain's European rivals contributed to its rising profile. As the editor of the *Times of India* during Curzon's viceroyalty remarked,

> British supremacy in India is unquestionably bound up with British supremacy in the Persian Gulf. If we lose control of the Gulf, we shall not rule long in India. . . . The moment it

> became known that Russia, or Germany, or France, or any other powerful nation, had planted a post within easy reach of the shores of India, an ineffaceable impression of the impermanence of British rule would be produced throughout Hindustan. . . . The appearance of a foreign Power anywhere in the Gulf, under however innocent a guise, would carry one irresistible conviction to the mind of every intelligent Indian.[25]

Indian sensibilities were particularly excited by French, German, Ottoman, and Russian activities in the Gulf. The French challenge was concentrated in Oman: the French flag was raised on smuggling dhows that resisted the Muscat ruler's authority; French arms dealers operated openly in Muscat's market, their wares destined for the North-West Frontier of India, where they were used against British forces; and Paris sought to undermine Britain's monopoly of influence over the sultan. The sultan was ordered aboard a British warship in Muscat harbor in 1899 and warned that his capital would be bombarded if he did not rescind his permission for a French coaling station in Oman.

The perceived German threat derived from the drive to build the so-called Berlin-to-Baghdad railway with a terminus on the Gulf, most likely in Kuwait. The issue was complicated by the uncertain status of Kuwait, which was claimed by the Ottoman Empire as part of its territory. Britain's refusal to recognize this claim was demonstrated by the treaty of protection signed with the amir of Kuwait in 1899 and, after years of sparring and negotiation, an Anglo-Ottoman understanding to terminate the line in Basra was reached in 1913. The Anglo-German agreement, however, had not been ratified by the onset of the First World War.[26]

The Ottoman role in Kuwait was seen as one menacing aspect of Istanbul's expansionist drive in the Gulf during the late nineteenth and early twentieth centuries. As early as the 1860s, claim was laid to Kuwait, Bahrain, central Arabia, Qatar, and even the Trucial Coast. Hasa was occupied in 1871 and became a permanent, if unruly, possession until its recapture by the Al Sa'ud in 1911. An attack on Qatar in 1892 ended in disaster and the effort a decade later to introduce Ottoman officials there was aborted by British representations in Istanbul. Ottoman claims to Qatar and parts of Abu Dhabi were eliminated only by the "Blue Line" Agreement of 1913. Recognition of Kuwait's autonomy, if not de facto independence, was not completely settled before the outbreak of war in 1914, but the war soon established its independence under British protection.

The Russian challenge was, at the same time, less direct but potentially more threatening. Russian expansionism throughout Asia was viewed warily in India. Not only was the Indian Empire threatened by perceived Russian designs on Iran and desire for a warm water port in the Gulf, but also Russian movement from Central Asia potentially imperiled the approaches to India through Afghanistan and Tibet. Through the decades on both sides of the turn of the century, rumors periodically surfaced of Russian planning for a railway with a terminus somewhere on the Persian shores of the Gulf, although such an endeavor never received serious consideration and Russia formally denied its intention to acquire a Gulf port. Russian warships and commercial shipping also appeared in the Gulf, and a Russian bank and consulate were established at Bushehr. In an effort to recognize Russian interests in the region and to control them, an accord was reached between London and St. Petersburg in 1907, dividing Iran into spheres of influence. In the end, the Russian threat to the Gulf, real or imagined, disappeared with the 1917 revolution.

The 1907 accord neatly illustrates the subordination of Indian foreign policy to Britain's broader international interests as seen in London. Curzon's victories in advancing his "forward policy," particularly the 1899 agreement with Kuwait, were few and, following his departure as viceroy, Whitehall assumed considerably closer control over Indian foreign policy. As a consequence, while British interests in the Gulf expanded in the years before the First World War—notwithstanding the declaration in 1903 of Lord Lansdowne, the Secretary of State for Foreign Affairs, that Britain would not tolerate the establishment of a foreign base in the Gulf—the extension of British supremacy in the region was of a subdued and largely passive nature.

The war, of course, brought its own dynamics. India's operations in the Gulf played a significant, if subsidiary, role in the larger war effort by tying up Ottoman forces on a front complementing British and French operations in the Levant. In addition, India was concerned as usual that India's Muslims might respond to a call for jihad from the Ottoman sultan in his capacity as caliph. Initial plans for the Indian expeditionary force sent to the Gulf were for the protection of the Iranian oil fields, a vital source of fuel for the Royal Navy. But as fears mounted that Istanbul might use the Gulf as another front or seek to undermine British influence there, and as considerations of the postwar political situation emerged, thoughts turned to the conquest of Mesopotamia. An easy start and quick occupation of Basra encouraged further advances, particularly as optimism gripped Delhi and Whitehall. But disaster struck with a serious setback at Ctesiphon in November 1915 and then the surrender of the British forces at Kut al-Amara where they had regrouped in April 1916.

Following this catastrophe, military operations in Mesopotamia reverted to the direct control of the Imperial General Staff in London, which resumed the campaign in early 1917 and captured Baghdad. Although political direction in Mesopotamia remained in Indian hands, there were considerable efforts to divorce it from India, particularly once the Arab Bureau was established in Cairo, with debate centering on whether administration of captured territories should be Arab or Indian in nature. In the end, the matter was settled by the metamorphosis of the Sykes-Picot Agreement into League of Nations mandates by which the French assumed control of Lebanon and Syria, and Britain did the same for Palestine, Transjordan, and Mesopotamia. There was no question of Iraq being incorporated into India, particularly once London replaced King Faisal al-Hashimi's lost throne in Damascus with another in Baghdad.

The new Iraqi mandate was the only place in the Gulf where Britain sought to rule directly. Indeed, while the reasons for Britain's assumption of control over the new state may have been less than compelling, the impact on Iraq was tremendous. For the first time, a single state emerged out of the three Ottoman provinces of Mosul, Baghdad, and Basra. The idea of direct rule was abandoned after the 1920 revolt and, after considerable deliberation in Whitehall, Britain thereafter chose to work through the Sunni establishment under the leadership of King Faisal.[27]

By this time, the British position in the Gulf was at its apogee. Britain controlled Iraq, supervised the smaller states of the Gulf, exercised considerable influence in Persia, and held the Al Sa'ud in check in Najd. But it is still surprising that Britain did not do more to consolidate its position and isolate the Gulf from the outside world. In part, this may be explained by the continuing bureaucratic war between Whitehall and India over control of the Middle East. When India lost the battle for Iraq, it withdrew bruised and unable to contemplate any new "forward policy."

Most surprising was the British attitude toward Gulf oil. The Anglo-Persian Oil Company and later the Iraq Petroleum Company operated the first oil-producing concessions in the Gulf and, since these provided sufficient oil for British needs, no concerted effort was made to prevent rival companies from gaining a foothold in the region. The Bahrain concession was acquired by Standard Oil of California (SOCAL), which registered the Bahrain Petroleum Company (BAPCO) in Canada (and later brought in the Texas Company (TEXACO) as an equal partner), apparently as a way to satisfy British objections to American involvement in Bahrain and Saudi Arabia. And what turned out to be the most important concession of all, in Saudi Arabia, was secured by American oil companies operating as the Arabian-American Oil Company (ARAMCO), largely because of British lack of interest and parsimoniousness.

RETREAT FROM THE GULF

The Gulf's experience during the Second World War introduced the first of two factors that marked the diminution of the British position. For the first time, the United States made its presence known in the Gulf, particularly through the shared role in resupplying the Soviet Union through the Persian corridor and in its use of British air bases in the Gulf (and along the southern rim of the Arabian Peninsula) in ferrying men and matériel to the Far East. American military advisers appeared in Iran for the first time. British complaints over American airplane damage to the landing field in Bahrain were a spur to the establishment of an American air base in Dhahran, Saudi Arabia. This marked the beginning of a change from Britain to the United States in providing the lion's share of military assistance, arms sales, and training efforts to the kingdom.

It should be noted that the American entrance in the Gulf, as tentative as it was for decades, came when the British Empire was collapsing and India was acquiring independence, thus eliminating one principal motive for British concern about the position of rivals in the Gulf. Still, the British government did not concede an American presence easily: U.S. diplomatic representation in the Gulf prior to British withdrawal was permitted only in Kuwait (from 1951) and then only grudgingly. The war also introduced a return of Russian influence to the Gulf, marked first in the abortive attempts to establish republics in Iran and later evolving into Russian political and military support to Iraq, Yemen, and Southern Yemen.

The other factor was the changing political atmosphere in the Middle East. Colonial empires were no longer fashionable and Arab and Iranian nationalism rendered European supremacy and bases in the region increasingly untenable. Indian independence in 1947 was only the first in a long line of colonial and political disengagements. Resistance to Iranian Prime Minister Musaddiq's nationalization of British oil assets in 1953 was unsuccessful. Britain was forced to abandon its bases in Egypt in 1954 and, in a futile attempt to regain its position, participated in the Suez debacle in 1956. The British privileged position in Iraq and its bases there were swept away in the 1958 revolution. Even Britain's provision of forces to defend newly independent Kuwait in 1961 deserved an asterisk: it is by no means clear that Baghdad was seriously contemplating backing up its verbal threats with military force against the shaikhdom.[28] The attempt to center British military forces in the Middle East in Aden in the 1960s, in compensation for the loss of Palestine, Egypt, and Iraq, foundered on the emergence of yet another nationalist movement that forced abandonment of Aden in 1967. The final British retreat from the Gulf—the withdrawal from its small air bases in Bahrain and Sharjah and the abrogation of the treaties of protection—was more of a whimper than an exclamation point. No foreign power or even local agitation forced the British withdrawal. It was prompted instead by minor budgetary calculations in Whitehall and a general sense that it was time to declare the empire dead.

It can be argued that the loss of India rendered British interests in the Gulf even more peripheral than before. To be sure, Britain continued to predominate in the Gulf oil industry, to exercise political overlordship in the smaller states, and to enjoy substantial commercial interests, particularly as oil exports first transformed Gulf states and when the oil price revolution dramatically increased their purchasing power. But despite the legacy of its privileged position, the British role in the Gulf was henceforth fundamentally little different from other outside powers. It traded commercial and cultural advantages and military support for recirculated petrodollars and a limited measure of influence.

THE LEGACY OF THE BRITISH EXPERIENCE WITH THE GULF

The long experience of British involvement with the Gulf produced lasting impact on both Britain and the Gulf. There are both tangible and intangible aspects to the impact on Britain. While the long decades of British intrigues in domestic politics, military interventions, political ultimata, and high-handed decisions are becoming largely and increasingly forgotten, the intangible bonds between the United Kingdom and the various Gulf states continue to remain vibrant. Despite its status as an oil-producing country (British oil production outstripped domestic demand by some 1,200,000 b/d as late as 1999 although consumption overtook production in 2006 for the first time), Britain is still heavily involved in Gulf oil matters. While Britain is not dependent on Gulf oil to meet its own needs, the fact remains that primarily British oil companies, such as BP and Royal Dutch Shell, are major players in the Gulf oil industry.

At the same time, the Gulf is an important market for Britain. British construction firms had the inside track in many Gulf states in the early years of the oil boom and they continue to hold a preponderant share of the industry today. British goods, from Land Rovers to household goods and foodstuffs, are ubiquitous imports in the Gulf. British expatriates remain highly visible in the smaller states—as managers in Gulf commercial firms as well as representatives of British industry, and in government and armed forces. Even in Saudi Arabia, the number of British expatriates is not far behind that of Americans. Britain continues to supply seconded military personnel to several Gulf states while others serve on private contract. Britain remains the United States' principal competitor in arms sales, even as British troops have backed up American forces in Iraq. During the period 2002 to 2005, Britain supplied some 27 percent of the total world arms deliveries to the Middle East, second only to the United States at just under 39 percent.[29]

The impact on the Gulf has been equally significant. Trading links remain strong and British industrial standards dominate throughout much of the region. British schools and universities draw large numbers of Gulf students and the British Council and private British firms provide much of the region's advanced English-language instruction. London and the British countryside remain a favorite summer destination for many Gulf visitors, particularly since September 11, 2001 made many Gulf nationals hesitant about traveling to or studying in the United States. The smaller Gulf states remain close politically to Britain. While the United States, as the world's leading military power, has assumed primary responsibility for Gulf defense, the smaller Gulf states hold fast to their military links with Britain, which is seen as less threatening than often unpredictable American military and political might.

It has also been observed in recent years that American policy in the Gulf has become reminiscent of past British policy. Like Britain, the American role began in a diffident manner but gradually increased in intensity and involvement. Since the mid-1980s, Washington has followed the British experience in engaging in active intervention in the Gulf and has acted for many of the same reasons that motivated Britain earlier: preventing rivals (the Soviet Union) from entering the region, protecting regional interests (supporting Iraq against Iran in the Iran-Iraq War, as well as reflagging the Kuwaiti tankers), propping up the Al Sa'ud despite opposition at home, entering into treaties of security protection with the smaller littoral states, marching into Afghanistan without achieving the objectives of the campaign, and invading Mesopotamia to oust an enemy and impose a subservient government only to find itself increasingly and fruitlessly entangled.

Whereas Britain's justification for such behavior was primarily India, that of the United States is overwhelmingly oil. Gulf oil has come to play a much greater role in American foreign policy than it did in Britain's, perhaps because concentration on the essential problem of keeping India secure tended to obscure other goals. It may be also because of the complacency of British oil companies in the first half of the twentieth century and Britain's self-sufficiency in oil in later years. Yet another reason may be the transformation of the international political environment in which the United States regards itself as having an obligation to protect worldwide access to oil supplies—and the Gulf with two thirds of the world's reserves is obviously the key—while Britain's horizon was more modest in its goal of securing adequate supplies for only its empire. In any case, American policy since 2001 has increasingly come to resemble Britain's imperial attitude: the U.S. government asserts its right to use its power as it chooses to deal with whatever enemies it discerns and local actors are subordinated to accepting and helping to execute this policy.

At the beginning of this chapter, British involvement in the Gulf was described as a triptych. The Gulf was seen as largely peripheral to British interests until the beginning of the nineteenth century when specifically Indian interests gradually created a preponderant British role in the region. It may be speculated that the transformation of British interests in India from commerce (the East India Company) to politics (the Government of India) was a determining factor in augmenting British power to protect the security of India and thus increase its role in the Gulf.

Still, although British power during this period was clearly capable of protecting and advancing British interests, London's concern with the impact on the larger arena served to confine, check, and even deny Indian strategy in the Gulf at nearly all points during the long period until the Second World War. Although perhaps not evident at the time, the British position in the Gulf began its decline from this point for a variety of reasons. The Gulf had been essentially peripheral to Indian interests during the empire. With India independent, its even more peripheral nature to Britain itself was masked only temporarily by the British retreat from its position in the wider Middle East. Nevertheless, the lessening of British supremacy in the Gulf coincided with Britain's declining ability to protect its interests and its friends there. Withdrawal in 1971 may have seemed fickle to some at the time, but in retrospect, it was clearly time to go.

Notes

1. I have used the terms "Britain" and "British" throughout this chapter for the sake of consistency, even though it would be more usual to speak of "England" and "English" in the first half of the period under review. Similarly, use of the terms "India" and "Indian" in this paper should be understood to mean the British government in India, unless otherwise indicated.
2. J. B. Kelly, *Britain and the Persian Gulf, 1795–1880* (Oxford: Clarendon Press, 1968), 1.
3. The short historical synopsis in this paper is derived principally from: J. G. Lorimer, comp., *Gazetteer of the Persian Gulf, 'Omân, and Central Arabia* (Calcutta, India: Superintendent, Government Printing, vol. 1: 1915; vol. 2: 1908; reprinted numerous times); Arnold T. Wilson, *The Persian Gulf: An Historical Sketch from the Earliest Times to the Beginning of the Twentieth Century* (London: George Allen and Unwin, 1928, reprinted 1954 and 1959); C. U. Aitchison, comp., *A Collection of Treaties, Engagements and Sanads Relating to India and Neighbouring Countries*, rev. ed., vol. 11, *Containing The Treaties, &c., Relating to Aden and the South Western Coast of Arabia, the Arab Principalities in the Persian Gulf, Muscat (Oman), Baluchistan and the North-West Frontier Province* (Delhi, India: Manager of Publications, 1933); Ravinder Kumar, *India and the Persian Gulf Region, 1858–1907: A Study in British Imperial Policy* (Bombay: Asia Publishing House, 1965); Abdul Amir Amin, *British Interests in the Persian Gulf* (Leiden: Brill, 1967); Kelly, *Britain and the Persian Gulf*; Briton Cooper Busch, *Britain and the Persian Gulf, 1894–1914* (Berkeley: University of California Press, 1967); Briton Cooper Busch, *Britain, India and the Arabs, 1914–1921* (Berkeley: University of California Press, 1971); Malcolm Yapp, "British Policy in the Persian Gulf," in *The Persian Gulf States: A General Survey*, gen. ed. Alvin J. Cottrell

(Baltimore: Johns Hopkins University Press, 1980); and J. E. Peterson, "The Historical Pattern of Gulf Security," in *Security in the Persian Gulf: Origins, Obstacles and the Search for Consensus,* ed. Lawrence G. Potter and Gary G. Sick (New York: Palgrave, 2001), 7–31. In addition, more specific sources have been referenced where appropriate.

4. Yapp, "British Policy," 71.
5. Halford L. Hoskins, *British Routes to India* (London: Longmans, Green, 1928; repr. London: Frank Cass, 1966; New York: Octagon Books, 1966).
6. Hoskins, *British Routes to India*, 373–97; Lorimer, *Gazetteer*, vol. 1, Appendix J, "The Telegraphs of the Persian Gulf in Their Relations to the Telegraph Systems of Persia and Turkey," 2400–38; and Christina Phelps Harris, "The Persian Gulf Submarine Telegraph of 1864," *Geographical Journal*, vol. 135, Pt. 2 (June 1969): 169–190.
7. J. E. Peterson, *Defending Arabia* (London: Croom Helm; New York: St. Martin's Press, 1986).
8. Phillip Darby, *British Defence Policy East of Suez, 1947–1968* (London: Oxford University Press for the Royal Institute of International Affairs, 1973); David Lee, *Flight from the Middle East: A History of the Royal Air Force in the Arabian Peninsula and Adjacent Territories, 1945–1972* (London: HMSO for the Ministry of Defence, Air Historical Branch, 1980).
9. For an overview see Rouhollah K. Ramazani, *The Foreign Policy of Iran: A Developing Nation in World Affairs, 1500–1941* (Charlottesville: University Press of Virginia, 1966). For specifics see Charles Issawi, ed., *The Economic History of Iran, 1800–1914* (Chicago: University of Chicago Press, 1971), 370 and Peter Avery, Gavin Hambly, and Charles Melville, eds., *The Cambridge History of Iran,* vol. 7, *From Nadir Shah to the Islamic Republic* (Cambridge: Cambridge University Press, 1991), 200.
10. On the development and structure of the system, see J. B. Kelly, "The Legal and Historical Basis of the British Position in the Persian Gulf," *St. Antony's Papers,* no. 4; *Middle Eastern Affairs,* no. 1 (London: Chatto and Windus, 1958; New York: Praeger, 1959), 119–40. For a study of the Gulf as an instance of Britain's "informal empire" as viewed through the employment of native agents in Bahrain, see James Onley, "The Politics of Protection in the Gulf: The Arab Rulers and the British Resident in the Nineteenth Century," *New Arabian Studies* 6 (2004): 30–92; as well as the same author's *The Arabian Frontier of the British Raj: Merchants, Rulers, and the British in the Nineteenth-Century Gulf* (London: Oxford University Press, 2007).
11. Edward Ingram, *In Defence of British India* (London: Frank Cass, 1984), 80.
12. Kelly, *Britain and the Persian Gulf,* 409.
13. Robert G. Landen, *Oman Since 1856: Disruptive Modernization in a Traditional Arab Society* (Princeton: Princeton University Press, 1967), 92.
14. Glen Balfour-Paul, *The End of Empire in the Middle East: Britain's Relinquishment of Power in Her Last Three Arab Dependencies* (Cambridge: Cambridge University Press, 1991), xviii.
15. J. B. Kelly in his introduction to S. B. Miles, *The Countries and Tribes of the Persian Gulf* (London: Harrison and Sons, 1919; 2nd ed., London: Frank Cass, 1966), 19.
16. Elizabeth Monroe, *Britain's Moment in the Middle East, 1914–1971,* rev. ed. (London: Chatto and Windus; Baltimore: Johns Hopkins University Press, 1981), 67.
17. Busch, *Britain, India, and the Arabs,* 483. An attempt to explain the actions and attitude of British representatives in the Gulf through their public-school education has been made by Paul Rich, *The Invasions of the Gulf: Radicalism, Ritualism and the Shaikhs* (Cambridge, UK: Allborough Press, 1991).
18. On these events, see Muhammad Morsy Abdullah, *The United Arab Emirates: A Modern History* (London: Croom Helm; New York: Barnes and Noble, 1978); J. E. Peterson, *Oman in the Twentieth Century* (London: Croom Helm, 1978); Frauke Heard-Bey, *From Trucial States to United Arab Emirates: A Society in Transition* (London: Longman, 1983; new ed., 1996); Abdullah Omran Taryam, *The Establishment of the United Arab Emirates, 1950–85* (London: Croom Helm, 1987); Mahdi Abdalla al-Tajir, *Bahrain 1920–1945: Britain, The Shaikh and the Administration* (London: Croom Helm, 1987); and Rosemarie Said Zahlan, *The Making of the Modern Gulf States: Kuwait, Bahrain, Qatar, the United*

Arab Emirates and Oman (London: Unwin Hyman, 1989; rev. ed., Reading: Ithaca Press, 1998).

19. Stephen H. Longrigg, *Oil in the Middle East: Its Discovery and Development*, 3rd ed. (London: Oxford University Press, 1968); Marian Kent, *Oil and Empire: British Policy and Mesopotamian Oil, 1900–1920* (London: Macmillan, 1976); Peter J. Odell, *Oil and World Power: Background of the Oil Crisis*, 8th ed. (New York: Viking Penguin, 1986); and Daniel Yergin, *The Prize: The Epic Quest for Oil, Money, and Power* (New York: Simon and Schuster, 1991).
20. Yapp, "British Policy," 93.
21. Ibid., 89.
22. Sultan Muhammad al-Qasimi, *The Myth of Arab Piracy in the Gulf*, 2nd ed. (London: Routledge, 1988); Charles E. Davies, *The Blood-Red Flag: An Investigation into Qasimi Piracy, 1797–1820* (Exeter, UK: University of Exeter Press, 1997).
23. The absence of any commitment to forsake other foreign relations in the Muscat agreement was due solely to the Anglo-French Declaration of 1862 in which both sides agreed to respect the independence of Muscat and Zanzibar. The texts of all these agreements are to be found in Aitchison, *Treaties*, vol. 11.
24. G. N. Curzon, *Persia and the Persian Question*, 2 vols. (London: Longmans, Green, 1892; repr. London: Frank Cass, 1966).
25. Lovat Fraser, *India Under Curzon & After* (London: William Heinemann, 1911), 112–13. See also the argument of American naval strategist Alfred Thayer Mahan, "The Persian Gulf and International Relations," *National and English Review*, no. 40 (September 1902): 27–45.
26. German activity in the Gulf also included the establishment of a German commercial firm along the Persian shore, the same firm's mining concession on the disputed island of Abu Musa, and the introduction of commercial shipping arrangements in the Gulf that undercut the prices of British lines.
27. On the mandate, see Stephen Hemsley Longrigg, *'Iraq, 1900 to 1950: A Political, Social, and Economic History* (London: Oxford University Press, 1953); Peter Sluglett, *Britain in Iraq 1914–1932* (London: Ithaca Press, 1976); and Charles Tripp, *A History of Iraq*, 2nd ed. (Cambridge: Cambridge University Press, 2002).
28. Mustafa M. Alani, *Operation Vantage: British Military Intervention in Kuwait 1961* (London: Laam, 1990).
29. Richard F. Grimmett, "Conventional Arms Transfers to Developing Nations, 1998–2005," U.S. Library of Congress, Congressional Research Service, *CRS Report* RL33696 (23 October 2006), 63.

Chapter 15

The United States and the Persian Gulf in the Twentieth Century

Gary Sick

It took half a century for the United States to become the major power in the Persian Gulf, and that process was characterized by evasions, indecision, and general reluctance to get involved. Initially drawn in during World War II to protect the Allies' supply lines to the Soviet Union, the United States then withdrew virtually all its military forces for more than a generation, content to leave commerce in the hands of the giant oil firms known as the Seven Sisters and most regional security responsibilities to the ministrations of its experienced and well-established British ally.[1]

Even when the British withdrew in 1971, the United States did not immediately rush to fill the vacuum, constructing instead an unusual proxy arrangement with Iran (and nominally Saudi Arabia) to fill the gap. When that, in turn, collapsed after the Iranian revolution, the United States began to build a military infrastructure in the region, a process that acquired its impetus from the internationalization of the Iran-Iraq War in the mid-1980s. But it was not until the Iraqi invasion of Kuwait in 1991 that the United States introduced major forces into the region that seemed destined to give it a dominant, sustained presence.

Throughout, U.S. interests in the Persian Gulf region were simple and consistent, conceived from the start in global, strategic terms: first, to ensure access by the industrialized world to the vast oil resources of the region; and second, to prevent any hostile power from acquiring political or military control over those resources. During the Cold War, the Soviet Union was seen as the most immediate threat to those interests; after the Soviet collapse, Iran and Iraq became the primary targets of U.S. containment efforts.

Other objectives, such as preserving the stability and independence of the Gulf states or containing the threat of Islamic radicalism, were derivative concerns and were implicit in the two grand themes of oil and containment. Preoccupation with the security of Israel was also a driving factor in U.S. Middle East policy during the half century of America's progressive entanglement in the Persian Gulf, and these two arenas interacted with each other despite heroic efforts by Washington to pretend that they were separate and unrelated issues.

For most of the twentieth century, the United States regarded the Gulf almost exclusively in the context of its global rivalry with the Soviet Union, and regional developments were perceived through the lens of larger strategic objectives. This helped to maintain the fiction that oil and Palestine could be separated, since each was understood to play a different role in the global struggle. However, when the Soviet Union was subtracted from the equation after the end of the Cold War, Washington increasingly came to view the Middle East in purely regional terms, and that artificial distinction began to evaporate.

The slow unfolding of U.S. policy contributed to (and occasionally was the victim of) the development of the modern Persian Gulf. The whole story is more than this chapter can hope to tell. Instead, this account will focus on a few key turning points, where seemingly unrelated U.S. policy choices eventually resolved themselves into an imperial presence that the imperium itself had scarcely anticipated.

THE TWIN PILLARS POLICY

Prior to World War II, U.S. involvement in the Persian Gulf was minimal. The first sustained encounter with the region was in the nineteenth century, in the days of the great clipper ships.[2] The United States regarded the Persian Gulf and Indian Ocean as a British preserve, and U.S. political, commercial, and military contact with the region was infrequent.[3]

The U.S. Middle East Command was established during World War II to oversee the supply route of war matériel to the Soviet Union. Its 30,000 troops constituted the largest U.S. deployment to the region from that time until Operation Desert Storm in 1991. The small U.S. naval contingent (Middle East Force) that was established in 1947 relied on British hospitality at Jufair on Bahrain Island.

Britain's announcement in 1968 that it intended to withdraw from its historic position east of Suez came as an unwelcome shock in Washington, which had long relied on the British presence as an essential component of its Soviet containment strategy along the immense arc from the Suez Canal to the Strait of Malacca. It also came at the worst possible moment, since U.S. forces were increasingly strained by commitments in Vietnam and Southeast Asia.

When the Nixon administration took office in 1969, it undertook a comprehensive review of U.S. Persian Gulf policy. This was part of a global effort to redefine U.S. security interests at a time of competing demands on U.S. military forces and a growing reluctance by the American public to support what were seen as potentially costly foreign commitments. The outcome of this review was the Nixon Doctrine, which placed primary reliance on security cooperation with regional states as a means of protecting U.S. interests around the world. In the Gulf, it was decided to rely heavily on the two key states of Iran and Saudi Arabia, a strategy that quickly became known as the "Twin Pillars policy."[4]

From the beginning, it was recognized that Iran would be the more substantial of the two "pillars" because of its size, its military capabilities, its physical juxtaposition between the Soviet Union and the Persian Gulf, and the willingness of the shah (unlike the Arab leaders of the region) to cooperate openly with the United States on security matters. This very special relationship between Washington and Tehran was sealed in May 1972 during the visit to Tehran of President Nixon and his national security adviser, Henry Kissinger.

In two-and-a-half hours of conversations over two days, a deal was struck in which the United States agreed to increase the number of uniformed advisers in Iran and guaranteed the shah access to some of the most sophisticated nonnuclear technology in the U.S. military arsenal. The shah, in return, agreed to accept a key role in protecting Western interests in the Persian Gulf region. All of this was summed up with startling candor at the end of the meetings, when President Nixon looked across the table to the shah and said simply, "Protect me."[5]

* * *

This moment was the culmination of several decades of tumultuous political relations between the United States and Iran. The overthrow of Muhammad Musaddiq in Iran in 1953 was arguably one of the key turning points in twentieth century Middle East politics. It cut short a nationalist experiment, returned the shah to the throne, demonstrated a willingness and ability of the United States (in collaboration with the British) to intervene in the affairs of a major state in the region and inadvertently laid the groundwork for the Iranian revolution a quarter of a century later.[6]

In a very real sense, this event marked the loss of America's political innocence in the region. Until that time, the United States was regarded, in Iran and elsewhere in the area, as an anticolonial power and potential bulwark against the predations of Britain and Russia, the cynical protagonists of the Great Game. The Musaddiq "counter coup" demonstrated that the United States could be just as self-serving and manipulative as the other external powers when its own interests were perceived to be at stake. There was one difference, however. Whereas the British in 1953 were concerned primarily about preserving their oil rights, the United States was more concerned about the perceived threat of Soviet political inroads into Iran.

By this act, the United States guaranteed that it would be held permanently responsible—at least by Iranian popular opinion—for the Iranian ruler's excesses and cruelties. In 1963, a fiery religious leader, Ruhollah Khomeini, led the opposition to a bill that, among other things, extended diplomatic protection to American military advisers. This rebellion, which in retrospect was a rehearsal for the revolution of 1978–79, led to Khomeini's exile for fourteen years. Although most Americans were scarcely aware of this incident, the Iranian opposition was convinced that the shah was acting on behalf of the United States.

The agreement between President Nixon and the shah in 1972 underscored the fact that Iran was no mere "client" state of the United States. Iran was on the brink of becoming a major power in the oil market and now had free access to the U.S. arsenal of modern weaponry. This was formally acknowledged with Iran becoming the protector of U.S. interests in the region, and the shah increasingly felt emboldened to lecture his great-power ally on politics, economics, and strategy. The United States in turn reduced its intelligence coverage of Iran's internal politics and relied on the shah for assistance: in putting down the Marxist rebellion in Dhofar; for an assured energy supply at the time of the oil embargo of 1973; and for support in a wide range of political and military operations ranging from the Middle East and Africa to as far away as Vietnam. Iran had become the irreplaceable linchpin of U.S. strategy in the Persian Gulf.

This role reversal, however, went almost unnoticed in the Persian Gulf and elsewhere. In Iran, the image of a compliant shah responding to orders dictated in Washington remained vividly implanted in the national psyche. As a consequence, when the revolution exploded in the late 1970s, the United States had the worst of both worlds. It had relinquished much of its independent capacity to assess and influence Iran's internal politics, but it was popularly suspected of orchestrating every move by the shah's regime.

Washington's cozy relationship with the shah also involved a tripartite covert action with Israel to destabilize Iraq by supporting a Kurdish rebellion against Baghdad. This plan was adopted in May 1972 during the Nixon-Kissinger visit; it collapsed in 1975 when the shah unilaterally struck a border agreement with Saddam Hussein and abandoned the Kurds. Despite its tragic elements, this secret war established a precedent for viewing the Persian Gulf as an extension of the Arab-Israel conflict and for U.S.-Israeli cooperation in the region.[7]

The collapse of the shah's regime in February 1979 was the death knell for the U.S. Twin Pillars policy. The United States, which at the time was locked in a high-risk effort to negotiate a peace settlement between Israel and the Palestinians, watched the shah's collapse with mounting dismay. Washington issued periodic public and private statements in support of the shah, but ultimately relied almost entirely on the shah to rescue his nation from a massive popular revolt led by Ayatollah Khomeini and Iranian clerics. Both the United States and the shah seemed incapable of understanding what was happening or mobilizing the policy instruments that might halt the collapse of the regime. By the time it became clear in Washington that the shah was incapable of acting decisively, it was too late. From the beginning, U.S. policy had been predicated on a close personal relationship between the American leadership and the shah. With his departure and the arrival of a hostile Islamist regime in Tehran, the United States was left strategically naked in the Persian Gulf, with no safety net.

The Carter Doctrine

This blow was compounded in February 1979 by reports of an incipient invasion of North Yemen by its avowedly Marxist neighbor to the south. This event, coming in the wake of the Marxist coup in Afghanistan in April 1978, the conclusion of the Ethiopian-Soviet treaty in November 1978, the fall of the shah, and the assassination of U.S. Ambassador Adolph Dubs in Kabul in February 1979, created the impression that the United States had lost all capacity to influence regional events. That impression was strengthened when Turkey and Pakistan followed Iran in withdrawing from the Central Treaty Organization in March.

Washington responded by dispatching a carrier task force to the Arabian Sea and by rushing emergency military aid to Yemen and the airborne warning and control system (AWACS) to Saudi Arabia. The United States also undertook a systematic effort to develop a new "strategic framework" for the Persian Gulf. By the end of 1979, the outlines of a strategy had been sketched in, including initial identification of U.S. forces for a rapid deployment force and preliminary discussions with Oman, Kenya, and Somalia about possible use of facilities. Nevertheless, when the U.S. embassy in Tehran was attacked in November and diplomatic hostages taken, a high-level review of U.S. military capabilities drew the sobering conclusion that U.S. ability to influence events in the region was extremely limited. In late November, when there were serious fears that the U.S. hostages were in danger of being killed, a second aircraft carrier was sent to the area and two additional destroyers were assigned to the Middle East Force.

The Soviet invasion of Afghanistan just before Christmas in 1979 reawakened fears of a Soviet drive to the Persian Gulf and Indian Ocean. The practical effect of the Soviet invasion was to terminate the efforts of the Carter administration to seek mutual accommodation with the Soviet Union, including support for the SALT II treaty on Strategic Arms Limitations. This policy shift was articulated by Carter in his State of the Union address of January 23, 1980, where he stated: "An attempt by any outside force to gain control of the Persian Gulf region will be regarded as an assault on the vital interests of the United States of America, and such an assault will be repelled by any means necessary, including military force."

This declaration, which quickly came to be known as the Carter Doctrine, bore a remarkable resemblance to the classic statement of British policy by Lord Lansdowne in 1903, when he said the United Kingdom would "regard the establishment of a naval base, or of a fortified port, in the Persian Gulf by any other Power as a very grave menace to British interests," an act that would be resisted "with all the means at our disposal."[8] The statement clearly established the United States as the self-proclaimed protecting power of the region and effectively completed the transfer of policy responsibility in the Persian Gulf from the British to the Americans.

When Carter made this statement, it reflected U.S. intentions rather than capabilities. By the time the Reagan administration arrived in Washington in January 1981, it would have been accurate to say that the U.S. security structure in the Persian Gulf region was more symbol than reality—at least as measured in purely military capacity.[9] Nevertheless, it was equally apparent that the developments of 1980 marked a major threshold in the evolution of U.S. strategy and a new conviction that this region represented a major strategic zone of U.S. vital interests, demanding both sustained attention at the highest levels of U.S. policymaking and direct U.S. engagement in support of specifically U.S. interests. That was without precedent.

The Reagan administration adopted the Carter Doctrine—in fact, if not in name—and over the following seven years succeeded in putting more substantial military power and organization behind its words. The Rapid Deployment Joint Task Force was reorganized in 1983 as a unified command known as the Central Command, with earmarked forces totaling some 230,000 military personnel from the four services. Its basic mission reflected the two themes that had wound through U.S. regional policy from the very beginning: "to assure continued access to Persian Gulf oil and to prevent the Soviets from acquiring political-military control directly or through proxies."

THE IRAN-IRAQ WAR (1980–1988)

Despite the shadow of Soviet military power, all physical threats to oil supplies and to regional stability came not from Russia and its allies but from political developments within the region. The first of these was the Arab oil boycott at the time of the Arab-Israeli war of 1973, which nearly tripled the price of oil and sent Western economies spinning into a serious recession. The second was the Iranian revolution, and the third was the Iran-Iraq war,[10] which Iraq launched with a massive invasion in September 1980.

The United States asserted its neutrality at the beginning of the war, and then later tilted unofficially in favor of Iraq as Iran drove back the Iraqi forces and counterattacked across the border. In 1985–86, as part of a "strategic opening" to Iran coupled with an abortive effort to free U.S. hostages in Lebanon, the United States and Israel undertook a series of secret contacts and substantial arms transfers to Iran that effectively shifted U.S. policy—at least at the covert level—toward Iran.[11] Funds from the arms sales were used to support the Nicaraguan counter-revolutionaries, or contras. When the revelation of the Iran-contra affair created consternation and threatened U.S. relations with the friendly oil-producing states of the Gulf, the United States reversed field sharply and adopted an openly pro-Iraqi position.[12]

During much of the war, the United States and many other powers adopted a hands-off posture, content to see these two abominable regimes exhaust each other on the battlefield, particularly since the war was having relatively little impact on oil supplies or prices.[13] That nonchalance began to fade in 1985–86 when Iran began to retaliate for Iraqi air attacks against its shipping in the Gulf by using mines and small, unmarked armed boats against neutral shipping en route to Kuwait and Saudi Arabia.

In late 1986, Kuwait asked both the United States and the Soviet Union to place Kuwaiti tankers under their flag and provide protection. The Soviet Union agreed to reflag three Kuwaiti tankers, and the United States quickly followed suit by reflagging eleven. The United States moved a substantial number of naval ships into or near the Gulf and began escorting tanker convoys to and from Kuwait.[14] Iran's indiscriminate use of mines led other NATO navies to send minesweepers and other escort ships to the Gulf to protect international shipping.

Although the reflagging decision was seen at the time as a temporary U.S. response to a specific problem, in retrospect it was a fundamental turning point. For the first time since World War II, the United States assumed an operational role in the defense of the Persian Gulf, with all that implied in terms of development of infrastructure, doctrine, coordination with NATO allies, and direct collaboration with the Arab states on the southern littoral. President Reagan's military intervention thus confirmed President Carter's assertion that the Gulf was of vital interest to the United States and that the United States was prepared to use military force in pursuit of that interest. Although the Carter Doctrine addressed the prospective threat from the Soviet Union, its first major implementation involved a regional state, anticipating the massive international coalition that repelled Iraq's occupation of Kuwait in January 1991.

From War to War

United Nations (UN) Security Council Resolution 598 was passed unanimously on July 20, 1987, calling for an immediate cease-fire between Iran and Iraq. This set off a full year of acrimonious debate, punctuated by sporadic missile bombardments of cities and further attacks on oil tankers.[15] A new element in this escalation of the war was the expanded use of chemical weapons by Iraq against civilian targets. Iraq had used poison gas extensively in earlier campaigns, but the targets had been Iranian military forces. On the evening of March 16, 1988, Iraq conducted two bombing raids against the village of Halabja, which Iranian forces were about to enter. The bombs caught the local Iraqi Kurdish villagers in their homes and in the street, killing at least 2,000 civilians.[16] The UN dispatched an investigating team that confirmed the atrocity. But Iraq was unrepentant. Foreign Minister Tariq Aziz wrote to the secretary-general that "in their legitimate, moral, and internationally approved self-defense, our people are determined to use all available abilities and means against the criminal invaders."[17] In fact, in the succeeding months, Iraq used poison gas more frequently and against a wider range of targets, including civilians, than at any previous time in the war. The UN Security Council passed Resolution 612 on May 9, 1988, mandating an immediate end to the use of chemical weapons in the war and holding out the prospect of sanctions against violators, but it was never implemented and had no effect.

During this same period, the Soviet Union announced its intention to withdraw its military forces from Afghanistan by early 1989. This resulted in the signing of an accord between Afghanistan and Pakistan on April 14 in Geneva, with the United States and the Soviet Union as co-guarantors.

Throughout this period, political cohesion in Iran was breaking down. The continued use of mines in the Persian Gulf set off a new round of clashes with U.S. forces, which attacked Iranian oil platforms on October 19, 1987, and April 18, 1988.[18] Iraq went on the offensive against Iran's disorganized and disheartened military forces, recapturing the Faw Peninsula in a lightning attack on April 18, then proceeding to push back Iranian forces all along the front. In mid-May, apparently with assistance from Saudi Arabia, Iraq carried out a devastating attack on the Iranian oil transfer site at Larak Island in the southern Gulf, destroying five ships, including the world's largest supertanker.[19] Antiwar sentiment began to appear openly in demonstrations in major Iranian cities. And most disturbing of all for the divided leadership, persuasive evidence began to accumulate that Khomeini was severely ill and virtually incapacitated.

On July 3, a commercial Iranian aircraft was shot down by the USS *Vincennes,* killing all 290 passengers and crew. This terrible accident, coming at the end of a seemingly endless series of defeats, underscored the despair of Iran's position. On July 18, the Iranian foreign minister sent a letter to the UN secretary-general formally accepting Resolution 598. Two days later, Khomeini sent a "message to the nation," read by an announcer, associating himself with the decision, which, he said, was "more deadly than taking poison."[20]

Iraq was taken by surprise and initially resisted accepting a cease-fire, while continuing its mopping-up operations. Iraq also continued to demonstrate a contemptuous disregard for the Security Council and for world opinion on the use of chemical weapons. A UN investigative team presented its report to the Security Council on August 1, finding that "chemical weapons continue to be used on an intensive scale" by Iraq. Only hours later, Iraq launched a massive chemical bombing attack on the Iranian (Kurdish) town of Oshnoviyeh. However, as international pressure mounted, Saddam Hussein finally agreed to accept a cease-fire on August 6. A UN observer force was rushed to the region, and a cease-fire went into effect on August 20, 1988.

The end of the war provided an opportunity for the Bush administration to reconsider its support for Saddam Hussein in the wake of revelations about Iraq's use of chemical weapons against its own population, the genocidal Anfal campaign against the Kurds, and efforts to develop nuclear and other weapons of mass destruction. The policy of limited cooperation with Iraq, however, remained intact. This policy became an embarrassment after the defeat of Iraq in 1991, when claims were leveled that the U.S. government had chosen to ignore warnings that agricultural credits might have been diverted to the purchase of military equipment. The most sensational charges of criminal responsibility were never substantiated, and the so-called Iraqgate scandal faded after the 1992 U.S. presidential elections. However, documents made available to the Congress and the media did demonstrate persuasively that the Bush administration had pursued a largely uncritical policy toward Iraq during the period between the end of the Iran-Iraq War and the Iraqi invasion of Kuwait.[21]

At a minimum, this policy of tolerance and inattentiveness may have contributed to a false sense of security on the part of Saddam Hussein as he prepared to invade his neighbor to the south. The U.S. ambassador to Baghdad, April Glaspie, was widely criticized for failing to warn Saddam Hussein about the possible consequences of an attack, but any fair-minded review of the record would reveal that she was accurately reflecting the policy of the president and secretary of state during this interwar period.[22]

The Second Gulf War

When Iraqi forces crossed the border into Kuwait at 1 a.m. on the morning of August 2, 1990, they set in motion a series of events that would transform U.S. policy in the Persian Gulf. It marked a turning point in U.S. relations with the Arab states of the Gulf, and the cooperation between the United States and the Soviet Union on a matter of high strategy and military policy, which would have been unthinkable only a few years earlier, marked the undeniable end of the Cold War. The successful creation of a very large international coalition under the auspices of the UN and under the direct leadership of the United States aroused expectations for both the UN and peacekeeping, some of which was expressed in President George Bush's use of the phrase "a new world order" in relation to the Gulf intervention.[23]

The eventual use of missiles by Iraq against Israel underscored the relationship between the Arab-Israel conflict and Gulf policy more clearly than at any time since the oil embargo of 1973. The immediate imposition of a draconian sanctions regime against Iraq, and its continuation over a period of many years, demonstrated both the extent and limitations of collective, nonviolent coercion by the international community. The combined use of air power, lightning ground mobility, and the use of high-tech weapons—many for the first time in combat—in a computerized battlefield environment wrote a new chapter in the conduct of modern warfare and raised some troubling new questions.[24] The media, and especially television, brought these events into the world's living rooms with an intimacy and immediacy that may have been unprecedented in its universality.

Saddam Hussein's forces were ejected from Kuwait with minimal combat casualties.[25] On March 3, U.S. General Norman Schwartzkopf met with an Iraqi military delegation at Safwan airfield in southern Iraq, and the Iraqis quickly agreed to allied terms. Almost immediately, revolts against Saddam Hussein's regime broke out among the Kurds in northern Iraq and among the Shi'i in southern Iraq. Initially President Bush declared that Iraq was violating the terms of the cease-fire by using military helicopters to put down the revolts. He reversed himself almost immediately, however, stating that "using helicopters like this to put down one's own people does not add to the stability of the area. . . . We are not in there trying to impose a solution inside Iraq."[26]

The distinction was critical. Over the following weeks, Iraqi forces brutally suppressed the uprisings and arguably preserved Saddam Hussein in power. The rationale for the change was spelled out two weeks later by White House spokesman Marlin Fitzwater, who noted, "There is no interest in the coalition in further military operations." Arab officials, he said, were telling Washington: "Let Hussein deal with this, then the dust will settle and he's going to have to pay the piper for the war over Kuwait. Or at least that is what we are counting on."[27]

In an interview with David Frost, General Schwartzkopf said he was "suckered" by the Iraqis into agreeing to permit helicopters to fly, ostensibly to move top officials between cities, when they really intended to use helicopter gunships against the rebels.[28] Five years later, also in an interview with David Frost, George Bush commented about Saddam Husain, "I miscalculated. . . . I thought he'd be gone." With regard to the Safwan meeting, Bush noted, "I think he took us by surprise. . . . We might have handled the flying of helicopters differently. . . . So I think there's room for some ex post facto criticism here."[29]

Whatever the rationale, the U.S. decision to permit Saddam Hussein to use advanced weaponry to suppress the internal revolts after the war made the United States an accessory after the fact to a massacre and ensured, whether inadvertently or not, that Saddam Hussein would retain power in Iraq. When the extent of the repression became known, and as Kurdish refugees began flooding across the border into Turkey, the United States, together with France and Great Britain, established so-called no-fly zones in the north and south. This gesture undoubtedly saved some lives and effectively prevented Saddam Hussein from reestablishing total control over the Kurdish territories. It was, however, much too late to save the many thousands of Iraqis who had spontaneously attacked the symbols of Ba'thist rule in the weeks after the allied victory.

In his testimony to the House Foreign Affairs Committee on February 6, 1991, Secretary of State James A. Baker III outlined the Bush Administration's postwar agenda for the Middle East. This included a revitalized peace process between Israelis, Palestinians, and Arab states, which led to a major conference in Madrid the following fall. In the Gulf, Baker made clear that all regional states—including Iran, and an Iraq without Saddam—could play a role in a future security arrangements.[30] By the time of writing, this had not happened.

The Clinton Administration and Dual Containment

On May 18, 1993, two months after President Clinton took office, Martin Indyk of the National Security Council staff spelled out the broad outlines of what he called America's "Dual Containment" policy in the Persian Gulf.[31] Traditionally, the United

States had pursued a policy of balancing Iran or Iraq against the other as a means of maintaining a degree of regional stability and to protect the smaller, oil-rich Arab states on the southern side of the Gulf. That was the purpose of the Twin Pillars policy, and it was implicit in subsequent tilts toward Iraq and (briefly) Iran during the Iran-Iraq War. Indyk, however, proclaimed the policy bankrupt and rejected it "because we don't need to rely on one to balance the other." Iraq was boxed in by UN sanctions, Iran was nearly prostrate after the eight-year war with Iraq, and the United States was the predominant power in the Persian Gulf with the "means to counter both the Iraqi and Iranian regimes."[32]

Although it was not necessarily Indyk's or Clinton's intention, the dual containment policy marked the formal entrance of the United States into the Persian Gulf as a resident political and military power. In the wake of the Iraq War, the predominance of the United States in the region was simply taken for granted, and there was no hint that this was a temporary state of affairs. Whatever one might have thought about the "New World Order," this new policy left no doubt about a new order at least in the Persian Gulf. The United States was the dominant power and was there to stay.

IRAQ

The objective of U.S. policy with regard to Iraq was to sustain the coalition that had defeated the armies of Saddam Hussein in Operation Desert Storm and to ensure that Iraq complied with all United Nations resolutions. The United States characterized the existing regime in Iraq as criminal and irredeemable and favored maintaining the sanctions until Saddam Hussein was gone.[33] This position created difficulties with other members of the UN Security Council, since Article 22 of the enabling Resolution 687 specified that the sanctions would be lifted once Iraq had eliminated and accounted for all of its weapons of mass destruction.

In the years after the adoption of the policy, the United States reportedly budgeted approximately $15 million per year for covert actions to destabilize the Saddam Hussein regime and for support of various Iraqi opposition groups.[34] The U.S. Central Intelligence Agency attempted to organize several operations to depose Saddam Hussein, including a major covert action just before the Clinton administration took office and at least two others in 1995 and 1996.[35] These operations were unsuccessful.

In June 1993 and in September 1996, the United States launched cruise missiles against targets in Iraq. The first case was retaliation for evidence of an Iraqi plot to assassinate former President George Bush in Kuwait. The second was in retaliation against Iraqi ground force incursions in northern Iraq in cooperation with the Kurdish Democratic Party.[36] On several occasions, the United States surged military forces into the region in response to Iraqi threats or failure to comply with UN Special Commission (UNSCOM) weapons inspections. In February 1998, when the Iraqi government refused to permit inspection of presidential sites, the United States appeared to be poised for a massive strike against Iraq. That crisis was resolved only when the UN secretary-general went to Baghdad and negotiated a memorandum of understanding with the Iraqi president.[37]

The bottom line, however, was that the United States, with significant help from a number of friends, allies, and the UN Security Council, was generally successful in keeping Saddam Hussein in what Secretary of State Madeleine Albright called a "strategic box." By mid-1998, this policy was losing support from the Arab states, which felt that the Iraqi people were being unfairly punished for the misbehavior of their rulers, and from states such as Russia, France, and China that had major political and financial interests in Iraq. The international consensus was preserved, however, primarily because of the unrelenting intransigence and belligerence of the Iraqi leader.

IRAN

The other target of dual containment, Iran, posed a very different set of problems. The dual containment policy called for Iran to: (1) cease its support of international terrorism and subversion, (2) end its violent opposition to the Arab-Israel peace talks, and (3) halt efforts to acquire weapons of mass destruction.

President Bush had referred to Iran in his Inaugural Address in January 1989, saying that "Goodwill begets goodwill. Good faith can be a spiral that endlessly moves on."[38] There was, however, no talk of goodwill by the Clinton administration. Instead, U.S. officials developed a special vocabulary in which Iran was routinely branded as a "rogue," "terrorist," "outlaw," or "backlash" state. This relentless drumfire of attacks—the mirror image of Iranian depictions of the United States as the "Great Satan"—had its effects in the media, in the Congress, among the public, and in the attitudes of lower-level bureaucrats. With a Democrat in the White House and the Republicans in control of the Congress, a domestic political contest developed over which party could be most vigorous in promoting U.S. policies to deal harshly with Iran. Apart from the intense rhetoric, this produced a series of stringent unilateral economic sanctions against Iran.[39]

In the presidential election year of 1996, the Congress attempted to extend the U.S. sanctions regimes internationally. They prepared and passed a bill that would impose sanctions on any foreign corporation that invested $40 million or more in the Iranian oil and gas sector. Libya was later added on the floor of the Senate, and the bill became known as the Iran-Libya Sanctions Act (ILSA).

In May 1997, Sayyid Muhammed Khatami was elected to a four-year term as president of Iran in a stunning electoral surprise. Khatami attracted the largest number of voters in Iranian history and won a decisive victory with 69 percent of the vote. Although Khatami was widely regarded as a candidate of domestic issues, it was his foreign policy moves that attracted the most attention during the first year of his term. In December 1997, Iran played host to the Organization of the Islamic Conference, where it won plaudits for its conciliatory positions and moderation. Iran called for closer cooperation with the UN, an institution it had shunned as a Western tool after the revolution. Iran began a concerted effort to improve its relations with Saudi Arabia and its other Arab neighbors in the Persian Gulf region, with some substantial initial success.

In January 1998, Khatami made an unprecedented "Address to the American People" in the form of an interview on the Cable News Network (CNN).[40] He praised the achievements of American civilization, went as far as an Iranian politician could go in expressing regret for the hostage crisis, and spelled out very clearly Iran's positions on all of the major issues of concern to the United States in positive terms.

Washington responded to the Khatami initiative cautiously but generally positively.[41] The United States toned down its rhetoric and took some small steps to improve relations. But problems remained. Less than sixty days after Khatami took office, the French oil major Total, together with state-owned partners Gazprom of Russia and Petronas of Malaysia, concluded a $2 billion deal to develop an Iranian gas field, which placed Total and its partners in apparent violation of ILSA.[42] In May 1998, however, the United States announced that it would waive the provisions of ILSA on grounds of national security. That decision was due almost entirely to pressure from America's European allies, but it was nevertheless received positively in Tehran.[43] The act was never enforced, but it had a significant deterrent effect on foreign companies considering investment in Iran, particularly those with major holdings in the United States that might be put at risk.

The United States also announced a major redeployment of its Persian Gulf forces, sharply reducing the number of ships and aircraft permanently stationed in the region.

This was due primarily to cost factors and personnel pressures, but again it was received positively by Tehran. There was growing awareness among Washington strategists that the initial assumption that the United States could alone confront both Iran and Iraq may have been exaggerated. At a minimum, as the threat from Iran appeared to be declining, the United States could ill afford to deliberately cultivate enemies.

On June 17, 1998, Secretary of State Albright delivered a major speech that responded almost point by point to the issues that Khatami had addressed in his interview six months earlier.[44] The speech was notable for its conciliatory tone and for the absence of the rhetoric that had characterized U.S. statements about Iran over the previous five years. The speech offered no specific new policies or initiatives, but it held out the prospect for a new beginning:

> We are ready to explore further ways to build mutual confidence and avoid misunderstandings. The Islamic Republic should consider parallel steps. If such a process can be initiated and sustained in a way that addresses the concerns of both sides, then we in the United States can see the prospect of a very different relationship. As the wall of mistrust comes down, we can develop with the Islamic Republic, when it is ready, a road map leading to normal relations. Obviously, two decades of mistrust cannot be erased overnight. The gap between us remains wide. But it is time to test the possibilities for bridging this gap.[45]

A speech by Albright on March 17, 2000, meant to appeal to moderates who triumphed in Iranian parliamentary elections the preceding month, went even further. In it the U.S. dropped economic sanctions against symbolic products such as carpets, pistachios, and caviar, but more importantly she went farther than any previous official in offering a qualified apology for the U.S. role in the overthrow of Prime Minister Muhammad Musaddiq in 1953.[46]

THE UNITED STATES AS A MIDDLE EAST POWER

By the end of the twentieth century, the United States had established a presence in the Persian Gulf that was more significant in terms of power and influence than any nation in the region. The military facilities that had begun to be developed during the latter stages of the Iran-Iraq War, and that had grown enormously during Operation Desert Storm, remained in place after the liberation of Kuwait.

It is not an exaggeration to say that the U.S. Gulf presence was the consequence of a single person, Saddam Hussein, the ruler of Iraq. It was his ill-fated attack against Iran in 1980, and the subsequent Iranian counterattack, that persuaded the regional Arab states to call officially for a U.S. military presence and to provide direct support, including facilities both on- and off-shore. That was a sharp contrast to their past position, which had officially called for the United States to leave the Gulf though, often unofficially, they let it be known that they were content that U.S. forces would be just "over the horizon" in the event of trouble. Saddam's invasion of Kuwait in 1991 accelerated that process enormously and convinced many Arab states of the region that they required palpable military protection that was neither part time nor largely invisible.

Of course, additional U.S. political and economic influence, which had been considerable for many years, flowed in with the military presence. Defense pacts were completed, often with a minimum of fanfare in a concession to Arab nationalist sensitivities, but with consequences for the intensity of economic (notably, but not exclusively, arms sales) and political interaction between the Arab states of the Gulf and the United States. Diplomatic presence was upgraded, and societal contacts, particularly access to U.S. education, blossomed. The sight of U.S. military personnel, especially in Persian Gulf ports, was no longer a rarity, and direct military-to-military contacts deepened. The United States quietly negotiated security agreements with all of the Arab states in the Gulf and built a string of operational military facilities—naval and air bases, pre-positioned storage facilities, and intelligence outposts—in locations throughout the Gulf. Although these facilities provided much greater flexibility for U.S. operations in the region, they were also a point of sensitivity for the Arab hosts, who feared being seen as U.S. dependencies.

At the millennium, the United States had overcome all of its initial hesitation and had begun to play a significant and sustained regional role. Curiously, Saddam Hussein remained the primary reason for the United States to maintain forces in the region and also the rationale for regional states to accept them. Saddam had failed to follow the U.S. script and simply fade away after his defeat in Kuwait. The United States continued to view him and his regime as a bone in the throat. The international sanctions were taking a high toll on the Iraqi people, and U.S. warplanes were involved in nearly daily armed sorties over the Kurdish areas of the Iraqi north and the largely Shi'i areas of the south. This policy was costly, both in terms of dollars and political capital in the region. The United States feared that regional states would become increasingly unwilling to provide the airbases and other support to sustain this armed sequestration of a fellow Arab country from the international community. Specifically, Saudi Arabia was under pressure from the dissident radical Osama bin Laden and his followers who denounced the presence of U.S. military forces on the sacred land of the Arabian Peninsula. All the Arab states in the region (except Kuwait) regarded the U.S. military presence on their soil as a sensitive issue and tried to minimize public attention and awareness.

As the United States entered the 2000 presidential elections, the dilemma of how to deal with Iraq was one of the few foreign policy issues to get much attention. In the second presidential debate, Governor George W. Bush gave some indication of the kind of policy he would prefer:

> MR. LEHRER: You could get him [Saddam Hussein] out of there?
>
> GOV. BUSH: I'd like to, of course. . . .He is a danger; we don't want him fishing in troubled waters in the Middle East. And it's going to be hard to—it's going to be important to rebuild that coalition to keep the pressure on him.[47]

Over the previous years, a number of prominent supporters of the Bush campaign had signed studies and open letters calling for the removal of Saddam Hussein from power, using force if necessary. In 1998 a group wrote to President Clinton arguing that "the only acceptable strategy is one that eliminates the possibility that Iraq will be able to use or threaten to use weapons of mass destruction. In the near term, this means a willingness to undertake military action as diplomacy is clearly failing. In the long term, it means removing Saddam Hussein and his regime from power. That now needs to become the aim of American foreign policy."[48] Virtually every signatory of that letter eventually became an official in the administration of George W. Bush.

At the turn of the millennium, the next act of U.S. engagement in the Persian Gulf had yet to be played out; but the stage was already set.

NOTES

1. The British certainly viewed the United States as a potential rival to their dominant influence in the region. This was particularly true following World War II, as the United States began to appreciate the strategic importance of oil, as the Persian Gulf emerged as a critical sector in the global doctrine of containment of the Soviet Union, and as British power began to wane. During this period, Britain maneuvered quite successfully to insure that

U.S. political presence in the region did not match its growing economic and military might. The United States was somewhat frustrated with these tactics, but its profound reliance on the UK as a strategic bulwark trumped any political ambitions until well after the British withdrawal in 1971. For a close look at part of this process, see Rosemarie Said Zahlan, "Anglo-American Rivalry in Bahrain, 1918–1947," in *Bahrain Through the Ages: The History,* ed. Abdullah bin Khalid al-Khalifa and Michael Rice (London: Kegan Paul International, 1993), 567–87.

2. These early contacts led to a treaty with the sultanate of Muscat and Oman in 1833, which is still recalled on occasions of state with Oman.
3. The following comments draw on the author's earlier published research. This includes "The Evolution of U.S. Strategy Toward the Indian Ocean and Persian Gulf Regions," in *The Great Game: Rivalry in the Persian Gulf and South Asia,* ed. Alvin Z. Rubinstein (New York: Praeger, 1983), 49–80 and "The United States in the Persian Gulf: From Twin Pillars to Dual Containment" in *The Middle East and the United States: A Historical and Political Reassessment*, 3rd ed., ed. David W. Lesch (Boulder, CO: Westview Press, 2003), 291–307.
4. For a more detailed account of this period, see Michael A. Palmer, *Guardians of the Gulf: A History of America's Expanding Role in the Persian Gulf, 1833–1992* (New York: Free Press, 1992) and Marc O'Reilly, *Unexceptional: America's Empire in the Persian Gulf, 1941–2007* (Lanham, MD: Lexington Books, 2008).
5. A detailed account of this episode and its implications can be found in Gary Sick, *All Fall Down: America's Tragic Encounter with Iran* (New York: Random House, 1985), 13–21, quote on 14.
6. For the most complete and succinct history and analysis of this event, see Mark Gasiorowski and Malcolm Byrne, eds., *Mohammad Mosaddeq and the 1953 Coup in Iran* (Syracuse, NY: Syracuse University Press, 2004).
7. Israeli-Iranian relations are discussed in detail in Trita Parsi, *Treacherous Alliance: The Secret Dealings of Israel, Iran, and the United States* (New Haven: Yale University Press, 2007), 23, 53–4. For a more detailed discussion of the sellout of the Kurds, see James A. Bill, *The Eagle and the Lion: The Tragedy of American-Iranian Relations* (New Haven: Yale University Press, 1988), 204–8. Israel had a well-developed strategy, known as the Doctrine of the Periphery, to outflank its hostile Arab neighbors by promoting relations with non-Arab states on the fringes of the conflict. In the case of Iran, this took the form of a very close strategic relationship for more than twenty years.
8. "British Position in the Persian Gulf: The Lansdowne Statement of Policy, 5 May 1903, (Document 163)," in *The Middle East and North Africa in World Politics: A Documentary Record,* 2nd. ed., vol. 1, *European Expansion, 1535—1914,* ed. J. C. Hurewitz (New Haven: Yale University Press, 1975), 506–07.
9. Former Secretary of Defense James Schlesinger drew attention to this fact in an article questioning whether the Rapid Deployment Joint Task Force was rapid, deployable, or even a force. See "Rapid(?) Deployment(?) Force(?)," *Washington Post,* September 24, 1980.
10. Gary Sick, "Trial by Error: Reflections on the Iran-Iraq War," *Middle East Journal* 43, no. 2 (1989): 230–44.
11. There was an interesting parallel in this second major U.S. collaboration with an outside power in Iran after the 1953 coup. Israel was interested in restoring its contacts and influence in Iran, which were lost during the revolution; the United States, however, saw this in Cold War terms, fearing that the USSR would exploit the post-revolution chaos to make political inroads into Iran.
12. For a detailed examination of this episode, see Theodore Draper, *A Very Thin Line: The Iran-Contra Affairs* (New York: Hill and Wang, 1991).
13. The casualty figures for the Iran-Iraq War are often exaggerated. Mohsen Rafiqdust, the former head of the Iranian Revolutionary Guard Corps, told Robert Fisk of the *Independent* (June 25, 1995) that 220,000 Iranians were killed and 400,000 wounded during the Iran-Iraq War. That is roughly consistent with Iranian official statements and with independent Western estimates. Iraq has never published any figures on its losses, but Amatzia Baram, a specialist on Iraq at the University of Haifa, has estimated that 150,000 Iraqis

were killed (*Jerusalem Quarterly* 49 [Winter 1989]: 85–86). If the standard ratio of two wounded for every man killed is applied, Iraq may have had 300,000 wounded. Thus, an informed estimate of total losses on both sides would equal approximately 370,000 killed and some 700,000 wounded, which is imprecise but plausible. In the case of Iraq, this casualty level is roughly comparable to U.S. losses in the Civil War.

14. The substantial deployment of U.S. forces to the Gulf was hastened—as was congressional approval—by the Iraqi missile attack on the USS *Stark* on May 17, 1987. Although the buildup was intended to counter Iran, the Iraqi attack galvanized public attention and underlined the threat to shipping in the Gulf.
15. Iraq was much better equipped than Iran, and it fired 3 to 4 missiles to every Iranian missile. The only confirmed use of poison gas was by Iraq—against Iranian troop formations and some civilian sites in Kurdish territory. For a more detailed examination of this armed negotiation, see Gary Sick, "Slouching Toward Settlement: The Internationalization of the Iran-Iraq War, 1987–88," in *Neither East Nor West: Iran, the Soviet Union, and the United States,* ed. Nikki Keddie and Mark Gasiorowski (New Haven: Yale University Press, 1990), 219–46.
16. For an authoritative account of Iraq's use of chemical weapons and the tepid international response, see Joost R. Hiltermann, "Outsiders as Enablers: Consequences and Lessons from International Silence on Iraq's Use of Chemical Weapons during the Iran-Iraq War," in Lawrence G. Potter and Gary G. Sick, eds., *Iran, Iraq, and the Legacies of War* (New York: Palgrave Macmillan, 2004), 151–66. See also Joost R. Hiltermann, *A Poisonous Affair: America, Iraq, and the Gassing of Halabja* (Cambridge, UK: Cambridge University Press, 2007).
17. Letter to the Secretary-General of March 28 (FBIS, March 30, 1988).
18. One mine struck the USS *Samuel B. Roberts* and on April 18, 1988, U.S. forces hit two Iranian oil platforms, Nasr (near Sirri Island) and Salman (in the joint Iran-Oman Lavan field), removing some 50,000 barrels per day from Iran's oil production. In the same action, two Iranian frigates were sunk, another was severely damaged, and four gunboats were damaged or sunk. Iran later brought a suit against the United States in the International Court of Justice seeking compensation for the loss of the oil platforms on the grounds that the attacks were a violation of international law and contrary to the terms of existing U.S.-Iranian agreements. The U.S. counter-claimed for damage caused by Iran to commercial ships sailing under the American flag. In 2003, the World Court ruled that the U.S. actions were unjustified, but did not grant compensation to either side. (International Court of Justice, Press Release 2003/38, 6 November 2003).
19. The bitter dispute between Iran and Saudi Arabia over Iran's participation in the annual hajj deepened the distrust between these two states. Saudi Arabia stepped up its direct support for Iraq, apparently permitting Iraqi aircraft to utilize Saudi airfields during raids on Iranian oil facilities in the southern Gulf. On April 26, 1988, Saudi Arabia broke diplomatic relations with Iran.
20. FBIS, July 21, 1988. On July 25, Khomeini made a six-minute appearance on television from the balcony of his residence. He appeared extremely frail and did not speak.
21. For example, see Murray Waas and Douglas Frantz, "U.S. Gave Data to Iraq Three Months Before Invasion; Persian Gulf: Documents Show Intelligence Sharing with Baghdad Lasted Longer Than Previously Indicated," *Los Angeles Times,* March 10, 1992, 1 (one of a series of investigative reports). See also "News Conference, Rep. Jack Brooks (D–TX), Rep. Charles Schumer (D–NY): Special Prosecutor Criminal Dealings with Iraq Prior to Iraqi Invasion of Kuwait," Federal News Service, July 9, 1992.
22. A verbatim text of Glaspie's meeting with Saddam Hussein on July 25, 1990 was later released by the Iraqi government and was published by the *New York Times* on September 23, 1990, 19. Glaspie, in testimony before the Senate Foreign Relations Committee on March 20, 1991, characterized the transcript as about 80 percent accurate, but with some key passages edited out.
23. Speech by President Bush from the Oval Office, January 16, 1991, two hours after the bombing campaign against Iraqi positions had begun.

24. See, for example, "Needless Deaths in the Gulf War: Civilian Casualties During the Air Campaign and Violations of the Laws of War," *Middle East Watch Report* (New York: Human Rights Watch, November 1991).
25. According to official counts, allied deaths were 146 Americans (35 by friendly fire), 24 British (9 by American fire), 2 Frenchmen, 1 Italian, and 39 among various Arab allies. Baghdad has never given an official count of its casualties, but postwar analyses concluded that Iraq's uniformed losses were far smaller than previously estimated, perhaps as low as 1,500 deaths. Estimates of civilian casualties were uncertain and varied greatly from one observer to another. See John G. Heidenrich, "The Gulf War: How Many Iraqis Died?," *Foreign Policy* 90 (Spring 1993): 108–25. The Associated Press on March 9, 1993 provided an overview of the various estimates.
26. *New York Times,* March 15, 1991, 13.
27. Ibid., March 27, 1991, 1, 9.
28. Ibid., March 28, 1991, 1, 18.
29. Dow Jones News, January 15, 1996.
30. Thomas L. Friedman, "Baker Sketches Future Gulf Role," in *New York Times,* February 7, 1991, A1.
31. The analysis in this section draws extensively on the author's article "Rethinking Dual Containment," *Survival* 40, no. 1 (Spring 1998): 5–32. See also Martin Indyk, "The Clinton Administration's Approach to the Middle East," Keynote Address to the Soref Symposium on "Challenges to U.S. Interests in the Middle East: Obstacles and Opportunities," *Proceedings of the Washington Institute for Near East Policy,* May 18–19, 1993, 1–8. At the time of this speech Indyk had just joined the National Security Council staff. He later became the U.S. ambassador to Israel (twice), separated by an appointment as assistant secretary of state for Near East affairs.
32. Indyk, "The Clinton Administration's Approach to the Middle East," 4.
33. See, for example, the remarks by Secretary of State Madeleine K. Albright at Georgetown University, Washington, D.C., March 26, 1997, as released by the Office of the Spokesman, U.S. Department of State.
34. Elaine Sciolino, "CIA Asks Congress for Money to Rein in Iraq and Iran," *New York Times,* April 12, 1995, 1.
35. All of these operations were publicly confirmed after the event by former senior officials of the U.S. government. See Don Oberdorfer, "U.S. Had Covert Plan to Oust Iraq's Saddam, Bush Adviser Asserts; Effort to Remove Leader Came 'Pretty Close,'" *Washington Post,* January 20, 1993, 1; and ABC News, "Unfinished Business—the CIA and Saddam Hussein," transcript no. 97062601-j13, June 26, 1997. There were also detailed reports in the *Los Angeles Times, New York Times,* and other media.
36. This attack was particularly controversial since the targets were in the south and unrelated to the ground attack in the north.
37. See "Memorandum of Understanding Between the United Nations and the Republic of Iraq," Associated Press, February 24, 1998.
38. See the text of the Inaugural Address in the *New York Times,* January 21, 1989, 10. Iran welcomed this remark and responded by helping to eventually free the U.S. hostages in Lebanon. It is a sore point with Iran that this gesture, in their view, was never reciprocated by the United States.
39. See Executive Order 12957 of March 15, 1995, and Executive Order 12959 of May 6, 1995. For a detailed analysis of the politics associated with the developments of Iranian sanctions, see Laurie Lande, "Second Thoughts," *International Economy* (May–June 1997): 44–49.
40. The transcript of this interview with Iranian President Muhammad Khatami was posted on the CNN web site immediately after it was aired on January 7, 1998. Large portions of the text were published in a number of newspapers the following day.
41. Even before the Khatami election, many senior policy observers and former U.S. officials were calling for changes in the Dual Containment Strategy. These voices included two former national security advisers, a former secretary of defense, three former assistant

secretaries of state for Near East affairs, and the former commander of U.S. forces in the Persian Gulf, among others.

42. The trigger level was reduced automatically from $40 million to $20 million on the first anniversary of the legislation in August 1997.
43. The European Union threatened to take the case to the World Trade Organization if the United States imposed sanctions on the French company, on grounds that the U.S. policy was in violation of international trade agreements. Although the third party sanctions of ILSA have never been formally enforced, the threat of possible U.S. action had a chilling effect on international investment in Iranian oil and gas, particularly by companies that had major commercial interests in the United States that might be the target of American retaliatory action. Iran inadvertently assisted this process by insisting on restrictive contracts that severely limited the profit margins that foreign companies could hope to realize, thereby reducing the incentive for the companies to defy the United States.
44. Secretary of State Madeleine K. Albright, Remarks at 1998 Asia Society Dinner, Waldorf-Astoria Hotel, New York, June 17, 1998, as released by the Office of the Spokesman, U.S. Department of State, June 18, 1998.
45. Ibid.
46. David E. Sanger, "U.S. Ending a few of the Sanctions Imposed on Iran," in *New York Times,* March 18, 2000, A1.
47. Transcript of the debate, hosted by Jim Lehrer of the PBS NewsHour. Posted at http://www.pbs.org/newshour/bb/election/2000debates/2ndebate1.html (accessed October 16, 2008).
48. See the letter to President Clinton produced by The Project For The New American Century on January 26, 1998, signed by many individuals who would later become key foreign and security officials of the Bush administration. (Available at: www.theindyvoice.com/politics/pnac [accessed October 16, 2008]) See also "A Clean Break: A New Strategy for Securing the Realm," a report prepared by The Institute for Advanced Strategic and Political Studies' "Study Group on a New Israeli Strategy Toward 2000," posted at http://www.israeleconomy.org/strat1.htm (accessed August 11, 2008).

CONTRIBUTORS

Lawrence G. Potter has been Deputy Director of Gulf/2000, a major research and documentation project on the Persian Gulf states, since 1994. He is also Adjunct Associate Professor of International Affairs at Columbia University, where he has taught since 1996. A graduate of Tufts College, he received an M.A. in Middle Eastern Studies from the School of Oriental and African Studies, University of London, and a Ph.D. in History (1992) from Columbia University. He taught in Iran for four years before the revolution. From 1984 to 1992, he was Senior Editor at the Foreign Policy Association (FPA), a national, nonpartisan organization devoted to world affairs education for the general public, and currently serves on the FPA's Editorial Advisory Committee. He specializes in Iranian history and U.S. policy toward the Middle East. He coedited (with Gary Sick) *The Persian Gulf at the Millennium: Essays in Politics, Economy, Security, and Religion* (St. Martin's Press, 1997); *Security in the Persian Gulf: Origins, Obstacles, and the Search for Consensus* (Palgrave, 2002); and *Iran, Iraq, and the Legacies of War* (Palgrave Macmillan, 2004). His most recent article is "The Consolidation of Iran's Frontier on the Persian Gulf in the Nineteenth Century," in *War and Peace in Qajar Persia: Implications Past and Present,* ed. Roxane Farmanfarmaian (Routledge, 2008).

* * *

Frederick F. Anscombe is Senior Lecturer in Contemporary History at Birkbeck College, University of London. He previously taught at the American University in Bulgaria (1994–2003). He earned a B.A. in History from Yale University (1984) and a Ph.D. in Near Eastern Studies from Princeton University (1994). His research interests lie in the Ottoman Balkans and Middle East. His work on the Gulf includes *The Ottoman Gulf: The Creation of Kuwait, Saudi Arabia and Qatar* (Columbia University Press, 1997) and "An Anational Society: Eastern Arabia in the Ottoman Period," in Madawi Al-Rasheed, ed., *Transnational Connections: The Arab Gulf and Beyond* (Routledge, 2005). He also edited *The Ottoman Balkans, 1750–1830* (Markus Wiener, 2006).

William O. Beeman is Professor and Chair of the Department of Anthropology at the University of Minnesota. He was previously Professor of Anthropology at Brown University and currently serves as the President of the Middle East Section of the American Anthropological Association. He has lived and worked for more than thirty years in the Middle East, including a number of years in the Gulf region. Author of fourteen books and more than one hundred scholarly articles, his publications include *Language, Status and Power in Iran* (Indiana University Press, 1986); *Culture, Performance and Communication in Iran* (Institute for the Study of Languages and Cultures of Asia & Africa, 1982); and *The "Great Satan" vs. the "Mad Mullahs": How the United States and Iran Demonize Each Other* (University of Chicago Press, 2008). A frequent commentator in the public media on Middle Eastern affairs, he has also served as a consultant to the U.S. State Department, the U.S. Department of Defense, the United Nations, and the U.S. Congress.

Mohamed Redha Bhacker (M.Sc., Ph.D. Oxon) is an Omani scholar who writes and lectures on the historical, economic, and political development of Oman, the Gulf and the Indian Ocean region. He is the author of *Trade and Empire in Muscat and Zanzibar* (Routledge, 1992) and coauthor of "Qalhat in Arabian History: Context and Chronicles" (*Journal of Oman Studies* 13 [2005]). He is on the editorial boards of the *Journal of Oman Studies* and *Journal of Colonial History* and is currently working on the Ibadi renaissance in East Africa and Oman and the emergence of modern Oman, its performance and prospects. He is also the founder of Al Mustadaama (Sustainability), a research consultancy that advocates the preservation of Omani culture.

João Teles e Cunha is a member of the teaching staff of the Institute of Oriental Studies, connected with the Catholic University in Lisbon, Portugal. He holds a degree in History from the University of Lisbon and a Master's degree from the New University of Lisbon. The topic of his master's thesis is "Economy of an Empire: The Economics of Estado da India in the Persian Gulf and Arabian Seas, 1595–1635." He is presently completing work on his doctorate on "Goa and the Creation of the Portuguese Inter-Colonial Market, 1660–1750." Among his publications are articles on the reigning family of Hormuz between 1565 and 1622, published in *Anais de Historia de Alem-Mar* 3 (2002), and on the consumption of tea in Portuguese society compared with China. He is on the editorial team of the new series *Livros das Monçoes* and is writing chapters on the economic history of Estado da India and of Goa from 1497 to 1830.

Touraj Daryaee is Howard Baskerville Professor of History of Iran and the Persianate World and Associate Director of the Dr. Samuel M. Jordan Center for Persian Studies and Culture at the University of California, Irvine. His specialty is Ancient Persian and World History. He attended schools in Iran, Greece, and the United States and received his Ph.D. in History from UCLA in 1999. In addition to a number of articles on the Persian Gulf in antiquity, he published *Shahrestaniha-i Eranshahr: A Middle Persian Text on Late Antique Geography, Epic and History,* translation and commentary (Mazda, 2002) and *Sasanian Iran (224–651 CE): Portrait of a Late Antique Empire* (Mazda, 2008).

Willem Floor is an independent scholar of the social and economic history of Iran, having published more than 150 books and articles, including about a dozen on the Persian littoral of the Gulf. Recent major works include *The Persian Gulf: A Political and Economic History of Five Port Cities 1500–1730* and *The Persian Gulf: The Rise of the Gulf Arabs—The Politics of Trade on the Persian Littoral, 1747–1792* (Mage, 2006 and 2007). He received his Ph.D. from Leiden University in 1971, after having studied sociology, economics, Arabic, Persian, and Islamology at Utrecht University (the Netherlands). After serving at the Middle East Desk (Dutch Ministry of Foreign Affairs) from 1968 to 1971, he worked in development projects in Africa from 1971 to 1974, before becoming a policy advisor to the Dutch Minister of Development Cooperation (1974–83). From 1983 to 2002 he worked worldwide as an energy specialist for the World Bank. He now writes about Iran full time.

Rudi Matthee is Unidel Professor of Middle Eastern History at the University of Delaware. He holds a B.A. and M.A. in Arabic and Persian Language and Literature from Utrecht University, and studied in Iran (1976–77) and Egypt (1981–83). He gained a Ph.D. in Islamic Studies from UCLA in 1991. Matthee is the author of *The Politics of*

Trade in Safavid Iran: Silk for Silver, 1600–1730 (Cambridge University Press, 1999), *The Pursuit of Pleasure: Drugs and Stimulants in Iranian History, 1500–1900* (Princeton University Press, 2005), and *Persia in Crisis: Safavid Decline and the Fall of Isfahan* (I.B. Taurus, 2009). He is coeditor (with Beth Baron) of *Iran and Beyond: Essays in Honor of Nikki R. Keddie* (Mazda, 2000); and coeditor (with Nikki Keddie) of *Iran and the Surrounding World: Interactions in Culture and Cultural Politics* (University of Washington Press, 2002). He has authored some thirty articles on Safavid and Qajar Iran (16th–19th centuries), dealing with issues of political, socioeconomic and material history.

Shahnaz Razieh Nadjmabadi has been a Research Fellow at the Institut für Historische Ethnologie at the Johann Wolfgang Goethe-Universität in Frankfurt/Main (Germany) since 2002. She has been a lecturer in the Department of Social Anthropology at the University of Heidelberg since 1986, as well as teaching at the Freie Universität Berlin and at the University of Maryland/Heidelberg. Dr. Nadjmabadi received a Ph.D. in 1973 in social anthropology from the University of Heidelberg, with a thesis on kinship systems among the nomadic populations of Luristan. After teaching at the University of Zürich, she worked at UNESCO in Paris from 1977 to 1986, where she was a project officer in the Department of Social Sciences supervising activities related to Human Settlement and Environment. She was also a member of the working group "Monde Iranien Contemporain" at the Centre National de la Recherche Scientifique, where she developed a project on the topic of identity among Arab and Iranian populations in the Iranian coastal province of Hormuzgan. She has published a number of articles on questions of identity, migration, and the historical development of the Hormuzgan area.

J. E. Peterson is an independent historian and author on the Arabian Peninsula and Gulf. He received his Ph.D. from Johns Hopkins University (SAIS) and has held various teaching and research positions in the United States. Recent positions have included Historian of the Sultan's Armed Forces in the Office of the Deputy Prime Minister for Security and Defence in the Sultanate of Oman; the International Institute for Strategic Studies in London; and Sir William Luce Fellow at the University of Durham. His most recent books include a *Historical Dictionary of Saudi Arabia* (Scarecrow Press, 1993, rev. 2003), *Historical Muscat: An Illustrated Guide and Gazetteer* (Brill, 2007), *Oman's Insurgencies: The Sultanate's Struggle for Supremacy* (Saqi, 2007), and *Oman Since 1970* (forthcoming).

Daniel T. Potts is Edwin Cuthbert Hall Professor of Middle Eastern Archaeology at the University of Sydney. He was born in New York and educated at Harvard (A.B., Ph.D.), and taught at the University of Copenhagen (1980–81, 1986–91), the Free University of Berlin (1981–86), and the University of Sydney (since 1991). He is the author of numerous books and articles on the archaeology and early history of eastern Arabia, Mesopotamia, Iran, and the Persian Gulf. He was the director of excavations at Thaj in Saudi Arabia and ed-Dur, Tell Abraq, Al Sufouh, Jabal Emalah, and Husn Awhala in the UAE. He is currently codirector of a joint Iranian-Australian archaeological research project in the Mamasani district of Fars province, Iran, excavating at Tal-e Nurabad and Tal-e Spid. He is the founding editor in chief of the journal *Arabian Archaeology & Epigraphy.*

Patricia Risso is Professor of History and chair of the department at the University of New Mexico, where she has taught since 1986. She holds an M.A. and Ph.D. from the Institute of Islamic Studies, McGill University, Montréal. Her research interests are cultural and economic contacts between India and the Middle East in the early modern period. In the last several years, she has focused on cross-cultural perceptions of maritime violence that affected commercial and diplomatic relationships. Her publications include *Oman and Masqat: An Early Modern History* (Croom Helm, 1986), *Merchants and Faith: Muslim Commerce and Culture in the Indian Ocean* (Westview Press, 1995), and a multiauthored two-volume text, *Sharing the Stage: Biography and Gender in World History* (Houghton Mifflin, 2008).

Abdul Sheriff is Executive Director of the Zanzibar Indian Ocean Research Institute. He was Advisor and Principal Curator of the Zanzibar Museums from 1992 to 2005, and prior to that Professor of History at the University of Dar es Salaam from 1969 to 1992. He studied at the University of California, Los Angeles, and at SOAS, University of London, from which he holds a Ph.D. He has specialized in the history of Zanzibar, with many publications, including *Slaves, Spices, and Ivory in Zanzibar: Integration of an East African Commercial Empire into the World Economy, 1770–1873* (Ohio University Press, 1987); *The History and Conservation of Zanzibar Stone Town* (edited) (Ohio University Press, 1995); and *Zanzibar Under Colonial Rule* (coedited) (Ohio University Press, 1991). Over the past few years his interests have broadened to include the dhow culture of the western Indian Ocean over the *longue durée,* on which he has published many articles and has completed a book.

Gary Sick served on the U.S. National Security Council staff under presidents Ford, Carter, and Reagan. He was the principal White House aide for Iran during the Iranian Revolution and the hostage crisis and is the author of two books on U.S.-Iranian relations. Mr. Sick is a captain (ret.) in the U.S. Navy, with service in the Persian Gulf, North Africa, and the Mediterranean. He was the Deputy Director for International Affairs at the Ford Foundation from 1982 to 1987, where he was responsible for programs relating to U.S. foreign policy. Mr. Sick has a Ph.D. in political science from Columbia University, where he is Senior Research Scholar and Adjunct Professor of International Affairs. He is also a former director of the university's Middle East Institute (2000–3). He is the Executive Director of Gulf/2000, an international research project on political, economic, and security developments in the Persian Gulf, being conducted at Columbia University with support from a number of major foundations. He is coeditor of three books on the Persian Gulf published by the Gulf/2000 project. Mr. Sick is a member (emeritus) of the board of Human Rights Watch in New York and founding chairman of its Middle East and North Africa advisory committee.

Mohammad Bagher Vosoughi, a native of Lar, is Associate Professor of History at Tehran University. He received his Ph.D. there in 2001 with a thesis on "Tarikh-i Muluk-i Hurmuz" (History of the Kings of Hormuz). He previously graduated from Teacher's College in History (1989) and served in the Literacy Corps. His many publications concerning the Persian Gulf area include *Tarikh-i muhajirat-i aqvam dar Khalij-i Fars* (The History of the Emigration of Peoples in the Persian Gulf) (Intisharat-i Danishnama-yi Fars, 1380/2002); *Jang-nama-yi Kishm by Anonymous and Jirun-nama by Qadri (d.1043 A.H.)* (The Conquest of Qishm and the Story of Jirun), ed. with Abd al-Rasul Khairandish (Miras-i Maktub, 1384/2005); *Tarikh-i Khalij-i Fars va mamalik-i hamjavar* (The History of the Persian Gulf and its Bordering Territories) (Intisharat-i Samt, 1384/2005); and *Tarikh-i mufassal-i Laristan* (Comprehensive History of Laristan), 2 vols. (Hamsaya, 1385/2006), with Manuchihr Abidi Rad, Sadiq Rahmani, and Kiramat-Allah Taqavi.

Donald Whitcomb has held the position of Research Associate (Associate Professor) at The Oriental Institute and the Middle East Center, University of Chicago, since 1981. He has a Ph.D. in Anthropology from the University of Chicago, an M.A. from the University of Georgia, and a B.A. in Art History from Emory University. Before this, he was Assistant Curator at the Field Museum of Natural History (1979–81) and has held research fellowships at the Smithsonian Institution (1981–82) and at the Metropolitan Museum of Art, New York (1977–79). Whitcomb's archaeological research includes direction of the excavations at Quseir al-Qadim, a Roman and Mamluk port on the Egyptian coast of the Red Sea (1978–82). Since 1986, he has been director of the Aqaba excavations in Jordan, investigating the early Islamic port of Ayla. Most recently, he has begun excavations at Hadir Qinnasrin, the early Islamic capital of north Syria near Aleppo. His earlier fieldwork included excavations and surveys in Jordan, Oman, Syria, and Iran. In addition to articles on the archaeology of Arabia, Oman, Iran, and Aden and the Hadhramawt, Whitcomb has published a monograph, *Before the Roses and Nightingales: Excavations at Qasr-i Abu Nasr, Old Shiraz* (Metropolitan Museum of Art, 1985) and coauthored two archaeological reports, *Quseir al-Qadim 1980* (Udena Publications, 1982) and *Quseir al-Qadim 1978* (American Research Center in Egypt, 1979). More recently, he edited a volume entitled *Changing Social Identity with the Spread of Islam: Archaeological Perspectives,* Oriental Institute Seminars 1 (Oriental Institute of the University of Chicago, 2004) and collaborated on an exhibition catalogue (with Tanya Treptow), *Daily Life Ornamented: The Medieval Persian City of Rayy* (Oriental Institute of the University of Chicago, 2007).

Index